Studies in Social Interaction

edited by DAVID SUDNOW
UNIVERSITY OF CALIFORNIA, IRVINE

THE FREE PRESS · NEW YORK
COLLIER-MACMILLAN LIMITED · LONDON

The Free Press
A Division of The Macmillan Company
866 Third Avenue, New York, New York 10022

Collier-Macmillan Canada Ltd., Toronto, Ontario

Library of Congress Catalog Card Number: 79-168542

Printing number 4 5 6 7 8 9 10

Contents

		page
	Preface	vii
HAROLD GARFINKEL	Studies of the Routine Grounds of Everyday Activities	1
HARVEY SACKS	An Initial Investigation of the Usability of Conversational Data for Doing Sociology	31
EMANUEL A. SCHEGLOFF	Notes on a Conversational Practice: Formulating Place	75
WILLIAM LABOV	Rules for Ritual Insults	120
MICHAEL MOERMAN	Analysis of Lue Conversation: Providing Accounts, Finding Breaches, and Taking Sides	170
AARON V. CICOUREL	Basic and Normative Rules in the Negotiation of Status and Role	229
DAVID SUDNOW	Temporal Parameters of Interpersonal Observation	259
HARVEY SACKS	Notes on Police Assessment of Moral Character	280

		page
GAIL JEFFERSON	Sides Sequences	294
SHELDON TWER	Tactics for Determining Persons' Resources for Depicting, Contriving, and Describing Behavioral Episodes	339
ROY TURNER	Some Formal Properties of Therapy Talk	367
MATTHEW SPEIER	Some Conversational Problems for Interactional Analysis	397
	Notes	428

Preface

This volume is not, in the usual sense of the term, a "reader," but a collection of original research papers by a group of anthropologists and sociologists who have been engaged in studies of everyday, naturally occurring social interaction. This research has been chiefly non-experimental in nature and has seldom involved the use of interview techniques. Rather, the research has proceeded mainly through the analysis of tape and film recordings made in actual settings of social interaction. It has been concerned to develop concepts and methods for the analysis of the details of such empirical materials. The volume is intended to furnish researchers in the field and their students with some of the results of our inquiries.

The sense in which the papers constitute the efforts of a "group" requires some comment. While none of the papers is a product of directly collaborative research, and while many excellent articles of direct relevance to the study of actually occurring social interaction could have been added to the present collection, the authors of these papers do share an intellectual perspective and periods of association together. All the authors, with the exception of William Labov, were associated with one another at the University of California at Berkeley and at U.C.L.A. within the past six or seven years as fellow graduate students and/or faculty colleagues. A central basis for their association was their involvement in Professor Harold Garfinkel's research in "ethnomethodology." Garfinkel's work on the phenomenological structure of ordinary settings of social activity provided and continues to provide an enormous intellectual stimulus for our researches. His insistence upon treating the member's perspective seriously in the analysis of social interaction is reflected in each and every paper in the volume, and may perhaps be seen as lending the present collection of articles its distinctive character. Garfinkel's paper, "Studies in the Routine Grounds of Everyday Activities," while previously published, is reprinted here because (at least to the editor) it contains the most systematic statement of the program and goals of ethnomethodological inquiry.[1]

While graduate students working with Goffman at Berkeley, Sacks, Schlegloff, Sudnow, and Turner became influenced by Garfinkel's work, introduced to his writings by Sacks. Sacks began his own research on the workings of the details of conversational activities upon his arrival at U.C.L.A. in 1963, and has come to stimulate considerable research in that area. All of those papers in the volume treating conversational structure grow out of Sack's work. His research on conversation has hitherto been available chiefly in the form of unpublished course lectures, which have been mimeographed and circulated each year since 1965. His reasearch on the sequential structure of conversational activities will appear shortly in a volume nearing completion.[2] Sack's dissertation at Berkeley, a version of which is presented here as "An Initial Investigation of the Usability of Conversational Data for Doing Sociology," established the problems of categorization as a central theme throughout his work and the work of Jefferson, Moerman, Schegloff, Spier, Sudnow, Turner, and Twer. It is recommended that the reader of this collection consider work by these people after studying Sack's paper first.

The paper in the volume by Aaron Cicourel, who has engaged in extensive methodological writing, presents an anlysis of the traditional concepts of "status" and "role" in interactional inquiries from the standpoint of the ethnomethodological perspective, and thus it furnishes the reader with a basis for locating and contrasting some of the research concerns found in this volume within the mainstream of sociological research. Cicourel's critical attacks upon social science methodologies and concepts has had widespread influence among sociologists since his volume *Method and Measurement in Sociology* appeared in 1964.[3]

The paper by William Laboy, "Rules for Ritual Insults," has been included in the volume for in addition to its excellence it provides the reader with a case in point of the articulation between the conversational research conducted by Sacks and his students and the form that analysis is beginning to take within linguistic anthropology.

Rather than employing the preface of the volume, as is customary, as an occasion for either summarizing the present collection of articles or arguing the implications of their perspectives for research on social interaction, we prefer to offer the collection to the reader without detailed

[1] Garfinkel's theoretical and empirical writings may be found chiefly in his volume *Studies in Ethnomethodology* (Englewood Cliffs, N.J.: Prentice-Hall, 1967). A collection of articles by persons involved in ethnomethodological research which does not overlap with the interaction studies collected here will appear as *Contributions to Ethnomethodology* (Bloomington, Indiana: Indiana University Press), in preparation.

[2] Harvey Sacks, *The Organization of Conversation* (Prentice-Hall), in preparation.

[3] Aaron Cicourel, *Method and Measurement in Sociology*, (New York: The Free Press), 1964.

characterization, the hope being that the articles' findings will suffice in themselves to generate further interest in such detailed interactional studies. That the style, methodology, topics, and theoretical interests of the papers have, within sociological inquiry, a distinctively "different" character, will be clear to the reader from the outset. From the editor's standpoint, however, in the final analysis the worth of whatever theoretical or programmatic statements we might make turns on the news about the world which the perspective embodied herein might make it possible to discover. We offer this collection to those concerned to learn more about the workings of everyday interactional activities. We believe the volume substantiates the position that studies of the details of particular conversational and bodily interactions can be given strong methodological warrant and that such investigations are productive of general and original sociological propositions. We hope the present collection will serve to stimulate basic research on the particularities of actually occurring interactional conduct.

David Sudnow
Laguna Beach, California

HAROLD GARFINKEL

Studies of the Routine Grounds of Everyday Activities*

THE PROBLEM

For Kant the moral order "within" was an awesome mystery; for sociologists the moral order "without" is a technical mystery. From the point of view of sociological theory the moral order consists of the rule governed activities of everyday life. A society's members encounter and know the moral order as perceivedly normal courses of action—familiar scenes of everyday affairs, the world of daily life known in common with others and with others taken for granted.

They refer to this world as the "natural facts of life" which, for members, are through and through moral facts of life. For members not only are matters so about

* Reprinted with permission from *Social problems*, Vol. 11, No. 3, Winter, 1964.

This investigation was supported by a Senior Research Fellowship, SF-81 from the U.S. Public Health Service. I am indebted to Egon Bittner, Craig MacAndrew, Edward Rose, Harvey Sacks, and Eleanor Sheldon for their many criticisms and suggestions.

(*Notes to this selection will be found on pp. 428–429.*)

familiar scenes, but they are so because it is morally right or wrong that they are so. Familiar scenes of everyday activities, treated by members as the "natural facts of life," are massive facts of the members' daily existence both *as* a real world and as the product of activities *in* a real world. They furnish the "fix," the "this is it" to which the waking state returns one, and are the points of departure and return for every modification of the world of daily life that is achieved in play, dreaming, trance, theatre, scientific theorizing, or high ceremony.

In every discipline, humanistic or scientific, the familiar common sense world of everyday life is a matter of abiding interest. In the social sciences, and in sociology particularly, it is a matter of essential preoccupation. It makes up sociology's problematic subject matter, enters the very constitution of the sociological attitude, and exercises an odd and obstinate sovereignty over sociologists' claims to adequate explanation.

Despite the topic's centrality, an immense literature contains little data and few methods with which the essential features of socially recognized "familiar scenes" may be detected and related to dimensions of social organization. Although sociologists take socially structured scenes of everyday life as a point of departure they rarely see[1] as a task of sociological inquiry in its own right the general question of how any such common sense world is possible. Instead, the possibility of the everyday world is either settled by theoretical representation or merely assumed. As a topic and methodological ground for sociological inquiries, the definition of the common sense world of everyday life, though it is appropriately a project of sociological inquiry, has been neglected. My purposes in this essay are to demonstrate the essential relevance to the program of sociological inquiries of a concern for common sense activities as a topic of inquiry in its own right and, by reporting a series of studies, to urge its "rediscovery."

MAKING COMMONPLACE SCENES VISIBLE

In accounting for the stable features of everyday activities, sociologists commonly select familiar settings such as familial households or work places and ask for the variables that contribute to their stable features. Just as commonly, one set of considerations are unexamined: the socially standardized and standardizing, "seen but unnoticed," expected, background features of everyday scenes. The member of the society uses background expectancies as a scheme of interpretation. In their terms, actual appearances are for him recognizable and intelligible as the appearances of familiar events. Demonstrably he is responsive to this background. At the same time he is at a loss to tell us what specifically the expectancies consist of. When we ask him about them he has little or nothing to say.

For these background expectancies to come into view one must either be a stranger to the "life as usual" character of everyday scenes, or become estranged from them. As Alfred Schutz pointed out, a "special motive" is required to make them problematic. In the sociologist's case this "special motive" consists in the programmatic task of treating a societal member's practical circumstances, which include from the member's point of view the morally necessary character of many of its background features, as matters of theoretical interest. The seen but unnoticed backgrounds of everyday activities are made visible and are described from a perspective in which persons live out the lives they do, have the children they do, feel the feelings, think the thoughts, enter the relationships they do, all in order to permit the sociologist to solve his theoretical problems.

Almost alone among sociological theorists, the late Alfred Schutz, in a series of classical studies[2] of the constitutive phenomenology of the world of everyday life, described many of these seen but unnoticed background expectancies. He called them the "attitude of daily life." He referred to their scenic attributions as the "world known in common and taken for granted." Schutz' fundamental work makes it possible to pursue further the tasks of clarifying their nature and operation, of relating them to the processes of concerted actions, and assigning them their place in an empirically imaginable society.

The studies reported in this essay attempt to detect some expectancies that lend commonplace scenes their familiar, life-as-usual character, and to relate these to the stable social structures of everyday activities. Procedurally it is my preference to start with familiar scenes and ask what can be done to make trouble. The operations that one would have to perform in order to multiply the senseless features of perceived environments; to produce and sustain bewilderment, consternation, and confusion; to produce the socially structured affects of anxiety, shame, guilt, and indignation; and to produce disorganized interaction should tell us something about how the structures of everyday activities are ordinarily and routinely produced and maintained.[3]

A word of reservation. Despite their procedural emphasis, my studies are not, properly speaking, experimental. They are demonstrations, designed, in Herbert Spiegelberg's phrase, as "aids to a sluggish imagination." I have found that they produce reflections through which the strangeness of an obstinately familiar world can be detected.

SOME ESSENTIAL FEATURES OF COMMON UNDERSTANDINGS

Various considerations dictate that common understandings cannot possibly consist of a measured amount of shared agreement among persons on certain topics. Even if the topics are limited in number or scope and every practical difficulty of assessment is forgiven, the notion that we are dealing with an amount of shared agreement remains essentially incorrect. This may be demonstrated as follows.

Students were asked to report common conversations by writing on the left side of a sheet what the parties actually said and on the right side what they and their partners understood that they were talking about. A student reported the following colloquy between himself and his wife:

HUSBAND:	Dana succeeded in putting a penny in a parking meter today without being picked up.	This afternoon as I was bringing Dana, our four-year-old son, home from the nursery school, he succeeded in reaching high enough to put a penny in a parking meter when we parked in a meter parking zone, whereas before he has always had to be picked up to reach that high.
WIFE:	Did you take him to the record store?	Since he put a penny in a meter, that means that you stopped while he was with you. I know that you stopped at the record store either on the way to get him or on the way back. Was it on the way back, so that he was with you, or did you stop there on the way to get him and somewhere else on the way back?
HUSBAND:	No, to the shoe repair shop.	No, I stopped at the record store on the way to get him and stopped at the shoe repair shop on the way home when he was with me.
WIFE:	What for?	I know of one reason why you might have stopped at the shoe repair shop. Why did you in fact?
HUSBAND:	I got some new shoe laces for my shoes.	As you will remember, I broke a shoe lace on one of my brown oxfords the other day, so I stopped to get some new laces.
WIFE:	Your loafers need new heels badly.	Something else you could have gotten that I was thinking of. You could have taken in your black loafers which need heels badly. You'd better get them taken care of pretty soon.

An examination of the colloquy reveals the following: (a) There were many matters that the partners understood they were talking about that they did not mention. (b) Many matters that the partners understood were understood on the basis not only of what was actually said but what was left unspoken. (c) Many matters were understood through a process of attending to the temporal series of utterances as documentary evidences of a developing conversation rather than as a string of terms. (d) Matters that the two understood in common were understood only in and through a course of understanding work that consisted of treating an actual linguistic event as "the document of," as "pointing to," as standing on behalf of an underlying pattern of matters that each already supposed to be the matters that the person, by his speaking, could be telling the other about. The underlying pattern was not only derived from a course of individual documentary evidences but the documentary evidences in their turn were interpreted on the basis of "what was known" and anticipatorily knowable about the underlying patterns.[4] Each was used to elaborate the other. (e) In attending to the utterances as events-in-the-conversation, each party made reference to the biography and prospects of the present interaction that each used and attributed to the other as a common scheme of interpretation and expression. (f) Each waited for something more to be said in order to hear what had previously been talked about, and each seemed willing to wait.

Common understandings would consist of a measured amount of shared agreement if the common understandings consisted of events coordinated with the successive positions of the hands of the clock, i.e. of events in standard time. The foregoing results, because they deal with the exchanges of the colloquy as events-in-a-conversation, urge that one more time parameter, at least, is required: the role of time as it is constitutive of "the matter talked about" as a developing and developed event over the course of action that produced it, as both the process and product were known *from within* this development by both parties, each for himself as well as on behalf of the other.

The colloquy reveals additional features: (1) Many of its expressions are such that their sense cannot be decided by an auditor unless he knows or assumes something about the biography and the purposes of the speaker, the circumstances of the utterance, the previous course of the conversation, or the particular relationship of actual or potential interaction that exists between user and auditor. The expressions do not have a sense that remains identical through the changing occasions of their use. (2) The events that were talked about were specifically vague. Not only do they not frame a clearly restricted set of possible determinations but the depicted events include as their essentially intended and sanctioned features an accompanying "fringe" of determinations that are open with respect to internal relationships, relationships to other events, and relationships to retrospective and prospective possibilities. (3) For the sensible character of an expression, upon its occurrence each of the conversationalists, as auditor of his own as well as the other's productions, had to assume as of any present accomplished point in the exchange that by waiting for what he or the other person might have said at a later time the present significance of what had already been said would have been clarified. Thus, many expressions had the property of being progressively realized and realizable through the further course of the conversation. (4) It hardly needs to be pointed out that the sense of the expressions depended upon where the expression occurred in serial order, the expressive character of the terms that comprised it, and the importance to the conversationalists of the events depicted.

These properties of common understandings stand in contrast to the features they would have if we disregarded their temporally constituted character and treated them instead as pre-coded entries on a memory drum, to be consulted as a definite set of alternative meanings from among which one was to select, under pre-decided conditions that specified in which of some set of alternative ways one was to understand the situation upon the occasion that the necessity for a decision arose. The latter properties are those of strict rational discourse as these are idealized in the rules that define an adequate logical proof.

For the purposes of *conducting their everyday affairs*, persons refuse to permit each other to understand "what they are really talking about" in this way. The anticipation that persons *will* understand, the occasionality of expressions, the specific vagueness of references, the retrospective-prospective sense of a present occurrence, waiting for something later in order to see what was meant before, are sanctioned properties of common discourse. They furnish a background of seen but unnoticed features of common discourse whereby actual utterances are recognized as events of common, reasonable, understandable, plain talk. Persons require these properties of discourse as conditions under which they are themselves entitled and entitle others to claim that they know what they are talking about, and that what they are saying is understandable and ought to be understood. In short, their seen but unnoticed presence is used to entitle persons to conduct their common conversational affairs without interference. Departures from such usages call forth immediate attempts to restore a right state of affairs.

The sanctioned character of these properties is demonstrable as follows. Students were instructed to engage an acquaintance or a friend in an ordinary conversation and, without indicating that what the experimenter was asking was in any way unusual, to insist that the person clarify the sense of his commonplace remarks. Twenty-three students reported 25 instances of such encounters. The following are typical excerpts from their accounts.

CASE 1

S) Hi, Ray. How is your girl friend feeling?
E) What do you mean, how is she feeling? Do you mean physical or mental?
S) I mean how is she feeling? What's the matter with you? (He looked peeved.)
E) Nothing. Just explain a little clearer what do you mean?
S) Skip it. How are your Med School applications coming?

E) What do you mean, How are they?
S) You know what I mean.
E) I really don't.
S) What's the matter with you? Are you sick?

CASE 2

On Friday night my husband and I were watching television. My husband remarked that he was tired. I asked, "How are you tired? Physically, mentally, or just bored?"

S) I don't know, I guess physically, mainly.
E) You mean that your muscles ache, or your bones?
S) I guess so. Don't be so technical.
(After more watching.)
S) All these old movies have the same kind of old iron bedstead in them.
E) What do you mean? Do you mean all old movies, or some of them, or just the ones you have seen?
S) What's the matter with you? You know what I mean.
E) I wish you would be more specific.
S) You know what I mean! Drop dead!

BACKGROUND UNDERSTANDINGS AND "ADEQUATE" RECOGNITION OF COMMONPLACE EVENTS

What kinds of expectancies make up a "seen but unnoticed" background of common understandings, and how are they related to persons' recognition of and stable courses of interpersonal transactions? Some information can be obtained if we first ask how a person will look at an ordinary and familiar scene and what will he see in it if we require of him that he do no more than look at it as something that for him it "obviously" and "really" is not.

Undergraduate students were assigned the task of spending from fifteen minutes to an hour in their homes viewing its activities, while assuming that they were boarders in the household. They were instructed not to act out the assumption. Thirty-three students reported their experiences.

In their written reports students "behaviorized" the household scenes. Here is an excerpt from one account to illustrate my meaning.

> A short, stout man entered the house, kissed me on the cheek and asked, "How was school?" I answered politely. He walked into the kitchen, kissed the younger of two women, and said hello to the other. The younger woman asked me, "What do you want for dinner, honey?" I answered, "Nothing." She shrugged her shoulders and said no more. The older woman shuffled around the kitchen muttering. The man washed his hands,

> sat down at the table, and picked up the paper. He read until the two women had finished putting the food on the table. The three sat down. They exchanged idle chatter about the day's events. The older woman said something in a foreign language which made the others laugh.

Persons, relationships, and activities were described without respect for their history, for the place of the scene in a set of developing life circumstances, or for the scenes as texture of relevant events for the parties themselves. Reference to motives, propriety, subjectivity generally, and the socially standardized character of the events were omitted. Descriptions might be thought of as those of a keyhole observer who puts aside much of what he knows in common with subjects about the scenes he is looking at, as if the writer had witnessed the scenes under a mild amnesia for common sense knowledge of social structures.

Students were surprised to see the ways in which members' treatments of each other were personal. The business of one was treated as the business of the others. A person being criticized was unable to stand on dignity and was prevented by the others from taking offense. One student reported her surprise at how freely she had the run of the house. Displays of conduct and feeling occurred without apparent concern for the management of impressions. Table manners were bad, and family members showed each other little politeness. An early casualty in the scene was the family news of the day which turned into trivial talk.

Students reported that this way of looking was difficult to sustain. Familiar objects—persons obviously, but furniture and room arrangements as well—resisted students' efforts to think of themselves as strangers. Many became uncomfortably aware of how habitual movements were being made: of *how* one was handling the silverware, or *how* one opened a door or greeted another member. Many reported that the attitude was difficult to sustain because with it quarreling, bickering, and hostile motivations became discomfitingly visible. Frequently, an account that recited newly visible troubles was accompanied by the student's assertion that his account of family problems was not a "true" picture; the family was *really* a very happy one. Several students reported a mildly oppressive feeling of "conforming to a part." Several students attempted to formulate the "real me" as activities governed by rules of conduct but gave it up as a bad job. They found it more convincing to think of themselves in "usual" circumstances as "being one's real self." Nevertheless one student was intrigued with how deliberately and successfully he could predict the others' responses to his actions. He was not troubled by this feeling.

Many accounts reported a variation on the theme: "I was glad when the hour was up and I could return to the real me."

Students were convinced that the view from the boarder's attitude was not their real home environment. The boarder's attitude produced appearances which they discounted as interesting incongruities of little and misleading practical import. How had the familiar ways of looking at their home environments been altered? How did their looking differ from usual?

Several contrasts to the "usual" and "required" way of looking are detectable from their accounts. (1) In looking at their home scenes as boarders they replaced the mutually recognized texture of events with a rule of interpretation that required that this mutual texture be *temporarily* disregarded. (2) The mutually recognized texture was brought under the jurisdiction of the new attitude as a definition of the essential structures of this texture. (3) This was done by engaging in interaction with others with an attitude whose nature and purpose only the user knew about, that remained undisclosed, that could be either adopted or put aside at a time of the user's own choosing, and was a matter of willful election. (4) The attitude as an intention was sustained as a matter of personal and willed compliance with an explicit and single rule (5) in which, like a game, the goal of the intention was identical with looking at things under the auspices of the single rule itself. (6) Above all, looking was not bound by any necessity for gearing one's interests within the attitude to the actions of others. These were the matters that students found strange.

When students used these background expectancies not only as ways of looking at familial scenes but as grounds for acting in them, the scenes exploded with the bewilderment and anger of family members.

Students were required to spend from fifteen minutes to an hour in their homes imagining that they were boarders and acting out this assumption. They were instructed to conduct themselves in a circumspect and polite fashion. They were to avoid getting personal, to use formal address, to speak only when spoken to.

In 9 of 49 cases, students either refused to do the assignment (5 cases) or the try was "unsuccessful" (4 cases). Four of the "no try" students said they were afraid to do it; a fifth said she preferred to avoid the risk of exciting her mother who had a heart condition. In two of the "unsuccessful" cases the family treated it as a joke from the beginning and refused despite the continuing actions of the student to change. A third family took the view that something undisclosed was the matter, but what it might be was of no concern to them. In the fourth family the father and mother remarked that the daughter was being "extra nice" and undoubtedly wanted something that she would shortly reveal.

In the remaining four-fifths of the cases family members were stupefied. They vigorously sought to make the strange actions intelligible and to restore the situation to normal appearances. Reports were filled with accounts of astonishment, bewilderment, shock, anxiety, embarrassment, and anger and with charges by various family members that the student was mean, inconsiderate, selfish, nasty, or impolite. Family members demanded explanations: What's the matter? What's gotten into you? Did you get fired? Are you sick? What are you being so superior about? Why are you mad? Are you out of your mind or are you just stupid? One student acutely embarrassed his mother in front of her friends by asking if she minded if he had a snack from the refrigerator. "Mind if you have a little snack? You've been eating little snacks around here for years without asking me. What's gotten into you?" One mother, infuriated when her daughter spoke to her only when she was spoken to, began to shriek in angry denunciation of the daughter for her disrespect and insubordination and refused to be calmed by the student's sister. A father berated his daughter for being insufficiently concerned for the welfare of others and of acting like a spoiled child.

Occasionally family members would first treat the student's action as a cue for a joint comedy routine, which was soon replaced by irritation and exasperated anger at the student for not knowing when enough was enough. Family members mocked the "politeness" of the students—"Certainly, Mr. Herzberg!"—or charged the student with acting like a wise guy and generally reproved the "politeness" with sarcasm.

Explanations were sought in previous, understandable motives of the student: the student was working too hard in school; the student was ill; there had been "another fight" with a fiancee. When explanations offered by family members went unacknowledged, there followed withdrawal by the offended member, attempted isolation of the culprit, retaliation, and denunciation. "Don't bother with him, he's in one of his moods again"; "Pay no attention but just wait until he asks me for something"; "You're cutting me, okay I'll cut you and then some"; "Why must you always create friction in our family harmony?" Many accounts reported versions of the following confrontation. A father followed his son into the bedroom. "Your mother is right. You don't look well and you're not talking sense. You had better get another job that doesn't require such late hours." To this the student replied that he appreciated the consideration, but that he felt fine and only wanted a little privacy. The father responded in a high rage, "I don't want any more of *that* out of *you* and if you can't treat your mother decently you'd better move out!"

There were no cases in which the situation was not restorable upon the student's explanation. Nevertheless, for the most part family members were not amused, and only rarely did they find the experience instructive as the student argued that it was supposed to have been. After hearing the explanation, a sister replied coldly on behalf of a family of four, "Please, no more of these experiments. We're not rats, you know." Occasionally, an explanation was accepted, but still it added offense. In several cases students reported that the explanation left them, their families, or both wondering how much of what the student had said was "in character" and how much the student "really meant."

Students found the assignment difficult to complete. But in contrast with on-lookers' accounts, students were likely to report that difficulties consisted in not being treated as if they were in the role that they were attempting to play, and of being confronted with situations but not knowing how a boarder would respond.

There were several entirely unexpected findings. (1) Although many students reported extensive rehearsals in imagination, very few mentioned anticipatory fears or embarrassment. (2) On the other hand, although unanticipated and nasty developments frequently occurred, in only one case did a student report serious regrets. (3) Very few students reported heart-felt relief when the hour was over. They were much more likely to report partial relief. They frequently reported that in response to the anger of others they became angry in return and slipped easily into subjectively recognizable feelings and actions.

In contrast to the reports of the on-looking "boarders," very few reports "behaviorized" the scene.

BACKGROUND UNDERSTANDINGS AND SOCIAL AFFECTS

Despite the interest in social affects that prevails in the social sciences, and despite the extensive concern that clinical psychiatry pays them, surprisingly little has been written on the socially structured conditions for their production, while the role that a background of common understandings plays in their production, control, and recognition is almost *terra incognita.* This lack of attention from experimental investigators is all the more remarkable if one considers that it is precisely this relationship that persons are concerned with in their common sense portrayals of how to conduct their daily affairs so as to solicit enthusiasm and friendliness or avoid anxiety, guilt, shame, or boredom. The relationship between the common understandings and social affects may be illustrated by thinking of the acting-out student-boarders' procedure as one that involved the production of bewilderment and anger by treating an important state of affairs as something that it "obviously," "naturally," and "really" is not.

The existence of a definite and strong relationship between common understandings and social affects can be demonstrated and some of its features explored by the deliberate display of distrust, a procedure that for us produced highly standardized effects. The rationale was as follows.

One of the background expectancies Schutz described concerns the sanctioned use of doubt as a constituent feature of a world that is being understood in common. Schutz proposed that for the *conduct of his everyday affairs* the person assumes, assumes the other person assumes as well, and assumes that as he assumes it of the other person the other person assumes of him that a relationship of undoubted correspondence is the sanctioned relationship between the actual appearances of an object and the intended object that appears in a particular way. For the person conducting his everyday affairs, objects (for him as he expects for others) are as they appear to be. To treat this relationship under a *rule* of doubt requires that the necessity and motivation for such a rule be justified.

We anticipated that because of the differing relationship of an exhibited rule of doubt (distrust)[5] that the other person was as he appeared to be to the legitimate texture of common expectancies, there should be different affective states for the doubter and the doubted. On the part of the person distrusted there should be the demand for justification, and when it was not forthcoming, as "anyone could see" it could not be, anger. For the experimenter, we expected embarrassment to result from the disparity that the distrusting procedure would create between the lesser thing that the experimenter's challenges of "what anyone could see" made him out to be under the gaze of his victim and the competent person he with others knew himself "after all" to be but which the procedure required that he could not claim.

Like Santayana's clock, this formulation was neither right nor wrong. Although the procedure produced what we anticipated, it also furnished us and the experimenters with more than we had bargained for.

Students were instructed to engage someone in conversation and to imagine and act on the assumption that what the other person was saying was directed by hidden motives that were his real ones. They were to assume that the other person was trying to trick them or mislead them.

In only 2 of 35 accounts did students attempt the assignment with strangers. Most students were afraid that such a situation would get out of hand, so they selected friends, roommates, siblings, and family members. Even so, they reported considerable rehearsal in imagination, much review of possible consequences, and deliberate selections among eligible persons.

The attitude was difficult to sustain and carry through. Students reported acute awareness of being "in an artificial game," of being unable "to live the part," and of frequently being "at a loss as to what to do next." In the course of listening to the other person experimenters would lose sight of the assignment. One student spoke for several when she said she was unable to get any results because so much of her effort was directed to maintaining an attitude of distrust that she was unable to follow the conversation. She said she was unable to imagine how her fellow conversationalists might be deceiving her because they were talking about such inconsequential matters.

With many students the assumption that the other person was not what he appeared to be and was to be distrusted was the same as the attribution that the other person was angry with them and hated them. On the other hand, many victims, although they complained that the student had no reason to be angry with them, offered unsolicited attempts at explanation and conciliation. When this was of no avail there followed frank displays of anger and "disgust."

Anticipated and acute embarrassment swiftly materialized for the two students who attempted the procedure with strangers. After badgering a bus driver for assurances that the bus would pass the street that she wanted and receiving several assurances in return that indeed the bus did pass the street, the exasperated bus driver shouted so that all passengers overheard, "Look lady, I told you once, didn't I? How many times do I have to tell you!" She reported, "I shrank to the back of the bus to sink as low as I could in the seat. I had gotten a good case of cold feet, a flaming face, and a strong dislike for my assignment."

There were very few reports of shame or embarrassment from students who tried it with friends and family. Instead, they were surprised, and so were we, to find as one student reported that "once I started acting the role of a hated person I actually came to feel somewhat hated and by the time I left the table I was quite angry." Even more surprising to us, many reported that they found the procedure enjoyable, and this included the real anger not only of others but of their own.

Although students' explanations easily restored most situations, some episodes "turned serious" and left a residue of disturbance for one or both parties that offered explanation did not resolve. This can be illustrated in the report of a student housewife who, at the conclusion of dinner and with some trepidation, questioned her husband about his having worked late the night before and raised a question about his actually having played poker as he claimed on an evening of the week before. Without asking him what he had actually done she indicated an explanation was called for. He replied sarcastically, "You seem to be uneasy about something. Do you know what it might be? This conversation would no doubt make more sense if *I* knew too." She accused him of deliberately avoiding the subject, although the subject had not been mentioned. He insisted that *she* tell *him* what the *subject* was. When she did not say, he asked directly, "Okay, what's the joke?" Instead of replying "I gave him a long hurt look." He became visibly upset, became very solicitous, gentle, and persuasive. In response she acknowledged the experiment. He stalked off obviously unhappy, and for the remainder of the evening was sullen and suspicious. She, in the meanwhile, remained at the table piqued and unsettled about the remarks that her statements had drawn forth about his not being bored at work "with all the insinuations it might or could mean," particularly the insinuation that he was not bored at work but he *was* bored with her and at home. She wrote, "I was actually bothered by his remarks . . . I felt more upset and worried than he did throughout the experiment . . . about how imperturbable he seemed to be." Neither attempted nor wanted to discuss the matter further. The following day the husband confessed that he had been considerably disturbed and had the following reactions in this order: determination to remain calm; shock at his wife's "suspicious nature"; surprise to find that cheating on her was liable to be hard; a determination to make her figure out her own answers to her questions without any denial or help from him; extreme relief when the encounter was revealed to have been experimentally contrived; but finally a residue of uneasy feelings which he characterized as "his shaken ideas of my (the wife's) nature which remained for the rest of the evening."

BACKGROUND UNDERSTANDINGS AND BEWILDERMENT

Earlier, the argument was made that the possibility of common understanding does not consist in demonstrated measures of shared knowledge of social structure but consists instead and entirely in the enforceable character of actions in compliance with the expectancies of everyday life as a morality. Common sense knowledge of the facts of social life for the members of the society is institutionalized knowledge of the real world. Not only does common sense knowledge portray a real society for members but in the manner of a self fulfilling prophecy the features of the real society are produced by persons' motivated compliance with these background expectancies. Hence, the stability of concerted actions that occur under the auspices of this compliance, as well as the extent and severity of disturbances in concerted actions, should vary directly with whatsoever are the real conditions of social organization that guarantee persons' motivated compliance with this background texture of relevances as a legitimate order of beliefs about life in society seen "from within" the society. Seen from the person's point of view, his commitments to motivated compliance consist of his grasp of and subscription to the "natural facts of life in society."

Such considerations suggest that the firmer a societal member's grasp of "what anyone like us necessarily knows," the more severe should be his disturbance when "natural facts of life" are impugned for him as a depiction of his real circumstances. To test this suggestion, a procedure would need to modify the *objective* structure of the familiar, known-in-common environment by rendering the background expectancies inoperative. Specifically, this modification would consist of subjecting a person to a breach of the background expectancies of everyday life while (a) making it difficult for the person to interpret his situation as a game, an experiment, a deception, a play, i.e. as something other than the one known according to the attitude of everyday life as a matter of enforceable morality and action, (b) making it necessary that he reconstruct the "natural facts" but giving him insufficient time to manage the reconstruction with respect to required mastery of practical circumstances for which he must call upon his knowledge of the "natural facts," and (c) requiring that he manage the reconstruction of the natural facts by himself and without consensual validation.

Presumably, he should have no alternative but to try to normalize the resultant incongruities within the order of events of everyday life. Under the developing effort itself, events should lose their perceivedly normal character. The member should be unable to recognize an event's status as typical. Judgments of likelihood should fail him. He should be unable to assign present occurrences to similar orders of events he has known in the past. He should be unable to assign, let alone to "see at a glance," the conditions under which the events can be reproduced. He should be unable to order these events to means-ends relationships. The conviction should be undermined that the moral authority of the familiar society compels their occurrence. Stable and "realistic" matchings of intentions and objects should dissolve, by which I mean that the ways, otherwise familiar to him, in which the objective perceived environment serves as both the motivating grounds of feelings and is motivated by feelings directed to it should become obscure. In short, the members' real perceived environment on losing its known in common background should become "specifically senseless."[6] Ideally speaking, behaviors directed to such a senseless environment should be those of bewilderment, uncertainty, internal conflict, psychosocial isolation, acute and nameless anxiety along with various symptoms of acute depersonalization. Structures of interaction should be correspondingly disorganized.

This is expecting quite a lot of a breach of the background expectancies. Obviously, we would settle for less if the results of a procedure for their breach were at all encouraging about this formulation. As it happens, the procedure produced convincing and easily detected bewilderment and anxiety.

To begin with, it is necessary to specify just what expectancies we are dealing with. Shutz reported that the feature of a scene, "known in common with others," was compound and consisted of several constituents. Because they have been discussed elsewhere,[7] I shall restrict discussion to brief enumeration.

According to Schutz, the person assumes, assumes that the other person assumes as well, and assumes that as he assumes it of the other person the other person assumes the same for him:

1. That the determinations assigned to an event by the witness are required matters that hold on grounds that specifically disregard personal opinion or socially structured circumstances of particular witnesses, i.e. that the determinations are required as matters of "objective necessity" or "facts of nature."

2. That a relationship of undoubted correspondence is the sanctioned relationship between the presented-appearance-of-the-object and the intended-object-that-presents-itself-in-the-perspective-of-the-particular-appearance.

3. That the event that is known in the manner that it is known can actually and potentially affect the witness and can be affected by his action.

4. That the meanings of events are products of a socially standardized process of naming, reification, and idealization of the user's stream of experience, i.e. are the products of a language.

5. That present determinations of an event, whatsoever these may be, are determinations that were intended on previous occasions and that may be again intended in identical fashion on an indefinite number of future occasions.

6. That the intended event is retained as the temporally identical event throughout the stream of experience.

7. That the event has as its context of interpretation: (a) a commonly entertained scheme of interpretation consisting of a standardized system of signals and coding rules, and (b) "What anyone knows," i.e. a pre-established corpus of socially warranted knowledge.

8. That the actual determinations that the event exhibits for the witness are the potential determinations that it would exhibit for the other person were they to exchange positions.

9. That to each event there corresponds its determinations that originate in the witness's and in the other person's particular biography. From the witness's point of view, such determinations are irrelevant for the purposes at hand of either, and both he and the other have selected and interpreted the actual and potential determinations of events in an empirically identical manner that is sufficient for all their practical purposes.

10. That there is a characteristic disparity between the publicly acknowledged determinations and the personal, withheld determinations of events, and that this private knowledge is held in reserve, i.e. that the event means for both the witness and the other more than the witness can say.

11. That alterations of this characteristic disparity remain within the witness's autonomous control.

It is *not* the case that what an event exhibits as a distinctive determination is a condition of its membership in a known-in-the-manner-of-common-sense-environment. Instead, the conditions of its membership are the attributions that its determinations, *whatever they might substantively consist of*, could be seen by the other person if their positions were exchanged, or that its features are not assigned as matters of personal preference but are to be seen by anyone, i.e. the previously enumerated features. These and only these enumerated features *irrespective* of any other determinations of an event define the common sense character of an event. Whatever other determinations an event of everyday life may exhibit—whether its determinations are those of persons' motives, their life histories, the distributions of income in the population, kinship obligations, the organization of an industry, or what ghosts do when night falls—if and only if the event has for the witness the enumerated determinations is it an event in an environment "known in common with others."

Such attributions are features of witnessed events that are seen without being noticed. They are demonstrably relevant to the common sense that the actor makes of what is going on about him. They inform the witness about any particular appearance of an interpersonal environment. They inform the witness as to the real objects that actual appearances are the appearances of, but without these attributed features necessarily being recognized in a deliberate or conscious fashion.

Since each of the expectancies that make up the attitude of daily life assigns an expected feature to the actor's environment, it should be possible to breach these expectancies by deliberately modifying scenic events so as to disappoint these attributions. By definition, surprise is possible with respect to each of these expected features. The nastiness of surprise should vary directly with the extent to which the person, as a matter of moral necessity, complies with their use as a scheme for assigning witnessed appearances their status as events in a perceivedly normal environment. In short, the realistic grasp by a collectivity member of the natural facts of life, and his commitment to a knowledge of them as a condition of self-esteem as a bona-fide and competent collectivity member,[8] is the condition that we require in order to maximize his confusion upon the occasion that the grounds of this grasp are made a source of irreducible incongruity.

I designed a procedure to breach these expectancies while satisfying the three conditions under which their breach would presumably produce confusion, i.e. that the person could not turn the situation into a play, a joke, an experiment, a deception and the like, or, in Lewinian terminology, that he could not "leave the field"; that he have insufficient time to work through a redefinition of his real circumstances; and that he be deprived of consensual support for an alternative definition of social reality.

Twenty-eight pre-medical students were run individually through a three-hour experimental interview. As part of the solicitation of subjects as well as at the beginning of the interview, the experimenter identified himself as a representative of an Eastern medical school who was attempting to learn why the medical school intake interview was such a stressful situation. It was hoped that identifying the experimenter as a person with medical school ties would make it difficult for students to "leave the field" once the expectancy breaching procedure began. How the other two conditions of (a) managing a redefinition in insufficient time and (b) not being able to count on consensual support for an alternative definition of social reality were met will be apparent in the following description.

During the first hour of the interview, the student furnished the "medical school representative" with the medical interview facts-of-life by answering for the representative such questions as "What sources of information about a candidate are available to medical schools?", "What kind of man are the medical schools looking for?", "What should a good candidate do in the interview?", "What should he avoid?" With this much completed, the student was told that the representative's research interests had been satisfied. The student was then asked if he would care to hear a recording of an actual interview. All students wanted very much to hear the recording.

The recording was a faked one between a "medical school interviewer" and an "applicant." The applicant was a boor, his language was ungrammatical and filled with colloquialisms, he was evasive, he contradicted the interviewer, he bragged, he ran down other schools and professions, he insisted on knowing how he had done in the interview. Detailed assessments by the student of the recorded applicant were obtained immediately after the recording was finished.

The student was then given information from the applicant's "official record." Performance information, and characterological information was furnished in that order. Performance information dealt with the applicant's activities, grades, family background, courses, charity work and the like. Characterological information consisted of character assessments by "Dr. Gardner, the medical school interviewer," "six psychiatrically trained members of the admissions committee who had heard only the recorded interview," and "other students."

The information was deliberately contrived to contradict the principal points in the student's assessment. For example, if the student said that the applicant must have come from a lower-class family, he was told that the applicant's father was vice-president of a firm that manufactured pneumatic doors for trains and buses. Was the applicant ignorant? Then he had excelled in courses like The Poetry of Milton and Dramas of Shakespeare. If the student said the applicant did not know how to get along with people, then the applicant had worked as a voluntary solicitor for Sydenham Hospital in New York City and had raised $32,000 from 30 "big givers." That the applicant was stupid and would not do well in a scientific field was met by citing A's in organic and physical chemistry and graduate-level performance in an undergraduate research course.

Students wanted very much to know what "the others" thought of the applicant and had he been admitted? The student was told that the applicant had been admitted and was living up to the promise that the medical school interviewer and the "six psychiatrists" had found and expressed in a strong recommendation of the applicant's characterological fitness which was read to the student. As for the views of other students, the student was told (for example) that 30 other students had been seen, that 28 were in entire agreement with the medical school interviewer's assessment, and that the remaining two had been slightly uncertain but at the first bit of information had seen him just as the others had.

Following this, the student was invited to listen to the record a second time, after which he was asked to assess the applicant again.

Results. Twenty-five of the 28 students were taken in. The following does not apply to the three who were convinced there was a deception. Two of these are discussed at the conclusion of this section.

Students managed incongruities of performance data with vigorous attempts to make it factually compatible with their original and very derogatory assessments. For example, many said that the applicant sounded like or was a lower-class person. When they were told that his father was vice-president of a national corporation that manufactured pneumatic doors for trains and buses, they replied like this:

> "That explains why he said he had to work. Probably his father made him work. That would make a lot of his moans unjustified in the sense that things were really not so bad."

When told he had a straight A average in physical-science courses, students began to acknowledge bewilderment openly.

> "Well! I think you can analyze it this way. In psychological terms. See—one possible way—now I may be all *wet* but this is the way I look at *that*. He probably suffered from an inferiority complex and that's an over compensation for his inferiority complex. His *great* marks—his *good* marks are a compensation for his failure—in social dealings perhaps, I don't know."

Attempts to resolve the incongruities produced by the character assessment of "Gardner" and "the other six judges" were very much less frequent than normalizing attempts with performance information. Open expressions of bewilderment and anxiety interspersed with silent ruminations were characteristic:

> (Whistles.) I—I don't think he sounded well bred at all. That whole tone of voice!! —I— Perhaps you noticed though, when he said "You should have said in the first place," *before* he (the recorded medical school examiner) took it with a smile.—But even so! No, no I can't see that. "You should have said that before." Maybe he was being funny though. Exercising a—No! To me it sounded impertinent!

Soon after the performance data produced its consternation, students occasionally asked what the other students made of him. Only after they were given "Dr. Gardner's" assessment, and their responses to it had been made, were the opinions of "the other students" given. In some cases the subject was told "34 out of 35 before you agreed with Dr. Gardner," sometimes 43 out of 45, 19 out of 20, 51 out of 52. All the numbers were large. For 18 of the 25 students, the delivery hardly varied from the following protocol:

> (36 out of 37) I would go back on my former opinion but I wouldn't go back too far. I just don't see it.—Why should I have these different standards? Were my opinions more or less in agreement? (No.) That leads me to think.—That's funny. Unless you got thirty-six unusual people. I can't understand it. Maybe it's my personality. (Does it make any difference?) It does make a difference if I assume they're correct. What I consider is proper, they don't.—It's my attitude—Still in all a man of that sort would alienate me, a wise guy type to be avoided. Of course you can talk like that with other fellows—but in an interview? . . . Now I'm more confused than I was at the beginning of the entire interview. I think I ought to go home and look in the mirror and talk to myself. Do you have any ideas? (Why? Does it disturb you?) Yes it *does* disturb me! It makes me think my abilities to judge people and values are way off from normal. It's not a healthy situation. (What difference does it make?) If I act the way I act it seems to me that I'm just putting my head in the lion's mouth. I did have preconceptions but they're shattered all to hell. It makes me wonder about myself. Why should I have these different standards. It all points to me.

Of the 25 subjects that were taken in, seven were unable to resolve the incongruity of having been wrong about such an obvious matter and were unable to "see" the alternative. Their suffering was dramatic and unrelieved. Five more resolved it with the view that the medical school had accepted a good man; five others with the view that it had accepted a boor. Although they changed they nevertheless did not abandon their former views. For them Gardner's view could be seen "in general" but it was a grasp without conviction. When their attention was drawn to particulars the general picture would evaporate. These subjects were willing to entertain and use the "general" picture, but they suffered whenever indigestible particulars of the same portrait came into view. Subscription to the "general" picture was accompanied by a recitation of characteristics that were not only the opposite of those in the subject's original assessment but were intensified by superlative adjectives, so that where previously the candidate was gauche, he was now "supremely" poised; where he had been boorish, he was "very" natural; where he had been hysterical, he was "very" calm. Further, they saw the new features through a new appreciation of the way the medical examiner had been listening. They *saw*, for example, that the examiner *was smiling* when the applicant had forgotten to offer him a cigarette.

Three more subjects were convinced that there was a deception and acted on the conviction through the interview. They showed no disturbance. Two of them showed acute suffering as soon as it appeared that the interview was finished and they were being dismissed with no acknowledgement of a deception.

Three others, by suffering in silence, confounded the experimenter. Without giving any indication to the experimenter, they regarded the interview as an experimental one in which they were required to solve some problems and thought therefore they were being asked to do as well as possible and to make no changes in their opinions, for only then would they be contributing to the study. They were difficult for the experimenter to understand during the interview because they displayed marked anxiety, yet their remarks were bland and were not addressed to the matters that were provoking it. Finally, three more subjects contrasted with the others. One of these insisted that the character assessments were semantically ambiguous and because there was insufficient information a "high correlation opinion" was not possible. A second, the only one in the series, according to his account found the second portrait as convincing as the original one. When the deception was revealed he was disturbed that he could have been as convinced as he was. The third one, in the face of everything, showed only slight disturbance of very short duration. However, he alone among the subjects had already been interviewed for medical school and had excellent medical school contacts. Despite a grade point average of less than C, he estimated his chances of admission as fair and had expressed his preference for a career in the diplomatic service over a career in medicine.

As a final observation, 22 of the 28 subjects expressed marked relief—10 of them with explosive expressions—when the deception was disclosed. Unanimously they said that the news of the deception permitted them to return to their former views. Seven subjects had to be convinced that there had been a deception. When the deception was revealed, they asked what they were to believe. Was the experimenter telling them that there had been a deception in order to make them feel better? No pains were spared and whatever truth or lies that had to be told were told in order to establish the truth that there had been a deception.

Because motivated compliance to the expectancies that make up the attitude of daily life consists from the person's point of view of his grasp of and subscription to the "natural facts of life," variations in the organizational conditions of motivated compliance for different collectivity members would consist of members' differential grasp of and subscription to the "natural facts of life." Hence, the severity of the effects described above should vary directly with the enforceable commitments of members to a grasp of the natural facts of life. Further, because of the *objective* character of the grasped common moral order of the facts of collectivity life, the severity should vary with their committed grasp of the natural facts of life and independently of "personality characteristics." By personality characteristics I mean all characteristics of persons that investigators use methodologically to account for a person's courses of action by referring these actions to more or less systematically conceived motivational and

Figure 1

Correlation of the extent of subject's subscription to the "natural facts" as an institutionalized order of knowledge about pre-medical circumstances and initial anxiety score.

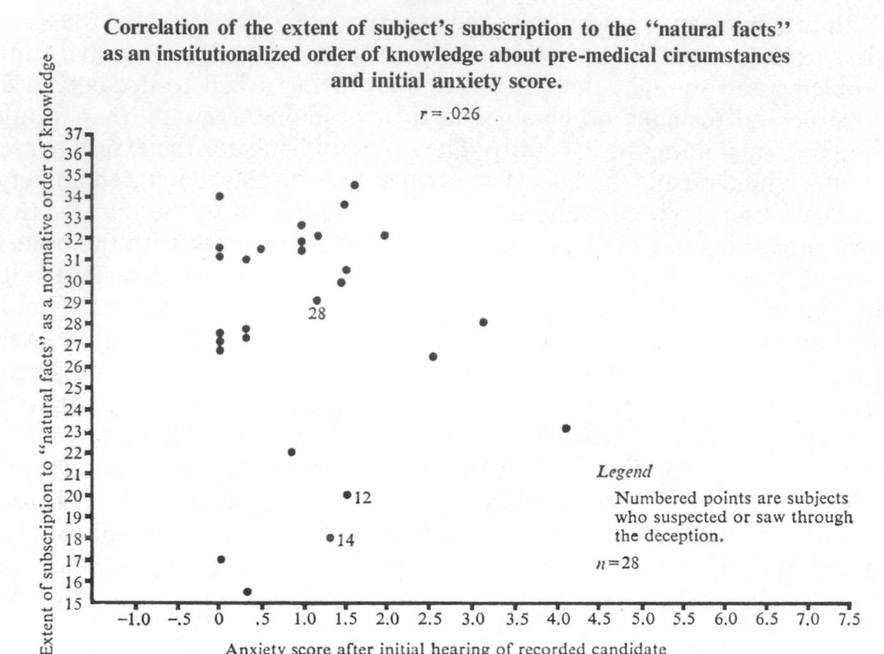

"inner life" variables while disregarding social and cultural system effects. The results of most conventional personality assessment devices and clinical psychiatric procedures satisfy this condition.

Thereby, the following phenomenon should be discoverable. Imagine a procedure whereby a convincing assessment can be made of the extent of a person's committed grasp of the "natural facts of social life." Imagine another procedure whereby the extent of a person's confusion can be assessed ranging through the various degrees and mixtures of the behaviors described before. For a set of unselected persons, and independently of personality determinations, the initial relationship between the committed "grasp of natural facts" and "confusion" should be random. Under the breach of the expectancies of everyday life, given the conditions for the optimal production of disturbance, persons should shift in exhibited confusion in an amount that is coordinate with the original extent of their grasp of the "natural facts of life."

The type of phenomenon that I propose is discoverable is portrayed in Figures 1 and 2, which are based on the study of the 28 pre-medical students reported above. Prior to the introduction of incongruous material, the extent of students' subscription to a common moral order of facts of pre-medical school life and the students' anxiety correlated —.026. After the incongruous material had been introduced and unsuccessfully normalized, and before the deception was revealed, the correlation was .751.

Figure 2

Correlation of the extent of subject's subscription to the "natural facts" as an institutionalized order of knowledge about pre-medical circumstances and relative anxiety score.

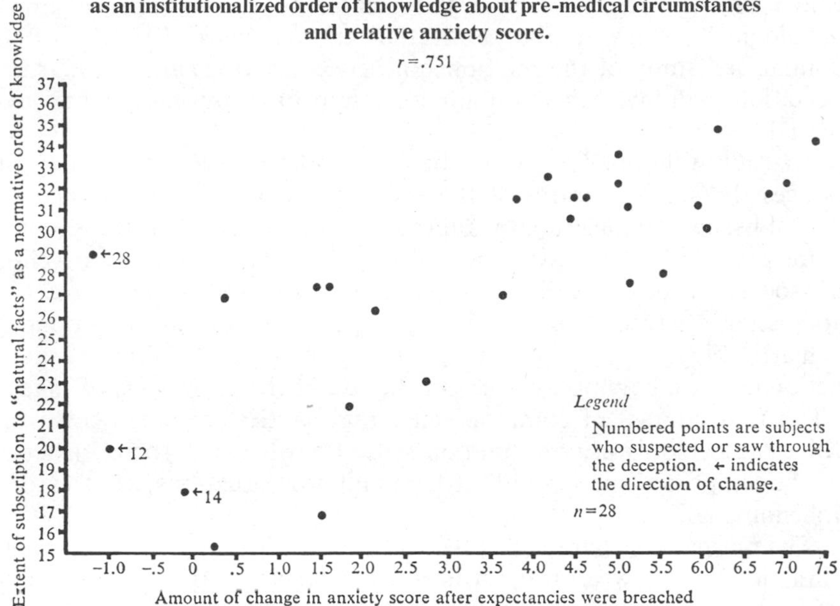

Because assessment procedures were extremely crude, because of serious errors in design and procedure, and because of the *post hoc* argument, *these results do no more than illustrate what I am talking about. Under no circumstances should they be considered as findings.*

THE RELEVANCE OF COMMON UNDERSTANDINGS TO THE FACT THAT MODELS OF MAN IN SOCIETY PORTRAY HIM AS A JUDGMENTAL DOPE

Many studies have documented the finding that the social standardiza- on of common understandings, irrespective of what it is that is standard- ed, orients persons' actions to scenic events, and furnishes persons the ounds upon which departures from perceivedly normal courses of airs are detectable, restoration is made, and effortful action is mobilized. Social science theorists—most particularly social psychiatrists, social chologists, anthropologists, and sociologists—have used the fact of dardization to conceive the character and consequences of actions that ply with standardized expectancies. Generally, they have acknow- d but otherwise neglected the fact that by these same actions persons ver, create, and sustain this standardization. An important and prevalent consequence of this neglect is that of being misled about the nature and conditions of stable actions. This occurs by making out the member of the society to be a judgmental dope of a cultural and/or psychological sort, with the result that the *unpublished* results of any accomplished study of the relationship between actions and standardized expectations will invariably contain enough incongruous material to invite essential revision.

By "cultural dope" I refer to the man-in-the-sociologist's-society who produces the stable features of the society by acting in compliance with pre-established and legitimate alternatives of action that the common culture provides. The "psychological dope" is the man-in-the-psychologist's-society who produces the stable features of the society by choices among alternative courses of action that are compelled on the grounds of psychiatric biography, conditioning history, and the variables of mental functioning. The common feature in the use of these "models of man" is the fact that courses of common sense rationalities[9] of judgment, which involve the person's use of common sense knowledge of social structures over the temporal "succession" of here and now situations, are treated as epiphenomenal.

The misleading character of the use of the judgmental dope to portray the relationship between standardized expectancies and courses of action goes to the problem of adequate explanation as the controlling consideration in the investigator's decision to either consider or disregard the common sense rationalities when deciding the necessary relationships between courses of action, given such problematic considerations as perspectival choice, subjectivity, and inner time. A favored solution is to portray what the member's actions will have come to by using the stable structures—what they came to—as a point of theoretical departure from which to portray the necessary character of the pathways whereby the end result is assembled. Hierarchies of need dispositions and common culture as enforced rules of action are favored devices for bringing the problem of necessary inference to terms, although at the cost of making out th
person-in-society to be a judgmental dope.

How is an investigator *doing* it when he is making out the member of
society to be a judgmental dope? Several examples will furnish some spec
fics and consequences.

I assigned students the task of bargaining for standard-priced m
chandise. The relevant standardized expectancy is the "institutionali
one-price rule," a constituent element, according to Parsons,[10] of
institution of contract. Because of its "internalized" character, the stude
customers should have been fearful and shamed by the prospec
assignment and shamed by having done it. Reciprocally, anxiety and a
should have been commonly reported for sales persons.

Sixty-eight students were required to accomplish one trial on any item costing no more than two dollars, and were to offer much less than the asking price. Another 67 students were required to accomplish a series of six trials: three for items costing two dollars or less, and three for items costing fifty dollars or more.

Findings. (a) Sales persons can be dismissed as either having been dopes in different ways than current theories of standardized expectancies provide, or not dopes enough. A few showed some anxiety; occasionally one got angry. (b) 20% of the single tries refused to try or aborted the effort, as compared with three percent of those who had been assigned the series of six trials. (c) When the bargaining episode was analyzed as consisting of a series of steps—anticipation of the trial, approaching the sales person, actually making the offer, the ensuing interaction, terminating the episode, and afterwards—it was found that fears occurred with the greatest frequency in both groups in anticipating the assignment and approaching the sales person *for the first try*. Among the single trials, the number of persons who reported discomfort declined with each successive step in the sequence. Most of the students who bargained in two or more trials reported that by the third episode they were enjoying the assignment. (d) Most students reported less discomfort in bargaining for high priced than low priced merchandise. (e) Following the six episodes, many students reported that they had learned to their "surprise" that one could bargain in standard-priced settings with some realistic chance of an advantageous outcome, and planned to do so in the future, particularly for costly merchandise.

Such findings suggest that one can make the member of the society out to be a cultural dope (a) by portraying a member of the society as one who operates by the rules when one is actually talking about the anticipatory anxiety that prevents him from permitting a situation to develop, let alone confronting a situation in which he has the alternative of acting or not with respect to a rule; or (b) by overlooking the practical and theoretical importance of the mastery of fears. (c) If upon the arousal of troubled feelings, persons avoid tinkering with these "standardized" expectancies, the standardization could consist of an *attributed* standardization that is supported by the fact that persons avoid the very situations in which they might learn about them.

Lay as well as professional knowledge of the nature of rule governed actions and the consequences of breaching the rules is prominently based on just such procedure. Indeed, the more important the rule, the greater is the likelihood that knowledge is based on avoided tests. Strange findings must certainly await anyone who examines the expectancies that make up routine backgrounds of commonplace activities, for they have rarely been exposed by investigators even to as much revision as an imaginative rehearsal of their breach would produce.

Another way in which the member of the society can be made a judgmental dope is by using any of the available theories of the formal properties of signs and symbols to portray the way persons construe environmental displays as significant ones. The dope is made out in several ways. I shall mention two.

(a) Characteristically, formal investigations have been concerned either with devising normative theories of symbolic usages or, while seeking descriptive theories, have settled for normative ones. In either case it is necessary to instruct the construing member to act in accordance with the investigator's instructions in order to guarantee that the investigator will be able to study their usages as instances of the usages the investigator has in mind. But, following Wittgenstein,[11] persons' actual usages are rational usages in *some* "language game." What is *their* game? As long as this programmatic question is neglected, it is inevitable that person's usages will fall short. The more will this be so, the more are subjects' interests in usages dictated by different practical considerations than those of investigators.

(b) Available theories have many important things to say about such sign functions as marks and indications, but they are silent on such overwhelmingly more common functions as glosses, synecdoche, documented representation, euphemism, irony, and double entendre. References to common sense knowledge of ordinary affairs may be safely disregarded in detecting and analyzing marks and indications as sign functions *because* users disregard them as well. The analysis of irony, double entendre, glosses, and the like, however, imposes different requirements. Any attempt to consider the related character of utterances, meanings, perspectives, and orders necessarily requires reference to common sense knowledge of ordinary affairs.

Although investigators have neglected these "complex" usages, they have not put their problematic character entirely aside. Instead, they have glossed them by portraying the usages of the member of a language community as either culture bound or need compelled, or by construing the pairing of appearances and intended objects—the pairing of "sign" and "referrent"—as an association. In each case, a procedural description of such symbolic usages is precluded by neglecting the judgmental work of the user.

Precisely this judgmental work, along with its reliance upon and its reference to common sense knowledge of social structures, forced itself upon our attention in every case where incongruities were induced. Our attention was forced *because* our subjects had exactly their judgmental work and common sense knowledge to contend with as matters that the incongruities presented to them as practical problems. Every procedure that involved departures from an anticipated course of ordinary affairs, regardless of whether the departure was gross or slight, aroused recognition in subjects that the experimenter was engaged in double talk, irony, glosses, euphemism, or lies. This occurred repeatedly in departures from ordinary game play.

Students were instructed to play ticktacktoe and to mix their subjects by age, sex, and degree of acquaintance. After drawing the ticktacktoe matrix, they invited the subject to move first. After the subject made his move, the experimenter erased the subject's mark, moved it to another square and made his own mark but without giving any indications that anything about the play was unusual. In half of 247 trials students reported that subjects treated the move as a gesture with hidden but definite significance. Subjects were convinced that the experimenter was "after something" that he was not saying, and whatever he "really" was doing had nothing to do with ticktacktoe. He was making a sexual pass; he was commenting on the subject's stupidity; he was making a slurring or an impudent gesture. Identical effects occurred when students bargained for standard-priced merchandise, or asked the other to clarify his commonplace remarks, or joined without invitation a strange group of conversationalists, or used a gaze that during an ordinary conversation wandered "randomly" by time to various objects in the scene.

Still another way of making the person out for a cultural dope is to simplify the communicative texture of his behavioral environment. For example, by giving physical events preferred status one can theorize out of existence the way the person's scene, as a texture of potential and actual events, contains not only appearances and attributions but the person's own lively inner states as well. We encountered this in the following procedure.

Students were instructed to select someone other than a family member, and in the course of an ordinary conversation and without indicating that anything unusual was happening to bring their faces up to the subject's until their noses were almost touching. According to most of the 79 accounts, regardless of whether the pairs were the same or different sexes, whether they were acquaintances or close friends (strangers were prohibited), and regardless of age differences except where children were involved, the procedure motivated in *both* experimenter and subject attributions of a sexual intent on the part of the other, though confirmation of this intent was withheld by the very character of the procedure. Such attributions to the other were accompanied by the person's own impulses, which themselves became part of the scene as their not only being desired but their desiring. The unconfirmed invitation to choose had its accompanying conflictful hesitancy about acknowledging the choice and having been chosen. Attempted avoidance, bewilderment, acute embarrassment, furtiveness, and above all uncertainties of these as well as uncertainties of fear, hope, and anger were characteristic. These effects were most pronounced between males. Characteristically, experimenters were unable to restore the situation. Subjects were only partially accepting of the experimenter's explanation that it has been done "as an experiment for a course in sociology." They often complained, "All right, it was an experiment, but why did you have to choose *me*?" Characteristically, subject and experimenter wanted some further resolution than the explanation furnished but were uncertain about what it could or should consist of.

Finally, the member may be made out to be a judgmental dope by portraying routine actions as those governed by prior agreements, and by making the likelihood that a member will recognize deviance depend upon the existence of prior agreements. That this is a matter of mere theoretical preference whose use theorizes essential phenomena out of existence can be seen by considering the commonplace fact that persons will hold each other to agreements whose terms they never actually stipulated. This neglected property of common understandings has far reaching consequences when it is explicitly brought into the portrayal of the nature of "agreements."

Apparently no matter how specific the terms of common understandings may be—a contract may be considered the prototype—they attain the status of an agreement for persons only insofar as the stipulated conditions carry along an unspoken but understood *et cetera*[12] clause. Specific stipulations are formulated under the rule of an agreement by being brought under the jurisdiction of the *et cetera* clause. This does not occur once and for all, but is essentially bound to both the inner and outer temporal course of activities and thereby to the progressive development of circumstances and their contingencies. Therefore it is both misleading and incorrect to think of an agreement as an actuarial device whereby persons are enabled as of any "here and now" to predict each other's future activities. More accurately, common understandings that have been formulated under the rule of an agreement are used by persons to normalize whatever their actual activities turn out to be. Not only can contingencies arise, but persons know as of any "here and now" that contingencies can materialize or be invented at any time that it must be decided whether or not what the parties actually did satisfied the agreement. The *et cetera* clause provides for the certainty that unknown conditions are at every hand in terms of which an agreement, as of any particular moment, can be retrospectively reread to find out in light of present practical circumstances what the agreement "really" consisted of "in the first place" and "all along." That the work of bringing present circumstances under the rule of previously agreed activity is sometimes contested should not be permitted to mask its pervasive and routine use as an ongoing and essential feature of "actions in accord with common understandings."

This process, which I shall call a method of discovering agreements by eliciting or imposing a respect for the rule of practical circumstances, is a version of practical ethics. Although it has received little if any attention by social scientists, it is a matter of the most abiding and commonplace concern in everyday affairs and common sense theories of these affairs. Adeptness in the deliberate manipulation of *et cetera* considerations for the furtherance of specific advantages is an occupational talent of lawyers and is specifically taught to law school students. One should not suppose, however, that because it is a lawyer's skill, that only lawyers are skilled at it, or that only those who do so deliberately do so at all. The method is general to the phenomenon of the society as a system of rule-governed activities.[13] It is available as one of the mechanisms whereby potential and actual successes and windfalls, on the one hand, and the disappointments, frustrations, and failures, on the other, that persons must inevitably encounter by reason of seeking to comply with agreements, can be managed while retaining the perceived reasonableness of actual socially organized activities.

A small-scale but accurate instance of this phenomenon was consistently produced by a procedure in which the experimenter engaged others in conversation while he had a wire recorder hidden under his coat. In the course of the conversation the experimenter opened his jacket to reveal the recorder, saying, "See what I have?" An initial pause was almost invariably followed by the question, "What are you going to do with it?" Subjects claimed the breach of the expectancy that the conversation was "between us." The fact that the conversation was revealed to have been recorded motivated new possibilities, which the parties then sought to bring under the jurisdiction of an agreement that they had never specifically mentioned and that indeed did not previously exist. The conversation, now seen to have been recorded, thereby acquired fresh and problematic import in view of unknown uses to which it might be turned. An agreed privacy was thereupon treated as though it had operated all along.

CONCLUDING REMARKS

The expectancies that make up the attitude of everyday life are constitutive of the institutionalized common understandings of the practical everyday organization and workings of society as it is seen "from within." Modification of these expectancies must thereby modify the real environments of the societies' members. Such modifications transform one perceived environment of real objects into another environment of real objects.

Each of many kinds of modifications of the background of everyday expectancies furnish an area of needed further work. Each modification has as its counterpart transformed objective structures of the behavioral environments that each modification produces. It is disconcerting to find how little we know about these different sets of background expectancies and the different objective environments that they constitute.

One such modification consists of the ceremonial transformation of one environment of real objects into another. Such modifications occur in play, theatre going, high ceremony, religious conversion, convention going, and scientific inquiry. A second modification consists of instrumental transformations of environments of real objects such as occur in experimentally-induced psychosis, extreme fatigue, acute sensory deprivation, brain injuries, prefrontal lobotomies, and the use of hallucinogenic drugs. A third transformation consists of neonate learning, which quite literally entails the growth of a world and is directed to the production of objective features of the persons' environment that "any competent member can see." The growth of the world is necessarily accompanied by the progressively enforced and enforceable compliance of the developing member to the attitude of daily life as a competent societal member's way of "looking at things." A fourth set of modifications is involved in adult socialization, distinguishable from neonate learning by the absence of radically naive expectancies. Other modifications are those of estrangement, which must include the various phenomena intended under the currently popular theme of "alienation," as well as the phenomena of the cultural stranger, of the major and minor forms of mental illness, of the degradation that accompanies charges of criminality and the fates of social incompetence found in mental retardation and old age. Modifications occur through mischief, playful and serious; through the subtle psychopathic effects of aging as one comes to learn that one may sin, cause others harm, and not "pay"; and through the discovery that the common societal orders that in adolescence appear so massive and homogeneous not only have their interstices but depend for their massiveness upon persons' continual improvizations. Finally, there is the modification that consists in the discovery and rationalization of the common sense world through the growth of social science as a social movement.

I have been arguing that a concern for the nature, production, and recognition of reasonable, realistic, and analyzable actions is not the monopoly of philosophers and professional sociologists. Members of a society are concerned as a matter of course and necessarily with these matters both as features and for the socially managed production of their everyday affairs. The study of common sense knowledge and common sense activities consists of treating as problematic phenomena the actual methods whereby members of a society, doing sociology, lay or professional, make the social structures of everyday activities observable. The "rediscovery" of common sense is possible perhaps because professional sociologists, like members, have had too much to do with common sense knowledge of social structures as both a topic and a resource for their inquiries and not enough to do with it only and exclusively as sociology's programmatic topic.

HARVEY SACKS

An Initial Investigation of the Usability of Conversational Data for Doing Sociology*

1.0 Among the basic resources we need in order to describe the materials we have collected are some *collections of membership categories*.[1] Our aim, which is to construct a description that provides the reproduceability of the conclusion a suicidal person may reach[2]—I have no one to turn to—involves us in attempting (a) to locate the collections of membership categories in terms of which the search for help for suicidalness is formulated, and (b) to describe the ways such collections are used to determine whether there are

* The materials used in this essay are almost entirely from transcribed telephone conversations between or on behalf of suicidal persons and staff

(*Notes to this selection will be found on pp. 430–431.*)

eligible persons available (to give "help"[3]).

1.0.1 The above formulation of our problem of description was arrived at in the course of the researches we are reporting here. Since that is so, and since we are explicitly introducing a way of doing sociology, it is appropriate to indicate how the formulation may be arrived at. Showing that will involve us in indicating the important sense in which this paper is necessarily a study in the methodology and relevance of Members'[4] activities of categorizing Members.

1.0.2 We may proceed to show how the formulation of (1.0) may be arrived at by developing a way of showing, first, that the task Members face of categorizing Members is completely general, and, second, how important this latter fact is.

1.1 It seems that the simplest way to show the generality of the categorization problem is by showing that no uncategorized population may be specified such that only one *categorization device* is available for categorizing the population's personnel.

1.1.1 By the term *categorization device* we mean that *collection of membership categories*,[5] containing at least a category, that may be applied to some population, containing at least a Member, so as to provide, by the use of some rules of application, for the pairing of at least a population Member and a categorization device member. A *device* is then a *collection* plus rules of application.

1.1.2 It is our task to show that for any population N (where N is equal to or larger than 1) there are at least two categorization devices available to Members, each of which (devices) (a) can categorize each Member of the population N in such a way that one does not get for any

members of an emergency psychiatric clinic. Transcriptions of the materials are collected in the appendix. In such transcriptions (C) refers to caller and (S) refers to staff.

The materials were collected and partially analyzed during the year I was a fellow of the Center for the Scientific Study of Suicide, Los Angeles (1963–64). I am greatly indebted to that institution and particularly its director, Dr. Edwin Schneidman, for financial and other support. The various drafts were written while I received financial support from the U.S. Air Force, AF-AFOSR-757-65, Harold Garfinkel, Principal Investigator. Acknowledging his support is a seriously synecdochal expression of what is a largely unacknowledgeable, merely pervasive impact on me.

A very much shorter version of this research was presented under the title "The Search for Help: No One to Turn To" in the collection *Essays in Self Destruction*, edited by Edwin Schneidman (New York: Science House). A more discursive version, also with the latter title, was submitted in partial fulfillment of the requirements for the Ph.D., to the Department of Sociology, University of California, Berkeley.

L. Churchill, E. Schegloff, D. Sudnow and D. L. Weider read and commented extensively on each of the various drafts the paper went through. Sudnow and Aaron Cicourel were especially helpful during the final stages of the work.

Finally, I should like to note that the draft here presented was completed in June of 1965. Without apologizing for it I do want to emphasize that it was an initial attempt to deal with conversational materials and is not directly representative of the state of work that I am now engaged in.

Member of the population the pairing (population Member + no category member), where (b) no member of either device is a member of the other.[6] Any device that satisfies constraint (a) will hereafter be called a Pn-adequate device, type 1.

1.1.3 While many devices that are categorization devices by reference to (1.1.1) are not Pn-adequate ones, it is perfectly obvious that there are at least two Pn-adequate devices that Members do have available to them and do use. For example, there are the devices whose collections are (1) sex (male, female), and (2) age (young, old).[7] There are of course others.[8,9]

1.1.3.1 The conclusion of (1.1.3) is of course not news. Our aim in developing it was not the assertion of a proposed piece of news. It was to show how an intuitively obvious fact might be established so as to secure a base for indicating what is news—the import of the conclusion.

1.1.3.2 Sociologists frequently treat some categorization that Members have done as providing the sociologist with materials that are descriptive in the sense that such materials may then be used—as they stand—for further sociological investigation. Alternatively, sociologists themselves frequently use Members' categorization devices to categorize Members as one step in doing sociological inquiries.[10] In both cases the presumptive warrant for this usage is or would seem to be that the demonstrable correctness of the categorization may properly be established by some such procedure as looking to see whether the object (person) so categorized was properly categorized, i.e. by observing, for example, that the Member categorized as "negro" is a negro.

While such sorts of assertions may seem to be adequate, may seem to employ a correspondence notion of the correctness of an assertion, the observation of (1.1.3) operates to prevent the use of their warrant. A demonstration of our claim that the presumptive warrant is inadequate, and consideration of when it might be adequate will be presented, first at (1.2). Further analysis is required before the features of that demonstration may readily be employed.

1.1.4 In the formulation of the notion *categorization device* (1.1.1), reference was made to rules of application of such a device's categories to a population. Rules of application will be presented at various places in this paper. A first rule is one that for a population N can only hold for the use of Pn-adequate devices.

Consistency Rule. If some population of persons is being categorized, and if a category from some device's collection has been used to categorize a first Member of the population, then that category or other categories of the same collection *may* be used to categorize further Members of the population. As a correlate of the consistency rule, the following may be proposed: *Category Relevance Rule 1.* If any Pn-adequate device is appropriate for categorizing some population, then any category of such a device may be used on each Member of the population to provide a count of how many are and how many are not Members of that Category.[11]

1.1.4.1 The relevance of the consistency rule may readily be established.[12] If any population N consists of at least two Members, i.e. requires at least two categorizations to do the job of categorizing its Members, then it is possible that although one device would do, two or more devices can be used. In other words, some Members could be categorized by reference to one device's categories, while other Members could be categorized by reference to another device. In short, for any population of two or more Members, the outcome reproduceability (of categorization) requires either the use of the consistency rule or some combining rules; and this is so even if we are dealing with the production of each categorizer separately or if there is only one categorizer.[13]

1.1.5 We have been talking of the activity of categorizing as involving the use of single categorization devices, and implicitly of a single category (e.g. "negro") being applied to single population Members. Let it be noted that one of the central features of the culture with which we are dealing is that single categories of single categorization devices can be referentially adequate.[14]

1.1.5.1 For Members, it is not absurd or insufficient in characterizing a Member to use a single category to refer to him. It is adequate reference on many occasions to say of someone no more than that they are "female" or "old" or "negro." It is not the case that such a usage is partial for every occasion or use whatever, though it is for some.

1.1.5.2 This fact (1.1.5) permits us to formulate another rule for the use of categorization devices.

Economy Rule. For any population N, on any occasion of categorizing Members, whether the consistency rule or some combining rules are necessary, the task may be complete if each Member of the population has had a single category applied to them.

1.1.5.3 The economy rule permits us to partially formulate one central socialization problem. Once a child has reached that stage of learning he makes utterances like:[15]

1) Once there was a baby pig. He played with his Mommy. He went to Mommy. Mommy went to Daddy.
2) The Daddy works in the bank. And Mommy cooks breakfast. Then we get up and get dressed. And the baby eats breakfast and honey. We go to the school and we get dressed like that. I put coat on and I go in the car . . .

From such a point, the child's task of becoming adequately socialized to doing categorization of Members consists in learning (a) what categories must be added to "Mommy," "Daddy," and "baby," to complete the collection of which they are members; (b) of adding to their apparatus of category collections, i.e. of learning collections other than the former one,[16] and (c) of learning proper occasions and rules of use of each of the devices. No longer need they face the task of learning what in principle adequate reference consists of. They've learned that. In principle their categorization is referentially adequate. The combinatorial tasks they face are of a different character, and a major combinatorial task has been solved (in principle) when they can make such utterances as:[17]

3) Pussy scratched. He cried. He's a *bad boy*. He banged. He stopped crying. He's a *good boy*. He cried again.

While the economy rule does not preclude the use of combinations of membership categories for single population Members, its presence does mean that the task of being socialized to doing adequate reference does not involve having to learn combinatorial possibilities for each pair, triplicate, etc., of categories as a prerequisite to doing adequate reference. The combinatorial problems are between classes of modifiers, of which (good, bad) are prototypes, and classes of membership categorization collections, of which (Mommy, Daddy, baby, etc.) is a prototype, and having learned the prototypes and their combinations the basic tasks have been accomplished.

1.1.6 Given the economy rule we can pose an initial formulation of the relation between categorization devices. Since a single device can be Pn-adequate, it is possible that on some occasion of doing categorization of a population N, a single Pn-adequate device can be exclusively appropriate. Such relations as mutual exclusion may obtain between particular devices or, indeed, the appropriateness of a given device may involve the exclusion of all others. This of course can only be possible if there are some single devices whose categories are referentially adequate, for example.

1.1.6.1 A central relevance of the foregoing possibility may be noted. Given the finding of (1.1.3), if two categorizers (or more) are in action, and they are dealing with any population N, if convergence between them is relevant, then a convergence problem exists. That is to say, it is possible that even if each of them need only categorize the same single Member, the fact that there are at least two devices available with no overlap of members means they might employ different categories to categorize that Member even if there was only a single proper solution to the problem of categorizing that Member when only one device was properly usable. By reference to (1.1.5–6), however, we may see that the economy rule providing for the possibility of single device adequacy, and exclusive appropriateness being possible, there are means for systematically providing for converging categorizations, perhaps without regard to either population size or number of categorizers.

1.1.7 Given the consistency rule and the economy rule, we have the:

Repeatable Use Rule. The application of a Pn1-adequate device to a population N involves determining for each Member of the population, in any sequence, which category is appropriate,[18] where any category may be repeatably used.[19]

1.2 Given the findings of 1.1.4–5–6–7 we are in a position to make the argument promised in 1.1.3.2.

It is possible in the first instance that the use of a single category to categorize some Member may be appropriate. Such a category may properly be chosen from a Pn-adequate device. However, the observational correctness criterion[20] of such a categorization would only be a warrant for the sociologist doing or using such a categorization, if: The sociologist could determine that the categorization device from which the category was selected was exclusively appropriate, i.e. by reference to a selection procedure for determining category device appropriateness. The foregoing is so because the observational correctness warrant focusses only on whether the category chosen from a given device is the appropriate one given that device's alternatives. If an uncategorized population were specifiable for which only one device could be found that would categorize it, then the selection problem would become trivial.

Since, however, we have shown that there are always at least two devices available, it follows that the correspondence-type criterion of correctness is only appropriate as a second step, i.e. after it has been determined that some particular exclusively appropriate device is to be used. The reproduceability of any categorization, whether done by members or by sociologists, requires, then, some method whereby the selection of the categorization device(s) to be used in making that categorization may be reproduceably provided for. While the manner in which that can be accomplished may well be problematic, the reader may now see how it is that the formulation of our research task (1.0) is arrived at. That accomplished, we may shortly proceed with our investigation of the "search for help."

1.3 We may say, introductorily, that if Members selected categorization devices methodically, then their selection activities might be describable. There are reasons for supposing that at least for some of the activities Members engage in they do proceed methodically.

1.3.1 "Methodical" and "describable" are equivalent both for the activities of doing science and the activities of the phenomena on which it is done. The fact of science tells us that some activities that humans do—for example, science—are methodical, and indicates as well that what is distinctive about social science may be just the fact that one is now dealing with an animal that is in principle capable of adequate self-description (and not that one is dealing with an animal whose activities are undescribably complex).

1.3.2 The fact, then, that some human activities are adequately describable (by which we mean describable by virtue of the methods whereby they are produced) means that we can, for any given activities, inquire as to whether they are describable in this fashion. Our task may then be formulated as follows: Let us see whether Members' activities of categorizing Members are methodical and, thereby, describable.

1.3.3 If, as I shall hope to show, Members' activities of categorization are not only describably methodical, but also that activities are done methodically is quite essential to the ways that they are seen as graspable by Members, then some ways whereby not only the describability but the simplicity of activities may be found, will be revealed. This, and no less, is our aim.

2.0 Let us introduce the two category collections we shall basically need in dealing with the materials this paper is concerned to describe.[21]

2.1 The two collections with which we shall be dealing may be called (1) R—a collection of paired relational categories, and (2) K—a collection constructed by reference to special distributions of knowledge existing about how to deal with some trouble (here, "suicidalness").

2.2 The members of collection R are such pairs of categories as husband–wife, parent–child, neighbor–neighbor, boyfriend–girlfriend, friend–friend, cousin–cousin, . . . stranger–stranger.

2.2.1 We find that the following rule provides for whether a pair of classes is a member of collection R: Any pair of categories is a member of collection R if that pair is a "standardized" relational pair that constitutes a locus for a set of rights and obligations concerning the activity of giving help.

2.2.1.1 To say that the pairs are "standardized" is to say the following:

1) If any Member X knows his own pair position with respect to some Member Y, then X knows the pair position of Y with respect to himself. X also knows that if Y knows what pair position Y has to X, then Y knows what pair position X has to Y.

2) If any Member Z (neither X nor Y) knows what X takes to be X's pair position to Y, then Z knows what pair position X takes it that Y has to X. Z also knows that X takes it that if Y knows that X stands to Y in the pair position X supposes, that Y takes it that Y stands to X in the pair position X supposes. Z knows too that the converse holds for Y. Z knows further, as X and Y know, what the rights and obligations are that obtain between X and Y given a convergence in their determination of their respective pair positions.

2.2.2 Since it is altogether central to the use of R in the search for help that it has the sort of standardization we have proposed,[22] let us here and now locate what in the materials the formulation permits us to observe, to see the culturally-provided-for orderliness of.

2.2.2.1 By virtue of the features of the standardization of R, any two Members, without regard to the pair positions they employ to locate each other and therefore even if they are unacquainted prior to the given conversation, are able to assess the treatment any third Member will expectably (1) give one of them, if one of them is suicidal, and the third Member's pair position to that one is determined, or (2) get from any other member, if it is someone other than one of the two who is suicidal, and if the pair relation of that third and any other Member is determined.

2.2.2.2 With the foregoing we can then partially[23] provide for some of the most recurrent occurrences of our materials, i.e. the various pairs of conversationalists are able to assess the expectable behavior of variously categorized third persons, where one participant to the conversation, and sometimes both, know only the pair position of the third persons whose expectable behaviors are being assessed. Such occurrences are then observably orderly across the various pair-positions from which they are done. See, for example, Quotations 2, 5, 10, 11, 17 in the appendix.

2.2.3 Having observed some central uses of knowledge of pair positions in collection R, we may explicitly propose what has heretofore been hinted at. Single categories may, for some items of Members' knowledge, be inferentially adequate. Members' knowledge of how Members behave is so organized that items of that knowledge may, discriminatively, be taken as expectably descriptive if no more than a single referentially adequate category has been asserted to hold for some Member in question.[24] It is that Members have such categorically localized knowledge that provides for what it is they employ to make the assessments just referred to.

2.2.4 Where R is relevant, its categories have what we shall call "programmatic relevance." By this latter term we intend the following: If R is relevant, then the non-incumbency of any of its pair positions is an observable, i.e. can proposedly be a fact. Furthermore, the various uses that may be made of the facts that Members locate and deal with obtain for this sort of fact also. For example, accounts of suicidalness may be constructed that employ the fact of some non-incumbencies as criterial. See Quotation 3 in appendix.

Category Relevance Rule 2. Given the relevance of some categorization device whose categories are programmatically relevant (whether or not the device is Pn 1-adequate), each category of the device is usable on the population being categorized such that the product of the device's application may consist of a set of observations (facts) that are formulable and usable not only vis-à-vis the product (category member + population Member) but also (category member + no population Member).

The outcome of the use of a device whose categories are programmatically relevant, given its relevance, may be proposed in terms of absences as well as presences, i.e. of categories for which there is not an incumbent as well as for those for which there is.

2.2.5 Apart from R, some prominent cases of devices whose categories have programmatic relevance (on the device's relevance) are the device "family," and various cases of the device-class "team," e.g. baseball team, football team, etc. For some of these devices, and perhaps for some categories of each of them, each category has a proper number of incumbents, such that not only may one observe that there are no incumbents for some category, but also how many are missing.

Those devices that are both (A) composed of programmatically relevant categories and (B) have for each category, either (a) some proper number of incumbents or (b) some proper minimal number of incumbents, may by a modification of (1.1.7) form cases of a class of Pn-adequate devices, (Pn2).

The modification, any device as specified above (A, B), may categorize any population N, where the device's categories are treated as a unit with reference to repeatable usage. The population then is construed in terms of the number of complete or incomplete units that its Members may be partitioned into.

2.2.5.1 One way that the modification operates to extend the size of the class of Pn-adequate devices is as follows: Some group of the categories of a Pn1-device, may by reference to the modification, constitute a Pn2-device. Some of the categories, which as pairs are collected in R, may be recombined, and under the label "family" become a Pn2-adequate device. By virtue of this modification we see (even more strongly than previously) that the class of devices usable on any population N is not merely larger than two, but that it is large indeed.

2.3 Collection K is composed of two classes (professionals, laymen). The bulk of our consideration of this collection will be offered elsewhere. Our aim in this section is to provide the minimal resources with regard to K necessary for the analysis in this paper. Let us first note that K is Pn-adequate[25] and provide, second, for how membership is distributed between its classes.

2.3.1 1) All those occupational categories for which it is correct to say that Members of the named occupations have special or exclusive rights for dealing with some trouble(s) are occasional occupants of K's class (professionals).

2) For any given trouble for which such an occupation exists as (1) above locates, that occupation (or occupations) constitutes the category exclusively occupying the (professional) class, where all who are not Members of it are undifferentiatedly occupants of the K class (laymen).

Thus, for any given trouble, incumbency in one of the classes excludes incumbency in the other.

3.0 In focussing on collection R, it might be asked:[26] How is it that when a search for help is being engaged in, the relevance of collection R is provided for? The formulation is, however, erroneous. For, as we shall observe, the very propriety of a search for help is provided for by the rights and obligations that are organized by reference to collection R. Our initial task is then to show how features of collection R provide for the propriety of occurrence of a search for help.

3.1 We have proposed (2.2.1) that the paired relational categories of collection R constitute loci for rights and obligations. Let us note that it is "programmatic R" (2.2.4) that provides the relevance of the category pairs, i.e. it is not the case that the relevance of the rights and obligations organized by reference to R is provided for by the fact of actual incumbency of some set of pairs.

For some pairs of categories:

1) X (a suicidal person, a programmatic incumbent of some pair positions) has a right to turn to Y (a programmatic incumbent of alternative pair positions) for help. Hence, any Member has a programmatic right to undertake a search for help, i.e. to at least determine whether any pair position to whose programmatic incumbent he has a right to turn is occupied by an actual incumbent.

2) If X chooses to undertake a search for help, and if that search involves telling those sought out who he is, what is wrong with him, and what he makes out the causes of his suicidalness to be, then X is obliged to turn to incumbents of these categories. Incumbents of these categories have a right that X not turn to incumbents of other categories.

3) If X sees that the alternative to engaging in a search for help is doing suicide, then X is obliged to seek help in alternative to doing suicide. It is a right of incumbents of these classes that X seek help as an alternative to doing suicide.

3.2 These three rules provide for the propriety of the search for help, where the alternative to seeking help is doing suicide. They provide also for its permissibility. They provide further that if the search is undertaken, it will, properly, be from classes to which the obligation to undertake a search is owed that helpers will be sought.

Since the rules provide from whom help may and may not be sought, they can be seen to distribute the classes of collection R into two subsets, Rp and Ri. Those classes that the rules locate as "classes whose incumbents are proper to turn to" are members of Rp, and those that the rules locate as "classes whose incumbents are not proper to turn to" are members of Ri.

3.3 It seems that subset Rp is properly used in an orderly fashion—that there is a proper sequence in the use of the classes it contains and that, furthermore, the rules (1–3, 3.1) hold not only with regard to the subset Rp but also with regard to the proper sequence for going into Rp. Then, if there is an incumbent of some "first-position" category pair, with respect to any incumbent of some "second-position" category pair, the rules provide that the incumbents of the first position should be turned to and not the second.

3.4 Given (3.1–2), and with respect to collection R, we are in a position to pose at least the form of the searcher's problem: "Anyone" means "any incumbent of a pair-position in subset Rp," and "no one" means "no incumbent of a pair-position in subset Rp." For any searcher, then, the problem is: Are there available persons who are incumbents of some pair position that is a member of the subset whose incumbents are properly turned to for help?

3.4.1 Assuming for the moment what we have yet to establish (cf. 7 ff.) that incumbency and availability are separate problems, we may observe that if for some suicidal person there are no incumbents of Rp, then the rules of 3.1 provide only that he is not obligated to turn to anyone for help. The rules do not provide, given that eventuality, that he cannot properly turn to anyone else. Compare, in this regard, Quotation 4 with Quotation 22 in the appendix.

3.5 With the preceding discussion (3.1 ff.) we have established (if that discussion is descriptive) the correctness of the assertion of 3.0. It is not the case that the search for help provides the relevance of collection R. Instead, the fact of suicidalness provides the relevance of a set of rights and obligations organized by reference to collection R. Collection R and the rights and obligations organized by reference to its categories provide the propriety of engaging in a search for help. As has been further indicated, collection R does more than that. It provides for the permissibility of the search and also the procedure for doing that search. But of these latter; more shall be said in the ensuing.

3.6 From the foregoing (3 ff.), several important results may be claimed. For the case of suicidalness, we have found that there is a solution to the problem posed in (1 ff.). A suicidal Member, when doing a search for help, will properly categorize Members by use of the categories of collection R. (See 5 ff. for a detailed consideration.) The use of R has been so established that if a Member who is suicidal and in the course of a search for help says of someone that they are "wife" or "friend" or "stranger," that assertion may be treated as reproduceably correct or incorrect. Before proceeding to see in detail how it is that R is used to organize the search for help, an attempt must be made to deal with the convergence problem, i.e. with the question of how it is that Members sought out by the use of R may or may not come to employ R to formulate their reponses.

4.0 In this section we shall deal with a problem about assertions (most particularly, such an assertion as "I am suicidal") that is similar to the Membership categorization problem dealt with in (1 ff. and 3 ff.). Can such an assertion as "I am suicidal" be, to use a term we shall shortly explicate, "definitive"? The import of the problem for the course of the search for help will be examined, most particularly with regard to the "convergence" (1.1.6.1) problem.

4.1 In our conversational materials, and in related and unrelated materials, it is recurrently noticeable that (1) when suicidal persons tell a Member of Rp that they are suicidal, the latter hears the assertion as a "joke," and (2) suicidal persons recurrently assert that they are afraid to tell Members of Rp that they are suicidal because they fear that the ones told will treat their assertion as a "joke."

We are of course not claiming that these possibilities are always actualized. It does seem that some assertions, such as "I am suicidal," can operate to provide, for one sought out by use of R and its rules of use, the relevance of R and its rules of use in formulating a response to the assertion. See Quotations 10, 11, 13, etc. Alternatively, Quotation 18 in the appendix.

4.2 We will say that an assertion is

1) "definitive" if, *that* a Member, A, proffers to another, B, *an assertion* which can operate to provide for B the relevance of the device employed by A to locate (a) who to locate, and (b) what to assert to them, *operates* as proper grounds for B to use the same device to control his response to the assertion. Such an assertion would then be definitive of the device its recipient would use to formulate his reponse.

2) "ambiguous," if we can clearly locate some set of consistently present alternative devices that its utterance provides as "proper alternatives" to choose between.

If, then, for some assertion A1, only device CD1 is properly usable by a recipient to formulate his response, and by the asserter to formulate it to the recipient, then assertion A1 is definitive. If, for some assertion A2, either device CD2, CD3 or some listable set of alternatives is properly usable to formulate who to offer it to and to formulate a response, then assertion A2 is ambiguous.

By a "proper alternative" we intend: Any alternative that a recipient may use both (a) to formulate his response and (b) to formulate an account of his response, where the account is acceptable even if the course of events that provides for his having to offer an account has involved the fact that the alternative he proposes to have used is by the course of events proved wrong. A proper alternative is then one that provides its user either with (a) the correct response to have taken, i.e. the correct collection plus its rules, or (b) an excusable error.

4.3 Now, given the fact that such an assertion as "I am suicidal" can operate to provide the relevance of R for some recipient, we may seek to see whether the assertion is definitive or whether it is describably ambiguous. Let us proceed first to present some relevant materials.

1) (husband of caller is suicidal)

C1. . . . But about two months ago when I was still home, he one Sunday, oh we have five children and I got home from church and he got a butcher knife and told the kids to go to the park and play. This is kind of unusual for him because he doesn't want them, especially the baby, to go anywhere unless we're there.

S1. Uh huh

C2. After they were all gone, I was laying on the couch just reading the Sunday paper and he came over there and started holding this butcher knife at my throat and I said what is the matter with you. He said I'm going to kill you. I'm going to end it all and I said oh for goodness sake put it down and go—I started to laugh it off and he sat there for about an hour. So I thought well he kept threatening to kill me and then he would pull it back as if to stab me and I just laid there, prayed. I almost believed that he was crazy. And then he has been acting fairly good since then. He doesn't have any religion and I'm Catholic but I said why don't you go down and talk to the priest, maybe he would talk to you. And he said No I don't have any friends, and I said honey you have lots of friends . . .

C3. . . . The last time he tried to kill me he sat and wrote a long suicide note or whatever—I don't know, I didn't read it. This was on a Sunday, when the kids and I got home from church and he wanted to know if I went to church with the kids, and they said of course she always goes to church with us. He said, I know she's got a boyfriend. I said quit acting silly in front of these kids. What's the matter with you? He says—oh and then I don't know, anyway, this time he tried to kill me. I didn't want him to think I was taking him seriously. He said well Joey run down to the police station before I do something I don't want to do. I says, Daddy quit it. Joey says, Daddy I don't want to go down there. They'll all look at me funny when they read the note. I says, Joey run outside, Daddy's only kidding. He says, No I'm not. You'd better let me do it. Then he got in the car and went tearing off. I looked for the note, last night, and he didn't have one so I thought oh, maybe he knew I'd wake up and maybe not. But I don't want to leave it go.

S3. I wouldn't let it go. It doesn't sound too good . . .

2) (from a coroner's report)

On the evening before she died she had dinner with LJ and Miss AB, close personal friends who live in the same building. She expressed feelings of discouragement . . . and made the following statement: "I get so damned disgusted sometimes that I think I will just commit suicide." Her friends thought she was kidding, and all of them had a few drinks and forgot about it.

3) See Quotation 18 in the appendix.

4) (mother, re. adult daughter)

S1. Now does she turn to you for help?

C1. Yes. When she gets all of this—when everything builds up in her so much, then she turns to me. One day here she was—and she was—we was standing at our sink washing dishes and she was crying and telling me. She says, mother, she says, I need help. She said, please help me. She said, mother, I've even got on my knees to Johnny [husband] and begged and cried for him to help me. And she said he would laugh at me like he thought I was crazy or something, I didn't need help or I was putting on or something. And her cousin that works over there—Elsie is her name, McKim, and she said that Elsie even told me herself—she's been over here since and said that she even cried for her to help me. She said, she told her, she says, Elsie I need help. She said I don't know where to go or who to turn to.

5) (friend)

C1. . . . and I haven't talked to her about calling anybody else, and the more I thought about it, you know, the more scared I got, really, because I would feel just terrible if she did anything to herself after telling me about it, and I don't want to cause trouble if she's just kidding and trying to . . .

4.4 In providing for such occurrences as the foregoing we seem to need first to recognize (1) that members employ a contrast set for categorizing assertions, where (2) it is by reference to a determination which member of the set an assertion is a case of that they find the relevance of alternative membership categorization devices.

4.4.1 Two central members of the assertion categorization contrast set which Members recognize and employ and for which they have names, are (serious, joke). Let us proceed to give an initial characterization of this set and these two of its members.[27]

4.4.2 For any assertion for which a recipient properly uses some membership categorization device (such as R) to formulate his response, the contrast set provides relevant categories, one of which is presumptively correct. The determination of which is apparently correct operates to locate the appropriate membership categorization device, i.e. the membership categorization devices are uniquely tied to assertion contrast-set categories. It is not an excusable error to hear an assertion as "serious" and use the device appropriate if the assertion were heard as "joke," and vice versa.

4.4.3 However, the category "serious" may be seen to be "complex," while the category "joke" is to be seen as "simple," i.e. if an assertion is heard as "serious," then depending on what the assertion proposes ("I am suicidal," "I offer you a job," "Let us get married") depends what particular categorization device is appropriate, where there are a variety of alternatives tied to different possible "serious" proposals. If an assertion is heard as "joke," then a single device is appropriate without regard to what the assertion might be seen to propose.

4.4.4 If a recipient cannot determine which category of the contrast set an assertion is a case of, that fact is relevant to the choice of a categorization device, where: The device then appropriate may be one not seen as appropriate, given either alternative clearly being seen as apparently correct.

4.4.5 The membership categorization device appropriate, given the determination that an assertion is a case of the category "joke," has (1) two members (audience, performer), where (2) the determination of which participant is a Member of which category is made by reference to who is a maker of the assertion (performer) and who the recipient(s) (audience). Given the assertion's categorization, laughter is the audience's appropriate response. The use of that response operates to (a) close the sequence which the assertion began and (b) to detopicalize the assertion. The fact that there is for some assertion a response that serves as (a) above does, means that there are both immediately available and conversational means of disposing of an assertion. It is obvious that for many actions, including many assertions, particularly those that are "serious," there may be neither immediately available nor conversational means for disposing of them. A question, for example, may remain live until an answer has been given:

1) A: Hey, did you talk Marcia into moving down here?[28]
B: Was she here?
A: Yeah.
B: When did she leave?
A: Bout half hour ago.
B: Yeah, I talked her into living here with me.

2) It should not be forgotten that about nineteen hundred years elapsed between the time when Pilate asked his famous question "What is truth?" (St. John, xviii. 38) and Tarski (285. 14) made a satisfactory reply: . . . J. C. C. McKinsey and Patrick Suppes: review of P. Destouches-Fevrier, "La structure des theories physiques," in *Journal of Symbolic Logic*, v. 19, no. 1, March 1954, p. 54.

The assertion "I am suicidal" may have not conversation, but hospitalization, as its appropriate response. If the assertion is heard as "serious," then the matter thereby raised may not be disposed of until its proposer has died. That the response of laughter operates also to detopicalize the assertion is equally important. For, given detopicalization, the assertion need not be counted as the first event in a history of suicidalness, a first warning, in terms of which both further and past events are to be assessed to decide the problem's proper treatment. To detopicalize is then to erase, and it may be noted there is some reason to suppose that, like alcoholism, once actually recognized, suicidalness is not erasable. Our conversations indicate, for example, that currently suicidal persons, on being asked for their history, will mention having been suicidal perhaps thirty years previously, though they do not intend thereby that the problem was continuously live.

4.4.6 It is well to note then that these ways that the categorization of an assertion as "joke" operates are centrally important alternatives to those operative, given the determination "serious." This being so, the possibility that an assertion is ambiguous as between the two categories is consequential. Let us look at some of the consequences.

4.4.6.1 If a Member knows that "serious" is a member of a contrast set of which "joke" is an alternative member, where an assertion relevant to that contrast set for its categorization faces the possibility of being categorized as one or the other, then it is understandable that Members considering how to get help via R may find themselves seeking more definitive means of invoking R than the use of an assertion. The so-called "attempted attempt" at suicide may be an action formulated out of such a search. The definitiveness of a body unconscious from an apparent overdose of pills may be seen as rather more secure than the assertion "I am suicidal," with regard to the likelihood of generating help.

4.4.6.2 The possibility of erroneous categorization by the recipient of an assertion provides the asserter with the basis for employing attempted correctives. Phrases such as "believe me" as in "And believe me, it's no joke because as I say, I just don't feel my life is worth anything at this point" seem directed to preventing or correcting the categorization "joke." Alternatively, the asserter may employ an attempted corrective that is methodically equivalent, for the asserter, to laughter for the recipient, i.e. such a line as "I was only kidding."

1) A: You always have an answer—just shut up.
   B: I don't want to.
   A: You don't have to. I was just kidding.

2) I would like to relate an incident that occurred with the man I was talking about earlier. At one stage he grew a beard, which was contrary to hospital rulings, and we got into a tangle over it. However, my patient grew a big, full beard. He stands five feet one. His father had not previously seen the beard and when I took him to visit his home, suddenly the father said, "Oh ho, So our boy is hiding behind a beard now, is he?" I said quietly, "Mr. B., I don't think that is true." There was an awful pause; the old man spluttered once or twice and left the room. When he came back 4 or 5 minutes later he said, "Oh ho! So it is a beard our boy is hiding behind now, is it?" I said, "Mr. B., you have said that twice. I don't think it is true." Then there was another ghastly pause before he said, "I was only kidding."[29]

4.4.7 An important general possibility was suggested in 4.4.6.1. For those assertions that can provide the relevance of some membership categorization device to which some procedures are tied, is it the case that for any assertion that can be "serious" the possibility exists that such an assertion can alternatively be "joke"? If this is so, then no such assertion can be definitive, and then all such assertions require, for a description of how they are categorized, a formulation that provides for a selection from among the alternatives (serious, joke).

4.4.7.1 A variety of procedures might be employed to resolve the problem of (4.4.7).

1) Each assertion that can be "serious" and each assertion that can be "joke" might be examined to see whether any that can be one cannot be the other.

2) It might be asked whether there is some component(s) intrinsic to the production of a possibly "serious" assertion that provides for the possibility that any such production could employ the component in such a fashion as to provide for the assertion as "joke."

3) The character of categorization devices might be examined to determine whether it is the case for a device that contains, say, two mutually exclusive categories that to produce an action for which one category may be appropriate involves producing an action for which the device is thereby relevant in such a way that both of its categories are thereby relevant if one is.

4.4.7.2 While the first alternative (of 4.4.7.1) is obviously the most conservative, and it was the fact that for a rather different group of assertions the alternative (serious, joke) was recognized as relevant that led me to ask whether the alternatives were general, that same alternative would hardly seem to provide us with sufficient means for formulating the problem in appropriate depth.

It is by reference to a combination of the second and third procedures that we came to see one import of the problem—which is nothing less than the structured way to which that "possible danger" gets oriented.

1) **Mr. Liebeler.** Tell us what happened as you took these pictures.

A. Well, as the car came in line, almost—I believe it was almost in line—I was standing up here and I was shooting through a telephoto lens, which is a zoom lens and as it reached about—I imagine it was around here—I heard the first shot and I saw the President lean over and grab himself like this (holding his left chest area).

Mr. Liebeler. Grab himself on the front of his chest?

A. Right—something like that. In other words, he was sitting like this and waving and then after the shot he just went like that.

Mr. Liebeler. He was sitting upright in the car and you heard the shot and you saw the President slump over?

A. Leaning—leaning toward the side of Jacqueline. For a moment I thought it was, you know, like you say, "Oh, he got me," when you hear a shot—you've heard those expressions and then I saw—I don't believe the President is going to make jokes like this, but before I had a chance to organize my mind, I heard a second shot and then I saw his head opened up and the blood and everything came out and I started—I can hardly talk about it. (The witness crying.)[30]

2) While walking along Pine Ave., in Long Beach, Fred W. Fox, a former Mirror colleague noticed a beer truck parked at the curb. Behind it on the street were half a dozen large cartons of beer, obviously just unloaded for delivery to a liquor store there.

As he went past it Fred imagined he heard a muffled voice calling, "Let me out, let me out of here!" No other passer-by seemed to hear it and he wondered if he were being bamboozled by a ventriloquist.

He stopped and turned back and the voice became louder. "Let me out—somebody let me out!" Then he noticed a slight tremor on the latch handle on the truck's rear door. He opened it and a large, red-faced teamster almost fell out. He'd locked himself in and there was no inside release for the latch. Fred wonders if the campaign to remove locks from abandoned refrigerators so children at play won't be trappèd should be extended to beer vans.[31]

3) 12. And the men said unto Lot, Hast thou here any besides son-in-law, and thy sons, and thy daughters, and whatsoever thou hast in the city, bring them out of this place:

13. For we will destroy this place, because the cry of them is waxen great before the face of the Lord; and the Lord hath sent us to destroy it.

14. And Lot went out, and spake unto his sons-in-law, which married his daughters, and said, Up, get you out of this place; for the Lord will destroy this city. But he seemed as one that mocked unto his sons-in-law.

15. And when the morning arose, then the angels hastened Lot, saying, Arise, take thy wife, and thy two daughters, which are here; lest thou be consumed in the iniquity of the city.

. . .

24. Then the Lord rained upon Sodom and upon Gomorrah brimstone and the fire from the Lord out of heaven;

25. And he overthrew those cities, and all the plain, and all the inhabitants of the cities, and that which grew upon the ground.[32]

4) Who could these men be? What were they talking about? What authority could they represent? K. lived in a country with a legal constitution, there was universal peace, all the laws were in force; who dared seize him in his own dwelling? He had always been inclined to take things easily, to believe in the worst only when the worst happened, to take no care for the morrow even when the outlook was threatening. But that struck him as not being the right policy here; one could certainly regard the whole thing as a joke, a rude joke which his colleagues at the bank had concocted for some unknown reason, perhaps because this was his thirtieth birthday, that was of course possible, perhaps he had only to laugh knowingly in these men's faces and they would laugh with him, perhaps they were merely porters from the street corner—they looked very like it—nevertheless his very first glance at the man Franz had decided him for the time being not to give away any advantage that he might possess over these people. There was a slight risk that later on his friends might possibly say he could not take a joke, but he had in mind—though it was not usual with him to learn from experience—several occasions of no importance in themselves, when against all his friends' advice he had behaved with deliberate recklessness and without the

slightest regard for possible consequences, and had had in the end to pay dearly for it. That must not happen again, at least not this time; if this was a comedy he would insist on playing it to the end.[33]

While we are not now in any position to determine whether the (serious, joke) alternative is general for assertion categorizations, the possibility that it is is one that ought to be given most serious attention, both with regard to the question of the ways persons do and might more effectively orient to possible danger and to the theoretical status of the phenomenon "joke," its sociological interest apart from theories of humor or non-serious activities. Let us summarize the discussion of this section.

4.4.8 The discussion of assertion categorization has relevantly indicated that the detection problem—what category an assertion is a case of—can be something oriented to by the (potential) asserter, and that one may find either (a) that those one ought properly to seek out, by reference to R, are not likely to hear one's assertions as "serious," i.e. by reference to what R would provide they do if they did so hear, or (b) that having made the assertion to them, they have failed to hear it as "serious," i.e. as signalling the propriety of use of R.

4.4.8.1 As a consequence of (a) above, the potential asserter may either seek a more definitive means of getting R operative—for example, the attempted attempt, or may attempt to see if there are not some hearers who may be turned to for whom the assertion is definitive. As a consequence of (b) above one may find the propriety of turning elsewhere, or the removal of the obligation to turn to Rp, by reference to the failure of those so located to use R in response. Alternatively, one may feel that he has done the tasks precedent to suicide, and with the illegitimacy of it removed as claimable against him by Rp members, he may feel free to do it.

5.0 Let us now see how the apparatus we have constructed out of our materials may permit us to analyze their production. Let us see how the foregoing categories and rules of use provide for the reproduceable occurrence of a variety of actually occurring pieces of conversation. Let us see further how solutions may be constructed to the problem we initially posed: How is it that the conclusion "I have no one to turn to" may be reproduceably provided for?

5.1 First, the fact that R classified any population N, and that the obligations to seek help and the rules for searching helpers out are formulated in terms of its categories, operates to provide that R is used to make an initial classification of the recipient (of the phone conversations we are examining) by the suicidal caller. This is so despite the fact that the recipient can be categorized by reference to categories organized in some other collection (e.g. K.). Suicidal callers recurrently talk of the recipient as a "stranger." (See Quotations 4, 22. cf. Quotation 21.) Also, non-suicidal callers recurrently report that it is by reference to the categories of R that a suicidal person came to locate them as someone to turn to for help. (Quotations 12, 14, 16.)

5.1.1 Such categorization is made (as we may put it) "even though" it may be the case that given the category employed to locate the recipient, the recipient is thereby—by reference to the subsets of R—formulated as improper to turn to.

5.1.2 If the recipient is not a member of Rp, it may be noticed that the explanations that involve reference to Rp features are offered without being sought, or are sought, and when sought are offered without being treated as irrelevant or improper. (See Quotations 1–4, etc.)

1) (Suicidal woman; no request for an account has been made by the recipient)

My sister came over on uh Sunday and she talked to me and I called her now to talk to her and she told me to please call these people and tell me what they say.

2) **S1.** . . . May I help you?
C1. Well, I don't know. My brother suggested that I call you.
S2. I see. Well, he must have had a reason for making this suggestion. Has there been some personal problem or difficulty that you're experiencing?
C2. Yes. I just lost my wife and I feel awfully depressed.

5.1.3 If an account has not been offered, then as an alternative to requesting one, the recipient may, by reference to the standardization of R, construct an account himself. He may infer the account—employing the features of R—where the fact of a contact having been sought with someone in Ri is treated as indicative of the situation of a caller with respect to Rp. See, for example, Quotation 2.

5.1.4 It is important to see, as our formulation proposes, that the caller may treat his having made the call as improper without regard to the fact that the recipient is one who holds himself out as proper to be called quite independently of the regulations of R. Recognized impropriety of a contact and the unwillingness of a recipient are quite separate matters. The fact that some persons or classes of persons are willing to give help, hold themselves out to give help, or propose their special competence to give help doesn't make them proper to turn to, if with respect to R they are members of Ri. (See Quotations 4, 13, 23.)

5.2 The fact of the standardization of R and of the programmatic relevance of its categories provides for discourse between Members about the categories and their incumbents "even though" the participants to the conversation are unacquainted previously to the analyzed conversations. The collection of programmatically relevant categories provides a set of topics. For one, the question of whether there are incumbents of these categories may be considered, where (a) the relevance of consideration of whether there are incumbents is not seen as problematic; (b) the way in which the fact of there being incumbents is dealt with is itself not disorderly.

5.2.1 So, for example, questions may be constructed employing the subset Rp as the object in the question—e.g. "Have you anyone to turn to?" Correlatively, answers to such questions may be formulated and recognized as possibly correct (recall 3.6), by constructing statements whose objects are categories that are members of Rp, e.g. "I have a husband." The reader may observe that interchanges composed of such questions and answers may be found throughout the materials included in the appendix.

5.3 Further, recalling the observation of (2.2.2.1), the standardization of R provides for the occurrence of aspects of almost all of the conversations collected in the appendix. To repeat: Two Members, without regard to the pair positions they employ to locate each other, and therefore even though they have no prior acquaintance, do engage in assessing the treatment some third Member(s) will expectably (1) give one of them, if that one is suicidal, and no more than the third Member's pair position to that one is in the first place determined, or (2) get from any other Member, if it is someone other than one of the two who is suicidal, and if the pair-relation between that third and any other Member may be determined. (See Quotations 5, 8, 10, 16, 17, 24.)

5.3.1 It is recurrently observable in the materials that the assessments of expectable behavior turn on the determination of the pair-positions in R of the Member whose expectable behavior is being assessed.

1) It is not the case that such discussions proceed by reference to Members formulated as "somebody" or to formulations by reference to collections other than R.

2) Sometimes neither participant to the conversation is acquainted with those they are talking about, but the pair-position information still seems adequate to them to provide assessments of expectable behavior.

3) Given the pair-position information, those who take it that they have information about the incumbent inconsistent with the inferences pair-position knowledge provides take it as those they are conversing with also take it that pair-position inferences are not simply superseded if "special knowledge" is held. Instead, special argumentation is required, and it may be insisted that the special knowledge will turn out to be incorrect where the pair-position inference will not. The inferences that pair-position knowledge provides are then to be treated seriously even if their correctness is to be denied. Acquaintanceship does not obviously provide superseding knowledge. (See citations to 5.3.)

5.3.2 If it is the suicidal person who is a third party to the conversation (i.e. not a participant) then their expectable reaction to proferred help is assessable. Again, in doing such assessment, the regulations with regard to R are relevant. The caller will recurrently propose that it is not expectable that the help of an outsider will be accepted; that, further, the suicidal person would be much disturbed to know that an outsider has been consulted. In several cases the caller proposed that the proper strategy would be for them to tell the suicidal that it is a "friend" that has been sought out and who ought to be contacted. The argument (considered below, see Quotation 4) that the recipient makes to a suicidal person who considers his own contacting "a stranger" improper is then made to the non-suicidal caller.

5.4 The standardization of R and the rules for distributing categories into its subsets provide the sense of one solution to the problem of this paper. A sense of "no one to turn to" can be stated thus: For the subset Rp, for some Member A, there are no incumbents of Rp categories.

5.4.1 The standardization only provides the sense of a solution. The possibility that such a situation may occur for some Member is another order of fact, one whose possibility is provided for by reference to quite a different apparatus. For some societies, the removal of an incumbent from a category—say the death of a husband—is the occasion for the operation of machinery that involves some other Member taking that place, if such another who is eligible is available. Among the Bemba, for example:[34]

> When a man dies, his name, his kinship duties and his hereditary bow are passed on to his sister's son or to her grandson through a daughter. The heir actually becomes the dead man in a social sense; he adopts the kinship terms the latter used, calling, for instance, "maternal nephew" the person he would previously have called "brother."

Again, among the people of the Shtetl:[35]

> If a man dies childless, his unmarried brother is obligated to marry the widow in order to perpetuate the line. Neither the widow nor the brother may marry anyone else without a formal release from the other.

Such machinery seems largely absent in this society. The fact of absence is of special importance because a variety of relations that Members treat—where the slots of a unit are filled, as named-person named-person and not unit-member unit-member relations—turn out, upon the occurrence of a pair having been rendered incomplete, to have been or now become unit-member unit-member relations. A widow finds that her friends are no longer her friends when she has not a husband any more, and finds then that she has lost (even) more than her husband by his death (or, in the case of divorce, by the divorce).

Our conversations include such interchanges as:

S1. How long have you been feeling the way you're feeling now? Since Christmas? [that was when her husband left her for another woman].

C1. Yes.

S2. Before?

C2. No. I had hope before Christmas. I had hope. I thought a love such as mine could overcome anything. I felt that I had everything there was in my love. And now it's turned against me. I don't feel like I have anything anymore. Nobody gives a damn, in other words.

S3. Nobody what?

C3. Gives a damn. What's the use?

S4. How about friends? Have you friends?

C4. I have friends. So-called friends. I had friends, let me put it that way.

S5. But you feel that since he left, everything—

C5. It's just like rats deserting a sinking ship. Nobody wants to talk to anybody that's in the condition I'm in. They all have their own family, their own problems. They all have their own husbands.

Another reports (a widow):

C1. And I'm just at the break. I said what have I got to live for? I said, Elsie, [daughter] tell me. If you could tell me something. She says, oh you going to take sleeping pills? Happy dreams. And this was it. And I says, I just can't find anything to go on for. I haven't—I had some friends, but not such close friends. I mean, they all have husbands. You can't push yourself in with them. I sit here day after day.

6.0 The preceding section might lead us to propose that device R provides Members with what could non-trivially be called a search procedure. To have found that Members have one, and perhaps have more than one, search procedure is of course extremely significant. First, it would not merely be a strong warrant for our supposition that the fact of science is not to be seen as extremely special—but indeed, since scientists very frequently do not by their own account have search procedures—other activities may be orderly in ways that we are not yet able to see that scientific activities are. Furthermore, if we can say that Members do have a search procedure, that device R constitutes one, then certain rather puzzling occurrences, which we shall consider below, might be clarified.

6.1 However, before any claim to have discovered that Members have search procedures may seriously be made, a problem must be posed: The analysis of 5 ff. dealt with (possible) reports of searches that were or were not undertaken. The question of how such conversations may be said to stand in relation to the occurrence of the search for help involves us in considering what sort of mapping there is between the talk about—more precisely, the talk within, for our conversations constituted parts of the search for help—a search for help and descriptions of the course of that search. Now, we know that there can be a one-to-one relation between a report of some action and the course of the action reported on. We know it because the methodical report of the scientist does just that. His report describes methodically how it is that some result may be reproduced, how in that sense it can be (was) arrived at. Such a coincidence for the possible reports that we are dealing with cannot merely be supposed.

6.2 Our task, however, does not seem to be to take some report and construct for that reporter a description of the course of his search; then see whether the two reports coincide. We have made no suggestion that for activities to be methodical their reports must consist of descriptions of the ways they are methodical. What we need is to see whether the procedure constructed in coming to terms with the reports the conversations contain usably describes search procedural activities for which such conversation does not exist.

6.3 We make no claim to have even begun a systematic investigation of such materials. Such materials as we have collected are, however, consistent with the analysis otherwise developed. On the occurrence of a death that officials take it may be suicidal, those concerned to determine whether it was suicidal engage in an attempt to locate and then interrogate Members whom they take it have relevant information.

6.4 It does seem that Rp and the rules of its use provide officials with the how of such an investigation. It does seem that they use device R such that knowing no more than the dead person's name they can feel confident as to who it is—that is, what potentially available possible persons—they need to discover and contact so as to determine whether the death was expectably suicidal. Officials can apparently suppose that if a suicide has possibly occurred and if there are Members of Rp available, then the possible suicider would (by reference to the rules of Rp) have informed such Members—some of them—that they were suicidal if they were. Rp is routinely used in this way by the police and coroners.

1) (from police report)

After we had completed our investigation at the hospital, we proceeded to the location and contacted victim's husband and her two sons. Upon questioning them, they repeated to the undersigned that it was their opinion that the victim had probably died of natural causes; that she had never threatened or attempted suicide, and that they felt that the capsule found near the body had nothing to do with her death.

2) (from coroner's report)

It is felt that the person who should be contacted is Mr. R.'s wife, who, however, is in New Mexico, apparently permanently.

3) (from coroner's report)

The evaluation of the personality of the victim must of necessity be limited because of the objection of the parents to revealing what was considered to be an important source of information about the victim. They refused to disclose the name of the victim's girlfriend with whom he had been out the night before, stating that she was upset enough and they did not want her to be involved.

6.5 In connection with the second part of the first quotation above, when Rp Members are located they do treat the fact (when it is a fact, or claimably so) that the dead person had not informed them of being suicidal as criterial for their not having committed suicide. The very relevance of such a claim—we are not of course considering whether it is in any particular case, correct—would seem to be further material that is most readily clarified by reference to the use of R as a search procedure.[36]

6.6 The quotations presented after (6.4) are obviously closely related to the discussion of (5 ff.). For as the conversations considered in the latter section involve the assessment of the expectable behavior of persons with whom at least one and sometimes both participants are unacquainted, so, too, the quotations indicate that officials take it that locatable persons with whom they are unacquainted, and who initially are not even known to exist, can be specified such that it is expectable that they will have information as to the possible suicidalness of a currently dead person. In both situations the working of the rules of R seems central.

7.0 Our aim in this section will be to develop another way that the conclusion "I have no one to turn to" may properly be arrived at. Our basic resources are, as before, the apparatus constructed in (2–4 ff.).

7.1 Let us first note that it seems that on the assertion of "I am suicidal," the offering of an account, an explanation, is relevant. Either it is offered or its absence is noticeable, and on not being offered it may be requested. The relevance of that request is not questioned: Either an account will then be offered or the recipient of the request may propose that they do not have an account—I don't know why—where both they and the Member they are talking to take it that that fact may be used in a similar fashion to the way a proffered account may be used.

7.2 Given our formulation of the detection problem (4 ff.), one basis for the request for help being requiredly accompanied by an account may be formulated. The basis seems to be of far more general relevance than the situation of suicidalness.

7.2.1 Where a Member's doing of some action (like giving help) is conditioned on his being informed of the presence of some state that (a) they cannot independently determine to be present and (b) where the assertion is not definitive of its correctness—i.e. can be made improperly, as a joke or lyingly—then Members take it that they may be placed in a situation where the request is made without proper basis. Members' orientation to possible misrequests in such situations are exemplified by the "Cry wolf" fable.

7.2.2 In the case of suicidalness, Members take it that the claim of suicidalness may be mis-asserted:

1) (an ex-girlfriend, with reference to a proposedly suicidal man)

S1. Do you know if he's had this kind of mood before?

C1. Not like that, no. But I mean as I tried to mention before, at first I thought that this was all part of an act, I mean not act, I shouldn't use that word. But it's just, he tries everything, you know, to patch things up and so . . .

This fear of what we may call the subversive use of a claim of suicidalness is clearly not without basis. For example, note the following conversation between a man referred to the clinic and a staff member.

1) **S1.** What did you do?

C1. It was an impulse because my wife was going to leave me, but it was only to steer her into going into reconciliation court. Do you understand what I mean?

S2. Yes. What did you do?

C2. I tried to shoot myself.

S3. How did you do it?

C3. I took the gun and loaded it, and tried to fire it.

S4. Then what happened?

C4. It went off, but actually I didn't aim it at myself. Maybe I can explain it better; it was to let her know that I had intentions of doing that.

. . .

S5. Well, what do you think about what you did?

C5. I got her to reconciliation court.

7.2.3 While there are a variety of ways that have been developed for dealing with this possibility of a subversive use of the request for help, one way seems to involve the following: Members take it that there are adequate and inadequate grounds for suicidalness, and that they may determine whether and what help they ought to do depending on whether or not an adequate, and determinedly present ground exists. Members take it (again, quite generally) that they may decide whether or not some proposed fact exists by determining whether or not a proposed explanation exists and is adequate.

1) The following quotation from a quite different area—part of an arbitration decision—may exemplify this procedure. Ford-UAW Arbitrations, case A-70, Harry Shulman, arbitrator.

> The story of the other discharged employees approaches the bizarre. Twelve of them testified before me. Each of them claims to be a completely innocent bystander wholly at a loss to understand why he was picked up for discharge. None of them admits being part of the crowd in any of the demonstrations. None of them admits even the normal curiosity of an innocent bystander. Each claims that he knew very little about the cause of the stoppages and cared even less after learning the cause. Each claims that

> when the lights went out, or the lines stopped, he asked his foreman what to do and, upon being told to stay or go home as he pleased but that his time stopped in any event, he left for home. One of the men, a lively young boxer, asserts that after seeing the crowd and the excitement he calmly repaired to a warm comfortable spot and went to sleep. He did this, he asserts, on two of the three days (being absent on the third) and slept the peaceful sleep of the just until the excitement completely quieted down. All, it seems, were veritable angels above and beyond contagion by the excitement in the Department.
>
> Now there unquestionably were serious stoppages in Dept. 84 on Nov. 5th, 6th and 8th. There were vociferous and angry men milling around and demanding action. Who were the incensed men who did take part? Who were the angry men whom it was so difficult to get back to work and who were so incensed, as the Union claims, that they turned against their own committeemen and even assaulted two of them? How indeed were these 14 chosen?
>
> The union advanced no explanations. There is no suggestion that these men were chosen by lot; and even such a method would normally be expected to catch some of the guilty. And there is no basis whatever in the evidence to suppose that the men were selected because of any personal animosity against them—with the slight possible exception of one man. Nor were the men generally regarded as "trouble-makers" of whom the Company would be glad to be rid.
>
> The Company's explanation is simple and without any contradiction other than the incredible stories related by the men themselves. The labor relations conciliator, with the help of his assistant, took the names or badge numbers of the most active men in the crowds that demonstrated in his office. This accounts for twelve of the fourteen . . . Under these circumstances I cannot give credence to the men's protestations of innocence.

In short, Members take it that they may choose among proposed competing facts by deciding that the fact is present for which there is an adequate explanation, and the fact is not present for which there is not an adequate explanation. Hence, where the action of giving help is properly conditioned on the presence of some state that is not independently determinable to be present by the one who ought to give help, the requirement that the request be accompanied by an explanation of the presence of the proposed state seems to be directed to permitting the determination to be made of whether the state is indeed present.

7.2.4 One who is contemplating the use of R to get help may then be faced with having to announce both that and why he is suicidal. And they may thereby be faced with considering the various treatments they may receive, given the announcement of their grounds—the account. It is then not merely the claimed fact of their suicidalness that provides for what it is that Rp Members ought to do. Instead, the account of their suicidalness provides those they seek out with an account for the latter's response, i.e.

the suicidal Member's account may provide an account for the potential helper's response. This being so, a procedure for assessing what a potential helper may expectably do is relevant and available. The suicidal Member may consider the various actions the potential helper may take for which the suicidal's account stands as the potential helper's proper account. The suicidal may use such a procedure in a circumscribed fashion, by reference to the standardization of proper actions the potential helper may take, given some account as the account of those actions.

7.3 We may recall that if there is a first Member available of Rp, it is to that Member that the suicidal ought to turn for help. Hence, the suicidal may use the above (7.2.4) procedure by reference to that first member. Suppose the suicidal person is a married woman. It seems that for such a one, the first Member of Rp is her husband. Now, suppose further that the account of her suicidalness involves the fact that she has been seduced into having an affair with another man—say, to keep as the prototype one that we have found in a suicide note, an acquaintance of her husband. She may then consider the various actions her husband may undertake given her adultery as the grounds of his action. On the one hand, he might treat the fact of her suicidalness as adequately accounted for and give her help. On the other, he might treat the fact of her adultery as an adequate ground for breaching their relation, for divorce.

She then faces the following dilemma. On the one hand, the fact that she is married and suicidal provides that her husband is the one to turn to for help. On the other, that which she tells him may operate to take him out of the slot that in the first place provides for him to be turned to. He is there (perhaps) so long as she doesn't speak; once she does, he may no longer be there. In that sort of dilemma she may well see that there is no one to turn to; where, furthermore, she is obliged to turn for help, to turn to him, and he is available.

7.4 The prototype may readily be generalized. If a suicidal Member has as the account of their suicidalness some action of theirs that for the first Member of Rp stands as the adequate grounds of a breach (e.g. of divorce, or disownment, or breaking-off, or indeed of death), then the suicidal person may, employing the categories according to the rules of use we have constructed, find themselves in the above described dilemma, and may see and report that "I have no one to turn to." (See Quotation 5 where the possible breach action is death of Rp members, Quotation 24.[37])

7.5 Having proposed that there are correct ways of arriving at "no one to turn to" the reader may ask whether, for us, any assertion of that conclusion stands only to pose the problem of how to show that the assertion is correct. There are, apparently, incorrect assertions of this type. Members recognize assertions as incorrect. And our analysis permits thei[r] location.

1) **S1.** Now you say you are contemplating suicide?
C1. That is right. I have been contemplating it now for three months. But I finally reached the end of my rope, I think.
S2. You think that the only pressure on you is financial?
C2. That is right. I don't think I'm insane. In order to think of suicide, I understand you've got to be insane.
S3. That's not necessarily true. Suppose we talk about your financial condition then.
C3. It's in a muddle, that's all. When I say it's in a muddle there is no embezzlement involved. It's just a lot of money that I have borrowed and I can't meet my obligations. A lot of it is personal, dear friends of mine, and a good portion of it I owe to the bank. The payments are due, and it's just pressing me and I have no other alternatives. I can't turn anywheres; that is, I still could. I could still go to friends of mine, but I've got a lot of pride and I don't want to do that anymore.

7.6 For Members, the fact that a breach may properly be undertaken given the suicidal's account does not necessarily mean that it will be undertaken. However, while suicidal persons do try to find out whether it will be employed, the attempt to find that out meets with special difficulties.

7.6.1 The problem is as follows: (1) There are known to be maxims that provide that for some actions for which a breach might be engaged in, breach is not engaged in. Thus there is a maxim to cover the case of unmarried pregnant daughters. While parents might propose in general that the pregnancy of unmarried girls is terrible, and drastic actions, say disownment, should be done to those who get "that way," if it happens that a daughter is in such a situation, then the maxim proposed, to quote its use in one of the conversations, is "parents close ranks around her, and give her the care she needs." There are such maxims for many breach-usable actions, but (2) they seem uniformly to be maxims for which there are no procedures available to determine whether, on any given occasion of their relevance, it will be the maxim or the breach that will provide the relevant Rp's actions.

7.6.2 How Rp will behave does not seem readily determinable as a condition of informing them (or not) of the action upon which they may proceed to act in drastically different ways. The various ways one in such a situation may attempt to find out what will be done are manifestly inadequate. They involve, for example, getting discussions going on the matter in general, or on current occurrences not within the given relational unit. For these, the proper conversational response seems to involve employing the breach alternative, whether one would use it or not were the proposed situation confronting one. (See Quotations 8, 20.)

8.0 It is apparent that central to the foregoing possibility (7 ff.) is the rule of orderly use of Rp, and of its correlate: If a first position of Rp has an incumbent, then the fact that a suicidal person has a good warrant for not turning to them does not mean that turning to some second position incumbent is thereby made proper.

The orderly use of Rp has a set of consequences that we may collect in this section—though some of them have been mentioned or suggested earlier. We may begin by reviewing earlier suggestions.

8.1 The considerations of (6 ff.) seem to indicate not only that it was R that provided the police with a search procedure, but further that they could take it that R had been operative with regard to the interactions between the suicidal person and others, i.e. that if someone had been suicidal, then they would have used R in its proper fashion to inform first position members of the fact of their suicidalness.

8.1.1 The fact that the first position member is standardized is obviously crucial to officials. The specifics of that standardization are that it is expectable that whether there is a first position member is something determinable by use of the dead person's name, such that parent or spouse is to be sought out, and where, furthermore, such possible persons are seen to be exclusively appropriate repositories, i.e. if they exist, then the question of the success of an inquiry turns first on their availability. We have seen that the fact that they are unavailable seems to have as its consequence that the inquiry is to proceed without further use of R—i.e. without seeking to locate persons who might otherwise know whether a declaration of suicidalness was made.

8.1.2 First position Members may be seen to agree with officials in this regard. Thus, as we shall indicate with some materials shortly, they take it that if a possible suicide did not inform them that they were suicidal, then the death is not to be seen as suicidal. The fact that they may propose that they were not so informed recurrently constitutes the basis for a claim on their part that a decision that the death was suicidal should not be made or should be reversed.

1) (in a letter asking coroner to reverse a decision of suicide)

> I know this may seem just a nuisance to you, but as I said I can't explain how much it means to me not to have my mother's memory marred by there being any question of her death. I also do not ever want any of her grandchildren, of which there are thirteen, to ever know or feel there was ever any doubt in her death, because I know there couldn't have been.
>
> My husband spent some time with her that evening and she was in good spirits. She went to work Saturday 6-2-62 morning and worked till 4:30 p.m. She stayed and had coffee with one of the women and was in good spirits. Later in the evening she talked to the lady in the connecting apartment, telling her how badly she felt *physically* and that she intended moving in with me and making her home with us. Later that evening my sister-in-law called her on the phone and she was coughing a lot and felt very tired but was completely herself mentally and she said she felt so bad she was going

right to bed and try to get some rest as she had to be to work early Sunday morning . . .

2) (from coroner's report)

On 4-4-63 I called Mrs. D. to arrange an appointment. She said that her husband never talked about suicide, and it was not like him to commit suicide.

8.2 Where a non-first-position incumbent is either turned to or happens on to information as to suicidalness, then even if they are unacquainted with first position incumbents they take it that their proper course of action consists in either locating and informing a first position incumbent as to the presence of the state that provides for the latter's relevance, or advising the suicidal person that a first position incumbent should be sought out. (See Quotations 10, 11.)

8.3 One difference between the variety of possible first positions in Rp and later positions in Rp is that alternative first positions, whether they be "parent," "spouse," or "boyfriend," each have a proper number of incumbents. Some further position Rp categories—for example, "friend" —do not. While, as noted in (8.2), incumbents of such further position categories do take it that first position incumbents are more proper to be turned to than they are, they also take it that the category "friend" is a member of Rp and that its incumbents with respect to each other stand in an orderly relation relevant to their alternatively being approached.

8.3.1 The treatment of the category "friend" as internally ordered seems to operate in several different ways.

1) A friend who is asked to help may, feeling that he is not a first-position friend, find (a) that as regards those he takes it are closer, his being turned to is an affront to them, and (b) that those whom he so locates may concur with him and treat the fact that he has been turned to as improper, as something that requires special explanation, and perhaps as evidence that they are not really in the position that they had supposed they were.

2) The latter fact suggests that a correlate to the proverb "when you need help you learn who your friends really are" is operative, i.e. the order in which friends are turned to in time of need indicates the order in which their closeness is otherwise felt.

8.4 It may be that there is an important consequence of the proper orderly use of Rp—to wit, that if first position Members fail to give help it is not expectable that any further position Members will do so.

9.0 We have observed (2.0) that both R and K can categorize any population N. Since the rules organized by reference to R provide for the propriety and the procedure of the search for help for suicidalness, and since by reference to R, one who is by reference to K "a professional" is (in our materials) a "stranger," i.e. a Member of Ri, the question must be posed: How is it that suicidal persons, or those they turn to for help by reference to R, come to treat as proper calling for a professional's help?

9.1 Since, as it seems, the restriction to use of Rp is an obligation that the suicidal have to Rp, several procedures consistent with the non-violation of that obligation may be found.

1) Members of Rp may tell the suicidal that they ought to turn to a professional. (See 5.1.2. (1), (2).)

2) Members of Rp, on being turned to for help, may themselves seek out a professional. (See, for example, Quotations 14, 15.)

3) If there are no Members of Rp, then while turning to a "stranger" may not involve turning to one who owes one help, it is at least not improper. (See Quotation 22.) In this case one is not replacing R with K, but using R beyond the point where one has claims to get help.

4) If there are Members of Rp, then perhaps one does not violate one's obligations to them if, while one does seek out a non-Member, one does it anonymously, i.e. without revealing who one is, and thereby without revealing who one's Rp are. Such an agency as the Suicide Prevention Center finds that suicidal persons who call it for help recurrently will not give their names. That fact is perhaps partially accounted for by reference to the fact that in contacting a stranger they are violating the rules of R if they do inform the stranger of their names. If a contact is made under these constraints, then it is obvious that a recipient, in seeking to extend the contact to a therapy relation, faces a special task. While we shall not here consider in detail how a professional can in such a situation get the contact extended, an outline of his solution may be sketched.

Just as the appropriateness of R provides for the inappropriateness of K, so the appropriateness of K provides for the inappropriateness of R. Those who are by reference to R, Members of Rp, are likely by reference to K, to be Members of Ki, where Kp is (professionals) and Ki (laymen) for any given trouble for which K is relevant.

The task of a professional, contacted initially as stranger, seeking to provide for both the propriety of his having been sought out, and a transformation of his status into the exclusively appropriate category to have been sought out, is then to show the suicidal person that his trouble is one for which the profession has special and exclusive competence such that it is not merely the case that it is not improper to turn to them, but that Rp cannot give help (See Quotation 4.)

9.2 Since the conclusion "no one to turn to" is arrived at by reference to Rp, it might be supposed that the replacement of R by K would in principle undercut the possibility of arriving at the conclusion. However, (1) to remove the appropriateness of R may serve to undercut the obligatory character of a search for help; (2) as a correlate of the "representativeness" feature (footnote 14) holding for K, if a first professional rejected the request for help, the requester might suppose that further requests to such persons would meet with the same response; (3) the criteria for use of K being seen by the suicidal as not merely need of help, but need of help plus ability to pay, then those who lack the latter might see themselves in even a weaker position if they saw K as exclusively appropriate.

1) (regarding another's suicidal wife)

C1. I said to him, since he was concerned about this, I wondered why he hadn't sought psychiatric help before. He said he couldn't afford private psychiatric help. If he could, you know, he would have done this. He evidently thought she would come out of it . . .

2) **S1.** . . . Have you seen a doctor?

C1. I have a doctor but he's a medical—in a clinic. I mean he has a medical center and he is so busy and I know that I've gone in there a lot of times with aches and pains and things and he says there is nothing wrong with me.

S2. Does he know about your depression?

C2. No. Well he should know, but I've never told him about that. We owe a bill and I couldn't go back there again to him until I got that bill paid and the last time I was there he had told me that there wasn't anything wrong with me and I really was full of aches and pains but he said he couldn't find anything.

3) (regarding previous psychological treatment)

S1. And were you feeling better during that time, or is it hard to evaluate?

C1. Yes and no. At times I was and at times I wasn't. I really didn't feel that I could open up to her, because she was seeing me free of charge and I think that this might have had a lot to do with it, but I was afraid that if I, you know, yelled at her or something like this, she would say: "I don't have to see you, or something like that."

4) **S1.** You've never seen a psychiatrist, though.

C1. No. They cost too much money.

Appendix

1.

S1. You don't have anyone to turn to?
C1. No.
S2. No relatives, friends?
C2. No.

2.

S1. Have you ever been married, Miss G—?
C1. No.
S2. And you're out here kind of on your own and things not going well?
C2. That's it.
S3. You have no one out here?
C3. Well, I have cousins, but you know they're cousins. They're third or fourth cousins . . .

3.

S1. Uh tell me. Is there uh is there anyone close to you, friend or family and so forth, that you could uh kind of be in contact with over this evening to kind of help you over the hump?
C1. If I had somebody like that I'd probably never b— never get to this point.

4.

C1. Maybe it was a mistake to call. I don't know. But I mean—
S1. Why do you think it might be?
C2. Well, you know, it seems to reach out for help from strangers is, I don't know. It seems to be very—like I shouldn't do it. Like my family and friends don't help me, I mean why should I go to a stranger for help, you know?
S2. Sometimes you need professional help.

. . .

C3. Well I'm going to tell you something. I have tried for many many years to get my family to help me. To understand and make myself clear to them. Try to tell them exactly what I was, and what I was trying and they refused to listen and oh, everything's all mixed up and now I've been just thrown over to my grandmother's, and of course I'm—oh, I don't know.
S3. You have parents in town?
C4. No. They're in Texas. I have nobody but my grandmother.
S4. Well, you know sometimes when the people close to us don't come through when we need them, we get sort of hopeless and feel as if no one will.

C5. Well, that's exactly how I feel. I feel today as though I would just like to go out and say—to hell with the whole thing and just flash away and be gone with me. That's exactly how—you know I shouldn't of called you to start with. I mean, I wanted to, to really wanted to. I thought maybe I might get a few answers, but I shouldn't have, because I feel as though it's a deceit. I really do.
S5. What? To ask for help?
C6. Yes. I really do, and because I—help, ask for help and somebody might say, he's mentally—well, he needs help or something. You know that type of thing.
S6. Well, let's get something straight. Anybody can get into a spot that he can't get out of by himself, where he needs some outside help.
C7. Yeah, so then we have to call strangers to get some help?
S7. Yes. If you break a leg, you wouldn't think anything of calling a doctor to have him help you.
C8. Yes, but that's different. But your own family should help you, don't you think?
S8. Maybe they should, but they're not.
C9. Yeah, but I really do think, I mean—
S9. Actually I don't think your family could help you with this. I think this is something you're going to have to struggle out inside yourself, and you will need professional help with this. Now are you afraid that this means you're crazy?
C10. No. I don't really think that I'm crazy.

5 (suicidal homosexual).

S1. Well I understand what these pressures are on you. Is there anyone you trust, anyone who can take care of you, because right now you need some taking care of. You need somebody to move in and take over.
C1. The only people I know are people just like myself. I don't have any regular friends.
S2. Well what about people just like yourself?
C2. They give me all kinds of things and they—
S3. What about your doctor?
C3. I don't have a family doctor.
S4. Well, somebody prescribed those pills.
C4. Well, he's just a doctor. I only called him up.
S5. You never saw him?
C5. A long time ago, for a little thing. I don't know him that well.
S6. You think he'd take over?
C6. I don't know.
S7. What about your parents?
C7. I can't tell them. I'd rather kill myself than tell them.
S8. You can't tell them what?
C8. Anything.
S9. Not even that you're suffering and need to be in a hospital?
C9. No.

S10. But they must have eyes. They probably have been sitting around worrying about this for a long time now.
C10. No. They haven't.
S11. I'd like to call them up and talk with them.
C11. I don't want them to know.
S12. I certainly wouldn't tell them anything that you told me. I'd just tell them that you're suffering, and that you're in bad shape, and you're thinking of killing yourself, and you need to be in the hospital, and I'd want them to get you there. You willing to have them know that?
C12. I don't want them to know anything. My dad's got heart trouble, and my mother ain't very good.
S13. And your mother what?
C13. And my mother isn't in good health either. If you called them and told them anything—
S14. I don't know. I've talked to a lot of people and I think I can handle them, so they won't fall over or anything. But you certainly need somebody to take care of you right now. I think this is part of the big problem that you have no relationships, you got nobody you can lean on. That's true, isn't it?
C14. Yeah. The only thing I can lean on right now is the floor.
S15. I think, well, what I've found from my experience is that people usually come through better than you think they will, even a stranger will come through for you if you say I'm sick and I've got to get to the hospital, but in any case, I would like to talk with your parents about this. You can be sure I won't tell them anything about your sexual problems, and I'm sure they're worried about your coming home drunk every night.
C15. They don't know, they're always in bed.
S16. Are they not very bright?
C16. They're all right. They've done too much for me actually.

6.

S1. And what brings the idea of suicide into your mind?
C1. Because. I don't know. A feeling of uselessness, persecution—oh just so many things. I can't put my finger on any one. I know it's a combination of all of them. I'm too weak to fight any of it, it seems. You know, I just don't really care. The only reason I'm doing this this way is because I don't want to involve my roommate in anything like this. Otherwise, if I were living alone I probably wouldn't have called anybody or anything.

7.

S1. Right. But you have thought about specific ways of doing it.
C1. Yeah. The only problem that seems to become involve—
S2. Is getting the means?
C2. No. No. The means are all there. It's just the amount of—if I could do it without involving other people, without leaving any traces, just nice and cleanly and not having the police involved and so forth and so on, this would be fine.

8.

S1. Is there anyone who you can lean on or turn to?
C1. Not in a situation like this.
S2. There is no one who knows what you're going through?
C2. No, and nobody—I'll explain this to you. I share an apartment with a fellow who is very close. However, this isn't the sort of thing I want to go into with him.
S3. Why?
C3. Well, let's say that this fellow is a very positive-thinking type.
S4. Sort of aggressive—
C4. Very aggressive type of person, and well, for one thing, this would rather dunk him and he's always had a great deal of faith and—and you name it and he has leaned against me a number of times. Now for me to turn around and tell him this had been going through my mind, and so forth and so on.
S5. You don't think he would understand?
C5. He would understand it, but it would mean that he'd feel that he couldn't lean upon me or trust me or so forth to the degree that he has been doing.
S6. I don't quite follow that jump in reasoning. You feel that if he finds out you have a weakness or that you're feeling upset, or despondent, that you would shake his faith in you?
C6. Yes. This is my feeling.
S7. Now sometimes we don't evaluate the people around us very well, and sometimes they respond better to a situation than we might imagine. But that's just a guess. I don't know him.
C7. Well, I have sort of tried to evaluate the situation as far as he is concerned; shall we say, by dropping subtle hints and referring to other people and so forth and so on, and this is the attitude that I get.
S8. He doesn't think much of anyone who feels this way?
C8. No. He's apt to consider them very weak and not able to handle problems and so forth and so on. And I don't want to create that impression in his mind that such a thing would happen to me.
S9. You'd rather be dead?
C9. Quite frankly, I think yes.

9.

C1. Does anyone need to know I've talked to you?
S1. Does anyone need to know?
C2. Yes.
S2. Such as who?
C3. Anybody. I wouldn't want anybody to know because if he [husband] found out or if anybody found out, his attorney found out—anything, they could always say that I was unstable and put me in an institution just like they did with his wife. That's what happened to his wife.
S3. What? That's what happened to his wife?
C4. Yes.

S4. Was she in a mental hospital?
C5. Yes.
S5. And you feel you're cracking up?
C6. This is what he's trying to do to me.
S6. Are you feeling that you're going out of your mind. Is that it?
C7. No. No. No. I don't feel like I'm going out of my mind.
S7. But he might be?
C8. But he would take advantage of this and say that I'm unstable.
S8. I don't know how he'd learn about this. Certainly not from us.
C9. Well that's all I wanted to know. Is this strictly in confidence? Is it strictly protective?
S9. Yes. Now as it happens it might be useful for us to see him, and I'm wondering about that.
C10. Oh. God forbid.
S10. Why do you say that?
C11. Oh, because he would use it against me in five minutes. I know that he would. He has an attorney that is that shrewd that he would.

10 (friend of suicidal is caller here).

C1. So then one day—one fine day—I went over there and I found him—a neighbor—standing there, didn't know what the hell to do next, and I'm sure I didn't. She was lying absolutely out on her bed with the Vodka right next to her and just miserable. Well, I thought, if I ever saw a human derelict with a good mind this was really pitiful, you know? Something has to be done. I'm not obligated but you just can't—I mean I just can't stand to see a human being in this condition and do nothing. So I called up her—I didn't know what to do with her. I didn't have the money or the place or anything else to take her in and do anything for her, so I called the—I called her sister . . . Well, anyhow I was over there and I called her sister—this woman who is so much older than she who lives down in Alhambra, and I said, now what am I going to do. This girl is lying here; she's drunker than a skunk. She doesn't have any money. Her husband left her. She's in a pitiful condition and I don't know what to do with her, and her sister said, "Well I'm sorry Miss Green, I'm afraid I can't help you. We're all packed and ready to go on a vacation tomorrow morning. This isn't the first time this kind of thing has taken place and frankly, I just don't feel that I should do anything about it." Well, I was absolutely astonished, and that left me holding this awful bag . . .

11.

C1. I wonder if you could give me a little bit of advice. Last Saturday I had a neighbor and friend who came over. She was very desperate about a family situation, and she told me that she just didn't want to live any more, and I really didn't take her seriously, but while she was here she took 18 sleeping pills.
S1. At your home?

C2. Yes. This was on Saturday—oh, about 5 o'clock, I'd say, and so I have advised her to—I didn't know that she did this, you know, because it was when I went out of the room. And I had advised her to go and see a relative. I thought it could give her more help than I could. You know, to stay with, everything . . .

12.

C1. . . . I'm calling for a friend who's had a history of mental disturbance; I believe attempted suicides were involved at that time . . .
S1. . . . What is your relationship to her?
C2. Just a friend.
S2. Just a friend. I see.
C3. Her family moved out about a year ago.
S3. No family. I see.
C4. Not in this part of the country.

13.

S1. What prompted you to call? You must have been concerned now, I suspect?
C1. Well, I don't know. Well, you know, I'm in a position where I feel like I'm a meddler, and then like somebody told me once, if you see something—you think they're drowning, and you jump in to save them, you wouldn't be meddling. So I don't know.
S2. Well, it doesn't sound to me that you're meddling. It sounds like you're concerned about a friend and an employee.
C2. Well she doesn't work for me any longer. She worked for me for a short while, and I like her very much . . .

14 (man, regarding suicidal girlfriend).

C1. Well, here is the situation. Now, first of all, I don't feel that I am adequately situated to be able to talk a person out of thinking their way in reference to suicide . . . I explained to her—I stayed up with her all night explaining to her that she just feels this way, and that these things do happen, but we accept them in the best faith possible, but now, I'm ready to give up and I want to turn it over to someone who can do a lot more good than I can.

15 (father of a suicidal son).

C1. The whole story is I'm the kind of fellow that if you were in my territory where you had difficulty with controlling a refinery or boiler plant, I would expect you to listen to me. When I'm outside of my territory and know it, I would expect to listen to someone who is qualified on it.

16.

S1. I see. Now this is your nephew?

C1. This is my nephew, and he resists any attempt to help him. Father K., an Episcopal minister, picked him up in a bar one night and took him outside and talked to him and then his wife took him home and he promptly beat his wife.

S2. I see. That makes it very difficult.

C2. It makes it just dreadful. And I think his mother—he will have nothing to do with any of us, of course. He says we are interfering with his life, which of course, we are, I suppose. But what do you do in a case like this. I am afraid to open a paper in the morning, I'm so afraid that he's gone rampant with a gun and, while they have taken the two guns he's had all the time away from him, you know those people could get guns anywhere.

17.

S1. You mentioned that your wife doesn't understand. Does she know you are sick?

C1. She—you're acting like a little boy. Mind his mother. I don't know if this is right.

S2. It doesn't help to throw something like that at someone. Didn't your doctor ever explain to her that you were ill?

C2. She wouldn't see him. You know what I mean. She doesn't feel there's any need for that sort of thing. I don't know whether she's a small person or whether she's normal. I don't know what it is. Maybe she doesn't have the capacity.

S3. Maybe she just doesn't know about these things . . .

18.

C1. . . . I mean the thing that makes it even more serious to me is the once or twice that I've mentioned it—not deliberately, but kind of slipping to the family or anything like that, they try to make a joke of it, you know.

S1. Well, no, see here we take all of that seriously.

C2. And believe me, it's no joke, because as I say, I just don't feel my life is worth anything at this point.

S2. Well we take that very seriously, and when someone feels that way, we try to do whatever we can to help them to work out of that feeling. And we'd like to help you.

C3. OK, fine then Mr. C——— . . .

19.

S1. Do you live alone?

C1. No. I have my mother with me. She's blind, has diabetes, and I can't talk to her. I have a son 26 years old by a previous marriage who's not with me. He has his own family and he's not very—of actions. He's strong minded. I remember I was too until this happened.

20 (man, regarding roommate).

C1. He doesn't know anything about this. I don't want to involve him in it at all.
S1. You ever talk to him about how you feel? About how discouraged you are?
C2. No.
S2. Why is that?
C3. Well he isn't the type of person who would understand anything like that, you know? I've seen other people—as a bartender he meets other people like this, and I've seen him at work and people will try to tell him something and he'll listen and then he'll make a big joke of it, and things like this, you know? He doesn't mean any harm by it, but—

21.

C1. Hello. I'd like to see a doctor right away. The state Mental Hygiene Clinic doesn't have anyone there this afternoon and they gave me your number and I need somebody to help me.
S1. Can you tell me what the trouble is?
C2. Yes. I'm going crazy. I'm cracking up right now, and I need somebody to say, yes, we'll help. Because I've been fighting for a long time, and I can't help myself and nobody can help me. I need professional help and right now there is no answer at all.
S2. OK. Why don't you come on in this afternoon.

22.

S1. Let me ask you another thing. We're very interested here. We get calls from people who often are very reluctant to give their names or just don't. Why is that? What prevents you or what makes you hesitate?
C1. Well. One feels like such a goddam fool you know?
S2. Why?
C2. I'm well over 21, and I should—you know—If I had a sister or a brother or a husband or somebody to talk to I'd talk to that person. But I feel like such an idiot when you have to call up a stranger and say will you please let me talk to you.

23 (not telephone, psychiatrist and woman).

Psych. 1 . . . Well I think I can see how we can help you . . . we will try to get you and your husband together to decide between you what's right. I think if you know what's right, you'll try to do what's right and that will be easier for you to get along.
W.1 You're going to have to tell my husband.
P.2 I think he'll come in.
W.2 No I mean if he comes in and if you talk about certain things. He's going to know that—
P.3 What?

W.3 Well, that I was talking about it.
P.4 He won't like that? You sound as though you're afraid of him.
W.4 No. But he just says that you're not supposed to talk about things that happen in the home.
P.5 Well, of course, coming here is like coming to a doctor, the professional relationship. While that's generally true, this is sort of the exception . . .

24.

S1. And do you have anyone to lean on? Anyone to help you at all?
C1. No one.
S2. There is no one you can talk to or turn to? No one who offers to help?
C2. No. I go with a fellow now, but he doesn't know anything about this.
S3. Why not?
C3. I don't know. I just can't tell anyone.
S4. Doesn't he notice how upset you are?
C4. Well, I didn't answer the phone Saturday and he finally came over and I was in bed, and he wanted to know what was the matter and I just told him I had the flu.
S5. Uh huh. But it sounds as if he's at least some worried about you, which means he may have picked up clues. You haven't said anything to anyone about wanting to harm yourself?

. . .

S6. Now you have your boyfriend. I think he is entitled to be let in on what's going on.
C6. Well, he's never had a problem himself in his life. I don't know. I just don't want to tell him about it. I know he's real kind, but I haven't gone with him that long. I've just been going with him for two months. Before that I went with someone for three years.
S7. What happened to him?
C7. He was afraid of problems.
S8. I see. So you're afraid you'll scare this fellow away?
C8. Yes.
S9. But if he does care about you at all, I think he would want to share your troubles, you know at least be a listener, because you—let me tell you something about what I think is going on with you . . .

. . .

S10. Another thing that helps clear a depression is being with people and talking. Besides your boyfriend is there anyone else? Do you have any other friends?
C10. Oh I have all kinds of friends. A lot of friends. But I just never have been able to talk. If I do, if I feel like talking about it, I'll say something that I don't mean. I can't explain it. Well, I mean it, I just don't really come out and say what's really troubling me.
S11. Why is that?
C11. I don't know.

S12. Are you afraid you'll be imposing on people?
C12. Yes, at times.
S13. Well, this is a time when you have to stop worrying about imposing on people. If you have a friend, this is what the friend is for. Is there anybody you can call in the middle of the night to just talk for a while when you need to?
C13. No.
S14. Why is that?
C14. Just maybe I don't have as good friends as I thought I did. I just know I don't think anyone would appreciate it.
S15. You say, maybe they're not so good. But maybe also you aren't willing to take advantage of them.
C15. Well of course I just never feel like talking to anyone in the middle of the night. I can't call somebody and say, gee, I had a bad dream, can't expect them to get up.
S16. I don't know. I think when you're in trouble, you need to use everybody around you. Could you call up your boyfriend?
C16. Oh I imagine so. I've never thought about it. He just called me a little while ago.

. . .

S17. Well I think there's too much your hiding from yourself. But this can come out in time. Right now, you know he knows there is something wrong and he wants to know what it is.
C17. Well I do recognize why I don't tell him. It's because I am afraid that he's just about the greatest person that I've ever known, and I'm just so afraid of losing him. I didn't lose the other one that way. He was just a selfish person. In fact we're still very good friends. But he admitted he was selfish.
S18. But this fellow seems to want to help. Sometimes the best thing you can do is to let him know you need him. I think you have some trouble about taking help, but that's just a guess. Anyway let's talk about this some more. You have a boyfriend; you have some other friends. There are some people you can be with. You shouldn't feel alone. When you're feeling really low, you ought to be in touch with somebody. Now you don't sound very convinced about your ability to do that. One thing in a depression is that people tend to be off by themselves.

25 (suicidal woman).

C1. . . . And I'm just at the break. I said, what have I got to live for? I said, Elsie [daughter] tell me. If you could tell me something. She says, oh you going to take sleeping pills? Happy dreams. And this was it. And I says, I just can't find anything to go on for. I haven't—I had some friends, but not such close friends. I mean, they all have husbands. You can't push yourself in with them. I sit here day after day. Even if I go to work, what am I working for? For what? I can't see anything to go on for. My daughter doesn't need me. My son doesn't need me. Everyone has to be needed by someone, and no one needs me.

S1. What about yourself?
C2. Well, do I need myself? Do I need my worries?

26.

C1. I am 49 years old and quite an active woman. I might possibly be menopausal, and this is doubtful. So what the hell, you know?
S1. How long have you been thinking about killing yourself?
C2. I was probably four or five. I tried to stab myself with a fork.

27.

S1. And you called Pelton [a state hospital] and they said they can't take you into the hospital. That's rather hard to believe if you really made clear it's an emergency.
C1. They think I'm kidding. I'm not.
S1. What makes them think you're kidding?
C2. I don't know.
S2. Anybody who knows about these things knows that you take something like this seriously . . .

EMANUEL A. SCHEGLOFF

Notes on a Conversational Practice: Formulating Place*

My aim in this essay is twofold. I hope to develop two problems of conversational analysis, each drawn from a different domain of problems. I shall develop a series of considerations that bear on one of the problems, and attempt to use those considerations in the understanding of the other. I shall proceed by sketching the first problem having to do with conversational sequencing, the problem of "insertion sequences," then abruptly shifting to the other problem, selecting formulations, which I shall call

* The research on which this discussion is based was supported by the Advanced Research Projects Agency, Department of Defense, through the Air Force Office of Scientific Research under Contract number F-44620-68-0040. An earlier version of some

(*Notes to this selection will be found on pp. 432-433.*)

the problem of "locational formulations". Next, a series of considerations relevant to the selection of a locational formulation will be developed, and some of those considerations will be brought to bear on a piece of data that presents an instance of an insertion sequence concerned with location, to show how this insertion sequence is ordered. I will try, in several concluding remarks, to explicate some underlying themes of the discussion.

I
INSERTION SEQUENCES

Elsewhere (Schegloff, 1968), I have described a kind of organization of utterances in conversation that allowed us to speak of them in non-trivial ways as a "sequence." Dealing there specifically with one way in which the initiation of conversational interactions is coordinated, attention was directed to a frequently occurring initial exchange, which was called a "summons-answer sequence." In order to use the term "sequence" in a strong fashion—to refer not merely to "subsequent occurrence" in the sense of the successive positions of the hands of a clock, but rather to a specifically sequential organization—a property called "conditional relevance" was proposed to hold between the parts of the sequence unit. When one utterance (A) is conditionally relevant on another (S), then the occurrence of S provides for the relevance of the occurrence of A. If A occurs, it occurs (i.e. is produced and heard) as "responsive to" S, i.e. in a serial or sequenced relation to it; and, if it does not occur, its non-occurrence is an event, i.e. it is not only non-occurring (as is each member of an indefinitely extendable list of possible occurrences), it is absent, or "officially" or "notably" absent. That it is an event can be seen not only from its "noticeability," but from its use as legitimate and recognizable grounds for a set of inferences (e.g. about the participant who failed to produce it).

A similar organization of utterances has been described more generally by Sacks (1967) for what he calls "utterance pairs." For utterances like "greetings," to say that they come in pairs, or that an exchange of them is an utterance pair, is to notice the same sort of observations as are reported in the discussion of "summons-answer sequences" under the notion of

parts of the paper was presented in a public lecture at the University of California, Berkeley, under the auspices of the Program on Language, Society and the Child in July, 1968. Both on that occasion and subsequently, I have discussed these matters with Harvey Sacks to my great profit. I have tried in various places to specify my indebtedness to him, but there are many others where I might have done so. While responsibility for the outcome is mine alone, I must thank Alan Blum for fruitful discussion in the early stages of this paper, and Erving Goffman and William Labov for critical reading and suggestions. Symbols used in the transcriptions are explained at the end of the bibliography. Each citation of transcript is followed by a code giving its source. A description of the bodies of material from which the data are drawn may also be found at the end of the bibliography.

"conditional relevance." I shall, therefore, use these terms interchangeably, referring to certain kinds of sequences as "utterance pairs," where one part of the sequence is conditionally relevant on the other.

Another kind of utterance sequence that has this structure is the pair "question-answer" (henceforth abbreviated to QA). The basic organization —by "basic" I intend that although other actual sequences may be found empirically, their analysis will be accomplished best by seeing them as modifications of this "basic organization"—involves the conditional relevance of an "answer" when a question has been asked. (Indeed, here—as Sacks has pointed out—this organization is even deeper, for the very recognition of an utterance as "an answer" may turn on its placement, its sequential relationship to "a question," there being no independent linguistic or logical criteria for distinguishing the status of an utterance as an assertion from its status as an "answer.") If this is the case, and if we seek to apply to QA sequences what we learn from other utterance pairs like SA (summons-answer) sequences, then upon the occurrence of a question an answer is relevant, and its non-occurrence is an event, upon which inferences can legitimately be based (by co-conversationalists). (Of course, the kinds of inferences drawn from the absence of an answer to a question can be expected to be different from those involved in SA sequences. The latter relate to physical absence, sulking, cold-shouldering, etc.; the former might concern ignorance, evasiveness, reticence, "covering up," etc.) For SA sequences, it was proposed that the conditional relevance of an answer was operative under a constraint of "immediate juxtaposition" or "nextness," i.e. in order to find the absence of an answer, a summoner did not have to wait indefinitely. If it did not occur as a "next" action (given some formulation of "units" of action), it could be found absent, and the range of possibilities that "absence" could warrant, e.g. the inferences of physical absence, etc., or a repetition of the first item, were thereby relevant. Applying these findings to QA sequences, we would expect that a Q followed either by silence or by talk not formulated as "an answer" would provide the relevance and grounds for repetition of the Q, or some inference based on the absence of an answer. Empirically this is not always so, and I shall be concerned as one part of this paper to show in the case of one kind of departure from this expectation that it should not be the occasion for rejecting the notions of "utterance pair" or "conditional relevance," or for rejecting the membership of QA sequences in that class. Rather, for the case I shall examine, the departure from the strict format that has been outlined stands in an orderly relationship to that format, and is adapted to its organizational requirements.

There are other kinds of departures from the utterance pair organization than the one to be dealt with here. We can mention at least those that turn on an analysis of the notion "question," and involve structurally different kinds of questions: e.g. questions that do not pass the conversational turn to another (some so-called "rhetorical questions"), questions whose sequencing format involves that the one to whom they are addressed return them to the questioner to be answered (e.g. riddles), and questions "answered" by another question. These will not be dealt with here. In the case we shall be concerned with, the initial question is followed by another question, not as an answer to it, and yet, though the talk following the question is not an answer, an answer is not seen to be "absent." One formulation of the problem then is as follows: given an utterance-pair structure where an answer is conditionally relevant on the occurrence of a question, how can one have, immediately following the question, an utterance (in the same conversation) that is not analyzable as "an answer" and yet does not allow the finding "no answer"? Alternatively, if we conceive a search procedure for "answers," in light of the seeming fact that "answers" may be discriminated by their sequential placement in relation to questions, one "place to look" indicated in such a search procedure would be in conversational turns following a question. How is it that one could look to such places, where the conditional relevance property allows the non-trivial finding of "absence" given non-occurrence, and although finding the "non-occurrence" of an answer (where the question is of a type allowing for and requiring an answer) nonetheless not find its "absence"?

The kind of occurrences we are concerned with here may be called "insertion sequences" or "inserted sequences," because between an initial question and its answer there is inserted another question-answer sequence.[1] For example:

*A: Are you coming tonight?
B: Can I bring a guest?
A: Sure.
B: I'll be there.
*A: Have you seen Jim?
B: Was he in today?
A: Yeah.
B: No, I didn't see him.

Such occurrences are not infrequent in actual conversations. If we represent question and answer pairs with the form QA, then we can represent such pairs with an inserted sequence as QQAA or

A: Q_b
B: Q_i
A: A_i
B: A_b

where the subscript "b" stands for "base" and the subscript "i" stands for "first insertion." A general formulation of this format might be as follows: a QA sequence can take a QA inserted sequence. If we take this general formulation without qualification, then we may note that Q_iA_i above, being a QA pair, can itself take an inserted sequence $Q_{ii}A_{ii}$,

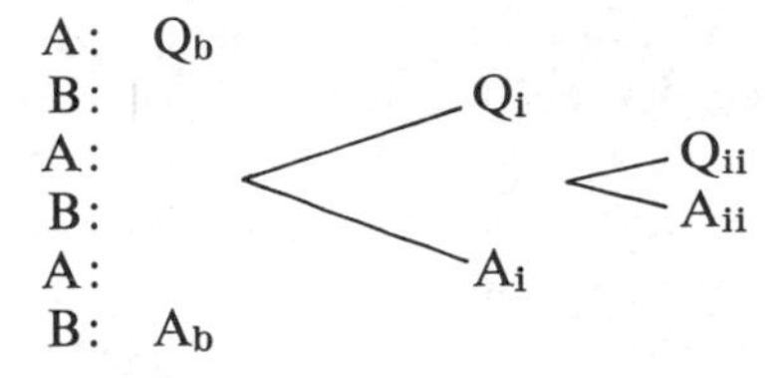

and Q_{ii} A_{ii} being a QA pair can take an inserted sequence Q_{iii} A_{iii}, and so forth indefinitely. Empirically, we do not find indefinite extensions of insertion sequences. It is possible to invent a conversational fragment with many insertion sequences; for example, one with three sequences might be as follows:

*A: Are you coming tonight? — Q_b
B: Can I bring a guest? — Q_i
A: Male or female? — Q_{ii}
B: What difference does that make? — Q_{iii}
A: An issue of balance. — A_{iii}
B: Female. — A_{ii}
A: Sure. — A_i
B: I'll be there. — A_b

However, such multiple insertions are rarely found in naturally occurring conversations. In many cases, a Q_{ii} or second insertion question will be a meta-question, requesting repetition of the Q_i (e.g. "Huh?" or "what?").

To understand how a Q_i can occur without being heard as the absence of an answer to Q_b, we shall want to look closely at it and see whether it stands in some orderly relationship to other utterances in the conversation. Perhaps such an examination will also shed light on the empirical limitation on multiplication of insertion sequences, yielding some specification of QA pairs that can or cannot take insertion sequences. To do this we shall look at a piece of actual conversation. Before doing so, however, I want to turn abruptly away from these questions to an entirely different area, consideration of which will be useful for the analysis of that datum when it is introduced, but which I shall also want to examine in its own right.

II
SELECTION OF LOCATION FORMULATIONS

It has been argued[2] that a central observation about "topic talk"—the argument is made initially about stories, more generally about "talk on a

* Indicates data invented for illustrative purposes.

topic," and perhaps holds more generally still—is "co-selection of features for topic." By this it is intended that if one looks to the places in conversation where an object (including persons) or activity is identified (or as I shall call it, "formulated"), then one can notice that there is a set of alternative formulations for each such object or activity, all the formulations being, in some sense, correct (e.g. each allowing under some circumstance "retrieval" of the same referrent). Furthermore, that the selections made at each spot are "fitted" to each other, or "go together." Rather than saying "they fit the topic," or are "appropriate to the topic," it may be preferable to say that in their co-selection they, at least in part, "constitute" the topic.

If this is the case, then it would clearly seem foolhardy to try to excerpt from its conversational surroundings some particular formulation, and examine how it was selected out of the set of terms that are, by a correspondence test of truth, equally "correct." The selection would seem understandable only as part of the co-selection of the variety of terms occurring in the conversational segment. Nevertheless, at the current stage of investigation, it may be advantageous to undertake just such an examination for certain kinds of collections of terms from which one is selected for use at some point in a conversation.

One such area is that of formulations of members. Because selection of identification of persons is a central resource for invoking common sense knowledge organized by reference to the collections of membership categories (Sacks, 1969, and n.d.), because it is nearly omnipresent in conversation, and because its unexamined co-optation into social science literature can be seen (for some social sciences) as a source of fundamental ambiguity, it appears useful to have considered the problem of the selection of formulations or identification terms for members in temporary isolation from topical context, where it might be analyzed best as part of a co-selection of terms for that conversational fragment. The yield is such as we find in Sacks' papers in this area (see "An Initial Investigation . . ." in this volume).

Although the warrant is considerably weaker, I propose to sketch some considerations relevant to the selection of formulations for another domain—locations. While in that domain also, and perhaps especially, the selection of a formulation or term must ultimately be analyzed in the context of co-selection of many terms, each from a collection of terms of which it is a member, I hope to derive some gains from some reflections on location-formulation selection divorced from conversational context. As I am proceeding here in explicit divorce from conversational context, I shall occasionally take a liberty not otherwise to be condoned of relying at various points on data easily enough recalled to have happened but not recorded and out of conversational context, or invented for the occasion.[3]

When speakers in a conversation make reference to a place, they use some term or formulation of it. This has taken work. I want to show here that this is so; to begin to investigate the character of that work, and its implications; and to suggest one way in which what we can learn about formulating locations can be of help in understanding seemingly quite unrelated conversational practices.

1. The Problem

The "problem"[4] of locational formulation is this: For any location to which reference is made, there is a set of terms each of which, by a correspondence test, is a correct way to refer to it. On any actual occasion of use, however, not any member of the set is "right." How is it that on particular occasions of use some term from the set is selected and other terms are rejected?

Were I now to formulate where my notes are, it would be correct to say that they are: right in front of me, next to the telephone, on the desk, in my office, in the office, in Room 213, in Lewisohn Hall, on campus, at school, at Columbia, in Morningside Heights, on the upper West Side, in Manhattan, in New York City, in New York State, in the Northeast, on the Eastern Seaboard, in the United States, etc. Each of these terms could in some sense be correct (if that is where my notes were), were its relevance provided for. On some occasion of use, for some co-conversationalists, under some conditions, in some conversational context, each of these terms (and undoubtedly many others) could, not only "correctly," but also "rightly," relevantly, appropriately, be used to formulate that place, while the others would not be used appropriately (or, if used, would be heard as possibly formulating some location, but in addition doing some other activity, such as "name-dropping," being arrogant, silly, etc.). I seek to direct attention to the sorts of considerations that enter into the selection of a particular formulation, considerations which are part of the work a speaker does in using a particular locational formulation, and the work a hearer does in analyzing its use.

Before turning to those considerations, however, it would be well to discriminate this problem from a related one. Aside from there being a range of place terms available to formulate a location, we should note that place terms can be used to formulate objects other than place. To choose but a few examples, terms that are place terms can be used to formulate occupation:

A: You uh wha 'dijuh do, fer a living?
B: Ehm, I work inna driving school. (1)
(BC, B, 20)

They can be used to formulate "stage of life":

A: When did this happen?
B: When I was in Junior High School. (2)
(GTS II, 23)

They can be used to formulate activities:

*A: What's Jim doing?
B: Oh, he's at the ballpark.

Where a place term is used to formulate something other than location, the first question may be not how that term was selected out of the set of terms that are correct for that place, but rather how a place term came to be used to do a non-place formulation. Such analyses cannot be undertaken here, but it can be noted that in (2) there follows an introduction into the story being told of persons formulated as "principal," "teacher," etc., and that in (1), although A understands from B's answer that he is a driving teacher (as the ensuing data makes clear), it later turns out that he is a messenger boy.[5] The analysis of how a place term was used to do non-locational formulation may have as its outcome the consequence that of the various terms that are correct for that place, only the one used was responsive to the problem that led to the choice of a location term in the first place (for example, street address would not have set the stage for a cast of characters formulated as school personnel, as in (2), nor would it have allowed inferences about occupation, as in (1)). Under those circumstances, the considerations relevant to using *some* place term, may without reference to other considerations select *which* place term. In such cases the central problem is not "which of alternative place terms" would be chosen, but rather "which of alternative ways of formulating X (stage of life, occupation, current activity, etc.)," one of which is a place term. Here, then, although location formulations are involved, the problem of the selection of location formulations is not the primary one. (The reverse case occurs when non-place terms are used to formulate a location, as in: "A: Is Terry there? B: No, he's teaching a class." While such cases will not be given much attention here, it is clear that they expand greatly the size of the set from which selection is made in choosing a locational formulation.)

There is a third form, in which place terms are indeed used to formulate location, but where some terms may do other work in addition. For example, "Good to be back home" may differ from "Good to be back in Chicago" in that the former is also an account, saying why "it's good," by reference to the kind of tie there is between members and "home," it being where one "belongs." Or to take another example, to report one's return from "The Catskills" (rather than Peekskill), from "The Cape"

* Indicates invented data; here the answer could indicate either work or leisure activities, depending on "Jim's" occupation.

(rather than Buzzards Bay), Zermatt (rather than Europe) can indicate simultaneously that it is a vacation one is returning from, and the sense of expectable answers to questions such as "who else was there.?" However, here we are dealing with terms that are properly seen as selected by reference to the problem outlined above, and show attention to the selection for topic of which we spoke earlier. They, therefore, properly fall within the domain we are investigating, and we shall have more to say below about the term "home," as well as those classes of terms that are "classes-for-a-topic" (as the class of "vacation place terms" just used). We turn now to several orders of considerations I shall argue are relevant to the selection of a location formulation and its hearing.

2. Location Analysis

A first sort of consideration relevant to the selection of a location formulation is a location analysis. By that I mean to suggest that the selection of a location formulation requires of a speaker (and will exhibit for a hearer) an analysis of his own location and the location of his co-conversationalist(s), and of the objects whose location is being formulated (if that object is not one of the co-conversationalists). One important dimension of such an analysis is whether, for some formulation, the objects of the analysis are co-present or not. For many conversational activities or topics, a formulation under which the co-conversationalists are co-present will be rejected. For example, the following segment is from a collection of calls to the police department of a mid-western city. Throughout this collection of conversations there is a great deal of inquiring and reporting of the location of various parties, events, directions, etc. Throughout, the name of the city, "Centurb," does not occur, never being the answer or part of the answer to questions like "Where are you?", "What is the address?", "Where is this?", "Where did this happen?" In this particular call, two police dispatchers are on the line with a lady who has reported a gas leak in her home. The conversation alternates between the precautions she should take (these points are omitted here) and finding where the help should be sent.

D: Radio, Jones.
C: Uh, this is Mrs. Lodge calling from one twenty one Sierra Drive/
D: One twenty one Sierra/
C: Yes.
. . .
D_2: Ma'am/where's Sierra located?
C: It's on the corner of Sierra and uh-hh Smith Drive.
D_2: Sierra and Smith/
C: Yes. . . .

D_2: Uh where is this Sierra and Smith located? We gotta know about this. (3)
C: One twenty one Sierra Drive. It's right on the corner.
D_2: [Right on the corner of Si—uh of what. Sierra/and Smith. Where is Smith?
C: [Sierra Drive. Sierra and Smith.
. . .
D_2: I wanna know where Smith is located.
C: Well it's uh right off Flint Ridge.
D_2: Off Flint Ridge.
C: Yeah.
D_2: Where're you at ma'am, are you in the County/
C: Uhm uh I'm in Exurb uhm.
D_2: (Alright)
C: Oh!!! Right near the A and P Shopping Center. Across— the creek. (3)
D_2: Alright, calm down now, you're—you're in Exurb/
C: Yes uh.
D_2: Alright, we'll get somebody out there then tuh one twenty one Sierra.
(CPD, 22–3)

In this segment, the failure to report as part of the formulation of place the city's name is heard as being produced by a finding of co-presence for that formulation. This is indeed the case in the other calls in the corpus. The failure to formulate the city leads then to hearing that the caller is in the city (co-present in it with the police, and thus not using it in her formulation), and to a search for her street on the city map. The formulation of place is not adequate (i.e. no further asking) until this is called into question and corrected.[6] The usual adequate formulation names some formulation for which the object being located and the conversationalists are not co-present.

A has offered B, both in Pacifictown, a nursing job.
B: And where is it? (4)
A[1]: Out in Edgetown, on Strawson Road.
(SBL, 1, 10, 2)

In some conversational contexts, for some conversational activities, finding a formulation for which the conversationalists are co-present may lead not to its rejection but to its selection. For example, in being "brought up to date" on the doings and whereabouts of old friends and upon learning of their wide dispersal, one might get, in New York, the exchange: "A: And where's Jim? B: Oh, *he's* in New York." Without speculating on the relevance for such an exchange of its placement in a series of locational formulations and its contrastive use in the series, or the relevance of such a discussion as prefiguring the possibility of reunions and their feasibility, it may nonetheless be noted that a finding of co-presence or non-co-presence is relevant, and requires as a consideration in the selection of a locational formulation a locational analysis by the speaker of the respective placement of the parties. And hearers take account of the use of that procedure to see how the formulation employed was arrived at (so that while it is the case that if Jim is in New York he is in the East, a report that he was in the East would be heard by A as reporting that he was not in New York).

Much of the preceding discussion relies on a notion of a "common sense geography" which many North Americans (at least) share. It is presumed by the interactants in their conversation with one another, and by me in reporting on their interactions and in inventing others for illustrative purposes. Because the terms in which locational analyses are conducted are supplied, at least in part (I say "in part" because some such analysis will be done in much more micro-ecological terms, e.g. "this room, that room"), by this shared ("everyman's") geography, it is to the point to remark on it briefly.

A considerable number of the terms suggested above as possible formulations for "where my notes are" seem to fall into a sort of concentric organization, each earlier term of the list being included in a later term. A similar relation holds between "the city" and "county" in (4). The same kind of structure seems to be relied on in an inference such as

A: Where did she train?
B: Uh I think in Oregon.
A: Oh. Mm mmm. (5)
B: Now, I'm not sure, Fran, but I think in Oregon, 'cause she's *from* Portland.

(SBL, 1, 12, 25.)

It is possible that the search for a term for which the conversationalist and/or referrent are or are not co-present is organized for some set of terms in a fashion ordered by such a concentric or hierarchic organization of terms.

What such a common sense geography is and how it is organized (hierarchically or in some other manner) and whether there is a single layman's geography or alternative geographies from which a selection is made on particular occasion of use—these are empirical questions, and not ones to be settled by consulting geography books. Such geographies are a cultural fact to be discovered[7] and perhaps subjected to a sort of "componential analysis" of place terms,[8] but have no necessary further consequences for the analysis with which we are concerned here. That there are such geographies in use, that some of them have a hierarchical organization, and that which one will be used may turn on current and recent respective locations of the parties, can be seen in the following:

A: who has recently returned to the country, has called B.
B: How *are* you?
A: I'm fine. How're you? (6)
B: Fine. Back from the wilds of Peru.
A: Yeah.

. . . (invitation talk)

B: *I*—oh I can't wai'tuh *see* you. (6)
A: Mmmhhehh heh!
B: That's really neat (1.0 sec. pause). Didje get tuh travel in South America a lot?

(TAC, 2, 5)

For Americans, it appears, one goes "to South America" not "Peru," just as one goes "to Europe" not "France." If one says one went to France, one is asked "where else?", rather than "where in France did you visit?" Persons who went "just to France" may have to account for it (e.g. via what they had to do, better and worse ways of travelling, etc.). And the same seems to hold for South America and countries in it; not "where in Peru" but "where else in South America." For Americans, the units parallel to the United States seem to be not France or Peru, but Europe and South America. On the other hand, when people "return" from any of these places, they return to "America." In giving the context for (6) above, I quite naively and automatically wrote "returned to the country." Typically, one who is said to have "returned to California" is heard to have returned from some other state.

These materials would seem to display elements of a common sense geography. They seem to display also a kind of hierarchic or concentric organization of units, which can be further appreciated by seeing that what is asked is "Didje get tuh travel in South America?", while "Did you get to Spain?" would be strange, though clearly for some classes Spain and Peru would be co-class-members. That persons may have more than one such geography and select among them according to a locational analysis is suggested by the possibility that for Americans spending a year or two in England, the response to "I was in France" may well be "where in France?" Similarly, for speakers in New York, a response to the report "I went to Philadelphia" of "Did you get to Boston?" might be strange, but for West Coast inhabitants it might not be.

These few notes on common sense geography may be helpful tools in trying to see how the remarks that have been developed on the relevance of locational analysis to the selection of a locational formulation may shed light on somewhat unrelated problems as a by-product. There are two such "throw-offs" to be suggested here.

The first has to do with one kind of circumstance in which a member makes what another might call an "overgeneralization." The datum involved is the following. An American, returned from a stay of several years in another country, writes a letter to a friend, a native of the country from which the writer has returned. At the beginning of the third paragraph he writes in connection with race relations: "Things here in the States are much worse than the press would have you believe." Having spent all his time since his return in New York City, persons might say that is an overgeneralization; he does not know what is going on in the rest of the country, he knows about New York. And there are lay theories to account for such overgeneralization: people do not think precisely; they are careless with language. Such views treat the utterance as if the speaker is, in the first part of the utterance, bounding the domain for which his assertion is true. One can then find that there is insufficient evidence to warrant the assertion for that domain. But we can take another view and ask: how is such an utterance assembled? It has parts; are all its parts produced in the same way? Instead of seeing the utterance as the defective or inadequate product of one procedure (e.g. a quasi-scientific one), can we see it as the proper outcome of some other? We can, perhaps, propose that different sets of considerations are relevant to producing the various parts of the utterance, and that the part "here in ———" may be produced, in part, by reference to such considerations of locational analysis that have been sketched above. In filling in some place formulation in such a phrase, the selection of a term will be guided by the respective locations of the parties (and not necessarily by a specification of the domain for which the assertion is proposed to hold). We noted above that with respect to other countries, persons return to "the United States." The "here" on which a recent returnee reports to his friend still abroad may then get as its formulation "the States." If persons use some such considerations to select a location formulation, while other parts of their utterance are produced by reference to other considerations, we can see one way in which statements which may come to be seen as "overgeneralizations" are generated.

The second "throw-off" has to do with the use and understandability of what could be called "locational pro-terms," most prominently, terms such as "here" or "there." These terms are prototypical members of a class logicians have called "indexical expressions,"[9] terms whose referrent varies with the context of its use. For terms like these it would appear that for the retrieval of their referrent to be possible, they should be used only after some referrent is named. On the occasion of their appearance, one could then search to find the term to which they refer. However, in some instances these pro-terms are used as first references, without prior place names and without causing difficulty. Utterances such as "How are things there?" or "Things here are going well" do not elicit responses such as "How are things where?" or "What do you mean 'here'?" One way in which a locational formulation that some location analysis by the speaker would yield as relevant, and hear that as the intended use of the pro-term.

Similarly, relational terms such as "downstairs," "in front," "across the street," etc., although they can be combined with place terms, are also used alone. When so used, they are purely formal and may be applied (for terms like "in front") to any structure, or (for terms like "downstairs" or "across the street") to any structure with certain properties (e.g., multi-leveled, or on a street). Agreements to "meet downstairs" or to "wait in front," insofar as they yield successful meetings, would seem to have involved the parties in finding the objects, never explicitly formulated, to which these relational terms were to be applied. And a locational analysis would seem to be involved in the adequacy of such usages, both in the making of arrangements (e.g. to meet) and in the recounting of tales, as in:

> A: En' I couldn' remember what I did with it so I said to Joan, "Go ahead uh an' I'll run *back*." An' I ran back and when I came down, uh, I uh—they said "you've missed all the ex*cite*ment" . . . (7)
>
> (Trio, 7)

or (for terms like "back," as in "going back") to any circumstances in which a "history of recent movement" is available.

Similarly, the term "home" has a shifting referrent; it is not used only for the house one normally occupies, but stands as an alternative term to a range of others. One can be "glad to be home" when one gets back to the United States, to New York State, New York City, the neighborhood, the house, etc. (With flights to the moon, a Soviet astronaut may soon announce the Russian equivalent of "it's good to be home" upon splashing down in the Pacific Ocean.) A locational analysis allows one to see how "home" is being used, i.e. in contrast to what kind of location formulation, and not necessarily to assume that all who express pleasure at being "home" when landing at Kennedy Airport live in the International Arrivals Building.

3. Membership Analysis

A second order of considerations in the selection of a locational formulation, which may be called "membership analysis," has to do with the categories of members of the society of which the hearer(s), in the first instance, but also the speaker, are members; that is, there are relationships between the identifications made (by the parties) of the parties to the conversation, on the one hand ("membership categorizations," as in Sacks, this volume), and the selection and hearing of locational formulation, on the other. Consider, for example, that members who are asked for directions or information may see that the inquiry was directed to them because the inquirer identified them in a particular way and saw their membership in some category as ground for seeking the information from them. In such circumstances, if the membership identification the "solution" of these pro-terms would be possible would be to look to the inquirer used as the warrant for the inquiry is incorrect, the request for information may be met not by an answer or plea of ignorance, but a denial or correction of the identification on which the inquiry was based. Something such as this is going on, it appears, when persons answer inquiries on the street with "I'm a stranger here myself"; or when shoppers, mistaken as sales personnel in department stores, answer inquiries about the whereabouts of "better dresses" not with "I don't know," but with "I don't work here." That the kind of place formulation involved in the inquiry is related to the membership categories is suggested by the likelihood that the question "what floor is this?", asked of the same persons, may be answered.

Seen from the point of view of an inquirer in such situations, the kind of formulation they have of the location about which they seek information may be used to decide on a search procedure for finding to which member of a population of possible answerers the inquiry should be directed. One New Yorker, for example, trying to find "Fillmore East" (a center for rock music) and knowing only its name, reports "looking for the hippiest looking person on the street" to ask for directions. Perhaps, armed with the alternative formulation "105 Second Avenue," the possibly helpful population would have not been so restricted. Similarly, someone looking for "Kent Hall" at Columbia University, a place which does not have a street address as an alternative formulation, may feel that he might need a person "from Columbia" to recognize his goal and help in finding it. I was, for example, stopped by such a person after getting off the bus at the University and asked "Are you going to Columbia?" "Yes." "Can you tell me where Kent Hall is?" (Of course, the initial question not only establishes my membership in a class whose members can be expected to be able to deal with "Kent Hall," it prepares me to recognize the name "Kent Hall" for the kind of thing it will be the name of, i.e. a Columbia thing.)

Furthermore, the use of certain formulations of a location will allow an interlocutor to hear that the speaker is for some membership class "a stranger," and that that identification is relevant in formulating a response. Examples here are difficult, because that some formulation marks its user as a stranger will (and this is what is at issue) be recognizable to non-strangers, and for any example chosen some readers will not be non-strangers. Nonetheless, one who asks in New York City how to get to the "Long Island Train Terminal" (instead of "Penn Station" or "Pennsylvania Station") will thereby be recognizable to New Yorkers (a class of members) as a non-New Yorker, a stranger (a non-class member). And although this is merely one membership identification of many that is correct for such a person (he being perhaps also a male, white, a father, a soldier, etc.), it is one that has relevance to the response, providing a sense of the sorts of locational formulations that can be used. (Where directions are asked for a place whose formulation does not allow a determination of the asker's status in this respect, it may be inquired into as a preliminary to answering. For example, if one is asked for the "Brooklyn Museum," the return may be "Do you know Brooklyn?" On the answer turns (1) which of alternative sets of directions will be given and/or (2) how the places the directions make reference to will be formulated. Will they, for example, refer to "where Ebbetts Field used to be"?)

Similarly, persons are marked as strangers when they call to check on the safety of relatives in Burbank upon hearing there are riots "in Los Angeles' Watts' section." The often-noted deluge of phone calls into areas of natural disaster and civil disturbances in contrast to the relatively little calling out to give reassurance (Fritz and Mathewson, 1957) appears to be related to the need of mass media to formulate the location of the events in terms recognizable to strangers, while their location is formulated locally in native terms. For Bostonians, both their relatives and the riots are in Los Angeles; for the relatives, the riots are in Watts, whereas they live in Burbank.

These remarks are intended to illustrate a variety of ways in which the relationship between members' categorizations of one another and selection or hearing of locational formulation manifests itself. To begin to spell out the features on which the linkage is based we must touch at least briefly on several more general issues.

It appears to be the case that persons (in this society, at least) in using names and in asking for them, claim their recognizability (an important variant omitted here is asking for a name to provide for its future recognizability). Persons introducing themselves use different "frames" in their introductions when claiming the recognizability of their name and when no such claim is made. On the telephone, for example, the frame "my name is ———" makes no claim to recognizability, while the frame "this is ———" does.[10] Where the claim to recognizability is warranted, but failure of recognition is anticipated, the "claim" form is used with assistance supplied for the recognition (e.g. "Professor Van Druten, this is Sally Bowes. I was in your course on German History."). When asking a name where the grounds for expecting its recognizability may not be apparent, grounds are given. Thus, in the classic ploy, "What did you say your name was again?", recognizability is based on a claim that the name has been already given. To cite actual data:

B has been talking about people she is having to lunch. (8)
A: Who didju say it was? I think you *told* me.
(SBL, 2, 1, 8, 5)

This is far from the only grounds that may be offered. For example:

A, who is visiting the city, has spoken of visiting a friend in Van Nuys.

B: Wh-what is yer friend's name, cuz my *son* lives in Van Nuys.
A: Glazer. (9)
B: Mmhmm no. And uh, if she uh . . .
A: She lives on Mariposa.
(1.6 second pause)
B: No, I don' even know that street.
A: Mm no.
(DA, 3)

Similarly, when a name has been asked for, the request can be rejected on the grounds of no expectable recognizability.

B: Who is that?
A: Uh she's uh not known here. She lives out in South town. (10)
B: Mm.
A: She's uhm-hum, just moved here about a year ago.
(SBL, 1, 10, 8)

For our concerns here, place names and personal names may be considered as of a piece, the issue of recognizability holding for both. "Name-dropping," for example, can be done with place names as well as with personal names, and depends for its operation on the recognizability of the name.

To speak of the "recognizability of the name" is insufficiently precise here. What is central is more than hearing once again a sequence of morphemes that have been heard before. What we mean by "recognizability" is that the hearer can perform operations on the name—categorize it, find as a member of which class it is being used, bring knowledge to bear on it, detect which of its attributes are relevant in context, etc. It is the ability to do such operations on a name that allow such responses as:

*A: Who did you go with?
B: Mary.
A: Oh, it was a family affair.

*A: I had lunch with Jones.
B: When's his book coming out?

*A: I saw Bundy.
B: Any chance of getting money?

Names themselves are on the whole neutral with respect to the categories of which their bearers are members. Whereas in English, personal names may indicate sex, ethnicity, and sometimes social class, they are otherwise mute. Recognition involves, then, the ability to bring knowledge to bear on them, to categorize, see the relevant significance, to see "in what capacity" the name is used.

In this respect, too, place names are like personal names.

A: And he said that some teacher, who's coming uhm from I believe he might have said Brooklyn, some place in the east. (11)

(SBL 1, 1, 12, 21)

Here, the particular place that had been mentioned is not clearly remembered, but the outcome of some operation (some analysis of the place that was mentioned) is. This sort of finding has wider import; however, our interest here is only in showing that on hearing, such operations, classifications (in short) "analyses" are done, and their outcome may be retained while the particular is not, and that what is meant here by "recognizability" is "analyzability" in this sense. Thus, names are to be used only when expectably recognizable, where that means "analyzable." When prospective users are not sure that some name will be recognizable in this sense, they may ask that about the name before using it:

A: Well tell me, do you—does the name Charles Weidman mean anything to you? (12)
B: Well, I should say so.

(SBL, 2, 2, 4, 11)

*A: D'ya know where the Triboro Bridge is?
B: Yeah.
A: Well make a right there . . .

And, if it is not recognizable, they may supply the relevant attributes:

*A: Do you know George Smith?
B: No.
A: Well, he's an artist, and he says . . .

Members treat the recognizability of particular names as variably distributed. For some names, recognition can be expected of the members of some membership categories. And not only recognition, but adequate recognition, i.e. not only can it be expected that they can perform some operations or analyses, but the ones that yield the adequate-for-the occasion outcome, the relevant recognition. Which categories of member can be expected to recognize a name turns on the kind of name. For place names, one relevant category is territorially based. Persons in a place, or in proximity to it, may be expected to be able to recognize place names in it or near it, and they may offer current or former proximity, or territorially based category membership, as evidence, warrant, or account for their recognitions.

D: . . . They're setting up emergency at uh uh the cattle barn.
Y'know where that is? (13)
C: Yeah. I live on 38th about 10 blocks east.
(IPD, #371)

And a show of knowledge about a place may prompt an inquiry "Oh, have you been there?" Knowledge of places is, in that sense, locally organized.[11] Although the structure of knowledge about a "sort of place" may be general and formal, everyone organizing knowledge in the same categories and on the same dimensions, the particulars that are so organized are assumed to vary with territorially-based memberships. Thus, most persons live similarly, in a place in an environment of places, in a house, in a neighborhood, in a "part of town"—which can be similarly talked of (and it is an important fact that some do not). Their place, and its environment of places, have characteristics, character, a population composition, etc. These categories are filled by persons with their particular situations, *their* house, *their* street, *their* neighborhood, *their* part of town, *their* city, *their* state, etc., on which they are knowledgeable and can speak, while others can respond accordingly. The sharing of particulars at one or another of these levels is perhaps one sense of membership in a "same community." It is by reference to the adequate recognizability of detail, including place names, that one is in this sense a member, and those who do not share such recognition are "strangers."

In this way, "right" selection and adequate recognition of place formulations can be seen to be one basis for demonstrations of, claims to, failings in, decisions about, etc. the competent membership of either speaker or hearer. Where "trouble" occurs, it can be seen either that the speaker's analysis was incorrect, or that the analysis was correct but the hearer is not a fully competent instance of the class of which he is (relevantly for the place term employed) a member. The occurrence of "trouble" can be most clearly recognized when the use of a place formulation produces a question or second question about the location of the initial place formulation as in (4) above or in

*A: I just came back from Irzuapa.
B: Where's that?

*A: Where are you?
B: Sloan Street.
A: Where's that?

In the first case, perhaps B can see the incorrect analysis A made of him to come up with that term as a claimedly adequate one, and can perhaps use

that incorrect analysis himself to see what sort of person A must be to have produced it. Alternatively, A can see B as a deficient version of some class in which B claims membership, for members of which "Irzuapa" ought to be an adequately recognizable place formulation. Insofar as friendships, reputations, marriages, collaborations, etc. may turn on someone's competent membership in some class of members (e.g. "swinger," "anthropologist," "good Jewish girl," "Africanist," etc.), each occasion of the use of a place formulation selected because of its presumed recognizability to a member of such a class is part of a never-ending potential test in which persons can be shown to be inadequate members of the class, and thereby inadequate candidates for the activity. Alternatively, each place term a person uses can be inspected to see if it is the term such a person, a member of a certain class of members, should use. The stream of conversation is thus full of places getting mentioned off-hand in some formulation, and requiring recognition. And much can turn on their being recognized and on their being "rightly" selected (where "right," as compared to "correct" may mean "not subject to further question, and not giving cause for a re-analysis of the membership of the user"). Aside from inferences about the membership and competence of the parties, trouble over a place formulation can lead to reparative work in the conversation to show that although the place formulation used was not recognized, the speaker's membership analysis used to choose that term was correct, and the hearer is not a defective member, but rather some particular account is available to explain the "momentary non-recognition."
Thus:

B: I played bridge today, and I—I was in the home—an awfully nice party down on El Ravina—El Ravina.
A: Yeah.
. . . (Talk regarding bad cards) . . .
A: This was a— This was a party, where *is* El Ravina.
B: Well, I'll tell you sum'n, the way I went, I went onto Pacific Boulevard, and I went up past El S— uh Prairie. *You* know,
A: Oh.
B: Rest Home. And then I turned to the left, and it's the very first street.
A: Oh! Of course. I know where it is,
B: Uh huh.
A: *I* know.
B: Uh huh. (14)
A: (Clears throat)
B: And it's a very nice little street,
A: Uh.
B: Close to the ocean.

A: I was getting it—mixed up with uh there's something like that out in uh Little *Falls*.
B: Well, that could be,
A: A—and uh like Ravina.
B: Mm hmm.
A: Maybe it's just Ra*vi*na, not *El Ravina*.
B: Mm hmm.
A: Out in Little Falls.
B: Mm hmm.
A: That's awfully—
B: Well this is E-l, R-a,v-i-n-a.
A: Yeah, *I* know where it is.
B: Uh huh. Yah—yeah, it's very easy to find. I was—I just got to the—got to the // first ( ).
A: It's the main one, to go down to,
B: Yeah.
A: Mm // hm.
B: Uh huh. And then when I was going to—you know, out, there I was facing the wrong way, so I thought etc.
(SBL 1, 12, 15–16)

A, having failed initially to recognize the name, eventually comes to say the speaker was not wrong to have used it; the membership analysis that might have produced this formulation was correct; it ought to have been recognized, and there is a reason why it was not.

Two further remarks on this point are relevant. First, the account given for the non-recognition is curious, i.e. "I was getting it—mixed up with uh there's something like that out in uh Little *Falls*." For why would the location of *El Ravina* have been a thing to ask for if she recognized it as being in *Little Falls*. The two can turn out to be "mixed up" only *after* she gets a formulation of *El Ravina* from B. Before that, she heard it as "in *Little Falls*," i.e. that *is* where it is. Why then ask where it is? And how can a "mix-up" that is possible only after the clarification that there are two different places involved account for the failure to recognize the name when it is first used. Perhaps it would have been strange to A that B would go to a party at "Little Falls," given some analysis of the "kind of place" that is and the "kind of person" B is. This lack of fit produced the failure of recognition. (On fit between places and persons, see below, section 4.) Second, throughout this segment A asserts several times her recognition of the place. But the discussion of where it is does not end until she demonstrates the recognition. We can note that transformations from one formulation to another can not only show a preferred formulation (as will be suggested below), but can demonstrate that the transformer has recognized and understood, by showing he can analyze the first formulation and find a correct transformation. Thus, for time formulations:

B: How long y'gonna be here?
A: *Uh* / not too long. Uh, just till uh Monday. (15)
B: Till—oh (yeh mean) like a week f'm t'morrow.
A: Yeah. (DA, p. 1)

So when A begins a transformation of El Ravina, exhibiting the product of an analysis, "It's the main one, to go down to," she demonstrates the recognition that B had a "right" to expect and relied on in employing the place name initially.

Of the variety and range of locational formulations from which a speaker selects, a significant number are place names (e.g. of parts of town, city, neighborhood, street, business, building, etc.). If the use of a locational formulation that is a place name requires, as a condition of use, its expectable recognizability; if recognizability involves the hearer's ability to categorize, bring knowledge to bear, analyze; if the hearer's ability to do so is seen to turn on his membership in some category of member, then selection of such a term will require a membership analysis of the hearer by the speaker. The analysis is to determine the availability to the hearer of that competence on which the speaker must rely if he is to use some locational formulation adequately, i.e. understandably, without further elaboration, with no further question. It is in the light of such considerations that the illustrative materials at the beginning of this section are to be understood, and the relevance of a membership analysis, in addition to the locational analysis discussed earlier, to the selection of place formulations is to be appreciated.

4. Topic or Activity Analysis

A third order of consideration that seems to be involved is an orientation to "topic" or to the activity being accomplished in an utterance; in short, a "topic analysis" or "activity analysis" is also relevant to the selection and hearing of a place formulation. This is suggested by the discussion above of the requirements of a hearer that he perform operations on names—categorize, analyze, etc.—to find the relevant respects in which it is used. Perhaps the central focus of relevance in this connection is the topic that is being built up or talked to, the activities being enacted in the utterance. In order to begin to get at this orientation to topic in the selection of place formulations, it will be useful first to consider whether the collection of formulations from which a selection is made is homogeneous and undifferentiated, or whether it is structured, and has sub-sets, or "sorts of formulations." I shall propose several "sorts of formulations" and propose that such sub-collection structures of terms are a resource in the sensitivity to topic of the selection of place formulations.

One sort of formulation I shall call G for geographical, and note it without discussion. Such formulations as street address (2903 Main Street) and latitude-longitude specifications are of this sort.

Another sort of term can be abbreviated as R_m, for "relation to members." Such forms as "John's place," "Al's house," "Dr. Brown's office" are among those intended. Terms such as "home," "the office," "the supermarket," "the store" are also of this sort, the first two (and ones like them) being formulated by their relationship to the speaker or hearer, the latter two, on some occasions of use, being heard as "the X to which we both know we go" (though in other conversational contexts they may be used as members of a class of places, a sort of place).

Of the R_m terms, ones of the form "the X" where it is used as "my X" or "your X," where the member by relation to whom the place is formulated is said "to have an X" (e.g. home, house, office, etc.) have special uses and properties. First, for most persons, there are relatively few terms that can be used in this way. "Home" and "office" (or some such work place equivalent) may exhaust the list for most persons. For those who have others, the character of the activity they are seen to do in using them may depend on whether their interlocutors knew they had such additional places.

> K: Oh I—I never saw it before, cause I was on the *ranch* when it first came *out*. And it was so funny. (16)
> R: Oh, do you own a ranch too?
> (GTS, 1, 13)

Note that the usage "the ranch" is recognized as K's ranch, K's "having" a ranch. And that can be seen, by those who did not know it before, as boasting, showing off, etc. Here, then, we have one way in which doing a correct membership analysis in picking a locational formulation can have consequences. "The ranch" can be used with persons who know you have one, while the talk continues to be focused on the movie that is under discussion. Alternatively, with those who do not know it, "away" would allow the same outcome. But here, "the ranch" becomes the focus of the conversation, and the "movie" topic is deflected.

These special R_m terms, "the X" type R_m terms, and especially the term "home," have the special character not only of "belonging to" the member in relation to whom they are formulated, but, as we noted earlier, such a place is for a member "where he belongs." One way of showing how this expresses itself in member's practices is to consider the use of terms like "out" or "not here."

Were someone to inquire at my home, by phone or in person, for "John Smith," there is a sense in which it would be true to say he was "out" or "not here." A search of the premises would reveal no one with that name. But that is not what would be said. What persons say in such circumstances is something like "You have the wrong number (address)." Being "out," or "not here," or "not here right now," is what people are with respect to a limited class of places, formulated typically as R_m places (where the m or member can be their name), especially of "the X" type, which might be called "base places" for them, places in which it is warranted to search for them without an account for looking for them *there*. It is for such places that when they are not there, they are "not here" or "out." And if a place stops having that relation to a member, others will normally be told upon inquiry "He doesn't work (live) here any more." In one case I know, someone was trying to reach an editor at "his office" for three weeks. Told each time he called that "Mr. Smith is out," he called back again. Only after some time did he learn that Smith had left his position, whereupon, of course, the caller discontinued his efforts.

The status of such places under R_m formulations as places where one belongs, whose presence there is not accountable, can be seen in another way. When a place is formulated by an R_m term, and especially as "X's home," persons calling on the telephone who fail to recognize the voice that answers as belonging to one by relation to whom the place can be formulated often ask "Who's this?" There are two kinds of answers to this challenge. One is "Who's *this*?" or "Whom do you want" (which children are often taught to ask, before answering); the other is some kind of self-identification by the answerer. It appears that in choosing between these kinds of answers, an analysis by the answerer of his relation to the place he is in is relevant. If he is a person by relation to whom the place can be formulated, if he "belongs" there, if his presence is not accountable, he will counter-challenge "Who's *this*?" If not, some self-identification will be returned and in many cases such a self-identification will be chosen as will also provide an account of the answerer's presence, e.g. "This is Mr. X's nephew" or "The babysitter," the latter showing not only why the answerer is there, but why she is answering the phone.

One further point before returning to R_m formulations in general. It was noted above that for most persons there is a restricted number of places of "the X" type. There are, however, resources for greatly expanding the set of terms that can be used to formulate such places. There is a set of terms mentioned earlier and discussed further below that are relationship terms such as "near," "with," "in front of," etc. When combined with some object, these terms generate a large set of terms that can stand as transformed formulations of an R_m term.

B: Uh if you'd care to come over and visit a little while this morning, I'll give you a cup of *co*ffee. (17)
A: Hehh! Well that's awfully sweet of you, I don't think I can make it this morning, hh uhm I'm running an ad in the paper and—and uh I have to stay near the phone.
(SBL, 1, 10, 14)

"Near the phone" seems here to be a place formulation chosen "for topic" to go with "running an ad." Clearly, selecting a term "for topic," given the resources of the collection of relational terms, can generate an extended collection of formulations that are transformations of "home" (e.g. "with the children," "in front of the stove," "working out back," "at my desk," "at the typewriter," etc.). I call them "transformations" for two reasons, neither to be supported by data here. First, if someone were to call B in (17) and ask where A was, the answer would probably not be "near the phone" (and might not be understandable if it were), but "at home." The basic formulation is "home"; "near the phone" is a topically-sensitive transformation. When removed from topical context, it is not a relevant transformation. Second, A, in selecting a place formulation, does not select from among "120 Main Street" (or whatever her address may be), "home," and "near the phone" to refer only to the sorts of formulations so far introduced into this discussion. It appears more likely, though there is no evidence, that she selects first between a G and R_m term, and having selected the latter, then modifies it for topic, or transforms it.

Why should she, however, have chosen an R_m term over a G term? Is there a preference rule for this choice? In general, it appears the rule is: use an R_m term if you can. The qualifier "if you can" refers largely to the earlier finding that names should be used only where expectably recognizable. The consequence here is that one should use an R_m term if one can formulate the place by relationship to a member the hearer(s) can be expected to recognize. So we find R_m forms used because the other knows the m, where that involves introducing a second or third formulation:

B: Euhhmm uh they live uh right at— They live on Oleander Street, and that's a street beyond Terrace Lane.
A: Yeah. (18)
B: Where Sarah lives.
A: Yeah.
(SBL, 1, 12, 9)

And where an R_m formulation is not used, it may be understood that it is because the other does not know the member involved, as in

B: I played bridge today, and I—I was in the home—and awfully nice party down on El Ravina—(1.0) (19)
El Ravina. (SBL 1, 12, 15)

And where a G term has been used to a hearer who knows the place by an R_m formulation, he may transform it.

*A: Meet you in front of one fifty three seventeenth avenue.
B: Oh, at Bill White's house?
A: Yeah. I didn't know you knew Bill.

On the whole, then, the preference rule appears to be: use an R_m formulation if you can. Clearly, this makes the choice of an R_m formulation turn on the outcome of a membership analysis, requiring an analysis of who knows whom, who are strangers, whether persons are members of such pair-relationships as would allow use of an R_m term. And since R_m terms are preferred, such a membership analysis may be required as a first procedure, if only to reject an R_m formulation and select another. The character of R_m terms and the preference rule thus suggests that a membership analysis has been done not only when an R_m term has been used, but when one has not but was possible.

Another expansion of the collection from which selection of a locational formulation is made can be seen to occur when we recognize that members may formulate members as being not "in" or "at" a place, but "between" places. Persons "on their way home," for example, may select that formulation in place of "in the station," "at 125th Street," "in the train," "in the third car," etc. A person dressed in a swimsuit in his car, may have a gas station attendant ask him "going to the beach?" Someone who will "return your call" wants to know if "you're in your office" and the answer may be "I'm on my way home." So another set of formulations is provided by the possibility of being "on the way to ———," "on way from ———," etc.

Similarly, there are places formulated so that their main character is not only, or not so much, where they are as where they are "on the way to," "between," i.e. where they are in relation to something else. Such formulations we will call R_l, or relation to landmark, where by "landmark" is not intended public buildings or monuments, but any object recognizable from description (here using "recognizable" not in the earlier sense of "analyzable," but as "capable of being seen as the place mentioned or described"). "Three doors from the corner," "three blocks after the traffic signal," "the last street before the shopping center," "behind Macy's," "to the left of the billboard," "next to the school building," "two houses down from Jack's place" are examples. Such terms are compounds of certain relationship terms and recognizable objects or place formulations of other sorts (being in this way like the transformation formulations for R_m places discussed earlier, e.g. "near the phone"). In such cases, whether or not the second part of the compound can be formulated as a place in its own right, it may also be formulated for what we may call its "relational" or "transitional" properties, as a point of reference. Conversely, a place that could be formulated in its own right may be formulated by using some other place as a point of reference. And if there are many such places that can be used for their transition value and be used as points of reference, then the size of the set of possible formulations from which selection is to be made is enormously increased. (For example, a place that can be formulated in its own right as Penn Station can then become "under Madison Square

Garden," "n blocks south of Macy's," "across the street from Hotel Q," etc.).

Landmarks, in the sense being used here, have as probably their most prominent use their inclusion in directions,[12] where they are used specifically as in-between places. Directions formulate getting from point A to point F by moving from A to B, B to C, C to D . . . to F, where B, C, D, E are used for their transition value. Any place can be so formulated for some places as "between them" for some class of members (for whom they would be recognizable; hence, again, the relevance of membership analysis).

Some places in the society may have almost solely transition value, and others will, for certain categories of members, have largely transition value. The phenomenon of seeing people "waiting" seems to rest on seeing them located in a transitional place, being thereby not in a place, but on the way to some other place. Places with high transitional value may thereby accrue great economic value, certain business seeking to be located precisely at places treated by members as transition places for many points of origin and many destinations. They are places, then, where people can meet, in some independence of where they may later be going. That members of this society could produce Schelling's results (1963, pp. 55–56), in which an absolute majority of persons told to meet someone in New York could agree on where to do it with no further information (e.g. where they were going to go after meeting, where the other was coming from, etc.), suggests their familiarity with the notion of a place in-between places, even where these are unknown, i.e. a place with absolute transition value, or maximum transition value (and further that they saw such a place as relevant to their task, and that an absolute majority could independently arrive at the same one). It is this feature that is central to the kind of formulation of location we are calling R_1.

Another sort of formulation might be called "course of action places," i.e. places that are identifiable places only by virtue of what goes on there and are so formulated (e.g. "where they leave the garbage"). In the history of the Western world, of course, that is how many places were made. (For example, where battle X was fought, etc., the latest being the spot, otherwise unidentifiable, where Kennedy was killed. The "otherwise unidentifiable" routinely leads to some mark of identification being put there, whether monument or city.)

Finally, a prominent sort of location formulation is place name, R_n, be it street, city, section, store or whatever. Names, we argued before, are used when analyzable, and so we should note that the indefinitely large collection of place names is organized into a variety of sub-collections, whose recovery is the work of analysis. The very terms just used to suggest kind of place names are themselves names of sub-collections or categories. Each place name may be a member of many sub-collections (for example, "Bloomingdale's" as a store, a department store, a "better" department store, an East Side store, a store on 59th Street, etc.) for each of which it is grouped with different co-class members. But even groups of names as a group may together be members of alternative collections ("Bloomingdale's," "Macy's," "Gimbel's" all being department stores, Manhattan stores, etc.). As a limiting case we should note those classes whose co-members are grouped together for a single attribute, and hence may be a class for a single (or limited range of) topic, as in the case used earlier of vacation places or, even more specifically, skiing places—perhaps for no other topic would Aspen, Zermatt, and Stowe be used and heard as co-class members.

Having suggested that locational formulations fall into types and collections, we can return to the concern with "orientation to topic" or "topic analysis" that occasioned this discussion.

The relevance of the organization of place formulations into collections is that where one has collections one has the possibility of attending, in the selection of formulations, to the collections of which they are members. One can, for example, use a consistency rule in selecting a set of formulations to be used (see Sacks, this volume), selecting formulations that are members of a same collection (or, otherwise put, using the collection membership of the first formulation used to locate the collection from which subsequent terms are chosen). For place formulations one can select terms that will allow selection of other terms by use of a consistency rule, and which will allow a hearer to observe that a consistent (i.e. from some same collection) set of formulations has been employed.

For example, the relationship terms discussed earlier have a collection usage, independent of the place terms with which they are combined. So "in front of ———," in back of ———," "to the right of ———," etc. can be seen, when used serially, to be drawn from a collection of such terms. And the place formulations to which this collection can be applied can have collection usages. We have already noted that place names can be analyzed as members of alternative collections. Here we can note that R_m terms are also capable of such organization, either by reference to the collection of places for some member (e.g. "He could be at home, at the office, or on the ranch"), or by reference to the places formulated by reference to members who are members of a single collection (e.g. "Should we play at Bob's place, or Arthur's, or Bill's?" for a "bridge circle"). Finally, the members of the collection of relational terms can be combined with a single place term ("in front of X," "across the street from X," etc.), thus formulating a set of places, each of which could be formulated in a variety of ways (even within the constraints of a location and membership analysis) by their respective relations to a single point of reference. In such a circumstance (but not only in such a circumstance) it would appear not only that the terms were being chosen for consistency, but that they had consistency for a focus. Thus, in the following data, all the place terms (which I have bracketed) appear to be formulated by reference to "Shepherd's."

JEANNETTE: Hello.
ESTELLE: Jeannette.
JEANNETTE: Yeah.
ESTELLE: Well, I just thought I'd—re—better report to you what's happen' at [Shepherd's] today /
JEANNETTE: What'n the world's happened // ed. (20)
ESTELLE: D'you have the day off /
JEANNETTE: Yeah /
ESTELLE: Well I—v—got outta my car at five thirty I drove aroun' an' at first I had t'go by [the front a' the store,]
JEANNETTE: Eyeah /
ESTELLE: An' there was two / p'leece cars [across the street], andeh-colored lady wan'tuh go in [the main entrance] [There where the silver is] an' all the // [(gifts an' things),]
JEANNETTE: Yeah,
ESTELLE: And they, wouldn' let'er go [in], and' he hadda gun / He was holding a gun / in 'is hand, a great big long gun /
JEANNETTE: Yeh.
ESTELLE: An'nen [over on the other side], I mean [to the *right* of there], [where the—emp*loy*ees come out], There was a whole—oh musta been tenuh eight'r ten employees stanning there, because there musta been a—It seem like they had every entrance barred. I don' know what was go // ing *on.*
JEANNETTE: Oh, my *God.*

(Trio, 1–2)

And in another conversation a few minutes later:

JEANNETTE: Maybe it was uh somebody from maybe—They wuh—was it [from the bank] / maybe there was a bank / holdup an' they were just you know—p—pre*pared* the—maybe there were—yiknow sometimes the—hh they—rob the bank, an' then they go [through Shepherd's 'r something like that]. (21)
ESTELLE: Where's the *bank*?
JEANNETTE: [Right on the corner.]

(Trio 14–15)

That the terms are selected by reference to Shepherd's is the outcome of work. The police cars "across the street" from Shepherd's were also "in front of" some other store, but the former formulation is selected; the "bank" is on the corner of some two intersecting streets (e.g. "on the corner of Main and Spring"), but is here formulated as "right on the corner," i.e. of Shepherd's block. Formulation selection *can* be done to focus *off* some object. For example,

B: Now for instance wu—she use to b*or*row from me. She borrowed twice, from me once.
A: Uh huh.
B: An', oh I was setting in 'er house, 'n Cal Major came 'n del*iver*ed something, and she w— said she didn't have the *change*. Would I loan 'er the money to *pay* 'im. . . . (22)
(SBL, 1, 1, 11, 1)

Here, "what was delivered" is focussed away from by being formulated as "something." So "focussing off" can be done conversationally. In the data of (20) and (21), "Shepherd's" can thus be focussed *off* or focussed *on*. The choice of formulations has done some work in focussing *on* it. And that focus is a focus on topic or oriented to topic, or partly constitutive of what the topic is. This, then, is an elaboration of one element of what we spoke of at the beginning of Part II (p. 79 above) as "co-selection of features (or descriptors) for topic"—namely selection of place formulations for topic.

As place formulations can have a collection membership and a consistency usage, so can membership identifications (see Sacks, this volume), i.e. one can use a membership term that allows a subsequent one to be selected for its consistency with the first. Is there any relationship between consistent selections of membership identifications on the one hand, and consistent selections of location formulations on the other? In other words, can there be not only "within type" consistency, but "cross-type consistency"? We cannot pursue such an inquiry here. It is part of the much larger question: what types of descriptors can be massed for consistency considerations (as between types and not only within them) so as to show that each term was not picked randomly, without reference to topic, but was picked for (or to constitute) that topic for which the cross-type consistency is relevant? And how is such co-selection done, i.e. is the selection for topic done within each type separately, or for one type initially, with subsequent types coordinated to the first, etc.? The data already introduced can offer at least a suggestion in this respect.

There are a number of collections of membership identification terms available for formulating the persons referred to in the story under discussion in the conversations from which (20) and (21) are taken. Consistent identifications would have been made, for example, by the terms "men" and "women." But although consistent among themselves, these member identifications would have stood in no relevant relation to the selection of place terms focussed on "Shepherd's." On the other hand, the collection whose terms include "employees," "customers," etc. would be relevant to that focus, to the type of place "Shepherd's" is. It seems that this is the collection of membership terms used. At the end of (20), "employees" is used to formulate the persons "stanning there" (persons who "could have been" formulate by sex, age, race, etc.). As for the term near the beginning of (20) "andeh-colored lady," it can be shown that it is used here as a description of a "kind of customer," where "customer" is not said.

That such "unspoken" primary categorizations are done can be seen in the use made of the identification "a blond." Although it appears that this term identifies as its primary category "color hair" or "type of member with blond hair," the term is used to specify a sub-class of female. "Female" is then the primary categorization, though unstated. Unstated primary categorizations, then, are possible. That "colored lady" is used here as a secondary sub-classification within a primary "customer" (or "non-employee") is suggested by the following data from "Jeannette's" call to a fellow employee at Shepherd's to find out "what happened" that occurred between the conversations from which (20) and (21) are respectively exerpted. Passing on what was reported to her, she says:

JEANNETTE: Well, she said that there was some *wo*man thet—the—they they were whh— had held up in the front there, thet they were pointing the *gun* at, 'n everything. A c-*ne*gro woman. (23)
PENELOPE: NO : : : ! *No.*
JEANNETTE: What.
PENELOPE: Dat was one of the emPLOYees.
JEANNETTE: Oh.
PENELOPE: He ran up to 'er an' she jus' ran up to 'im an' sez "What's happ'n what's 'app'n'" W'l the kids were laffing abou//t it,
JEANNETTE: Oh/ heh heh heh heh//heh heh.
PENELOPE: An' she wuh—That was somebody thet worked in the *sto//re.*

(Trio, 10)

It appears, then, that there can be links of consistency or relevance between types of descriptions, e.g. for personnel and for place; that one gets an adaptation to "Shepherd's," that given the type of place "Shepherd's" is there are constraints on the kind of identification that will be made of personnel, and that selection of each kind of term can be produced with an orientation to topic. Aside from location and membership analysis, then, "topic analysis" seems to be relevant to the selection of a locational formulation. It is relevant to a speaker in building or assembling "a topic," and relevant to a hearer in analyzing what is being talked to, what the focus is. Indeed, as a hearer must analyze place formulations that are used to find their relevance, place formulations can be used to focus his analysis; their co-selection with other descriptors creates the relevance that he finds in his analysis. It may be in the light of this co-selection that we should appreciate that the use of "Junior High School" to answer "When did this happen" in (2) above is followed by the introduction into the story of characters formulated as "principal" and "teacher," and the answer "I work in a driving school" to the question "Wha' dijuh do for a living?" in (1) occurs in the middle of a conversation that began

B: I like tuh ask you something.
A: Shoot.
B: Y'know *I* 'ad my licen'suspendid fuh six munts. (24)
A: Uh huh.
B: Y'know for a reaz'n which, I rathuh not mensh'n tuh you, in othuh words,—a serious reaz'n, en I like tuh know if I w'd talk to my senator, or—somebuddy, could *they* help me get it back.

(BC, B, 20)

It may be that co-selection for topic is relevant not only for selection of *a* place term given the relevance of *some* place term; it may also be relevant to the selection of a place term to formulate a non-place descriptor.

I have urged that in the selection and adequate hearing of a locational formulation, at least three orders of consideration are relevant—a location analysis, a membership analysis, and a topic analysis—and I have tried to sketch the dimensions of the selection problem, and the kinds of work subsumed under the analyses that are involved. I now return to the problem of insertion sequences introduced in Part I to see if, as a "throw-off" from the notes on locational formulation, we can make any progress in elucidating what is involved there.

III
AN INSERTION SEQUENCE TYPE

Insertion sequences, it will be recalled, are sequences occurring between the two parts of an utterance pair, i.e. between two utterances the second of which is conditionally relevant given the occurrence of the first. Most broadly posed, the problem of insertion sequences would be concerned with what kinds of insertions various kinds of utterance pairs could take. A more limited inquiry would be directed to the various kinds of insertions (if there are various kinds) the utterance pair QA (question, answer) could take. Here, we are more specifically concerned with one kind of sequence we find inserted into QA pairs, i.e. a QA insertion. We have asked: what are the constraints on QA insertions, such that one does not find indefinite expansions? What must the second question (i.e., the inserted question) have to show that it is attentive to the first, that while after the first question an answer is relevant, and that the following utterance is not an answer, nonetheless the finding "no answer" is not warranted and is not made?

We shall proceed by examining some data with an insertion sequence. It will be useful to reproduce a large segment of the data. The utterances are broken up and numbered for convenience of reference.

B_1: You know, I have // a house, a big garden—
A_1: Yes.
B_1: Why don't you *come* and see me some//times.
A_2: I would like to.
B_{3a}: I would like you to.
B_{3b}: Let me // just—
A_3: I don't know just where the—uh—this address // *is*.
B_{4a}: Well where do—
B_{4b}: Which part of town do *you* live.
A_4: I live at four ten east Lowden. (25)
(2.0)
B_{5a}: Well, you don't live very far from me.
B_{5b}: If you go on the State (1.0) High—no if you go out past the court house // to Elmhurst.
A_5: Yeah.
B_6: [[Okay?
A_{6a}: [[Yes—
A_{6b}: Yes.
B_7: Go to Elmhurst, pass the court house and go to Elmhurst. And then go Elmhurst, uh north.
A_7: Mm hm.
B_8: Towards Riverton, til you come to that Avilla Hall.
A_{8a}: Oh, yes.
A_{8b}: [[Uh huh,
B_9: [[Dju know where that // is?
A_9: Oh, surely.
B_{10}: Avilla Hall on the corner of Bor//don.
A_{10}: Uh huh.
B_{11}: Well there, on Bordon you turn back to town, left,
A_{11}: Uh huh,
B_{12}: A very short block.
A_{12}: Uh huh,
B_{13}: And the very first street from Elmhurst there, crossing Bordon is called Avenida del Mar.
A_{13a}: Yes.
A_{13b}: I know where that is.
B_{14}: And uh there's a mailbox on the corner of ( ). You turn right, (after that).
A_{14}: Mm hm,

B_{15}: And the very first house after that corner is—the corner house, is the corner of Junipero Serra,
A_{15}: Mm hm,
B_{16a}: —and Avenida del Mar.
B_{16b}: And that's my house.
A_{16}: Oh!
B_{17}: Mm hm.
A_{17}: Mm yes I know exactly where it is.
B_{18}: Now the house has some uh fruit trees, on the corner, orange trees, (25)
A_{18}: Mm hm.
B_{19a}: It's the corner house.
B_{19b}: First there's the corner house of Bordon and Avenida del Mar, it has uhm geraniums and roses.
A_{19}: [[Mm, hm,
B_{20}: [[And then the next house, there's a driveway and then there's the—you go onto Avenida del Mar, uh right.
A_{20}: [[Mm hm,
B_{21}: [[And it goes straight—uh there's a corner right away, and that corner house is mine.
A_{21}: I see, uh huh,
B_{22}: The front faces on Junipero Serra.
A_{22a}: Uh huh,
A_{22b}: That isn't far at *all.*
B_{23}: It's uh within uh a one minute's walking distance from Avilla Hall.
A_{23}: Mm hm,

(SBL, 1, 10, 12–14)

I shall argue for the following mapping of the data onto the insertion sequence format, QQAA.

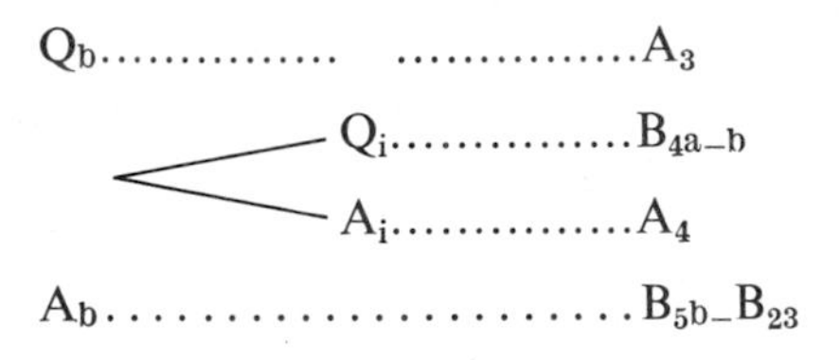

Although A_3 is not constructed syntactically as a question, it appears to be used here (a) as a question and (b) as a request for directions. As for (a), note that B_{4a-b}, "Well where do— which part of town do *you* live," is produced as a "second" or "return" question by its placement of accent (a procedure whose most commonplace occurrence is *A: How *are* you. B: Fine, and how are *you*. That "seconds" are done with special accent or intonation can also be seen when the second is not a "return" but a "repeat." Thus, if A summons B by calling his name and gets no answer, he may repeat the summons.[13] Thereupon, B may respond "I didn't hear you," which appears puzzling, since if he did not hear him, how can he know *that*, and if he did, he is lying. It is the distinctive accent and intonation of "seconds" that allow such a finding (Sacks, lectures). If B produces her utterance as a second or return question, then A_3 is being treated as a "first question."[14] As for (b), it is being claimed that the "where" question here requires for its answer not some formulation of, e.g. the part of town (a formulation whose possible relcvance can be seen by its use in B_{4b}), but rather a procedural account, i.e. directions. That A_3 is a "possible request for directions," that it would be relevant for a hearer to inspect it to see if that is what it is, rather than to inspect it to see what it is, may be claimed because of its placement after the sequence B_2–A_2. For sequences of actions whose first actions are an invitation and an acceptance, direction-asking-giving (and generally, "making arrangements") is a sequentially relevant next action. (So, for example, where the invited one does not make an inquiry, the inviter may nonetheless ask "Do you know how to get here?" We cannot know, but B_{3b} may have been the beginnings of direction-giving.) Therefore, although A_3 may be doing other things as well (as will be discussed below), it is at least a request for directions. We have, then, a scgment, including in it an insertion sequence, which begins with a request for directions. How does the insertion sequence fit?

One way to examine this matter would be to look for some orderliness in the relation of the Q_i to the Q_b. In other work, it has regularly appeared that one crucial aspect of what an utterance does in a conversation turns on its sequential placement and, most importantly, what it follows. We have already seen that the Q_i is produced with attention to the preceding utterence, i.e. in being produced as a second question. We shall, however, focus on the relation between the Q_i and A_b, and argue that the insertion sequence Q_iA_i is a "pre-sequence" for the activity done in A_b.

"Pre-sequences" [discussed in Sacks, (1967), #8 and #9, and Schegloff (1968)] are utterances produced as specifically prefatory to some activity. The term "pre-sequence" is an aggregating term to collect various specific cases, such as pre-invitations, pre-offers, pre-warnings, etc. In data such as

A: Hello?
B: Judy?
A: Yeah. (26)
B: Jack Green.
A: Hi Jack.
B: How ya doin. Say, what're ya doin.
(Sacks, 1967, lecture 8)

*A: Hello.
B: Hi. Are you doing anything?

"What're ya doing" and "are you doing anything" are heard as pre-invitations, i.e. are heard by reference to what they have been inserted before. Pre-sequences, then, are produced and heard via their sequential placement, but as placed not after some utterance, but before one. (For further discussion, see the cited references.)

In the present case, it is being urged that the Q_iA_i insertion sequence is a pre-sequence for the activity of A_b. Such a proposal seems to fit nicely to the very notion of an insertion sequence. For it could be asked: how is it an insertion? When it is produced, the A_b has not yet been produced. In what sense can something be inserted between one item and another that has not occurred? Does that not treat the conversation as an accomplished product, rather than as a developing process for the conversationalists who produce it? No. The Q_b utterance makes an A_b utterance conditionally relevant. The action the Q_b does (here, direction-asking) makes some other action sequentially relevant (here, giving directions by answering the Q_b). Which is to say, after the Q_b, the next speaker has that action specifically chosen for him to do, and can show attention to, and grasp of, the preceding utterance by doing the chosen action then and there. If he does not, that will be a notable omission, an event, on which inferences of their lack of attention or grasp may be based.

We are asking: is there some talk that the next speaker after Q_b could produce that would not be the action chosen by the Q_b, but would nonetheless exhibit an orientation to that action, and thereby to the Q_b that requires it? One way would be to do an action that, although not the one chosen, was a pre-sequence to the one chosen. This would exhibit an orientation to, and understanding of, what action was conditionally and sequentially relevant at that point. Here we want to show that B_{4a-b} is a pre-sequence for "giving directions," where "giving directions" is a sequentially relevant next action to the Q_b A_3 "asking directions" (and that is at least one thing that A_3 is).

How B_{4a-b}–A_4 is a pre-sequence to direction-giving may be shown by seeing what sorts of resources "direction-giving" may require, and how the B_{4a-b}–A_4 sequence is addressed to those requirements. The materials that have been developed on locational formulations may be useful here, for they have suggested that where selection of location formulations is done, various analyses are relevant. Giving directions requires (at least for the sort of directions involved in getting some place) location formulations. Where the one who is to give directions does not have the materials for the required analyses, or seems not to have them, the possibility of asking for them becomes relevant, and a pre-sequence can be a way of doing that and can be seen to be doing that.

In the data we are concerned with here, two requirements for direction-giving that seem relevant are (a) regarding locational analysis, what would be a relevant first segment of directions and a right formulation of it, e.g. a first landmark or transition place, and (b) regarding membership analysis, what sorts of places and formulations would the other know, recognize, be able to analyze, as the base on which directions can be built.

The first issue involves that where A is starting from is relevant to (though not necessarily identical with) where B starts the directions. This issue is related to the point made earlier that not every place is "in-between" any two places, or has transition value for them, and, hence, can be used as a landmark. To choose a set of transition places for use in the directions, as places the other is to be "brought to" serially in reaching the goal, one may need the points of origin and destination. If a direction-giver knows them for the hearer, he can proceed. In face-to-face interaction, the direction-giver may derive it from a locational analysis; when asked "how do I get to X?" it is heard as "from here" and "now." (And if the directions involve walking east and the asker wants to make a phone call first and the phone booth is in the opposite direction, an explanation will frequently be offered, or the direction-giver will try to make a "correction.") Or, as is often the case in telephone inquiries, the asker will build that information into the question. (Thus, I have heard persons ask a travel information service, "How do I get to X from the Upper West Side?") Where the information is not available, a crucial resource for formulating the directions is lacking.

The second consideration should be familiar from the previous discussion. We have already suggested that recognizability of locational formulations is related to membership, and particularly to the locally organized knowledge attributable to territorially based membership classes. Where someone lives can be informative about what they know, what formulations of what places will be right for them. Independently of what places will have transition value, there is the issue of what formulations of those places will be right and recognizable, and this turns on membership analysis (as does the issue of what transition places can be omitted, i.e. for what do directions not need to be given, as here in B_{5b}, getting to the "State Highway," or to the "Court House." The direction-giver must know the asker's "base knowledge," i.e. for what formulations of places that might be used in the directions there would not be the re-asking "where's that." This kind of knowledge is seen to be organized via territorially organized membership.

A direction-giver must, then, have the materials for a locational analysis and a membership analysis. Frequently, he will have such materials; if not, he can use a pre-sequence to get them. B_{4a-b} is the sort of question that seeks those materials. The "part of town" can be a locus of knowledge; it can be grounds for choosing a set of transition points, and a right formulation for them. (For that work, it may be superior to "where do [you live]?", if we can for a moment presume that that is what B_{4a} started to be. The latter question asks an address, and B may be as unknowing about the location of A's address as A is about B's. An "address" answer might then occasion a re-asking by B, "where's that?" And no basis for formulating directions would have been elicited. Whereas "address" may be known only to people in "that part of town," "parts of town" are presumed known to people in the town, and would be adequate for doing the required analyses. It happens that A answers with an address, and B can use it, but that does not change the contingencies.) The selection of transition places and formulations of them based on B's analyses—"Elmhurst" (B_7), "Avilla Hall" (B_8), "Avenida del Mar" with its "mailbox" (B_{13}, B_{14})—turn out to be "right," a matter to which both parties orient themselves throughout the direction-giving, B with inquiries ("O.K.?" B_6, "D'ja know where that is?" B_9), A with reassurances both in response to inquiries and unsolicited ("Uh huh's" throughout, "Oh yes," A_{8a}, "Oh surely," A_9, "I know where that is," 13_b, "Yes I know exactly where it is," A_{17}).

I have argued, then, that A_3 is a (base) question, asking for directions; that B_{4a-b}, the beginning of an insertion sequence, is a pre-sequence for direction-giving, gathering materials for analyses required for the selection of location formulations to be used in the directions; that A_4 adequately supplies those materials; and that B_{5b}–B_{23} give the directions requested by A_3, and are thus the (base) answer (omitting here the checking of the adequacy of the directions and rightness of the formulations woven into the direction-giving). For completeness, a few remarks should be made about B_{5a}, "Well, you don't live very far from me," which has so far been left out.

It could be proposed that A_3, rather than or in addition to, being a request for directions, begins a decline of the invitation. Although I can see no argument for this as the activity A_3 is doing (especially in view of the acceptance in A_2), such a suggestion seems responsive to the possible relevance of A_3 to such an action. And B_{5a} can be interpreted as responsive to that possible relevance as well.

The relevance is this. For offers and invitations, distance may be grounds for accepting or declining. Thus, in the middle of a major disaster, distance can be one of the grounds cited by the police (D in the data below) for declining the offer of a doctor's services.

D: Is this Dr. ———?
C: No, I wanted to know if you got a hold of him.
D: No, we didn't, uh since he's that far away we don't uh since we have uh since I talked to you the Army has volunteered to send some out. (27)
C: Uh huh.
D: So, doctors uh . . . well we don't need 'em bad enough to call 'em in from out of town.

(IPD, #59)

And earlier in the conversation we have been examining, A declines B's offer of a nursing job, using distance as a relevant ground.

A: Yeah, but this—this is a nice case // an I just—
B: Is it? Are *you* on it now?
A: I relieve. It's the one I've been relieving on ever since March. (28)
B: Ah uh what kind of a case is it.
A: Uhm it's the uh post-brain surgery.
B: Mm hm.
A: And uh it isn't hard work.
B: I see. And *where* is it.
A: Out in Edgerton, on Strawson Road.
B: Oh and it's *quite* a drive from here too. Well you know, uh seven days a week is just too much for me . . . (etc.)

(SBL, 1, 10, 2)

A finding of "far" can, therefore, be relevant to declining an offer or invitation, though it should be noted that "far" and "near" are formulations of place chosen with an orientation to topic. So "far" for a job may be "near" or "not far" for a friend. Because directions can serve as an indication of distance, a finding of "far" or "near" may be relevant to whether or not they will ever be followed. The "assessment in advance" ("you don't live very far from me") may then provide some way of hearing the directions.

As the directions are produced "piece by piece" and are analyzed by hearer "piece by piece," and at each point the hearer may not know how many more steps there may be, an assessment may be assembled over the course of the directions as to how far/how complicated they are, and the relevance of that to the invitation considered. An assessment in advance can be useful in trying to cut that off. It may lead, perhaps, to hearing at each step of the directions that there is not likely to be too much more to come. It may control the assembly of the assessment over the course of the development of the directions. Finally, it makes an assessment by the hearer at the end of the directions not a "free assessment." For the hearer to find at the end of the directions that "it's far," given the "assessment in advance," would not be just an assessment, but a disagreement, and one might not want to respond to an invitation with that. In the data here, A's assessment at the end (A_{22b}) echoes B's, "That isn't far at all." (Sacks has pointed out that speakers beginning an extended utterance may supply their hearers with the remark appropriately made at its end. Speaking in the first instance of stories, he notes that they frequently are begun "The funniest thing happened" or "I heard the strangest story" or "I have wonderful news," and hearers chime in at the end with "how funny," "how odd," "how wonderful," thereby letting the speaker see they have correctly noted the end of his extended utterance. The data under consideration here suggests that directions are another sort of extended utterance on which these bounds can be used.) If we recall that location formulations are selected with an orientation to topic or activity, then we can appreciate that the use of "not very far" rather than "near" may be chosen for its fit to such "preventive measures" as are being taken here.

We started by asking how insertion sequences in QA pairs were possible without a violation thereby being committed, without the absence of an answer being found—that is, how do people see when a question follows a question that it is not *any* other question, not an evasion? (We speak of those cases where it is not seen as an evasion by the speaker of the first Q. Of course, some second questions are so seen, and *their* features should be investigated.) We have suggested one way, where the inserted question is a pre-sequence for the activity that the initial or base question makes relevant. Since the insertion sequence is specifically done and heard as prefatory to the activity made conditionally relevant by the question, attention both to that activity and to the question is thereby exhibited.

More generally, conversationalists are on the whole required to exhibit attention to last prior utterances [Sacks, (1967)]. Questions are specially "demanding" in that respect, because they make an answer conditionally relevant. However, if a question requires an answer that will include parts that themselves require exhibiting attention to some set of considerations (as place formulations require attention to respective location, respective membership, and topic or activity), then what follows the question can exhibit attention to the question by exhibiting attention to those considerations required by the activity the question makes relevant. In the materials at hand, our exploration of the considerations relevant to selecting a locational formulation have allowed seeing that the insertion sequence under examination did that. For other materials, we can now look to see to what degree insertion sequences are pre-sequences to the second part of the base utterance pair, and what sorts of work relevant to the activity of that second part the insertion sequences are doing.

IV
CONCLUDING REMARKS

I have argued that for any "place" there is a set of terms or formulations that are "correct." On any occasion of employing a term for that "place," much less than the full set is "right" or adequate (i.e. not producing questions, or further questions, requiring reformulations).[15] It happens, on the whole, that speakers select "right" or adequate formulations, and do preliminary work if it is required in order to do so. The selection of a "right" term and the hearing of a term as adequate, appear to involve sensitivity to the respective locations of the participants and referrent (which can change over the course of the interaction); to the membership composition of the interaction, and the knowledge of the world seen by members to be organized by membership categories (where the composition can change over the course of the interaction); and to the topic or activity being done in the conversation at that point in its course, and which is, at least in part, constituted as "that topic" or "that activity" by the formulations selected to realize it.

If this is so, then it seems to follow that on each occasion in conversation on which a formulation of location is used, attention is exhibited to the particulars of the occasion. In selecting a "right" formulation, attention is exhibited to "where-we-know-we-are," to "who-we-know-we-are," to "what-we-are-doing-at-this-point-in-the-conversation." A "right" formulation exhibits, in the very fact of its production, that it is some "*this* conversation, at *this* place, with *these* members, at *this* point in its course" that has been analyzed to select *that* term; it exhibits, in the very fact of its production, that it is some particular "*this* situation" that is producing it.[16]

* * *

It is one lesson of these materials that formulation of locations accomplish and exhibit the particularities of an interaction, and they do this through general, formal structures. (By the last phrase I mean that the problem of selecting a term from a collection of terms, or of selecting a collection from a set of collections, is a general, formal procedure, although its outcomes can be particular to the circumstances in which the operation is done. The contrast might be where particularities of situation would be exhibited by unique markers for a situation or class of situations.) We can now look to see for what other domains this lesson is relevant. Are there kinds of conversational practices that cannot do this? Are there many others designed for that kind of use, which permit conversation to operate within very tight constraints, while each one can be at each point a matter for analysis as the outcome of a general practice and part of a general structure?

As for the former question, it appears that the most general sequencing structures of conversation for which we have descriptions hold across such variations as place formulations reflect.[17] As for the second question, it seems to invite a detailed, empirical examination of the gloss "context."

These notes may be read as pertinent to some ways in which "contextual variation" affects interaction. It is being proposed that the much invoked "dependence on context" must be investigated by showing that, and how, *participants* analyze context and use the product of their analysis in producing their interaction. To say that *interaction* is context-sensitive is to say that *interactants* are context-sensitive, and for what and how that is so is an empirical matter that can be researched in detail. One dimension has to do with the ways in which interactants particularize their contributions so as to exhibit attention to the "this-one-here-and-now-for-us-at-this-point-in-it" character of the interaction. I have tried to suggest that place formulations particularize at least for location, composition (at least with respect to those membership categories relevant to the selection of place formulation) and place in conversation (topic, activity). It is now in order to see what range of conversational practices are subject to similar usage, what kinds of organization they have, whether or not they are fitted to one another, etc.

That others await description seems clear. One need only note that selection of age terms for members (see Sacks, this volume), and the selection of collections of age terms from which to select a term seems to exhibit attention to particularities, especially of membership (although other categories of member seem to be involved than in the case of place-formulation selection). Thus, terms like "older man" or "young woman" cannot be divorced from the age composition of participants in the conversation in which they occur, as "he's 45" may on occasion be. So the alternative collection of age terms—the one being the set of terms of the form "n years old," the other the set of terms including "young, old, younger, older, middle-aged, not so old, . . ."—may have different potential for exhibiting attention to particularities of membership composition, and may be selected accordingly. If a term is chosen from the latter collection, it may then be used to exhibit attention to the specific membership composition of an interaction.

More directly parallel to discussion of place formulation are temporal formulations. Although this is certainly not the place to develop an analysis, a few observations may suggest that temporal formulations may particularize in their domain in a manner congruent with location formulation. Note that an event may be formulated as occurring at "2:06; about 2; in the afternoon; Monday afternoon; Monday; the third week in January; January; January 23; January 23, 1964; January 23, 1964 A.D.," providing a seeming calendrical parallel to what were called G terms above. Or an event can be formulated as "before we met," "after the baby was born," "a month after your grandfather died," etc., forms that appear to be for temporal formulations similar to R_m terms in place formulations. Formulations such as "the day after the Kennedy assassination," "a week before the election," "the day of the storm," etc., are for various membership groups located by "reference to landmark," in this case "landmark" dates. There seem to be preferred temporal formulations and transformations to them (as is the case with place formulations), as in the following data:

(29)

A: You know when the next meeting of the curriculum committee is?
B: Friday morning at 10:00.
A: Tomorrow.
B: Right.

in which B's choice of formulation is found not "right" in not exhibiting a grasp of the "when" of the conversation in relation to the object being talked of.

In short, there is reason to believe that a search for other conversational practices that exhibit attention to the particularities of the interaction in which they occur will find others; some perhaps with a structure similar to that discussed here in connection with place formulations, others perhaps quite different. As more such practices are subjected to analysis, we may be able more fully to document empirically an argument that can be suggested only tentatively from this discussion, concerning the "efficiency" of language as a resource in interaction. Various investigators have claimed that language is overbuilt for the kind of use it ordinarily gets (see, e.g. Sapir (1921), p. 13; Weinreich (1966), p. 147); that it would be more efficient to have a single term for each referrent, and each term refer to but a single referrent, and not have synonyms; that there is much redundancy built into human communication because of the defectiveness of language or of humans as senders and receivers of messages, and redundancy allows messages to get through anyhow [Colin Cherry (1957), p. 117]. If one takes conversational interaction among a society's members as one's domain (rather than characteristics of communication channels or linguistic structures exempted from daily use), then the major interest may be in the way alternative available formulations of objects allow the exploitation of members' analytic skills to accomplish a fundamental feature of everyday, organized social life. For it is through such resources that the production of a world of particular specific scenes through a set of general formal practices is accomplished and exhibited.

REFERENCES

CHERRY, COLIN, *On Human Communication* (Cambridge: The M.I.T. Press). 1957.

CONKLIN, HAROLD, "Hanunoo Color Categories," *Southwestern Journal of Anthropology*, XI, 4, 339–43. 1955.

FRAKE, CHARLES O., "The Diagnosis of Disease Among the Subanum of Mindanao," *American Anthropologist*, LXII, 1, 113–32. 1961.

FRITZ, CHARLES E., *and* MATHEWSON, J. H., *Convergence Behavior in Disasters*: A Problem in Social Control) Washington: National Academy of Science—National Research Council). 1957.

GARFINKEL, HAROLD, *Studies in Ethnomethodology* (Englewood Cliffs, N.J.: Prentice-Hall). 1967.

GARFINKEL, HAROLD, *and* SACKS, HARVEY, "On Formal Structures of Practical Actions," in John C. McKinney and Edward Tiryakian (eds.), *Theoretical Sociology: Perspectives and Developments* (Appleton-Century-Crofts, forthcoming). 1969.

GARFINKEL, HAROLD, *and* SACKS, HARVEY (eds.), *Contributions to Ethnomethodology* (Bloomington: Indiana University Press, forthcoming).

GOODENOUGH, WARD, "Componential Analysis and the Study of Meaning," *Language*, XXXII, 195–216. 1956.

GREENBERG, JOSEPH (ed.), *Universals of Language* (second edition, Cambridge: The M.I.T. Press). 1966.

LOUNSBURY, FLOYD, "A Semantic Analysis of the Pawnee Kinship Usage," *Language*, XXXII, 158–94. 1956.

LYNCH, KEVIN, *The Image of the City* (Cambridge: The M.I.T. Press). 1960.

MCKINNEY, JOHN C., *and* TIRYAKIAN, EDWARD (eds.), *Theoretical Sociology: Perspectives and Developments* (Appleton-Century-Crofts, forthcoming). 1969.

MOERMAN, MICHAEL, "Being Lue: Uses and Abuses of Ethnic Identification," American Ethnological Society, *Proceedings* of 1967 Spring Meetings. 1967.

PSATHAS, GEORGE, *and* KOZLOFF, MARTIN, "The Structure of Directions: An Analysis of an Everyday Activity" (mimeo). 1968.

SACKS, HARVEY, "On a Device Basic to Social Interaction" (mimeo). n.d.

SACKS, HARVEY, Transcribed Lectures (mimeo). 1967.

SACKS, HARVEY, "An Initial Investigation . . ." (this volume). 1969.

SACKS, HARVEY, *The Organization of Conversation* (Englewood Cliffs, N.J.: Prentice-Hall, Inc., forthcoming).

SACKS, HARVEY, "The Baby Cried," in Harold Garfinkel and Harvey Sacks (eds.), *Contributions to Ethnomethodology* (Bloomington: Indiana University Press, forthcoming).

SAPIR, E., *Language* (New York: Harcourt, Brace & Co.). 1921.

SCHEGLOFF, EMANUEL A., "The First Five Seconds: The Order of Conversational Openings," Ph.D. dissertation, Department of Sociology, University of California, Berkeley. 1967.

SCHEGLOFF, EMANUEL A., "Sequencing in Conversational Openings," *American Anthropologist*, LXX, 6, Dec., 1968, 1075–95. 1968.

SCHELLING, THOMAS, *The Strategy of Conflict* (New York: Oxford University Press). 1963.

SUTTLES, GERALD D., *The Social Order of the Slum:* Ethnicity and Territory in the Inner City (Chicago: University of Chicago Press). 1968.

WEINREICH, URIEL, "On the Semantic Structure of Language," in Joseph Greenberg (ed.), *Universals of Language* (second edition, Cambridge: The M.I.T. Press). 1966.

DATA SOURCES

BC Telephone conversations on a radio "talk show."
GTS Group psychotherapy sessions with teenagers.
CPD Phone calls to the emergency desk of the police department of a midwestern city.
SBL Phone conversations in a western city.
Trio A series of three phone conversations, A to B, B to C, B to A.
DA Phone conversation.
IPD Phone calls to midwestern police department in immediate aftermath of a disaster.
TAC Phone conversations among young adults in a western city.

SYMBOLS USED IN TRANSCRIPTS

/	indicates upward intonation
//	indicates point at which following line interrupts
(n.o.)	indicates pause of n.o. seconds
[	indicates simultaneous utterances when bridging two lines
( )	indicates something said but not transcribable
(word)	indicates probably what said, but not clear
but	indicates accent
em*PLOY*ee	indicates heavy accent
: : :	indicates stretching of sound immediately preceding, in proportion to number of colons inserted

WILLIAM LABOV

Rules for Ritual Insults

Linguists have not made very much progress in the study of discourse. By and large, they are still confined by the boundaries of the sentence. If *discourse analysis* is not a virgin field, it is at least technically so in that no serious penetration of the fundamental areas has yet been made. There is of course a well-known publication of Harris entitled *Discourse Analysis Reprints* (1963), but it is concerned with rearrangements of sentence structure that are not related to the general questions to be raised here.[1] Although there are linguists who are beginning to make contributions to the study of discourse—Gunter, Grimes, Stennes and others—it is somewhat startling for linguists to discover that the major steps have been taken by sociologists. Sacks and Schegloff, whose contributions

(*Notes to this selection will be found on p. 434.*)

appear in this volume, have isolated a number of fundamental problems, and made some progress toward solution: the selection of speakers, the identification of persons and places, and the isolation of that social competence that allows members of a society to engage in talk. The influence of their work on my own essay will be apparent in the focus on sequencing in ritual insults, and on the social knowledge required for their interpretation.

Linguists should be able to contribute their skill and practice in formalization to this study. It would not be too much to say that the concepts of invariance, and rule-governed behavior, are more fully developed in linguistics than in any other field of social study. Yet there may be such a thing as premature formalization, which Garfinkel, Goffman, Sacks and Schegloff are anxious to avoid: the categorical model of linguistic behavior may indeed lead linguists to set up paradigms of discrete features, mutually defined by their oppositions, for fields where only open sets are to be found in reality. But formalization is a fruitful procedure even when it is wrong: it sharpens our questions, and promotes the search for answers.

Some General Principles of Discourse Analysis. The first and most important step in the formalization of discourse analysis is to distinguish *what is said* from *what is done*. There is a small number of sentence types from a grammatical viewpoint—principally *statements*, *questions* and *imperatives*—and these must be related by discourse rules to the much larger set of actions done with words. It is commonplace to use these terms interchangeably with the names of certain actions: *assertions*, *requests for information*, and *commands* respectively. But there is no such simple one-to-one relationship; it is easy to demonstrate, for example, that requests for information can be made with statements, questions, or imperatives:

I would like to know your name.
What is your name?
Tell me your name!

Furthermore there are a great many other actions that are done with words and which must be related by rule to the utterance: refusals, challenges, retreats, insults, promises, threats, etc. The rules that connect what is said to the actions being performed with words are complex; the major task of discourse analysis is to analyze them, and thus to show that one sentence follows another in a coherent way. If we hear the dialogue

A: Are you going to work tomorrow?
B: I'm on jury duty.

we know intuitively that we are listening to coherent discourse. Yet there is no formal basis in sentence-grammar to explicate our reaction to this well-formed sequence. A *statement* follows a *question*; the question is a *request for information*; but in what way does the statement form an *answer* to that request? Some fear that linguists will never be able to answer such questions, because one would have to enter into our grammars every known relation between persons and objects—in this case, that people on jury duty are not able to work.[2] However, the form of discourse rules is independent of such detail. In answering A's request for information Q–S_1 with a superficially unrelated statement S_2, B is in fact asserting that there is a proposition known to both A and B that connects this with S_1. When A hears B say "I'm on jury duty," he searches for the proposition B is asserting; in this case, he locates "If someone is on jury duty, he cannot go to work." B's answer is then heard as "I'm not going to go to work tomorrow."

The rule of discourse that we can then formulate will read as follows:

If A *makes a request for information* Q–S_1, *and* B *makes a statement* S_2 *in response that cannot be expanded by rules of ellipsis to the form* X S_1 Y, *then* S_2 *is heard as an assertion that there exists a proposition* P *known to both* A *and* B:

If S_2, then (E) S_1

where (E) *is an existential operator, and from this proposition there is inferred an answer to* A'*s request:* (E) S_1.

This is a rule of interpretation that relates what is said (S_2) to what is done (the assertion of P and the answer to Q–S_1). Note that there is no direct connection between the two utterances Q–S_1 and S_2, and it would be fruitless to search for one.

The over-all relation of discourse rules to utterances shows several levels of abstraction. Consider a conversation of the following superficial form:

A:	Are you going to work tomorrow?	(U_1)
B:	I'm on jury duty.	(U_2)
A:	Couldn't you get out of it?	(U_3)
B:	We tried everything.	(U_4)

To understand the connections between these four utterances, they must be expanded to a scheme such as the following:

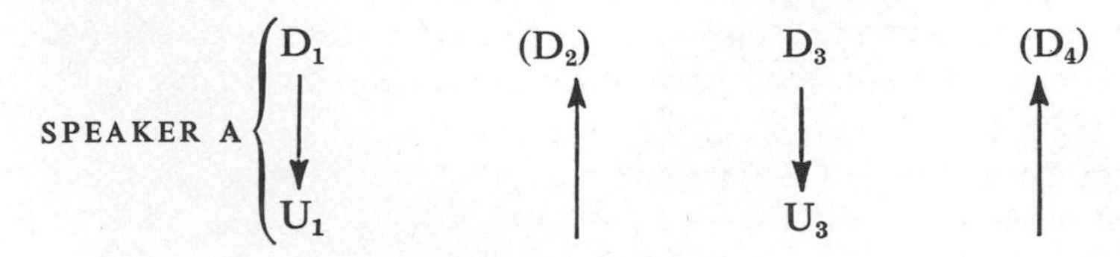

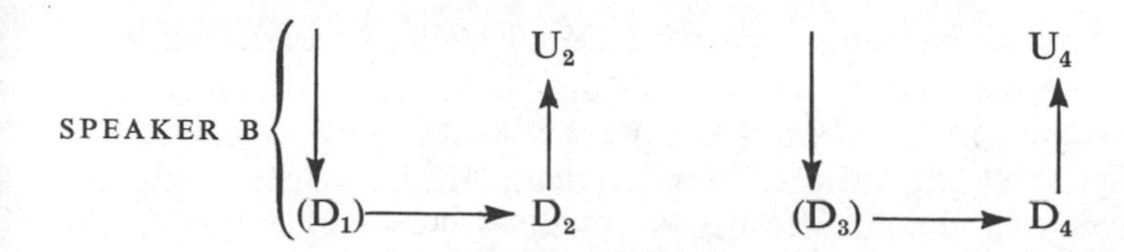

Speaker A begins with the intention of performing the action D_1; by a production rule, he does so with the utterance U_1. Speaker B uses the inverse interpretation rule to interpret U_1 as A's action D_1, and then applies a sequencing rule to decide his response D_2. He then codes D_2 into the utterance U_2 by a production rule, and Speaker A interprets this—in this case, by the rule cited which tells him that the statement *I'm on jury duty* is a response to D_1 to be interpreted as "I'm not going to work because I'm on jury duty." The other sequences follow in the same manner.

There are two types of discourse rules here: rules of interpretation UD (with their inverse rules of production DU) and sequencing rules DD which connect actions. There are of course other rules that connect actions at higher levels of abstraction. The diagram may actually show such structures as

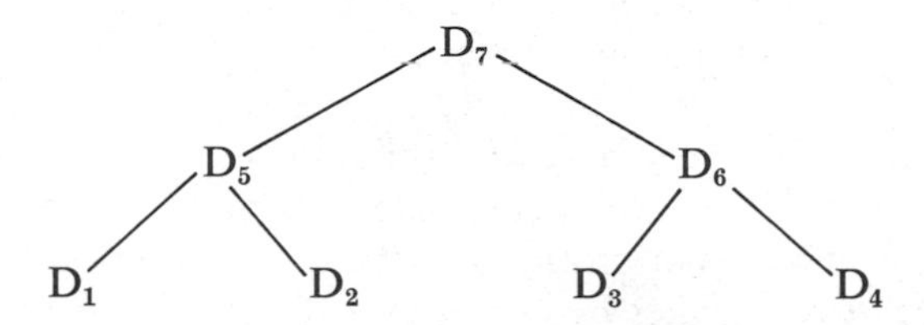

where D_5, D_6 and D_7 may be considered exchanges, encounters, inquiries, or even challenges and defenses depending on the larger context of interaction and higher level rules.

Any statement S_2 will not do in these sequences. If B had replied "De Gaulle just lost the election," A could reasonably complain "What has that to do with your going to work tomorrow?" The rule tells A to search for a proposition P that will make the connection; if he fails to find it, he will reject B's response. But the operation of the rule is invariant. A *must* inspect S_2 as a possible element in a proposition *if* S_2 *then* $(E)S_1$, before he can react. Failure to locate such a proposition may reflect a real incompetence: younger members of a social group may not be able to find the proposition being asserted. Thus Linus knocks at Violet's front door and says[3]

LINUS: Do you want to play with me, Violet?
VIOLET: You're younger than me. [Shuts the door.]
LINUS: [puzzled] She didn't answer my question.

The unstated proposition being asserted here by Violet is presumed to be part of the communal *shared knowledge*, but it has not in fact reached Linus yet. This concept of "shared knowledge" is an essential element in discourse analysis; to illustrate its importance further, we may consider examples in which statements are heard as *requests for confirmation*. The following exchanges are taken from a therapeutic interview.[4]

THERAPIST: Oh, so she *told* you.
PATIENT: Yes.
THERAPIST: She didn't say for y*ou* . . .
PATIENT: No.
THERAPIST: And it never occurred to her to prepare dinner.
PATIENT: No.
THERAPIST: But she does go to the store.
PATIENT: Yes.

These four instances are typical of a great many examples, where the first utterance is a statement and the second is *yes* or *no*. It seems that a statement is functioning as equivalent to a yes-no question—that is, a *request for information*. These statements have the same compelling force as requests made in question form: we frequently see that the patient is not allowed to continue until a yes or no answer is given.

A great many speakers habitually use statements to ask for confirmation. How is it that we regularly and reliably recognize these as requests, and not as assertions? There is a simple and invariant rule of discourse involved here; it depends upon the concept of "shared knowledge", which I will introduce into the rules by classifying all reported events as A-events, B-events, or AB-events. Given any two-party conversation, there exists an understanding that there are events that A knows about, but B does not; and events that B knows about but A does not; and AB-events that are known to both. We can then state simply the rules of interpretation:

If A makes a statement about a B-event, it is heard as a request for confirmation.

If A makes a statement about an A-event ("I'm sleepy"), it is not heard as such a request. But if he utters a statement about a B-event ("You were up late last night") it is heard as requesting a confirmation, "Is it true that . . ."[5]

In addition to these concepts of shared and unshared knowledge, there are other elements of discourse that are based on sociological concepts: notions of role, rights, duties and obligations associated with social rules. Now consider the following exchange from a narrative of the patient, Rhoda, in the therapeutic sessions cited above.

RHODA: Well, when are you planning to come home?
RHODA'S MOTHER: Oh, why-y?

In the face of such a sequence, it is common to say that "a question is answered with a question." But questions do not answer questions, any more than statements do. *Answers* are given to *requests*; they may occasionally take the form of questions. Closer examination of this sequence shows that Rhoda's question is a *request* for action, not information, and her mother's question is a *refusal* of that request. But what are the rules that allow us to make this interpretation?

A parallel case can be observed in the following extract from one of our group sessions with the "Jets."[6] The speakers involved here are Stanley, the president of the Jets, and Rel, a Puerto Rican member who is also one of the officers (prime minister). At one point Rel called for quiet:

REL: Shut up please!
STANLEY: . . . 'ey, you tellin' *me*?
REL: Yes. Your mother's a duck.

Rel's first remark—an imperative—is clearly a command or *request for action*. Stanley's response is formally a *question*, but it is certainly not a *request for information*; again, we intuitively recognize that Stanley is refusing[7] but by what regular rule of interpretation do we recognize this? The general form of the answer may be outlined as follows. The underlying rules for *requests* for action appear to have the form: A *requests* B *to do* X *for the purpose* Y *under conditions* Z. For this to be heard as a valid command, it is necessary for the following additional pre-conditions to hold: B *must believe that* A *believes that*

1. X needs to be done.
2. B has the ability to do X.
3. B has the obligation to do X.
4. A has the right to tell B to do X.

There are many ways to perform this request, and many ways of aggravating or mitigating the force of the command. One device involves making statements or asking questions that refer to any of the four pre-conditions. The same mechanism can be used to refuse the request. In both of the examples just given, B refuses by asking a question concerning the relation of A, B, and X, which is heard as a question about (and a challenge to) pre-condition 4.

These brief illustrations from current work on discourse analysis show that the form of discourse rules is independent of the particular propositions being asserted, challenged, or denied. These rules have to do with invariant relations between the linguistic units and actions intended or interpreted. Discourse rules also contain references to unstated assumptions about social relations, which we are only beginning to work out. These involve the concepts of shared or social knowledge, the roles of speaker, addressee and audiences, their rights and obligations, and other constraints that have not appeared before in the array of linguistic primitives. Some linguists who are currently analyzing the deep structure of sentences have come to realize that one must posit elaborate presuppositions to explain syntactic data, but they have not yet attempted to incorporate such presuppositions into their formal rules.

The questions we have posed so far have been based upon examples relatively transparent to our intuitive sense of what was being done (especially when larger sections of the text are taken into account). But in the last example, Rel's closing remark is not at all clear in this sense. Why did Rel tell Stanley that his mother was a duck? Does this have any cognitive meaning, and if so, what rules of interpretation are operating? Rel's remark performed some kind of work, because Stanley then retired from his threatening posture and he apparently considered the incident closed. Stanley regularly insists on his status as president of the Jets; he never backs down from a challenge or backs away from a fight. There are a number of times in this group session when sequences such as these led to fights—semi-serious, but none the less real. If Rel had just said "Yes," there would certainly have been some punches traded. But his last remark was accepted as appropriate, coherent discourse, which established some kind of closure to the incident. To those outside this sub-culture, Rel's utterance (and the action intended) are as opaque as the previous examples were transparent. Those who have some knowledge of urban ghetto culture will recognize Rel's remark "Your mother's a duck" as a ritual insult, and they will connect it with the institution of *the dozens*, *sounding*, or *signifying*. *Sounding* is a well-organized speech event that occurs with great frequency in the verbal interaction of Negro adolescents we have studied, and occupies long stretches of their time. This speech event is worth describing as part of the general program of "the ethnography of speaking" outlined by Hymes (1962). Here we have an opportunity to go further, and hope to establish the fundamental rules that govern this sounding, and use this investigation to achieve some deeper understanding of discourse analysis. If the rules for sounding are appropriate and well constructed, it should be possible to throw light on the particular problem cited here: why does Stanley retire when Rel says to him "Your mother's a duck"?

Studies of Non-standard Negro English. For the past four years, we have been engaged in a study of the non-standard English of Negro speakers in urban ghetto areas, principally in South Central Harlem.[8] Our purpose was twofold: (1) to examine the differences in structure between non-standard Negro English and the standard English of the classroom, and (2) to examine the differences in the use of language in these two sub-cultures—to understand the speech events and standards of verbal skill which governed language in the vernacular culture. Our study of ritual insults is drawn from this second part of our work.

Although we used a variety of means of studying and recording speech including surveys of adult speakers, our basic approach was through long-term interaction with adolescent peer groups. We first made contact with the group through our participant observer, John Lewis, who was located in the area. Several leading members were interviewed individually, and a number of trips and group sessions were held in which the members were recorded in spontaneous interaction with each other. Most of the important material for grammatical analysis was recorded at group sessions, where each person was recorded on an individual track. We also obtained a great deal of valuable material on sounding from recordings made en route in a Microbus, where it is difficult to say at all times who has said what. Both kinds of data will be used in the analysis to follow. We finally interviewed all members of each group in individual sessions, so that we can compare speech styles in individual and group styles, for the pre-adolescent "Thunderbirds" and "Aces," and the adolescent "Jets," "Cobras" and "Oscar Brothers," as well as the comparable white groups from Inwood. All of the data on sounding, however, is drawn from group sessions where members are talking to each other.

The following pages will present a large body of information about this speech event. There should be very little difficulty in understanding the literal meaning of the sounds as English sentences. The grammar used (non-standard Negro English, NNE) presents no particular difficulty to most Americans; the vocabulary is not especially hip or esoteric; the trade names and personalities mentioned are a part of the general American scene. But the activity itself is not well known, the point of the whole proceeding will escape many readers. The ways in which sounds are delivered, and the evaluation of them by the group, follow a well-established ritual pattern that reflects many assumptions and much social knowledge not shared by members of other sub-cultures. To understand the significance of sounds and the function of this activity for members of the vernacular NNE culture, it will be necessary to write explicit rules of discourse for producing, interpreting and answering sounds. In our original investigation of sounding, we were much concerned with the syntactic structures involved. Much of this material is preserved here, since it adds considerable depth to our understanding of the abstract operations involved.

Terms for the Speech Event. A great variety of terms describe this activity: *the dozens*, *sounding*, and *signifying* are three of the most common. The activity itself is remarkably similar throughout the various Negro communities, both in the form and content of the insults themselves, and in the rules of verbal interaction which operate. In this section we will refer to the institution by the most common term in Harlem—"sounding."

Sounding, or "playing the dozens," has been described briefly in a number of other sources, particularly Dollard (1939) and Abrahams (1962). Kochman (1968) has dealt with sounding in Chicago in his general treatment of speech events in the Negro community. The oldest terms for the game of exchanging ritualized insults is *the dozens*. Various possibilities for the origin of this term are given in Abrahams (1962: footnote 1), but none are very persuasive. One speaks of "the dozens," "playing the dozens," or "putting someone in the dozens." The term *sounding* is by far the most common in New York, and is reported as the favored term in Philadelphia by Abrahams. *Woofing* is common in Philadelphia and elsewhere, *joning* in Washington, *signifying* in Chicago, *screaming* in Harrisburg, and on the West Coast, such general terms as *cutting*, *capping* or *chopping*. The great number of terms available suggests that there will be inevitably some specialization and shift of meaning in a particular area. Kochman suggests that "sounding" is used in Chicago for the initial exchanges, "signifying" for personal insults, and "the dozens" for insults on relatives. In New York, "the dozens" seems to be even more specialized, referring to rhymed couplets of the form

> I don't play the dozens, the dozens ain't my game
> But the way I fucked your mama is a god damn shame.

But "playing the dozens" also refers to any ritualized insult directed against a relative. "Sounding" is also used to include such insults, and includes personal insults of a simpler form. Somebody can "sound on" somebody else by referring to a ritualized attribute of that person.

It seems to be the case everywhere that the super-ordinate terms that describe a verbal activity are quite variable and take on a wide range of meanings, while the verbal behavior itself does not change very much from place to place. People talk much more than they talk about talk, and as a result there is more agreement in the activity than in the ways of describing it. A member of the NNE subculture may have idiosyncratic notions about the general terms for sounding and the dozens without realizing it. He can be an expert on sounds and be quite untrustworthy on "sounding."

The Shape of Sounds. As noted above, some of the most elaborate and traditional sounds are "dozens" in the form of rhymed couplets. A typical opening dozen is cited above. Another favorite opening is:

> I hate to talk about your mother, she's a good old soul
> She got a ten-ton pussy and a rubber asshole.

Both of these initiating dozens have "disclaiming" or retiring first lines, with second lines that contradict them. They are in this sense typical of the usage of young adults, who often back away from the dozens, saying "I don't play that game," or quoting the proverb, "I laugh, joke and smoke, but I dont' play" (Abrahams, p. 210). There is a general impression that sounding is gradually moving down in the age range—it is now primarily an adolescent and pre-adolescent activity, and not practiced as much by young men twenty to thirty years old; but we have no exact information to support this notion. The rhymed dozens were used by adolescents in New York City twenty years ago. In any case, most young adolescents do not know many of the older rhymed dozens, and are very much impressed by them. To show the general style, we can cite a few others that have impressed the Jets and Cobras (and not included in the twenty examples given by Abrahams):

> I fucked your mother on top of the piano
> When she came out she was singin' the Star Spangled Banner.
>
> Fucked your mother in the ear,
> And when I came out she said, "Buy me a beer."

The couplet that had the greatest effect was probably

> Iron is iron, and steel don't rust,
> But your momma got a pussy like a Greyhound bus.

The winner in a contest of this sort is the man with the largest store of couplets on hand, the best memory, and perhaps the best delivery. But there is no question of improvisation, or creativity when playing, or judgment in fitting one sound into another. These couplets can follow each other in any succession, one is as appropriate as the other. The originators certainly show great skill, and C. Robins remembers long hours spent by his group in the 1940's trying to invent new rhymes, but no one is expected to manufacture them in the heat of the contest. The Jets know a few rhymed dozens, such as "Fucked his mother on a red-hot heater/ I missed her cunt 'n' burned my peter," but most of the traditional rhymes are no longer well known. One must be quite careful in using the rhymed dozens with younger boys, if they cannot top them, they feel beaten from the start, and the verbal flow is choked off. To initiate sounding in a single interview or a group session, we used instead such primitive sequences as: What would you say if someone said to you, "Your momma drink pee?" The answer is well known to most peer group members: "Your father eat shit." This standard reply allows the exchange to begin along conventional lines, with room for elaboration and invention.

For our present purposes, the basic formulas can be described in terms of the types of syntactic structures, especially with an eye to the mode of sentence embedding. I will draw most of the examples from two extended sounding sessions in which sounds were *used* rather than simply *quoted.* One was on a return trip from an outing with the Jets. Thirteen members were crowded on a single microbus; one hundred and eighty sounds were deciphered from the recording made in a thirty-five minute ride. The other was a group session with five Thunderbirds in which Boot, Money, David and Roger sounded against each other at great length. For these sixty sounds, the record is complete and exact identification of every utterance is possible.

There are of course many other sessions where sounds are cited or used; included in the examples given below are some from a trip with the Cobras in the Microbus, where thirty-five sounds were deciphered from one short section of a recording.

(a) *Your mother is* (*like*) . . . Perhaps the simplest of all sounds is the comparison or identification of the mother with something old, ugly or bizarre: a simple equative predication. The Jets use great numbers of such simple sounds:

> Your mother look like Flipper . . . like *Hoppity* Hooper . . . Your mother's a Milk Dud . . . A Holloway Black Cow . . . a rubber dick . . . They say your mother was a Gravy Train . . . Your mother's a bookworm . . . a ass, period. . . . Your mother James Bond, K.C. . . . Your mother Pussy Galore.

The Cobras use a number of sounds of this type:

> Your momma's a weight-lifter . . . a butcher . . . a peanut man . . . a iceman . . . a Boston-Indian. Your mother look like Crooked-Mile Hank! . . . like that piece called King Kong! . . . Quahab's mother look like who did it and don't want to do it no more!

Note that the mass media and commercial culture provide a rich body of images. Such sounds were particularly appropriate on the Jet outing because every odd or old person that passed on the way would be a stimulus for another sound.

> Your mother look like that taxi driver . . . Your mother a applejack-eater . . . a flea-bag . . . the Abominable Snowman . . . Your mother is Phil D. Basket [calypso accent] . . . Your mother's a diesel . . . a taxicab driver.

Another passer-by sets off a train of simple identifications at the very end of the Jet outing:

—There go Willie mother right there.
—Your mother *is* a lizard.
—Your mother smell like a roach.
—Your mother name is Benedict Arnold.

One passing lady is the focus of a whole series of sounds. One can sound on someone simply by saying that "There go your mother."

—Hey-ey! [whistle] . . . That's your mother over there!
—I know that lady.
—That's your mother.
—Hell, look the way that lady walk.
—. . . she sick in the head.
—Walk like she got a lizard-neck.

(b) *Your mother got* . . . Equally simple, from a syntactic point of view, is the series of sounds with the form *Your mother got so and so.* The Thunderbirds use long sequences of this type:

BOOT: Your mother got a putty chest.
BOOT: Your mother got hair growin' out her dunkie hole.
ROGER: Your mother got a .45 in her left titty.
MONEY: Your mother got a 45 degree titty.
BOOT: Your mother got titties behind her neck.

The Jets use simple sounds of this sort as well: The first statement here is not a sound; it simply provides the base on which the sound is built, in this case the verb *got*.

—You got the nerve to talk.
—Your mother got funky drawers.
—Your mother got braces between her legs.

Again:

—Your mother got boobies that shake . . . hangdown lips . . .
—Bell mother got a old beat-up boot . . .
—Her mother got a face like a rubber ass . . .
—Junior got a face like a clown . . .

From an adolescent Chicago group:

Your momma got three titties: chocolate milk, white milk, and one half-and-half.

The Cobras show the same style; note that *wear* does as well as *got* where clothes are concerned:

—Your mother got on sneakers!
—Your mother wear high-heeled sneakers to church!
—Your mother wear a jock-strap.
—Your mother got polka-dot drawers!
—Your mother wear the seat of her drawers on the top of her head!

The Cobras sounds on clothes gradually drift away from the basic sounding pattern to a more complex structure that plays on the names of New York City Department stores:

—Your momma got shit on . . .
—Bra's mother bought her clothes from Ohrbach's. All front and no back!
—You get your shit from Bob Hope—Bob give it to you and you hope they fit!
—You got your suit from Woolworth! All wool but it ain't worth shit!
—You get your shoes from Buster Brown—brown on the top and all busted on the bottom!

Note that one of the Jets or Cobras can appear as the subject of a sound, though the majority are directed against someone's mother. In some ways, sounds of the *X got* . . . type are more complex when directed against a member, possibly because the comparisons are not as ritualized. Some of these are original and/or complex similes:

—He got a head like a water-hydrant, and shit . . .
—He got a head like a water-pump . . . a mailbox . . . like the front of a bus.
—You got a nose like a car fender!

The Thunderbirds say:

BOOT: Money got a head like a tornado mixed with a horse.
MONEY: You got a head of a motor.

(c) *Your mother so* ——— *she* ———. More complex comparisons are done with a quantifier, and adjective, and an embedded sentence of the type (b) or other predication.

DAVID: Your mother so old she got spider webs under her arms.
BOOT: Your mother so old she can stretch her head and lick out her ass.

Such sounds can be made freely against a member of the group:

ROGER: Hey Davy, you so fat you could slide down the razor blade without getting cut . . . an' he so thin that he can dodge rain drops.

These are traditional "fat" and "thin" similes; they take on a particular value here because David *is* fat (a ritualized attribute for him). Boot continues with ritual sounds along these lines:

BOOT: Eh eh, your mother's so skinny she could split through a needle's eye.
BOOT: Your mother's so skinny, about that skinny, she can get in a Cheerioat and say, "Hula hoop, hula hoop!"

This last variant is one step more complex, with two clauses subordinated and two commercial products conjoined into one rhetorical figure. The same simile appears with a different breakfast cereal in a Jet sound (Stanley's):

—Your mother so skinny, she do the hula hoop in a Applejack.

Other Jet similes are somewhat more advanced than the T-Bird ones.

—Bell grandmother so-so-so-ugly, her rag is showin'.
—Bell mother was so small, she bust her lip on the curve.
—Your mother so white she hafta use Mighty White.
—Your mother so skinny, she ice-skate on a razor blade.
. . . so skinny she can reach under the doorknob . . .
. . . so low she c'play Chinese handball on a curve.
. . . so low, got to look down to look up.
. . . so ugly, she got stinkin' with a glass of water.
. . . so black, she sweat chocolate.
. . . so black that she hafta steal to get her clothes.
. . . so black that she has to suck my dick to get home.

Sometimes these similes have clauses subordinated within them: "your mother is so ——— that when she ——— you can ———." To get all of this into one proposition is sometimes difficult in the heat of the moment.

—Your mother's so small, you play hide-and-go-seek, y'all c'slip under a penny.

Here the conjunction *when* is omitted (not uncommon in the speech of children), but the *y'all* seems out of place, and it would not be too unfair to say that this syntax is just beyond the range of performance available to the speaker. Boot of the Thunderbirds can handle constructions of this complexity, but he is the only one who can: the following sound of Boot is even more complex, since the *when* clause conjoins two other clauses:

BOOT: His mother was so dirty, when she get the rag take a bath, the water went back down the drain.

Here the only flaw in the surface structure is perhaps the absence of *and* before *take a bath*. The underlying structure of this sentence might be shown as:

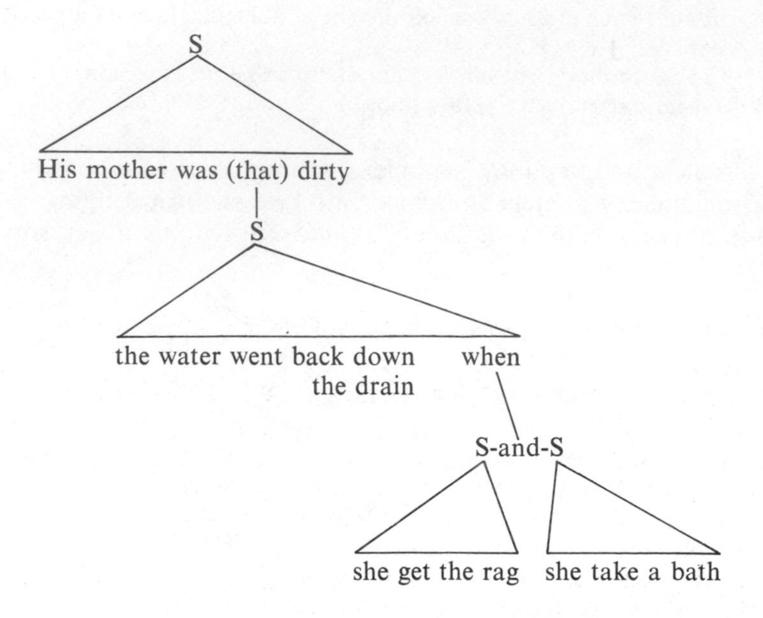

The structure of the sound makes it necessary to foreground the *when*-clauses, so that the action which makes the insult be last rather than end with a condition. This means that two clauses interpose between the quantifier and the predication *went down*—a type of left-hand embedding in the surface which is indeed rare in colloquial speech. Boot uses a similar construction without the initial *so* clause in the following sound, which again is well beyond the syntactic competence of most members:

BOOT: Your mother, when she got to work and she had—those, you know—open-toe shoes, well, her stockings reach her—be sweeping the ground.

Notice that the following sound is much simpler, since the main point is made by a subordinated clause which can therefore appear in final position:

BOOT: His mother go to work without any drawers on, so that she could get a good breeze.

Some of the Jets can use constructions of a complexity equal to those of Boot just given. The most complex syntax occurs in sounds of the type *Your* X *has* Y with attributive quantifiers dominating several sentences.

—Who father wear raggedy drawers?
—Yeh, the ones with so many holes in them when-a-you walk, they whistle?

This sound is received with immediate enthusiasm.

—Oh, shi-it! When you walk they whistle! Oh shit!
—Tha's all he got lef' . . . He never buys but one pair o' drawers.

And shortly afterwards, this sound models another of the same form:

JR: Ronald got so many holes in his socks, when he walks them shoes hum!
Them shoes say MMMM!

Again, it may be helpful to show some of the abstract structure which underlies sounds of this complexity:

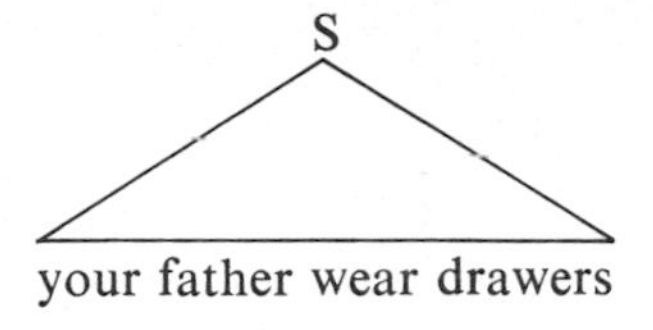

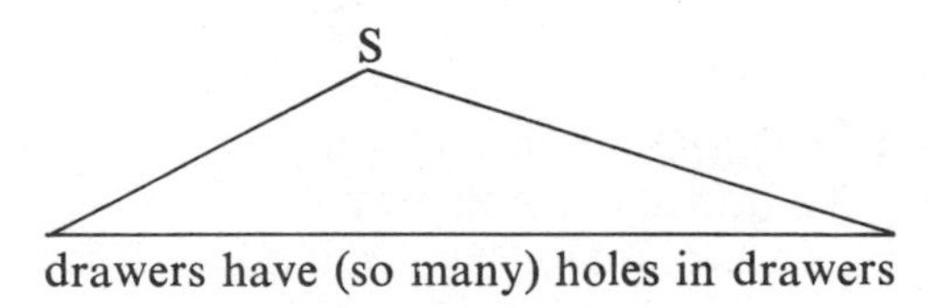

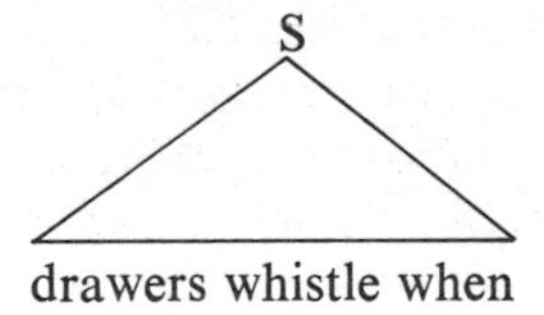

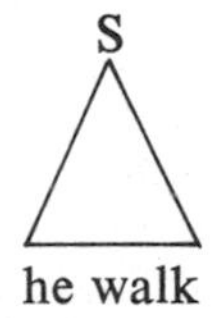

The comparative node *so many* is contained in a relative clause, and it dominates in turn a sentence which dominates a time clause. It cannot be accidental that all of these complex structures are positively evaluated by the group: we can argue that only an idea of exceptional merit would justify for the originator the effort of using such syntax, and that the evaluation refers to the idea; or we can argue that the complexity of the structure itself is impressive for the listener.

(d) *Your mother eat* ———. We now return to a different type of sound which does not involve similes or metaphors, but portrays direct action with simple verbs. The power of these sounds seems to reside in the incongruity or absurdity of the elements juxtaposed—which may be only another way of saying that we do not really understand them.

BOOT: I heard your mother eat rice crispies without any milk.
ROGER: Eat 'em raw!
BOOT: Money eat shit without puttin' any cornflakes on.

The Jets use such constructions freely as well.

—His mother eat Dog Yummies.
—Somebody said your mother's breath smell funny.
—They say your mother eat Gainesburgers.
—Your mother eat fried dick heads.
—Your mother eat coke-a-roaches.
—Your mother eat rat heads.
—Your mother eat Bosco.
—Your mother a applejack-eater.
—Your mother eat scumbag.

One obvious recipe for constructing sounds of this type is to mention something disgusting to eat. Yet most of the items mentioned here are not in that class, and as we will see below less than half of the examples we have could actually be considered obscene. Dog Yummies are not disgusting (they are edible but not palatable) but it is plainly "low" to eat dog food. Elegance in sounds of this type can also involve syntactic complexity. *Your mother a applejack eater* seems intuitively to be a more effective sound than *Your mother eat applejack*. (Applejack, a new breakfast cereal at the time, may be favored because it suggests applejack whiskey.) If so, it is a further piece of evidence that syntactic complexity is a positive feature of sounds.

(e) *Your mother raised you on* ———. This is a specific pattern with fairly simple syntax, particularly effective in striking at both the opponent and his mother. In the Thunderbirds' session, a series of such sounds was initiated by one of the investigators.

WL: Your mother raised you on ugly milk.
BOOT: Your mother raised you on raw corn.
DAVID: Your mother raised you with big lips.

BOOT: Your mother gave you milk out a cave.
BOOT: Your mother gave you milk out her ass.
. . . When you just born, she say "Take a shot."

(f) *I went to your house* . . . A very numerous and important series of sounds are directed against the household and the state of poverty that exists there. Some of these are complex rhymes, quite parallel to the rhymed dozens:

BOOT: I went to your house to ask for a piece of cheese.
The rat jumped up and say "Heggies, please."

Heggies is the claiming word parallel to *dibbs*, *halfsies*, *allies*, *checks*, etc. which was standard in New York City some twenty years ago. Today *heggies* is a minor variant, though it is still recognized, having given way to *thumbs up*.

Most sounds of this type are in prose. Many are directed at the strong position of rats and roaches in the household. They may take the form of anecdotes disguised as true stories.

BOOT: Hey! I went up Money house and I walked in Money house, I say, I wanted to sit down, and then, you know a roach jumped up and said, "Sorry, this seat is taken."
ROGER: I went in David house, I saw the roaches walkin' round in combat boots.

Several sounds from a session with the "Aces" may be quoted here, in which the members noted where they had learned various sounds.

TONY: A boy named Richard learned me this one: When I came across your house, a rat gave me a jay-walkin' ticket.
RENARD: When I came to your house, seven roaches jumped me and one search me.
TED: And I made this one up: I was come in your house; I got hit on the back of my head with a Yoohoo bottle.

Ted's original sound seems weak; it leans upon the humor of specifying a Yoohoo bottle but does not connect with one of the major topics of sounding. One such topic is the bathroom, or lack of one, a strong point to sound on:

BOOT: I went to your house and ask your mother, could I go to the bathroom. She said, "The submarine jus' lef'."
ROGER: I went to his house—I wanted to go to the bathroom, and her mother—his mother gave me a pitchfork and a flashlight.
ROGER: I ringed his bell and the toilet stool flushed.

Remarks about someone's house, how poor it is, are apt to become quite personal, as we will see below. The Jets did not produce many of the "I went in X's house . . ." sounds, but the following occurred in quick succession:

—I went in Junior house 'n' sat in a chair that caved in.
—You's a damn liar, 'n' you was eatin' in my house, right?
—I went to Bell's house 'n' a Chinese roach said, "Come and git it."
—I brought my uncle—I brought my uncle up Junior house—I didn't trust *them* guys.

The tendency to take "house" sounds personally shows up in the second line of this series. As we will see below, the charge that "you was eatin' in my house" returns the accusation of hunger against the originator, and this can have a solid basis in real life.

(g) *Other anecdotal forms.* There are many other anecdotal sounds which do not fall into a single mold. Some are quite long and include the kind of extra detail which can give the illusion, at the outset, that an actual story is being told. From the Jets' session we find

—I ran over Park Avenue—you know, I was ridin' on my bike—and—uh—I seen somebody fightin'; I said lemme get on this now. I ran up there and Bell and his mother, fallin' all over: I was there first xxx gettin' it—gettin' that Welfare food xx.

The incoherent sections are filled with slurping noises which are an important part of such food sounds—indicating that those involved were so desperately hungry and so uncivilized that they behaved like animals.

One can also deliver an anecdote with the same theme as the rhymed dozens quoted above:

—Boah. I'm not gonna say who it was, boah. But I fucked somebody's mother on this bridge one night, Whooh! That shit was so good, she jumped overboard in the river.

There are any number of miscellaneous sounds that can be disguised as pseudo-anecdotes.

ROGER: One day, Money's mother's ass was stuck up and she called Roto-Rooter.

On the other hand, there are anecdotes which take the form of rhymes:

BOOT: I went down south to buy a piece of butter
I saw yo' mother layin' in the gutter.
I took a piece of glass and stuck it up her ass
I never saw a motherfucker run so fas'.

Such narratives typically use the simplest type of syntax, with minimal subjects and preterit verb heads. The anecdotal type of sound appears to be most effective when it is delivered with hesitations and false starts, rather than with the smooth delivery of the other types of sounds. The technique is therefore closely associated with certain types of narrative styles in which the point is delayed to the final clause, where the Evaluation is fused with Result and Coda, as in a joke (Labov and Waletzky, 1968). It is generally true that all sounds have this structure: the evaluative point must be at the very end.

(h) *Portraits.* Just as narrative calls for simple syntax, sounds which present elaborate portraits demand syntactic complexity. The most common are those which place someone's mother on the street as a whore.

—Willie mother stink; she be over here on 128 St. between Seventh 'n' Eighth, waving her white handkerchief: [falsetto] "C'mon, baby, only a nickel."
—Hey Willie mother be up there, standin' the corner, be pullin' up her—her dress, be runnin' her ass over 'n' see those skinny, little legs.

(i) *Absurd and bizarre forms.* The formal typology of sounds presented so far actually covers the great majority of sounds used. But there are a number of striking examples which are not part of any obvious pattern, sounds which locate some profoundly absurd or memorable point by a mechanism not easy to analyze. There is the darkly poetic sound used by Eddie of the Cobras:

—Your mother play dice with the midnight mice.

Rhyme also plays an essential part in this uncommon sound:

—Ricky got shot with his own fart [fat].

We might also cite the following exchange:

—Your mother take a swim in the gutter.
—Your mother live in a garbage can.
—Least I don't live on 1122 Boogie Woogie Avenue, two garbage cans to the right.

The attraction of trade names like *Right Guard* or *Applejacks* may be largely based on their bizarre and whimsical character. Any kind of un-feminine or outlandish behavior on the part of one's mother can be charged:

—Willie mother make a livin' playin' basketball.
—I saw Tommy mother wearin' high-heel sneakers to church.

(j) *Response forms: puns and metaphors.* Sounds are usually answered by other sounds, and the ways in which they follow each other will be discussed below. But there is one formal feature of a sound which is essentially made for responses: "At least my mother ain't . . ." Although these forms cannot be used to initiate sounding, several can succeed each other, as in these sequences from the "Aces" session:

—At least I don't wear bubblegum drawers.
—At least his drawers ain't bubblegum, it's not sticky like yours.
—At least my mother don't work in the sewer.
—At least my mother don't live in the water-crack, like yours.

There are a series of traditional responses of this form which incorporate complex puns. Abrahams cites a dozen from South Philadelphia, including five common in Harlem. Perhaps the best known is:

—At least my mother ain't no railroad track, laid all over the country.

Such forms frequently occur as simple similes, such as

—Your mother's like a police station—dicks going in and out all the time

Although puns such as these seem to have been part of the original dozens tradition, they are no longer common among adolescents in Harlem. They seem to have been adopted by white groups, in the city, where they are quite well known. When our white interviewers used some of these in sounding sessions, they were admired, but they did not initiate a series of other sounds as in the case of "Your momma drink pee" or "Your mother raised you on ugly milk."

This presentation of the "shape" of sounds has also given the reader some idea of the range of topics sounded on. Our own exploratory interviews in other parts of the country show that this scheme applies quite well to other cities and other Negro communities. Kochman and his students have provided descriptions of the Chicago patterns which are very similar to those of Harlem (1968). O. C. Wortham in San Francisco has collected a large body of pre-adolescent sounds, many of which might have been quoted directly from the Thunderbirds, Jets or Cobras: "Your mama got a cast on her right titty," "your mama wears a jocky strap," "your mother wears holy drawers," "Ricky's mama eat shit," "your mother named Mike," "your mother wears tennis shoes to work," "he say his mama plays Batman," "hey, it's so cold in your house the roaches walk around with fur coats on," "man I done busted you so low, you can walk up under that piece of paper with a top hat on."

Ritual insults among white peer groups. While some elements of the dozens and other Negro ritual insults have appeared among white peer groups in the urban centers, the typical forms used among whites are quite different from those of Negroes. The personal experience of several of our own investigators (Paul Cohen and Benji Wald) drawn from different areas of New York City, shows firm agreement on ritual insults. Whereas the NNE practice of sounding ranges over a wide variety of forms and topics which are combined with great flexibility, the white forms are essentially a limited set of routines. Two of the most common begin with "Eat shit":

A: Eat shit.
B: What should I do with the bones?
A: Build a cage for your mother.
B: At least I got one.
A: She *is* the least.

A: Eat shit.
B: Hop on the spoon.
A: Move over.
B: I can't, your mother's already there.

These are indeed ritual and impersonal insults, directed in part against the opponent's mother. But the sequencing occurs in a fixed form, and there is little room for individual choice. These are essentially "snappy answers" which show how knowledgeable rather than how competent the speaker is. It is the aptness of the rejoinder which is looked for:

A: Kiss my ass.
B: Move your nose.

A: Fuck you.
B: Yeh, that would be the best one you ever had.

A: You motherfucker.
B: Your mother told.

A: Got a match?
B: My ass against your face.

These are trick responses. The first speaker may say something aggressive (but not particularly clever) or he may be tricked into a routine such as:

A: How tall are you?
B: Five foot seven.
A: I didn't think shit piled that high.

The white groups also use a certain number of comparisons of the "You are so X that Y" type: "You're so full of shit your eyes are brown." Furthermore, there are similes directed against one's mother that overlap those cited under (b): "Your mother so low she could play handball on a curve . . . walk under a pregnant cockroach without stooping."

The white material is limited in content as well as form and quantity. *Shit* is the most common topic, and in general the insults are based on the taboo words rather than taboo activities. One does not find the proliferation of odd and bizarre elements and the wide range of choice characteristic of the NNE forms. Furthermore, this activity does not occupy any considerable time for the white groups—in a word, it is not a speech event for white groups in the sense that sounding is a speech event for the Negro groups.

There is some evidence that Southern whites (for example, from the Mississippi Delta area) show the same range of ritual insults as Northern whites, and that the rich development of sounding described here is indeed a characteristic of the Negro speech community.

Attributes and Persons Sounded On. A review of the content of the sounds given above under (a–j) will show that a wide but fairly well-defined range of attributes is sounded on. A mother (grandmother, etc.) may be cited for her age, weight (fat or skinny), ugliness, blackness, smell, the food she eats, the clothes she wears, her poverty, and of course her sexual activity. As far as persons are concerned, sounding is always thought of as talking about someone's mother. But other relatives are also mentioned—as part of the search for variety in switching, or for their particular attributes. In order of importance, one can list the opponent's relatives as: mother, father, uncle, grandmother, aunt. As far as number of sounds is concerned, the opponent himself might be included as second most important to his mother, but proverbially sounds are thought of as primarily against relatives.

One of the long epic poems of the NNE community ("toasts") called "Signifying Monkey" gives us some insight into the ordering of relatives. Signifying Monkey stirs up trouble ("signifies") by telling the lion that the elephant had sounded on him:

> Mr. Lion, Mr. Lion, there's a big burly motherfucker comin' your way,
> Talks shit about you from day to day.

The monkey successively reports that the elephant had talked about the lion's sister, brother, father and mother, wife and grandmother.

> The monkey said, "Wait a minute, Mr. Lion," said, "That ain't all,"
> He said, "Your grandmother," said "she was a lady playin' in the old backyard,
> Said evertime he seen her, made his dick get on the hard."

Even more relatives are brought in, which bring the monkey to the inevitable conclusion:

He said, "Yeah he talked about your aunt, your uncle and your cousins,
Right then and there I knew the bad motherfucker was playin' the dozens."

What is said about someone's mother's age, weight, or clothes can be a general or traditional insult, or it can be local and particular. The presence of commercial trade names in the sounds is very striking: Bosco, Applejacks, Wonder Bread, Dog Yummies, Gainesburgers, Gravy Train, as well as the names of the popular figures in the mass media: James Bond, Pussy Galore, Flipper. The street culture is highly local, and local humor is a very large part of sounds. As noted before, one of the best ways to start a loud discussion is to associate someone with a local character who is an "ultra-rich" source of humor. Trade names have this local character—and part of the effect is the superposing of this over-specific label on the general, impersonal figure of "your mother" as in "Your mother look like Flipper." Local humor is omnipresent and overpowering in every peer group—it is difficult to explain in any case, but its importance cannot be ignored.

The odd or whimsical use of particular names can be illustrated by a sequence that occurred when John Lewis left the microbus at an early stop. As a parting shot, he leaned back in the window and shouted genially "Faggots! Motherfuckers!" This set up a chain of responses including a simple "Your mother!" from Rel, "You razor blade bastard!" from someone else, and finally an anonymous "*WINNIE THE POOH*!"

Obscenity does not play as large a part as one would expect from the character of the original dozens. Many sounds *are* obscene in the full sense of the word. The speaker uses as many "bad" words and images as possible —that is, subject to taboo and moral reprimand in adult middle-class society. The originator will search for images that would be considered as disgusting as possible: "Your mother eat fried dick-heads." With long familiarity the vividness of this image disappears, and one might say that it is *not* disgusting or obscene to the sounders. But the meaning of the sound and the activity would be entirely lost without reference to these middle-class norms. Many sounds are "good" because they are "bad"—because the speakers know that they would arouse disgust and revulsion among those committed to the "good" standards of middle-class society. Like the toasts, sounds derive their meaning from the opposition between two major sets of values: *their* way of being "good" and *our* way of being "bad."

The rhymed dozens are all uniformly sexual in character, they aim at the sexual degradation of the object sounded on. But the body of sounds cited above departs widely from this model: less than half of them could be considered obscene, in any sense. At one point in the Jet session, there is a sequence of three sounds concerning fried dick-heads; this is immediately followed by

—Your mother eat rat heads.
—Your mother eat Bosco.
—Your mother look that taxi driver.
—Your mother stinks.
—Hey Willie got on a talkin' hat.
—Your mother a applejack-eater.
—Willie got on a talkin' hat.
—So, Bell, your mother stink like a bear.
—Willie mother . . . she walk like a penguin.

This sequence of nine remarks contains no sexual references; the strongest word is *stink*. Many sounds depend upon the whimsical juxtaposition of a variety of images, upon original and unpredictable humor which is for the moment quite beyond our analysis. But it can be noted that the content has departed very far from the original model of uniform sexual insult.

Only someone very unfamiliar with the NNE sub-culture could think that the current generation is "nicer" and less concerned with sex than previous generations. The cry of "Winnie the Pooh!" does not mean that the Jets are absorbing refined, middle-class wit and culture. Its significance can only be understood by a deeper study of the nature of this ritual activity.

Evaluation of Sounds. One of the most important differences between sounding and other speech events is that most sounds are evaluated overtly and immediately by the audience. In well-structured situations, like the Thunderbird sounding session, this is true of every sound. In wilder sessions with a great many participants, like the Jet session in the Microbus, a certain number of sounds will follow each other rapidly without each one being evaluated.

The primary mark of positive evaluation is laughter. We can rate the effectiveness of a sound in a group session by the number of members of the audience who laugh. In the Thunderbird session, there were five members; if one sounded against the other successfully, the other three would laugh; a less successful sound showed only one laugh, or none. The value of having a separate recording track for each speaker is very great indeed.

A really successful sound will be evaluated by overt comments: In the Jet session, the most common forms are: "Oh!" "Oh shit!", "God damn!" or "Oh lord!" By far the most common is "Oh shit!" The intonation is important: when approval is to be signalled the vowel of each word is quite long, with a high sustained initial pitch, and a slow-falling pitch contour. The same words can be used to express negative reaction, or disgust, but then the pitch is low and sustained. The implication of the positive exclamations is "That is too much" or "That leaves me helpless."

Another, even more forceful mode of approving sounds is to repeat the striking part of the sound oneself: In the Jet session for example:

JOHN L.: Who father wear raggedy drawers?
WILLIE: Yeh the ones with so many holes in them when-a-you walk they whistle?
REL: Oh . . . shi-it! When you walk they whistle! Oh shit!

Negative reactions to sounds are common and equally overt. The most frequent is phony: "Tha's phony!," "Phony shit!" But sounds are also disapproved as *corny*, *weak* or *lame*. Stanley, the president of the Jets, elaborates his negative comments quite freely:

JUNIOR: Aww, Nigger Bell, you smell like B.O. Plenty.
BELL: Aww, nigger, you look like—you look like Jimmy Durante's grandfather.

STAN: Aw, tha's phony [bullshit] . . . Eh, you woke me up with that phony one, man . . .
BELL: Junior look like Howdy Doody.
STAN: That's phony too, Bell. Daag, boah! . . . Tonight ain't your night, Bell.

At another point, Stanley denounces a sound with a more complicated technique: "Don't tell 'im those phony jokes, they're so phony, you *got* to laugh."

The difference between these negative terms is not clear. For our present purposes, we may consider them equivalent, although they are probably used in slightly different ways by different speakers. The Cobras do not use the same negative terms as the Jets. They will say "Sh—you fake—take that shit outa here!" or, most often, "That ain't where it's at."

These evaluative remarks are ways of responding to the over-all effect of a sound. There is also considerable explicit discussion of sounds themselves. In the case of a traditional sound, like a rhymed dozen, one can object to an imperfect rendition. For example, Stevie answers one of our versions with "Tha's wrong! You said it wrong! Mistake!" Members are also very clear on who the best sounders are. Among the Thunderbirds, it is generally recognized that "Boot one of the best sounders . . . he's one of the best sounders of all." This very reputation will interfere with the chances of getting other members to initiate sounding—they know in advance that they will be outdone. In general, sounding is an activity very much in the forefront of social consciousness: members talk a great deal about it, try to make up new sounds themselves, and talk about each other's success. Sounding practices are open to intuitive inspection. It is possible to ask a good sounder, "What would you say if somebody said to you . . ." and he will be glad to construct an answer. Members will also make meta-comments on the course of a sounding session: "Now he's sounding on you, Money!!" or announce their intentions, as Roger does: "Aw, tha's all right. Now I'm gonna sound on you pitiful."

Furthermore, members take very sharp notice of the end result of a sounding contest, as noted below. In a sounding session, everything is public—nothing significant happens without drawing comment. The rules and patterning of this particular speech event are therefore open for our inspection.

The Activity of Sounding. We can distinguish two very different uses of sounds: (1) ritual sounding and (2) applied sounding. The quotations given above are taken from sounding sessions which are examples of the first: rituals in which the sounding is done for its own sake. Applied sounding involves the use of sounds for particular purposes in the midst of other verbal encounters, and follows a very different set of rules. We will consider ritual sounding first, beginning with the general rules which apply, and then the operation of these rules in the two sessions which have been cited.

There are three participants in this speech event: antagonist A, antagonist B, and the audience. A sounds against B; the audience evaluates; B sounds against A; and his sound is evaluated. The general structure is then more complex than most ABABAB exchanges: it is

A-1 e B-1 e A-2 e B-2 e . . .

A-1 almost always contains a reference to B's mother. B-1 should be based on A-1; to the extent that it is an original or well-delivered transformation of A-1, B may be said to have won. A-2 may be an entirely new sound. But if A-2 is a further transformation of B-1, it is usually evaluated even more highly. Whereas we may say that A-2 "tops" B-1 if it is intrinsically better, A may be said to "get" B most often if A-2 is a variant or clearly related to B-1. This is what is meant by "topping" B—the exchange is held open. A skillful sounder can hold an exchange of variants open beyond the point where it would normally be considered ended by conventional estimates. The series may be terminated by one antagonist clearly winning over the other. Thus in that part of the Thunderbirds' session following Ricky's collapse, Boot clearly beats Money. The exchange starts with Boot's long story of how Money was tricked into thinking that a jar of urine was ice tea, and he drank it. Money objects, rather incoherently: "I know you love thuh—ice tea . . . I know you love to pee—i—ice cream tea." Boot then begins sounding:

A-1	BOOT:	His mother go to work without any draws on so that she c'd get a good breeze.
B-1	MONEY:	Your mother go, your mother go work without any, anything on, just go neked.
e	DAVID:	That's a lie.

In the first exchange, Money clearly fails, as evidenced by his hesitation: he simply exaggerates Boot's well-constructed and witty sound without the corresponding wit. David's comment is negative—particularly in that it takes Money's sound to be a factual claim.

A-2 BOOT: Your mother, when she go to work and she had—you know th-toe shoes, well her stockings reach her be—sweeping the ground.
e {RICKY: [laughs]
e {ROGER: Ho lawd! [laughs]

Boot's A-2 is stretching the limits of the syntax available to him, and he has considerable difficulty in getting it out. It is clearly an extension of A-1 and B-1, of the form "Your mother go to work with . . ." But instead of the conventional wit of A-1, or the reduced variant of B-1, A-2 enters the field of the unconventional and absurd. Boot scores two strong responses from Ricky and Roger.

Money cannot build further on the syntactic model, but he does attempt to respond to the theme of holes in shoes. There is no audience response.

B-2 MONEY: Your mother have holes—potatoes in her shoes.

Since Boot has won this exchange, he now begins a new sequence:

A-3 BOOT: Your mother got a putty chest [laugh].
B-3 MONEY: Arrgh! Aww—you wish you had a putty chest, right?

Money responds, but he does not sound. Boot continues with another sound of the "got" type; now, however, the pattern is complicated as Roger joins in, sounding specifically against Money. This is a second stage which occurs when one antagonist is clearly losing ground: he becomes the object of group sounding.

A-4 BOOT: Your mother got hair growing out her dunkee hole.
C-4 {ROGER: Money your mother got a 45 in her left titty.
{MONEY: Awwww!
e RICKY: [laughter]

Money now responds to Roger's sound with a variant which strikes us as a very able one.

B-4 MONEY: Your mother got a 45° titty.

Now it is Roger who answers Money, and gets a strong response. Boot then adds a sound which is rather incoherent and gets no response.

C-5 ROGER: Your mother got baptised in a whiskey bottle.
e MONEY: [laughs]
e RICKY: [laughs]
e DAVID: [laughs]
A-5 BOOT: Your mother sail the seven seas in a sardine can. [laughs]

The situation has become unclear. Sounding is defined for members as one person sounding upon another, but three are involved. Money's laughter indicates that he thinks Roger's sound is not against him, but against Boot. David now explicitly says that the antagonists are Boot and Roger, but Roger denies this: he is still sounding against Money. Boot adds a further dig which recognizes that Roger's *him* means Money, not Boot.

DAVID: Now you and Roger sounding [laughs].
ROGER: I'm sounding on him.
BOOT: That half of a motor. [laughs]

Given the sanction of a group attack against Money, David now begins his own. But Money turns to us suddenly and says "Can we sing now?" (The formal recording of singing was one of the purposes of the session.) Money's question is interpreted as a transparent attempt to escape, and a storm of abuse descends on his head from the leaders of the group. He is forced to acknowledge his defeat explicitly.

D-6 DAVID: Everytime Money looks at the moon, everytime
MONEY: Could we sing now?
BOOT: [laughs]
ROGER: [laughs]
DAVID: Money look at moon, he say "Ooo, look at the moonshine."
ROGER: He changing the subject!
RICKY: Awww! Tryin' to change thuh-ih-subject!
ROGER: What's the matter, you feeling all right, or you want some more sounding?
MONEY: Uh-uh.

The sounding sessions goes on, with Money saying nothing. When he speaks up later on, Ricky says "Hey Money, you better keep quiet, if you don't want 'em soundin' bad on you." It should be quite clear that there are winners and losers in sounding sessions.

The speech event we call sounding is not isolated from other forms of verbal interaction: it can merge with them or become transformed into a series of personal insults. When ritual insult changes into personal insult, the difference between the two becomes quite clear. We take as an instance the beginning of the sounding session with the Thunderbirds. To save space, evaluative reactions to each sound will be put in brackets after it.

In this session, we can observe the difficulty that members have in distinguishing between hypothetical and actual sounding. The question "What would you say if . . ." is quickly transformed into actual sounding. The series was initiated by an effort of C. Robins to get Money to sound.

CR: (to Money) What would you say if Boot said "Your father look like Funjie!"? [ROGER: "Oh Lord, oh Money . . . oh ho . . . Funjie . . . ooo!" ROGER, BOOT, RICKY, DAVID: laugh].
MONEY: Hunh?
CR: That's like Funjie's your father. [ROGER: Ohh! BOOT, RICKY: laugh]
BOOT: He's sounding on you, Money!
CR: No, no, if *Boot* said it . . .

At this point, other staff members join in and try to make it clear that we are only asking what Money would say *if*. Money tries to answer, but Boot takes over with the support of the rest of the group. Our efforts to push Money to the fore do not succeed.

DAVID: Boot one of the best sounders.
MONEY: I say, uh—uhm—
BOOT: Now if you said that to me . . .
CR: No no no no, you sound him, tell him, say say that . . .
MONEY: He's one of the best sounders of all.
CR, WL: Money sounds good too.
BOOT: Now if he said that to me, know what I'd say? I'd say—

Boot is irrepressible. Money's failure to sound well in the face of Boot's dominant position is precisely the same phenomenon that W. F. Whyte observed in Doc's corner gang (1955). Followers did not bowl as well against the leader of the group as they could by themselves. In other situations we have seen Money sound very well.

"B-1" BOOT: I'd say, "His father got four lips."
"A-2" MONEY: I'd say, "Your mother got four lips." [BOOT: "That ain't nothin'." CR: "What does that mean?"]

Boot's sound hits on the familiar topic of thick lips, part of the self-derogatory pattern of NNE. (Cf. Jets: "Your father got lips like a—Oldsmobile.") Money's hypothetical A-2 is the weakest kind of switch: substitution of one relative for another, and it is properly and immediately derogated. Money has failed again. The part of second antagonist is now taken up by David: a small, fat boy who is continually being pushed aside by Boot and is the constant butt of jokes. On the other hand, he has a great deal of courage, and unlike others in the group, never gives up in the struggle to establish his position, and never allows Boot to dominate the situation entirely. In the following sounding session, Boot applies his verbal skill with ruthless force to crush David, but David's verbal resources are greater than one would have predicted.

A-3 DAVID: So your . . . So then I say, "Your father got brick teeth."
B-3 BOOT: Aw your father got teeth growing out his behind! [MONEY, RICKY, ROGER laugh.]

Boot's response is a clear example of a winning effort. He takes David's hypothetical A-3, and adds to it elements of absurdity and obscenity that obtain positive evaluation from all three members of the audience. Note that Boot's sound is no longer hypothetical: it is the first "real sound" of the series. David attempts to top this by staying with the "behind" theme, but he fails to get a coherent thought out. He is not fluent in this area, at least in the face of Boot's ability.

A-4 DAVID: Yeah, your father, y-got, your father grow, uh, uh, grow hair from, from between his, y'know. [MONEY laughs.]
B-4 BOOT: Your father got calluses growin' up through his ass, and comin' through his mouth. [BOOT, MONEY and RICKY laugh.]

Boot builds further on the original model, and crushes David with a display of virtuosity that leaves him with nothing to say. Boot is not willing to leave it there; like many a good sounder, he can seize his advantage by piling one sound on another. He switches abruptly to:

B-4′ BOOT: Your father look like a grown pig. [BOOT, MONEY and RICKY laugh.]

David wants to respond, and he reaches out for a sound which breaks the rules. It is not a ritual insult at all, but a personal remark that hits on a failing of Boot's step-father.

a-5 DAVID: Least my—at least my father don't be up there talking uh-uh-uh-uh-uh-uh!

The fact that this is a personal insult and not a ritual insult is shown by the fact that Boot answers it. Since ritual insults are not intended as factual statements, the allegations of sounds are not denied. But Boot vigorously responds to David's taunt. Roger's comment acknowledges that Boot has been hit.

BOOT: Uh—so my father talks stutter talk what it mean? [ROGER: He talk the same way a little bit.]

Now Boot responds to David's insult with a comparable one, which is related to A-5 in exactly the way that one sound is related to another. Boot's father stutters; David's father is old and has gray hair: a simple fact, but Boot makes a great deal of it.

A-6 BOOT: At least my father ain't got a gray head! His father got a big bald spot with a gray head right down there, and one long string . . .

David is hurt, and he too feels it necessary to deny the personal insult. But Boot doesn't stop: he picks up the point of "one long string" and grinds it in over and over, to the amusement of Roger and Money.

DAVID: Because he'old, he's old, that's why! He's old, that's why! . . .
BOOT: . . . and one long string, that covers his whole head, one, one long string, about that high, covers his whole head. [ROGER: ho lord, one string! MONEY, BOOT laugh.]

Boot brings tears to David's eyes. Boot's side-kick Money does not mind, but Ricky objects.

DAVID: You lyin' Boot! . . . You know 'cause he old, tha's why!
RICKY: Aw man, cut it out.

Boot has won the day, but he has no sense of restraint. He now returns to ritual sounding: his next insults are not intended as allegations of fact, but David continues to take them as personal.

What follows now is no longer the controlled counterpoint of sounding, of the form A e B e, but rather an excited argument, in which both parties are in strident overlap most of the time. It is mostly David against Boot now: Boot's insults do not draw much response from the others, and one can sense the group support ebbing from him.

B-7 BOOT: Your father look like this—with his butt coming out, and he go [slurp] he look like . . .
DAVID: You a liar!
B-8 BOOT: You know one time I came over his house, I saw some slop in the garbage, you know, and then, and I left it there, and David say, David say [slurp, chomp, chomp, chomp] [MONEY laughs.]

David is ready to take up any weapon at hand. He seizes upon the poverty theme, and a personal charge that hits home. It takes some time for David to be heard: finally Boot stops his chomping effect to issue a vigorous (but ineffective) denial.

A-9 DAVID: So! and you always come over my house and say, yeah, Boot always come over my house and say, Boot always coming over my house to eat. He aks for food, and Ohhh lawww . . .

BOOT: I don't come over your house—I don't come nuttin! I only come over your house on school days and from now on I do.

David senses his advantage and pursues it.

DAVID: . . . and when we go swimmin', we go, you aks for food, and ever ti—and you come over my house—

Boot can no longer deny the factual truth of David's charge, but he tries to mitigate the facts: foolishly perhaps, because David is ready with a crushing response.

BOOT: Yeah, I only be playin', I only be playin'!
DAVID: *Yeah, but you sure be eatin'*!

Not every story ends with the underdog showing as well as David. David's momentary success is all the more striking because Boot is without doubt in verbal control of the group. As we have seen, Boot continues his triumphant progress sounding against others, in no way daunted by this reversal. In these extracts, we have the full weight of evidence for the important point that Boot is *the verbal leader* of the Thunderbirds—that he excells at all the verbal skills of the NNE sub-culture. It is not only that Boot has a larger store of sounds at his disposal, and can draw upon them more readily. His syntax is also more complex, and he can deliver sounds that no one else can. All of the more complex examples from the Thunderbirds cited above are those of Boot.

The Rules for Ritual Sounding. In the presentation of sounding so far, we have seen that this speech event has a well articulated structure. These rules can be broken: it is possible to hurl personal insults and it is possible to join in a mass attack on one person. But there is always a cost in stepping out of the expected pattern—in the kind of uncontrolled and angry response which occurs, or in the confusion as to who is doing what to who.

As we examine these examples of sounding, the fundamental opposition between ritual insults and personal insults emerges. The appropriate responses are quite different: a personal insult is answered by a denial, excuse or mitigation, whereas a sound or ritual insult is answered by another sound. Sounds are then necessarily chained into longer sequences, since a sound and its response are essentially the same kind of thing, and a response calls for a further response. The complexity of sounding is actually the result of this comparatively simple structure, so that our semantic diagram of sounding might be reduced to:

S-1 e S-2 e S-3 . . .

On the other hand, personal insults produce dyads of interaction: insult (I) and denial or excuse (D). We observe a chain in this last exchange between Boot and David:

I_A D_B I_B D_A I_A D_B . . .

but there is no inherent, structural reason for chaining as in the case of sounds. These are DD sequencing rules in the scheme on pages 122–123.

There is an invariant rule operating here which is not subject to violation. What is normal and automatic for a personal insult is unthinkable with sounds. We have the exchanges A: *You come over to my house and ask for something to eat*. B: *I do not*! and A: *Your father got grey hair and one long string* . . . B: *That's cause he's old, that's why*! But we do not have such exchanges as A: *Your momma drink pee*. B: **That's a lie*! Instead the response is *Your father eat shit*. If this was merely a semi-categorical rule we would expect joking responses with denials, deliberate misinterpretations of the sounds, parallel to those we sometimes hear with requests: *Would you mind opening the window*? *No. Can you give me the time*? *Yes*. Since responses to sounds are so automatic and deep-seated, we must pre-suppose a well-formed competence on the part of members to distinguish ritual insults from personal insults. On the face of it, it does not seem easy to make this distinction. It is a question, among other things, of how serious the antagonist is: does he want to start a fight? does he mean it? are people going to believe this is true? What is the internal competence which allows Boot to recognize immediately David's personal insult, and to respond with a denial? How can the Jets sound on each other for hours without anyone being insulted?

To answer this question, it is necessary to specify more precisely the structure of sounds. The superficial taxonomy given above under (a–j) merely charts the differences in the syntactic forms of sounds as they are uttered. If sounds are heard as one kind of utterance, there must be a uniform mode of interpretation which shows all of these forms as derived from a single underlying structure. We propose that this structure is

T(B) is so X that P

where T is the target of the sound, X is the attribute of T which is focussed on, and P is a proposition that is coupled with the attribute by the quantifier *so . . . that* to express the degree to which T has X. The target T(B) is normally B's mother or other relative. (It may seem as if there are more complex targets such as "Your mother's clothes" or "Your mother's face" but these may best be seen as derived from constructions such as "Your mother is so ugly that her face . . .") The attribute X is drawn from the range of features or topics outlined above: age, weight, clothes, etc. It is limited to a specifically *pejorative* value: *age* is specifically *old*, *weight* is *skinny* or *fat*, *clothing* is *ragged* or *dirty*, *appearance* is *ugly* or *dirty*, *sexual behavior* is *loose* or *immoral*; *smell* is *stink*, *wealth* is *poor*, *food* is *poor* or *disgusting*. The proposition P may have a wide variety of forms, although there are lower-level sequencing rules and standards of excellence that govern its form. Thus we have a typical sound, *Your mother* [T(B)] *so old* [X], *she fart dust*. [P].

It will be observed that there are a great many sounds with simpler forms than this, and some that are more complex. We might consider that the simpler forms such as *Your mother the Abominable Snowman* are derived from a full form T(B) *is so* X *that* P by rules of deletion parallel to syntactic rules for ellipsis. However, it seems more plausible to write discourse rules for making sounds indirectly, parallel to the rules for making commands or requests. One can make commands by statements which mention only the conditions or pre-conditions for such commands. Thus someone can request a glass of water by stating that he is thirsty. A sound may be made by simply stating the proposition P. The delection of T(A) *is so* X *that* . . . is recoverable in the interpretation of the listener, who has the competence to know what attribute is being sounded on. For example, *Your mother look like Flipper* must be understood as "Your mother is so ugly that she looks like Flipper," whereas *Your mother name the Black Boy* will be interpreted as "Your mother is so black that she is named 'Black Boy'." *Your father got teeth growing out of his ass* is one of many sounds that must refer to an attribute *odd*, *crazy*, or perhaps most literally, *fucked-up*.

Of the simpler forms listed under (a)–(d) above, the only types which offer serious difficulty in this interpretation are the equative forms. Type (a), *Your mother the abominable Snowman* can be understood as either "Your mother is so ugly that she looks like the abominable Snowman" or ". . . that she is named the abominable Snowman." If one takes a more mystical approach—that the speaker is asserting "Your mother is in fact the Abominable Snowman"—this is equivalent to saying that the insult is directed against the opponent himself, rather than his (ritual) mother. If we hold the notion that the sound is intended to insult or degrade the opponent's mother, rather than to claim he has an altogether different mother, then the interpretations of "like" and "is named" are called for.

Sounds of the (d) *Your mother eat* . . . type are usually interpreted as referring to the attribute "poor" (or "hungry" which may be subsumed under "poor"). Thus *Your mother eat corn flakes without any milk* may be understood as "Your mother is so hungry that she eats cornflakes without any milk!" or as "Your mother is so poor that she has to eat cornflakes without any milk."

On the other hand, the following sequence of sounds must be given a different interpretation:

—His mother eat Dog Yummies . . .
—Somebody said your mother's breath smell funny.
—They say your mother eat Gainesburgers.
—They say your mother was a Gravy Train.

These are plainly based on the traditional mode of insulting someone's mother by calling her a *dog*. The direct insults *Your mother's a bitch . . . a dog . . . You're a son of a bitch* do not have any weight in sounding today. But the existence of this model makes it plain that the underlying interpretation is not "Your mother is like a dog" or "Your mother is named *dog*" but rather "Your mother is a dog." On the other hand, Boot's sound *Your father looks like a grown pig* is not equivalent to saying *Your father is a pig . . . a swine!* but rather must be taken to mean "Your father is so fat that he looks like a grown pig."

The type (e) *Your mother raised you on ugly milk* is unique in this series, because it must be interpreted as a sound directly against the opponent: "*You* are so ugly that your mother [must have] raised you on ugly milk." But we might add that the mother is also being insulted here, so that the sound adds in effect "and it's your mother's fault!"

The more complex sounds such as the anecdotal (f) *I went to B's house* . . . type must be taken as directed against the whole family: "B's family is so poor that . . ." On the other hand, complex comparisons such as *Your father drawers have so many holes in them that when he walk they whistle* can be interpreted as "Your father's drawers are so ragged that . . ." or as one step further, "Your father is so ragged that his drawers have so many holes in them that when he walks they whistle."

There are, of course, a certain number of miscellaneous sounds which are difficult to interpret in any scheme: *Your mother play dice with the midnight mice* is many-ways ambiguous.

It is clear that the formal definition given does not include the rhymed dozens, which have the underlying structure *I fucked your mother so much that* . . . A number of other sounds, such as *I took your mother* are based upon the model in which the sounder asserts that he sexually insulted or degraded the opponent's mother. This model must be added as an alternative mode of sounding to the one outlined above. But the great majority of sounds used by the Jets, Cobras and Thunderbirds fit the T(B) *is so* X *that* P model. We must presuppose that members have the competence to make such interpretations if we are to explain their behavior.

The capacity to interpret sounds frequently depends on the ability to locate the underlying negative adjective X when only the proposition P remains. What does it mean to say

Your mother eat Bosco!

It requires native competence to decide if this is a sound against your mother's blackness (Bosco is a chocolate product; cf. *Your mother so black she sweat chocolate*); or her poverty (cf. *Your mother eat corn flakes without any milk*); or her decency (cf. *Your mother eat scumbag*).

We can now write rules for sounding that will account for the interpretation of a sound and selection of an appropriate response to it. The following rule (1) begins with the listener B's position, as he hears what is said and interprets it to decide what has been done: a rule of interpretation UD in the scheme given on pages 122–123.

(1) If A makes an utterance S in the presence of B and an audience C, which includes reference to a target related to B, T(B), in a proposition P, and

(a) B believes that A believes that P is not true and

(b) B believes that A believes that B knows that P is not true . . .

then S is a *sound*, heard as T(B) *is so* X *that* P where X is a pejorative attribute, and A is said to have *sounded on* B.

This rule can (and must) be abbreviated by identifying conditions (a) and (b) as conditions for shared or social knowledge. These are only the first of an infinite series of recursive conditions which represent the fact that there is shared knowledge between A and B that P is not true. In the terminology of discourse analysis now being developed, an A-event is one known to be known only to A [in A's biography] and a B-event is one known to be known only to B, whereas an AB-event is one known to be known to both. We may summarize conditions (a) and (b) as *it is an* AB *event that* P *is not true*.

The audience C is an essential ingredient here. It is true that one person *can* sound against another without a third person being present, but the pre-supposition that this is public behavior can easily be heard in the verbal style. Sounds are not uttered in a direct, face-to-face conversational mode. The voice is raised and projected, as if to reach an audience. In a two-person sounding situation, the antagonists treat each other as representing the audience.

Note that rule (1) does not require the attribute X to be explicitly mentioned. On the other hand, the proposition P must be present. We rarely hear sounds of the form T(B) *is* (Q)X where Q is a simple quantifier, and it is doubtful if they are to be classified as sounds. *Your mother is very fat*; *your father is real black* are not heard as sounds. Indeed, we can explain the non-deletability of P as we return to the question of the conditions for recognizing sounds as opposed to personal insults. The rule (1) is designed to answer the original question: how does B recognize a ritual insult? First, he recognizes an appropriate target. Secondly, he recognizes the *sounding situation*: a remark is made by A in a loud voice designed to be heard by the audience C. Thirdly, he judges the proposition P to be appropriate to a ritual insult in that everyone present plainly knows that it is not true. The Jets' mothers do not look like Flipper or Howdy Doody; they are not the Abominable Snowman; they do not eat Dog Yummies or fried dick-heads. Furthermore, it is a matter of human competence to know that everyone knows that these propositions are not true. On the other hand, the attributes X may justly be attributed to one's mother: she may very well be fat, or skinny, or ugly, or black, or poor, or old. If the proposition P were deleted, the ritual insult would become a personal insult. *Your family is poor!* is not a ritual insult, but a personal one. We have noted that Boot's stepfather does stutter; David's father is old and has gray hair—and all the Thunderbirds know this.

Outsiders would of course be able to recognize ritual propositions P, but without the shared knowledge of members as to whose family was poor, which family was poorest, and which mother was blackest, the outsider could not as readily recognize a personal insult. He would have to suspend judgment. The group does not share all knowledge equally, and sounding is not confined within a single peer group or hang-out group. Therefore sounds must be recognized as ritual insults in themselves, without presupposing any specific knowledge of the sounder's family. For this reason, the propositions P tend to become more and more bizarre and unlikely. *Your mother so low she c' play Chinese handball on a curve* (curb) is a safe sound. Nobody is that low. On the other hand, there is something dangerously personal in *Your mother look like his father, boy; 'n' you know how HE look, boy.* There are other cases, some noted below, where weak sounds can be interpreted as personal insults. They are then denied, and conflict follows. But if one reviews the sounds quoted above, it will be immediately obvious in almost every case that the propositions P are known to be untrue.

The same argument applies to the rhymed dozens. Among young adults, to say *I fucked your mother* is not to say something obviously untrue. But it is obviously untrue that "I fucked your mother from tree to tree / Your father said, 'Now fuck me!'" The situation can become difficult in some neighborhoods. In the Puerto Rican barrio of East 111th Street, it is a common sound to say "Your mother's on Fifth Avenue!" meaning that she is a prostitute. To the question, "What about the kids whose mothers *are* on Fifth Avenue?" members reply "They don't say much."

The danger of sounds being misinterpreted as personal remarks cannot be overstated. One real incident is worth citing.[9] A group of musicians were returning to New York City on a bus, and they started sounding on the wife of one member of the band who lived in Detroit: jumps into the hay with the ice man, and so on. When they got to the hotel, they noticed he was missing. Later they found out that he went back to Detroit; and he did find his wife in bed with someone. A short while after, he committed suicide.

There is no need to compile a great many such incidents to demonstrate the danger of ritual sounding that is not obviously untrue. In dealing with strangers it is considerably harder to say what is a safe sound, and there are any number of taboos that can be broken with serious results. Generally speaking, extended ritual sounding is an in-group process, and when sounding occurs across group lines, it is often intended to provoke a fight. One such case has been documented by Swett (1966). A young musician named Young Beartracks killed another young man known as Chicago Eddie outside a poolroom in East Palo Alto. In the court testimony it was said that there had been an argument between the two preceding the shooting. Swett, who knew the situation quite well, points out that they were engaged in the dozens, and that there was considerable tension already present between the two—Eddie was a member of an urban gang and Young Beartracks a recent member of a rural gang. The role of the dozens in this situation was plainly relevant to the shooting that followed—actually a case of verbal aggression by Eddie against Young Beartracks—but the judge and jury did not understand this point[10]:

> The first witness for the prosecution, the poolroom attendant and a member of the urban gang, did state in cross-examination that "Eddie put him [Young Beartracks] in the dozens," but the effort of the defense counsel to procure a clarification of the term "dozens" was objected to by the prosecution on the grounds that the witness had not been qualified as an expert in semantics. (Swett, 1966)

First it is worth noting that P *can* be deleted if X is also missing; we then have *Your mother!* This is a very common sound; as cited above,

JOHN LEWIS: Faggots!! Motherfuckers!!
REL: Your *mother*!

Here of course there is unrecoverable deletion—that is, there is no X or P that can be reconstructed. We can interpret *Your mother* as signaling either a generalized insult, or as referring to the intention to sound on someone. It may also be used in public places as an elliptical form where behavior is not as free as normally. I observed the following sequence used by two ten-year-olds entering a delicatessen:

—Your mother!
—Your father!
—Your uncle!

We can now give rule (2) for responding to a sound.

2) If A has sounded on B, B sounds on A by asserting a new proposition P′ which includes reference to a target related to A, T(A), and such that it is an AB-event that P′ is untrue. P′ may be embedded in a sentence as a quantification of a pejorative attribute X′ of T(A).

This is a DU production rule in the scheme outlined on pages 122–123. It also contains reference, in the first clause, to the DD sequencing rule, which may be stated independently as (3) *the response to a sound is a sound.* We have thus filled out the original paradigm for discourse analysis, which may be shown as

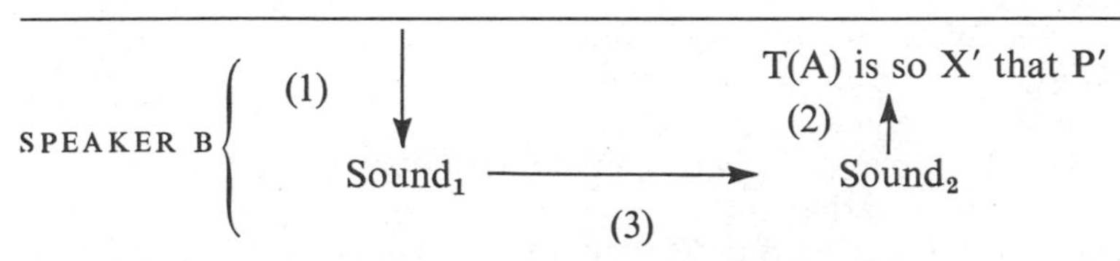

There is an interesting condition here on P′ which is that *If* X′ ≠ X, *then* P′ ≠ P. In other words, if A says, *Your mother so old she fart dust*, B cannot say *Your mother so skinny she fart dust*, or *Your mother so black she fart dust*. But if X′ = X, then it is possible for P′ = P, if the target T is shifted, although this is the weakest kind of response. Among young children who do not sound well, one will hear such sequences as:

—Your mother got funky drawers.
—Your father got funky drawers.

But one does not hear as an answer, "*Your* mother got funky drawers," for this would be equivalent to a denial of the sound. We can now see why denial of ritual sounds is impossible; for to deny a sound is to admit that it is *not* a matter of general knowledge that it is obviously untrue, just as to excuse or mitigate the sound is to admit it as factually true.

The description of P as being obviously untrue—that its untruth is an AB event—is equivalent to deciding that the sounder is not "serious." This decision must be made in any conversational exchange—whether it is a matter of commands, requests, assertions or sounds—it is the first act of interpretation which the listener must make. As Harvey Sacks has pointed out (1966) there are important consequences of this decision: if the speaker is judged serious, a suitable response must be constructed to fit the situation. If the speaker is joking, then all that is usually required is a laugh—no matter what was said by the first speaker. In the case of sounding, the judgment is made that the speaker is not serious—the insult is a ritual one —but the answer will be governed to a certain extent by the nature of the proposition P. Excellence in sounding, and the winning of the contest, will depend upon the relation of P′ to P.

The following more general formulation of the interactional structure of sounding is based upon the suggestions of Erving Goffman, in response to an earlier presentation of this analysis. Goffman's framework isolates four basic properties of *ritual* sounding, as opposed to other types of insult behavior:

1. A sound opens a *field*, which is meant to be sustained. A sound is presented with the expectation that another sound will be offered in response, and that this second sound may be built formally upon it. The player who presents an initial sound is thus offering others the opportunity to display their ingenuity at his expense.

2. Besides the initial two players, a third-person role is necessary.

3. Any third person can become a player, especially if there is a failure by one of the two players then engaged.

4. Considerable symbolic distance is maintained and serves to insulate the event from other kinds of verbal interaction.

These properties, illustrated in the previous sections, are the means by which the process of insult becomes socialized and adapted for play. They may eventually be formalized in higher-level rules of verbal interaction. In the following discussion, we will see in greater detail how the first principle operates in ritual sounding.

Sequencing in the Content of Sounds. The rules given in the sub-section above are all that are needed to generate a series of sounds between two antagonists. There are further complications involved when a third person enters the exchange, and when a number of members join in sounding on one antagonist who is falling behind. But sequencing is much more than the fact that speakers take turns and succeed each other: sequencing involves the substance of sounds which succeed each other—how one sound is built on another, and how a series of sounds are brought to a conclusion. Above all, we are concerned with the standards of excellence in sounding—what makes one person a better sounder than another, and how the group evaluates the performance of an individual. This topic will provide us with the best insight into the factors which control the use of language in the street culture. In settings far removed from the classroom, under standards of performance that are alien to those of the school, peer group members develop a high level of competence in syntax, semantics and rhetoric. One part of this competence was seen in the toasts developed by adults: in this discussion of sounding, we will observe the creative use of language by adolescents. We will consider first simple sequences of the type AB, where B builds on A's sound to achieve a greater level of complexity, and may be judged in some sense to have surpassed it.

The extensive selections from the Thunderbirds' session show a number of such AB sequences. We cited:

DAVID: Your father got brick teeth.
BOOT: Your father got teeth growin' out his behind.

Note that both sounds feature the same attribute: odd or misshapen appearance, and the same target (relative to the speaker). Boot also preserves the same surface form: that is, in neither sound does the T *is so* X *that* . . . sentence appear. We do not in fact find sequences of the form:

A: Your father got brick teeth.
B: Your father got such long teeth that they growin' out his behind.

We also note that the most superficial syntax of the proposition P is preserved: *Your father got* . . . Finally, Boot builds his sound on the same specific notion of misshapen teeth that David introduced. But Boot does not limit himself to mere exaggeration, such as *Your father got teeth a mile long*. Instead, he adds a new theme which combines anal interest with absurdity. We will not attempt to explore here the question of how "original" Boot's effort is. Most sounds are repetitions or re-combinations of elements that have been used before. But it should be clear that sheer memory will not do the trick here, as it will with rhymed dozens. The reply must be appropriate, well-formed, it must build upon the specific model offered. It was observed before that Boot clearly won this round, judging by the response of the audience.

Turning to the Jet session, we find that the targets usually shift more rapidly, since more than two members are involved and there is more overt play to the audience. The sequence AB is illustrated by many examples such as:

A: Eh man, Tommy mother so little, look like she got hit by lightning.
B: Your mother so small, you play hide-and-go seek, y'all c'slip under a penny.

Here the target and attribute are preserved by B, who adds another clause, going far beyond A in syntactic complexity (and apparently to the limits of his syntactic competence). The same pattern prevails when two different sounders are sounding on the same third man.

A: Bell grandmother so-so-so ugly, her rag is showin'.
B: Bell grandmother got so many wrinkles in her face, when they walk down the street, her mother would say, "Wrinkles and ruffles."

In the second sound, the attributes of age and ugliness overlap. The proposition is embedded in a more complex way in the T *is so* X *clause*; the embedded P combines three sentences as against the one sentence of the A model, and again shows the left hand embedding which is so rare in colloquial speech. The underlying structure of this sentence is certainly as complex as any we have seen:

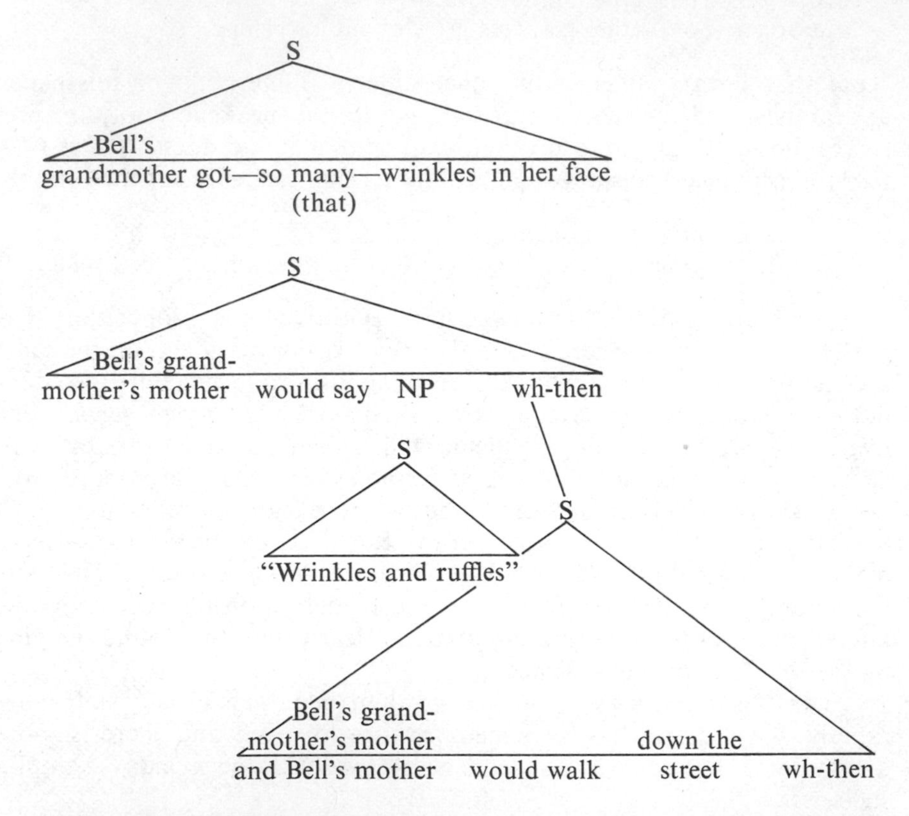

Most of the sequences in the Jet session are more complex than this, but throughout we see the general pattern that B builds on A. We do not find sequences which reverse this order—in which the same target and attribute are preserved, but in which the proposition P is simpler—as would be the case, for example, if B and A were reversed above.

In the Cobras' sounding, we get many long sequences of comparable structure until someone arrives with a more complex form that ends the series:

—Your momma's a peanut man!
—Your momma's a ice-man!
—Your momma's a fire man!
—Your momma's a truck driver!
—Your father sell cracker-jacks!
—Your mother *look* like a cracker-jack!

The last sound in this series cannot be topped, and the sounding goes off in a completely different direction: "Your father named Theodore . . ." Here is another example of Cobras building on each other:

—Your mother got on sneakers!
—Your mother wear high-heeled sneakers to church!
—Your mother wear high-heeled sneakers to come out and play on the basketball court!

The complication which B adds is often a semantic one—an additional pejorative attribute is inserted, as in the following:

A: Your mother name Black—Black Boy.
B: Your mother name the Black Bruiser.

The attribute attributed to the target is now not only blackness, but also masculinity or lack of femininity (as in *Your mother James Bond*).

When a sound becomes too ordinary—too possible—we can then observe a sudden switch in the pattern of response to that appropriate for a personal insult. This can happen by accident, when a sound is particularly weak. For example, in the Jet session:

A: I went in Junior house 'n' sat in a chair that caved in.
B: You's a damn liar; 'n' you was eatin' in my house, right?

This is the only instance in the Jet sounding session where a statement is denied, and it is plainly due to the fact that the proposition P is not appropriate for a ritual insult. Its untruth is not at all a matter of general knowledge—it is quite possible that a chair in somebody's house would cave in, and that the chair in Junior's house *did* cave in. It is interesting that Junior takes the same line that David took in countering Boot's personal insult. First Junior denies the charge; second, he hits back with another proposition that is again a personal, not a ritual statement: "You came over to my house to eat [since there was no food in your own], and so what right have you to complain?" Of course, the second part implicitly contradicts the first—if no chair caved in, how does Junior know what occasion is being talked about? Just as Boot was forced to concede the truth of David's point, so Junior here is plainly speaking of an actual event.

There is no immediate response to contradict Junior's last remark. Instead, the theme of sounding is continued, based on A as a first element in the series.

B: I went to Bell's house 'n' a Chinese roach said, "Come and git it."
A: I brought my uncle—I brought my uncle up Junior house: I didn't trust *them* guys.

Triads. There are many triads in the Jet session, where B tops A, and a third person adds a sound against B. This third sound often has a different target, attribute and/or form of proposition: it is shorter and more pointed, and acts as a coda which terminates the series.

A: Your mother got funky drawers.
B: Your mother got braces between her legs.
C: Looks like your mother did it 'n' ran.
A: Bell mother got a old beat-up boot.
B: Her mother got a face like a rubber ass.
C: Junior got a face like a clown.

In both of these cases, the final sound is contributed with authority by Bell, a senior member of the 100's group. In the second triad, it is Bell who is sounded against by A, and again by B, and Bell who answers as C. A short, firmly-delivered sound of this sort, with heavy stress on the last monosyllable, seems to close off debate effectively. After the first two members of a series, the closing element provided by a third person will usually show formal simplification. Thus we have:

A: Your mother eat coke-a-roaches.
B: Your mother eat fried dick-heads.
A: Your mother suck fried dick-heads.
C: His mother eat *cold* dick-heads.

The theme here from the beginning is "so hungry that she eats . . ."; the sounder is engaged in a search for something as disgusting to eat as he can find. B certainly tops A in this respect; note the complex noun phrase with an embedded participle. But A does not lose: he keeps the series open, capitalizing on the sexual element introduced by B. A's reply does not depend upon syntactic complication. In simply changing the verb, he introduces semantic complexity by introducing the implicit attribute of sexual immorality. *Sex* takes a higher place on the implicit agenda of relevant topics than *hunger* or *poverty*, so that we now have to read the sound as "Your mother is so hot that . . ." Thus A's reply achieves semantic change with a minimum of formal change. The third man achieves closure by returning to the original verb and shortening the form with a much simpler noun phrase. The absurdity of C's sound is based upon the assertion that the substitution of cold for hot food can be relevant at this stage in the search for disgusting attributes. This is a very low-ranking item on the agenda or relevance which governs discourse. It is a common source of humor to make such a sudden, incongruous claim to reverse the order of relevance.

We have seen that one way to achieve excellence in sounding is to develop complex comparisons with a high degree of left-hand embedding which suspends the final proposition. Another is to learn to close off sequences with short sounds which abruptly change the prevailing form. The third, and perhaps the subtlest method has been illustrated here—bringing about striking semantic shifts with minimal changes of form, a "minimax" solution. This is best illustrated by the following sequence at the very beginning of the Jet session.

JOHN L: I'll take you to the last man.
JUNIOR: I'll take your mother.
REL: I took your mother.

The initial remark of John Lewis is not a sound; he is simply "louding," or "granning." Junior's counter is a sound of the "dozens" model. The introduction of the target *your mother* also introduces the sexual meaning of *take*, so that ambiguity is achieved with a minimum formal change. Rel's final addition seems to us an even more adept example of semantic shift with a minimal effort. By changing from the challenge of the future form to the simple assertion of the past tense, Rel resolves the ambiguity in favor of the sexual meaning. (The semantic machinery operating here is not obvious, but the effect is.). As a third element in the series, Rel's sound also fits the pattern of a short, decisive closure.

There are other forms of sounding which use the same targets and attributes, but very different formal structure. For example, questions are not common as sounds, but the following series begins with two:

A: Hey didn't I see . . . shit on your mother bed?
B: A shot gun . . .
C: Did you see me under your mother bed when your father came in?
D: No I saw your uncle.
C: Oh my uncle was there too.

This whole series is positively evaluated by the group with great enthusiasm. But we will not explore the formal side of sounding further in this discussion.

Applied Sounding. So far, we have been considering the speech event called "sounding" as the principal focus of verbal activity.

But sounding also occurs as an element in other kinds of interaction. Members with great verbal "presence of mind" are able to use sounds at critical moments to channel the direction of personal interaction in a direction that favors them. We may call such a use of ritual insults "applied sounding." It will be immediately apparent that applied sounds do not follow the rules set forth for ritual sounding—they are embedded in other rule sequences and other higher level structures of verbal interaction. But rule (1) for interpreting utterances as sounds will apply. Of the four more general properties of the ritual sounding situation on pages 122–123 above, only the fourth property is preserved—that symbolic distance is obligatory. But this property will prove essential to the analysis and ultimately to the solution of the initial problem posed in this paper.

First it must be understood that verbal interaction among the Jets requires great verbal "presence of mind." Sounding is only one of the many ways of putting someone down. For example, the sounding session in the microbus cited above was initiated when Junior called out:

JUNIOR: Hey what's your name! When a we goin' on the next one, KC?

This was out of line in two respects. First, in using "What's your name" with someone whose name was as well known as his own. By adding "KC" (the usual term of address for John Lewis), the insult was only compounded. Secondly, this remark was out of line in that there had been no promise of a second outing, and Junior was showing extreme hubris in demanding it. John Lewis turned around and replied without hesitation:

JOHN L: Next time you give me some pussy!

There was considerable uproar at this—it was evident to one and all that Junior had been put down decisively.

John Lewis's remark is one of a large class of ritual insults that impute homosexuality to the antagonist by indirection. Here it catches Junior in a double bind. If he wants to refute the ritual charge of homosexuality, then he has to interpret Lewis's reply as meaning "Never!" But that is his decision—John Lewis has neatly left it up to him. If Lewis had said "You're not going!" he would have been faced with a roar of injured innocence and fierce denunciation: "You cheap bastard!" etc. He has sidestepped the problem and put Junior down decisively: "Got you Junior—got you that time!"

Among the Jets, Rel is one of the most skilled at using sounds in this way. At one point in the Jets session, 13-year-old Stevie was trying to push his way into a fight developing between Larry and Rel by warning Larry, "He gon' getchyou with 'is legs . . . he got legs—he got leg like—lik—"

Larry gave Stevie no more than a withering look, but Rel said:

Aah, your *mother* got legs on 'er *nose*!

This sound crushed Stevie, and he made no effort to reenter the higher status group for some time. Rel's sound was as apt and crushing as Stevie's effort was bumbling and ineffective. Note, however, that Stevie is ordinarily a verbal leader of his own age group—another instance of the dominance of power relations over verbal skill.

We are now in a position to return to the original problem posed by Rel's sound, "Your mother's a duck." How is this a coherent response to Stanley's challenge? A closer examination of the context will help. First of all, we can note that when Rel first called for quiet, he was talking to the group as a whole, especially the younger, lower-status members at the other end of the table.

REL: Shut up, please!

It was a deliberate, half-serious decision on Stanley's part to interpret Rel's request for action as being directed at *him*. As president, it was quite in order for him to challenge Rel's right to tell *him* to be quiet.

STANLEY: . . . 'ey, you tellin' *me*?

Stanley put his elbow on the middle of the table, and stretched out his long forearm towards Rel. His emphasis on *me* indicated that he was choosing to take this request personally. At this point, neither Rel nor Stanley could retreat.

REL: Yes.
STANLEY: Come a li'l closer.

Now Rel applied a simple sound against Stanley:

REL: Your mother's a duck. Get outa here.
STANLEY: Come a li'l closer an' say—
REL: Your mother's a duck.

At this point, Stanley withdrew his arm, looked around, and became involved with someone else. Our understanding of why Stanley retreated is based on the definition of a sound as a ritual insult—one that is obviously not true. Though Stanley chooses to say "I take this personally," Rel puts him down by redefining the situation as a ritual one. Informally, the message is "What are you carrying on for? This is just a game we're playing and you know it—unless your mother *is* a duck." If Stanley insisted on taking the situation seriously, then he would be saying that it *could* be true—his mother could be a duck.

The logic of Rel's sound is the same as that of John Lewis's reply to Junior. The skill of the sounder leaves the ultimate decision up to the challenger: if he insists on taking the matter personally, the fight will go on, but he has already condemned himself and will find it very hard to regain his lost ground.

Thus the answer to the original problem we posed lies in the concept of a ritual event as one that is formulated without regard to the persons named. Sounds are directed at targets very close to the opponent (or at himself) but by social convention it is accepted that they do not denote attributes that persons actually possess; in Goffman's formulation, symbolic distance maintained serves to insulate this exchange from further consequences. The rules given above for sounding, and the development of sounds in a bizarre and whimsical direction, all have the effect of preserving this ritual status. As we have seen, the ritual convention can break down with younger speakers or in strange situations—and the dangers of such a collapse of ritual safeguards are very great. Rituals are sanctuaries; in ritual we are freed from personal responsibility for the acts we are engaged in. Thus when someone makes a request for action in other sub-cultures, and he is challenged on the fourth pre-condition, "What right have you to tell me that?," his reply may follow the same strategy:

It's not my idea—I just have to get the work done.
I'm just doing my job.
I didn't pick on you—somebody has to do it.

Any of these moves to depersonalize the situation may succeed in removing the dangers of a face-to-face confrontation and defiance of authority. Ritual insults are used in the same way to manage challenges within the peer group. An understanding of ritual behavior is an important element in constructing the general theory of discourse, and this analysis of sounding is submitted with that end in view.

REFERENCES

ABRAHAMS, ROGER D. (1962). "Playing the Dozens." *Journal of American Folklore* 75: 209–18.

DOLLARD, JOHN. (1939). "The Dozens: The Dialect of Insult," *American Imago* I: 3–24.

HARRIS, ZELLIG S. (1963). *Discourse Analysis Reprints*. The Hague: Mouton and Co.

KOCHMAN, THOMAS. (1968). "Language Behavior in the Negro Ghetto." Chicago: Northeastern Illinois State College, Center for Inner City Studies. Mimeographed.

LABOV, WILLIAM, *and* JOSHUA WALETZKY. (1967). "Narrative Analysis." In *Essays on the Verbal and Visual Arts*. Proceedings of the 1966 Annual Spring Meeting of the American Ethnological Society, Seattle: University of Washington Press, pp. 12–44.

LABOV, WILLIAM, PAUL COHEN, CLARENCE ROBINS, *and* JOHN LEWIS. (1969). *A Study of the Non-Standard English of Negro and Puerto Rican Speakers in New York City.* Vol. I: "Phonological and Grammatical Analysis." Volume II: "The Use of Language in the Speech Community." Final Report, Cooperative Research Project No. 3288. Washington, D.C.: Office of Education.

SACKS, HARVEY. (1967). Lecture notes, U.C.L.A., mimeographed.

SWETT, DANIEL. (1966). "Cross-Cultural Communications in the Courtroom: Applied Linguistics in a Murder Trial." San Francisco State College, mimeographed.

WHYTE, WILLIAM F. (1955). *Street Corner Society: The Social Structure of an Italian Slum.* Chicago: University of Chicago Press.

WORTHAM, O. C. (1966). "Negro Culture in the Americas." Mimeographed.

HYMES, DELL. (1962). "The Ethnography of Speaking," *Anthropology and Human Behavior.* Washington, D.C.: The Anthropological Society of Washington, pp. 13–53. Reprinted in Fishman, Joshua (ed.) *Readings in the Sociology of Language.* The Hague: Mouton, 1968.

MICHAEL MOERMAN

Analysis of Lue Conversation: Providing Accounts, Finding Breaches, and Taking Sides*

Social science assumes, as our human experience daily confirms, that social life is orderly. No one can take *professional* credit for that order, however, for it is a members' accomplishment. In this essay, I propose to

* The research on which this paper is a partial report was supported by grants from the Division of Behavioral Sciences, Advanced Research Projects Agency, Department of Defense (Order #836) monitored by the Directorate of Information Sciences, Air Force Office of Scientific Research as AFOSR-66-1167 and AFOSR-68-1428.

(*Notes to this selection will be found on pp. 435–439.*)

(a) document the detailed orderliness of actual conversational[1] interaction;

(b) show that participants orient to this orderliness;

(c) explicate the knowledge—together with the rules for situated use of this knowledge—that members actively use in accomplishing this orderliness. The procedures used for doing this are constantly controlled by the actual data of the on-going social activities for which they attempt to account. The data are public,[2] and consist of tape recorded natural conversations in the Lue dialect of Thai, transcriptions of those recordings, and word for word glosses and translations of the transcriptions.[3] The procedures are sufficiently explicit for readers to follow, correct, and independently apply them to my data and other data of natural interaction in Lue and other societies.[4] This is rather different from conventional social science which, instead of directly examining the data of social life, either "refines" (which requires cooking and condensing) some of that data to be used as an assumed index of the rest, or understands some arbitrary segment of it as standing for some more real social order (e.g., economic [Marx], genealogical [Radcliffe-Browne], political [Leach], sexual [Freud]) that it hides.

The essay, exclusive of appendices to it, is divided into two main sections. The first presents an analysis of a fragment of a conversation in which stories were being told. The second discusses some implications of that analysis for the social sciences in general and for ethnography in particular. In order to evaluate that discussion, the reader will have to attend to the analysis and its data.

ANALYSIS[5]

I will concentrate on utterance[6] VIII.1 #204 and show its appropriateness as an account, that it recognizes a breach, and that it provides a culpable reason for that breach and thereby allies its speaker with the storyteller. I claim for each of these cumulative features and their analytic components that they are oriented to by participants in the conversation. In analyzing #204, I will make use of perspectives and concepts that are generally useful for the analysis of natural interaction.

VIII.1	**1**	**2**	**3**	**4**	**5**
#204	ɛ̆·w	phôb	kă·t	pûn	ɛ
W	visit	all over	market	D	PRT
					CT:kramaŋ

(So), [She] (must have just) went visiting around the market.

Providing Accounts. One prominent feature of conversations is that their participants orient to the sequential placement of the utterances which compose them. The situated intelligibility that an utterance has for participants frequently depends upon the particular ways in which they tie that utterance to particular preceding ones.[7] Since at the present stage of our[8] work "tieing" is a gloss for a number of different relationships (some unanalyzed) among utterances, it might prove helpful to point informally to an instance of tieing without analyzing its specific features. Consider the conversational fragment III.1 #333–5. The speaker of #335 clearly made use of #334's status as an answer to the question asked by #333.

III.1
#333

M	bá	kɛ̂w	myŋ	pín	sa·	nân
	T	N	PRN	to be	what	D

Ba Kaew, what's wrong with you there?

#334

W_1	tŭm
	pimples

#335

W_2	tŭm	mɛŋ	pôŋ	khwāt
	pimples	chiggers		dig

[Probably] pimples (from) chiggers burrowing in.

For #334 to have this status, its speaker presumably attended to and analyzed #333 sufficiently to know that it was (a) a question that (b) *she* might answer by (c) saying *tŭm*. My purpose in presenting this fragment is to take advantage of the reader's intuitive recognition of tieing. It might well be the case that an adequate analysis of the specific ties among III.1 #333–5, their interactional work, and the member knowledge they imply would require a paper no less elaborate than this one. This should not be discouraging, however, since I hope that the analysis of #204 will show that an adequate account of a single stretch of talk provides procedures and results that tell us things we would otherwise not know about other talk, about conversation, and about the societies in which both occur.

The reader will observe that #204's ties (both forward and back) to other utterances are essential to all of the analytic features that I will develop in this paper.

Regardless of initial lay notions to the contrary, it is not the case that stretches of talk are typically transparent with respect to topic. Without analysis, III.1 #333–5, for example, might equally well be taken as being "about" pimples, chiggers, or (a boy named) *bà kɛ̂w*. This observation implies that it can be a participant's task as speaker to constrain and as listener to analyze the topic or focus of an utterance or of a stretch of talk.

In the utterances preceding VIII.1 #204, C repeatedly calls attention to a single feature of his story, the elapsed time for which the speaker of #204 accounts. That C does this in #196b:11–17, #196d, #198:8–12, and #201 was pointed out to me by a graduate student.[9] I mention this not

VIII.1	**1**	**2**	**3**	**4**	**5**	**6**	**7**
#196b	caj	páj	sŷ·	nǎm pa·	káp	bâ·w li·	káb
C		to go	buy		CNJ	cigarettes	and
	8	**9**	**10**	**11**	**12**	**13**	**14**
	an	ka? fa·j	ni	kó·	bǎ·	le·w	jaŋ
		matches	PRT	fear	NG	fast	even
	15	**16**	**17**				
	sý·	lot thi·p	hŷ·				
	buy	bike	INDR				

[He sent her] to go buy *nampla* and cigarettes and matches. [He was] afraid (that) [she] wouldn't be quick, so [he] bought [her] (a) bike.

	1	**2**	**3**	**4**	**5**	**6**	**7**
#196d	kân	luk	bá·n ma·ŋ	hân	paj	kǎ·t	na
C		from	N	D	go	market	PRT
	8	**9**	**10**	**11**			
	paj	pin	cō·mo·ŋ	ni			
	go	is	hour	PRT			

Although (as far as) from Ban Maŋ here to the market, it took [her] an hour.

#198	**1**	**2**	**3**	**4**	**5**	**6**	**7**	**8**
M	mɔ̂·	xɛ·	mɔ̂·	kɛ́·ŋ	kɔ·	tâŋ	wâ·j	bá·
	pot	curry	pot	curry	CNJ	put	AUX	NG
	9	**10**	**11**	**12**	**13**	**14**	**15**	**16**
	thâ·	paj	hýn	nə·	páj	sȳ·	nām pá·	nì
	must	go	long	PRT	go	buy		PRT CT:na

The soup pot, the curry pot is set down [all ready]. Don't be long(!) [Just] buy some *nampla*.

#201	**1**	**2**	**3**	**4**	
M	á·w	pín	cō·mo·ŋ	wa·	ni
	PRV	be	hour	chiaw[CT]ná	
				[PRT]	

[But she] really took (a whole) hour!

merely to be generous, but as evidence of our claim that public data and procedures permit cooperative work, and to support my hope that analysis of a conversation need not require conventional ethnographic knowledge of the language or culture of its speakers. This is a hope, not a conviction, because it seems likely that participants themselves require detailed knowledge of their language and culture in order, in this instance, to analyze C's utterances for their references to elapsed time. That an American reader can also recognize the focus on elapsed time does not imply that he must have used the same cultural and linguistic resources in order to do so. My understanding of what the Lue resources are is presented in Appendix A. I have segregated them there as a convenience to the reader and, more importantly, because as a facsimile member of Lue society I must rely upon the reader's judgment of whether or not they are central to the analysis offered here. In the *Discussion* section of this essay I will return to the issue of whether the analysis of conversational interaction requires ethnographic knowledge.

That participants notice the focus that C provides is suggested by #202 (whether that utterance is given its literal or idiomatic reading[10]) and implied by #204's ascription of an intervening activity to the actor who went to market.[11]

VIII.1

#202	kɔ·	wā·	nân	lɛ
W	CNJ	say	D	PRT

Just like that. (Idiom)
Said already. (Literal)

#204 provides an account of what "must have" happened between going to market to buy things and returning. It does this by supposing a temporally extensible activity (ɛ̌*w*, #204:1) to have occurred between going and returning. I will show how participants knew an account to be appropriate, and how they knew that it was a delay (for this is what an interposed temporally extensible activity would account for) that was to be explained.

Although #202 and #204 are both appropriate, they differ in what they accomplish interactionally and in what they show their speakers to have taken account of. There is no need to suppose the speaker of #202 (literal) to have taken account of more than C's repetition[12] or (given the idiomatic reading) of C's focusing on some topic in what he has said so far. Uttering #204, on the other hand, requires knowing that there has been an accountable delay in a particular actor's returning from market.

VIII.1

	1	2	3	4	5	6	7
#196d	kân	luk	bá·n ma·ŋ	hân	paj	kă·t	na
C	although	from	N	D	go	market	PRT

	8	9	10	11
	paj	pin	cō·mo·ŋ	ni
	go	is	hour	PRT

Although (as far as) from Ban Maŋ here to the market, it took [her] an hour.

#196e

	1	2	3	4
C	[phái	wā·	sak	tə·]
	who	says	any	time
		can't be		

(It) can't [take as long as an hour].

How could participants know that it would be appropriate to provide an account? For this, I think, C's use of "can't happen" (#196e) for a feature of his own story is specially informative. For "can't happen" to be intelligible at all, participants must tie it to some other utterance(s). According to my informant, what C says "can't happen" is precisely what he has just said (in #196d) did happen. My analysis of #204 indicates that its speaker and other participants (on the basis of what they subsequently do with #204) also analyze #196e for its ties to #196d:9–11. Their understanding, then, is something like, "(It) took an hour (and) can't [have taken an hour for her to make that trip]." Since #196e must be tied to some other utterance(s) to be intelligible, and since the utterance to which it is tied is #196d:9–11, it seems fair to suppose the speaker of #204 to have oriented to the commonplace paradox contained in my expanded translation. As a commonplace paradox, the tied pair of utterances means something like:

"If things were as they should have been, this couldn't have happened. Yet it did happen." It may be generally the case that a commonplace paradox makes providing an account or giving an explanation appropriate. The explanation that #204 proposes, and this may be generally true of explanations of commonplace paradoxes, is an account of "What wasn't as it should have been." It must, however, be observed both that (as #202 indicates) such a paradox does not require[13] an explanation and that its status as a paradox (and not, for example, a dispute) depends upon the inconsistent utterances having both been made by the same speaker, C.

Producing #204 requires having attended to and analyzed more than #196e, its ties to #196d, and that C said both. Before turning to the orientation, analyses, and cultural knowledge #204 requires, let us consider who can be said to have the capacity for those things.

The conversational events analyzed in this section are interactive in the minimal sense that accounting for an utterance requires us to suppose that its speaker had oriented to and analyzed other utterances (often spoken by other participants) and oriented to the analyses made of utterances by other participants. There is therefore no reason for supposing that the knowledge explicated is unique to a specific individual. Who, then, can be said to possess it?

As a consequence of having lived in the village and in the house where recording VIII.1 was made, I know many things about the individual who spoke #204. There is no *a priori* reason to suppose that any one (or any combination) of these things (such as sex, age, wealth, genealogical position, weight, religion, complexion, native language, order of birth, cooking skills) is required to account for the utterance. Except as developed by the analysis itself, there is no reason to suppose that considerations of personal motivation, social class, or ethnicity are involved in producing or accounting for an utterance, a conversation, an interaction. For the anthropologist, the main interest of this observation is that there is no reason to suppose that the common culture of participants in these conversations is either completely shared by or restricted to the set of individuals to whom it is correct and sometimes convenient to assign a single ethnic label (Moerman 1967, 1968a). Some of this common culture may be restricted to the persons who produced this very conversation, some shared by their fellow villagers, some peculiar to the Tai-Lue, some to the normal members of every society. There is some reason to hope that the techniques used in this essay will permit our learning the incidence (including the universality) of the rules they develop. There is even more reason for regarding them to be immune from some problems of sampling (by region, sex, role, and other social categories).

First, the constraint of natural interaction requires us to show more than one native actively using some piece of knowledge so as to permit them to interact. Restricting our touchstone of common knowledge to that shown to be known and used in actual interactions precludes our having any initial concerns or claims about whether that knowledge is also shared by other actors who happen to be correctly categorizable with the same ethnic name.

Second, and in part out of recognition of the obscurantism of an enterprise that limited its subject matter to a "tribe" or to what W said to K on tape VIII, we must build a model of the speaker/listener that tells us how much of what transpires on our tapes could be accomplished only by those individuals whom we happened to record. I have already argued that the knowledge required for properly speaking #204 cannot be restricted to the individual woman who spoke it. Let us consider whether it is reasonable to suppose that knowledge to be restricted to individuals who "occupy" a particular "role."

In Lue materials, as in American ones, there seem to be some asymmetrical conversational activities (e.g. inviting-accepting) bound to reciprocal pairs of actors (e.g. host-guest) in such a way that for the activity to take place at all there must be actors categorized appropriately to it. I propose that for III.1 #14 to be an invitation, W must be taken as a host,

---

III.1

#13	náŋ	tí nî	kɔ	dâj	ka·
Mr	sit	D	CNJ	PRV	Q

Can (I) sit here?

III.1

#14	ý·	dâj·	xŷn	mə·	hən	lɔ̄
W	NG	can	rise	go, come	house	PRT

No. Come on up to the house.

VIII.2

#898	ā·	cân	nân	lɔ̄·	phúm	ĭ·	páj	lɛ̄ nə·
M	EXCLM	like	D	PRT	PRN	FTR	go	PRT

Well! That's it. I'm going.

#899
Mr ə·

#900			
W	ĭ·	mə·	hôn
	FTR	go	already

Are [you] going already [?]

I.1
#1563*

NA	phŏm	cà	klà·p	kɔ̀·n	lá		
	PRN	FTR	return	first	PRT		

I'm leaving now.

#1564

Mr khàp
Yes.

#1565

NA	lɛ́w	kɔ	wa·ŋ	wa·ŋ	cà	ma·	jîam
	CNJ	CNJ	free	free	FTR	come	visit

And when I have free time I'll come visit you.

* in CT

#1566

M_3 khàp

#1567

M_2 khàp

VIII.1
#188

K	ə·	déw	déw	déw	nāŋ	û·	nî·	kɔ̆n
		moment	moment	moment	sit	talk	D	first

Hey, wait a minute, wait a minute, come sit down and talk here first.

#189

K	ə·	xâ·w	ka·ŋ	nî	ɛ·
		enter	middle	D	PRT

Sit down right here in the middle.

VIII.1
#228

W	ĭ·	mə̆·	kɔ·	mə·	lɔ·
	FTR	go	CNJ	go	PRT

If you're going, then go.

Mr as a guest. As between the pair guest-host, it is guests who say or otherwise indicate that they are leaving (VIII.2#898; I.1#1563/5), hosts who acknowledge their departure (VIII.2#899–900; I.1#1564, 1566, 1567). I am suggesting that there is sometimes a bonding between activities (and consequently the situated utterances which accomplish those activities) and actors (and consequently the situated individuals so formulated) which would provide members with these resources and constraints:

(a) In some circumstances, making a host's utterance can be a bid for being considered a host (VIII.1 #188/9).

(b) In some circumstances, the individual formulated as host may be able to prevent an activity from getting done by not himself doing it.

(c) An individual who is a guest may be able to get something done by means of making it a host's duty to do it. So, for example, a speaker may utter the first of an utterance pair anticipating that if no one else offers the second, then the host must as host do so.

These candidate observations suppose that there are scenes recognizable to members as having hosts, that members have knowledge that permits them to recognize a host, and that such a host in such a scene can always be called upon to do a host-like activity. If it is such a host-like activity to acknowledge leave-taking, then VIII.1 #228 makes its speaker a host.[14] It is possible (although I doubt) that #204 is somehow the kind of utterance that a proper host will have to make if no one else does. This would permit those present to regard #204's speaker as predictable and its absence as interpretable.

Even if VIII.1 #204 is a host's remark in these senses, our model of the listening required to speak it is nevertheless not unique to the individual named W. If

1) (a), (b), or (c) above hold, or

2) if the absence of a host's remark is noticeable or interpretable to whomsoever, or

3) if any individual might sometime talk as host, then any host component of our model of the speaker of #204 is general to competent members.

I make this point somewhat elaborately because it is typical but wrong for anthropologists to suppose as a working practice that there is a one-to-one correspondence between individuals and "roles" and to further suppose that the only role knowledge that they must explicate is that peculiar to a given individual. To put the issue epigrammatically, for a society to have a king, the king must know how to act like a man (since he is not always kinging) and all men must know how kings act (so that his proper behavior is recognizable). For the present data, even if "doing hosting" is involved in accounting for VIII.1 #204, we cannot suppose the knowledge needed for uttering #204 to be restricted to some set of individuals who (and who alone) are always and merely hosts. Performing such an activity requires that those who are audience to it also know how to recognize and interpret such a performance. It further requires common detailed knowledge of how such a performance is properly done on the particular situated occasions that make it appropriate and provide the relevance of the member categorizations the performance uses.

In this section I have attempted to show that the intelligibility and appropriateness of an account depend upon, and are visible to, analysts and participants through orienting to and analyzing sequential utterances, their speakers, and the ties among them. In subsequent sections I shall examine the "content" of #204 as an account in order to see the knowledge its speaker must have used and what he accomplished interactively by saying it.

Recognizing a Breach. I must now return to two features of #204 that the preceding section merely took for granted. How does its speaker know and show that a delay in returning from market is to be accounted for? How does its speaker know and show whose delay it was?

Consider, with respect to the second question, that #204 does not specify any actor to whom the activity (#204:1) is ascribed. I think that it is nevertheless quite clear that for #204 to be the account for which participants take it, there is no mystery about who went *ĕw*. My general argument about this accomplishment is that natural conversation wherever it has been examined shows its participants to orient to an alignment among the actions and the actors talked about. English pronouns provide speakers of that language with a linguistic resource for doing this. Lue utterances often lack pronouns or other lexical indicators of actors.[15] In both Lue and English (and presumably in other languages as well),[16] linguistic resources are insufficient for the conversational task of aligning actions and actors. To accomplish this task, members[17] additionally use shared and sanctioned knowledge of the social world. At the present state of our work, I propose that some of this knowledge is conveniently handled by the analyst as *category-bound activities* and as *context-bound typifying ascription.* Both of these concepts make use of the notion of *categorization labels* (CL). All three of these concepts are useful beyond the present data. Since they have utility for the analysis of conversation and interaction by both Lue and Americans, my depiction of them will be somewhat more elaborate than my immediate purposes (accounting for VIII.1#204) require.

The actor whose tardiness #204 explains must be one who went to market. Producing #204 therefore requires participant analysis of the utterances which indicated who that actor was. The requisite participant analysis may be elaborate in that #196b, which tells of going shopping (#196b:1–10):

(a) is syntactically ambiguous for subject,
(b) names no actors,
(c) even if regarded as a single utterance with #196a, names an actor (#196a:1) who has not been mentioned before.

The course of the story[18] and, specifically, #215 and #217:1–9, 19–27 indicate that participants take it that the actors who performed the actions

VIII.1

#196a	**1**	**2**	**3**
C	lá·n	nî·	ni
	grandchild	D	PRT
	nephew/niece		

Now this *lan*

#196a[1]

K	bɔ caŋ	hý
	NG can	Q

[You] can't?

#196b	**1**	**2**	**3**	**4**	**5**	**6**	**7**
C	caj	páj	sŷ·	năm pa·	káp	bâ·w li·	káb
		to go	buy		CNJ	cigarettes	and
	8	**9**	**10**	**11**	**12**	**13**	**14**
	an	ka? fa·j	ni	kó·	bă·	le·w	jaŋ
	he's	matches	PRT	fear	NG	fast	even
	15	**16**	**17**				
	sý·	lot thi·p	hŷ·				
	buy	bike	INDR				

[he sent her] to go buy *nampla* and cigarettes and matches.
[He was] afraid (that) [she] wouldn't be quick, so [he] bought [her] (a) bike.

mentioned in #196b are those mentioned in #190. Specifically, *ĭ·naŋxam*, hereafter termed A_2 (as the second actor mentioned in #190), was the person who went (#196b:2) to buy (#196b:3) some items (#196b:4, 6, 9). It is also A_2 whom the speaker of #204 supposes to have *ɛ̆w*'d. The *pɔ̄·ló·ŋ* (hereafter termed A_1 as the first actor mentioned in #190) was the person who feared[19] (#196b:11). VIII.1#196b:11–17 then reads, "[He] feared (that) [she] wouldn't be quick, so [he] bought [her] (a) bike." These ascriptions between actors and actions were also made by my informant and me. What resources do the teller, audience, analyst and informant use for naturally and automatically making these ascriptions?

Lexical and syntactic knowledge is insufficient for these ascriptions. The word *caj* (#196b:1), if it appears in the conversation at all,[20] can be used here as a verb ("to use, to make use of, to send"), to mark a passive form, or as both ("A_2 was used or sent to . . ."). My informant and I understood both that it meant "was sent by" and that it was A_2 who was sent by A_1. It is clear that participants made the same actor provisions. Let me propose two Lue norms (E_1 and E_2) that provide for the actor

---

VIII.1

#215	**1**	**2**	**3**	**4**	**5**		**6**
C	kun	thâ·w	câ·j	ni	ni	(Insert #216)	lōt
	people	old	use	D	PRT		bike

7	**8**	**9**	**10**	**11**	**12**
m̌	mi·	kɔ·	sỹ·	hŷ·	nǐ?
NG	have	CNJ	buy	INDR	PRT

Old people send [her/them on errands]. Insert #216. [She/They] don't have a bike (so) [old people] buy one for [her/them].

#217	**1**	**2**	**3**	**4**	**5**	**6**	**7**	**8**
C	xǐ·	páj	lew	kā	lūk	ni·	páj	kǎ·t
	ride	go	fast	PRT_Q	from	D	go	market

9	**10**	**11**	**12**	**13**	**14**
káb ma·	lɛ̄w kɔ·	[á·w ma·]	hŷ·	hé	lɛ̄·w
return	CNJ	[bring]	INDR	PRT	
				CT:sǐa	

15	**16**	**17**	**18**	**19**	**20**	**21**
kɔ·	hŷ?	pɔ̄ thâ·w	hə̌·j	xá·j	páj	náj
CNJ	here!	T	VCTVE	want to	go	where
		old man				

22		**23**	**24**	**25**	**26**
(kɔ)	(Insert #218)	sǎŋ	kun	thâ·w	lɛ·w kɔ
		tell	person	old	CNJ

27	**28**
páj	lɔ̄·
go	PRT

["?] Did [you/she] ride fast? From here to the market and back and then give [it to him, saying], ["]Here dear grandfather,["] when [I/you] want to go anywhere, INSERT #218 [I will] tell the old people first.

---

ascriptions participants make for #196b. At this point in the argument, I propose them less out of serious interest in their content than in order to discuss the concept, of which E_1 and E_2 are examples, of context-bound typifying ascriptions.

E_1. If there is a *pɔ̄·ló·ŋ* who has a *lá·n* and one uses the other to go buy such things as those listed by #196b:4–9, then it is typically the former who so uses the latter and typically the latter who goes to buy such things.

E_2. If a *pɔ̄·ló·ŋ* has a *lán* and one buys a bike for the other, then typically the former buys it for the latter.

Later in this essay I will consider E_1 and E_2 as specific ethnographic statements about the Lue and as instances of how members and analysts of any culture make use of norms. In order to explore the notion of context-bound typifying ascriptions, however, let us consider, first, the American sequence:

01 The woman heard the baby cry.
02 She picked her up.

I do not believe that Americans will find the subject and object of 02 ambiguous with respect to the actors given by 01. This lack of ambiguity is based on members' knowledge of category-bound activities (Sacks 1966–1967)—that is, there are some activities (e.g. crying) so bound to actors (e.g. baby) that a member hearing that the activity was done when the actor was present supposes that the actor did the activity. In addition to such activities which are, in the context of a conversation, uniquely bound to an actor, there are some pairs of actors (e.g. mother/daughter) and some asymmetrical paired actions (e.g. spanking) such that a member hearing the activity transpired between the actors knows which performed and which received it. My analysis offers no reason not to believe that the Lue make similar use of such context-bound typifying ascriptions.[21]

In the data under examination, A_2 is retained as the actor who "was used to go shopping" through means other than her pronominalization (as *xáw* or *man*) or repetition, whether partial (*ǐ·nî·*) or complete (*ǐ·naŋxam nī*?). Rather, she is categorized as *lán* and this categorization, I shall argue, is basic to the way in which the story was understood generally and to the way in which #204 was used specifically.

The actors mentioned by or provided for the utterances in my corpus are only very occasionally merely human—that is, individuals are typically formulated by such labels as male, peasant, headman, Lue, etc. I call such formulating labels *categorization labels* or CLs.[22] Since most, perhaps all, individuals can correctly (by the rules of the culture that does the labelling) be assigned more than one non-synonymous CL,[23] the correctness of a CL is never sufficient to account for its actual use on situated occasions (Moerman 1968a, cf. Moerman 1965). For this, we will need rules (which presumably take correctness into account) of relevance and appropriateness.

Section 1 of Appendix A is intended to show that an individual categorized as *ǐ·* can and (in the context of this conversation) must also be a *lán*; an individual categorized as *pɔ̄·ló·ŋ* can and (in the context of this conversation) must also be the *pɔ̄·ló·ŋ* of that *lán*. Although, the demonstration is relegated to an appendix, three of its features have sufficient potential for further work on my Lue corpus and sufficient detailed resemblance to features of American conversation for me to discuss them here.

The first productive feature is the mutual relevance of CLs from the same collection. Sacks (1966–1967) has demonstrated for American conversation that when one speaker uses a CL from a collection (e.g. "I'm a doctor" from the profession collection) subsequent speakers will typically use CLs from the same collection (e.g. "I'm a lawyer," not "I'm from Milwaukee"). Without conversational data, I have pointed to the same phenomenon among the Lue (Moerman 1968a). Moerman has also (a) remarked on the phenomenon of "teams" of CLs. These I formulate as small, closed sub-sets of CLs, all from the same collection, with the property that the correct categorization of an individual with a member CL implies that there exists some other individual who can be correctly categorized with some other member CL (e.g. Correct categorization of some individual as "short-stop" requires that there be some other individual who is correctly categorizable as "pitcher."), and (b) demonstrated that co-membership in a team is a resource used to resolve collection-ambiguity (e.g. Should "baby" be heard as a CL from the family collection or from the stage-of-life collection?) by hearing CLs that could come from the same team as members of that team (e.g. Hear "the baby" of "The baby cried. The mommy picked it up" as a member of the family collection because "mommy" is a team-mate in that collection). I would argue that the Lue do much the same and thereby hear #190:3, (*pɔ̄·ló·ŋ*) which is collection ambiguous, as a kinship term by virtue of (*lán*) #196a:1, its team-mate. At least, A_1 and A_2 are heard to be in a relationship, and kinship may be its form.

The second productive feature concerns actors in stories. In C's story, as in others I have examined in my Lue corpus, the actors to whom actions are ascribed are limited to those specifically mentioned and to their team-mates (like the *mɛ̄·thâw* [#208:2] of the present story).

The third feature, like the first discovered by Sacks in American conversation, is *category consistency* by which, at this point in the analysis, I mean no more than that alternative interpretations of the relationship between A_1 and A_2 (i.e. uncle-niece, prominent man-young girl, patron-client) are consistent with one another and all are consistent with the run of the asymmetrical paired actions between them (e.g., A_1 scolds A_2, A_1 sends A_2 shopping, A_2 goes shopping for A_1, A_1 buys a bike for A_2).

I take it that I have now (partially through Section 1, Appendix A) established how it can be and that it, indeed, is the case that the *lán* of 196b:1 is the same actor (A_2) as the *ǐ·naŋxam* of #190 and that she is the *lán* of the *pɔ̄·ló·ŋ* (A_1) of #190. It is more interesting to consider the interactional relevance and consequences of this categorization, since I will argue that the categorization must be oriented to and used by participants in order for them to have made the sense the data show them to have made of C's story, and specifically needed by the speaker of #204 in order for that speaker to know that A_2 has delayed. The most general observation is that conversation requires alignment of actors with actions, that such alignment is done here with a CL (a "mere descriptor," if you like), and that this CL (and, I would assert, every categorization label or "mere descriptor") is not interactionally neutral.

Appendix A, Section 2 identifies some of the linguistic and (unsituated) cultural resources that participants have and may have used in order to know that C's focus was on

(a) the trip to market,
(b) the time the trip took,
(c) and that the time was long.

I argue there, however, since the distance (#196d:2–6) and especially the time (#196d:8–10) are ambiguous, that this information—while perhaps necessary—is insufficient for participant knowledge that A_2's sloth, not her alacrity, is to be accounted for.[24] In order to account for participants knowing that it is A_2's delay that is to be explained, I must suppose them to have oriented to and relevantly analyzed[25] that

(a) this is a story in which A_1 scolded A_2 (#190:3–8),
(b) that A_1 and A_2 are in the relationship analyzed above,
(c) and (some of that:) A_1 feared (#196b:11–13), obviated (#196b:14–17), forbade (#198:8–12), and was inconvenienced by (#198:1–7; #203) just such delays.

VIII.1

#198	**1**	**2**	**3**	**4**	**5**	**6**	**7**	**8**
C	mɔ̂· pot	xɛ· curry	mɔ̂· pot	kɛ́·ŋ curry	kɔ· CNJ	tâŋ put	wâ·j AUX	bá· NG
	9	**10**	**11**	**12**	**13**	**14**	**15**	**16**
	thâ· must	paj go	hýŋ long	nə· PRT	páj go	sŷ· buy	nām pá·	nì PRT CT:na

The soup pot, the curry pot is set down [all ready]. Don't be long(!) [Just] buy some *nampla*.

VIII.1
#196d

	1	**2**	**3**	**4**	**5**	**6**
C	kân	luk	bá·n ma·ŋ	hân	paj	kă·t
	although	from	N	D	go	market

7	**8**	**9**	**10**	**11**
na	paj	pin	cō·mo·ŋ	ni
PRT	go	is	hour	PRT

Although (as far as) from Ban Maŋ here to the market, it took [her] an hour.

#196b

	1	**2**	**3**	**4**	**5**	**6**
C	caj	páj	sŷ·	năm pa·	káp	bâ·w li·
		to go	buy		CNJ	cigarettes

7	**8**	**9**	**10**	**11**	**12**	**13**
káb	an	ka ? fa·j	ni	kó·	bă·	le·w
and		matches	PRT	fear	NG	fast

14	**15**	**16**	**17**
jaŋ	sý·	lot thi·p	hŷ·
even	buy	bike	INDR

[He sent her] to go buy *nampla* and cigarettes and matches. [He was] afraid (that) [she] wouldn't be quick, so [he] bought [her] (a) bike.

VIII.1
#203

C	bâ·w lì·	tì·	su·b	kɔ·	bá·	mi
	cigarettes	RLTV	smoke	CNJ	NG	have

[The old folks] didn't have any cigarettes to smoke.

That is, locating that trip time as excessive (or, at least, that there has been a relevant and sanctionable delay) depends upon participant knowledge that

(a) there is a relationship between A_1 and A_2,
(b) that the relationship has been breached (which is what the story, as announced by the scolding [#190], is about), and
(c) that delaying—given the circumstances narrated between the actors as the story categorizes them—constitutes just such a breach.

I had already argued that Lue discourse permits terms other than #196b:1 to be used for A_2, and that the term which is used establishes a relationship between A_1 and A_2 which permits E_1 and E_2. My argument here is that the relationship provided by the CLs allows participants to use what C narrates in order to know that the relationship has been breached. This permits participants to know that C is focusing on, and that it is appropriate to account for (see preceding section), A_2's delay.

Features of the immediate interaction (perhaps along with abstract cultural knowledge of geography, taxonomic opposition, and time)[26] are needed for participants to make the sense that they do make of C's story. It is only through the relationship established by the categorization labels that the events of the story show that A_2 had dawdled although A_1 is anxious that she be prompt (#196b:11–13) and has provided her with a bike so that she can be (#196b:11–17); that A_1 has specifically ordered her not to take a long time (#198:8–12); that A_2's meal awaits her return (#198:1–7, 13–16). Through her *ɛ̆w* A_2 has committed the breaches of annoying and inconveniencing A_1, and of being disobedient, selfish, and ungrateful. These breaches, and the notion of breach itself, are located by participants legitimately expecting A_2 to do things specifically other than and opposite to what she has done. This expectation is based upon members' notions of what kinds of behavior are proper between A_1 and A_2.

That A_1 could have scolded A_2, that he did so justly,[27] that she could in general have behaved improperly to him and could specifically have been annoying, selfish, disobedient, ungrateful, and inconveniencing all depend upon there existing between A_1 and A_2 a relationship she has breached and which breach his scolding notices and punishes. Participants' ability to find the story as intelligible as they do find it depends upon their having a notion—and rules for applying it here—of proper role behavior in such a relationship, of how that relationship is violated, and of how such violations are sanctioned. In this simple Lue tale, we and the participants can see Lue society working at the task of making sense of itself.

The reflexivity of the phrase is not accidental. Hearing that A_1 scolds A_2 is a listeners' basis for supposing them to be in such a relationship that A_1 can scold A_2. Knowing them to be in such a relationship makes it sensible for participants to address themselves to the justice, not the possibility, of such a scolding and provides criteria of justness. Hearing that he has given her a bike provides for their being in just such a relationship that he might do so. This relationship, in turn, provides criteria of gratitude that are involved in the justness of the scolding. Hearing that he sends her to do casual shopping provides for their being in such a relationship that he may do just that. Only a relationship that allows him to give her orders permits disobedience; only one in which he gives her a bike permits ingratitude.

The CLs used for the actors, together with the actions that transpire between them, specify the relationship between A_1 and A_2; through that relationship, human and moral sense is made of their actions. For participants to have made sense of the story, in just the ways in which they did make sense of it, they must have normative notions—confirmed and conveyed by the story itself—of just how people like A_1 and A_2 should behave. Connected to these notions are expectations of how such persons typically misbehave.

Just what is this relationship, which the CLs tell participants should obtain between A_1 and A_2 and which provides the *productive*[28] form for the very detailed and context-bound typifying ascriptions? Those who write about Thai society give great attention to a paired relationship, commonly called "patron-client" when not in the context of kinship and *phî·-nɔ́·ŋ* in the context of kinship. The first member is said to be senior to the second, his junior. The senior controls, directs, and materially rewards the junior who obeys, respects, and performs minor services for his senior. I claim that E_1 plus E_2 shows this description of patron-client to be a norm known, needed, and used by members and to also show that *pɔ̄·ló·ŋ* and *lán* are proper possible CLs for patron and client, respectively. Disobedience, ingratitude, selfishness, lack of concern are breaches typically ascribed to clients of patrons, to junior of seniors. *ɛ̌w*'ing, commonplace for everyone, is perhaps "proverbially" expectable of young persons and of journeys to towns and other places of interest—that is, committing just these breaches by means of *ɛ̌w*'ing is "normal" in exactly the American sense that members know "the typical manner in which offences of given classes are committed, the social characteristics of the persons who regularly commit them, the features of the settings in which they occur, the types of victims often involved" (Sudnow 1965:259).

Categorization labels, like the *lán* of #196b:1, are not merely descriptors, but do the interactional work of formulating individuals into actors and of invoking norms. It appears that normative ascriptions, the entailment of moral qualities, the provision of typifying activities, and other components of the sociology done by members are done on and by means of categorization labels and their known-to-member properties. In order to participate in interaction (or, at least, to tell and be audience to stories) members must orient to and make active constant use of the properties stereotypically associated with CLs.

In C's story, participants have only the properties of *ǐ·*'s, *láns*, and *pɔ̄·ló·ŋ*s to bring under the norms (and, specifically, under the typifying ascriptions) they know in common. In order for their conversation to be coherent, just as participants find it coherent, *they* must *know* and *actively use* just these norms. Locating breaches and normative expectations depends upon the social relationship that participants, through the resources of the story—and crucially through the CLs—know exists between A_1 and A_2 and, since the events and characters of the story are typifications, between "people like them."

Whatever participants might otherwise know about some *i·naŋxam* and her *pɔ·ló·ŋ* is irrelevant to C's story. Participants need no knowledge of whether A_1 or A_2 exists as an individual. If either does exist, there must be further predicates (e.g. fat, dark, homely, fond of betel) with which it would be culturally correct to describe him. Neither the analyst, to account for the interaction, nor those present, to have participated in it, need know any of these. More important than its being limited to the actors it announces, C's story is limited not to the correct predicates for those actors as individuals, but to the known-in-common properties of the CLs that have been used to formulate them plus information specifically given in the story. What participants must know is told them by the ways in which the actors are labelled and by stated details. By virtue of being given the CLs, participants know and use the normative properties of those CLs and of the relationships between individuals so labelled. To make situated sense of C's tale they need, additionally, just as we do, stated information: especially the scolding, and also gifts of a bicycle, motives for that gift, running errands, etc. Given the relationship established by the CLs, participants use this additional information in order to know that this relationship has been breached.

A_1 and A_2 are inference-rich solely through the titles (including the informative θ) that Lue usage requires precede names. It is sometimes understood about titles, including kinship terms, that they—or their semantic components—reflect and arise from what is somehow important in the society that uses them. I propose, alternatively, that it is unnecessary to suppose the existence of some "real" independent social order that lies behind the words used to talk about it, and to which those words provide access as its indeces. The social importance of the entailed properties and semantic components of titles consists of the required use of titles as CLs. The importance of sex, relative age, and normative expectations between patrons and their clients to participant understanding of this conversation can be seen directly in the conversation itself. To put it baldly, relative age is important to Lue society in that it is a semantic component of titles like *ǐ·* and *pɔ̄·ló·ŋ*. The work of understanding an interaction in order to participate in it, is done on CLs. A participant always has, and—as in this instance—sometimes has no more than, the title CL on which to work.

Taking Sides. I have shown *that* and how #204 was both produced through and indicates participant analysis of A_2 having delayed. In this section I will argue that its speaker provides a culpable reason for that delay, which thereby justifies A_1 having scolded, and consequently allies with the story-teller. The general interest is in the interactive properties of telling and being audience to stories. Specifically, I will argue that the particular activity (*ĕw*) #204 ascribes to A_2 is explanatorily adequate, intelligible, commonplace, and politic. In terms of these considerations, I find it strikingly elegant and perhaps uniquely apt.

As an activity that is temporally vague (but extensible), *ĕw* is adequate for explaining A_2's having taken a longer time than she might otherwise be expected to. There are activities, like plowing or eating, that are temporally specific in the sense that members regard them to typically take some known amount of time. *ĕw*, which one can gloss as "traipsing about, wandering about, visiting around, goofing around, sight-seeing," etc., does not present itself as one of these. This makes the activity a useful one to interpose in order to explain almost any normal (see p. 188) yet noticed delay in returning from market. Interposing it suggests[29] that the speaker of #204 must have attended sufficiently well to know the order of delay that #204 assumes the task of explaining.

Further features of the ascribed activity that make it an adequate explanation of A_2's delay are generality and lack of category-boundness. By "generality" I mean to observe that any action that involves moving from place to place can involve *ĕw*'ing.[30] By "lack of category-boundness" I mean to observe that the members of any CL for humans (except infants) can *ĕw* and so, therefore, could A_2 have. This generality and lack of category-boundness does not show the speaker of #204 to have been inattentive, since it would have been possible (in some unsituated, but otherwise culturally available sense) to have ascribed specific (e.g. ran out of gas, stayed overnight) or category-bound (e.g. delivered a sermon) activities inconsistent with the actions or actors of the story.

The generality and lack of category-boundness of *ĕw* are related to its intelligibility as an activity all are likely to have regarded themselves as having done and to therefore be able to ascribe to others, in almost all situations. It is this that also makes the interposed activity commonplace.

The features of #204 I have located so far (i.e. that it provides an account, accounts for a delay, and ascribes an activity that is general, commonplace, and always ascribable) do not require categorial knowledge about its speaker. If they are correct at all, they impute orientations and analyses unrestricted among participants. While recognition of the culpability of what is ascribed by #204:1 is similarly general, the politicness of making such an ascription involves the co-categorization of its speaker with C via the events and actions of the story.[31] I have less confidence in the merits of the following analysis of specific co-categorizations than in the general observation that story telling is interactive stuff. Informal observation of Lue and American stories suggests that story teller and audience orient via the story to their co- and cross-categorizations. This may be one resource that members have for sometimes feeling that a story teller has mistaken them by the stories he tells, for a story's potential for insulting and correcting its audience, and for judgments of the propriety of a story to the occasions on which it is told. These matters, however, are only suggested by my analysis.

In order to indicate that ascribing an activity that is as commonplace, normal, general, etc. as *ĕw* can be interactionally pointed, consider that among the Lue, English (Austin 1961) and Americans there are ways to account for a blameable action (such as delaying in this context) that serve, or are offered, to excuse, justify, or "explain away" that action. #204:1 is not one of these. First, it recognizes that there was a delay[32] which, given the story as analyzed so far, might justify a scolding.

Secondly, it assumes the normal operation of the relevant institutions that justify the scolding.[33] I find it quite striking that knowing the normal operations of society permits such sparse information as the speaker of #204 is given to produce a "correct" explanation of A_2's delay.[34] In some purely logical (and hence fantastic) way she might have supposed A_2 to have been abducted, elected Prime Minister, evaporated, transformed into a chicken, etc. Just as an American father who wonders, "What on earth could have happened," to his daughter who is twenty minutes late from school does not, in fact, suppose that any thing on earth could have happened to her, but knows quite well the few things that might have, so W assumes the normal operations of her society in making the ascription she makes.

Thirdly, #204 does not propose an excuse or justification for the delay. Consider some activities my familiarity with the village make me think would be possible (unsituated) excuses or justifications. A girl cyclist might take a long time returning from market because the bike broke, the bike was stolen, she lost her money, she lost the goods, the goods were unavailable, she was detained against her will, something happened to her, she delayed in order to do a good deed, she had an accident, etc. In contrast to these events, A_2's having *ĕw*'d is in this instance culpable, and *specifically scoldable*.

The speaker of #204 could have proposed some culturally available culpable activity (e.g. arson, conversion to Christianity, murder, prostitution) for which scolding would be a travesty of punishment. Instead, she proposes an activity:

(a) that is properly scoldable;

(b) the scoldability of which is tied to in subsequent utterances by C and others;

(c) and which conforms with the story, as the story turns out, in that those who scold A_2 (#'s 230, 232, 234) are those who should scold her and do not are themselves both blamed[35] (#220) and punished by A_2's resultant probable incorrigibility (#s 236, 237, 237a).

VIII.1

#230

	1	2	3	4	5
C	[ĭ· ni·]	kun	thâ·w	câ·j	páj
	[T, PRN]	person	old	use	go

6	7	8	9
[páj kə̆t	páj xám]	[cín dáj]	[pa·lăm pa·lə́·]
to stop off		how / why	very much

10	11
sam	nî
like	D

[The old man said to the girl, " Kid, when elders send [you] on an errand, why do [you] stop off and (waste) so much (time) like this?"

#232

M	an	cīn	nî·	bà·	da·j	khwa·m	ō·
	thing	like	D	NG	get	meaning / content	EXCLN
	jă·ŋ	ni·					
	like	D					

["Acting] like this is bad.["]

#234

	1	2	3	4	5	6	7
C	cámpín	páj	lew	ma·	lew	kā·	cín
	necessary / urgent	go	fast	come	fast	PRT	example

8	9	10	11	12
nî·	kun	thâ·w	câ·j	nì?
this	persons	old	use	PRT

["]It's urgent to go and come back fast! (It's) old people (who) [you are] doing (things for).["]

#235

C (?)	[di· wā·]	dă·
	good say / appropriate to	curses

It would be good to bawl [her] out.

Any ascription #204 could have made, including the one it did make, is interactionally consequential. The immediately relevant consequences of #204:1 are to provide justification and content for the yet undescribed scolding of A_2 and to maintain (or perhaps provide) direction and coherence for C's story. In referring to this coherence, I mean to hint at the observation that, like more fragmentary stretches of talk,[36] stories are (to members) "about something" but that knowing what they are about requires analysis. Let us first observe that the content of the scolding (#s 230, 232, 234) is specifically for A_2 dawdling (#230:6–7) and not hurrying (#234:1–6) and thereby ties to and signals the appropriateness of #204:1. In the scolding, A_2 is not abstractly told "never to dawdle." Rather, she is told that errands for *elders* (#234:9–11) are urgent (#234:1) business and that she should not dawdle when *old people* (#215:1–2;

VIII.1
#215

	1	2	3	4	5		6
C	kun	thâ·w	câ·j	ni	ni	(Insert #216)	lōt
	people	old	use	D	PRT		bike

	7	8	9	10	11	12
	m̌	mi·	kɔ·	sỳ·	hŷ·	nī?
	NG	have	CNJ	buy	INDR	PRT

Old people send [her/them on errands]. Insert #216. [She/They] don't have a bike (so) [old people] buy one for [her/them].

VIII.1
#213

	1	2	3	4		5	6
C	ah	lêŋ	xá·w	ja·j	ma·	pín	có·n
	EXCLM	care for	PRN exclusive	big	come	be	thief
				grow			

7	8	9		10		11	12	13
sáŋ	i	ma·		caŋ	pɔ	ǐ·	ma·	xôb
which	PRT	come	CT:kɔ	jaŋ		T	dog	bite

14	15	16		17
ho·	kun	thâ·w	nī?	wā·
head	person	old		Q

Oh, take care of them until they're grown up, then why do they become crooks, [why do they] become dogs that bite heads (i.e., ingrates who return evil for good) of old people.

#230:2–3) send her on errands (#215:3; #230:4–5; #234:11). If specific ingratitude is relevant, it is toward *old people* (#215:1–2) who have bought her a bike (#215:10–12). It is wrong to assume that any of these features, or any data, is casual.

Of the possible characterizations of A_1 (e.g. male, kinship title, generous, inconvenienced, disobeyed) only one "old person" is selected. The scolding specifically concerns the duties of children to their elders. The story, like the ones that precede and follow it,[37] "concerns" ingratitude and disrespect of youngsters for their elders. In this story (as in those) one generation raises (#213:2) the other (#213:3) to become disrespectful (#236:15–18) criminals (#213:6) and ingrates who return cruelty for kindness (#213:11–16). This is a bad way for them to behave (#232). It is specifically a feature of this story that young people should be scolded (#235) so that this won't happen. A *mɛ̄ thâw* appears as an actor in the story exclusively (#208:2; #220:4) as a female elder who sympathizes with (#208:4–5; #220:6; #222) and protects (#208:8–24; #211) A_2. C (#220:8–16; #236) and other participants (#219; #237; #238;? #241) focus on the idea that what the *mɛ̄ thâw* does and fails to do will make A_2 (#220:8–16) more incorrigible and disrespectful when she grows up (#236; #237; #237a; #238; #241). The *mɛ̄ thâw* should therefore have scolded her (#227).

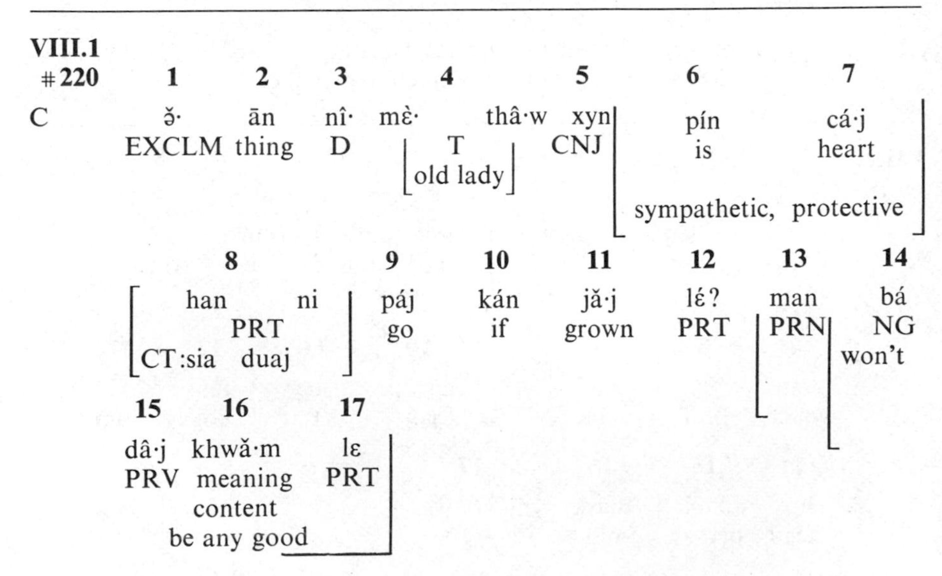

VIII.1
#220

	1	2	3	4		5	6	7
C	ɔ̆·	ān	nî·	mɛ̀·	thâ·w	xyn	pín	cá·j
	EXCLM	thing	D	T		CNJ	is	heart
				old lady			sympathetic, protective	

8		9	10	11	12	13	14
han	ni	páj	kán	jă·j	lɛ́?	man	bá
PRT		go	if	grown	PRT	PRN	NG
CT:sia duaj							won't

15	16	17
dâ·j	khwă·m	lɛ
PRV	meaning	PRT
	content	
	be any good	

So here the old lady really went along with [her]. [But the old man said, "If you're permissive like this now, the kid] won't be any good when [she] grows up.["] [Don't act like this."]

VIII.1

#236	1	2	3	4		5	6
C	nî·	bá·	wa·	ñăŋ	knock	xá·w	dâ·j
	D	NG	say	anything NT		PRN	PST PRV

7	8	9	10	11	12	13
dâ·n	xá·w	dâ·j	nân	páj	thən	nì?
stubborn	PRN	PRV PST	D	go	CMPLVE	PRT

14	15	MM	16	17	18
man	bă·		pin	ká·n	ko·
PRN	NG		to be	a thing of / a work of	fear

(The old woman) didn't say anything. Knock. [The girl] was unteachable, (couldn't be taught). [She] just had no respect.

#237	1	2	3	4	5	6	7	8
S	y·	bă·	kó·	sáŋ	hən	lὲ	phá·j	wā·
	yeah	NG	fear	anything	PRT	PRT	who	says

9	10	11				12
sáŋ	kɔ·	[tyk	mâ·w	ân	lɛ	
anything	CNJ	stop / stays as is		only]		

Sure [she] didn't respect anything. Whatever anyone says, [she] just stays as [she] is.

#237a	1	2	3	4	5	6	7	8
C	bà·	tēn	jă·j	ni	jaŋ	hēd	cân	nân
	NG	in time for	grow big	PRT	still	PRV	variety	D

9		10
[jă·j	ma·]	tho
grow big		EXCLM

[If she] acts like that (when) [she's] still small, when [she] grows up, Buddha!

#238

M2	tho
	EXCLM
	Buddha!

VIII.1

#208

	1	2		3	4	5		6
C	hə̂·*	mɛ̀·	thâ·w	nî·	hâk	lá·n	ni	khyn
	EXCLM	T		D	love	grandchild	CT:lɛwkɔ	
		old lady					CNJ	

7	8	9	10		11		12
hə̂*	bǎ·	mi·	bâ·w	li·	[ə·	àn]	bǎ·
EXCLM	NG	have	cigarettes		[mis-spoke]		NG

13	14		15	16	17	18	19
mi·	ka?	fa·j	kɔ·	jǔ·	nî·	kab	nȳŋ
have	match		CNJ	stay	here	CLSFR	one

20	21		22	23	24	
lu?	[á·w	mə·]	hŷ·	pāt	hé·	lɔ·
PRT	[take	go]	to	strike	PRT	PRT
	[bring over to]					

* Approximate tone.

So. That old lady loved her grandchild. "Here" [she said] There are no cigarettes—oh, no, no—There are no matches. There's still a box (of them) here, go light them." [Alt.: and [she] lit (one) for [him].]

#222

C	hǎk	hǎk	lá·n	clears throat	ni
	love	love	grandchild		PRT

[She] loved the grandchild.

#241

M	y·	xá·w	tyŋ	bá·	nân	[hé	kam	lɛ̄·w]
	yeah	PRN	to the extent of	NG	D	[	PRT	]

Yeah, they go as far as not [teaching her] at all.

VIII.1
#227

C	kan	wā·	[mɛ̀·	thâ·w]	dǝ̌t	nǎ	o·
	suppose			T	scold	PRT	EXCLM
				old lady	complain		

Suppose the old lady had complained (or scolded).

It seems reasonable to suppose that C knew what kind of story he intended to start by #190, and that he and other participants had available to them and oriented to the preceding story and the categorizations of the individuals present which that story and #190 made relevant. Consider that the culturally correct dimensions for categorization made relevant by the CLs of the story are ambiguous for the speaker of #204.

For the speaker of #204, is the scolding of #190 to be understood as "we women" (including A_2 and excluding C) against "you men" or "we elders" (excluding A_2 and including C) against "you kids"? Insofar as justifying the scolding amounts to taking sides (and is in that sense political), the speaker of #204 takes sides with old vs. young and thereby aligns herself with C.[38] It is reasonable to suppose that C would have told his story differently (if he told it at all), and would specifically not have called for an account, had he not been able—on the basis of categorizations of participants made relevant by the story and story series—to anticipate that the account would align itself with him. Had he not gotten such an account as #204:1, he might have focused differently (if at all) on the *mɛ̄ thâw* with

Figure 1

Actor	*Sex*	*Age*
C	+	+
A_1	+	+
A_2	–	–
W	–	+
mɛ̄ thâw	–	+

Key: + = male, elder
– = female, junior

whom, had she proposed a different account, the speaker of #204 might have co-categorized herself. His anticipation, like my being able to point to choice among correct and relevant categorization devices, provides hard and situated meaning to the otherwise orphic observation that age is more important than sex in the Lue and Thai social and kinship systems. The observation further suggests that stories are political in the sense that they can, and perhaps must, be used to publicize category alliances. This is supported by ethnographic accounts of parables and anecdotes being used in judicial proceedings and institutional political councils. In contrast to such accounts, finding politics in C's story does not rely upon advance knowledge that some situations must by their nature be institutionally and dramatically political, while others are not. I would propose, more generally, that teller and audience to a story orient to their co- and cross-categorizations *via* the CLs and activities of the story in such a way as to publicize their category alliances. This is a constant feature of story telling everywhere; its conventionalized (but otherwise accidental) consequence is the practical utility of telling stories in order to accomplish politics, decision making, and adjudication. A further consequence of the proposal would be to direct future work toward making visible how stories and story telling interactionally accomplish the instructing and sociability students of folk literature claim for them.

DISCUSSION

As an ethnographer practicing in 1968, I have professional and perhaps transient interests in the procedures and results of the preceding analysis itself. A reader whose concerns are different from mine will have a different structure of relevancies. A "symbolic interactionist," for example, might find as the main interest of our work that it provides procedures for the description and analysis of conversation, which is so crucial, yet so vacant, in the theories of Simmel and of Mead. Linguists might view our work as demonstrating that discourse analysis—by participants and thus by analysts—requires extra-linguistic resources. Students of Kenneth Burke might consider our work an explication of his thesis that "language is an implement of action" (1936:220). Although the suggestions of many social theorists have sometimes been helpful, our work is now both too empirical to "follow from" a theory of society and too young to propose one. Nevertheless, the following discussion takes into account more general implications of our work than are demonstrated in my analysis.

Ethnoscience and Ethnography. Tracing the detailed orderliness of actual interaction involved me in examining how members made use of what they know. So, for example, knowing that *lán* can be a correct label for someone who is also correctly an *ǐ·* is insufficient to account for the situated use of *lán* to so categorize her or for its conversational consequences. Knowing that an individual so categorized can *ěw* is insufficient to account for the situated interactive features of ascribing that activity to her. It is possible to use these observations for distinguishing between my interest in categorization and what has come to be called "ethnoscience" (Sturtevant 1964, Colby 1966). Ethnoscience is principally concerned with rules which will permit those who investigate a society to write a dictionary of lexemes that members of that society will recognize as providing correct categorizations. I am concerned with rules that can handle the considerations (that sometimes include correctness) that members actively use to orient to and recognize the appropriateness of categorizations, norms, and utterances on the situated occasions of their use, and to interpret, and sanction their interactive consequences. As Hymes (1966:5) points out, a member who knew only rules for correctness would be judged incompetent by his fellows.

The orderliness of conversation makes it apparent that the conversational situation in which an utterance occurs has a major influence upon its appropriateness. Two classes of situational features to which members can be shown to orient are conversational sequencing (e.g. "tieing rules") and conversational activities (e.g. "taking sides"). Our contributions here, then, are:

(a) to share in and provide substance for the observation that rules of correctness are insufficient to account for the member knowledge that produces social action;

(b) to observe that participants in a conversation do not necessarily orient to the correctness of each utterance. This implies that rules of correctness are sometimes unnecessary and suggests that the analyst must show (and cannot assume) member orientation to the correctness of the stretch of talk which he is analyzing;

(c) to point to conversational setting as a major influence upon appropriateness;

(d) to locate sequencing, activity, and relevant co-categorization as components of setting;

(e) to delineate and demonstrate some of the ways in which sequencing, activity and relevant co-categorization work.

The preceding analysis shows that the members of a society make active use of categorizations and thereby accomplish such tasks as invoking norms, taking sides, etc. Members can also mis-categorize,[39] presumably deliberately, so as to accomplish insult, praise, and other activities. The use, social consequences, member knowledge, participant analysis, and other components of the "meaning" of a word are all so heavily influenced by the setting—and particularly by the sequence of tied utterances—in which a word occurs that lexical definitions are only obscurely informative. This observation, which I am certainly not the first to make, provides building blocks, not stumbling blocks, for our work because we take account of, rely upon, and provide access to the settings which influence situated meanings.

The procedures used here do not rely upon knowledge of a real world external to the conversations analyzed. I do not have to assume that natives constantly orient to and maintain the position of a lexeme within a discrete semantic domain and a structured taxonomy. I do not rely upon asking natives questions. All of us, I think, even in the culture of which we are members, cannot be sure of the relationship between the question one intends to ask and the answer which one gets in response to it. As Fowler and Leland (1967:393–401) have observed, even taxons for ontologically identical referents within a demarcated domain can form a taxonomy distorted from native taxonomies by a striving for consistency, as well as by other unknown pressures of the situation in which questions are put to informants. Our techniques permit enquiry into the very properties of the chained question/answer sequences upon which both ethnoscience and conventional fieldwork are based.

A further, but perhaps inessential, distinction between our enterprise and ethnoscience is the kind of linguistic theory to which each is superficially analagous. Ethnoscience, and particularly the analysis of the semantic components of lexemes, resembles immediate constituent grammar. Our enterprise, despite its radically different ontological assumptions (cf. Moerman *in press*, note 15), vaguely resembles generative grammar. This resemblance results from and is warranted by our data, not our program. All competent members are able to—and to show their competence must—participate in a large number of proper non-replicate conversations. This implies that the rules by which they do so are probably finite, and even small, in number and certainly generative and abstract in form.

In order to account for the detailed orderliness and the interactive accomplishments I have traced in a petty conversation, one could suppose that Lue villagers memorize very detailed sets of rules and long lists of the occasions for their appropriate use. However, it is difficult to imagine the grandfatherly guardians of Lue tradition instructing their small charges, "If you ever hear a story about a *pɔ̄·ló·ŋ* who scolds an *ǐ·* . . ., then just jump in and say, . . ." Since interactive events are mutually oriented to for their orderliness, the knowledge that produces them must be stateable in the form of rules. Since the events are more detailed than the rules, the rules must be more abstract than the events, and generative of them. As a more intuitively familiar example than the data used here, consider the stunningly detailed regularities which Sudnow (1967:127–48) observed in the sequence of actions that transpire between doctors announcing to inquirers that a relative was dead upon his arrival at the hospital—regularities that extend to such minutae[40] as conversational topics, eye contact, and posture. If such regularities are instinctive, we would expect—which is not the case—that all peoples everywhere transact the same business in just the same way. If we wish to account for the regularities through simple learning theory, we would have to suppose that the unfortunate woman who enquires about her husband on Wednesday must have come in to ask about her dead-on-arrival father on Tuesday. Clearly the most reasonable supposition is that members know, orient to, and sanction highly abstract (or primitive) rules that generate actual action in an orderly and sanctioned manner. The abstractness or generativity of these rules means that we do not need to seek them solely in their most dramatic expression. It also suggests that the rules that are distinctive of gross institutions or elaborate rituals may, in their lack of productivity, be quite trivial, and, in their historical particularity, quite limited when compared to the rules that account for quotidian and universal actions like conversation. Furthermore, from the strikingly detailed correspondences between Lue and American conversation, there is reason to hope that the principled ways in which members make interactional use of their abstract knowledge is not only more interesting, but also more universal than the concrete norms and rules ethnographers traditionally collect.

One component of our work is the sometimes tedious, but quite necessary, task of discovering, documenting, and demonstrating the existence and content of culturally invariant procedures for language use. Some of the detailed correspondences between features of Lue and of American conversation which we have located may turn out to be crude or mistaken. Further, our enterprise is too young for us to know the theoretical statuses of such analytic objects as CLs, asymmetrical paired activities, question-answer pairs, sequencing rules, etc. We are nevertheless confident that we have begun the important task of building a science that can replace vacuous belief or unprincipled insight into the procedures, some of them culturally invariant, whereby members use talk to accomplish their social order. My use of findings from American conversation represents confidence in our joint enterprise rather than personal diffidence. We claim for our procedures an ability to distinguish among the loci (e.g. personal, household, community, role, ethnic, universal) of the features they describe. The discovery of normative expectations between *láns* and *pɔ̄·ló·ŋ*s, or even between Lue patrons and clients, is of only passing interest compared to the observation—subject to disconfirmation by using the same procedures on fresh materials—that it is a culturally invariant component of conversational orderliness for participants to be required to tie their utterances to other utterances in a conversation. I further suggest as culturally invariant that such tieing commonly requires alignments among the actors and activities talked about, that categorization labels (CLs) are typically used as a resource for maintaining such alignments, that the CLs used invoke norms, and that these norms must be oriented to by participants if they are to make the sense which the analyst can show them to have made of the conversation. Even if this compound suggestion should be shown wrong in detail, its form recommends new tasks for ethnographers. They should:

(1) come to control the CLs, norms, and other abstractly correct specific units of particular societies so as to be able to

(2) trace the principled ways in which members of a society know which specific norms, CLs, etc. are relevant on the situated occasions of their use and the interactional consequences of using them, so as to

(3) determine the extent to which the principles discovered [in (2), above] are culturally invariant.

Abstract Principles and Native Knowledge. It is commonplace to observe that rules for correct behavior are somehow important to orderly social life. It must also be observed that such rules—whether the maxims or proverbs stated by natives or the structural principles or themes stated by the anthropologist—are, even when correct, insufficient to account for the actual activities under which they are retrospectively subsumed. Among the difficulties presented by even superficial observation or introspection are: How is it known which rule is to be brought to bear in what manner on which aspects of all moments of every action? How are rules "brought to bear?" That is, what is the relationship between an abstract rule and the actual activities members bring off so as to confirm it? Through demonstrating the orderliness of actual interaction, I could point to the ways in which participants in that interaction were informed of which abstract rules were relevant. By examining the actual interactional consequences of these rules being used, I could show how otherwise inert rules are actively used and sanctioned.

Contemporary ethnography contains no explicit and consistent procedures for relating actual on-going interactions to the abstract roles, norms, rules, institution labels, etc., which the interactions are supposed to somehow represent. There is characteristically no reason other than professional orthodoxy for supposing that what transpires between two individuals is, for example, relevantly genealogical and not sexual, political, economic, etc. Anthropologists, like other people, make their world orderly by means of the language they use to describe it. Although the best of them recognize that labels matter more for the native than other facts do (e.g. Leach 1954:97), anthropologists typically use labels in a manner unmotivated by native orientations to them. The reader of a field "note from an *abangan* informant" (Geertz 1960:27) is made to suppose that the speaker, who must have other culturally correct CLs as well, is talking as a spokesman for the category with which the anthropologist labels him. The reader who encounters the observation that, "of the fifteen plots acquired by gift, most were given by brother or by father to son" (Moerman 1968b:95) is seduced by anthropological concern with kinship into supposing that genealogical connections motivated and explain the transactions. Only an overpowering faith in the omnirelevance of one's professional scheme of classification could recommend editing away the undoubtedly large number of social scenes which must have transpired between one event and "the next stage of this social drama [which] followed the month of the *Chipenji* gathering" (Turner 1957:270). Writing about one's own society (as inspection of the sociological literature confirms) offers no protection from the unmotivated use of norms and categorizations. Were it not for her sensitive, but inexplicit and perhaps accidental, use of what natives actually said to one another, Powdermaker's account[41] of a traffic accident as an instance of race relations (1939:49) might just as well be an instance of norms about lawyers and laymen, townsmen and countryfolk, old cars and new.

The relation between norms and actions is a central problem for which the "ideal vs. real behavior" distinction is obviously too gross and naive. The real issue is: How are norms made operative on the situated occasions of their use? How can abstract notions (whether the natives' or the anthropologist's structural/functional ones) constrain the variegated motility of concrete situated behavior? Perhaps an informal example will be helpful for showing that this cannot be discovered by asking natives questions about it.

In order to develop the point that the Lue, like the Americans, take it that a conversation must be about something, I asked my informant (in Lue), "If Mr. A tells Mr. C that he has talked with Mr. B, can C always ask what they talked about?" The answer was, "Yes, always." In asking Mr. Wongyai this question I was obeying the canons of good fieldwork by using his native language and by transforming my abstract concerns into specific details which he could follow yet presumably not deliberately adapt to his idea of what answer I wanted. Nevertheless, his answer, like any informants' abstract norm, is a puzzle, not a solution. I suppose that if a Lue ethnographer were silly enough to ask me the same question about the Americans, I too would answer, "Yes, always." A more accurate answer would be, "Yes, and no," for clearly the propriety of the question, "What did you talk about?" depends crucially upon how the question was placed in the conversation between A and C.[42] If the question has already been asked of A during his conversation with C, it could probably not be asked again. Unless the question is asked soon after A's announcement, it probably cannot be asked at all. It may be that the question is permitted or required only as the second utterance of a conversation that begins with a report of some other conversation. The general difficulty is excising one social event (the imagined question, in this instance) from its context (the imagined conversation between A and C) in order to use it as a criterion for some other event or class of events. Although we seem quite able to do this as members ("Tell me, did he propose to you?"), and although much of the social sciences rests upon its unexamined use, investigators do not have procedures for de-contexting one event for use as a criterion of other events and classes of events. Our work hopes to make explicit the contexted features of natural interaction to which members orient in making use of their productive abstract social knowledge.

In the data discussed, one can see precisely how (as E_1) normative expectation of *pɔ̄·ló·ŋ*'s was actively used, to what effect, and with what probable sanctions (maintaining one's appearance as a competent member through being able to analyze the coherence of, and thereby properly participate in, a conversation.) The very feature of this data which initially makes the sanction appear only probable—it is a "story" told principally by a single individual—is also the feature that simplifies the member's task of recognizing some event as an instance of a particular norm. Every abstract rule requires for its effective use some way of knowing whether the immediate situation is to be handled as an instance of it. My interest in abstract norms is directed primarily toward members' situated use of them and only incidentally toward an inventory of correct ones. Some of the reasons for this should be apparent. If norms can be as specific and detailed as E_1 and E_2, an ethnography whose task is their collecting would be uninteresting and endless. To judge from the ways in which participants used the norms for patrons and clients, and knew from the stated categorizations that they were to so use them, the meaning, use, sanction, and interest such norms have for members is embedded in the conversational sequences making those norms relevant.

Native and Analytic Knowledge. A dichotomy between "folk-models" and "analytic models" is basic to much contemporary cultural anthropology (Bohannan 1963), but the properties of these constructs, the differences between them, and their mutual relationships are obscure. Although I do not endorse the simple dichotomy, it provides a convenient way for discussing some features of my work.

Goodenough (1956) is usually credited with the signal observation that members do not necessarily order their affairs with respect to anthropological concerns. However, his proposal (1957) that ethnographers can master native principles by learning to emulate natives in a manner satisfactory to them fails on a number of grounds. One difficulty is that native standards for satisfactory behavior by a stranger may (for lay reasons as divergent as "politeness" or "prejudice") be quite different from the standards they hold themselves to. A further difficulty can perhaps best be presented through linguistic analogies of the sort that Goodenough and other "ethnoscientists" use. I am able to speak acceptable English partially through the use of grammatical rules I am unable to state. I can speak Thai, more or less acceptably, under a similar disability. One's introspectively based accounts of his behavior in his native society provide data for analysis, but are not themselves analyses. I see no reason why this is not equally true of how one accounts for his behavior as a facsimile member of another society. (cf. Moerman, *in press*). My accounts of how I "made it" among the Lue are neither complete (in the sense that all analytic components needed to generate the behavior are stated) nor correct (in the sense that natives perform exactly the same analysis, and that the analysis generates an activity which, were one of them to do it, would be interactionally equivalent to mine). Our studies of conversation, on the other hand, accept the constraint of showing participants to orient to the analytic objects of the analysis, which accounts for the features of their talk which we examine. We can therefore hope that the components of our models of the speaker/listener are relevant and active parts of member productive knowledge. The work represented by this essay permits me to propose that it is possible to distinguish between knowledge based on co-membership and knowledge based on formal analysis of conversation, but that doing such analysis relies upon having some member knowledge.

At the outset of the research of which this is a partial report, I had hoped to distinguish between the results of analysis and of member knowledge (and fieldworker facsimiles of such knowledge) in such a way as to permit ethnographic analysis of cultures known only through conversations recorded in them. Because of the normative and abstract correctness rules needed both for translation and in order to trace member relevancies,[43] I no longer think this possible. This paper was partially intended to explicate some of the ways in which participants made normative, shared, and sanctioned use of what they know. By virtue of having lived and studied among the participant individuals, I have come to know some of the things they know. In principle there is thus nothing wrong with my making use of having acquired some of the knowledge they have. Nevertheless, the present implication of these observations is that unless natives are trained to do analyses, the procedures used here can merely supplement but never replace conventional ethnography. It is my own conviction that these procedures are sufficiently superior to conventional ethnography[44] to recommend that natives be trained to perform analyses that will explicate their own (and universal) interactional intuitions.

There is, however, some anecdotal evidence to support belief in the possibility that interactions can be analyzed by strangers to the societies in which they occurred. Consider that untrained graduate students who knew no Thai (and who were told only that the tape they were given was a segment of a normal conversation) were able to make some sense of it. They assigned utterances to speakers and developed a notion (largely acoustic) of "interruption." When provided with a transcript (including gloss and translation), some students were able to formulate, develop, and investigate such analytic notions as "interruption," "acting as a host," "giving commands," etc. and to use these both to criticize one another's work and challenge the translation. More advanced students and colleagues, none of whom know Thai, have made independent observations (informed, however, by the ethnographica contained in draft analyses) upon the data which have required me to modify my analysis. I would suggest that such episodes support our conviction that—in marked distinction to the rest of anthropology—the procedures we are using lend themselves to cumulative and cooperative progress, as well as supporting my now somewhat diminished hopes for sensitive and informative analyses of cultures by non-members.

In studying a stretch of talk, one concentrates on its features which prove most amenable to analysis. This essay is concerned to some extent with an analytically acceptable reformulation of rather traditional notions of cultural norms. An analyst who approached the same data without my professional biases might well be able to describe more interesting and productive features which make no use of conventional ethnographic knowledge. He would, however, be constrained by the faults and the unexplicated strengths of my data.

The difficulties of translation, which affect all ethnography are especially apparent in the methods used here. Although the data analyzed and the procedures for analysis are more public than in any competing kinds of ethnography the reader must rely upon my transcription gloss, and translation.[45] Its phonemic inconsistencies and my reference to the possible non-existence of #196b:1 reveal that the transcription itself is imperfect. It would have been misleading for me to "clean it up" since it was in this form that it provided the data for the analysis. Moreover, even were it perfectly phonemicized, it would, of course, provide only a pale facsimile of what participants had to work with, lacking, as it does, kinesthetic, paralinguistic, and extrasituational information. I think it impossible either for participants to analyze their own interaction or for analysts to know everything that participants take account of. The methodological caution is that we can never hope to explain all the features of an interaction to which members might orient; we must avoid false explanations (e.g. by a lexical demonstration of a feature for which participants used intonation) of the features we do analyze.

SUMMARY

It is possible to subject entirely public data of actual social interaction to explicit analytic procedures without either reliance upon private or conventional knowledge about such things as culture, class, role, motive, etc. or assumptions that some actual data are less informative than others.

These procedures and their results:

(a) tell us things we would otherwise not know about how members of a society make use of their cultural resources;

(b) are cumulative. A result of procedural refinement obtained at one time informs analysis of further data;

(c) are productive in that results obtained from analyzing one piece of data can be tested against and used to account for further data.

The utility of identical procedures on Lue and American conversation, together with the close-grained similarities of the results obtained, indicates that it is possible to discover detailed and powerful universals in the ways in which members of any society do conversation and therein mutually orient to, confirm, and sanction their cultural knowledge.

Competent conversational participation requires member orientation to and use of abstract generative social knowledge which can be explicated through such analytic objects as categorization labels, typifying ascriptions, etc.

Analyzable features of conversation are used by participants so as to accomplish interactive tasks the analyst can thereby locate.

It is possible to isolate some features of natural settings to which members orient. This permits distinguishing between correctness and appropriateness, tracing the operation of appropriateness rules and their interactive consequences, and confusing neither set of rules with the extrinsic concerns of the social science professions.

It is possible to distinguish between knowledge based on co-membership and knowledge based on formal analysis of conversation, but doing such analysis relies upon having some member knowledge.

Appendix A

Cultural and Linguistic Resources

Section 1: A_2 = *ĭ·naŋxam* = *lán*; A_1 = *pɔ̄·ló·ŋ*; A_1 is reciprocal to A_2. This demonstration is required for my observation that participants take the actor labelled *ĭ·naŋxam* in #190 to be the same actor as the *lán* of #196b and also for the other alignments of A_1 and A_2 made in my analysis.

The demonstration makes use of and develops the notion of a *collection* of categorization labels. For the moment, the reader can regard a collection as a set of CLs which seem, semantically, to belong together. Insofar as the notion proves useful to our work, it would be desirable to show that a collection belongs, for members, to a single delimitable semantic field and has, for the analyst of native activities, a distinctive set of properties to which members interact. An example of such a set of properties would be those prematurely claimed (Moerman 1968a) for ethnic CLs as used by the Lue: exhaustive, egalitarian, eternal, non-optative.

E_1 supposes that the *lá·n* is A_2, that there is some regular and contextually possible meaning in the relationship *to have* between a *pɔ̄·ló·ŋ* and a *lá·n* and that #196b:4–9 are not just items mentioned in sequence, but constitute *a list* which has properties. Let us consider the first two suppositions.[1]

How can it be shown that the *lá·n* is A_2? First, a *lá·n* (#208:5) who might have gone to town to buy such things riding (#217:1) a bike remains a character in the story, so showing a possible constancy of A_2 = *lá·n* for the story's subsequent continuity. Second, I hear and have no reason not to suppose that others including C hear #196 as part of a sequence that begins with #190 and is tied directly back to #190. As a basis for hearing this tie to #190, it is possible that NOUN *nî· nī*? or NOUN DEMONSTRATIVE *nī*? is used only when the noun has already been referred to in the same conversation.[2] If this hypothesis is confirmed by consulting the corpus, how was *lán* not stated before #196a, been referred to? If the hypothesis is disconfirmed, how might #196a nevertheless be tied to #190 through common actors?

The title *pɔ̄·ló·ŋ* (#190:3) is restricted to mature male individuals; the title *ĭ·* (#190:7) restricted to individuals who are female and junior.[3] *pɔ̄·ló·ŋ* is a CL which may come from more than one collection of such labels: kinship based, wealth based, residence based, and perhaps others. *lá·n* ("nephew/niece," "grandchild") is a CL in the kinship and age collections.

What of the relationship between A_1 and A_2? In the kinship collection, *lá·n* is reciprocal[4] to *pɔ̄·ló·ŋ* in the sense that:

(1) anyone whom x properly calls *pɔ̄·ló·ŋ* can properly call x *lá·n*.

(2) if y is said to be the *pɔ̄·ló·ŋ* of x, x will be said to be the *lá·n* of y.

(3) for y to be properly labeled a *pɔ̄·ló·ŋ*, there must be some individual x who refers to y as his *pɔ̄·ló·ŋ* and to whom y refers as his *lá·n*.

(*Notes to this Appendix will be found on p. 440.*)

pɔ̄·ló·ŋ, a member of more than one collection, shares the kinship collection with *lá·n*; *lá·n*, a member of more than one collection, shares the kinship collection with *pɔ̄·ló·ŋ*. Within the kinship collection:

- **(i)** *lá·n* and *pɔ̄·ló·ŋ* are in the relation *to have* in the sense (listed above as (1)–(3)) in which they are reciprocals
- **(ii)** every *pɔ̄·ló·ŋ* must have at least one *lá·n*
- **(iii)** a young girl can be a *lá·n* to a *pɔ̄·ló·ŋ*; a *pɔ̄·ló·ŋ* cannot be a *lá·n* to a young girl.

Within all relevant collections of CLs: an individual categorized as *ǐ·* (and named *naŋxam*) must be a young girl; an individual categorized as *pɔ̄·ló·ŋ* cannot be a young girl.

Section 2: Knowing what C focused on.

What resources do participants have for knowing that C's focus is on: a) the trip to market, b) the time of this trip, c) that the time is accountably long?

a) The construction (#196d:.2–.7) "*luk* place y *páj* x" means, minimally, from "place y to place x." It can also mean "to go from place y to place x." The second reading is presumably confirmed by #196d:.9–.11 which is made a comment on .2–.7 through the particle *na* (#196d:.8). Adding actors, #196d: .2–.11 translates as "To go from Ban Mang here to market [and back?] took [her] an hour."

#196d:.1 (*kân*), is difficult to translate, important for the translation of the rest of #196d, and conversationally quite important. Here and in other occurrences my informant glosses *kân* as both (Central Thai) *phieŋtɛ̀·* meaning "only, merely" and as [CT] *mɛ́· tɛ̀·* meaning "even, including." The ambiguous gloss would permit translation of #196d as both "even though it was fully as far as . . ." and as "even though it was only as far as . . ." This ambiguity suggests that the best uninterpreted translation for "*kân* A B" is "although A, B." That is, the use of *kân* indicates that A and B are mutually relevant, that A and B both occur, and that this (mutual relevance and co-occurrence) are commented on. Somewhat more specifically, I take *kân* (and some situations of "but" and "although" in English) [Pollner and Zimmerman, 1967] to mean: "Despite some of the implication of A, B." The question, now, is "despite which of the implication of A?"

b) Traveling time. Assume for the moment (as will be discussed under c, below), that participants hear both "Ban Mang" and "the market" to refer to the nearby Ban Mang and market which they often visit. The route between the two is frequently travelled, dusty safe, short, a well marked route, bordered by rice fields, and has a large (though presumably not infinite) number of other properties and implications. Which of these implications are we told, by *kân*, does not hold? The implication with which B is inconsistent. That is, #196d: .9–.11 states traveling time. Operating as B in the *kân* A B construction, it tells us that it is the traveling time implication of A (.2–.7) which is commentably disconfirmed. "An hour" is either too long or too short for the trip since the trip was

no { further than
more difficult than
less familiar than
more a place of sudden time-consuming dangers
closer than
less difficult than
less a place of time-consuming dangers
. . . } than a trip

from *ban maŋ hân páj kǎ·t.* That is, # 196d:.1 and .9–.11 means that it is the time spent on the trip which is commentable on. The comment on it (in addition to the *kân* itself) is made as # 196e, "can't be!" which thus ties to, comments on, and thereby demonstrates the commentability of, the hour trip of # 196d. It is the *kân* in its situated use which tells us what (elapsed time) both is and can't be.

c) Long traveling time. I have now provided for participants knowing the relevance of travel time in the formulation: "despite all those things which make you expect this trip to have taken time$_x$, it took time$_y$." How might it have been known that "all those things . . ." make time$_y$ accountably great, not accountably small? More specifically, what non-context resources do participants bring to bear on # 196d:2–7 which lets them know, as they evidently do, that # 196d:11 is a long time?[5] On the basis of my conventional ethnographic knowledge of the society in which the recording was made, I can suggest some such resources, but think them insufficient.

For these villagers "an hour" is an approximate, even vacuous, unit of time which may be long, short, or just right depending upon how it is interpreted. A "real time" trip from the real Ban Mang to the real marketplace and back takes somewhat less than ten minutes by bike, about twenty minutes by foot. This indicates that elapsed time of one hour to go, shop, and return is not—for any unsituated sense—noticeably long.

(i) Even if an hour were a long time because participants are familiar with the distance in space and in traveling time from the known, real and local Ban Mang to the known, real and local market, villagers know that personal names and village names are not unique specifiers. It is often possible and frequently known to be the case that more than one person or more than one village has the same name. Specifically, for the names of Lue villages in Chiengkham and for the particular name "Ban Mang" it is known that villages with identical names are to be found in the Sip Song Panna. It is also known that stories are frequently set in the Sip Song Panna. The audience for this story knows that C comes from the Sip Song Panna.

These considerations are intended to

(a) recognize the referential ambiguity of proper names for persons and places

(b) stipulate that some usages of such names requires that their ambiguity be resolved.

(c) posit that the instanced usage (VIII.1: # 196d:.1–.8) is of the kind that requires such resolution.

How is the resolution accomplished here in order to give the reading "the known, real, and local Ban Mang and market, between which we know the distance in time and space"? I suggest that it is done by the demonstrative, *hân* (#196d:5), and thereby imply that demonstratives, even when syntactically required, are conversationally informative.

(ii) Even if the distance between the two real places of Ban Mang and the Chiengkham market is simple and universally known, an analyst's use of it creates a number of problems. What right has anyone, even a member, to assert analytically (and not just as a stereotypic commonplace) that "everyone knows" something? Is there some general rule, like "always look near home first," which recommends my assuming that *kă·t*, "market" is here taken to mean "the Chiengkham market at which we do our shopping?" Must the analyst make, rely upon, and assume the members to also make a reality test, or may he hope for purely conversational resources?

It is to make this hope slightly more reasonable that I prophesy[6] that inspection of some corpus of conversations in this village will show that someone going to Ban Mang sometimes says that he's *mə· kă·t*. That is, Ban Mang is counted part of the *kăt*, in the sense of "town," and all villagers know this and use it somewhat independently of the physical proximity between the two.[7] The resource for doing this is one of taxonomic opposition between a circle and its center. *kă·t* can mean the town area, the shopping section, or the area of the daily market (*kă·t mò·*)-place. The distinction of Ban Mang from the central *kă·t* by means of the "from A to B (of which A is sometimes counted a part)" construction is like "from the [UCLA] campus to Westwood" in that the UCLA campus is sometimes counted as being in Westwood.

Appendix B

UNEDITED SEQUENCED DATA (VIII.1 # 187-243)

English words added to the gloss for intelligible translation are enclosed in parentheses when I judge them to be provided by Lue syntax. Words bracketed in the translation are extra-grammatical. They were usually provided by the informant, either volunteered (e.g. # 193) or in response to such questions from me as *pháj* ("who?") or *sáŋ kɔ*? ("what's that?"). Additional conventions observed in the gloss are as follows.

Form in Gloss	*Meaning*
AUX	auxiliary verb
CLSFR	classifier
CNJ	conjunction
CT	Central Thai
D	Demonstrative
DW	Mr. Dheerawatan Wongyai, the informant. Used to indicate a disagreement between him and MM.
EXCLM	exclamation
FTR	future particle
INDR	marker of indirect object
Mr or MM	Michael Moerman, both as conversation participant and translator.
N	proper name of persons and places.

Form in Gloss	*Meaning*
NG	negative particle
PRN	pronoun
PRT	grammatical particle unglossed but incorporated in translation
PRV	pro-verb
PSE	hesitation or pause marker
Q	question particle
RCP	reciprocal particle
RLTV	marker of relative clause
T	title
VCTVE	vocative—Somewhat like American, "dear."
W	woman speaker
(?)	speaker identification uncertain.

VIII.1
 # 187

WS	pɔ̄·	sɛ́·ŋ	xá·j xó·	isa·	nân
	T	N	laugh	what	D

Pɔ Sɛŋ, what are you laughing at?

#188

K	ə·	déw	déw	déw	nāŋ	û·	nî·	kə̆n
		moment	moment	moment	sit	talk	D	first

Hey, wait a minute, wait a minute, come sit down and talk here first.

#189

K	ə·	xâ·w	ka·ŋ	nî	ɛ·
		enter	middle	D	PRT

Sit down right here in the middle.

#190

	1	2	3	4	5	6	7	8
C	wan	nân	pɔ̄· ló·ŋ	kɔ·	də̆t	hŷ·	ĭ·	na·ŋ xam
	day	D	T	CNJ	scold or curse	INDR	T	N

That day, *pɔloŋ* scolded *i* Naŋxam.

#191

K	ā·w,	ì·	sī·	xáb	phɔ̀·	du
	PRV	T	N		PRT	PRT

Have *i* si *xab* a bit.

#192

Child	xāb	lɔ
		PRT

(Go ahead and) *xab.*

#193

W	bá·	cà·ŋ	nɛ·	(knock)
	NG	able	PRT	(knock)

[say that you] can't. (not person asked)

VIII.1
#194

K	xâb	lɔ́·	xâb	hŷ·	pɔ̄· cá·n	faŋ	lu?
		PRT	sing	so that	[(MM) T]	listen	PRT

Go ahead and *xab, xap* so *Pɔ·an* can listen.

#195

W	bá·	cà·ŋ	ba·	cà·ŋ	nɛ·
	NG	able	NG	able	PRT

[say] "I can't, I can't." DW: (Not the person asked. Without *nɛ* would probably be person asked)

#196a

	1	2	3
C	lá·n	nî·	ni
	grandchild	D	PRT

Now this *lan*.

#196a[1]

K	bɔcaŋ	hý
	NG can	Q

[You] can't?

#196b

	1	2	3	4	5	6	7
C	caj	páj	sỳ·	năm pa·	káp	bâ·w li·	káb
		to go	buy		CNJ	cigarettes	and

8	9	10	11	12	13	14	15
an	ka? fa·j	ni	kó·	bă·	le·w	jaŋ	sŷ·
PSE	matches	PRT	fear	NG	fast	even	buy

16	17
lot thi·p	hŷ·
bike	INDR

[he sent her] to go buy *nampla* and cigarettes and matches. [He was] afraid (that) [she] wouldn't be quick, so [he] bought [her] (a) bike.

VIII.1
#196b[1]
MM ə·

#196c
M hy hy

chuckles

#188

K	ə·	déw	déw	déw	nāŋ	û·	nî·	kə̆n
		moment	moment	moment	sit	talk	D	first

Hey, wait a minute, wait a minute, come sit down and talk here first.

#189

K	ə·	xâ·w	ka·ŋ	nî	ɛ·
		enter	middle	D	PRT

Sit down right here in the middle.

#190

	1	2	3	4	5	6	7	8
C	wan	nân	pɔ̄· ló·ŋ	kɔ·	də̆t	hŷ·	ǐ·	na·ŋ xam
	day	D	T	CNJ	scold or curse	INDR	T	N

That day, *pɔloŋ* scolded *i* Naŋxam.

#191

K	ā·w,	ì·	sī·	xáb	phɔ̀·	du
	PRV	T	N		PRT	PRT

Have *i* si *xab* a bit.

#192

Child	xāb	lɔ
		PRT

(Go ahead and) *xab.*

#193

W	bá·	cà·ŋ	nɛ·	(knock)
	NG	able	PRT	(knock)

[say that you] can't. (not person asked)

VIII.1

#194

K	xâb	ló·	xâb	hŷ·	pɔ̄· cá·n	faŋ	lu?
		PRT	sing	so that	[(MM) T]	listen	PRT

Go ahead and *xab*, *xap* so *Pɔ·an* can listen.

#195

W	b[illegible] cà·ŋ	ba·	cà·ŋ	nɛ·
	N[illegible] able	NG	able	PRT

[s[illegible] "I can't, I can't." DW: (Not the person asked. Without *nɛ* would probably be person asked)

#196a

	1	2	3
C	lá·n	nî·	ni
	[illegible]andchild	D	PRT

[illegible]ow this *lan*.

#196a[1]

K	bɔcaŋ	hý
	NG can	Q

[You] can't?

#196b

	1	2	3	4	5	6	7
C	caj	páj	sỳ·	năm pa·	káp	bâ·w li·	káb
		to go	buy		CNJ	cigarettes	and

8	9	10	11	12	13	14	15
an	ka? fa·j	ni	kó·	bă·	le·w	jaŋ	sŷ·
PSE	matches	PRT	fear	NG	fast	even	buy

16	17
lot thi·p	hŷ·
bike	INDR

[he sent her] to go buy *nampla* and cigarettes and matches. [He was] afraid (that) [she] wouldn't be quick, so [he] bought [her] (a) bike.

VIII.1
#196b[1]
MM ə·

#196c

M	hy	hy

chuckles

#188

K	ə·	déw	déw	déw	nāŋ	û·	nî·	kə̆n
		moment	moment	moment	sit	talk	D	first

Hey, wait a minute, wait a minute, come sit down and talk here first.

#189

K	ə·	xâ·w	ka·ŋ	nî	ɛ·
		enter	middle	D	PRT

Sit down right here in the middle.

#190

	1	2	3	4	5	6	7	8
C	wan	nân	pɔ̄· ló·ŋ	kɔ·	də̆t	hŷ·	ĭ·	na·ŋ xam
	day	D	T	CNJ	scold or curse	INDR	T	N

That day, *pɔloŋ* scolded *i* Naŋxam.

#191

K	ā·w,	ì·	sī·	xáb	phɔ̀·	du
	PRV	T	N		PRT	PRT

Have *i* si *xab* a bit.

#192

Child	xāb	lɔ
		PRT

(Go ahead and) *xab*.

#193

W	bá·	cà·ŋ	nɛ·	(knock)
	NG	able	PRT	(knock)

[say that you] can't. (not person asked)

VIII.1

#194

K	xâb	lɔ́·	xâb	hŷ·	pɔ̄· cá·n	faŋ	lu?
		PRT	sing	so that	[(MM) T]	listen	PRT

Go ahead and *xab*, *xap* so *Pɔ·an* can listen.

#195

W	bá·	cà·ŋ	ba·	cà·ŋ	nɛ·
	NG	able	NG	able	PRT

[say] "I can't, I can't." DW: (Not the person asked. Without *nɛ* would probably be person asked)

#196a

	1	2	3
C	lá·n	nî·	ni
	grandchild	D	PRT

Now this *lan.*

#196a[1]

K	bɔcaŋ	hý
	NG can	Q

[You] can't?

#196b

	1	2	3	4	5	6	7
C	caj	páj	sỳ·	năm pa·	káp	bâ·w li·	káb
		to go	buy		CNJ	cigarettes	and

8	9	10	11	12	13	14	15
an	ka? fa·j	ni	kó·	bă·	le·w	jaŋ	sŷ·
PSE	matches	PRT	fear	NG	fast	even	buy

16	17
lot thi·p	hŷ·
bike	INDR

[he sent her] to go buy *nampla* and cigarettes and matches. [He was] afraid (that) [she] wouldn't be quick, so [he] bought [her] (a) bike.

VIII.1
#196b[1]
MM ə·

#196c
M hy hy

chuckles

#188

K	ə·	déw	déw	déw	nāŋ	û·	nî·	kə̆n
		moment	moment	moment	sit	talk	D	first

Hey, wait a minute, wait a minute, come sit down and talk here first.

#189

K	ə·	xâ·w	ka·ŋ	nî	ɛ·
		enter	middle	D	PRT

Sit down right here in the middle.

#190

	1	2	3	4	5	6	7	8
C	wan	nân	pɔ̄· ló·ŋ	kɔ·	də̆t	hŷ·	ǐ·	na·ŋ xam
	day	D	T	CNJ	scold or curse	INDR	T	N

That day, *pɔloŋ* scolded *i* Naŋxam.

#191

K	ā·w,	ì·	sī·	xáb	phɔ̀·	du
	PRV	T	N		PRT	PRT

Have *i* si *xab* a bit.

#192

Child	xāb	lɔ
		PRT

(Go ahead and) *xab.*

#193

W	bá·	cà·ŋ	nɛ·	(knock)
	NG	able	PRT	(knock)

[say that you] can't. (not person asked)

VIII.1

#194

K	xâb	lɔ́·	xâb	hŷ·	pɔ̄· cá·n	faŋ	lu?
		PRT	sing	so that	[(MM) T]	listen	PRT

Go ahead and *xab, xap* so *Pɔ·an* can listen.

#195

W	bá·	cà·ŋ	ba·	cà·ŋ	nɛ·
	NG	able	NG	able	PRT

[say] "I can't, I can't." DW: (Not the person asked. Without *nɛ* would probably be person asked)

#196a

	1	2	3
C	lá·n	nî·	ni
	grandchild	D	PRT

Now this *lan*.

#196a[1]

K	bɔcaŋ	hý
	NG can	Q

[You] can't?

#196b

	1	2	3	4	5	6	7
C	caj	páj	sỳ·	năm pa·	káp	bâ·w li·	káb
		to go	buy		CNJ	cigarettes	and

8	9	10	11	12	13	14	15
an	ka? fa·j	ni	kó·	bă·	le·w	jaŋ	sŷ·
PSE	matches	PRT	fear	NG	fast	even	buy

16	17
lot thi·p	hŷ·
bike	INDR

[he sent her] to go buy *nampla* and cigarettes and matches. [He was] afraid (that) [she] wouldn't be quick, so [he] bought [her] (a) bike.

VIII.1

#196b[1]

MM ə·

#196c

M hy hy

chuckles

#188

K	ə·	déw	déw	déw	nāŋ	û·	nî·	kə̆n
		moment	moment	moment	sit	talk	D	first

Hey, wait a minute, wait a minute, come sit down and talk here first.

#189

K	ə·	xâ·w	ka·ŋ	nî	ɛ·
		enter	middle	D	PRT

Sit down right here in the middle.

#190

	1	2	3	4	5	6	7	8
C	wan	nân	pɔ̄· ló·ŋ	kɔ·	də̆t	hŷ·	ĭ·	na·ŋ xam
	day	D	T	CNJ	scold or curse	INDR	T	N

That day, *pɔloŋ* scolded *i* Naŋxam.

#191

K	ā·w,	ì·	sī·	xáb	phɔ̀·	du
	PRV	T	N		PRT	PRT

Have *i* si *xab* a bit.

#192

Child	xāb	lɔ
		PRT

(Go ahead and) *xab*.

#193

W	bá·	cà·ŋ	nɛ·	(knock)
	NG	able	PRT	(knock)

[say that you] can't. (not person asked)

VIII.1
#194

K	xâb	lɔ́·	xâb	hŷ·	pɔ̄· cá·n	faŋ	lu?
		PRT	sing	so that	[(MM) T]	listen	PRT

Go ahead and *xab*, *xap* so *Pɔ·an* can listen.

#195

W	bá·	cà·ŋ	ba·	cà·ŋ	nε·
	NG	able	NG	able	PRT

[say] "I can't, I can't." DW: (Not the person asked. Without *nε* would probably be person asked)

#196a	**1**	**2**	**3**
C	lá·n	nî·	ni
	grandchild	D	PRT

Now this *lan*.

#196a[1]

K	bɔcaŋ	hý
	NG can	Q

[You] can't?

#196b

	1	**2**	**3**	**4**	**5**	**6**	**7**
C	caj	páj	sỳ·	năm pa·	káp	bâ·w li·	káb
		to go	buy		CNJ	cigarettes	and

8	**9**	**10**	**11**	**12**	**13**	**14**	**15**
an	ka? fa·j	ni	kó·	bă·	le·w	jaŋ	sŷ·
PSE	matches	PRT	fear	NG	fast	even	buy

16	**17**
lot thi·p	hŷ·
bike	INDR

[he sent her] to go buy *nampla* and cigarettes and matches. [He was] afraid (that) [she] wouldn't be quick, so [he] bought [her] (a) bike.

VIII.1
#196b[1]
MM ə·

#196c
M hy hy

chuckles

#205

C	ká fa·j	í·	pāt	kɔ·	bă·	mi	thâ·
	matches	PRT	strike	CNJ	NG	have	wait

	jŭ·	cân	nân
	exist	like	D

There weren't any matches to strike. Just waiting around like that.

#206

W	ka fa·j	na·j	hən	han	lu
very quiet	matches	in	house	D	PRT

There are matches in the house.

#207

Child	hiŋ	fa·j	han	lɔ·	nɔ̂·j
F	against	fire	D	PRT	N

They're on the *hiŋfaj*, Noi.

#208

C	1	2	3	4	5	6	7
	hə̂·*	mὲ· thâ·w	nî·	hâk	lá·n	ni khyn	hə̂*
	EXCLM	T old lady	D	love	grand- child	CT: lɛwk CNJ	EXCLM

8	9	10	11	12	13	14
bă·	mi·	bâ·w li·	[ə· àn]	bă·	mi·	ka? fa·j
NG	have	cigarettes	[mis-spoke]	NG	have	match

15	16	17	18	19	20	21	22
kɔ·	jŭ·	nî·	kab	nȳŋ	lu?	[á·w mə·]	hŷ·
CNJ	stay	here	CLSFR	one	PRT	[take go bring over to]	to

23	24	
pāt	hé·	lɔ·
strike	PRT	PRT

So. That old lady loved her grandchild. "Here" [she said] There are no cigarettes—oh, no, no—There are no matches. [?] There's still a box (of them) here, go light them." [Alt.: and [she] lit (one) for [him].]

---

* Approximate tone.

VIII.1

#209

Child	pə̄n	í·	phɔ̂·
	PRN	FTR	look

off
mike I'll go look.

#210

WS	m	páj	tə̄·	à·	cɛ́n fɔ·ŋ
	NG	go	yet	Q	N

Haven't you gone yet, Cɛnfɔŋ?

#211

C	nǎm pá·	kɔ·	mi·	ní·	[nɔ̂·j	nȳŋ]	á·w	thɔ̌k
		CNJ	have	D	very	little	take	pour
	sǎ·j	wǎ·n	ma·	hŷ·	kín			
	into	cup	come	INDR	to eat			

["] There's (still) a drop of nampla. ["] [She] poured it into a plate (for) [him] to eat.

#212

little Child	cɛ́n fɔ·ŋ
	N

#213

	1	2	3	4		5	6	7
C	ah	lêŋ	xá·w	[ja·j	ma·]	pín	có·n	sáŋ
	EXCLM	care for	PRN	big	come	be	thief	which
				grow				

8	9	10	11	12	13	14	15
ǐ	ma·	caŋ pɔ	ǐ·	ma·	xôb	hó·	kun
PRT	come	CT: kɔ jaŋ	T	dog	bit	head	person

16	17
thâ·w	nī? wā·
old	Q

Oh, take care of them until they're grown up, then why do they become crooks, [why do they] become dogs that bite the head (i.e., ingrates who return evil for good) of old people?

VIII.1
#214
M1 y·

#215

C	1	2	3	4	5		6
	kun	thâ·w	câ·j	ni	ni	(Insert #216)	lōt
	people	old	use	D	PRT		bike

7	8	9	10	11	12
m̌	mi·	kɔ·	sỳ·	hŷ·	nī?
NG	have	CNJ	buy	INDR	PRT

Old people send [her/them on errands]. Insert #216. [She/They] don't have a bike (so) [old people] buy one for [her/them].

#216

Child	ə̄m	mὲ·	á·w	hŷ·	pən	lɔ·	pə̄n	xá·j	dâ·j
F	T	T	take	to give	PRN	PRT	PRN	want	

man	nε·
PRN	PRT

Oh mother, give it to me. I want it.

#217

C	1	2	3	4	5	6	7	8
	xî·	páj	lew	kā	lūk	ni·	páj	kǎ·t
	ride	go	fast	PRT_Q	from	D	go	market

9	10	11	12	13	14	15
káb ma·	lε̄w kɔ·	[á·w ma·]	hŷ·	hé	lε̄·w	kɔ
return	CNJ	[bring]	INDR	PRT CT: sia		CNJ

16	17	18	19	20	21
hŷ?	pɔ̄· thâ·w	hə̌·j	xá·j	páj	náj
here!	T (old man)	VCTVE	want to	go	where

22		23	24	25	26
(kɔ)	(Insert #218)	sǎŋ	kun	thâ·w	lε·w kɔ
		tell	person	old	CNJ

27	28
páj	lɔ̄·
go	PRT

[" ?]Did [you/she] ride fast? From here to the market and back and then give [it to him, saying], ["]Here dear grandfather,["]when [I/you] want to go anywhere, INSERT #218 [I will] tell the old people first.

VIII.1

#218

Child	y·	mὲ·	paj	sá·
	[T	]	go	where what

Mommy, where are you going?

#219

S	me·n	lɛ
	correct	PRT

That's right.

#220	**1**	**2**	**3**	**4**		**5**	**6**	**7**
C	ɔ̆·	ān	nî·	mὲ·	thâ·w	xyn	[pín	cá·j]
	EXCLM	thing	D	[T old lady]		CNJ	[is sympathetic,	heart protective]

8		**9**	**10**	**11**	**12**	**13**	**14**
[han	ni]	páj	kán	jă·j	lέ?	man	bá
PRT		go	if	grown	PRT	PRN	NG
[CT: sia duaj]							[won't

15	**16**	**17**
dâ·j	khwă·m	lɛ
PRV	meaning content	PRT
be any good]		

So here the old lady really went along with [her]. [But the old man said, "If you're permissive like this now, the kid] won't be any good when [she] grows up. ["Don't act like this."]

#221

W	há	há	há	(laughing)
	laughing			

#222

C	hăk	hăk	lá·n	clears throat	ni
	love	love	grandchild		PRT

[She] loved the grandchild.

VIII.1
#223

W	hák	pha·j
	love	who

Loved who?

#224

Young boy	(?)páj	i· sáŋ	nă	sɛ́·ŋ
	go	what	PRT	N

Where are (you) going, Sɛŋ?

#225

C	ə·	ní·	(continuous talking)
	EXCLM	D	

So then (continues talking)

#226

Child (?) in NT	cá·w Sir?

#227

C	kan wā·	[mɛ̀·	thâ·w]	dɔ̆t	nă	o·
	suppose		T	scold	PRT	EXCLM
		old lady		complain		

Suppose the old lady had complained (or scolded).

#228

S	ĭ·	mə̆·	kɔ·	mə·	lɔ·
	FTR	go	CNJ	go	PRT

If [you're] going, then go.

#229

Young boy	xɔ·ŋ
	N

VIII.1

#230

1	2	3	4	5
[ĭ· ni·]	kun	thâ·w	câ·j	páj
T, PRN	person	old	use	go

6	7	8	9
[páj kə̆t	páj xám]	[cín dáj]	[pa· lăm pa· lɔ́·]
to stop off		how	very much
		why	

10	11
sam	nî
like	D

[The old man said to the girl,"] Kid, when elders send [you] on an errand, why do [you] stop off and (waste) so much (time) like this?"

#231

W

[paj xam]
stop off

Stop off.

#232

C (?)

an	cīn	nî·	[bà·	daj	khwa·m]	ō·	jă·ŋ	ni·
thing	like	D	NG	PRV	meaning	EXCLM	like	D
				no good	content			

["Acting] like this is bad.["]

#233

W

ĭ·	saŋ
what	

#234

C

1	2	3	4	5	6	7	8
cámpín	páj	lew	ma·	lew	kā·	cîn	nî·
necessary	go	fast	come	fast	PRT	example	this
urgent							

9	10	11	12
kun	thâ·w	câ·j	nì?
person	old	use	PRT

["]It's urgent to go and come back fast! (It's) old people (who) [you are] doing (things for).["]

#235

C (?)	[di·	wā·]	dă·
	good	say	curses
	appropriate to		

It would be good to [her] out.

VIII.1

#236

	1	**2**	**3**	**4**		**5**	**6**	**7**
C	nî·	bá·	wa·	năŋ	knock	xá·w	dâ·j	dâ·n
	D	NG	say	anything		PRN	PST	stubborn
				NT			PRV	

	8	**9**	**10**	**11**	**12**	**13**	**14**	**15**
	xá·w	dâ·j	nân	páj	thə̂n	nì ?	man	bă·
	PRN	PRV	D	go	CMPLVE	PRT	PRN	NG
		PST						

MM	**16**	**17**	**18**
	pin	ká·n	ko·
	to be	a thing of	fear
		a work of	

(The old woman) didn't say anything. Knock. [The girl] was unteachable, (couldn't be taught). [She] just had no respect.

#237

	1	**2**	**3**	**4**	**5**	**6**	**7**	**8**
S	y·	bă·	kó·	sáŋ	hə̆n	lɛ̀	phá·j	wā·
	yeah	NG	fear	anything	PRT	PRT	who	says

	9	**10**	**11**	**12**		
	sáŋ	kɔ·	tỳk	mâ·w	ân	lɛ
	anything	CNJ	[stop	[only		]]
			stays as is			

Sure, [she] didn't respect anything. Whatever anyone says, [she] just stays as [she] is.

#237a

C	**1**	**2**	**3**	**4**	**5**	**6**	**7**	**8**
	bà·	tɛ̄n	jă·j	ni	jaŋ	hēd	cân	nân
	NG	in time	grow big	PRT	still	PRV	variety	D
		for						

9 **10**

[jă·j ma·] tho
[grow big] EXCLM

[If she] acts like that (when) [she's] still small, when she grows up, Buddha!

Begin series of simultaneous utterances

#238

M2 tho
EXCLM
Buddha!

VIII.1

#239a

Child kap faj ni
matches PRT

(Here are) the matches.

#239b

W [á·w sa·j] lɔ́·
[PRV] PRT

Put it down.

#239c

W2 [á·w săj] nî· ni
[PRV] DMNST PRT

Put it down here.

#240

W2 kam déw kɔ̆n ỹ tə
moment single first NG yet

Just a minute, not yet.

#241

M y· xá·w tyŋ bá· nân hɔ́ kam lɛ́·w
yeah PRN to the extent of NG D [PRT]

Yeah, they go as far as not [teaching her] at all.

 # 242

W	nî·	nε·	hɔ́mɛ́εn
	D	PRT	N

Here (you are) Hɔmεen.

 # 243

W2	má·j	ni·	bǎ·	ot	ka·
	silk	D	NG	durable	Q

This thread isn't strong, is it?

End series of simultaneous utterances.

Appendix C

PART 1. TRANSLATION OF STORY WHICH PRECEDES VIII. 1:187–241.

167 This thing, I say, is [worse] than [ignoring] parental words; [worse] than [ignoring] the old people's words, what the elders say who saw the sun before him, the old people of those days. Nowadays [our] knowledge, cleverness, intelligence—who do we learn it from? [We] don't learn from [our] fathers or [our] mothers, do [we]? Money and cash, how many hundreds and thousands do [we] spend? It's ten thousand, more than ten thousand, in order to (learn to) understand English, European of any kind, of all sorts—in order to be able to know them.
169 [Young people think that] if (one) doesn't have the money circulate again, (he) can't become a teacher, a policeman, a soldier, any kind [of official]. And if [the young people nowadays] come to their village, come to their home and see their parents speaking the old way (i.e., Lue), [they think,"] ridiculous these old people, it's no use, speaking with those old fashioned words![",]
172 Like this: ["]How can [you] get by?[", says the young man."]What do you mean, how can [I] get by, boy? I plow my fields, and the fields are big to the extent of over ten *rai*.[", the old man answers.]
174 [I] plowed to raise my children to be big enough and tall enough already. [You] are big enough, everything enough already. [But] now, nowadays [you] use a tractor and in just a minute 'brrrrrrr' it's done.["]
177 In the time of the old people, (they) did it little by little, hurting their hands, plowing, hurting (their) hands, (working as) everyone's slave. Hurting (their) hands little by little, a little at a time, a little at a time, [Comfortable in believing that] someday it would be finished.
178* [For them,] enough to eat [was sufficient], wasn't it?
179 Yes, enough to eat. Nowadays they consider only speed, wanting to go like a jet. Go zoom, go zoom, come zoom, come back zoom—like that.
182 [They] don't just want a bicycle, don't just want to ride a bicycle, isn't that so? [They want first] a Honda, a Honda, and then (demand) an 850 cc. Suzuki.
184 In addition.
185* [They] only want to use fast things, right?
186 Yeah, [they] consider only speed.
186a* Yeah.

PART 2. TRANSLATION OF STORY FOLLOWING VIII. 1:187–241.

244 Kɛw's fields still weren't finished. [No one helped one another.] Everyone just ran off [and the head of the household cursed them saying, "] mother cunt![""]
246 If [they] hired a servant to cook for them, [they] might be afraid that (she) would poison them.

* Utterance spoken by an individual other than C.

248 [Children whom no one has corrected] are dogs that bite heads (i.e., ingrates who return evil for good).
249* Yes, they do whatever they want to do, nowadays. They ignore what their parents say. (They) don't want to listen to anybody at all.
249a Yeah, (they) don't listen at all.
253 When they ask (their) parents for money and aren't given it [because the parents really don't have any [they] complain, saying, "[They] didn't give (us) any money."
254* Yeah.
255 [And if] they get money, (they) just disappear [with it].
256 [They] really use up a lot [of money].
257 [They] eat it up without ever feeling full. [They] don't ever let (their) mouths or throats miss (anything). (It's just) not normal.
258a Where can [so much] money come from [for them to spend it like that]?

REFERENCES

AUSTIN, JOHN LANGSHAW, "A plea for excuses," in *Philosophical papers* (Oxford: Clarendon Press). 1961.

BOHANNAN, PAUL, *Social Anthropology* (New York: Holt, Rinehart & Winston). 1963.

BURKE, KENNETH, *Permanence and change: an anatomy of purpose* (New York: New Republic). 1936.

COLBY, R. N., "Ethnographic semantics: a preliminary survey," *Current Anthropology*, 7: 3–32. 1966.

FOWLER, CATHERINE S., *and* JOY LELAND, "Some northern Paiute native categories," *Ethnology*, 6: 381–404. 1967.

GEERTZ, CLIFFORD, *The religion of Java* (The Free Press of Glencoe (paperback edition)). 1960.

GOODENOUGH, WARD H., "Residence rules," *Southwestern Journal of Anthropology*, 12: 22–37. 1956.

"Cultural anthropology and linguistics," Georgetown University Monograph Series on Language and Linguistics, no. 9, Paul Garvin, ed. (Washington). Repr. in *Language in culture and society*, Dell Hymes, ed. (New York: Harper and Row). 1957.

HYMES, DELL, "On communicative competence," in *Research planning conference on language development in disadvantaged children* (New York: Yeshiva University). 1966.

KATZ, JERROLD R., *and* JERRY A. FODOR, "The structure of a semantic theory," in *The structure of language*, Jerry A. Fodor and Jerrold J. Katz, eds. (Englewood Cliffs, New Jersey: Prentice-Hall). 1964.

LEACH, EDMUND R. Political systems of highland Burma. Boston: Beacon Press. 1965.

MOERMAN, MICHAEL, "Ethnic identification in a complex civilization: who are the Lue?" *American Anthropologist*, 6: 1215–30. Reprint 214 of the Institute of International Studies, University of California, Berkeley. 1965.

"Reply to Narroll," *American Anthropologist*, 69: 512–13. 1967.

*Utterance spoken by an individual other than C.

"Being Lue: uses and abuses of ethnic identification," American Ethnological Society, *Proceedings* of 1967 Spring Meeting, pp. 153–69. Reprinted as #275, Southeast Asia Series, Institute of International Studies, University of California, Berkeley. 1968a.

Agricultural change and peasant choice in a Thai village (University of California Press). 1968b.

In press: "A little knowledge," in *Cognitive anthropology*, Stephen A. Tyler, ed. (New York: Holt, Rinehart, & Winston).

POLLNER, MELVIN, *and* DON H. ZIMMERMAN, "Making sense of making sense: explorations of members' methods for sustaining a sense of social order. Unpublished manuscript. 1967.

POWDERMAKER, HORTENSE, *After Freedom* (New York: The Viking Press). 1939.

SACKS, HARVEY, Unpublished lectures. 1966–67.

SCHEGLOFF, EMANUEL A., "The first five seconds: the order of conversational openings," unpublished Ph.D. dissertation (in sociology) (University of California, Berkeley).

SHUTZ, ALFRED, "Collected papers II: studies in social theory" (The Hague: Martinue Nijhoff). 1964.

STURTEVANT, WILLIAM C., "Studies in ethnoscience," in *Transcultural studies in cognition*, A. Kimball Romney and Roy Goodwin D'Andrade, eds. *American Anthropologist*, Vol. 66, No. 3, Part 2. 1964.

SUDNOW, DAVID, "Normal crimes: sociological features of the penal code in a public defender office," *Social Problems*, 12: 255–76. 1965.

"Passing on: the social organization of dying" (Englewood Cliffs, New Jersey: Prentice Hall). 1967.

TURNER, V. W., *Schism and continuity in an African society* (Manchester University Press). 1957.

WIJEYEWARDENE, GEHAN. "Address, abuse and animal categories in northern Thailand," *Man*, n.s. 3: 76–93. 1968.

AARON V. CICOUREL

Basic and Normative Rules in the Negotiation of Status and Role

INTRODUCTION

It is commonplace in sociology for writers to acknowledge the ultimate importance of the interacting situation between two or more actors. The assumed relationship between structure and process, however, often is no more than an expression of faith rather than the integration of social process with social structure (or role theory with institutional theory). The present essay seeks to modify and build upon some recent literature by re-examining the utility and meaning of current conceptions of "status," "role," "norm," and "social interaction," to suggest a more explicit foundation for integrating social

(*Notes to this selection will be found on pp. 441–442.*)

process with the structural or institutionalized features of everyday life.

Goode suggests that "when the social analyst refers to a social position which is definitely institutionalized, (e.g. mother, physician), he is more likely to use the term 'status.' By contrast, he is more likely to use the term 'role' when referring to a social relation which is *less* institutionalized (e.g. peer relations in play groups)." Thus, statuses are defined "*as the class of roles which is institutionalized*," and this leads to the suggestion that "the analysis of social change must treat of the processes by which roles do become institutionalized—that is, become statuses."[1]

In this essay I argue that any reference to the actor's perspective must cover both the researcher's and the actor's attempts to negotiate field work and everyday activities, and not become an abstract label removed from the work necessary for recognizing and organizing socially acceptable behavior we label the social structures. Thus, the researcher's model of the actor must rest on interpretive procedures common to both the actor's and observer's methods for evaluating and generating appropriate courses of action. Goode's formulation and the many papers on the subject do not clarify the following distinctions:

1. Terms like "status" and "role" are convenient for the observer as a kind of an intellectual shorthand for describing complex arrangements and activities in social life, but of limited utility for specifying how the actor or observer negotiates everyday behavior. Such terms seem to provide only a general *orientation* for describing behavior and, as Goode notes, "no line of theory has been developed from the distinction."[2] The usual imagery associates "status" with wider community relationships like kinship and occupational structure, and the assumption is that more stability is implied than when the term "role" is used to speak of behavioral expectations.

2. Can we say that individual actors employ such terms in defining social situations for themselves and others? How does the actor in everyday life order and assign meanings to objects and events in his environment? The point is whether the social analyst is using the terms as a convenient shorthand to describe what he thinks is the actor's perspective or whether the actor's vocabulary includes the same terms and meanings or their equivalents as those of the observer.

3. When the researcher seeks to analyze written documents, he must decide on the level of abstraction of the materials so as to know the extent to which they are "coded" by the writer and the extent to which they represent verbatim or edited versions of observed activities, imputations, and implied or explicit inferences by the writer or others. Here the researcher must reconstruct the context of interaction and its "status-role" components. Such reconstruction is dependent, however, upon some solution to the following points.

4. When interviewing or participating within some group or com-

munity, the social analyst must decide on the relevance of the vocabulary he uses for asking questions and the language used by the actor for responding. The empirical question here is how do observer and actor interpret each other's verbal and nonverbal behavior and the context-restricted setting?

5. When the researcher seeks to establish contacts for field research in his own or some foreign country, how does he acquire, and to what extent does he employ, specifiable notions of "status" and "role" in carrying out his field work? What conceptions does he impute to respondents? Does he decide their "statuses" and "roles" as a condition to developing strategies of entering, maintaining and terminating (perhaps temporarily) his relationships with informants? Does he employ different conceptions with those who "run interference" in contacting respondents and informants, as opposed to subjects with whom he conducts actual interviewing or participant observation? Does he (and if "yes" how does he) distinguish between vocabularies he uses for "maximum" communication with others of different "status" in field research, and are such vocabularies different from the language of social research used to communicate theoretical and empirical findings and conclusions to colleagues?

The general question is, how do respondents and observer-researchers conduct themselves during social interaction with various types of "others," and whether or not such conduct is governed by conceptions congruent with terms like "status" and "role"? The terms as currently defined do not allow for explicit shifts between the social analyst's concepts of social organization as used in published communication with his colleagues, the social analyst's common sense conceptions used for managing his own affairs, the observer-researcher's tacit working conceptions when engaged in participation and observation in field studies, and the researcher's model of how the actor's common sense perspective is used for understanding and taking action in some environment of objects.

Anyone engaged in field research will find that the shorthand vocabulary of social science is very similar to the general norms stated in some penal code: they do not correspond to explicit sequences of events and social meanings, but the fit is "managed" through negotiated socially organized activities of the police, prosecution, witnesses, the judge, and the suspect or defendant.[3] It is not clear that terms like "status" and "role" are relevant categories for the actors nor relevant for the observer's understanding of the action scene he seeks to describe.

STATUS AS STRUCTURE AND PROCESS

Goode notes that even interaction between strangers involves some minimum normative expectations, and hence some kind of social organization is presumed by participants ignorant of their "actual" statuses and roles. Thus, some set of minimal "boundary conditions" informs our actors of each other even if their imputations are seen as mistaken during subsequent reflection. The basis for social interaction among strangers, therefore, is presumably those properties attached to the most institutionalized activities of everyday life. Thus, "whether a given relationship can be characterized as a status *is a matter of degree. Statuses are, then, the role relationships which are more fully institutionalized* or which contain a greater number of institutionalized elements."[4]

What emerges, then, is that status relationships are based upon norms (external to immediate interaction) that have a broad consensus by "third parties" in ego and alter's social networks or some larger community. This suggests that the more spontaneous or intimate the relationship, and hence the interaction, the less "institutionalized" the behavior of each. Thus, strangers will respond to more impersonal or "safe" definitions of the situation in interacting with one another. Close friends would be more likely to innovate before each other during social interaction, or they would be less constrained by "third parties." In order for individual actors to innovate as "loners" they would presumably reject the social network of "third parties" or the community. By way of analogy we can refer to G. H. Mead's distinction between the "I" and the "me" or "generalized other" and make the obvious link here between the impulsive features of the "I" or the less institutionalized features of the role. On the other hand, we have the reflective, community-at-large, reference group connotation of the "me," and its links to norms viewed as commonly accepted in some group or community sense, or backed by "third parties."[5]

The general problem is that we know very little about how persons establish "statuses" and "roles" in everyday social interaction. Initial social encounters are based upon "appearance factors" and/or general "background" information. The initial encounter may lead to an acceptance of individuals qua individuals before or in the process of exchanging information about membership in "legitimate" or "acceptable" status slots. Empirically, we must know how introductions and identifications are accomplished, the ways in which actors employ sequencing rules to order their exchanges, infer and establish relevant "facts," over the course of interaction.[6]

The presumed conformity or nonconformity of actors to norms raises the question of how does the actor decide what "norms" are operative or relevant, and how does some group or "community" (or its representatives) decide that actors are "deviant" and should or should not be punished or sanctioned negatively? The following quotation illustrates one set of difficulties when seeking conceptual clarification and empirical evidence on conformity and deviance:

> When the individual's norms and goals are in accord with those of the group, his behavior will meet approval. However, if the individual finds

> that his behavior deviates from the group norms, he has four choices: to conform, to change the norms, to remain a deviant, or to leave the group. Of course, he may also be removed from the group without his consent.[7]

The statement by Hare provides us with a set of abstract concepts based upon small group research which does not allow for the negotiated and constructed character of interpersonal exchanges in daily life. In a laboratory setting we can easily lay down some general and specific rules governing play in some game or simple task. But even here there is negotiation *vis-à-vis* rules or instructions, and this latter environment of objects cannot be tied easily to notions like status, role, and norms, employed by actors in less structured or controlled everyday situations.[8] Establishing "norms and goals for the actor," much less for some group or wider community, is not exactly obvious theoretically, nor procedurally clear methodologically. The fit between abstract community and legal categories of deviance and reported or observed behavior is an exceptionally difficult one to describe with any accuracy, and its empirical status remains only partially clarified.[9]

References to conformity and nonconformity are not clear because social scientists have not made explicit what they mean by normative and non-normative conditions, and role and non-role behavior. Presumably, the various statuses that one occupies cover a wide range of identifying characteristics and conduct, most of which would be subsumed under "status" categories like "male," "female," "student," "father," "husband," "mother," etc. "Non-role" behavior might then refer to scratching one's head, picking one's nose, "some" laughing or crying (assuming there are no imputations about a "sick" role), etc. But when would walking "too fast" or laughing "too loud" or smiling "too often" or dressing in "poor taste" be considered as a "normal" feature of some set of "statuses" and corresponding "roles" taken singly or in some combination, as opposed to the generation of imputations that suggest or demand that the actor be viewed as "sick" or "criminal," and so forth? The sociologist's model of actor competence and performance remains implicit and does not address how the actor perceives and interprets his environment, how certain rules govern exchanges, and how the actor recognizes what is taken to be "strange," "familiar," "acceptable," etc., about someone so as to link these attributes with a preconceived notion of status or role.

Goode suggests alternatives when he states:

> If "role" includes only that part of behavior which is an *enactment* of status obligations ("idea"), then there is little point in studying role behavior. In his role behavior the actor cannot face any moral problem, and there can be no deviation from the norm; else by definition there is no role behavior. Necessarily, all the important data on roles would then be contained in a description of statuses. The alternative interpretation is also open—that the actor *can* face a moral problem, whether to enact the status demands, (i.e.,

> role behavior) or not. Then the study of role behavior versus non-role behavior would be a study of conformity versus non-conformity. However, this interpretation is not followed by Linton or, to my knowledge, by anyone else.[10]

The issue is one of specifying those sectors of the actor's actions the social scientist wishes to "explain" or leave untouched by terms like "status," "role," and "norms." Statements to the effect that "statuses" are "roles" that are "institutionalized" do not indicate how the observer decides that the actors are able to recognize or make evaluations about "appropriate" status obligations and then act on them in some way, or that the actors engage in procedures which can be interpreted as evaluations of action scenes in ways that are "more" or "less" institutionalized.

I want to underscore the necessity of linking the strategies of interaction among actors, with the structural framework employed by the social analyst. The observer must make abstractions from complex sequences of social interaction. How does he decide the role-status-norm relevance of the exchanges about which he observes or interviews? To what extent must he take the actor's typifications, stock of knowledge at hand, presumed appearance to others, conception of self, strategies of self-presentation, language, and the like into account in deciding the institutionalized character of status relationships, role relationships, and the normatively based expectations employed or imputed?

Some examples may help illustrate the conceptual complexity here. In a large university a new faculty member who arrives to assume his new duties has already been told what classes he is to teach and may be shown his office by a secretary who addresses him as "Mr." or "Dr." He may have met the other members of the department during an interview some months earlier. His initial contacts with other members of the department may occur in the hallways or at some party given by the chairman early in the fall semester. He is faced with a number of status dilemmas because of how his colleagues introduce themselves or the way he introduces himself to them. Do they (or he) use first names, last names, formal titles, or "Mr." or do they call out their full name and refrain from calling him by his name when calling on the telephone or receiving a call? If at the chairman's party he is introduced as "Mr." is it because of an initial superficial formality or because he has yet to terminate his degree? How does he address the secretary, answer the phone, and sign his mail? The interaction sequences with non-academic personnel, administration officials, colleagues inside and outside of his department, constitute encounters which may be quite fragile for our new instructor. His imputations as to "what is going on" and how should he explain his relationships within the university may also depend upon age differences, whether he has a regular appointment or temporary one, how his colleagues and others address and speak to him, and how his wife (if married) might react to her (perhaps sudden) elevation to "faculty status" even though she may have recently completed her undergraduate work. The young instructor will probably encounter the same type of difficulties with his new neighbors. Does he introduce himself as "Joe" or "Dr." or "Professor" or "Mr.?" What if his wife engages in first name introductions and he with more formal usages independently? How or when does his occupational status enter the neighborhood scene?

The ways in which our young instructor "presents" himself will convey different connotations to different "others" depending on his physical appearance, clothing, language, etc., and more importantly, how his occupational status is revealed and when it is revealed after or during the initial encounter. But in what sense are the "old hands" now looking at our new instructor as someone fulfilling or not fulfilling the "rights and duties" of his new status? What evidence do they have about his teaching and research or contacts with students? How do they observe his conduct in their presence as "adequate" or "inadequate" "role" behavior? Who is keeping score and how?

In his new status as professor, therefore, our colleague must generate "adequate" performances commensurate with his position, through a continued sequence of encounters and exchanges with others, despite having been officially granted his degree. New acquaintances may accept and impute considerable importance to him, but he must somehow "carry it off," and often without any explicit "norms" or "rules" to go by. We obviously do not hand our new instructor a "script" outlining his "role" in detail. Use of terms like "anticipatory socialization" or "on-the-job-training" add little more to our understanding of actual encounters, for research on such matters is missing or weak.

Successive encounters may not "achieve" the status expected by others in that those with whom he shares formal status-equality in the institutionalized sense of "college professor" may invoke extra academic criteria that we loosely call "personality factors" in everyday life, while others may invoke publication or conversational ("is he bright?") criteria in "granting" or withholding the treatment they give to instructors who "come on" and "do well." The fragility or precariousness of our new colleague's status as seen by him and by others cannot be ascertained without reference to the interactional sequences of everyday life where our young instructor must "bring it off."

The social analyst who goes to a foreign country (or does research in his own) encounters similar problems. Explaining yourself as a "professor of sociology" in your own country in order to gain access to a police department for a study of juvenile justice can be a difficult problem. In another country the problem can be compounded by many additional elements.[11] For example, making the necessary field contacts may be the most difficult part of the study. How does the field researcher go about doing it? Can he pass himself off as simply an "American professor" of anthropology, sociology or political science? Obviously, "it depends." Some groups really might not care what his credentials are, but only want to know if he is some equivalent of a "good guy," a "nice guy," or a "right guy"—that is, trustworthy in their eyes. For others, his official credentials might be invaluable and some nice letters of introduction with large gold seals affixed even impressive to many. If our researcher is based at a foreign university, problems always revolve around how "official status" is handled or managed in subsequent interaction with foreign colleagues who work within quite a different university atmosphere, where students are a powerful and vocal group, and most professors earn their living by "moonlighting." Dealing with big-city bureaucrats and village functionaries may require quite a different set of strategies for gaining information or further access. Finally, interviews and/or participant observation with informants and subjects at work or at home may require further strategies and/or modifications of earlier procedures. The general problem of how we can establish, maintain and successfully terminate our contacts in field settings cannot be resolved with existing social science role theory, although there are many works that are very informative about how people manage their presence before others.

Social scientists working in their own country take for granted their own vocabulary and common sense or implicit conceptions of others, places, and things, and also take for granted the vocabulary and implicit conceptions of the people they study. In another country, working in a village or a large city, the social analyst becomes painfully aware of the inadequacy of social science status and role concepts in guiding his own research and the necessity of negotiating his own status and role behavior *vis-à-vis* informants or respondents. There is no adequate theory of social process by which to guide his establishment of contacts, informants, subjects, and simultaneously inform him of strange patterns of bureaucratic life in foreign areas. Each researcher must decide these matters for himself. There is, therefore, the inevitable problem of sorting out (and perhaps coding) large quantities of information and ambiguously subsuming such material under commonly used and accepted concepts like "status," "role," "norm," "values," etc. The *grounds* for deciding the "appropriate" recognition and what is an adequate description of different "statuses," "roles," and "norms" are seldom discussed.

Conceptions of Status. The notion of status as a structural feature of social order leads to formal definitions and some abstract examples, but seldom point to interactional consequences. References to the literature usually begin with Linton's definition: "A status, as distinct from the individual who may occupy it, is simply a collection of rights and duties. Since these rights and duties can find expression only through the medium of individuals, it is extremely hard for us to maintain a distinction in our thinking between statuses and the people who hold them and exercise the rights and duties which constitute them."[12] Linton's definition presupposes consensus as to the meaning of "rights and duties," and he does not make the observer's and actor's indicators for recognizing status an integral part of the concept. Even if we could agree on formal positions within the table of organization of some kinship system or firm, the empirical evidence is not plentiful and does not make problematic variations in how individuals perceive and interpret formal statuses. The fact that we must always observe individuals and/or obtain reports about them from others or these same individuals means that we are always confronted with the problem of knowing how to evaluate what we observe, how we ask questions, and what to infer from the answers.

Kingsley Davis' work is another well-known source on the meaning of "status."

> A person therefore enters a social situation with an identity already established. His identity refers to his *position*, or *status*, within the social structure applicable to the given situation, and establishes his rights and obligations with reference to others holding positions within the same structure. His position and consequently his identity in the particular situation result from all the other positions he holds in other major social structures, especially in the other structures most closely related to the one he is acting in at the moment.
>
> To aid in establishing the identity of the person, external symbols are frequently utilized. A common indicator, for example, is the style of dress. . . .
>
> In the course of an individual's life very broad positions are first acquired . . . as he goes through life he acquires more specific positions, and his actual behavior in the various situations to which these positions apply serves to refine and modify the initially assigned identity. . . .
>
> The normative system lays down the formal rights and obligations in connection with a position. Though it permits a certain amount of legitimate variation within the limits imposed, it also lays down rules to be followed in case the individual oversteps the limits. A right is a legitimate expectation entertained by a person in one position with respect to the behavior of a person in another position. From the point of view of the other person this claim represents an obligation. . . .
>
> An individual carries his social position around in his head, so to speak, and puts it into action when the appropriate occasion arises. Not only does he carry it in his head but others also carry it in theirs, because social positions are matters of reciprocal expectation and must be publicly and commonly conceived by everyone in the group. . . . The term status would then designate a position in the general institutional system, recognized and supported by the entire society, spontaneously evolved rather than

> deliberately created, rooted in the folkways and mores. Office, on the other hand, would designate a position in a deliberately created organization, governed by specific and limited rules in a limited group, more generally achieved than ascribed.[13]

Davis' comments presume information carried "in the head," some unstated principles for recognizing when "appropriate" action is necessary and suggest the importance of changes over time and situated action. His remarks refer to specific and vague attributes associated with the concept "status." On the "specific" side persons enter situations with readily recognized "identities" and "rights and obligations." Further, actors acknowledge the "rights and obligations" and are supported by the "normative system." Finally, "statuses" are spontaneously evolved and recognized and supported by the entire society, while "offices" are more explicitly known in deliberately created organizations. The "vague" elements include the fact that over time the actor's status may well be refined, broadened, and modified in unspecified ways. The norms governing behavior may vary with the actor's status and situations he encounters. Finally, since actors "carry" social positions around in their "heads," each interaction scene presumably is a potentially problematic state of affairs. The dialectic between what appears as "obvious" and structurally or institutionally invariant and that which depends upon the actor's perception and interpretation-implementation of his status or statuses is stressed as important by Davis, but not conceptually clear. It is necessary to show how the "vague" features that unfold and become concretized over the course of interaction, alter, maintain, or distort the "specific" or "institutionalized" features of "status." The interesting question is, how do we "integrate" the apparent discrepancy between the processes necessary to understand the structure, and whether the structure is in fact an invariant set of conditions for "explaining" or "knowing" the significance of the processes. Or, does the process re-create the structure continuously during the course of interaction? A necessary complex set of properties for understanding status and its behavioral components requires a model of the actor that includes how "external symbols" and appropriate rules are recognized as relevant to the actor and interpreted by him over the course of interaction. Cognitive procedures (in the head) and a theory of social meaning are presupposed when the terms "status" and "role" are used. But our model of the actor refers both to the researcher as observer and actor as participant.

Parsons' usage of "status" refers to role-expectations.

> Role-expectations, on the other hand, are the definitions by *both* ego and alter of what behavior is proper for each in the relationship and in the situation in question. . . . Sanctions are the "appropriate" behavioral

> consequences of alter's role-expectations in response to the actual behavior of ego.
>
> Both role-expectations and sanctions may be institutionalized to a greater or lesser degree. They are institutionalized when they are integrated with or "express" value-orientations *common* to the members of the collectivity to which both ego and alter belong, which in the limiting case may consist only of ego and alter.[14]

Parsons' position in *The Social System* is similar to that of Linton, though he refers to the "status-role bundle."[15] Parsons' formulation includes the actor in some interaction scene, but the observer and actor appear to be locked in the same social arena in unknown ways, and it is difficult to know how the observer or actors perceive "proper" "role-expectations," how the observer decides on the "fit" between ego and alter's perspectives, and what ego and alter and the observer take into account that is based upon the "institutionalized" features of the interaction. Thus, in focusing upon the interactional context for structural properties of social order, Parsons directs our attention to "common" value orientations. But this apparent conceptual "answer" avoids the crucial questions of what passes as "common" and how our actors decide on their own or some collectivity's "common" value-orientations; how consistent are actors in honoring or excepting such orientations if we assume they exist; and how would varying degrees of institutionalization refer to value-orientations "more" or "less" common to a group? Explicit cognitive procedures and a theory of meaning are absent from Parsons' formulation.

According to Homans, "A man's status in a group is a matter of the stimuli his behavior toward others and others' behavior toward him—including the esteem they give him—present both to the others and to himself, stimuli that may come to make a difference in determining the future behavior of all concerned."[16] The "stimulus" view presented by Homans is rather general and apparently everything depends upon the actors' interpretation of implicit stimuli. But later Homans clarifies his position as follows:

> In their private speculations, some sociologists were once inclined to think of the small informal group as a microcosm of society at large: they felt that the same phenomena appeared in the former as in the latter but on a vastly reduced scale—a scale that, incidentally, made detailed investigation possible. . . . But to say that the two phenomena have points in common is not to say that one is a microcosm of the other, that the one is simply the other writ small. The two are not alike if only because in an informal group a man wins status through his direct exchange with the other members, while he gets status in the larger society by inheritance, wealth, occupation, office, legal authority—in every case by his position in some institutional scheme, often one with a long history behind it.[17]

While the stimuli, to use Homans' term, that are available to actors in face-to-face exchanges are usually quite different from stimuli available through indirect means such as the mass-media, a biography or *Who's Who* interpretation of the stimuli according to typified conceptions occurs in both cases. It is not clear how the actor utilizes "external symbols" (including structural information about occupation, age, wealth) when engaged in direct exchanges with others. Nor does Homans clarify how the actor infers "what is going on" over the course of interaction. A model of the actor that presupposes inductive procedures and a theory of meaning is also evident in Homans, but such notions remain implicit features of his discussion.

Work by Blau contains an elaborate analysis of social process, more realistically rooted in empirical studies, but it also suffers from implicit references to the actor's use of inductive procedures and a theory of meaning when engaged in social exchanges. Blau, like the others cited above, does not disentangle the observer's interpretations (requiring inductive procedures and a theory of meaning) from those of the actor, preferring to tell the reader about social life through the eyes of a detached observer armed with many complex abstract notions that subsume a rather impressive range of activities. Thus, his central notion "of social exchange directs attention to the emergent properties in interpersonal relations and social interaction. A person for whom another has done a service is expected to express his gratitude and return a service when the occasion arises. Failure to express his appreciation and to reciprocate tends to stamp him as an ungrateful man who does not deserve to be helped."[18] Precisely how actors recognize appropriate services and establish rates of exchange, how the observer and actor assess their significance, and decide their "normal" management are not explicit features of Blau's framework.

Basic concepts of social interaction that presuppose tacit notions of induction and meaning are not discussed at their own level, but taken for granted as "obvious" and meaningful. Consider the following:

> The internal differentiation of status and the associated distribution of rewards in substructures may be based on standards that are, from the perspective of the encompassing social structure, universalistic or particularistic, although these standards are, by definition, universalistic within the narrower compass of each substructure, that is, they are generally accepted criteria of achievement *within the subgroup.* If internal status in substructures is governed by standards universally accepted as valid throughout the macrostructure, as is typical for criteria of instrumental performance, superior internal status indicates assets that are valued in other collectivities too. . . . If, however, internal status in substructures rests on diverse standards that are particularistic from the perspective of the macrostructure, the higher a person's status is in one collectivity, the less likely are his

qualifications to make him acceptable in another with different value standards.[19]

Blau's remarks seek to integrate social process with social structure, but he begins and ends with propositions considerably removed from theoretical and empirical clarification of the elements of process as seen by both the actor and social analyst. His theorizing does not specify how actor and researcher learn, recognize, and use standards as universalistic or particularistic, nor the kind of interpretive procedures the actor must possess to carry out social exchanges that enable him to recognize what standards are appropriate for particular social settings.

Goffman's work brings us closer to the kinds of events in everyday life from which social analysts make inferences about process and structure. Goffman's descriptions also convey the idea of a fully informed third party who has intimate knowledge of social exchanges. There are times when the reader feels Goffman has perhaps observed or experienced (from the "inside") some of our more delicate and/or embarrassing encounters in daily life. While he fails to clarify whose point of view, and by what procedures, the observer is to infer the details of everyday life social encounters, Goffman gives the reader a very convincing impression of being on the spot and "knowing" what takes place from the perspective of an "insider." Implementing Goffman's perspective is difficult because (1) Goffman's assumptions about the conditions of social encounters are substantively appealing but lack explicit analytic categories delineating how the actor's perspective differs from that of the observer, and how both can be placed within the same conceptual frame; and (2) all of Goffman's descriptive statements are prematurely coded—that is, interpreted by the observer, infused with substance that must be taken for granted, and subsumed under abstract categories without telling the reader how all of this was recognized and accomplished. Consider the following:

> When an individual enters the presence of others, they commonly seek to acquire information about him or to bring into play information about him already possessed. They will be interested in his general socio-economic status, his conception of self, his attitude toward them, his competence, his trustworthiness, etc.[20]

How the actor acquires information (the interpretation of external symbols, the use of language categories) or utilizes information already possessed so as to link the presumed knowledge "appropriately" to a particular setting, requires explicit reference to inference procedures and a theory of how the actor assigns meaning to objects and events. But Goffman's model of the actor does not reveal how the actor (or observer as actor) negotiates actual scenes, except through the eyes of an ideally situated and perceptive "third party." The wider community relevance of the notion of "status" is provided in the following quotation:

> Society is organized on the principle that any individual who possesses certain social characteristics has a moral right to expect that others will value and treat him in a correspondingly appropriate way. . . . In consequence, when an individual projects a definition of the situation and thereby makes an implicit or explicit claim to be a person of a particular kind, he automatically exerts a moral demand upon the others, obliging them to value and treat him in the manner that persons of his kind have a right to expect.[21]

Goffman's implicit reference to status as process alludes to many possible (but unexplicated) rules the actor might use, provides a vivid glimpse of the action scene itself, and how the interacting participants might treat each other in "more" or "less" institutionalized ways. But the idea of projecting a definition of the situation and hence a claim to being a certain type of person demands rules that both actor and observer follow in generating behavioral displays, and assigning the meanings to which Goffman endows the action scene.

ROLE AS PROCESS

The idea of "role" as the dynamic aspect of "status" or the "less" institutionalized class of statuses implies a problematic or innovational element in behavior. The problematical elements of "role" are underscored by Goffman and exemplified in his remark that "Life may not be much of a gamble, but interaction is."[22] A notion like "status" provides us with an ideal normative label for understanding how both actor and observer subsume initial impressions based on appearances and verbal identifications and introductions to establish some preliminary basis for mutual evaluation. At the level of interaction, actors are constrained by the possible formality of ritualized introductions, whereby the communicants (or some third party) provide verbal material to support or detract from the appearance.[23] I am suggesting that labels designating a range of features that we call "status" are used by observer and actor as practical language games for simplifying the task of summarizing a visual field and complex stimuli that are difficult to describe in some precise, detailed way.[24] This means that the labels do not recover the appearances and imputations subsumed by the participant unless imagined details are supplied by an auditor during the course of interaction. Whereas this elaboration by the actor—an elaboration not subject (by him) to verification—serves his practical interests, the scientific observer cannot afford to rely on the same tacit elaboration; his model of the actor must clarify how his observations are necessarily deficient. Films or video-tapes can provide access to the original source of observations and the possibility of improving the common sense observer's limitations. We are faced with the problem of deciding the actor's "logic-in-use" versus his reflections or "reconstructed logic" after he leaves the scene.[25] Even though Goffman provides rich "third party" descriptive accounts of the course of social exchanges, he does not tell us how the social analyst as observer and/or participant translates the "logic-in-use" of his field work into the "reconstructed logic" of his theorizing. The works of others cited above have also avoided this problem. Goffman, however, makes more of a frontal attack on the "notion" of "role-expectation" and the "definition of the situation."

> To summarize, then, I assume that when an individual appears before others he will have many motives for trying to control the impression they receive of the situation. This report is concerned with some of the common techniques that persons employ to sustain such impressions and with some of the common contingencies associated with the employment of these techniques.... I shall be concerned only with the participant's dramaturgical problems of presenting the activity before others.[26]

Goffman's remarks presume that the actor possesses well-developed procedures for coping with his environment, procedures employed by the actor when satisfying what the observer (with unstated procedures) loosely labels "role" behavior, if it stems from or is "oriented by" some set of more formalized imputations and claims about kinship relationships, positions in groups, communities, and work organizations. The perceptive remarks by Goffman extend conceptions of role generally found in the literature. The critical feature of role, as stressed by Goffman, among others, lies in its construction by the actor over the course of interaction. This construction makes status-emitting stimuli problematic for the actor because of situational constraints.

This notion of construction, despite a lack of conceptual clarity, can be seen in the following quotation from Mead.

> The generalized attitude of the percipient has arisen out of co-operative activities of individuals in which the individual by the gesture through which he excites the other has aroused in himself the attitude of the other, and addresses himself in the generalized attitude of the other, and addresses himself in the role of the other. Thus he comes to address himself in the generalized attitude of the group of persons occupied with a common undertaking. The generalization lies in such an organization of all the different co-operative acts as they appear in attitudes of the individual that he finds himself directing his acts by the corresponding acts of the others involved—by what may be called the rules of the game.[27]

Mead's remarks stress the problematic features of how two participants evoke a kind of cooperative exchange. Ralph H. Turner has stated the constructive elements of role behavior clearly in the following passages:

> Roles "exist" in varying degrees of concreteness and consistency, while the individual confidently frames his behavior as if they had unequivocal existence and clarity. The result is that in attempting from time to time to make aspects of the roles explicit he is creating and modifying roles as well as merely bringing them to light; the process is not only role-taking but *role-making*.
>
> The actor is not the occupant of a position for which there is a neat set of rules—a culture or set of norms—but a person who must act in the perspective supplied in part by his relationship to others whose actions reflect roles that he must identify. Since the role of alter can only be inferred rather than directly known by ego, testing inferences about the role of alter is a continuing element in interaction. Hence the tentative character of the individual's own role definition and performance is never wholly suspended.[28]

Turner's exposition of role behavior underscores the creative and modifying elements of role-taking and role-making. As noted in the earlier quote from Mead, the participants of an action scene emit stimuli that each must identify as relevant for taking (while perhaps modifying) the role of the other, or making (creating) the role. The role of each participant can only be inferred and never known directly, and the role behavior displayed is always tentative and being tested over the course of interaction.

But the model of the actor implied here lacks explicit statements about how the actor recognizes relevant stimuli and manages to orient himself (locate the stimuli in a socially meaningful context) to the behavioral displays so that an organized response can be generated that will be recognized as relevant to alter. The actor must be endowed with mechanisms or basic rules that permit him to identify settings that would lead to "appropriate" invocation of norms, where *the norms would be surface rules and not basic to how the actor makes inferences about taking or making roles.* The basic rules or interpretive procedures are like deep structure grammatical rules; they enable the actor to generate appropriate (usually innovative) responses in changing situated settings. The interpretive procedures enable the actor to sustain a *sense of social structure* over the course of changing social settings, while surface rules or norms provide a more general institutional or historical validity to the meaning of the action as it passes, in a reflective sense. To the Meadian dialectic of the "I" and the "me" is added the explicit requirement that the actor must be conceived as possessing induction (interpretive) procedures, procedures designed to function as a base structure for generating and comprehending the behavioral (verbal and nonverbal) displays that can be observed. An implicit base rule or interpretive procedure in Mead's theory would be the notion that participants in social exchanges must assume that their use of verbal and nonverbal signs or symbols are the "same," or this "sameness" (in an ideal sense) must at least be assumed to hold.[29]

The social analyst's use of abstract theoretical concepts likc role actually masks the inductive procedures or interpretive rules whereby the actor produces behavioral displays others and the observer label "role behavior." Without a model of the actor that specifies such procedures or rules, we cannot reveal how behavioral displays are recognized as "role-taking" or "role-making."

The extensive coverage of the research literature by Sarbin employs the following definitions of "status" (called "position" by Sarbin) and "role."

> In other words, a position is a cognitive organization of expectations, a shorthand term for a concept embracing expected actions of persons enacting specified roles. These expectations, organized as they are around roles, may justifiably be called role expectations. Thus, a position is a cognitive organization of role expectations. . . .
>
> A *role* is a patterned sequence of learned *actions* or deeds performed by a person in an interaction situation. The organizing of the individual actions is a product of the perceptual and cognitive behavior of person A upon observing person B.[30]

Sarbin's remarks stress the learned elements of "role" in everyday life, and refer to various studies which suggest the ambiguities of "roles" for different actors. But Sarbin leans on the short-hand concepts of sociologists and anthropologists, taking for granted the "positions" and "roles" in society that social scientists treat as "known" and "clear," but which do not specify the mechanisms or procedures or rules employed by the actor to recognize and attribute expectations to others. While Sarbin's discussion of "role" and "self" takes us beyond the focus of this paper, his remarks on the self changing over time, based upon experience, are important for underscoring the significance of actual "role-enactment" on "position" over time. But the construction of role behavior over the course of interaction would stress learning mechanisms that would be selective in scanning the visual field or behavioral displays, rather than simply learning actions the observer labels patterned sequences or roles. Memory would always be contingent upon procedures or rules that identify or recognize objects and events as socially meaningful.

In summarizing this section I want to stress two problems that preclude our present use of the concept role: (1) It is difficult to say what role taking and role enactment is all about if the "statuses" or "positions" to which they refer are not clarified (how they come to be recognized) from both the actor's perspective and that of the observer, and the problem may be confounded if "non-role" behavior (that is, not following from some recognized "status") as opposed to "role" behavior, is not clarified as a residual category, for such information could be a more important complex attribute in the evaluation of the actor's role behavior by others (including the observer); and (2) to what extent does our understanding of conduct subsumed under the label "role" depend upon a clarified analysis of the perception of "norms" inasmuch as many writers shift their structural argument about "status" as institutionalized to the idea of "role" as a set of implicit "norms?"

What we have failed to learn since the impact of Mead's work are the "rules of the game," how many "games" are there? and how do actors (and the observer) come to treat some sequence of events as a "game" or legitimate social activity? Presumably, the actor's perception and interpretation of an environment of objects is established and continually reestablished, in unknown specificity and vagueness, but according to some set of "standards," "rules," or "norms." A closer look at the concept "norm" is the next order of business.

NORMS AND THE PROBLEMATIC CHARACTER OF EVERYDAY LIFE

A major difficulty in analytically based accounts of "role" lies in "norms" or "rules" by which the actor is presumably oriented in perceiving and interpreting an environment of objects. The literature reveals continual reliance on some notion of "status" to suggest stable meanings about "position" *vis-à-vis* others in some network of social relationships. There is an implied consensus about the "rights and obligations" of actors occupying some commonly known and accepted "status." The variability attached to "role" (its innovative or "less institutionalized" character) appears to stem from the various actors who may come to occupy a given "status." The actor's differential perception and interpretation of "statuses" implies ambiguity for all participants.

The notion of "norms," including legal norms, is a variable element of social interaction. The common view is to characterize our theoretical conceptions of "norms" as stable features (with acknowledged differences between the mores and folkways) of society that evoke consensus in groups.

Norms are problematic to all interaction scenes because our reflective thoughts, as participants or observers, reify and reconstruct the "rules of the game." The analogy that fits here is that of Mead's distinction between the "I" and the "me." Although interaction is always a gamble for all concerned, we have managed to exempt that abstract entity called "society." The reflective "me" of the participants and observers (including the social analyst) imputes meanings and re-interprets perceptions and actions, after the social scene unfolds, but it is the "I" that is "leading the way" with potentially impulsive, innovative, spontaneous interpretations of the situation. Another way of characterizing the problem is to speak of role-taking as "logic-in-use" and status as "reconstructed logic." The rehearsal elements of role-taking involve "logic-in-use" because the actor is taking more than "internalized norms" or stored information into account, for it is the appearance, behavior and reactions of others in a particular setting that activates normative categories. The "reconstructed logic" comes into play after the interaction as a way of evaluating "what happened" and connecting it to others or some wider group or community. The particular action scene the actor must attend requires that he locate emergent (constructed) meanings within the wider context of general rules or policies.[31] The general rules or policies are norms whose meaning in emergent (constructed) action scenes must be negotiated by the actor.

Statuses, like general rules or policies, require recognition and interpretation when interacting participants must elicit and search appearances for relevant information about each other. Role taking and role making require that the actor articulate general rules or policies (norms) with an emergent (constructed) action scene in order to find the meaning of one's own behavior or that of some other.

With our present conceptions of status, role, and norms we would be hard-pressed to explain role behavior by simulation techniques. We would fare better consulting theatrical directors. Suppose that the government printing office began publishing manuals, prepared by the U. S. Office of Education, and based upon the "expert" advice of social scientists, that purport to contain detailed descriptions of all the important "statuses" of the society, complete with "role variability" permitted regionally, nationally, and qualified for such categories as "nuclear family," "extended family," "close friends," "casual friends," "acquaintances but not friends," "strangers," "foreigners," and "children up to pre-teens." Presume that the "norms" or "rules" governing interaction are described for each "status" and "role," and the various settings in which variation is permitted. Suppose that another manual outlines "role-playing procedures" beginning with children who can speak, and covering all adult possibilities, including "old age." Assume that grants to adult education centers and school systems by the government provide an organizational basis for implementing the program.

The obvious point to our example of writing simulation manuals is that the human organism must possess basic rules or interpretive procedures that emerge developmentally and continue to provide innovations late in the life cycle. The dramaturgical metaphor of the stage is defective in explaining how actors are capable of imitation and *innovation* with little or no prior rehearsal, just as a child is capable of producing grammatically correct utterances that he has never heard, and capable of understanding utterances that have never been heard before. Terms like "attitudes," "values," "need dispositions," "drives," "expectancies" are inadequate because there is no explicit attempt to formulate basic rules the actor must learn to negotiate novel experiences as well as be able to construct constancy in his environment. The language and meaning acquisition principles that would permit basic rules to emerge must allow for the operation of memory and selection procedures that are consistent with pattern recognition or construction, active (searching for documentary evidences) and passive (taking the environment for granted, until further notice, as "obvious" or "clear") hypothesis testing, and be congruent with the actor's ability to recognize and generate novel and "identical" or "similar" behavioral displays.[32]

The distinction between basic rules and norms is tied to the difference between consensus or shared agreement, and a sense of social structure. Basic or interpretive rules provide the actor with a developmentally changing sense of social structure that enables him to assign meaning or relevance to an environment of objects. Normative or surface rules enable the actor to link his view of the world to that of others in concerted social action, and to presume that consensus or shared agreement governs interaction. The shared agreement would include consensus about the existence of conflict or differences in normative rules. The following two quotations from Goode and Shibutani reveal the negotiated or constructed character of consensus or shared agreement that exists in normative behavior:

> Perhaps the social structure is under no threat under modern conditions of apparently weak consensus if the conformity to which ego is pressed is merely of a "general" nature, that is, the norms permit a wide range of rough approximations to the ideal. But whether norms in fact are general is not easy to determine. Which is in fact "the" norm? You should not lie (only a loose conformity is demanded); or you may not tell lies of the following types in these situations but not in others, and the wrongness of other lies is to be ranked in the following order. The first is a general norm, and of course there will be only a rough conformity with it, but it is not a correct description. The second would be empirically more accurate, but no one has established such a matrix of obligations on empirical evidence.[33]

> In recurrent and well organized situations men are able to act together with relative ease because they share common understandings as to what each person is supposed to do. Cooperation is facilitated when men take the same things for granted. We are willing to wait in line in a grocery store on the assumption that we will be waited on when our turn comes up. We are willing to accept pieces of paper of little intrinsic value in return for our labors on the assumption that money can subsequently be exchanged for the goods and services that we desire. There are thousands of such shared

assumptions, and society is possible because of the faith men place in the willingness of others to act on them. Consensus refers to the common assumptions underlying cooperative endeavors.[34]

The quotations from Goode and Shibutani underscore the necessity of viewing normative behavior as including variations in the interpretation of general rules, as well as tacit assumptions about how ego and alter will trust their environment in the absence of cumbersome and redundant details about the meaning of "familiar" activities. Persons will recognize the grocery store line as a particular instance of a general case and not ask the clerk or other persons standing in line if the "general rule" holds in "this grocery store." The idea of basic rules employed by actors is implicit in how the actor decides a general rule is implied or operative.

The basic rules provide a sense of social order that is fundamental for normative order (consensus or shared agreement) to exist or be negotiated and constructed. The two orders are always in interaction, and it would be absurd to speak of the one without the other. The analytic distinction parallels a similar separation in linguistics between the surface structure utterance (the normative order of consensus statements), and the deep structure (the basic social order or sense of social structure).[35] The distinction is necessary and presupposed in a reference to how the actor recognizes social scenes as normatively relevant, and in the differential perception and interpretation of norms and action scenes *vis-à-vis* role behavior. But unlike the rather static notion of internalized attitudes as dispositions to act in a certain way, the idea of basic or interpretive rules must specify how the actor negotiates and constructs *possible* action and evaluates the results of *completed* action. Our model of the actor must (1) specify how general rules or norms are invoked to justify or evaluate a course of action, and (2) how innovative constructions in context-bound scenes alter general rules or norms, and thus provide the basis for change. Hence, the learning and use of general rules or norms, and their long-term storage, always require more basic interpretive rules for recognizing the relevance of actual, changing, scenes, orienting the actor to possible courses of action, the organization of behavioral displays and their reflective evaluation by the actor.

Terms like "internalized norms" or attitudes appear inadequate when we recognize how socialization experiences revolve around our use of language, and linguistic codifications of personal and group experiences over time. Our perception and interpretation of social reality is continually modified by the acquisition of new and different context-bound lexical items. The educational process is designed to teach us how to think abstractly and utilize language to order our experiences and observations. Linguistic structures enable us to extend our knowledge and subsume a wide spectrum of experiences and observations, but it also filters these activities both as inputs and outputs. For those with less educational experience, the world of everyday life takes on different meanings.[36] The study of language use is important for understanding how actors routinize or normalize their environments, perceive and interpret them as threatening or disruptive or new or strange.

Structural arrangements provide boundary conditions by way of that which the actor takes for granted: typified conceptions that make up the actor's stock of knowledge, ecological settings, common linguistic usage, and bio-physical conditions. The interaction remains structured by such boundary conditions, but is also problematic during the course of action. But the actor's typified orientation to his environment minimizes the problematic possibilities of social encounters: the fundamental importance of common sense ways of perceiving and interpreting the world is the taken-for-granted perspective that reduces surprise, assumes that the world is as it appears today, and that it will be the same tomorrow. The actor constructs his daily existence by a set of tried and proven recipes.[37]

A more refined conceptual frame for understanding norms will have to specify basic rules as a set of invariant properties governing fundamental conditions of all interaction so as to indicate how the actor and observer decide what serves as definitions of "correct" or "normal" conduct or thought. The basic rules would suggest that the nature of minimal conditions that all interaction presumably would have to satisfy for actor and observer to decide that the interaction is "normal" or "proper" and can be continued. The acquisition and use of interpretive rules or procedures over time amounts to a cognitive organization that provides a continual sense of social structure.

SOME FEATURES OF BASIC RULES AND THEIR FIELD RESEARCH RELEVANCE

In this final section of the essay I want to outline some of the elements that the notion of basic or interpretive rules would possess if terms like "status," "role," and "norm" are to retain any usefulness. In presenting my discussion I will lean heavily on the writings of Alfred Schutz because I believe he has made more explicit the ingredients of social interaction also discussed by James, Mead, Baldwin, and others. I find Schutz' writings to be quite compatible with the linguistic theory known as generative-transformational grammar, and hence will draw upon elements of both in my discussion of some of the features of basic or interpretive rules.

Both Chomsky and Schutz stress the importance of the *intentions* of speaker-hearers. In transformational grammar considerable emphasis is placed upon the speaker-hearer's competence to generate and understand acceptable (grammatically correct) utterances. This competence presumes a deep structure whereby the speaker's intentions are first formulated according to base or phrase structure or rewrite rules. The base structure utterance, therefore, can be viewed as an elaborated (before the fact) version of what is actually spoken (and heard by a hearer). Transformational rules operate on the deep structure so as to delete or rearrange the utterance so that a surface structure comes out as a well-formed or grammatically correct sentence. For present purposes we can say that speakers and hearers possess two common sets of phonological and syntactic rules whereby each is capable (possesses the competence) of generating and comprehending deep and surface structures.

Schutz is concerned with the semantic or meaning component of social interaction. The linguist is not interested in focusing on interaction itself, but his statements can be extended logically to include conditions formulated by Schutz for understanding how social order or social interaction is possible. I consider the following passage from Schutz to be central to the problem of social order, as well as compatible with the formulations of the generative-transformational linguists.

> More or less naively I [referring to the common sense actor's view of things] presuppose the existence of a common scheme of reference for both my own acts and the acts of others. I am interested above all not in the overt behavior of others, not in their performance of gestures and bodily movements, but in their intentions, and that means in the in-order-to motives for the sake of which, and in the because motives based on which, they [others] act as they do.[38]

The notion of a common scheme of reference includes the idea of action that is motivated by a plan of projected behavior that Schutz calls an "in-order-to" motive, and the possibility of reflective behavior whereby some reason is assigned to the past, completed action (called a "because motive" by Schutz). Many readers may not feel that Schutz has presented material that goes beyond the work of James, Baldwin, Mead, or others, but I believe the extension by Schutz of ideas by these writers can be found in several features making up the "common scheme of reference" which can be viewed as basic or interpretive rules capable of being studied empirically. The following features are proposed as basic to all interaction, but not exhaustive, yet a necessary first step in clarifying the fundamental base structure of social interaction.

1. The first rule refers to a *reciprocity of perspectives* which Schutz divides into two parts. The first part instructs the speaker and hearer to assume their mutual experiences of the interaction scene are the same even if they were to change places. The second part of the rule informs each participant to disregard personal differences in how each assigns meaning to everyday activities; thus each can attend the present scene in an identical

manner for the practical matter at hand. Schutz uses a question and answer format to further illustrate this rule. The question-answer sequencing requires a reciprocal rule whereby my question provides a basis (reason) for your answer, while the possibility of a future answer from you provides a basis (reason) for my question. When I ask a question I have intentions (a deep structure) or a more elaborated version in mind than what I actually ask you. My "pruned" or "deleted" surface question, therefore, presumes a more elaborated version that I assume you "fill in" despite receiving only my surface message. Your answer, therefore, is based upon both the elaborated and surface elements of my question, and I in turn "fill in" your answer so as to construct your elaborated intentions. Both participants, therefore, must presume that each will generate recognizable and intelligible utterances as a necessary condition for the interaction to even occur, and each must reconstruct the other's intentions (the deep structure) if there is to be coordinated social interaction.

2. The reciprocity of perspectives rule or interpretive procedure cannot operate unless additional rules or sub-routines accompany its use. One sub-routine consists of the actor's ability to treat a given lexical item, category, or phrase, as an index of larger networks of meaning as in normative development of disease categories, color categories, and kinship terms.[39] The appearance of a particular lexical item presumes the speaker intended a larger set, and assumes the hearer "fills in" the larger set when deciding its meaning. A related sub-routine allows the actor to defer judgment on the item until additional information is forthcoming. Or, an item or category may be assigned tentative meaning and then "locked-in" with a larger collection of items retrospectively when a phrase appears later in the conversation. This *et cetera* rule and its sub-routines permit the speaker-hearer to make normative sense of immediate settings by permitting temporary, suspended, or "concrete" linkages with a short-term or long-term store of socially distributed knowledge.

3. To introduce a third rule or interpretive property, the idea of *normal form* typifications, I quote again from Schutz:

> But as I confront my fellow-man, I bring into each concrete situation a stock of preconstituted knowledge which includes a network of typifications of human individuals in general, of typical human motivations, goals, and action patterns. It also includes knowledge of expressive and interpretive schemes, of objective sign-systems and, in particular, of the vernacular language.[40]

Interaction participants presume normal forms of acceptable talk and appearances, or if discrepancies appear, attempt to normalize the action scene. The rule provides the actor with a basis for rejecting or reducing a range of possible meanings to a collapsed typification of the social structures. The rule instructs the actor to reject or recognize particular instances as acceptable representations of a more general normative set. The collapsing, typifying activity of immediate action scenes is context-bound, but enables the actor to make use of short- and long-term store (socially distributed knowledge) so as to subsume the particulars of an unfolding setting under more general normative rules. Hence notions like status, role, and norm cannot be relevant to an understanding of everyday social interaction unless the actor possesses a rule for recognizing normal forms or subsuming particulars under general normative or surface rules, and thus establishing a basis for concerted action. Asking the actor what he "sees" or has "seen" in experimental or field studies requires that the researcher know something about how the actor typifies his world, according to what kinds of linguistic categories and syntactic rules.

When the observer seeks to describe the interaction of two participants, the environment within his reach is congruent with that of the actors, and he is able to observe the face-to-face encounter, but he cannot presume that his experiences are identical to the actors; yet both actors assume their experiences are roughly identical for all practical purposes. It is difficult for the observer "to verify his interpretation of the other's experiences by checking them against the other's own subjective interpretations," because while there exists a congruence between them, it is difficult to "verify" his interpretation of the other's experiences unless he (the observer) becomes a "partner" and/or seeks to question the other along particular lines.[41] The observer is very likely to draw upon his own past experiences as a common sense actor *and* scientific researcher to decide the character of the observed action scene. The context of our interpretations will thus be based upon "logic-in-use" and "reconstructed logic," and therefore include elements of common sense typifications and theorizing.

> The observer's scheme of interpretation cannot be identical, of course, with the interpretive scheme of either partner in the social relation observed. The modifications of attention which characterize the attitude of the observer cannot coincide with those of a participant in an ongoing social relation. For one thing, what he finds relevant is not identical with what they find relevant in the situation. Furthermore, the observer stands in a privileged position in one respect: he has the ongoing experiences of *both* partners under observation. On the other hand, the observer cannot legitimately interpret the "in-order-to" motives of one participant as the "because" motives of the other, as do the partners themselves, unless the interlocking of motives becomes explicitly manifested in the observable situation.[42]

The complexity of perspectives involved in direct interaction and observation depend, therefore, upon subtle shifts by the researcher requiring his use of basic or interpretive rules and common sense typifications. The observer cannot avoid the use of basic or interpretive rules in research for he relies upon his member-acquired use of normal forms to recognize the relevance of behavioral displays for his theory. He can only objectify his observations by making explicit the properties of basic rules and his reliance on them for carrying out his research activities.

When our interest in the sources of information provided by direct participation in interaction and observation is shifted to interaction by telephone, an exchange of letters, to messages we receive from third parties or read or hear about via the news media, the actor's perspective for "knowing" his partner or "other" progressively narrows. If the telephone conversation is between acquaintances, friends or kinship elements, our model of the actor must include the situation described by Schutz as follows:

> I hold on to the familiar image I have of you. I take it for granted that you are as I have known you before. Until further notice I hold invariant that segment of my stock of knowledge which concerns you and which I have built up in face-to-face situations, that is, until I receive information to the contrary.[43]

The ways in which the actor retains an image of the other based upon prior face-to-face experiences is a fundamental feature of how we can interpret interview material from respondents. Knowledge of what Schutz calls the "constitutive traits" of the other by the actor is presupposed in making inferences about the meaning of respondents' utterances. Hence, when we become interested both in the actor's comprehension of a world divided into different sectors of immediacy, as opposed to others or objects not in face-to-face contact, then our theory and methodology must reflect the many transitional ways of "knowing" for the actor which fall between "direct" and "indirect" experiences of others, objects, and events. The experience of others not in face-to-face contact Schutz refers to as the actor's perspective of a "contemporary." The immediate apprehension of the contemporary is accomplished by typifications, even though the "other" may have been known in the past through face-to-face communication.

> The act by which I apprehend the former fellowman as a contemporary is thus a typification in the sense that I hold invariant my previously gained knowledge, although my former fellowman has grown older in the meantime and must have necessarily gained new experiences. Of these experiences I have either no knowledge or only knowledge by inference or knowledge gained through fellowmen or other indirect sources.[44]

Schutz' remarks suggest the elements necessary for understanding the basic processes that generate role behavior or the actor's point of view *vis-à-vis* some "other," and also point to a more general model whereby we can decide how the observer-researcher obtains data about the actor-other, and how such data are to be interpreted. Schutz notes how the simultaneity of ongoing interaction means that the actor follows a step-by-step constitution of the other's conduct and its experienced meaning, and, wherefore, when faced with "an accomplished act, artifact, tool, etc., [the actor views the end-products] as a pointer to such subjective step-by-step processes" experienced in direct interaction.[45] The observer-researcher, therefore, cannot always take utterances by respondents as evidence unless he has some confidence that they reflect the step-by-step processes of the original or mediate experiencc, thereby lessening the possibility that "coded" substantive responses are distorting, altering or truncating, the meaning of the activities, objects or events for the actor. Schutz' comments on how the actor utilizes "personal ideal types" as a means of comprehending what is experienced directly and indirectly, provide the observer-researcher with a fundamental element for any model which seeks to understand how the actor manages to perceive and interpret his environment in spite of apparent discrepancies, and the fact that the "norms" are not clearly understood "directives to action," and that "consensus" emerges through the constructions of participants using basic rules in the course of interaction. The "stability" of the world of contemporaries for the actor refers to the typifications employed by him and the fact that they are detached from an immediate and hence emergent subjective configuration of meaning, because "such processes—typical experiences of 'someone'—*exhibit the idealizations*: 'again and again,' i.e. of typical anonymous repeatability."[46] In the case of direct interaction the personal ideal types are modified by the concrete "other" given in direct experience to the actor. Hence, the actor can deal effectively with an environment which carries with it ambiguity and gaps in "directives to concrete action" because the typical is rendered homogeneous, non-problematical, and, therefore, taken for granted. The actor establishes equivalence classes subject to the modifications inherent in direct and indirect contacts with others. The observer-researcher's equivalence classes cannot be established without reference to the actor's use of basic rules and the common sense equivalence classes constructed during interaction.

Thus, when the observer-researcher questions respondents about the "social structures," he must distinguish between various events and objects and how they are known to the actor. Schutz claims that a typifying scheme is inversely related to the level of generality of the actor's experiences, and the experiences are rooted in the stock of knowledge possessed by the actor, from which he derives the scheme.

> These rcmarks make it obvious that each typification involves other typifications. The more substrata of typifying schemes are involved in a given ideal type, the more anonymous it is, and the larger is the region of things simply taken for granted in the application of the ideal type. The

> substrata, of course, are not explicitly grasped in clear and distinct acts of thought. This becomes evident if one takes social realities such as the state or the economic system or art and begins to explicate all the substrata of typifications upon which they are based.[47]

If our observer-researcher is studying a family unit, a small village, a small group of elite leaders, he may interview A about X, where X may be an individual or some collectivity. The ideal-typical characterization of X by A keeps invariant A's direct experiences of X, making them typifications. A's description of X may be punctuated by examples designed as "evidence" and motivated by various interests, stock of knowledge, etc. The observer-researcher refers the information (depending upon how it is interpreted *vis-à-vis* the strata of meaning suspected and/or probed for) to his own stock of knowledge about X, his interest in X, etc. The more removed (by "institutionalized" law, by physical and social distance, by tradition, etc.) X is from A, the more standardized a given typifying scheme will be, the more careful will be the required probing and the inferences drawn. If the respondent A is referring to documents he has read, or his information is based upon others' interpretations of documents, the observer-researcher will have to decide the meaning of the sign system used by A, for the "distance" of the document is likely to lead to more "objective" use of signs—that is, without benefit of "inside" knowledge. If A was the member of some audience witnessing a village fight, and was face-to-face with the participants, his remarks shift to that of an observer as described earlier.

SUMMARY

Throughout this chapter I have tried to discuss terms like "status," "role," and "norm" within a general model for characterizing social interaction, and the perspectives employed by participants. Everyday experience for the actor is at any particular moment partitioned into various domains of relevances whereby common sense equivalence classes of typifications taken for granted are employed. The correspondence between the social analyst's terms, "status," ("role-expectation," etc. "role,") and the world as experienced by our constructed actor-type, does not refer to the same sets of typifications, nor are the two sets of categories used by our actor and observer-researcher, or the experiences upon which they are based, arrived at by the same inferences and reasoning. In the ideal the actor and observer-researcher employ different kinds of constructs and their procedural rules are distinct. In actual practice, however, the actor's everyday theorizing is probably not much different from the observer-researcher. Both employ the same basic rules and similar typifications, and neither may clarify (during interaction) the particular vernacular or rules used to communicate the domains of relevance each describes, nor delineate the strata or layers of meaning intended or suggested by the linguistic categories and connotations used. Differences between our "practical theorist" and "academic theorist" may all but disappear when both describe everyday activities. The observer-researcher must rely upon basic or interpretive rules when subsuming "recognized" behavioral displays under concepts derived from his scientific vocabulary. Hence, unless the researcher clarifies, conceptually and empirically, his reliance on basic rules, he cannot make claims to "objective" findings. Most of the above discussion can be summarized by the following remarks:

1. Participants in social interaction apparently "understand" (by elaboration of verbal and nonverbal signals) many things even though such matters are not mentioned explicitly. The unspoken elements may be as important as the spoken ones.

2. The actors impute meanings that "make sense" of what is being described or explained even though at any moment in clock time the conversation may not be clear to the partner or independent observer by reference to the actual terms being used. Through the use of basic or interpretive rules the participants supply meanings and impute underlying patterns even though the surface content will reveal these meanings to an observer unless his model is directed to such elaborations.

3. A common scheme of interpretation (the basic rules) is assumed and selective background characteristics are invoked to account for and fill in apparent "gaps" in what is described or explained. The participants seem to agree even though neither has indicated any explicit grounds or basis for the agreement. Each may choose to "wait and see."

4. The participants do not typically call each other's utterances into doubt, demanding independent evidence, so long as each assumes he can receive "details" (or that "details" are available) on discrepancies detected in the conversation. But even when there are doubts, the partner will seek to "help" the other get through the conversation. Direct confrontations require radical shifts in the perspective each participant employs; but as a first approximation they both take for granted that each knows what they say and mean by their utterances.

5. The basic rules activate short- and long-term stored information (socially distributed knowledge) that enables the actor to articulate general normative rules with immediate interaction scenes. The basic and surface (normative) rules provide the actor with a schema for partitioning his environment into domains of relevance.

6. The basic or interpretive rules govern the sequencing of interaction (the basis for social order) and establish the conditions for evaluating and generating behavior displays the researcher labels as appropriate status and role attributes or conduct. The articulation of basic and surface (normative)

rules establish a basis for concerted interaction we label the social structures.

7. Notions like status, role, and norm, therefore, cannot be clarified unless the researcher's model explicitly provides for features enabling the actor to recognize and generate "appropriate" behavioral displays. Nor can we explain the observer's ability to recognize behavioral displays as falling under such rules, unless we have a model of interaction that provides for basic or interpretive rules and their interaction with normative or surface rules.

DAVID SUDNOW

Temporal Parameters of Interpersonal Observation*

This essay will sketch some temporal features of interpersonal settings which seem to constrain, for members of a society, the production and recognition of relevant appearances, gestures and moves where an orientation to "glancing" observation is required as a condition of concerted action. For a vast number of routinely accomplished social interactions, the ability of persons to "make out" each other's actions, features of scenes, categorical statuses, etc. "at a glance" is crucial. I should like to consider some possibly interesting features of glance-based interpretation.

Not only is it the case that persons seem able to "formulate" features of

* The research project on which the present paper is based has been funded by PHS grant #MH 16196–01. I am grateful to Harvey Sacks for his comments on an earlier draft of this paper.

(*Notes to this selection will be found on p. 443.*)

another's appearance, of a scene, gesture, etc. "at a glance"—as the successful occurrence of a wide variety of interactional sequences attests—but for many interactional sequences there seems to exist a *requirement* for interpretation with "no more than a glance," and, in many situations, with no more than a single glance. That is to say, for many activities, the single glance is a maximally appropriate unit of interpersonal observation.

The basis for this requirement may sometimes appear predominantly physical as, for example, in the coordination of automobile or sidewalk pedestrian traffic where single-glanced monitoring of others' actions is an often required procedure, or, in other situations chiefly ceremonial and social, as in the numerous activities where the immediate, spontaneous, glance-based recognition of another's moves, categorical status, gestures, etc. is strongly sanctioned and violations sometimes harshly noticed (e.g. "Hey, I was in line here," "Why are you staring," etc.). Whatever its particular situational structure, the obligated sufficiency of the single glance for furnishing information relevant to coordinating concerted actions is clearly both empirically widespread and of great import for routinized, non-verbal interactional order.

At the outset I shall leave the precise nature of the glance, as a form of looking, undefined. Differentiation of the glance from other forms of looks—in terms, for example, of length, directionality, and intensity—will concern me here only in passing and later in the discussion. For the while, precise definition is unnecessary, the observations I shall make being readily recognizable to any reader who thinks of the glance in a common-sense way, as a quite short look. Our intuitive grasp of what the glance is like will suffice for most of this discussion.

I shall suggest that persons exhibit through their actions an orientation to so constructing appearances of self, activities, relationships, moods, etc. that there will be a correspondence between the intended sense of a conveyed portrayal and what is observable in that portrayal to a glancing observer. I shall argue below that one confronts special tasks of appearance production when he orients to his appearance's availability to a glancing other, and I shall try to suggest some possibly interesting features of those tasks. As the other side of the coin, a glancing viewer confronts special tasks in his observational procedures. I shall suggest that the situation of the "glanced at" party and the "glancer" place them each in a position of interactional sensitivity to the other.

The interest in "glancing" is part of a general research interest I have in social situations of observation, particularly in circumstances where persons are behaving with explicit orientation to the possible observation of another, and where the fact that their behavior might be so oriented is an inference which, in turn, they seek to control. "Glancing," as a mode of looking actors attend and do, is here regarded as a case of interpersonal observation in general, an observational procedure, which I propose is especially interesting because its structure reveals various basic temporal parameters of interpersonal settings. My concern is thus with features of "timing" in interpersonal conduct, "glancing" considered as a type of observation that brings those features into sharper focus.

First some broad remarks. One feature of many interpersonal settings—those referred to as "public places"—is that an orientation to an observer or performer in such settings is an orientation to an "unknown" observer or performer, to a "stranger." If "interpretation" at a glance is possible, then in such "public places" that possibility must be attended by producers and viewers of appearances as a standardized one. That is to say, for many actions in many settings one need not and can not know who another is personally to know if his glance will yield what one seeks to have it yield. The orientations we will discuss are in part, then, orientations to "anyman's glance."

Another general remark. It seems that in doing a glance there is the presumption, in a wide range of settings, that the glance will furnish not merely a "hypothesis" regarding some other's appearances, but will yield expectably correct and sufficient, interactionally relevant information. The glance is not regarded by members as an imperfect, poor substitute for preferred extended looking. Rather it is, for members of this society at least, a natural, non-incomplete, normatively governed unit of observation, often a maximally appropriate monitoring procedure, known and known in advance to be sufficient and sufficient for "anyman" for furnishing interactionally relevant information. The unit "glance," then, is not an analytic unit but a member's one.

The above observations are altogether obvious. What I shall do is explore some features of the operation of glances, and especially, their "timing." If glances are routinely and correctly sufficient for a vast range of concerted actions, their timing and, moreover, the production of appearances under an orientation to their timing might be expected to be a quite relevant issue.

That the timing of a glance might be consequential for its informational adequacy may be suspected in light of the fact that many of the aspects of scenes whose glanced-at "observability" and "interpretation" seem regularly achieved are aspects that may be regarded as organized as "courses of action," having spatially and temporally extended dimensions. Insofar as many observed features of scenes might be viewed as continuous over time and mobile in space, unfoldingly revealing themselves, grasping such aspects of scenes, we might in some theoretical sense suppose, would seem to require witnessing the developing progress of a scene over its spatially and temporally extended course. We see a person engaged in some movements, the sense of which becomes available to us as we observe and construct those movements, observed through their unfolding progress, into a recognizeable course of social action. Now we see him step off the curb onto the pavement, now gesturing with finger pointed on an extended hand, now approaching a slowing vehicle, now entering a stopped taxicab. It *comes* to: "Man getting a cab"; "Man embarking on a cab ride"; "cab-getting in Manhattan"; or some related activity formulation.

While it is quite apparent that persons routinely engage in both viewing others' actions over their course and, conversely, producing appearances with an orientation to the fact that they will be observable and interpretable to others as they progress, it seems equally true that for many witnessed activities and in a wide range of interactional circumstances, alternative procedures of interpretation and action production operate. The obvious useability of the glance for "making out" necessarily grasped features from ongoing courses of action, attests members' ability to "short circuit" retrospective-prospective observation and inference. If it were recurrently required that extended witnessing and analysis of courses of action was a requisite for characterization and subsequent adjustive action, such a requirement would seemingly make for a radically different world of action possibilities. The issue of "timing" in observation, as an intrinsic dimension of the "glance," is obviously critical, given the essentially unfolding, developmental character of scenes and bodily behavior.

Now we may not initially assume that the order of information about some scene, action, person, gestures, etc. that a glance will furnish is equivalent, in "depth," to those aspects of scenes, persons, actions, etc. discernible under more temporally extended inspection. I shall consider below the issue of "orders of information" glanced viewing seems to afford. To the extent, however, that the glance is capable of furnishing some order or level of information about *courses* of action whose temporal extension, theoretically speaking, exceeds that of their observation, and to the extent that varieties of courses of action are organized such that only at certain and not all points in their course is such an order of information potentially made available to a viewer, as we shall see seems to be routinely the case, then the "timing" of the glance in the course of such a course of action might be somewhat critical. And, as we might expect and hope to show, the production of an appearance under an orientation to the interpretive availability of that appearance to a glancing viewer, would expectably be sensitive to synchronizing certain features of the production to its to-be-glanced-at observation. The chief hypothesis of this essay is that the recognition and production of appearances of persons in social situations routinely requires sensitivity to such temporal arrangements and to the internal time structure of activities. Moreover, such sensitivity as is required for the conduct of a vast range of concerted actions in public places must somehow be organized in a standardized way, such that it operates for "strangers."

In this essay I shall introduce some considerations for the study of such sensitivities by employing a "non-natural" situation of observation—

the activity of "posing" for a still photograph—as a heuristic point of departure. This situation affords the opportunity for highlighting some aspects of observational timing. After having so utilized that situation I shall suggest the relevance of aspects of its temporal organization for the analysis of naturally occurring situations of appearance production and interpretation. Such suggestions will involve offering some rather commonplace examples, intended to simply remind the reader of temporal features of interactional settings which are, in the first instance, altogether intuitively apparent. In doing so, several parameters of interpersonal settings of nonverbal interaction will be specified as invariantly relevant features of interactional settings.

A central feature of photographic depiction, from the standpoint of an interest in natural observation, is the fact that the camera is an instrument of instantaneous recording, i.e. it captures only a tiny instant, routinely much less than a second in duration, from the ongoing progress of some scene. It might be initially suggested that the fleetingness of the camera shutter's glimpse makes it formally (and roughly) analogous to the fleetingness of the naturally occurring glance. I shall begin by considering such an analogy and see how it might enable me to introduce some apparently descriptive features of everyday temporal constraints on observation.

First, I must specify a perspective from which to consider the analogy profitably.

1. While only the briefest instant is exposed to view in front of the still camera, a noteworthy and definitive feature of the photographic process—one that seems to clearly distinguish that process from the situation of "natural" human observation—is that that instant is recorded. That is to say, while we may conceive of a look of the briefest duration at some scene, it is unclear what model of the perceptual process might be implied by suggesting that such a look "preserved" or "recorded" or rendered a "document" of that scene. It is clear that the shutter and film of the camera produce an extraordinarily "detailed" record of the object of the operator's attention. This feature of the photograph—its "permanence" "despite" the fleetingness of the process which produces it—has a consequence that will be considered below.

2. A second feature of "photographic glancing" is that while only a brief second is "selected" from some ongoing scene or course of action for preservation, the ongoing course of action is, in a cameraman's enterprise, viewed over a temporal course with an orientation to that selection. Stated alternatively, the cameraman scrutinizes a scene from behind his viewer; he does not glance at that scene but views it more or less extendedly, making a selection of a "recordable instant" from the unfoldingly appreciated and analyzed course of action. From the standpoint, then, of the observer of an action, the analogy between the "glancing" of the camera

and the "natural" glancing of a human does not straightforwardly apply. The relevance of this difference, where the cameraman holds within his visual-temporal field the material from which he will select a "recordable" instant, and the natural viewer, at least in many situations, not observing his subject prior to the "glance" at it, will be suggested below. Note now simply that a difference exists between the situation of photographic scrutiny under the auspices of capturing a recordable instant and those situations of glanced viewing that do not involve continuous pre-glance monitoring. Variations with respect to this variable will be discussed below.

3. While I shall return to consider some of the issues posed in (1) and (2) above, let me first consider the analogy from the perspective not of an observer but a subject of the photographer's attention. Whatever might be the basis for the felt "realism" of a photographic depiction, persons seem to routinely regard the attention that they are getting when in front of a camera as capable of capturing them "as they really are" or "as they can make themselves appear." Persons regard the photograph to be produced by the camera as a document of their appearances, actions, movements, relationships, aspects, moods, etc., and attend the production of such a document seriously. While they may engage in antics, gestures of contempt, or indifference in front of a camera, that such displays will be accurately preserved and read as evidence of their intent seems to be the concern and orientation of camera subjects. "Having a picture taken" is, in some senses, a serious activity, and the properties of the attended product of that activity are routinely accorded authenticity.

I want to consider whether the fact of the instantaneousness of the recording procedure is attended by camera subjects, how it might be attended, how the fact that a camera viewer is viewing the subject's appearances over some course to make a selection structures the subject's actions, and how the temporal features of this "posing" situation might be generalized and modified to non-camera specific, i.e. ordinary appearance production situations.

To briefly recapitulate the camera situation: We have in the ideal typical case a subject or subjects orienting to the observation of a photographer viewing appearances so as to select from the course of a presentation some instantaneously recordable instant which will preserve, for later viewing, an intendedly conveyed appearance, gesture, relationship, aspects, etc. Two features of the subject's orientation are of special interest:

1. While in the ideal-typical "posed" case the subject is aware of the cameraman's presence and scrutiny, the precise moment of expected exposure is routinely not known. That is to say, while the scope of a relatively narrow range of viewing time within which the exposure will occur is known, the instant of exposure is uncertain.

2. The subject's behavior exhibits a close orientation to the fact that the exposure will be instantaneous, and so produces an appearance as to provide that when that instantaneous exposure occurs, his actions will be readily interpretable to some later viewer as the gestures, movements, appearances, relationships, aspects, modes, etc. that the subject, in collaboration with the photographer, seeks to make observable.

I would suggest first that an orientation to the uncertainty of "exposure time" has analogies in non-photograph specific situations of observability, where, in varieties of settings and under a variety of interactional arrangements, a range of possible observation time may be known to a person and/or controllable by him, but the precise "point" of observation may be relatively unclear, if it is a "point" of observation that is attended. And secondly, an orientation to providing for the "definiteness" of some fleetingly capturable appearance, gesture, movement, relationship, etc. can be seen in a wide variety of "natural" interactional circumstances of appearance production where an orientation to the likelihood of a very brief look on the part of another is manifestly and requiredly attended, and where the interactional context provides conditions that necessitate the "clear" communication.

What is generally involved in the camera situation is the production of an appearance which at some or any of a set of possible instantaneous viewings will be equally and sufficiently "definitive," for a viewer, of that appearance, such that the appearance intendedly portrayed by the subject will be interpretively available, at that instant, to a later viewer of the portrayal.

As a rough description, we may suggest that one characteristic manner in which subjects behave when under the scrutiny of a "camera glancer" under the temporal situation described above is for them to strike a "well chosen pose" and "hold it," keeping themselves relatively immobile at some position for a "non-natural" period of time, i.e. for a period of time which, if their actions were being continuously viewed or continuously recorded, would be seen as "strange," "transfixed," "stilted," or otherwise peculiar. Routinely, the "frozen pose" is held in advance of the actual camera exposure and, especially where the camera poser is too far from the camera to hear the actual exposure made, the "pose" is held after actual exposure.

I shall suggest that this "frozenness" of the adopted pose, to be examined in detail below, is designed to handle both the uncertainty of the actual moment of exposure within a relatively narrow range of possible observation time, and the anticipated brevity of the expected "look." I shall suggest that the pose itself, i.e. what "point" in the course of such action is held, is oriented to providing for the "definitiveness" of the portrayed appearance. These two features of orientation are, as we shall see, intimately related. I shall argue additionally that such orientations and adaptations are observable in non-camera specific settings of appearance production where

(a) the occurrence of a brief look is oriented to;
(b) there is an orientation to the occurrence of a brief look within some relatively narrow expectable range of time within which an observation will occur;
(c) the intendedly portrayed action is such that a brief look may criterially discriminate that action from other actions, and
(d) there is an interest in so behaving as to insure the adequacy of the brief look for the conduct of some interactional sequence.

Let us consider some commonplace activities, e.g. "walking across the street," "having a conversation," "window shopping," "entering a doorway," "looking at a watch," etc. Consider having to produce an appearance of such actions in natural settings under the constraints of (a) anticipating only the briefest look of another and (b) seeking to provide that that anticipated brief look will suffice for that other to see us as "walking across the street," "having a conversation," "window shopping," etc. Let us begin by considering the production of such appearances under that simple concern alone, i.e. to provide for an "unambiguous" interpretation.

Now we may suggest that a strong orientation to such a task is not at all a routine way in which we seem to attend our environmentally situated activities; that, recurrently, say in "window shopping" or "conversing," our orientation to others' watching is such that either they will see our actions over their course, or if they only look very briefly at us; that they get a "definitively clear" grasp of the "details" of our actions may be unimportant. In explicitly posing for a photograph, persons are routinely heightenedly concerned with providing for the "definitiveness" of their actions at a "glance." To imagine a natural situation of some heightened concern for such observability, let us conceive a possible actual scene, simply to concretize the discussion. Consider, for example, a situation, quite familiar in its general form, where we seek to provide that an acquaintance whom we seek not to have to greet will observe us absorbed in "window shopping" as he passes by on a sidewalk, and will take that activity as warranting our not having noticed him.

Some features of this hypothetical, familiar situation can be offered:

Assuming that we have seen the acquaintance without making eye contact with him, so we can take it that he hasn't seen us see him, one possible issue is that in his approach toward our direction we don't know at what points he will notice us. That uncertainty provides that in attempting to appear "absorbed" we must so appear over some range of time. We are in a position to assess, judging from his distance from us when we first see him and his likely pace (or the likely pace of "sidewalk walkers"), when he will likely be no longer watching us. We may perhaps also feel comfortable with an inference about when, given some starting point in his approaching path, he may first see us. The uncertainty of his looking time within this standardized expectancy range provides that within that range our actions are relatively inflexible; we must maintain what he will see as our engrossment for the duration of the likely observation period, our main alternative being, by trying to secretively observe his approach, to better estimate his looking time, that procedure, however, increasing the risk of eye contact and the requirement to then display recognition.

By "inflexibility" I mean that our concern to appear to be "window shopping" may involve us in a more engrossing attitude toward the window in front of us than we might otherwise exhibit were the issue of observability for such purposes not relevant. While we may routinely, in "actual" window shopping, look back and forth between the window and the street, stroll from one window to another, etc., our orientation in this situation to not meeting the acquaintance's eyes and, simultaneously, to appearing properly unavailable for eye contact, will somewhat restrict the range of our movements and actions. For all of the time we feel it likely that we might be observed we shall, perhaps, find it necessary to at least be faced toward the window.

Now the inflexibility of our actions in this sense, their relatively unidirectional focus, is somewhat diminished in such a hypothetical situation by virtue of the fact that we have no reason to expect that our potential viewer will merely glance at us. Rather we have strong reason to suppose that our acquaintance will look at us for a rather extended period of time as he moves down the street toward our location. Secondly, while he might only glance, at the point he should glance it may be unimportant to us that he see us as specifically "window shopping," but simply required that he see us engaged in some activity from a class of actions which may legitimately hold our attention and thereby account for our unavailability for greeting. We have to provide that we are not seen "ignoring" him.

A consequence of that possible extended viewing situation and the uncriticalness for the purposes, within some range of activities, of the specific activity he sees us engaged in, is that while it provides for the inflexibility of our actions over an extended or relatively extended period of time it provides, simultaneously, for "internal flexibility" within the overall expected observation range. We may, for example, in ways to be suggested below, light a cigarette, scratch our head, tie a shoe lace, adjust our clothing, look at some notes, etc., so long as we can do so without appearing to be making ourselves purposefully unavailable for eye contact. While we are perhaps locked into a position oriented toward the window, the range of actions we can allow ourselves to be seen as engaged in is considerable. The additional feature of the situation above, that should our acquaintance see us at all his expected recognition of us will warrant more than glance looking, such that accountability of our actions does not hinge on their mere glance availability, further relaxes the temporal constraints upon our appearance production.

Let me elaborate some features of this hypothetical temporal situation, which upon closer examination becomes more complicated. First it may be suggested, about the specific appearance of "engrossment," that not *any* activity may appropriately serve as an occasion for the demonstration of that order of involvement which would be seen to warrant unavailability for eye contact. While one seeking to provide that he is too engrossed to notice an approaching acquaintance may properly do so by looking in front of a window at displayed merchandise, or by perhaps browsing through notes or having a conversation with another, should his engrossment be portrayed by *intense* involvement, say, in lighting a cigarette, the possibility that he will be seen as purposefully avoiding eye contact may arise.

It seems, however, that the suitability of an appearance for conveying sufficient engrossment, in our hypothetical situation, turns not as much on the nature of the action being conveyed as on the temporal situation of observation. Should only a glance be expected, and a single glance, then involvement may, in fact, be sufficiently and appropriately conveyed by the lighting of a cigarette, scratching the head, watching another pass, tying a shoe lace, etc. Such actions which are, as these, brief in duration, may serve as occasions for demonstrating unavailability for eye contact if their brevity is in some way conveyed. When only a glance is expected it is possible that a staging may occur where a fixed, posed position sustains the appearance of involvement in such actions, and, by virtue of the occurrence of only the single glance, evidence of the staged, posed, "held" character of the appearance display is not revealed, such revelation ideally occurring only when the pose is seen, over some period of time, to have been assumed. That is to say, the anticipated occurrence of the mere and single glance affords the opportunity to express involvement via an action which, if the action were otherwise (i.e. continuously) viewed, would serve to express not appropriate involvement but feigned involvement, i.e. in this case, purposeful avoidance. In our hypothetical situation, of course, such an expectation would not be warranted.

There seems, then, to be a relationship between the adequacy of some appearance or activity for conveying a state of the actor's attention and involvement and the temporal situation *vis-à-vis* some observer for whom he finds himself producing such an appearance. In a situation of continuous, relatively continuous, or expectably repeated observation, or, at least, in one where the extent and manner of observation is uncertain, an interesting appearance production problem is presented. While in glancing situations, frozenness of poses may, as we shall see, provide an appropriate means for attempting to definitively convey certain actions, some *movement* seems expressly *required* when one's actions are viewed over their course, at least in the deceptive situation we have been discussing. When an involved, immobile, observably posed appearance is held and witnessed over a period of time, the inference of purposeful staging becomes possible, and, consequent upon that inference, one which, in some situations, may question the motives of the actor.

The problem of appearance production in the window shopping example, or, for instance, in such situations as that which students confront when taking an examination in front of a monitoring proctor, involves the production of an appearance or set of appearances for an observer who may either merely glance or watch more extendedly. The structured anxiety of such situations seems to partially reside in the fact that the scope and duration of possible observation time is sufficiently unpredictable to make it difficult to avoid appearing posed (i.e. staged) on the one hand and too mobile on the other. It appears that enough mobility is required to insure that "posing" is not seen to be occurring (as, for example, a "cover" for an illicit activity) if more than a glance should occur, and not such a degree of movement that the activity or set of activities one is up to becomes questionable should only a glance occur and occur at a point or points over which the actor has little control. It may be noted, of course, that excessive movement itself may, in such situations, convey the impression of an illicit motive.

Let me now turn to consider more specifically the timing of the glance. We have thus far introduced some temporal aspects of a situation where undercover work of some sort is going on. Let us focus now on situations of coordinated interaction where single glance monitoring occurs and where persons must rely on the effectiveness of the appearance production work they do in order to insure that an interactional sequence proceeds properly.

Let us consider the situation of "walking across the street," where an orientation to being clearly so seen is held by virtue of the noted presence of a rapidly approaching vehicle. Here a familiar traffic situation may be readily imagined where a mere and single glance is expected, where the sufficiency of the mere and single glance is criterial for bringing off safe passage (we can conceive a situation where the driver's speed and position are such that he will have to adjust his behavior to the pedestrian rapidly), and where, as a consequence, the concern for a correspondence between the "details" of what we are doing and what we are seen at a single glance to be doing, may be of paramount concern.

Unlike the situation of appearing non-purposefully unavailable for eye contact, where "window shopping," for example, is only one of a set of actions that may equally well serve such a purpose, and where the occurrence of more than a glance or more than a single glance is expectable, in such a dramatic traffic situation we are immensely concerned that the driver's mere and single glance locates our actions unambiguously as the single activity "walking across the street." The orientation to the possible mere and single glance, in such a circumstance, requires that we so produce an appearance that at any point at which that single glance occurs within the expected (and hoped for) observation period, we are immediately and clearly seen "walking across the street." The immediate, transparent, glanced-at recognition of our singular action is desired, and the situation has, if we conceive of a particularly crucial (but altogether common) traffic situation, extreme temporal inflexibility. To the extent that the range of the expected glance time is narrow (and it is to be importantly noted, as we shall consider below, that for such coordination persons must be able to closely anticipate the point of glancing with a narrow range), this situation most approximates some of the features of the camera posing circumstance.

Before considering glance timing directly, some complications must be introduced. We noted above (p. 12, c.) that one expected condition for or constraint upon the tightness of the temporal structure of situations of observability was the relationship between the *organization* of an action and the *criteriality* of a glance for providing access to it. To state that relationship more fully we may say that the discriminative criteriality of a glance will vary both (a) depending upon the action under expected scrutiny and (b) the purposes at hand. These features are related, which is to say that what particular action is observed, requiredly observed, performed so as to be observed, will be a feature of the interactional requirements of the situation, and, in turn, the criteriality of a glance will be a function of the oriented-to-action.

To consider this relationship, return to the situation of "window shopping" where the orientation to the possible extensiveness of a look or repetition of a glance, by the observer, warranted on the basis of mutual acquaintanceship, may serve to permit, and, as we noted, require, the performer to be relatively flexible in the manner of his performance, more flexible than would be the case if a single glance would expectably occur and would be requiredly sufficient to yield, as the witness' assessment, the conception that the shopper is "involved."

Now we may note that numerous instants within a course of "appearance engrossed" in some activity may be interchangeable with respect to the criteriality of a look, at such instants, for furnishing the inference of "engrossment underway." Whatever particular action the "engrossed" party seeks to demonstrate his state of involvement through, be it looking into the window, having a conversation with another with his face aligned away from the oncoming acquaintance, reading a book, etc. the "engrossingness" of his appearance does not stand or fall, within some limitations, on *all* that he is doing at some particular instant in time. Nor does it apparently hinge on some *particular* item of behavior at any instant in time. If, while having his "engrossing" conversation with another he scratches his head, adjusts his clothing, shifts his bodily position slightly, and the like, the "engrossing character" of his conversation is potentially available so long as the fact of the primacy of his conversational involvement is conveyed. That requires of him that his bodily alignment be generally attuned in a conversational position *vis-à-vis* some other. If all that is required is that he be seen as "with" another, he must organize his appearance such that whatever "else" he might be doing, the "withness" feature will be observable.

As we have suggested above, the expectation, in our hypothetical avoidance situation, of more than a mere glance, considerably aids our actor in the assumption of his appearance in one respect, permitting him to be somewhat non-artificially posed in the adoption of his appearance, and may perhaps constrain him in another respect, in that it may require work to foster that impression. Over and above that order of consideration is the fact we have just introduced—namely, that the bodily requirements of "being engrossed," given, I would suggest, the fact that "engrossment" characterizes not a particular activity but the state of involvement of a person in some range of activities, establishes less than completely rigid demands upon appearance production. Only the "withness" features—if a conversation or feigned conversation is employed as the occasion of engrossment—need be managed.

We are confronted then with two simultaneously operative orders of constraint upon appearance production: (a) the temporal situation of observation and (b) the order of information about an action, status, relationship, person, etc. that is intendedly portrayed to an observer. These factors do not seem, in any concrete interactional situation, to be entirely separable, on one hand, nor entirely interdependent on the other. If we imagine a hypothetical situation where "appearing to be with" another is required and where that impression must be conveyed to a merely glancing other, we can expect to find some tightening, by performers, of the temporal structure of their presentation. If it is critical that their "withness" be picked up at a glance; we expect to find them sustainedly engaged, in expectation of the glance, in those actions that are especially definitive of that state of a relationship. By the same token, however, "being with" another may be seen via a variety of different visually available facts: bodily alignment *vis-à-vis* those not in the relationship, or bodily contact, or facial expressions, or, in some situations, mere physical proximity. The organization of the "course of action" "being with" is such that various particular physical actions interchangeably serve to provide the impression of the state of the relationship. If a glance should miss, in time, some of those aspects of an appearance which aid in conveying that impression, other perceived features of the persons' appearances *vis-à-vis* one another will frequently suffice to provide the material for a correct identification.

Contrastively, the situation of being definitively seen as "walking across the street," not only if a mere glance is expected but even if slightly extended viewing is likely, seems to require a more rigid internal time order, such that close attention must be given to assuring that all features of the conveyed impression are consistently in accord with the sought after identification. Should a walker, in the course of such a sequence of actions as are involved in making it across the street, stand momentarily still and scratch his head before entering the line of traffic and should a glance occur at that instant, the possible equivocality of his actions may, to his danger, be seen.

Consider the following contrast, as another example of the varying criteriality of glance timing. Compare being seen as "engaged in a conversation," with being seen as "looking puzzled at what another has said." It can be readily seen that the activity of "being engaged in a conversation" may be available at any of a series of glances directed toward the conversational unit at some point in the course of the conversation's progress. If a glance occurs even when neither of the parties are currently speaking, their bodily alignments, facial positions, distance, etc. will likely be so organized (and un-selfconsciously so) as to permit determination of the conversational status of their encounter. So that, for example, if A seeks to speak to B who is involved in "conversation" with C, that B is so involved, and hence, for example, not to be interrupted, may be observable at numerous points at which A might glance at B and C within the course of their conversational encounter. For that activity, or better stated, for that formulation of some set of observed affairs—"having a conversation" or "he is busy now"—the criteriality of the timing of the glance may be relatively weak. We can, of course, imagine a particular interpersonal situation where the fact of "talk in progress" might be requiredly shown, and the constraints would be presumedly greater. For the activity being "puzzled," whose observation may involve the noticing of what might occur as a relatively brief event, e.g. the knotting of the eyebrows, the timing of a look adequate to furnishing such a formulation might expectably be quite critical. From the standpoint of the producer of an observed action, appearing in "conversation," like appearing "unavailable for eye contact" involves less strenuous attention to the temporal structure of his action's organization *vis-à-vis* a glancing observer than appearing "puzzled."

We may thus appreciate that given some purpose, i.e. some situational structure specifying the need for making some activity observable, the purpose, e.g. "to appear engrossed," to "appear to be about to enter the traffic flow," to appear "busy with another in conversation," to appear "puzzled," etc., will structure and be structured by the temporal relationship to the producer's activities and observer's witnessing. The sufficiency of a glance will thus partially depend upon the order of determination of order of activity formulation which is sought and the temporal structure of that activity, i.e. its internal temporal organization. We can appreciate the performer's perspective, where seeking to produce an appearance that will be definitive of a particularly formulated course of action, he will orient to the relationship between the temporal viewing pattern of an observer and the temporal structure and temporally discriminative criteriality of the intendedly conveyed action.

It may be noted that one way of considering the issue of glance timing importance is to ask the question: How critically timed must a photographic snapshot be to yield an image clearly definitive of some desired state of affairs? If we seek to photograph an "orchestral performance in progress" we need only so time our photograph that the fact of music in progress is conveyed, that being, perhaps, achievable at any point where the conductor's hands can be captured in some state of movement, or the musicians can be seen to be holding their instruments in a state of play. If we alternatively wish to convey "a rising crescendo," our temporal sensitivity is increased and we must await a point where the conductor's and musicians' bodily attitudes are at a particularly strenuous phase.

The situation of camera posing constitutes a particularly tight attention to the relative but only slight uncertainty concerning the moment of observation, an orientation to the extreme brevity of the moment of observation, and, quite frequently the intention, say in posed advertising photography, of conveying highly specific levels of activity formulation at a brief observation moment. To the extent that the criteriality of a brief look is attended for capturing the intendedly conveyed action, and to the extent that the exact time of observation is uncertain but only uncertain within a narrow range, then the "pose holding" we routinely observe in photographic situations becomes a particularly effective, though partial solution (and partial for important reasons to be suggested below) to the problem of "definitive" recognition.

We may here note that in posing for a photograph whose main interest is presenting a good likeness or flattering version of the subject, the timing of the exposure may be quite critical, and the orientation to that criticalness on the part of subjects is readily observed. A slight movement, a slightly wrong timing, may give away unwanted features, since the organization of facial appearance is such that at any given instant it may be relatively radically changed, as by a slight grimace, blink of the eyes, or other minor movement. Insofar as when persons seek to control such minor alterations by constructing fixed facial poses they appear to increase their likelihood, photographers often prefer to rely upon their own timing ability rather than their subjects' self control and assistance. Be that as it may, persons who in natural environments seek, for whatever reasons, to present a controlled appearance of self under an orientation to the glanced availability of that appearance, can be observed to adopt relatively immobile and well-planned facial and bodily presentations. The point of that fact is that faces have, in a sense, "courses of action," as do what we ordinarily think of as activities, and their presentation is often subject to the same order of temporal sensitivity as is the presentation of an activity appearance.

Let me now consider some features of "frozen stances" in the photographic situation in more detail. If we examine advertising photographs, particularly those that are designed to present persons engaged in some specific activity, we can see some of the aspects of the production of an "unambiguous" or "definitive" appearance. We regularly find that the *co-present features* of such scenes are highly and purposefully organized with respect to each other. In a picture of a man using a piece of equipment the moment of exposure has captured him fully engrossed in that action. His eyes, hands, facial composition, bodily tonus and alignment, all aspects of his appearance and demeanor are accountable for by reference to the activity we see him engaged in. Now in using such a piece of equipment—for example, a "gardening tool"—it would obviously be the case that over the course of his activities with the equipment numerous "other" activities would occur. Or, stated alternatively and more accurately, using a gardening tool in a setting where instantaneous observability of *that* particular action is not at issue, entails doing a variety of things; such a worker may sneeze, scratch his nose, lean against the equipment, converse with another, use the equipment in a distracted way, etc., etc. In a photographic depiction, however, the interest of which is often in directing a viewer's attention to this activity "in progress," all of the observable features of the subject's stance, attention, focus, etc. are explainable by reference to and organized with respect to the single activity "using a gardening tool." So, too, a photograph of a teacher conducting class will show him captured at that point where his extended arm, with chalk in hand, is about to write on a blackboard while the angle of his body and face is approximately half way oriented to the blackboard and half way toward the class, some members of which are seen, from behind, intently attending his performance.

A routinely observed feature, then, of appearances produced under the expectation of their definitive single glance availability, where such appearances are of activities where the timing of a glance may relevantly discriminate them from appearances of other activities, is such an accountability of the features of the scene, where each of a set of particular behavioral features is produced so as to converge on the generic, intendedly portrayed singular activity. Providing for the instantaneous availability of a single recognizeable action, for those actions whose organization is such that some particular gestures or stances or movements are most unambiguously definitive of them, gestures, stances, etc., which are, to use the linguist's image of phonemic discrimination, contrastive with respect to that activity, involves the assemblage, into one held instant, of an integrated set of aspects, the momentary integration of which at any given time over the course of the continuously observed performance of that action might likely occur only quite intermittently, if ever so perfectly and coherently co-present.

Photographic depiction as a skill involves, in dealing with candid as well as posed subjects, the selection of just such maximally engrossing, maximally organized, epitomizing moments from ongoing actions, the selection of what has been termed by the famous photographer Cartier-Bresson as the "decisive moment." And the posed photograph subject may assist the photographer in making such a selection less arduous and more "perfect" by cooperatively assuming and sustaining an integrated activity or appearance position.

In natural interactional settings the momentary freezing of a position, awaiting some indication, usually felt to be guaranteed by the occurrence of eye contact, that what is being portrayed has been seen, is recurrently found in such coordination situations as the hypothetical traffic situation sketched above. Interactionally speaking, the frozenness of the pose is designed, in such situations, to compensate for the glance-timing's criteriality, providing that within some limited time span the action will, in being held constant, be (unambiguously) available. For actions whose organization is such that the timing of a glance is particularly critical, we find producers of actions actively cooperating with the anticipated viewers of such actions by seeking to lessen the criticalness of the observer's glance timing. That collaboration is accomplished by holding constant features of the appearance which, with an improperly timed glance, might in many cases by virtue of the ordinary serial organization of the appearance of critical features, be missed, where a miss would likely lead to unwanted equivocality of interpretation. To the extent that the consequences of misinterpretation are important, as for example in numerous traffic situations, collaborative work in dealing with these temporal facts seems to increase. For interactions where the import of assuring a correct interpretation is considerable, special signalling efforts will be made to insure that a look will occur in the first instance.

We noted above that in the case of photographic depiction the cameraman does not in fact merely glance at the scene he intends to photograph but, rather, watches it over its course in anticipation of an appropriate moment for exposure. It appears crucial for much of interactional coordination in public places that persons be able to rely on the fact that considerable pre-glance monitoring work routinely goes on. There is strong reliance, for example, upon the effectiveness of peripheral vision in monitoring the environment for situations requiring more directed looking.

Not all "glances" yield the material for the kinds of formulations of actions and appearances we have been considering. Rather a significant difference seems to obtain between the "look" that is of such a character that it is sufficiently "focussed" to permit "seeing" such actions as "person crossing the street," "man window shopping," "man and woman conversing," and a "look" that is hardly a "look at" anything at all, but rather constitutes a relatively unfocussed, "un-motivated," "un-directed," relatively random behavior of the eyes. It can be suggested that some special or situated interest is required before persons "focus" their eyes upon some scene, before they "look at it" with an interest in making it out, and that much of our eye behavior involves continual and rapid shifts from partial focussing on some object to another, many objects that fall within the visual field not being "seen" at all.

What we have been treating as a "glance" and as orientations to the occurrence of a "glance" is properly classified as a "focussed look," analogous in that sense to the highly focussed "looking" of the photographer's camera. The production of appearances under an orientation to the occurrence of such "focussed" looks, where there are attempts to make the "details" of such appearances available, can be seen to differ from the production of appearances under an orientation to the occurrence of relatively unfocussed looks, where it may be the case that an initial requirement to have such looks furnish the material for detailed formulation of actions and persons is that such looks must first become "focussed" in nature.

By "detailed formulation" I mean the specification of such features of scenes as their actors as categorized actors, their activities as nameable activities, actors' appearances as types of appearances, and the like. So the information that that is a "man crossing the street" or a "pretty girl," or a "pair of conversants," and the like, is what I mean by a "detailed" formulation of some witnessed scene. "Unfocussed" looks, occurring not out of some "interest" in a scene but as peripheral monitoring eye behavior, do not seem to furnish such information about the objects that are encompassed within their view. Rather, such "looks" yield, it may be speculated, such properties of scenes or persons or collectivities as "normal," "strange," "nothing happening," "weird," "striking," etc. It can be suggested that a sequence of "looking" behavior occurs, where the initial "look" or first part of a "look' furnishes information about such properties of scenes or persons and where a later look or the later part of some first look (and we are probably talking here of milli-seconds) focusses in on, "looks at" the scene, person, activity, etc., permitting more detailed formulation of categorizeable actors, activities, appearances, and the like. And, moreover, we might suggest that whether or not a "focussed look" (of which a glance is one type) occurs depends upon what the "unfocussed look" yields as such normative properties of a visually encountered scene.

If such distinctions prove to be in any way descriptive of interpersonal looking, we might profitably direct attention to consideration of the way appearances are produced so as to provide for such sequences as: (a) unfocussed look—no further look, or (b) unfocussed look—focussed look.

The situations of glance observability we have discussed all involve, implicitly, sequence (b). Yet it is clear that persons may orient to producing an appearance so as to insure that "nothing" gets seen in their activities. Or, at least, the issue of the generation of a look, whether a glance or more, can be treated as problematic. "Glances," unlike photographs, are clearly interactional phenomena, their occurrence and the degree of "interestedness" they exhibit is a matter persons seek to control as a normative requirement. To do a "glance" is to demonstrate some order of interest in the glanced-at-object, and there are familiar techniques regularly employed that operate to influence the degree of informativeness of that order of interest. Persons can, for example, by doing glances in the course of "scans," attempt to make them appear "unmotivated" and "unfocussed" (since "scans" are seen as specifically disinterested ways of visually taking in some environment, by fitting a glance within a scan, the attempt to have that "glance" not appear as a "glance" at all but as a "non-look" is made).

We can expect that considerable attention is given by persons to deciding about the looks they receive and, in turn, in controlling their appearances for those looks, whether or not, to what extent, and in what respects they are seeing what is intendedly presented. Further investigations of interpersonal observation will explore the ways in which such decisions are made and controlled. For example, we have here not considered the ways in which appearance production might be controlled and structured by virtue of an orientation to the fact of an observer glancing out of a "scan." If we consider the coordination of freeway traffic, and consider, for example, the use of turn signals, and the occasions where enormous stake is put on the fact that the turn signal will be seen, we can see that the orientation to the fact that an observer will do his glancing with some repetition, and in the course of scanning in front of him, provides a basis for dealing with the otherwise imaginable overly critical significance of a glance timing.

In the traffic example introduced above we suggested that to the extent that the import of insuring a correctly definitive glance increases there is a corresponding concern to insure that the glance-timing's relevance be a matter whose *responsibility is shared*, where the producer of the to-be-glanced-at-action, by "posing," seeks to minimize the import of the timing's relevance. We noted that an additional interest may exist to get a look generated in the first place, to have the "pose" seen. In the language of the above discussion, the interest is to insure getting a "focussed" look and, as we mentioned in passing, that interest may be sufficiently strong in some settings and sufficiently crucial for the interaction, that special efforts will be directed to generating it. The task of "getting noticed" often involves so producing an appearance that an unmotivated look will pick up those features of a scene which will warrant bringing the eyes into focus and seeing the intendedly portrayed appearance. The use of arm signals, waving, and the like seems to have, say in traffic situations, such an interest. And, generally, a way of generating a "focussed look" is to produce the kind of "eye catching" movements that an unfocussed, peripheral monitoring procedure locates.

I have spoken of appearance production under temporal constraints as being oriented to providing a solution to various categorization problems. We can say, as has been said by Sacks with respect to the classification of persons[1] and Schegloff with respect to the classification of locale,[2] that a categorization problem exists with respect to the classification of *activities.* Howsoever "clearly" some particular activity may appear to be available by virtue of the nature of the appearance a person presents, there always exist numerous alternative activities in terms of which that appearance may be formulated. Our hypothetical window shopper, no matter how unidirectionally he is seen to be absorbed in what may be called that activity, may, quite obviously, be said to be doing literally an infinite range of things. It is no guarantee and in fact impossible that the effort he puts to maximizing the availability of some interpretation in his activities will result in that interpretation being uniquely fitted to those activities. Aside from possibilities that he will be seen to be feigning, covering up, and the like, we have available as alternative ways of describing his appearance, such possibilities as "spending the day," "getting fresh air," "turned with his back toward the street," "the typical American businessman on a lunch break," etc. etc. The list can be indefinitely extended. We can readily imagine interactional and other determinants that would make each of the above and many other formulations of our "window shopper" appropriate. While *vis-à-vis* the "acquaintance" he seeks to establish an appearance of "engrossment," *vis-à-vis* a "stranger" he may be simultaneously concerned to appear to be keeping to his own business," and to a friend whom he does not see, who is in turn identifying him to another he does not know, he may be "that guy in the blue sweater looking in the window across the street." To the bulk of passers-by he may simply be a blurred figure, not otherwise noticeable.

In what sense then are we to treat the above remarks about "definitiveness," "solutions," "unambiguity," when with little imagination we can offer numerous alternative formulations of his appearance? Are we prepared to say, given the above observation, that appearance work is essentially irrelevant to the issue of categorization? Certainly it is the case that when persons set about constructing appearances of self, and when they do so with cognizance of and sensitivity to the temporal features of their witnessed character, they strongly feel that they are directly controlling the categorization of their activities for others, despite our ability to theoretically and quite simply show the existence of a multiplicity of simultaneously available alternatives as an inescapeable fact.

Now it is quite clear that there is no way one can, via the way he uses his body—for example, when sitting in an office—present an appearance for one who looks in while passing by of being simply "at work" as against being "the office worker spending his day at the office," or "the white man," or "American industriousness in action," or "at work on a paper under preparation for publication in a volume," etc. Control over applicability of such alternatives lie beyond the physiological capabilities of the actor.

Clearly, considerations other than physical appearances we encounter and produce are responsible for establishing circumscribed collections of relevant activity-categorizations from which a selection of a particular activity formulation will be made. We have not nor shall we at this point explore such considerations, except to note that the interactional situation would seem to be the chief source of relevance. For the driver of a vehicle, "pedestrians" at crosswalks have (as candidate activities they may be seen to be engaged in) such courses of action as "crossing the street" and "not crossing the street." Given the relevance of that or a similar pair or otherwise constituted collection of activity terms, appearance production and detection is constrained to deal with those possibilities. Persons no more formulate the categorical status of others' actions apart from the relevancies established by contextual features than they formulate the categorical status of persons and places apart from the situated contexts in which such formulation matters. To speak of temporal constraints on appearance production apart from concrete interactional contexts is as incorrect as to refer to a person as a "man" in the abstract, for in the "abstract" he is no more or less a "man" than he is a variety of other objects as well.

It would seem that a fundamental set of tasks confronts students of nonverbal behavior—namely, the investigations of the ways interactional environments establish activity relevancies and how, in turn, the relevant collections of alternative activity formulations in some setting constrain both the kinds of appearance production work that go on and the kinds of monitoring procedures that are employed in that setting. I have attempted to simply introduce, as one significant parameter concrete interactional interpretation and bodily activity must be geared to, the temporal structure of interpersonal settings. It can be proposed that there is more than a casual relationship between the formulational relevancies of some interactional setting and rules pertaining to observation in such settings. Aspects of settings that have been characterized as formal as against informal, as "tight" and "loose,"[3] may be perhaps given a temporal basis. To the extent that the nature of relevant activity formulations in some setting constrain temporal aspects of appearance production and recognition, we can perhaps characterize those settings in terms of institutionalized temporal structures and sensitivities.

HARVEY SACKS

Notes on Police Assessment of Moral Character*

INTRODUCTION

1. For Western societies, at least, being noticeable and being deviant seem intimately related. The notions that one is suspect whose appearance is such that he stands out, and correlatively that the sinner can be seen, have the deepest of foundations. Indeed, in Judeo-Christian myth-

* Formerly titled "Methods in Use for the Production of a Social Order: *A Method for Warrantably Inferring Moral Character*." This paper was written about seven years ago as a paper for one of Erving Goffman's courses at UC Berkeley. It is heavily indebted to a reading of his work and also to materials he presented in lectures, some of which he has since published in his books *Encounters*, *Stigma*, and *Behavior in Public Places*. It was also, and equally much indebted to those writings of Harold Garfinkel which were then available, and which have now been collected and published in his volume *Studies in Ethnomethodology*. During the period of its writing I received financial support as a Pre-Doctoral Fellow of the National Institutes of Mental Health, U.S. Public Health Service, and from the Center for the Study of Law and Society, University of California, Berkeley.

(*Notes to this selection will be found on pp. 444–446.*)

ology, human history *proper* begins with the awareness by Adam and Eve that they are observables.[1] The next bit of social information they thereupon learn is: To be observable is to be embarrassable.[2] The first social technique they learn is: They can by mutual regard achieve privacy.[3] And then they learn the first terrible norm: The retention of privacy is conditioned on *naive* conformity.[4]

1.a If, in American society, it is the case that the inferences as to moral character which particular appearances may warrant is a matter of central concern, then: We expect that there are specialized methods for producing from the appearances persons present such inferences as to moral character as can warrant the propriety of particular treatments of the persons observed.

1.b It is the case that the relation of observability to deviance is of central concern. In public places persons are required to use the appearances others present as grounds for treating them. Persons using public places are concurrently expected by others to present appearances which can be readily so used, and expect others to treat their own appearances at face value.

1.c While the regulation of inferences (hence of treatments) by reference to appearances determines an elegant means for routinizing casual public interaction, it obviously has characteristic problems. First, what is to be done about those persons whose appearance suggests no clear inferences, i.e. whose appearance does not warrant particular treatments?

Second, what is to be done about those persons whose appearance is projected to take advantage of the enforced inferences others make in order to do the latter ill?

Third, what is to be done about those persons who consistently or blatantly fail to properly read appearances, who consequently produce inappropriate treatments?

Fourth, what is to be done about those persons for whom the problem of properly reading appearances is dramatically tortuous?

In this paper I shall not consider "what is to be done." Rather, I am concerned with how those about whom that question may properly be raised are located.[5]

1.d As the appearances persons present are of central concern, so too are there specialized methods for producing the inferences that appearances warrant.

The concern of this essay is to move towards their description. I shall proceed in this direction by attempting a description of a method used by specialists—the police—for inferring from appearances such a probability of criminality as warrants the treatment of search and arrest.

My grounds for the choice of the police are as follows. First, the police are engaged, with others, in locating persons about whom the question may properly be raised: can they give a legitimate accounting for their appearance?

Second, they are, in contrast to others so engaged, specialized in the locating of candidates on the basis of the appearances presented in public places.

Third, as specialists, certain problems of the relation of the first two and the last two problems of 1.c. above need not be examined. That the police are specialists means that they are accredited for regularly recognizing possible deviants. Since the regular recognition of possible deviants, quite as much as the failure to produce a proper appearance, constitutes evidence for deviance (e.g. paranoia), the professional accreditation of the police provides a quick and easy test as to whether a claimed recognizer of deviants should be given diagnostic examination. The "public-spirited" citizen receives special and ambivalent attention.[6] Since, then, I want only to deal with the location of persons presenting improper appearances, choice of the police avoids in general the question of the possibly symptomatic status of recognizances. Fourth, as specialists their methods ought to be reasonably easy to discover.

1.e Since I am only interested in the police instantially, I shall restrict the investigation to a domain of their work involving a special concern for matters with which persons in general are, albeit less intensively, also concerned. I shall describe a method used for recognizing "suspicious persons," and shall not be concerned with methods used for recognizing either "wanted persons" or those seen in the commission of an offense. While some evidence will be offered that the method the police use for recognizing suspicious persons is in general use,[7] a demonstration of its general use will not be presented in this paper.

A FIRST SIMPLIFIED STATEMENT OF THE POLICEMAN'S PROBLEM

2. Among the Americans, the police are occupational specialists on inferring the probability of criminality from the appearances persons present in public places. Since a mutual orientation to appearances defines a means for producing and accepting the appropriate proprieties by which casual public encounters are routinized, it is important that these means be protected from exploitation. One central role of the police involves protecting the viability of these means. Patrolmen are intensively oriented to the possibly improper appearances persons may present.

2.a The decisional problem faced has the following form: Maximize the likelihood that those who will turn out to be criminals and who pass in view are selected, while minimizing the likelihood that those who would not turn out to be criminals and who pass in view are selected. This problem is faced under the conditions:

1. that the persons seen are (differentially, to be sure) oriented to the character of their own appearances as grounds of inference as to probable criminality[8];
2. that the value of correct and incorrect inferences are neither equal nor uniformly calculable prior to a treatment decision.[9]

2.b Others—for example, homosexuals while cruising—face a similar problem. For our purposes the latter differ from the police in the following way: The police are concerned to recognize persons concerned to make themselves unrecognizable as criminals. The homosexual is concerned to recognize homosexuals and to inform them of the presence of a colleague; he is also concerned not to be recognized as homosexual by others, particularly by the police. The issue reaches maximal complexity when police seek to have homosexuals recognize them as colleagues for the purpose of having the latter engage in a move that constitutes grounds for arrest.

The police face a similar problem with prostitutes, junkies, and the like, and that class of persons also faces the problem of differentially communicating, by way of their appearances, with potential clients, the public and the police.

THE METHOD IN USE: AN INCONGRUITY PROCEDURE: ITS BASIS

3. The method that the police are trained to employ may be called an "incongruity procedure." It constitutes an attempt to refine a method for observing persons based on the wisdom noted above (1).

3.a It begins with the fact that persons within the society are trained to naively present and naively employ presented appearances as the grounds of treatment of the persons they encounter in public places.

The treatments for which appearances are ordinarily used as grounds of selection vary widely, from, for example, deciding whether "that one" is such a one as one can pass in the street without fear of attack, illegitimate approach, etc., to how it is that one may properly pass, follow, or approach "that one."

3.b Since mutual orientation to appearances determines a means for producing and accepting the appropriate proprieties by which casual public encounters are routinized, it is important for the continuing viability of these means that they be protected from exploitation.[10] The incongruity procedure takes recognizance that the facts of 3.a determine a weapon by which inappropriate treatments may be garnered. Persons may exploit an ability to present appearances to which they are not otherwise entitled.

3.c If a group can be trained to (1) avoid routinely treating appearances at face value, and (2) alternatively to view the persons they see as presenting possibly improper appearances, they can (3) attend to a variety of features, such as the ease with which an appearance is presented, which may (4) warrant empirical investigation of the propriety of the presented appearance. Some comment on these points is appropriate.

First, that a warrant is necessary, i.e. that conditions are restricted under which an empirical investigation may be pursued as to the propriety of a presented appearance, is expectable.[11] The elegance of the use of appearances depends primarily on the fact that appearances in general are not to be questioned.

Second, users of the method do not propose that they are able to state definitively what features they will use to decide that an appearance may be improper, i.e. does warrant investigation. It is perhaps obvious why this should be so. As the police are oriented to using appearances as evidence of criminality, so criminals are oriented to using appearances as fronts, i.e. as hindrances to recognition. Were a definitive list compiled, one to which the police would themselves be bound, it would provide criminals with definitive information on the appearances to avoid in order to assure safe passage across the policeman's line of vision.

Given the latter two points, one central problem of the use of the procedure may be exposed: How is the proper use of the procedure to be decided in any particular case?

While I shall consider this problem further below,[12] because of their general relation to the above discussion I note here the general features of its solution. Instead of the proper use of the procedure being decided by reference to the correctness of the inference of probable criminality, the propriety of the inference constitutes the condition for determining whether the persons selected are possibly criminal. And whether the inference was proper is decided in the courts by having the policeman state what it was that aroused his suspicions; the judge (or jury) then considers whether an ordinary person would have been roused to suspicion on such grounds. Only if so is the person selected by the policeman convictable.

A PRELIMINARY DISCUSSION OF THE INCONGRUITY PROCEDURE IN USE

4. Given that police ply a route, they must, in order to use the incongruity procedure, learn to treat their beat as a territory of normal appearances. The learned normal appearances are to constitute background expectancies in terms of which the beat is observed during particular patrols. Given these expectancies the patrolman must so sensitize himself as to be arousable by whatsoever slight variations appear which seem to be warrantable bases for making of the explanation of presented appearances a matter for investigation.

4.a The novice policeman is obviously not in position to use the procedure. First he must learn how to see as a patrolman. By having a novice patrol with a mature officer, the former can be shown what it is that one can see by way of the method. The demonstration that may be offered can have a quite considerable charm.[13]

As he walks through his beat with a mature officer, persons who to him appear legit are cast in the light of the illicit activities in which the latter knows they are engaged. The novice is shown that he ought to see persons passing him in terms of the activities in which they are engaged. And the activities in which they are engaged are often more prurient than he might suppose. The lovely young lady alighting from a cab is now observable as a call-girl arriving for a session. The novice is shown how to see the streets as, so to speak, scenes from pornographic films. And what is more, he is able to see the illicitnesses under the conditions that few, if any, who observe him passing through the streets are able to see either that the officer is in such a scene or what it is that he is indeed observing. The policeman, then, has the privacy of the stag show theatre, while parading the streets in full uniform, and, further, there is no noticeable entry or exit at which, if he is seen, embarrassment might be called forth.

4.b Training manuals provide the novice with lists of features constituting good grounds for treating persons who pass in his view.[14] As we have noted,[15] these lists are intendedly not definitive. They have an extremely interesting status. Aside from providing examples of the sorts of features any policeman ought to be attuned to,[16] they operate as records in an expandable history of police success and failure. The import of those parts of the lists that consist of "great recognizances" or "great boners" is, to use Moore's term, autotelic.[17] The policeman can attend to his route with an awareness that he can, by making an especially subtle recognizance, take a place within department history. That is to say, he is encouraged to engage, even when patrolling alone, in playing observation games; for example, glance at a store window, note to himself all the items that he can recall within it, then check back to see what he has missed or noted incorrectly. While such games are more readily played when police patrol in pairs, the attended history of recognizances permits the lone patrolman to play the games against the department's historical figures.

The persons on his beat can also reinforce the playing of observation games by expressing their amusement at his awareness when they make slight deviations from their normal habits. Then, too, the fact that one cannot pre-determine what information may turn out to be useful encourages the collection of seemingly trivial details because awareness of such details has occasionally paid off with an unexpected arrest which was heavily rewarded.

4.c What is normal for a place is normal for the place at a time. The meaning of an event to the policeman at a place depends on the time it occurs. The time at which it occurs is furthermore a matter of an overlapping and changing group of cycles—that is, the meaning of an event is not merely a matter of the hour, but the day too is involved in deciding its significance; furthermore, the season counts, and then finally "while it didn't used to be that way here," now "such a thing is typical."

While in a sense these facts are obvious, it is obvious as well that sociological theories of deviance are not now constructed to deal with them. Yet even for demographic analysis such facts may be of real importance. For example, given the use of learned normal appearances as the grounds of locating suspect persons, we would expect that territories in transition will have higher crime rates than stabler territories simply because the policeman geared to the normal appearances of a beat may, not adjusting exactly to the rate and character of transition, be ready to see newer arrivals as suspicious for the beat seen as an area in which they are not normal features.[18]

The time-ordered character of normal appearances poses a touchy strategic problem for the police. A patrolman can best be attuned to normal appearances by so scheduling his route such that he appears at places at the same significant time.[19] In doing so he gets the closest awareness of the constancies and variances at that time for that place. But if his behavior is so scheduled, it provides criminals with definitive information about where he will be at a particular time, and consequently permits the scheduling of illegal events. In order to reduce the information criminals can gain by observing his course, the policeman is therefore concerned to randomize his path through a beat, i.e. to proceed through different ways each time, to double back occasionally, to take his breaks at different times and in different places. But doing this of course reduces his sensitivity to the normal appearances he uses to detect the presence of something awry or, to avoid that perhaps unfortunate phrasing, reduces his confidence that he can discriminate the peculiar because the range of what he uses as normal becomes more extended.

4.d The police treat the normal ecology of territories as a normative ecology. As sociologists describe them, cities typically consist of discrete ecological areas of socio-economic segregation. Juvenile gangs tend to treat the borders of ecological areas as boundaries. Persons who "don't belong" are seen as foreigners, and are subject to treatment as such. Their safe passage depends on the deference of the local lords. The police too treat ecological borders as of normative import. Persons whose appearance indicates that they are not normal members of an ecological area, e.g. whites in negro areas, the apparently poor in wealthy areas, etc., are subject to having a request made for "their papers" and an interrogatory made as to the reason of their presence.[20]

Furthermore, as the police treat territories as a set of normal appearances, so they expect others to treat them.[21]

> . . . Coming to a street intersection, the officers observed a man crossing the intersection who did not appear to know where he was going. The officers alighted from the car, questioned this man, and searched him. He provided the police with full credentials and indicated that this was the first occasion on which he had ever been questioned by a police officer. His answers satisfied the officers that this man was quite "legitimate." They thanked him for his cooperation and sent him on his way.

4.e Two related features of the use of the procedure involve the policeman's appearance.

1. Those who treat the presence of the police as other than normal are seen as other than normal themselves.[22]

> They were in search of "house jumpers"—who are individuals collecting current bet slips and who turn them in at a "drop" station . . . The officers indicate that they can determine who a collector is as a result of their experiences in dealing with these people. As an example, they indicate that if an individual gives them a "double look," they'll check him. By this the officers mean that if an individual sees them in their unmarked car and then turns to look at them once again, chances are the individual has some gambling paraphenalia on his person. In such cases, the officers leave their car and search the person in an attempt to uncover the current bet slips.

2. Conversely, as the police enforce on persons that they treat their presence as normal, so it is enforced on the police that they appear as they are expected to appear, i.e. that if they are present, their presence be apparent.[23]

> An officer attempted to develop an accosting and soliciting case through the use of a private and expensive vehicle. This case was thrown out of court upon the basis that "everyone knows that the police officers use cheap cars," and for a police officer to resort to the use of a Cadillac in order to develop an accosting and soliciting case constitutes entrapment.
>
> Some time ago a handbook operation was going on in a downtown building. Since the handbook was located near the medical building, doctors dressed in white jackets sometimes frequented the place. An officer therefore disguised himself in a white coat and managed to place a bet. The case was thrown out of court on the ground that entrapment was involved.

4.f Given the orientation of the police to the beat as a territory of normal appearances, a notion of "normal crime" may be constructed. We may talk of the normal crime of an area not in terms of the statistical constancy of certain crimes for time units, but as that crime that is so managed within an area that those so engaged appear while so engaged as features of its normal appearance.

The notion of normal crime has the following import: given the orientation of the police, those routinely engaged in illegal activities will attempt to construct a front such that their routine appearance in a territory will (or can) be treated as a normal appearance of the territory by its patrolmen. Organizers of the numbers racket will, for example, employ those who have a reason for going through a neighborhood several times a day and stopping at a wide range of places. The newspaper deliverers and the mailmen are ideal.

Whether or not the numbers racket has happened to fix the patrolmen, it must adopt a front for its routine collections and dispersals so that (a) public-spirited citizens and (b) various detective groups do not on observing the area interpret their routine presence as "numbers men making pick-ups and deliveries." They must adopt this front not simply to avoid being noticed, but because if by some chance they happen to be noticed, the beat patrolmen who has failed to arrest must be able to reasonably claim that they simply appeared to him to be routine features of the territory, i.e. that they gave him no good grounds for an aroused suspicion.

4.g We have noted above (3.c) that it is not the case that the proper use of the method is determined by the demonstrable correctness of the inferences produced.

The general warrant of the method is not based on the professional status of the police; its general warrant is that anyone can see its plausibility. Its warrant in particular cases is that the inference made is one which ordinary persons would make. This means that the policeman is not simply concerned to develop his sensitivity. He must balance his sensitivity against his ability to verbalize, i.e. to present descriptions of how he became aroused. And what is more, though he is a specialist on the normal appearances of his beat, his inferences are judged by those who lack both his special knowledge and his developed sense of the unusual.

While the police would like their special skills in observation to constitute grounds of a recognition of their professional status, and their professional status to then operate as a preliminary warrant of their observations, the fact that the warrant of their observations is decided by a test of reasonableness for an ordinary man is not only irking but also places them in a severe bind.

Apart from the fact that they then tend to see the courts as hindering them in their work and in their search for professional status, they feel required to adopt a series of unpleasant adaptations.

1. The method of recognition and the method of presentation may

become separate issues. The policeman may feel himself forced to "rationally reconstruct" what happened.[24]

> A court officer noted that a particular police officer would behave in the following manner:
>
> He would state that he saw defendant come down the street, knew him as a long time police game operator, stopped him, searched him, found policy tickets, and brought him in. The prosecutor would advise he had no case as the search was not legal, and unless the search was made pursuant to a lawful arrest, the evidence was inadmissible. The officer would then say "put me on the stand." When on the witness stand, he would testify he was standing under a street light when the defendant came by, a man known to him to have been previously convicted of policy violation, and that he saw his policy ticket sticking out of the defendant's coat pocket. Thereupon he arrested him, searched him, and found a number of such tickets and brought this prosecution.
>
> The court officer noted, in this case, that in one year two individuals each obtained $5,000 damages against this officer for false arrest. He was encouraged to resign from the force with his pension rights intact.

2. Once information has been gathered about criminal activities, the police may engage in staging observable crimes. For example, if the police know that someone is selling dope, they may—because they cannot say that the fellow was seen selling dope, only that an exchange of something was seen—arrange through the use of hired addicts for a purchase to take place which is sufficiently observable for recounting in court.

The staging of crimes is especially messy. First, the police may have to employ persons who would otherwise be institutionalized. In doing so they assure these persons at least a temporary freedom, sometimes indeed to pursue their illegal endeavors.[25] Second, where they are unable to get hired hands, they may themselves have to spend time in such activities as smiling in public toilets, making time with the lonely women who frequent bars, etc.

A SECOND SIMPLIFIED STATEMENT OF THE POLICEMAN'S PROBLEM

5. A policeman takes it that the persons he sees engaged in passing through the streets are oriented to a social order in terms of whose features they select the proper or improper courses of action which bring them to use the streets. His aim is to find a way of making activities observable in the particular sense of allowing him to see the passing of persons in terms of the courses they have selected.

Typically, he is in a position merely to observe persons passing in the street and does not engage in fully tracking their paths from entry to the streets to exit therefrom. In locating persons who are to be candidates in a test of their possible criminality he does not begin with information about the courses in which they are engaged. That they are possibly engaged in illegal activities must first be decided by way of the incongruity procedure, i.e. by way of a device for locating candidates from the set of observed persons.

Once located, his concern is to produce information about the paths candidates select and then to transform the information about the paths they select into evidence of the courses they have selected. He seeks, that is, to transform information about the paths candidates select into a description of a set of acts which may be seen as the assembly of a crime.

His problem then seems to be:
Given that

1. he encounters persons in and by way of the streets, persons engaged in undetermined activities;

2. the activities are taken to be parts of selected courses of action constructed with an orientation to their propriety;

3. candidates for investigation are located prior to tracking their paths or knowing the course of action in which they are engaged;

Then:

How, by way of their street activities can one look at persons so as to be able to use their appearances to isolate candidates for investigation, and

How can one then use what candidates do both as materials for discovering the courses of action in which they are engaged, and for determining in terms of those courses, that sense of their observable acts on the basis of which a strategy may be generated for demonstrating the observable character of their activities as the assembly of a crime?

5.a While the police might treat the streets as merely incidental locales of the persons they encounter, in fact they treat the streets with great seriousness. The police take it that what takes place in the streets stands in a determinable relation to that organization of concerted courses of action which involves persons in using the streets. If they discover who to investigate, then by tracking him they can at least determine the strategic problem that exposing the course to which he is oriented poses. Exposing the course itself will not be a problem patrolmen will be concerned with. But it is their job to determine who is to be tracked.

5.b As the police take it that those engaged in illegal activities do not randomly use the streets, so too persons routinely engaged in illegal activities are concerned to regulate the activities of those of their agents who use the streets in the course of work so that the use does appear random.

Persons who organize illegal activities are concerned to minimize the clues that use provides to those who might, by analyzing street activities, expose the organization regulating those activities.

However, the strategic problem they face in doing so involves them in a bind similar to that the police were shown to face (4.c). Organizers of a numbers operation will, for example, regularly move the stations to which route-men go in delivering their slips. They may also attempt to have route-men vary the way they proceed through a territory. But the attempt to randomize has its drawbacks. Persons making purchases are kept in a far more viable mood if those they deal with keep a regular schedule. Then, too, those who keep a regular schedule will, if they are not held in suspicion, be less likely to arouse suspicion.

For the police, the problem of locating the persons using the streets as parts of coordinated illegal activities has a different purport than that of locating persons engaged in sole crimes. In the former case it is the organizers they seek to make observable, and the persons using the streets constitute not the sought-for criminals but possible resources by which organizers may be located. The police are oriented to the organizers, and are by and large willing to let the street operatives alone, because they are aware that those who use the streets are readily replaceable, and because, insofar as the organizers are not located, arrest of street operatives means only that the work of exposing the organization must begin again from the beginning, i.e. with an attempt to locate and track their replacements. Organizers, on the other hand, cannot rest content with the fact that their street operatives are not being bothered. For, even if this is so, it may be the case that the police are accumulating information that may soon be sufficient to crack the organization itself.

5.c Encountering by way of the streets what is taken to be a managed social order has a wide range of other imports.

1. Police seem often to treat an area as an "expressive unit." Suppose they see a group of persons standing on a street corner. The meaning they attach may be neither behavioral (e.g. how crowded they are) nor be conceived in terms of the conduct of those persons (e.g. what *they* are up to). A group of persons on a street corner may be seen as "the neighborhood is restless tonight," i.e. as a gesture of the territory. Conversely, in producing their own responses to neighborhood gestures they see their own actions as an answer to the neighborhood. Thus a policeman, having felt that the young toughs are getting over-rowdy, may pick one out and rough him up, taking it that this will be seen as instantial, as a remark that such persons had better get back in line. While such remarks often seem to be understood, i.e. the one that was beaten up takes it that he is incidental, and the others take it that police intend them to calm down, it seems also to be the case that when communication failures occur, the recipients of a gesture may experience both puzzlement ("why me, I was just standing on

the corner?") and may have a hostility towards the police reinforced ("they have to maintain a quota of arrests, and don't care who they take in" or "they just pick on us, so what is the use of playing straight?").[26]

2. They also take it that the appearance of a neighborhood is attended to by those who pass within it as the shape in which it is maintained by the police. Thus, they may feel called on to make arrests because they feel that persons passing can see that the police see unshapely activities going on.[27]

> The wretched man positively insisted on being arrested. I'd been watching for a long time. And I didn't see how I could let him carry on much longer like that. He might get killed. Or someone might make a complaint at the police station. Then where would I be? There were a lot of people watching him and I thought most of them knew I had seen him. They would be thinking it was time I did something about it. They couldn't be expected to realize that I was a policeman who had never made an arrest. I could almost feel them looking at me, wondering how long it would be before I went into action.
>
> If only he would actually get on to a bus it would be all right. He would be whirled away, out of my uncomfortable little world, in no time at all. But he never did get on to a bus. He tried often enough, but usually the conductor waved him off, or he waited too long, grabbed wildly at the handrail as the vehicle drew away and, losing his balance, went reeling into the gutter. What a skinful he must have had! He was as tight as an owl.

3. For the police, the range of sights, sounds and the like which they observe while going through the streets is conceived in terms of the access these might give to private places. If the private places of a territory are the dominant setting for its activities, then the police attend to the streets with a highly refined sensitivity. Persons living in suburban areas report that "the only way" they can walk in the streets at night without being stopped by the police is if they can get a dog to accompany them. And the police chief of Beverly Hills notes that even this may not be sufficient, since his police are familiar with the persons and dogs who make a habit of walking at night.[28]

4. For the police, objects and places having routine uses are conceived in terms of favorite misuses. Garbage cans are places in which dead babies are thrown, schoolyards are places where molesters hang out, stores are places where shoplifters go, etc.

5.d For the police, each patrol of a beat is conceived as potentially adding items to a cumulative set of values; they want a patrol to count. What any patrol may, however, add to (or subtract from) an assembled body of knowledge, reputation, security, opportunity, etc. may vary considerably.

Given that some sort of mathematics seems attended to in the patrol as an occasion within a continuing set of occasions, we can appreciate the police concern with the matters that are seen as unordered, for example, the fact that "breaks," i.e. unexpected large accumulations (or losses) of units occur at undetermined points within a career. A policeman may, whether rookie or oldster, happen upon a crime in its course which, because of the public attention it gets, assures him then and there of fame and promotion. Or an old policeman, having assembled a large collection of units of value, may suddenly be caught in a compromising situation, and see himself stripped at a point when re-assembly cannot be looked forward to. Or a policeman who knows the habits of the crooks he usually deals with may encounter a young hood who, being unaware of the business relations regular crooks and regular cops arduously establish, on being caught, fires and kills the cop.

The import of these unordered contingencies are, quite simply, that talk of the "course of a policeman's career" must recognize that the policeman is never able to say at what point he currently is in his career. Where he is now is radically a matter of where he will have turned out to be. This corner he approaches may be the corner at which he will have been killed.

5.e That the police seek to be professionals is well known.[29] While this might be accounted for in terms of a general search for status, one basis for the status seems to be their concern, and the concern of those they deal with, i.e. criminals, to develop means for establishing their relation as business-like, i.e. as impersonal, code-governed, etc.

The police claim that crime is a business is not merely a cry on their part for more adequate means to attack crime. It is as well an attempt to suggest, given quite limited means, that if criminals behave reasonably the police, too, will try to do so. The persons feared most by either side are the green groups of the other. The new criminal is felt to be most dangerous; the old pro, trustable, almost a partner. And the criminal, too, is much more afraid of the rookie cop than of the veteran.

Throughout this century, each generation of oldsters seems to see the young members of the other as over-ready to engage in unwarranted violence, and to remark to their co-generationists about the businesslike relation they might have were it not for the young hot-heads.[30] A business-like relation need imply no bribery, of course; merely that minimizable risks be minimized.

GAIL JEFFERSON

Side Sequences*

In the course of some on-going activity (for example, a game, a discussion), there are occurrences one might feel are not "part" of that activity but which appear to be in some sense relevant. Such an occurrence constitutes a break in the activity—specifically, a "break" in contrast to a "termination"; that is, the on-going activity will resume. This could be described as a "side sequence within an ongoing sequence."

The following fragment is a verbatim report of such an occurrence in the midst of a game called "Marco Polo" which three children are playing in a swimming pool. The three participants are Steven (age 6), Susan (Steven's older sister, age 8) and Nancy (Susan's best friend, age 8). The game involves, in part, that It shuts his eyes and counts to ten while the Not-Its

* This paper comes out of several years association with Harvey Sacks, in the capacity of "data recovery technician" at UCLA and UCI. A reader familiar with Sacks' work will recognize its indebtedness to him throughout.

(*Notes to this selection will be found on pp. 447–451.*)

use that time to "hide"—in this case, to position themselves somewhere in the pool. When the ten-count is completed, It, keeping his eyes shut, attempts to locate and tag one of the Not-Its by a "sounding" technique: It yells *Marco*! and the Not-Its are obliged to respond *Polo*! When one of the Not-Its is tagged, he becomes It, and the cycle is repeated. The report picks up at a point where Steven has been tagged and thereby becomes It:

> As he begins to count to ten, Susan and Nancy move to about halfway across the pool.
>
> STEVEN: One, two, three, ((pause)) four, five, six, ((pause)) eleven, eight nine ten.
> SUSAN: "E*le*ven"?—eight, nine, ten?
> STEVEN: Eleven, eight, nine, ten.
> NANCY: "E*le*ven"?
> STEVEN: Seven, eight, nine, ten.
> SUSAN: That's better.
>
> Whereupon the game resumes.[1]

(The report offers no description of the "resumption" procedure.)

Steven's ". . . eleven, eight, nine, ten" may be the sort of error or violation which people often report to be a "trivial matter," as an account for not having initiated correction procedures for it.[2] There are ways to justify such a claim; for example, in that the rules of Marco Polo do not contain provisions for such an event, i.e. it is not a game-relevant error or foul or illegality; or perhaps in that, insofar as the purpose of the count goes—to provide a more or less standard time interval which the Not-Its use to "hide" themselves—the substitution of "eleven" for "seven" does not alter that interval as would, for example, an ommission.

As it happens, such "trivialities" are often taken to task, and there may be an interesting relationship between objects that have as an account for their not being corrected that they were "not worth bothering about," and the sort of issues involved in correcting them. This essay will attempt to characterize the "bother"—that is, to discover some of the issues involved in correcting such an error. For example, how it is that, upon a remarking by one of the three players, the halting of the game is cooperatively and instantly accomplished and attention is shunted from game activity to the dealing-with of a single word, such that further progress of the game awaits an outcome. To accomplish that, an analysis of "side sequences" will be undertaken, which will involve an attempt to describe in detail some of the resources available to these three children.

The analysis will begin with Susan's "'E*le*ven'?—eight, nine, ten?" which will now stand as a proposed case of a device which can generate a side sequence.

"'E*le*ven'?—eight, nine, ten?" is, in part, a "repeat." A "repeat" is a conversational object identifiable whether or not one has heard something twice in succession. One can apparently hear a piece of talk, and without having heard some prior piece of talk (actually not hearing it, for example, not being present on the occasion of its occurrence; or, having heard it, not understanding it, not "catching" it) hear that the talk is a "repeat" and thereby hear that something was said "before," that it is that item which is being said now, and that, being said now, it is being said "again."[3]

A "repeat" is differentiatable from such a similar object as a "frame" or "locator," which may also be replicating that which has been said before. That is to say, in "Eleven?—eight, nine, ten?" it is "eleven" which is being "repeated," and the "repeat" is "framed" by replications of the digits eight, nine, ten.[4]

The differentiatability of a "repeat" from other replications derives from the distinctive work that they do; "repeats" have as a specific consequence of their occurrence and recognition that, for example, further talk will be done, whereas the work of the other replications, as in this case, may be directed to locating precisely the repeated item and perhaps emphasizing its noticability by providing the "ground" on which it stands out.

A "repeat," then, may be said to have a specific prior object as its "product-item." For a hearer to understand what is being done with, for example, "E*le*ven?—eight, nine, ten?", he must find that "eleven" has been selected out, and is being noticed via its occurrence in "One, two, three, four, five, six, eleven, eight, nine, ten."

There is another set of conversational objects, "interrogatives": things like "What?", "Who?", etc., which may also be talked of as having prior objects as their product-items. For these, however, the work of selecting a prior object as a product-item is actualized in the talk, in contrast to a "repeat" which in effect *is* its product-item. This may be observed in the following fragment.

A: If *Per*cy goes with—Nixon I'd sure like that.
B: *Who*?
A: Percy.[5]

Here it can be seen that, indeed, the operation that yields a product-item involves the issue of selection. Whereas in the case of the "repeat" it might appear that it is the entire replicated series that has become the product-item of a "repeat" as an undifferentiatable device from "replication" in general, and that, for example, there is an ambiguity that Nancy then clarifies by producing only the intended product-item, "E*le*ven?," in the case of the interrogative, of two possible "who"-relevant objects (Percy / Nixon), one is yielded. The recipient of "Who?" apparently has no problem finding which "who" is the intended product-item.

Just *how* that selection is accomplished is an issue that will be at least alluded to later. However, for the selection problem itself, there is a possible solution having to do with issues of "timing" or "placement." Selection of the product-item could be accomplished by placing the "repeat" or "interrogative" immediately adjacent to the object—that is, the instant it has occurred. This does not happen for the two fragments so far considered. However, that the repeat and interrogative do not occur immediately adjacent to the intended product-item does not mean that they occur just anywhere. Specifically, it can be observed that they occur immediately adjacent to the *utterance* containing the intended product-item. There is a "recognizeable complete utterance"[6] which is immediately followed by the repeat or the interrogative.

STEVEN: One, two, three, ((pause)) four, five, six, ((pause)) eleven, eight, nine, ten.
SUSAN: "E*le*ven"?—eight, nine, ten?

and

A: If *Per*cy goes with—Nixon I'd sure like that.
B: *Who*?

It might be argued that this apparent "utterance-adjacency" is happenstance, that, for example, the next speaker couldn't arrange his utterance "in time" to follow the intended product-item. However, in other places various sorts of immediate juxtapositions can be found.

A: Uh, how early is she gunnuh pick [you up.
B: [I have no idea.[7]

and in the following, "Uh" signals that the next speaker is starting to talk, where perhaps his utterance is not completely arranged at the moment he starts talking.

DESK: Which hospital.
CALLER: Uh, it-it to uh, ih-well, bring 'em, over to Doctor Tower's o[ffice, or Presbih—
DESK: [*UH : : :* that's—we can't take to a,
CALLER: Well, Presbyterian emergency room.[8]

The capacity for immediate juxtaposition is observable in both cases above, and such items as "uh" provide that it can be done whether or not an utterance is delivery-ready at the moment speech begins. In the second instance there is a suggestion of the sort of reasons for an adjacency lapse such as is found in the initial data and the Percy fragment; it might be that the one who is going to do the interrogative or the repeat is permitting the one who is currently speaking to remedy the troublesome item without that remedy being solicited. In the "UH : : :" case above, A's juxtaposition was done "too soon" since B's ". . . or Presbih—" is the beginning of a remedy to "Doctor Tower's office" *vis-à-vis* the initial question, "Which hospital?"

By permitting an utterance to go to completion, upon completion it may be assumed by the one who is going to do the interrogative or repeat that there is no unsolicited remedy forthcoming. Such an assumption may be legitimatized by the fact of a recognizeable completion having occurred, where the placing of a repeat or interrogative prior to completion might be claimed by its recipient to be unwarranted.

Since such items as repeats and interrogatives appear to be specifically selective of their product-item, it may not be necessary to place them immediately adjacent to the intended product-item for a recipient to be able to locate it. Since there is the capacity for item-adjacency, where utterance-adjacency occurs the issue may be interactional; the "adjacency lapse" a means of permitting the current speaker to do an unsolicited remedy. Conversationalists might be seen to be orienting to that issue in the Percy fragment where there appear to be two possible "who" items such that item-adjacency would seem to be necessary. In such a case, the one who does the interrogative or repeat might feel that its recipient in some sense "already knows" that it is a possibly troublesome item; that a minimal noticing will be sufficient to locate it.

This is not to say that placement does not matter. If in fact Susan's "E*le*ven?—eight, nine, ten?" generates a "side sequence," it is at least imaginable that had this remark been placed "too late" it might be bypassed in the interests of other activities that are on-going. Consider the following fragment.

A: We stole—okay d—we'll *tell* him. We stole all the uhm
B: I stole the Mama Lisa.
A: No we didn't,
B: [[And sold it to a pusher.
A: [[Well, *you* may've—
A: I came in last night // and I stole all the reco(hh)rds.
C:→The *Ma*ma Lisa?
D: The—
A: —from here.
D: Oh you did huh?
A: heh heh
D: Good luck.
A: heh I burned it in a large pile.[9]

In this case, where a repeat is not placed adjacent to the utterance in which its product-item occurs, it might be guessed that D, in his first, cut-off utterance, "The—" might be posing a response to C's repeat; for example, starting to say "The *Mo*na Lisa I think is what he means," and retracts that in favor of continuing the on-going activity.

For the interrogatives, of course, placement can be crucial. If items such as "Who?", "What?" are not in recognizable following-adjacency to the utterance in which the intended product-item occurs, they may be heard in recognizable following-adjacency to some other item, not the intended product-item.

"Repeats," then, are differentiatable from initially "similar" objects—for example, "replications"—and have features comparable with features of initially "dissimilar" objects—for example, interrogatives. Among repeats themselves are sub-classes, each with differentiatable, comparable, sometimes converging features.

The repeat in the initial data has an intonation that is regularly characterized as "disbelief," "surprise," etc. For convenience it is being referred to as a "questioning repeat." This type of repeat characteristically signals that there is a problem in its product-item, and its work is to generate further talk directed to remedying the problem.[10] (Further instances of this type of repeat will be considered, and its work detailed, shortly.)

Another type of repeat is that procedure whereby one demonstrates "appreciation," "enjoyment," etc. of the product-item; where "laugh tokens"[11] alternate with syllables of the repeat. For example:

AL: Then th'r gonna dismantle the frame 'n see if the frame's still there.
LOUISE: hh//heh heh heh!
AL: Got *ter*mites.
(0.6)
KEN:→"T(hh)er(h)mite(h)s" hhh
LOUISE: Well y'know wi—n—*fall*out. Who knows what they'll eat now.
(0.6)
KEN: hhhh
(1.5)
KEN: hh hh
(1.0)[12]

ROGER: He's a politician.
AL: Yes. I'm a politician. I think I'm greater than all of you.
(1.0)
KEN: [[I think yer out of yer fuckin *mind* heh
ROGER: [[*I* beg to differ with you,
AL:→hehh heh hhh "I b(h)eg to differ with you."
( ): ((sniff))
( ): ((cough))
ROGER: Yer better'n *most* of 'em. Cept me.
(4.0)[13]

Roughly, the "laugh token" repeat differs from the "questioning" repeat not only in that they do not "mean" the same thing (for example, that the former demonstrates some sort of approval and the latter demonstrates some sort of disapproval), but in that they do not do the same work. Laugh tokens in general are regularly associated with termination of talk[14] and it can be proposed that the laugh token repeat is regularly associated with termination of talk with reference to its product-item.

That may appear to be directly contradicted by the data—that is, immediately following the laugh token repeat is an utterance that refers to the product-item of the laugh token repeat: "Well y'know wi-n-*fall* out. Who knows what they'll eat now.", and "Yer better'n *most* of 'em. 'Cept me." However, immediately following that referential utterance there is an appreciable pause (where a standard between-utterance pause is something like 0.3 to 0.6 seconds, and in these cases the pauses are at least 3.0 seconds), and it is possible that the referential utterance is produced specifically by reference to the fact that laugh tokens are associated with termination, such that, for example, an attempt to "keep the topic going" may be seen. In the first case, such an attempt is in some sense successful, but the utterances that follow the long pause are specifically observable as attempts to keep things going via, for example, the problem in selecting which aspect of the prior talk is now being "continued."

KEN: hh hh
(1.0)
LOUISE: They sh'd really take the upholstery apart, tuh see if there's any money in it. hh
(1.0)
LOUISE: At'sa firs'in(hh)g // they do.
ROGER: Funny if termites starded eatin steel,
(1.4)

In the second case, "closure" is in a sense marked by the occurrence of an "assessment"[15] which incorporates laugh tokens.

ROGER: Yer better'n *most* of 'em. 'Cept me.
(4.0)
KEN: Go(h)d. Damn I haven't seen this group this bitchin in *yea(hh)rs* hehh

An alternative account for the possible "delay" utterance involves an ambiguity which inheres to laugh tokens. A laugh token in following-adjacency to an item such as "Got *ter*mites" or "*I* beg to differ with you"—objects that are intendedly jokes and can be "appreciated" via laughter—can alternatively and equivocally be another sort of object; that is, it can be "laughing at" and not "laughing with" the joker. A laugh token can then converge with a questioning repeat if it is found to be possibly non-appreciative; that is, it may then call for some remedial work (cf. p. 303, "heh heh 'Mother' hah hheh hhehh" and p. 316, I, "Well illuminate(h)d?"). Further, there seems to be a uni-directionality to the hearing of "at"/"with"; where "at" may be heard unequivocally, but "with" is also possibly "at." For example, in the following fragment there appears to be no ambiguity for the recipient of a laugh token.

A: See Judy was a Soshe. And we both said "We're not Soshes" yet she was. And she would say "I'm not a Soshe, I'm not a sho—s—*I'm* not a Soshe." Y'know, this—and she was so Soshey.
B: heh hehhehh
A: That was a tongue twister,[16]

In this case it is clear that B's laughter is "at" A's tongue-tiedness in "I'm not a sho—s—. . . .," which A attends with "That's a tongue twister." On the other hand, where there is an intended joke that is surely hearable as such, there is apparently still an open possibility that the repeater is otherwise dealing with it. This possibility is attended via a sort of hedging, where a more or less remedial, explicatory item is produced, say, "just in case."

Apparently, the proper way to handle a laugh token repeat is to ignore it (and regularly it is handled in just that way), since, if it is heard as an object signalling appreciation via laughter, then it is a terminator. If it is heard as its alternative possibility, then the problem it raises ought to be talked about—if the item is acknowledged at all. In a sense it is a compliment which enforces modesty upon its recipient, in the interests of continuing the on-going sequence. Specifically, even if the laugh token repeat is taken as a compliment, it is not properly returned with "Thank you." Compare that to another way of doing "appreciation" which may specifically elicit further talk from the one who did the "appreciated" item:

LOUISE: What's wrong with *you* t'day.
. . . . .
. . . . .
. . . . .
. . . . .
DAN: *Yea:h.* That's a good *ques*tion.
(1.0)
LOUISE: *Thank* you.
(0.3)
DAN: *Does // he have—?
LOUISE: °I get an A?
(0.5)
DAN: *D'z'e have some//thing (   )?

LOUISE: °(I c'd use another A,)
KEN: 's gotta com//plex.
ROGER: Am *I* hiding something,[17]

(For clarity, certain liberties are taken with the transcripts. The dots indicate omitted utterances.)

In this case, via "That's a good question" being a possible compliment (where it is also—and here clearly is being used as—something else, for example, a way to impress upon Roger the import of the question, to urge him to answer it), it generates for one of its hearers an acknowledgement series in which the complimenter ought to then acknowledge her thanks with "You're welcome," and is then, for that device, talking competitively with the very person he engaged in talk.

There is still another type of repeat, the sort that "recognizes correctness" or does "affirmation"; which does not generate further talk directed to the product-item, nor does it raise issues of possible termination, but provides that the one who was speaking before the "side sequence" occurred will, upon its completion, continue.

A: Uh, she asked me to stop by, she bought a chest of drawers from um
(4.0)
A: What's that gal's name? Just went back to Michigan.
(2.0)
A: Helen, um
B: Oh I know who you mean,
(1.0)
B: Brady— *Bra*dy.
A:→Yeah! Helen Brady.
B: Mm hm,
A: And, she—she says she's uh never had a new bedroom set so she's fixed this all up . . .[18]

and

B: No, *I* had the *queen* Cora. And uh Ray uh that Morgan, or—no their names aren't "Morgan," but Ray an' Lisa or Lah—um oh whoever they // are,
A: Yeah I-I keep saying "Morgan"—*Smith.*
B:→Yeah, Smith.
A: Uh//huh,
B: Uh—that Ray had the ace-king.[19]

These various repeat procedures are also available to a single speaker, such that one can remark on one's own talk. In the first of the two above cases, B's "Brady—*Bra*dy" is such a same-speaker repeat; an affirmative repeat. In the following report there is also an affirmative same-speaker repeat:

As the play ends, Patrick says "That was my point," casually.
Ernie objects, "No it wasn't!"
"Yes it was!" says Patrick with determination. "You hit it there. It bounced right there," says Patrick, pointing to a spot near the net on Ernie's side. "It hit there."
→Patrick points and repeats with certainty, "It bounced right there."[20]

And here, a repeat that attends a troublesomeness of its product-item, following a remedy plus a characterization of the trouble:

The mother isn't holdin—the father isn't—ah Freudian slip heh heh "Mother" hah hheh hhehh[21]

The preceding was not intended as an exhaustive list of the kinds of repeats, or an analysis of their workings. There are other sorts of repeats—for example, questioning repeats that do not have "surprise" associated with them, but are more nearly straight requests for information:

A: I didn' get tuh vote I declined tuh state this time, when I registered, so, I just uh, didn't get tuh vote fer president so,
B:→You // declined—
A: I think I—
B: What—whaddiyou mean.
A: Well, I vote Republican *and* Democrat.
(1.0)
B: Oh : : : yea : : : h.[22]

and

A: I got in a phone booth, it w'about two o'clock in the morning. We w—comin home—I w'z comin home from a party. I got on the phone and I started—I started hearin this tick tick tick tick an' the heh I just hung up an' ra(h)n heh God uh // I didn't know
B:→"Tick tick tick"?
A: Thought it was a time bomb or—you know,[23]

There are doubtless others. The intention here is to provide a sense of the sort of object a "repeat" is: an object that has as its product-item a prior occurrence of the same thing, which performs some operation upon that product-item. Focus is directed to "questioning repeats" which, it will be shown, provide that the one who produced the object which is repeated is obliged to talk some more with reference to that object, contrasted to, for example, directly continuing with the on-going talk.

In effect, Susan's questioning repeat is a juncture point between the game and non-game activity. It provides that the talk that precedes it, Steven's count to ten, is not only a game action, but "becomes" the first part of the series of utterances which comprise the non-game activity.

The dual status of Steven's utterance will not be directly considered, but the assertion that it is "part" of a series of utterances will be examined; that is, the claim that it is a unit in a "sequence." Since the notion "sequence" is crucial to this analysis, it will be given detailed attention.

The term "sequence" refers to events that occur as a "serial unit," which belong together and follow one after another. They do not just happen to occur one after another. One can go through a corpus of transcribed conversations and pick out many "similar" one-after-anothers, which can be found upon closer observation to be characterizeably cases of a "same" sort of sequence.

For example, one can find a Misapprehension Sequence of three parts. The parts will be named for convenience, and, as is the case with other names of objects in this paper, are not intended as definitive of the objects, but a way to handle them readily. In the Misapprehension Sequence there is a statement of sorts, a misapprehension of sorts, and a clarification of sorts: (s)–(m)–(c). Following are a few cases of the Misapprehension Sequence.

(1.a)	A:	(s)	Are you serious or are you—kidding.
	B:	(m)	No I'm serious he said I could have the room if I wanted it.
	A:	(c)	No I mean uh about beating you up.[24]

(1.b)	A:	(s)	Her whole room she's got it wallpapered. She just—she just got done rewallpapering it about a month ago,
	B:	(m)	—with the pictures of the Beatles.
	A:	(c)	No. A month ago Mom had it done in this grasscloth. . . .[25]

(2.a)	A:	(s)	Does he own my house? // hehhehh
	B:		eheh heh heh
	C:		Yeah he bought it last—a week ago. I don't know, probably does.
	D:	(m)	What are you getting at Roger?
	A:	(c)	*No*thing. Every week he tells us something else h(h)e owns or i—or is involved in you know . . .[26]

(2.b)	A:	(s)	. . . there was these three girls and they just got married,
	B:		ehh hehh hhh hhh Hey waita se(h)cond.
	C:		heh!
	B:	(m)	Drag tha(h)t by agai(h)n hehh hehh
	A:	(c)	There—there was these three *girls*. And they were all *sis*ters. An' they'd just got married to three *bro*thers.[27]

These sequences have an orderliness which—if this were a game—could readily be seen as the product of participants' acting according to a rule, and for the purposes of this paper it will be assumed that conversationalists do behave according to such rules.[28] In the case of the Misapprehension Sequence the rule seems to provide that if a statement is made and is followed by a demonstration/assertion that a hearer did not understand, then the one who made the statement may/must provide a clarification.

The preceding fragments will be independently examined to see the distinction between alternative forms ("may" and "must") of the "clarification rule." These considerations will have some relevance for the "questioning repeat" as it will be later developed that the talk generated by such an object is indeed a "sequence," and that sequence involves the "must" form of an expanded version of the clarification rule.

Cases 1.a and 1.b are instances of the "may" form clarification and cases 2.a and 2.b are instances of the "must" form. Roughly, for the first two, the "clarificatory" (c) utterances ("No, I mean uh about beating you up" and "No. A month ago Mom had it done in this grasscloth") stand in a relation to the "misapprehensions" (m) (". . . he said I could have the room if I wanted it" and "—with the pictures of the Beatles") where it is the business of the (c)-speaker to show that the (m)-speaker's utterance was a misapprehension of (s). That is to say, in 1.a and 1.b (m) is a *product* of (c), and not necessarily a "misapprehension" in its course. As it is occurring it is intendedly or proposedly a correct apprehension of (s), and "becomes" (m) as a result of the work the (c)-speaker does upon it.

In this "may" form clarification, the option is the clarifier's in the sense that (m) could just as well be something else, but for the fact that the clarifier shows that an (m) occurred. Thus, some item that precedes a clarification in the "may" form sequence is an *either-or* object. (An "either-or" object can be briefly characterized here as something which may be *intended* as one thing—for example, a "correct interpretation," a "strike" thrown by the pitcher, a "pressuring" of Roger by Dan; and may *turn out* to be something else—for example, a "misapprehension," a "home run" hit by the batter, a "compliment" received by Louise.)

Cases 2.a and 2.b are instances of the "must" form clarification. The relationship between (m) and (c) here is one where it is the business of the (m)-speaker to show that (s) requires clarification, and (c) is then an obliged utterance. This means that, first, the (m) is a non-equivocal object —as in the initial data, being tagged is being tagged, unequivocally; and second, one either produces a "clarification" or is observably not producing it (as contrasted with observably doing some other action altogether).

The "must" form (c) is an "*if-then*" object which can be briefly characterized by reference to the initial data, where "counting to ten" is an "if-then" object in the sense that, having the "counting to ten" as the action name for the reported utterance "One, two, three, four five six, eleven eight nine ten," a reader of that report can—knowing the rules of Marco Polo—know what game action *preceded* it, i.e. that preceding Steven's counting to ten, Steven was tagged. One can know it because "counting to ten" is a piece of behavior which abides by one of the rules of the game, that rule being an if-then, "must" form rule: if Steven is tagged, then Steven is It and will now therefore close his eyes and count to ten. Further, if Steven does not count to ten he is not doing an alternative game action, he is in violation of the rules, i.e. is "not counting to ten."

The option in the "must" form is not the clarifier's as it is in the "may" form, but the misunderstander's in the sense that (s) could just as well be understandable but for the fact that the (m)-speaker asserts that a misapprehension (or no comprehension) has occurred. In case 2.a it appears that at least for some of the participants (s) is understandable; that is, someone other than the (s)-speaker or the (m)-speaker produces laugh tokens which could be a demonstration that he "got" (s), and still another participant finds (s) understandable in that he can produce an answer to it.

In short, whereas in the first two cases it is the clarifier who could "let it go," in the second two cases it is the misunderstander who could "let it go." The option in the "must" form is to "misunderstand", a second speaker's option, where in the "may" form the option is to "clarify", a first-speaker-again option.

Having "options" as analytical resources, the data might be examined to begin to develop a sense of "talk control." Specifically, in case 2.a and 2.b it might be seen that the (m)s ("What are you getting at?" and "Drag that by again") can be designated as Bs for which the (s)s are A, but are in some sense becoming As for which the speaker who produced the (s) will now do a B. There are various other occasions of this shifting relationship; for example, upon a statement by an A-speaker, say, an "announcement" which has as an expectable B for it some sort of comment, the B-speaker produces a question, which is now an A for the answer which is its B, and the initial A-speaker becomes a B-speaker.[29]

Further, as can be seen in 2.a, there is not only this linear working of talk, but, so to speak, horizontal working. The first utterance, "Does he own my house?" is, among other things, a "question" for which an "answer" will be its B: "Yeah he bought it last—a week ago . . ." However, the "question" that elicits an "answer" from one party as its B, also elicits laugh tokens, i.e. what is, directed to one person, a "question," appears to be, for another person, a "wisecrack" which has "laughter" as its B. This "question-wisecrack" also receives, as its B, a statement of misapprehension, providing that the A is an "unclear object."

This is not merely to point out that conversational activities are complex, but to focus on at least one feature of these bits of talk, a feature that matters not only for the immediately prior data, but for the initial data and for consideration of the "questioning repeat" in general, i.e. to focus on objects that are B to a prior A and A for an expectable—perhaps obligated—B. Specifically, they can generate a sequence of talk involving the initial A-speaker as a B-speaker; a sequence which that initial A-speaker did not necessarily intend to generate, and at least did not directly provide for.

There appears to be a series of specifically B-type actions which may be produced upon the occurrence of various A-types, where those A's cannot be seen, for example, to require such a B in the sense that a "question" requires an "answer" or "Marco!" requires "Polo!" So, one option on some statement is to produce a one-line wisecrack which in variously characterizable ways stands as a B to the statement, that wisecrack then generating a sequence that consists at least of a B, say, a "retort," for which the wisecrack is its A:

KEN: (A) The new fad in about seven years will be women smokin cigars, you—because be*fore* it used to be all men were s-smoking cigar*ettes,*
AL: (B/a)→Well so you'll be smoking a ci*gar* in seven *years* I don't care.
(1.0)
KEN: They had a—
ROGER: (b) heh! hh//hh hhh hehh
KEN: (b) *Thanks.*[30]

In this particular case, and in general, a "wisecrack" sets up among its next utterances things like laughter and retorts. These next utterances stand as B's for which the wisecrack is an A, where the wisecrack was produced as a B to some prior A.

The possibility for a B-to-some-prior-A, A-for-the-next-B object provides that an A-speaker cannot necessarily control what will be done with some utterance he makes. He can—merely or however—project a possible sequence.

It is the case for wisecracks as B-to-A, A-for-B objects (and it remains to be determined whether it is so for all or some of the other such objects, including the "questioning repeat"), that they cannot guaranteedly control what will be done with *them.* On the occurrence of a wisecrack, which is now an A for the sequence that may be generated upon its occurrence, a B-speaker to that wisecrack now has an option, involving the "either-or" formulation. A B-speaker can hear something other than the intended wisecrack, such that some item which is upon its occurrence clearly a wisecrack, may turn out to be transformed by a B-speaker into a "misapprehension" to which a (c) will be its B; that is, instead of a wisecrack getting a retort, a misapprehension gets a clarification.

(3.a) A: (s) Why didn't they do anything about that bullet cause that was another wound.
B: (m) Well what are they gonna do about it, ((pause)) except remove it.

A: (c) No! But that means that there was another bullet, from a different direction, shot.[31]

(3.b) A: (s) . . . I shave around Saturday night y'know, cause goin out Saturday night. hhh
B: (m) You—you know—The rest of the week you don't shave but Sa(h)turday night.
A: (c) No, I mean I usually shave in the morning except on Saturday when I shave at night.[32]

It might be noted that whether in fact or for anyone's observation, some, or all, or any of the six cases that involve objects that receive clarificatory utterances are "really" misapprehensions or wisecracks, that is not the issue. The point is that there are objects that can be either wisecracks or misapprehensions, such that an object like an "intended wisecrack" can be treated as a "misapprehension" and is not a non-transformable object in the sense that the game-action "tagging" is non-transformable; and also that the clarifier's option is not necessarily contingent upon a determination as to whether some object was a "real" misapprehension. They all may receive clarifications. Possibly the phrase "No, I mean . . ." which introduces some of the clarifications can be seen to specifically occur when the (c) is produced via the "may" form clarification rule; that is, given that for this version of the rule the (c) is optional, then it may be necessary to signal, with "No I mean . . ." that the prior utterance was indeed an (m) for which this is a (c).

On the other hand, it appears that a clarification occurring as a B to a misapprehension (intended, transformed, joking, etcetera), is a non-transformable object—that is, when a clarification occurs it is treated as something that means what the speaker was trying to say before. (Extended versions of cases 1.a through 3.b appear in the appendix. No analysis has been done on occurrences following the clarifications, but perhaps it can be observed that there is nothing in that talk to suggest that the participants are manipulating the clarificatory utterance, or examining it to see if it is indeed a clarification, or if not, what then.)

At this point it will be proposed that one of the utterances in the initial data, the one in which Steven at last provides a correction for "eleven," belongs to the same class of actions as "clarifications," i.e. a "clarification" may be a sort of "correction," and/or both of these are members of the class of actions which can be called "remedies."

Using this extended collection, it may be observed that, as a statement of misapprehension—such as, in 2.a "What are you getting at?" and 2.b "Drag that by again"—involves the "must" form of the clarification rule and is a second speaker's option, so the questioning repeat involves a remedy as its if-then, must-form obligated next action.

It is being proposed, then, that the questioning repeat, as a B-to-a-prior-A, A-for-a-next-B object is generative in the ways that a statement of misapprehension is, is generated by work that a B-speaker performs on some A, and can set up a sequence that is not necessarily intended by the A-speaker, and which is not subject to the possibility of transformation that the otherwise similar wisecrack is.

At this point also, it must be noted that the various utterances that have so far been identified as initial A-type objects, are in some sense or another regularly B-type objects for some sequence of talk which has been on-going. So, as a specific instance, the question-wisecrack-unclear statement in 2.a ("Does he own my house?") is clearly in reference to something that has been said before, and now this question is asked about some "he," where that pronoun directs attention to that prior piece of talk as its source. And, returning to the initial data, Steven's "counting to ten" belongs to the on-going sequence, whereas the sequence generated by a B-speaker to it does not belong to the game sequence. It will be developed here that the latter sequence is not merely "another" sequence, but that it and others like it are, in a series of ways, *subsidiary* to the former sequence.

The action "counting to ten" is provided for by the structure of the on-going sequence, the game of Marco Polo. It is also the case that *how* the action is done is not controlled by the structure nor legislated by the rules of that game. So, for example, where "counting to ten" might be preferably done by producing "One, two, three; four, five, six; seven, eight, nine, ten," it might be adequately done by producing "Wuhtoothree-fawfisisenayniten," and there is nothing wrong, in terms of game action, with a count to ten that includes "eleven" as one of its digits (cf. p. 295). However, there are procedures for—and apparently reasons for—dealing with such characterizably "trivial" matters. Several procedures have been sketched. The issue of "reasons" for initiating procedures to generate remedies can be focused on via the demonstrated capacity of the recipient of a questioning repeat, an interrogative, a laugh token, to locate the intended product-item of such an object. The recipient can then provide further talk directed to clearing up what *he* can see to be the problem with it, without any further delineation of that problem, and this holds even for places where there is possible ambiguity, such that "heh hehhehh" is treated by its recipient as noticing the stammer and not expressing amusement at the anecdote, and an explication is offered (cf. p. 301). In the Percy fragment, not only is the product-item of "Who?" located, but there is further talk directed to identifying Percy for the interrogator.

B: *Who*?
A: Percy. That young fella thet uh—his daughter was murdered.
(1.0)
B: Oh *yea : : h. Yeah.*[33]

It would seem that, given not much more than an indication that there is a problem, the recipient can "also" find that there is a problem, can locate that problem, and can offer a remedy for it. By producing a remedy, the recipient legitimatizes the complaint.

Earlier it was mentioned that completion of an utterance that has a problematic item in it might, for its hearer, legitimatize his assumption that an unsolicited remedy was not forthcoming, whereupon he may initiate remedial procedures. It might also be seen that with the offering of a remedy, the act of initiating remedial procedures is observably a legitimate one. It is, then, the recipient's action that demonstrates that there was good reason for someone to do, for example, a questioning repeat. This is not to say that any given recipient of such an object can decide whether or not he will do an action to warrant that object, since the remedy appears to be sequentially obligated given the complaint (cf. p. 305 ff). The point is that once a remedy is offered, no further justification is needed for the object that elicited it, and no further attention is given that object *per se*. Even when a remedy is not done, and the complaint is argued, it is with, for example, an "affirmative repeat" of the initial product-item, and not, for example, with a questioning repeat of the questioning repeat, for one, because such an object does not exist in this culture.

Consider the following fragment, a telephone call for which A is a female at a private residence, B is male:

A: Hello,
B: "He*llo* : :"?!
A: Yeah. "He*llo*."
B: Wuh—Is this 293-4673?
A: No it's 293-4637.
B: Oh I'm awfully sorry.[34]

Here it might be briefly noted, with reference to earlier considerations of the differentiatability of the questioning repeat from similar and dissimilar objects (p. 295 ff), that "hello" as an appropriate next item, for a first "hello" might cause some difficulty in hearing that the object which follows this first "hello" is a questioning repeat and not a return. However, there is apparently no such problem. The object was instantly recognized as a questioning repeat and, as it turns out, was correctly recognized, since, when it is challenged with the affirmative repeat, B then requests information that will tell him whether his complaint was legitimately challenged; that is, whether he has reached the number he intendedly dialed.

Moreover, the interchange continues with:

A: Am I supposed to be a business firm?
B: Yes. That's right. That's exactly right. I'm calling my office. They *ne*ver answer with "he*llo* : :".

This suggests that independent of issues of "correctness," the remedial procedure generated by the questioning repeat is operative. Although in her particular case A correctly used "hello," she can nevertheless locate a way in which the complaint is legitimate which she offers to B, in effect finding that his action was but incidentally incorrect, since as far as B knew he was correctly applying the questioning repeat to an occurrence at his office.

The fact that some item can be "wrong" in such a way that how it is possibly "right" is available (in the environment of a residence, "Hello" is right, "He*llo : : ?!*" is wrong; in the environment of an office, "Hello" is wrong, "He*llo : : ?!*" is right, and B can check to see if he has contacted a residence and A can check to see if B was calling his office), suggests that it is insufficient to say, for example, that "eleven" is noticed to be wrong because it *is* wrong, and that its correction is accomplished by replacing it with "seven" because "seven" is the correct item in the ten-count. A hypothetical description of how Steven's count might be "right" is if it were a quotation of something he encountered on television the night before; it would then be a perfect quotation, recognizable as such by someone who had also seen the program. The "correction," then, would be a matter of his finding that for this environment his quotation was a *non sequitur*.

Further, for any given product-item of a questioning repeat there might be more than one problem, since for any spoken object one problem can always involve pronunciational issues. Nevertheless recipients of questioning repeats select an issue and provide a remedy by reference to that issue. The selection of the issue intended by the one who noticed a problem may have to do with a convergence of the noticer's intentions and relevancies provided by the on-going activity. This might be outlined with a hypothetical example. If an umpire in the midst of a baseball game says "Strike t'ree!" and the batter turns and exclaims "'*T'ree : :' ?!*", the umpire will perhaps feel obliged to respond to that, to affirm or correct his utterance. However, the problem the umpire selects may not be something which the noticer can control, but something which the on-going activity—the baseball game—will control; that is, the umpire may not hear that the batter is taking issue with his pronunciation of "three," but will more likely hear that perhaps he should have said "Strike two."

The following interchange might stand as a version of the situation offered above. It takes place on a two-way radio talk show, A is the caller, B is the moderator.

A: . . . and I want to know what you think about it.
B: I am appalled.
A: Yer—((pause)) a *paul*?
B: That's right sir, I am appalled.
A: Yeh. Uh ((pause)) what's that?[35]

B's hearing of "Yer—a *paul*?" seems to have been controlled by the on-going activity, which for two-way radio shows is frequently "argument." A questioning repeat occurring in the course of an argument may be an expression of "surprise" at some stated point of view, initiating remedial procedures involving that B explain why he is "appalled" at something about which A (and presumably everybody else) is "delighted." By producing an affirmative repeat B is "challenging a questioning repeat" where perhaps he ought to have been responding to a request for information. And it is in a sense incidental that A actually intended a request for information. The procedure generated by a questioning repeat, controlled by the on-going activity, has yielded for B that he has been "argued with."

Not only, then, are such items as questioning repeats subsidiary to the particular utterances from which they draw their sense, which serve as their source, via a relationship to which they have their completeness as actions; but they are subsidiary to the on-going activity of which those utterances are a part.

Still another sense of the term "subsidiary," as a descriptive term for side sequences, can be arrived at in the following way. It was noted at the outset, and is perhaps directly observable in some of the conversation fragments, that upon the occurrence of such things as the questioning repeat, the on-going activity is halted. There are other ways to halt an on-going activity, for example, by initiating what will be called "competitive" activities. These are things that—intendedly or consequentially—not only halt the on-going activity but terminate it. A model of a "competitive" event is found in this excerpt from a report of a baseball game which has been in progress for some thirty minutes:

> *32′18″* ((The pitcher)) turns and throws another ball in to ((the batter)).
> ((The batter)) swings for strike two.
> The ball is thrown back out to ((the pitcher)).
> ((The runner)) takes another long lead and teases ((the pitcher)), trying to get him to throw the ball to ((the baseman)).
> ((The pitcher)) just looks, however.
> *32′35″* Mrs. Turner blows the whistle, signalling the termination of the recess period.
> The game ends suddenly. The children turn away, and many of them run eagerly for the schoolroom.[36]

Termination of an on-going sequence occurs frequently in conversation, although on a less dramatic scale. It is not necessary for a crowd to disperse or dead silence to occur for it to be a noticeable fact that an on-going activity has terminated. There can be, for example, a "change in topic" or, on a finer scale, within a recognizably "same topic," a shift of focus. These provide to varying degrees that what has been on-going is now no longer on-going. Such termination can be observed to be at least associated with the occurrence of competitive activities at juncture points in conversation. A particular sense of the term "competitive" may be seen in the very production of talk at such junctures; specifically, utterances belonging to two different sequences occur simultaneously, where one of the sequences is picked up and the other is terminated. Following are two instances of that sort of event:

A: Yeah, it's been a rough week, I—everbuddy is—yihknow,
B: Mm—
A: —talkin about it, 'n everbuddy, course *I* don't know whether it's that, er just thet we're just—completely bogging down et work, ·hhhhm
A:→Er [WHAT A WAYTUH—WAYTUH TAKE, MY FINALS?
B: [OH : : : WELL EV'RYBODY'S SA : D.
B: *Oh : :* ! Howjuh *do* with yer finals.[37]

and

A: They wan'tuh git me in the r-*swing* a' things hnh
B: →How-HOW [OLD WERE YOU WH'NY'FIRST WENT.
A: [BY TH'TIME I'M NINETEEN 'M A GENUINE NEUROTIC. heh! hh heh
B: How old were you when y'first went.
(0.3)
A: *Oh : :*, I'd say about, thirteen,[38]

(the fragment at footnote 15 might also be examined for this issue.)

A characteristic feature of competitive activities is that the two simultaneous utterances each go to completion. This can be directly contrasted with a case of the subsidiary type of utterance, in this case the questioning repeat which is perhaps a request for information (p. 303). Here, the utterances may start simultaneously, and at least one of them—specifically for this issue, the utterance for which "You declined—" is a subsidiary object—stops, permitting the other to continue:

A: I didn' get tuh vote I declined tuh state this time, when I registered, so, I just uh, didn't get tuh vote fer president so,
B: YOU [DECLINED—
A: [I THINK I—
B: What—whaddiyou mean.

To enrich the description of "competitive" events, it might be noted that the occurrence of a stressed "*Oh : :*" in each of those fragments might be specifically accountable as affiliates to competitive talk. It appears that for cases of competitive simultaneous talk, the one whose talk is part of the terminated sequence not only, then, responds to the talk of the other with a "continuation" of that other sequence, but demonstrates that he sees its legitimacy as a competitive object to his own. The stressed "*Oh : :*" is then, similar to other expressions of "special interest" or "special attention," like "Oh *really*?". Such items frequently appear at juncture points which consist of simultaneous competitive talk.

LOUISE: . . . I *hate* it. Twelve and a half years old and I—seventeen and a half we look the same.
(2.0)
KEN: You know, my brother and I have come to one a- mutual agree[ment that—that we—
LOUISE: [SHE'S TALLER THAN I AM TOO.
KEN: She *is*? She's taller'n you?[39]

In this case, after a two-second pause and a fairly well-established utterance in what might be a new sequence, Louise overlaps—and turns out to have interrupted—Ken's talk with a proposal that she is "still talking." Ken demonstrates the legitimacy of her proposal with an utterance which, by "expressing heartfelt interest" in what she has said, "urges" her to continue.

"Competitive" sequences seem to yield readily to description. On the other hand, "subsidiary" sequences might appear to be characterizeable only after the fact—that is, perhaps anything that gets started could go on for some amount of time, over an indeterminate number of actions, and if it turns out that a given sequence at some point is no longer going on, that does not warrant giving it a name that implies at least a structural potential for closure such that the on-going sequence will be guaranteed its resumption. As a first step in developing a description of "subsidiary" sequences it can be noted that for formal events such as games there is frequently an alternative to the on-going activity which is not a competitive activity, does not result in termination of the on-going sequence. That alternative resides in the various sequences called "time-outs."

Time-outs are formal subsidiary sequences. They are known to be, are set up to be, and are initiated by virtue of the fact that, at the very least, they are of shorter duration than the game itself, by actual clock time, or because they consist of a nameable sequence with a set of parts, and specifically with a recognizable "last part." So, for example, the sequence generated by an injured player on the field has as its last part the action "player is removed from field," whereupon, expectably, the on-going sequence will resume.

Time-outs also have a recognizable "first part" by which the subsidiary sequence is generated. It can be found that conversationalists have access to "first parts" of specifically subsidiary sequences. For example, an object like "By the way" or "Oh incidentally" when it occurs at the end of a conversation, can be readily observed to be a "first part" of some subsidiary sequence. "By the way" can specifically signal that the "goodbyes" will be halted and will resume when the matter at hand has been dealt with. It is at least a promise that the sequence it will generate will be a subsidiary sequence and not a competitive sequence. So, in this fragment from a two-way radio talk show, "By the way" is placed in following-adjacency to a "goodbye":

A: F'give me sir, I'm gunnuh haftuh go.
B: O:kay.
A: Nice // talkin tuh you.
B: I enjoyed talking.
A: [[Thank yeh very *much.*
B: [[Thank y'very much. Okay,
A: Buh bye.
B:→ Uh—by the way : : :, Have a-a—Good luck in the hospit'l.
A: Thank you.
B: [[Okay buh bye.
A: [[Mm buh bye.[40]

It is by way of this fragment that a key point about side sequences in particular, and perhaps interactional phenomena in general, is raised. That is, "goodbye" would seem to be—if anything is—a structural part which is specifically a "last part." That "By the way" can be placed in following-adjacency to, and as a replacement for, "goodbye" suggests that there is a distinction between structural provisions and participants' work; where a given segment of talk is the result of the cooperation of those two; that is, is the result of participants' work in carrying out structural provisions. This point will be developed below.

Data has been used to locate places in which participants are engaged in "side sequences." These are demonstratedly subsidiary sequences for some on-going sequence, at least insofar as the objects that generate them are subsidiary objects. They are also possibly subsidiary sequences in that on-going sequences frequently can be found at some point, to pick up again. It remains to be seen if there are ways in which this second sense of "subsidiary" is a built-in feature of the relationship of side sequences to on-going sequences. One way to find that it is "built-in" is to find that there is a cooperating of structural provisions and participants' work.

Returning to the initial data, the verbatim report of the Marco Polo incident, it appears to be at least an *observer's* accomplishment that he found something he could call a "resumption" of the on-going sequence. Whatever did happen next, the observer's work has been to formulate it as a "resumption." This piece of observer's work will be used to suggest that "resumption" is an accomplishable object—that is, that there might be a kind of conversational work which provides for side sequence closure so that the on-going sequence can "resume."

A series of fragments will be examined by reference to the possibility of "resumption of an on-going sequence" as participants' work. These fragments are presented as cases of the same phenomenon that occurs in the initial data, with one difference—the ensuing events are available for examination. Thus, a possibility that could only be an observer's assertion in the initial data is something that can be looked for as an activity by participants.

To begin with, the structural provisions will be considered. What will be looked for is a triplet structure, analogous to the (s)–(m)–(c) triplet in the Misapprehension Sequences. As with the (s)–(m)–(c), ordered letters will be used to mark a possible "sequence" where, then, it will remain to be shown that something more than arbitrary notation is involved; that these "sequences" are mechanisms in which orientation to parts and to the relationship of these parts is involved.

The "sequence" here will be (O)–(S)–(R): On-going sequence, side-sequence, return to on-going sequence. Again, in order to more clearly exhibit the processes, liberties will be taken with the transcripts. Complete versions will be built up in the course of the discussion, and intact extended versions are supplied in the appendix.

I	A:	O	Wouldju call somebody like that a *nut*?
	B:		No,
	A:		Whaddiyuh *call* 'em. You can't say they're nuts,
	B:		He's a person who's well illuminated.
	. .	S	. . .
	C:		"Well illuminate(hh)d"?
	. .		. . .
	. .		. . .
	. .		. . .
	. .		. . .
	B:		Well eh well he's freed from all the eh inhibitions society imposes on him.
	A:	R	Listen. When he had the responsibility—when he had the responsibility to take—take charge of—he was second in charge of the dorm . . .[41]
II	A:	O	They crank this thing down at th'bottom. 's funny lookin.
			(1.0)
	B:		But the *air's* gotta come in there and the air is sorta infiltrated with little uh pixy dust.
	. .	S	. . .
	C:		"*Pi*xy dust"!?
	. .		. . .
	. .		. . .
	D:		"Radioactivity" I *think* is what he means.

C: (hh)Oh. Okay.
.. ...
C: I don't see what a bomb shelter—
.. R ...
C: Ey you know I don't see—I think it would be a great feeling y'know sit around there . . .[42]

III A: An' everybody's askin 'im t'dance.
B: An' because he's scareda dancing he's gonna dance in private til he
O learns how.
A: And a goodlooking girl comes up to you and asks you, y'know,
B: "Gi(hh)rl asks you to—"
.. S ...
C: Well it's happened a lotta times,
B: Okay okay go ahead.
(1.0)
B: So he says "no."
(1.0)
B: R Cause he's scared to admit that he can't dance an' he's scared to *try*. Cause he's gonna make a fool of himself.[43]

That participants orient to such things as (O)–(S)–(R) as "parts," and parts in relation to one another, might be initially suggested by pointing out the use of items like "Oh. Okay" (II); items that can signal "satisfactory termination" of the action they follow. That the satisfactory termination of *an* action provides for the initiating of another action, and that participants produce actions according to that fact, might be seen via the "By the way" fragment (p. 315), where "Okay" is something like a "pre-final" object—that is, it at least *occurs* immediately prior to "Buh bye." That it is *placed* immediately prior to "Buh bye," i.e. provides for the initiating of "goodbyes," can be observed in that both parties use it that way, in one case one party using the other's "Okay" to provide for his "buh bye":

B: Thank y'very much. Okay,
A: Buh bye
.. ...
.. ...
B: Okay buh bye.

In (III) "Okay okay go ahead" not only signals satisfactory termination, but instructs that there now be a return to the on-going sequence.

Terms like "Oh, Okay" are so frequently associated with these side sequences that they might be included into the sequence as a potential component. Such a four-part sequence occurs in the initial data:

1) One, two, three, ((pause)) four five six, ((pause)) eleven, eight, nine, ten.
2) "E*le*ven"?—eight, nine, ten?
.. ...
.. ...
3) Seven, eight, nine, ten.
4) That's better.

It occurs in (II):

1) But the *air's* gotta come in there, and the air is sorta infiltrated with little uh pixy dust.
.. ...
2) "*Pi*xy dust"!?
.. ...
.. ...
3) "Radioactivity" I *think* is what he means.
4) (hh)Oh. Okay.

and in the fragment below:

1) He likes that waiter over there.
2) Wait-"*er*"?
3) Waitress. Sorry.
4) That's better.[44]

The four-part version occurs in side sequences generated by other objects, for example in the Percy fragment:

1) If *Per*cy goes with—Nixon I'd sure like that.
2) *Who*?
3) Percy. That young fella thet uh—his daughter was murdered.
(1.0)
4) Oh *yea : : h. Yeah.*

Where there is *not* a four-part sequence there may be characterizable reasons for its non-occurrence, and those will be considered shortly.

Orientation to "parts" and their relationship might be most directly observable on the larger part-scale of the (O)–(S)–(R), in the relationship of (R) as specifically a "third part" to (S) as a "second part." It is not merely that there *occurs* a return to the on-going sequence, but that to return to the on-going sequence from (S) is a task performed by participants, resulting in a sequence-part (R). It is performed in distinctive, characterizable ways.

Specifically, (R) is either attempted as a "resumption" or a "continuation," each of which is an apparatus with distinctive components and techniques, which provide that—and which—return procedure is being initiated. In (I) and (II) there is an attempted "resumption," with "Listen" and "Hey you know" as first terms in utterances which in various ways implicate the talk constituting the on-going sequence. Such objects are regularly "attention getters" and signal, for example, that something that has been going on will now be re-attended. In (III) there is an attempted "continuation" with "So" as first term in the utterance which implicates the on-going sequence.

Where "resumption" might readily be seen to be of some interactional interest, the workings of "continuations" are such that they provide for their own interactional uninterestingness; that is, "resumption" *marks* that there is a problem in accomplishing a "return," while "continuation" is specifically directed, for example, to "covering up" the problem. In (III), however, that a "continuation" is an interesting matter becomes observable in that it is, in a strong sense, B's particular task to return to the on-going sequence; that is, he brought it to a halt, and apparently without good grounds, and he is now attempting to accomplish a return as a "continuation." In a sense, with the "continuation," he is attempting to "delete" the side sequence and tie directly to the on-going sequence.

Other data can then be examined for the occurrence of "continuation" as someone's attempt to get something done, where otherwise it simply appears that some sequence is continuing as a matter of course and not as the result of a particular technique. So, for example, a fragment introduced as an instance of the "affirmative repeat" yields an (O)–(S)–(R) structure with the (R) accomplished by the "continuation" apparatus, with the term "and" as a component. A glance at the fragment on page 318 will probably suffice to see the (O)–(S)–(R) structure; what will be shown here is the working of the device "continuation."

A: Uh she asked me to stop by, she bought a chest of drawers from um
. . . . .
A: Helen, um
. . . . .
. . . . .
A: Helen Brady.
. . . . .
A: And she—she says she's uh never had a new bedroom set so she's fixed this . . .

The work of "continuation" is specifically to incorporate the *content* of the side sequence into the syntax of the on-going sequence, but in effect deleting the *sequence* in which, for example, the name Helen Brady was found. In an exchange such as the Helen Brady fragment, this work is not readily seen, as compared to (III) where the intendedly deleted sequence involves a challenge. And perhaps "continuations" are differentiatable from "resumptions" in the sense that, had A for the Helen Brady fragment used "Listen" or "Hey you know," she might be seen to be overdoing her return to the on-going sequence; a "continuation" is sufficient in that case, a "resumption" unnecessary; and the B for "Gi(hh)rl asks you to—", by using a "continuer" might be seen to be improperly using a "continuer," where "resumption" was appropriate; that is, "acting as if" the sequence had proceeded:

A: An' everybody's askin 'im t'dance.
B: An' because he's scareda dancing he's gonna dance in private til he learns how.
A: And a goodlooking girl comes up to you and *asks* you, y'know,
.. ...
.. ...
.. ...
B: So he says "no." Cause he's scared to admit that he can't dance an' he's scared to *try*.

Again, note that the content of the side sequence (for which "And a goodlooking girl comes up to you . . ." is in a sense, the first unit) is preserved, while the syntax of the on-going sequence is invoked via the switch back from "you" to "he."

It may then be seen that a "return" to the on-going sequence is a task which, for alternative contingencies, is accomplished with alternative devices: "resumption," "continuation"; where the availability of such devices provides for manipulation of the talk in the sense that by using "continuation" participants can be proposing that there is no trouble, i.e. no "resumption" necessary, where that may not be the case. (cf. p. 300, where the first case may be an attempt to avert termination by proposing that talk is "continuing"; and p. 314, the issue of "still talking.")

Having raised "return to the on-going sequence" as a possible task, it can be noted that certain tasks have an assigned doer. Earlier the phenomenon of "time-outs" was mentioned. It can be further noted that for games that have formal time-outs it is specifically the task of an official to resume the game, in independence of the potential for closure within a time-out sequence. The game is resumed on an official's signal and resumed, for example, despite anybody or everybody's continuing interest in an injured player, beyond the moment when the player has been removed from the field.

That is to say, the potential for closure of the time-out sequence is enforced by someone whose task it is to accomplish a return to the on-going sequence, where in the first place the termination of the time-out may not be convergent with, for example, that the player has recovered. For game-activities, the issue is that he has been removed from the field of play. (And so it is for side sequences in conversation. The issue is to "resolve the problem," and that is done by going through a certain sort of sequence. Although this procedure is strictly an abstract, formal procedure —that is, does not involve inquiries into why someone said a thing like "Pixy dust" or whether they are likely to say it again—it will be shown shortly that no such inquiries are necessary, no promises need be elicited. The procedure appears to be effective beyond its immediate occurrence.)

One way to locate the enforcer of side sequence closure, i.e. the assigned doer of the return to the on-going sequence, might be to apply a notion of "relative status" to the data, using items like "big sister"–"little brother," "therapist"–"patient," etc., to see if, for example, it is the higher status or lower status category which applies to the person who did a return, and whether there is any consistency across fragments. However, on some of the fragments there is insufficient information to set up such categories.

An alternative procedure would be to examine the materials at hand to see if there is some orderliness in the relationship of the return—and any given doer of it, to other action-units of the sequence and doers of them. A set of letters can be assigned to retain information on "which person," i.e. as a direct replacement for his name; a separate set of letters can be assigned to action-units within the (O)–(S)–(R) sequences, analogous to the (s)–(m)–(c) units within the Misapprehension Sequence.

This device will be applied to the three sequences initially selected as being "identical" to the Eleven fragment. In this case the action-units will not be "named," but will be designated simply "a" and "b." Thus, for example, Aa(O) will indicate that person A is doing action-unit "a" for sequence-part (O). There is reason for separately designating speakers and actions in that it can be found that more than one person is doing what appears to be an "a" or "b" action for some sequence-part. For example, in (III):

A*a*(O): An' everybody's askin 'im t'dance.
B*a*(O): An' because he's scareda dancing he's gonna dance in private til he learns how.
A*a*(O): And a goodlooking girl. . . .

and (as will eventually be shown), in (I):

Aa(O): Whaddiyuh call 'im. You can't say he's nuts,
B*b*(O): He's a person who's well illuminated.
. .   . . .
D*b*(O): He'll do anything for kicks.

For better accessibility, the utterances accompanying the lettered designations will be supplied.

I	Aa(O):	Wouldju call somebody like that a *nut*?
	Bb(O):	No,
	Aa(O):	Whaddiyuh *call* 'em. You can't say they're nuts,
	Bb(O):	He's a person who's well illuminated.
	..	...
	Ca(S):	"Well illuminate(hh)d"?
	..	...
	..	...
	..	...
	..	...
	Bb(S):	Well eh well he's freed from all the eh inhibitions society imposes on him.
	Aa(R):	Listen. When he had the responsibility . . .
II	Aa(O):	They crank this thing down at th'bottom. 's funny lookin.
	Bb(O):	But the *air's* gotta come in there and the air is sorta infiltrated with little uh pixy dust.
	..	...
	Ca(S):	"*Pi*xy dust"!?
	..	...
	..	...
	Db(S):	"Radioactivity" I *think* is what he means.
	Ca(S):	(hh)Oh. Okay.
	..	...
	Ca(R):	Ey you know, I don't see what a bomb shelter . . .
III	Aa(O):	An' everybody's askin 'im t'dance.
	Ba(O):	An' because he's scareda dancing he's gonna dance in private til he learns how.
	Aa(O):	And a goodlooking girl comes up to you and *asks* you y'know,
	Ba(S):	"Gi(hh)rl asks you to—"
	..	...
	Cb(S):	Well it's happened a lotta times,
	Ba(S):	Okay okay go ahead.
	Ba(R):	So he says "no."

Glancing over the lettered sets *vis-à-vis* the doer of the return to the on-going sequence, it can be noted that: For (I) A is "a" for (O) and A is "a" for (R); for (II) C is "a" for (S) and C is "a" for (R); for (III) B is an "a" for (O), B is "a" for (S), and B is "a" for (R). Considering that for each of these exchanges there are co-present at least four possible speakers, that one person is found to do the "a" for (O) or (S) and the "a" for (R) seems to be the result of an orderly relationship between those sequence-parts and the doers of them.

Further, there are two specifically observable "non-occurrences": (1) No non-speaker-so-far is "a" for (R), and (2) no "b" speaker for (S) does the "a" for (R). It may be that the workings of who shall do the return to the on-going sequence are more delicate and particular than has been sketched, but *vis-à-vis* the locating of whose task (R) might be, it is roughly and at least, a person who has done some "a" and has not become the doer of a "b" for (S).

Having as a possibility that "return to the on-going sequence" is a designatable task for some particular person, then it must be inquired whether it is a task that matters for its doer, i.c. is he "responsible" for its accomplishment. That might be suggested by noting that in each case the one who does the return gets it done "despite" some difficulty—that is, it apparently matters to the doer—if the amount of effort he is willing to expend to get it done is any measure. In none of the cases is the return simply and readily accomplished. In (I) and (II) the resumer works through competing talk, and in (III) the continuer works through others' silence, that silence following his instruction to "go ahead."

I Bb(O): He's a person who's well illuminated.
Aa(O): Well, he's—
Ca(S): "Well illuminate(hh)d"?
Bb(S): hehhehh
Aa(R): *Waita minute. When he—
Db(O): He'll do anything for kicks.
Aa(R): *No! No listen.
Bb(S): Well eh well he's freed from all the eh inhibitions society imposes on him.
Aa(R): *Listen. When he had the responsibility . . .

II Db(S): "Radioactivity" I *think* is what he means.
Ca(S): (hh)Oh. Okay.
Db(S): hmh hmh
Ca(R): *I don't see what a bomb shelter—
Bb(S): From that big bonfire in the sky hehh
Ca(R): *Ey you know, I don't see . . .

III Ba(S): Okay okay go ahead.
(1.0)
Ba(R): So he says "no."
(1.0)
Ba(R): Cause he's scared to admit that he can't dance an' he's scared to *try*. Cause . . .

An extensive consideration of how a task can be seen to "matter" to its doer will not be attempted here. However, Sacks has offered some preliminary remarks, by reference to the doing of "introductions"[45] as the sort of task for which there is some designatable doer, which is taken up by someone who finds that he is the one who ought to do it—without hesitation, without deliberation, and without any further "motivation" than that he is the one who ought to do it; that is, that the social organization that provides for his finding that it is his task to do "introductions" may also provide that the doing of it should matter to him. "Return to the on-going sequence" might be considered analogously; that is, for the purposes of this essay it will be suggested that however it has come about that a task can be an assignable task for some person, so it has come about that the task will matter to him, specifically in the sense that having initiated it, or having done a single attempt is not sufficient, but he will attempt to accomplish it.

Having the person who does an "a" for (O) and/or (S) as the "responsible party" for (R) guarantees that there will be a return, in the same way that having an official present guarantees a return to the game after a time-out. In the case of games, the official is hired for a job that includes doing returns; in conversation the "official" is locally selected and is in a sense, self-selected—is, so to speak, a volunteer.

That the doer of the return is presented with difficulty in the accomplishing of the return is an issue that requires some consideration, and which may come about in the following way. As far as can be seen by examining long series of transcripts, for example, the group therapy sessions from which these particular side sequences were excerpted, which consist of five consecutive two-hour sessions, it can be noted that for various sorts of events there is recurrence of talk with reference to them, over the course of one session, or across sessions. These might be specifically nameable events—for example, "the time Al got into an argument with Ken." In general, one consequence of such a reference is that the argument may be re-generated. Such is not the case for the side sequences generated by a questioning repeat. Once the side sequence is terminated, i.e. once the on-going sequence is successfully resumed, there is no recurrence of talk with reference to the side sequence. Once terminated, it is done with, once and for all.

That may be consequential for events within a side sequence, in that one result of a side sequence generated by a questioning repeat is that the particular item dealt with is extinguished for that environment. It ought not—and in these data does not—occur again. And it may be noted that talk with reference to some prior event can be done with a single term, say, a "key" term. For example, in the fourth of the taped therapy sessions, reference to an event in the first is done with a single word, "Beatle."

ROGER: . . . I mean we don't have claws, or fangs or fur,
JIM: Some // do hhhehhh!
ROGER: —so we have guns.
KEN: hheh
ROGER: heh
KEN: You don't have // fur?
ROGER: I'm speakin of th'average human.
KEN: Hey—you don't have fur? Wh-what's that on yer head?

ROGER: Oh, n-n-
KEN: D'you call that a mop?
JIM: Yeah
ROGER:→It's a Beatle.
KEN: "It's a Beatle." Ohh *no(hhhh)o*![46]
(4.0)

If a single word can do that sort of work, then it is unlikely that the non-recurrence of the words dealt with in side sequences can be explained with, for example, that it is just one single word among the multitude of words which were produced in some ten hours of talk. Instead, its non-recurrence may be an accomplished fact.

Difficulty in accomplishing a return to an on-going sequence from a side sequence may derive from the issue of extinguishing the product-item of a questioning repeat in the following way: As long as the side sequence is in progress there might be a possibility that the one who did that item can provide that it is, in fact, acceptable, and may then recur. If the side sequence is terminated and acceptance has not been granted, then that item is extinguished. This would provide good reason for the "b" speaker in a side sequence to attempt to keep the sequence open, perhaps resulting in talk that overlaps the first attempt at a return to the on-going sequence. Consider (II) in which C performs action "a" for the side sequence and action "a" for the return, where B is observably proposing that he is "still talking" (cf. p. 314), such that the "a(R)" is initiated before B, the selected "b" for the side sequence has "finished."

Bb(O): But the *air's* gotta come in there and the air is sorta infiltrated with little uh pixy dust.
. . . . .
Ca(S): "*Pi*xy dust"!?
Bb(S):→YOU KNOW FROM THE BIG BOOM?
Ca(S): "*Pi*xy dust"?
Db(S): "Radioactivity" I *think* is what he means.
Ca(S): (hh)Oh. Okay.
Db(S): hmh hmh
Ca(R):→I don't see [what a bomb shelter—
Bb(S): [FROM THAT BIG BONFIRE IN THE SKY hehh
Ca(R): Ey you know, I don't see. . . .

That is to say, the item C selects as "Okay," and via its being acceptable initiates the return, is D's replacement for "pixy dust," "radioactivity"—and not B's whimsical explication "You know from the big boom?" Possibly, had "(hh)Oh, Okay" been placed after "You know from the big boom?", it would provide that "pixy dust" was, for example, accepted in light of B's explication, and therefore might recur in this place among these people. Instead, a second questioning repeat is placed there, is "correctly" followed by an acceptable remedy which is followed by "Oh okay." And it can be noted that the term "pixy dust" does not recur. B's equally whimsical "continuation" of his explication, "From that big bonfire in the sky hehh," which overlaps C's attempted return to the on-going sequence may be produced specifically as an attempt to avert the closure of the side sequence so that "pixy dust" can be found to be, after all, acceptable.

The task of returning to the on-going sequence appears then to be not only a matter of "getting things going again," but also of enunciating whether some problematic object, after having been processed, is or is not acceptable for the given environment. Note, for example, in (III), the challenge having been done, it is in effect interrupted by the same speaker attempting to retract the uncompleted challenge with an acceptance.

Aa(O): And a goodlooking girl comes up to you and *asks* you, y'know,
Ba(S): "Gi(hh)rl asks you to—"
Ba(S):→ALRIGHT,
Cb(S): Well it's happened a lotta ti[mes,
Ba(R): [OKAY OKAY GO AHEAD.
(1.0)

Despite the attempted retraction, an appropriate "b" for (S) occurs, and B's "Okay okay go ahead" is characterizably not an acceptance of "Girl asks you to dance" after consideration of supporting material, for example; it is part of the attempted retraction. One possible reason for the noticeable balking of the others at taking up B's offered "continuation" return to the on-going sequence might be that, having been initiated the side sequence ought to have been gone through, and *then* a finding (acceptable / not acceptable) delivered.

It can be seen, then, that the one who initiates a side sequence is not thereby in a position to control certain features of it. As was mentioned earlier, he cannot control what will be made of some noticing of a prior item, where that is controlled by the on-going sequence of which that item is a part (p. 311). Here it is observed that co-participants may, by their talk or their silence, have some effect on the working out of a side sequence which the initiator did not necessarily intend, nor directly provide for.

Having mentioned the work of those co-participants who are not initiators of the side sequence, a further observation on the initial data can be made: that Nancy did not immediately, also, query Steven's "eleven." This can be proposed as an observable feature of the interaction in that people do produce simultaneous talk, and in the footnotes there is an instance of simultaneous production of a questioning repeat:

The first boy gets up and says, "If I'm elected vice-president I'll keep the room quiet, I'll be a good sport, and I'll help other people, and I'll ask questions . . ." finishing lamely.

several children say with disbelief, "*Ask* questions, *ask* questions!"[47]

The issue is somewhat more interesting than that perhaps Nancy does not do a questioning repeat when she should or could. It will be proposed that Nancy is doing a "continuation" of the on-going sequence. Again, the initial data is not transparent in this respect, since Nancy's appropriate action happens to be her silence—that is, her present game action is to be silent and stay away from Steven. Her next game action will be to yell "POLO!" when Steven has yelled "MARCO!" Therefore there is nothing to look at to see that by saying nothing she was doing something, specifically a "continuation of the game sequence." The excerpts under consideration, however, provide something to look at such that "continuation" can be a directly observable activity, as a "continuation" in contrast to a "break."

I Aa(O): You can't say they're nuts,
Bb(O): He's a person who's well illuminated.
Aa(O): °WELL HE'S—
Ca(S): *"Well illuminated(hh)d"?
. . . . .
. . . . .
Db(O): °HE'LL DO ANYTHING FOR KICKS.
. . . . .
Bb(S): Well eh well he's freed from all the eh inhibitions society imposes on him.

II Bb(O): But the *air's* gotta come in there an' the air is sorta infiltrated with little uh pixy dust.
Aa(O): °DOESN'T BOTHER ME ANY, [I AIN'T GONNA LIVE IN IT,
Ca(S): * ["*Pix*y dust"!?
Bb(S): You know from the big boom?

III Aa(O): And a goodlooking girl comes up to you and *asks* you, y'know,
Ba(S): *"Gi(hh)rl asks you to—"
. . . . .
. . . . .
Ba(R): °So he says "no."

IV (Not submitted previously as it is not a case of the "questioning repeat")
Aa(O): Like yesterday there was a track meet at Pallisades. Rees was there. Isn't that a reform school? Rees?
Bb(O): Yeah.
Cb(O): Yeah.
Aa(O): Buncha niggers an' everything?
Cb(O): °YEAH.

Aa(O): He went right down on that field, an' he was just sittin there talkin like a nigger, an' all the guys, an' y'know all these niggers are all up [there an'—
Ba(S): * [YOU MEAN "NEGRO", DON'CHA?

(Note for this case the issue discussed on p. 297, of an adjacency-lapse permitting the one who is currently speaking to do an unsolicited remedy.)

Co-occurring within each fragment are two sorts of utterances, each of which stands as a possible "second" to the same prior utterance:

I) "Well, he's—", "He'll do anything for kicks" : : "Well illuminated?"
II) "Doesn't bother *me* any, I ain't gonna live in it" : : "*Pi*xy dust!?"
III) "So he says 'no'" : : "Gi(hh)rl asks you to—"
IV) "Yeah" : : "You mean 'Negro' don'cha."

And in these terms, events in the initial data might be set down as: ((proper next game action)) : : "'E*le*ven'?—eight, nine, ten?"

The co-occurrence of provision for continuation and provision for break does not mean that (a) there is ambiguity as to whether or not something "wrong" occurred, or that (b) one hearer heard something wrong and another did not. The alternative actions are available to someone who *did* hear something wrong. It can at least be suggested that these are "either-or" options for someone who did hear something wrong; that doing a provision for continuation does not necessarily derive from not hearing something wrong, by noting that in the initial data Nancy provides a seconding of Susan's questioning repeat, i.e. says "E*le*ven?", and in (II) the replacement item for "pixy dust" is provided by one who is not selected to do the "b" for (S), i.e. D says "Radioactivity I *think* is what he means." In these cases, a participant other than the one who initially provided for a break in the on-going sequence, and who is at the very least by an omission providing for continuation, demonstrates his hearing of something wrong. In (III) some other than the selected "b" offers an explication—in this case supporting the contended utterance, "Well it's happened a lotta times"—but in doing so, he demonstrates that without further talk he knows what the issue is (cf. the "Hello" fragment, p. 328).

Since the focus of this paper has been the generating and terminating of side sequences, the issues involved in the availability of "continuation" as a pervasive alternative to the questioning repeat are somewhat ancillary. They are, however, relevant, and will be briefly sketched.

Hopefully the foregoing discussion will warrant a replacing of the terms "provision for continuation" and "provision for break" (and "questioning repeat," etc.) with the terms "pass" and "challenge" as more transparent and readable than the terms they are replacing. It can be suggested that one of the things a conversationalist must consider upon the occurrence of something he feels he ought to challenge is the task he will be imposing on himself and his co-participants. That is to say, the choice of whether to pass some item or to challenge it is not a matter of selecting from among two equivalent actions. Decision to challenge is something conversationalists can know to be a matter of immediate consequence, in contrast to a decision to pass. Further, this is known —in the same way it is known by other participants—by the one who produces the item which, then, is either challenged and/or passed.

In looking over the data one might have a feeling that for some of the incidents, that item which becomes the product-item of a questioning repeat was, in the first instance, done "on purpose." A warrant for that feeling might be arrived at in the following way. Earlier it was proposed that such objects as the questioning repeat can select a product-item "despite" an adjacency-lapse (p. 297, ff). In examining the four fragments, one thing that is observable is that the adjacency-lapse is either minimal or non-existent, i.e. "utterance-adjacency" turns out to be, also, "item-adjacency":

I Bb(O): . . . well illuminated.
Aa(O): °Well, he's—
Ca(S): *"Well illuminate(hh)d"?

II Bb(O): . . . pixy dust.
Aa(O): °Doesn't bother *me* any,
Ca(S): *"*Pi*xy dust"!?

III Aa(O): . . . girl comes up to you and *asks* you, y'know,
Ba(S): *"Gi(hh)rl asks you to—"

IV Aa(O): Buncha niggers an' everything?
Cb(O): °Yeah.

It can be briefly noted that objects like "y'know" and "an' everything" are standard completion signals, whereupon someone else may speak. In effect, then, in each of the four cases the problematic item happens to occur at the end of the utterance. And in (IV), participants' orientation to the uses of an adjacency-lapse, to permit an unsolicited remedy, may be seen in that A, upon an initial "passing" of the term "nigger," is exhibiting the consequences of that term's being passed—that is, he is not merely then "using" that term again, but can be seen to be "pushing" it, specifically, for example, by correcting the term "guys" to "niggers": ". . . an' all the guys, an' y'know all these niggers are . . ." Note in the appendix that upon being challenged he re-corrects "niggers" to "guys." In effect he is using what is not an empty place to talk, but somebody's adjacency-lapse, to demonstrate that he takes "Yeah" as an acceptance of the term "nigger," and will not provide an unsolicited remedy.

This does not directly demonstrate that such items are being *set up* to be challenged, but, for one, there are ways to do something wrong which are not so readily challenged; some utterance might require picking apart piece by piece (cf. the extended version of IV in the appendix). A corollary note is that to propose to be providing for a correction by repeating an error rests on an assumption that the one who did the error knows what constitutes its correction. Further, it might be asked, since there is at least someone who is willing to "continue," why does the "wrongdoer" not talk to that one, and perhaps provide that the challenge will be bypassed in the interests of the on-going activity (cf. p. 311).

In a sense, the production of an item which is not only wrong but is challengeable is a task which someone might accomplish. It provides for the relevance of a challenge where there is an available device for doing the challenge, for which there is a pervasive alternative—pass—and where a choice must be made, that choice being, so to speak, weighted in favor of not doing a challenge by virtue of the immediate consequences that will have—the initiating of a side sequence that sets up the problem for the challenger of accomplishing a return to the on-going sequence. (Here, "immediate" consequences in contrast to "long range" consequences," i.e. to pass some heard-as-wrong object, to not initiate procedures directed to extinguishing it, may result in later difficulties.)

The issue at the moment of the occurrence of a "challengeable" is: Will it be passed (and this appears to mean specifically, not challenged by anyone) or will it be challenged. Since it is available to all participants including the one who produces a challengeable, what sort of work a challenge will involve, this can be a way to discover, to measure, the import of any such item for a given environment, insofar at least as what is said in a place, among people, is a component of environment.

Appendix

1.a (GTS:2:2:7)

KEN: 'N I'm gonna keep *my* same place,
(1.5)
AL: Oh, that's good. Glad fer you, showing yer authority.
KEN: Yah. Told Daddy I wanted it.
AL: You tol' Daddy. Big Daddy. *Mm* hm.
KEN: Daddy almost beat me up!
(1.5)
AL: [[Good!
KEN: [["Yuh c'n have it if yuh wannit. Damn kid," mhh
DAN: Are you serious, or are you—kidding?
KEN: No I'm serious. He said I could have the room if I wanted it, he didn't kid me,
DAN: No I mean uh // about beating you up.
AL: ((sung)) How dry I am,
KEN: Oh no hehhehh He just said uh,
(1.0)
AL: I heard a real nasty // joke.
KEN: "I don't care, if you wannit you can have it."
ROGER: Hey you know I d-almost didn't make it here this morning.
(1.0)
AL: Too bad,

1.b (GTS:1:2:15)

DAN: Well you seem as*toun*ded t'find that somebody could be that involved in something.
(1.0)
KEN: hhheh hh In *the:m*?
(1.5)
LOUISE: Some people *like* them,
ROGER: ((deep breath))
KEN: Wuh-d- // her whole *room* jus' got it wallpapered.
ROGER: ((cough))
(0.7)
KEN: She jus'—she jus' got done rewallpapering it about a *month* ago,
(0.3)
LOUISE: —with the pictures of the Beatle//s.
KEN: No. A-a month ago Mom had it done in this gra: sscloth, like junk *yih*know it looks like //Hawaiian—
LOUISE: Yeh I know we have it.
KEN: She came in there the other night with *Scotch* tape, an' (0.5) *E*very inch of the room. (0.3) You couldn'—the *roof* I think she's got done, in Beatle pictures.

2.a (GTS:1:2:31)

KEN: Oh I-I-I never saw it before cause I was on the *ranch* when it—first came *out*. And it was so fun//ny,
ROGER: Do you own a ranch too?
(0.7)
KEN: Well my father, *doe*sn' *own* it, No it's just uh,
(1.5)
KEN: —at a frien//d's ( )
AL: —just owns the state.
(0.3)
LOUISE: ehhh t'heh
(0.2)
KEN: ehheh No.
(0.5)
KEN: No. 'e // jus'—he owns the—
ROGER: Does he own my hou//se?
(KEN): hhhh
(0.5)
(ROGER): heh//heh! hh hh // hh heh
AL: hhh! hhhh!
KEN: Yeh he bought it last—// (a week ago),
AL: hhh hhh
(0.5)
KEN: I don't know,
(0.7)
KEN: Prob'ly does.
(0.6)
KEN: In fact I'm (al//ready)—
DAN: Wha//t're you expretting at Roger?
AL: Whh : : : : :
(0.7)
ROGER: *No*thing. Every week 'e tells us something else h(h)e owns. 'r i-is in*vol*ved in y'know, an' ih—
(1.3)
KEN: What. Seeing a movie? I don' *own* it. I cross my heart.
ROGER: Well i : : z (*dumb*) yihknow there's a lotta factories aroun' my house yihknow,
(0.7)
ROGER: An' then I meet Ken an' founds out 'is father *ow*(*h*)*ns* 'em a(hh)ll hh/hehh!
(KEN): hehheh
ROGER: hmhh He owns muh whole neighbuhood y'know heh hhh!
KEN: They've *all* got Norman Goss an' Com//p'ny written in big black wr—letters on 'em.
ROGER: Kind of—petrifyin'.
(1.5)
KEN: And my *grand*father finally stepped out,
(1.5)

2.b (GTS:2:2:16)

KEN: You wanna hear muh—eh my sister told me a story last night.
ROGER: I don't wanna hear it. But if you must,
(1.0)
AL: What's purple an' an island. Grape—Britain. That's what 'is sis//ter—
KEN: No. To stun me she says uh there was these three girls an' they just got married?
ROGER: ehh/hehh hhh hhh // Hey waita se(h)cond.
KEN: An' uh—
KEN: ( )—
AL: heh!
ROGER: Drag tha(h)t by agai(h)n hehh//hehh
KEN: There—there was these three *girls*. And they were all *sis*ters. An' they'd just got married to three *bro*thers.
ROGER: You better have a long talk with your sis//ter.
KEN: Waita—waita min//ute.
ROGER: Oh. // Three brothers.
AL: eheh
AL: eh//heh!
KEN: And uh— // so—
AL: The brothers of these sisters.
KEN: No they're different—mhh//hh
AL: You know *di*fferent families. // (No link up.)
ROGER: 'S closer th'n be*fore*, // hhh
KEN: So—
AL: heh! hh hh
KEN: *Qui*et.
AL: hh hh // hhhh
KEN: So, first of all, that night . . .

3.a (GTS:1:1:35)

LOUISE: Hm—Now they're not even sure. You know there was another bullet? A little colored kid was brought in, you know when this happened I was watchin it, a little colored kid was brought in to the hospital with a bullet wound. And they never said anything after that.
ROGER: Why should it? It's in Dallas. heh (y'know?)
KEN: hhh
LOUISE: heh//heh
ROGER: Bullets are *intended* for little colored kids hehhehh
KEN: heh heh
ROGER: To keep 'em from growing up into big colored *men*.
LOUISE: heh
KEN: heh heh
LOUISE: No but I wonder what hap—why didn't they do anything about that bullet cause that was another wound. And // they said the only bullets had been—

ROGER: Well what are they gonna do about it? —Except remove it.
LOUISE: No! But that means that there was another bullet from a different direction, shot. That he // there was only two bullets could be *shot* from his gun.
KEN: Man, a colored kid?
ROGER: They rationalized it. They say heh heh
LOUISE: "It wasn't there it was all i(h)n his imagination."
ROGER: "It's a colored kid so somebody else was shootin' 'im" you know,
(2.0)
ROGER: Just so happens somebody was out coon hunting at the time.
KEN: hehhehhh You know in uh—
ROGER: Which is forgivable in Dallas.
KEN: In—
LOUISE: "For*give*able"? You get an honor.
KEN: In Vegas I heard . . .

3.b (GTS:1:1:47)

AL: You know what Roger does he comes to a um—
ROGER: I must do something, // (   ),
AL: Yeah well you don't shave every once in awhile I think it's to show that you're older than us, isn't it?
ROGER: No, that's not I shave that's not I shave around Saturday night y'know cause going out Saturday night hhh // I mean—
LOUISE: You-you know—the rest of the week you don't shave but Sa(h)turday night.
ROGER: No I mean I usually shave in the morning except on Saturday when I shave at // night.
LOUISE: Mm
(2.0)
ROGER: Does it look bad?
AL: [[heh heh it looks terrible!
LOUISE: [[heh heh
KEN: hehh
ROGER: hehh I'll shave for you next // week.
KEN: [[You dirty grub!
LOUISE: [[You look like a common slob.
ROGER: Anybody got // a razor on 'em? hehhh
AL: He's gotta lotta company hehh
DAN: Well this fear, this fear of not being distinct . . .

I (GTS:4:22)

KEN: No but—I mean—people like this—wouldju call somebody like that a *nut*?
ROGER: No
KEN: Whaddiyuh *call* 'em? You can't say they're // nuts,
ROGER: He's a person who's well illuminated.

KEN: Well // he's—
DAN: Well—"Well illuminate(hh)d"?
ROGER: hehhehh
KEN: Waita minute // when he—
JIM: He'll do anything for *kicks*.
KEN: No! // No listen.
ROGER: Well eh well he's freed from all the eh // inhibitions society imposes on him.
KEN: Listen. When he had th' responsibility—
KEN: When he had th' responsibility to take—take charge of—he was second in charge of the dorm. When I'd leave that j-dorm // that dorm would act perfect. No shit he-he'd rule with an // iron hand. Waita minute.
ROGER: hhh heh!
ROGER: Well then he was well in command of his—eh situation and all of his faculties and he knew when to ac' like an asshole an' when to uh
(1.0)
KEN: Well I don' know
ROGER: uh sober up, an' he—an' // he had his own feelings of right an' wrong,
JIM: He-he—

II (GTS:2:2:19)

ROGER: I-*I* been thinkina buildin a fallout shelter.
(1.0)
KEN: hh
ROGER: But I'd just throw parties th(hh)ere anywa(hh)ys hehh it'd be a fall *in* shelte(h)r heh//hh
AL: heh
KEN: Hey—
(0.5)
AL: heh
KEN: Have you seen some a' these—fallout shelters?
ROGER: Yeah, I've seen so : : me,
(1.0)
ROGER: Be a // *nasty* place tuh hide fro(h)m the // co(h)ps
KEN: The lady—
KEN: Well— // the lady up the street just-just had one put in? About four days ago?
AL: hehh hh hh hhh! ha
(DAN): Mm hm?
KEN: And there's so // many—
ROGER: An' she threw a house war//ming! hh!
KEN: Waita minute
(   ): ((cough))
AL: heh heh
KEN: Waita minute
ROGER: hh a // *bomb*! hehh hh hehh hh

KEN: She's gotta *gun* in it.
KEN: She's gotta gun hangin' there? And I said what's the gun for she said in case any a' my *neigh*bors wanna come in. // Yuh know?
AL: heh
ROGER: hehhh An' she invi(h)tes you i(h)n to // see it. hehh
KEN: Y'know?
KEN: I s'd—well— // well you know, / all yer neighbors 've gotta do is just put a little *mud* in that little air hole up there in the top an' *yer* all done. eheh
AL: Oh : :
AL: ("Come to my *nest*.")
(1.0)
ROGER: That's wonderful little air hole an' all the radi//ation comin inna li'l ai(h)r // hole,
(DAN): ((clears throat))
KEN: No they *crank* this thing down at the bottom. It's funny lookin.
(0.5)
ROGER: But the *air's* gotta come in dere an' the air is sorta infiltrated with little uh pixy dust.
(1.0)
KEN: Doesn' bother *me* any,
AL: *Pi*//xy dust!?
KEN: *I* ain't gonna live in it,
ROGER: Y'know from the big boom?
(2.0)
DAN: Ra//dio—
AL: *Pi*xy dust,
KEN: heh hh
DAN: Radioactivity I *think* is what he means,
AL: (hh)OH. Okay,
KEN: hh
(2.5)
DAN: hmh hmh
AL: *I* don't see // what the bomb shelter's—
ROGER: From that big bonfire in the sky heh
AL: 'Ey you know I don't see—I think it'd be a great feeling y'know, // sit around there while everybody—
ROGER: It's a : : sinine.
ROGER: It's really *a*sinine, I (swear).
AL: I s—I do *too* because i-uh just think. It—*I* don' wanna walk out there you know, an' see all these—I wanna come out there, an'—might as well have one final bla : st you know,

III (GTS:5:37)

DAN: Well what about the guy that gets up on the dance floor, who feels that he can't dance.
ROGER: He's sca : red,
(2.0)

ROGER: *Oh : :* wait. Mayb—he-he can't really dance. An' he doesn't wanna make an ass of himself.
(1.0)
JIM: He wants to // dance but he can't dance.
ROGER: He doesn't want pee—
ROGER: Yea//h. An' he's—
JIM: An' everybody's askin' 'im t'dance.
ROGER: An' because he's scareda dancing he's gonna dance in private til he learns how.
JIM: And a goodlooking girl comes up to you and *asks* you, y'know,
ROGER: Gi(hh)rl asks you to—
ROGER: Alright,
KEN: Well it's happened a lotta ti//mes,
ROGER: Okay okay go ahead.
(1.0)
ROGER: So he says "no."
(1.0)
ROGER: Cause he's scared to admit that he can't dance, an' he's scared to *try*. Cause he's gonna make a fool of himself.
KEN: *I* can't dance, and—hell every time, every time the-the dance play—er every time there's a dance I'm always at it, an' I'm always dancin',
ROGER: An' yer al—yer dancing?
KEN: Sure. I can't dance worth shit, I just move around hehh 's all you gotta do,
DAN: There *are* images, evidently that any—every one of you have about yourselves though at any rate.

IV (GTS:4:23)

JIM: Like yesterday there was a track meet at Pallisades. Rees was there. Isn't that a reform school? Rees?
ROGER: Yeah.
KEN: [[Yeah.
JIM: [[Buncha niggers an' everything?
KEN: Yeah.
JIM: He went right down on that field, an' he was just sittin there talkin like a nigger, an' all the guys, an' y'know all these niggers are all up // there an'—
ROGER: You mean Negro, don'cha?
JIM: Well an' they're // all—
KEN: An' Jig // hehh
JIM: They're-they're *all* up in the stands you know, all, the—these guys are just completely radical *I* think—I think Negroes are cool guys, you know?
KEN: *Some* of 'em, yeah.
JIM: Some of 'em, // yeah, but when they get in groups look out uh you know? heh

KEN: The others would just as soon slash yer face as see yuh.
JIM: He // gets up there, an'
ROGER: W-why d'yuh put 'em all in one group? "I think—Negroes are cool guys."
JIM: I do *too*.
ROGER: Y-you // wait. You just said y—
JIM: But, *some*. But some *whites*'re a lotta, y'know, // some—
KEN: Yeah, some whites//'ll come up an' slash yer face.
ROGER: Well they're individuals. You // *know* that.
JIM: Yeah! They're *cool*. They're—bitchin guys.
ROGER: "Negroes are cool people and some of 'em are bad."
JIM: Y'know, some *whites* are bad, an' some— // are cool, so?
ROGER: Well—they're just individuals.
JIM: Yeah?
(4.0)
KEN: But—Really. What wouldju call somebody like that. Wouldju call 'im a nut?
ROGER: No, I wouldn't.
JIM: No.
KEN: No—I mean—from what we've said. What wouldju call it.

SHELDON TWER

Tactics for Determining Persons' Resources for Depicting, Contriving, and Describing Behavioral Episodes

I PROBLEMATIC OBSERVABLES

The following discussions are directed to the investigation of persons' facilities for making sense out of and talking about observable sights in which other persons are apparently active. Our interest is turned in particular to occasions in which persons talk about "behavioral episodes." Such occasions may appear in a newspaper reporter's description of a riot,

(Notes to this selection will be found on p. 452.)

in congressional reports containing eye witness accounts of a presidential assassination, in a conversation in which one of the conversants tells what he saw on his way to work, in an ethnography which describes a native ceremony, in a letter in which a wife describes her husband's behavior in some party incident, etc. It shall be proposed that these descriptions are themselves studiable phenomenae whose research permits a formulation of a set of fundamental features of behavior that people seem to attend when they make sense out of and relate such incidents or "behavioral episodes."

Two particularly auspicious research materials containing "descriptions of behavioral episodes" have been *Reader's Digest* "Cartoon Quips" and a group of transcribed two-party conversations. The "quips" are one line representations of cartoons that have appeared in various magazines; usually the cartoon's caption and a brief description of the cartoon are included in that line, e.g. "Nurse to co-worker in hospital nursery as she holds up baby for proud father to see: 'I've shown this one to twelve new fathers today and it's a chip off the old block to each one of them.'"[1] The conversations[2] in which the conversers talk at some length about several specific cartoons and photographs are between college freshmen and sophomores that I happened to be tutoring and who had been asked and permitted that a number of their tutoring conversations be tape recorded. Having previously agreed to have their tutoring conversations recorded (for some "research reason" unknown to them), they did not object when they were asked to go through some magazines and describe to each other the jokes and photographs they came across in full knowledge of the tape recorder's operating presence.

It is conceivable that the collected materials do not reflect the ways in which people "naturally," "spontaneously," "on their own" relate cartoons or describe photographs that they have seen. Possible issues surrounding the relationship between the cartoon discussions in the data and those occurring in the natural course of "ordinary conversation," however, have not arisen in the research thus far, and contentions on such issues do not as yet demonstrably affect the research's general proposal or its findings: a close examination of the conversation and the quip materials helps us to represent and formulate a set of persons' methods, common practices, collective knowledge, and procedures for describing behavioral episodes. Moreover, warrant will be forthcoming for presenting these formulations of persons' practices as some of "*describers' resources*" for investigating, describing, explaining, and contriving observable scenes.

How the data are considered and what they might yield is suggested by the following observations on one of the excerpts from the conversations[3]:

.01 F. Sit on a couch (   )
.02 M. They were both sitting on the couch

.03 [F. In an exceedingly modern sterile room . . . Yeh
.04 [M. Yeh
.05 F. Uh . . . both eh sitting on a couch and she apparently had moved to the other end practically off the couch and he was ((pause)) well, couldn't imag . . . well she
.07 said to him as she was at the other end of the couch
.08 she said to him uh that she wasn't far sighted that she did really love him. As he
((extracted from data supplement page 359))

From F's utterance beginning on line .05, we gather that the captioned drawing F is purportedly describing "says" several things, e.g. that the caption is a quote of what one figure says, that the figure had "moved," the direction in which it moved (or where the figure was before), which figure it was, etc. Though the remarks that do this reporting may appear rather ordinary, unexceptional, or obvious, that they are and can be made on a cartoon arouses some research curiosity: how does one come to see that the caption is someone in the cartoon's talk, and the "*woman's*" rather than any other figure's? How is one able to tell that the "woman" had "moved"? that the two figures are "a couple"?

The conversants' remarks can themselves bear the researching of these questions: embedded in them are the conversants' solutions to a number of observation/description "problems" and puzzles posable and resolvable by reference to a cartoon. Some of the work that the cartoon describer does to locate and attempt to resolve these puzzles we can formulate by examining these solutions (which will, by the way, eventually recommend the nature of the aforementioned "describers' resources").

Even though cartoons are so often described routinely and without issue, such conversational remarks as "I don't understand," "I don't get it" and their conversational consequences, found throughout the transcript, offer a warrant for characterizing cartoon descriptions as the product of some figuring. Such remarks seem to indicate the status of a conversant's talk on a cartoon which they follow, and are themselves usually followed by revisions and/or additions to that previous talk. Discussions of such troublesome cartoons frequently end with some indication of whether or not the conversants consider it solved, e.g. "Now I get it," "It still don't make sense," etc. These closing remarks and "I don't understand"[4] remarks both announce there is something to be "gotten" or "figured out" and that only certain talk gives the cartoon away. A conversant, in fact, may offer a considerable amount of talk on a cartoon without describing it to another's understanding or satisfaction.

Cartoons and photographs are far from exhaustive of the varieties of observables on which people seem to do figuring to solve problems. Recall, for example, street scenes or other behavioral episodes where understanding what was "going on," "who" did "what," what it "means," etc. were clearly topics of witnesses' conversation. In addition, persons' descriptions of paintings, advertisements, dramas, movies, inkblots, etc., are probably partially analyzeable as solutions to "observation problems."

Though people do not always *verbally* announce their own solutions to observables by describing them, observers do on occasion otherwise show that some figuring has been, can be, or is expected to be done. Circumstances in which one person directs another's attention to a scene with a remark like "Look at that!" seemingly expecting the "that" will be made out to be a specific scene (e.g. the way someone is dressed, a dog fight, a sunset, etc.) are examples of such occasions. The utterer of a remark like "Look at that!" expects that another can solve problems such as what is to be noticed and what to make of it after simply directing his gaze toward the sight.

Later on we propose through some data that people hold expectations that persons engaged in interaction are constantly noticing, figuring out observables, and performing actions that are in accord with what they "see." Certain occurrences demonstrate that a behavior can indicate that its behavior oriented to an observation "problem" whose nature and solution are at least inferentially available to witnesses of the behavior.

Cartoon descriptions that demonstrably contain explicit verbal solutions to what describers themselves treat as problematic observables are one place to begin a close examination of persons' procedures for deciphering some of their pictures of the world. The work here will perhaps lay the groundwork for an investigation of the nature of the work people do when they "make out" actual pictures of the world with which they are frequently confronted.[5]

II
THE "PROBLEM" OF LOCATING AND IDENTIFYING BEHAVIORS

Consider the line 4.6.2 in the following excerpt:

4.5.7 M. huh Oh in this eh ((whispers)) (match) . . . In this eh caricature there's—there's this troop uh of Boy Scouts—uh there's 4 of them and their scoutmaster and what it is it's a paper drive.
C. Mhm
M. An heh heh the funny thing about it is that they're all in back of the ah the truck with all the-the magazines and uh
[he's (   )
C. [en all
4.6.2 M. the stuff and instead of working they're eh reading huh reading comics.

C. Yeah
((excerpted from data supplement page 360))

The terms "working" and "reading" occupy two positions in the utterance; call them "A" and "B" respectively. The "instead of" sets up these two positions, "instead of A, B," which are to be filled by a class of A's and B's whose members can stand as alternatives to each other. Besides showing what people take as alternatives in this case, the A and B chosen show what things can be classified together. Apparently names of "activities" or "actions" can be classified together as a group whose members can stand as alternatives in an "instead of A, B" construction.

If "B" tells what is "done," the number of possibilities for what is done "instead of B" are *theoretically* as large as the number of actions, e.g. "instead of sleeping, swimming, running, etc., they're reading" are all conceivable. Again theoretically, the choice of "reading" for B does not, or very limitedly, constrains the choice for what is to be put in the A position —that is, "they" may be said to be doing several things other than "reading." "Reading," for that matter, can be called "working": a figure seated in an office at a desk "reading" may be said to be "working."

It is, nonetheless, at least intuitively clear that for this cartoon other possible choices for what "they" are "not doing" are not so "suitable," "relevant," or "sensible" as "working." Evidently, the A, "working," is not arbitrarily chosen, but chosen for some reason which permits it to be a relevant sensible alternative to the B, "reading."

These observations lead to the proposal that describers sometimes probably have criteria for choosing one action rather than another, or in alternative to another to describe a figure's behavior. Furthermore, actions ascribed to figures tentatively "belong" or can be made to belong where they occur in descriptions. In other words, names of actions occupying positions or "action spots" in descriptions encourage, demand, or suggest that the describers know, find, or suggest provisions for that behavior's occurrence.

"Action spots" are characteristically filled by saying what is *being done in particular*. The A and B actions in this case are distinguishable alternatives to each other by a variation in this feature that they share, i.e. names of actions imply, or directly propose what is "*being done in particular*." "Doing" aspects of actions are clearly invoked when names of actions answer questions like "what is he doing?" and an action's "doing" properties are used when distinctions like (he is "doing") A "rather than," "in addition to," "instead of" ("doing") B are made.

Action spots need not be, and frequently are not, filled by naming an action: remarks like "he is doing nothing" or "not doing anything" exhibit typical alternative ways the spot can be filled. The "doing nothing" in a remark of this form may be a claim that the figure it speaks of ("he") is not engaging in a *specific* behavior that was in some way provided for. It is easy to recall instances, for example, where a young subject of an "accusation/demand" like "Stop molesting your sister" forms a denial by pleading, "But I didn't do nothing." Evidently, nothing is not "nothing" in any absolute sense, but represents the non-occurrence of a "specific something" (like "molesting one's sister") for the occasion of its use. This "localized" use of "nothing," then, vents the user's recognition that there are specific forms of behavior that are relevant to some occasion and that they were "not done."[6]

Before investigating how cartoonists can provide "specific action relevancies," note that although verbal identification of behaviors are usually not contested (by hearers) as something cartoon describers ought not to do, this is not generally so wherever people verbally identify behaviors: "interactants'" explicit identifications of their own or other interacting parties' behavior uttered in the course of that interaction may be "contestable", especially when the behavior mentioned is perfectly obvious to the utterer and its recipient(s). Remarks like "He is talking!", "He is handing you something!", etc. in such circumstances are probably not heard as "informers" but as demands for "response," or "recognition," etc. An interactant receiving such a remark and not recognizing or not caring to recognize its warrant might respond with "Do you think I'm blind!", "No kidding!", or the like. Such responses hint of the "seeableness" of (certain) behaviors in witnessed scenes, and sanction "unwarranted" attempts at pointing out what one can "see for himself."

However, the possibility that interactants treat utterances of this nature as "primarily informative" is not precluded: for example, when it is established that some interactant was not "aware of," did not "notice," or could not observe a behavior. Furthermore, there are occasions in which interactants announce their behaviors in the course of performing them, probably for persons outside of the episode. For example, appearing in the transcription of a federal hearing are remarks like "I hand you a document which we will mark . . ." which evidently preserve the action for the record.

These latter circumstances and others, namely cartoon discussions, in which people "permit" verbal deciphering of behavior in the course of their observation, provide specific material with which to investigate the problematic nature of selecting and identifying actions and actors; the research can then proceed to examine two related "central" tasks: the describers' task of selecting actions for characters, and the cartoonists' task of contriving scenes which in ways can be expected to "control" the selection's outcome. In the discussion immediately following, data in which actions are "ascribed" is consulted to formulate what may be describers' and cartoonists' resources for orienting to their respective tasks of finding and providing for a scene's action.

III
ASCRIPTIONS OF "RELATED" ACTIONS

.01 G. And the salesman probably asked him "well how d'ya like the book?"
.02 D. the book
((both laugh))
.03 G. He says, "I was not only able to put it down, I was able to throw it"
D. throw it huh huh huh
((page 362 data supplement))

Here G apparently says that line .03, the quoted caption, is the "man's" "answer" to the "salesman's" "question" (line .01). G's utterance tells one that among the things available in the cartoon are: that one figure talked, then a second talked; that they were talking to each other; and what each said. Cartoons have provisions for indicating that "talk" is being exchanged between two or more figures. Before inquiring into these provisions, note one case of a recurrent class of phenomenon arising in this excerpt: a depicted/described episode can be regarded as part of, the result of, or related to some *antecedent* event, action, or episode. G proffers the "history" of the captioned talk ascribed to the "man"; this talk is said to "answer" some "question" which, though not quoted in the cartoon, is nonetheless quoted by G as the depicted scene's antecedent. One of the following analyses' findings is a way to account for the fact that scenes are described as including their history without the hearers objecting on grounds of the unreasonableness of doing such "historical reconstructions."

Quip writers' manner of ascribing talk is usually some variation of three forms:

1) "X to Y, 'caption'" ascribes the caption as "X's" talk, e.g. "nurse to co-worker . . ."
2) "X at Z: 'caption'" names X as the talker and Z a place or "circumstance," e.g. "Soviet official, at meeting . . ."
3) "X while doing N: 'caption'," e.g. "Minister exhibiting his paintings . . ."

In a few of the conversers' descriptions, the caption is something that "X" "reads" from somewhere; for most cases, however, if the caption looks like somebody's talk, describers tend to ascribe it to one of the cartoon figures. A "cartoon reading rule" corresponding to these observations might be: read the caption as the possible talk of one of the figures. To address the question of how a particular piece of "talk" has, or can be made to have, some place in the cartoon it helps describe, describers' actual managing of this particular activity will be consulted.

Quips having the "X to Y 'caption'" form designate a figure, "Y," at whom the talk is directed. One might thereby consider that the depiction/description tasks are respectively to provide for and find both a "talker" and his "intended recipient."

A variety of actions other than "talking" can be said to engage a multiplicity of actors in some fashion; the second action ascribed to the "nurse" (quip p. 340) is one of this variety, e.g. "holds up baby for proud father to see"; "smiling at Y," "shaking hands with Y," "holding door for Y," "giving a package to Y" are just a few others.

Describers are not always obliged to find a plurality of figures engaged every time one of these actions are ascribed. There is nothing in principle exceptional about saying that a figure "smiles" at something other than another figure or is just "holding up a baby," etc. "Talk," and other "*related actions*" like "shaking hands," "greeting," on the other hand are intrinsically describable by this property; their occurrences *expectedly* engage a plurality of figures.

Describers' handling of these "related actions" in the recorded descriptions recommend a proposal that they and their hearers or readers consider, rely upon, and invoke this group of actions' "relatedness" property when they are ascribed: when "talking" is ascribed to an "X," it is relevant that there be some "Y" noted, accounted for, or asked about by either or both the ascriber and hearer. Furthermore, ascriptions of related actions can form a structure with which to aggregate and organize the member figures of a multi-figured scene—that is, second, third, etc., figures can all become intended recipients, or "interactants," via the related actions of a first, e.g. "X to Y_1, Y_2, . . .," "X at meeting," etc.

Relatedness properties typically characterize ordinary "X to Y" ascriptions as well as allowing that certain exceptions, novelties, oddities be understood and recognized as such. For instance, there are a number of conceivable ways that a talker can discernibly intend his talk for a "non-person" and be marked peculiar, under stress, or in an "unusual circumstance" as a result (e.g. "talking to" a wall, a horse, or nothing at all). Aside from the fact that explanations for this behavior can preserve or undermine witness' notions of the talker's sanity, they are, above all, *usually relevant and perhaps warranted.*[7]

IV "PAIRED RELATED" ACTIONS

Describers exercise some choice when, for multi-figure drawings, they ascribe the captioned talk to one figure and designate another as its intended recipient. The significance of the choice of "who" says what to "whom" and that of the selection of identification categories for those characters comes up in another excerpt:

001	G.	heh ok this joke . . . it's a man talking on
002		a phone while his wife is coming down the steps in a formal. And it says, "Listen to me Francine,
003		stay at Wellsley. We can discuss who you are and who I am over the vacations"
004	D.	heh heh
005	G.	Golly
		I don't—I don't exactly get that one
	D.	hehhh
006	G.	"We can discuss who you are and who I am . . ." Oh, his wi—he doesn't know his wife is
007		coming down and he's planning uh w—a weekend with another girl, and the wife
008		hears it.
009	D.	Oh I see
010	G.	And th-they're gonna you know uh change their name or something
011	D.	Oh and she calls or something like that
012	G.	Yeah that's right
013	D.	Uheh he ok what does his wife think
		[what about that
014	G.	[( )
		From her expression she looks you know
		utterly shocked
015	D.	heh heh
016	G.	He'll probably be utterly shocked too when
		he sees her

One figure can be said to "not know what another figure is doing" (e.g. "coming down the steps"), yet know that the other figure is in earshot. Furthermore, a figure can be said to direct its talk to some figure (e.g. "Francine"), yet intend it for another (e.g. the "wife"). Nonetheless (it may be argued) that the captioned talk is not *intended* for the "wife."

A possible distinction between a "hearer" and a "figure at whom talk is directed" constitutes one basis for this argument. "Hearing" is ascribed to the "wife"; and, at this point in the inquiry, it is at least suspected that "hearing" has something to do with, or can be made to have something to do with, the scene it helps to describe. Part of the relevance of "hearing" can be shown to derive from its membership in a "pair" of related actions that usually go together or occur concomitantly, e.g. "talking-hearing."

The "paired relatedness" feature of "hearing" is reflected in its use and describes its relevance here in the following ways: when "talking" is ascribed to a figure, a second figure and his "hearing" are relevant, though "hearing" need not be mentioned. In remarks like "She kept talking though no one was listening," and "I don't think anyone heard his comment" the activities mentioned are probably not randomly or arbitrarily juxtaposed—that is, evidently when someone "talks," it is relevant that another or others "listen," or when someone "comments" it is relevant that other(s) "hear" it.

Paired relatedness properties describe a number of actions and their use, e.g. "questioning-answering," "giving-taking," "apologizing-pardoning," "greetings," and others. Moreover, a structure delineated by this action feature instructs the research of a variety of phenomena. For instance, combining the paired relatedness feature of "talk" with the "cartoon reading rule" yields a mechanism which can generate the "X to Y, caption" form so frequently found in the quips: the "reading rule" prescribes a "talker"; the "paired relatedness" property of "talking" suggests a "hearer."

In addition, this action property permits us to establish a framework of depicter/describers' resources for reconstructing "histories" or "temporally extending" a depicted scene to include its antecedents. Recall that G (in data, p. 362) found that the caption for the scene depicted could be spoken of as a later occurrence in an episode some figure initiated by asking a "question." G treats the caption as an "answer"; and describers probably know that "answers" are "responses" and occupy a "paired" position, so that when they are recognized and/or ascribed to a figure, the second member of the pair, a "question," and its asker, are relevant. Knowing whether an action is a "response" or something that "ought" to be "responded to" is an adjunct competence to knowing the bindingness of pairs and what regulates their attendance in acting scenes.[8] And this knowledge of the "paired relatedness" features of some depicted/described responsive actions is a resource by which describers can know when and how to mention a response's antecedent and thereby at least begin to interpret a scene's "history."

"Paired relatedness" properties form bases for describing and understanding portions of sundry familiar interaction episodes. For example, the warrant for and construction of "excuses" or "denials" of someone's "ignoring/avoiding" the first action of a pair can derive from the paired nature of that "ignored/avoided" action. One may deny that "Y ignored X's question" by claiming that "Y answered it"; or deny that "Y ignored X's greeting" by claiming that "Y returned the greeting." Evidently, saying that "Y ignored X's action" can be tantamount to saying that Y performed some other action, or no action, in the place where the responsive member of a pair is expected to occur; one can undermine the credibility of a claim that "Y ignored or avoided X" in this manner, by a cogent claim that Y has performed the "responsive act." Such claims regarding the occurrence or non-occurrence of a paired action not only reflect the bindingness of a pair in providing for an obligatory series of actions but again reveal the status of the pairedness property of some actions as a resource for elaborating on "what is going on" as well as for directing inquiries for finding out what is going on. An "intended recipient's" behavior may be measured, accounted for, or noted with respect to its "responsiveness"; and, what is more, it seems to be a describer's business to know when and how to locate, account for, or explain "unresponsive" behavior.

For some reason, people do not ordinarily *explicitly* ascribe both actions of a pair when their occurrence is otherwise (implicitly) indicated (i.e. by ascribing one member of a pair); for example, the quips' "talking"-ascription forms mentioned earlier may ascribe "talking" to an "X," but rarely, though with certain exceptions, is the activity "hearing" also ascribed or actually mentioned—that is, it is not usual to find remarks like "and Y hears." An exception in the "Wellesley joke" discussion ("and the wife hears") lends reason to the argument introduced earlier: a "hearer" and an "intended recipient" of some talk are possibly distinct categories. Remarks designating a "hearer" by mentioning "hearing" (e.g. "and she hears him") are distinct from those that merely designate an intended recipient in that they can and usually do signal some "hearing" difficulty. There may be some issue as to whether the talk "could have been heard," "was supposed to have been heard," "was intended to have been heard," and other variations. Thus, when a figure is actually said to "hear," the description of the scene in which it "hears" most likely provides a circumstance in which that figure's hearing may entail an issue of this type. Explicitly saying a figure "hears" can be tantamount to saying that he "overhears"; G's version of the Wellesley cartoon, for example, lends itself to interpreting the wife's "hearing" as "overhearing."

V
"APPROPRIATE" IDENTITIES FOR FIGURES

As noted above, G's locating an intended recipient other than the "wife," and commenting that the "husband" does not know that his wife is "coming down the stairs" do not necessarily in themselves imply that the wife is not a second intended recipient for the "husband's" talk. However, a line of reasoning taken from the data, which turns on the "*wife*"'s being an inappropriate "hearer" favors the "overhearing" or unintended recipient possibility, and will be outlined for its interesting implications.

Although theoretically any physically capable "X" can be said to "talk" to any physically capable "Y," in practice there may be constraints on either the "X" and "Y" chosen or explanation of the fact that "X" said what he did to a particular "Y." One gets some feeling for these constraints by substituting the "wife" as the intended recipient in G's description of the Wellesley joke, and noticing the difficulty or awkwardness that results. This "non-interchangeableness" of figure identifications supports a suspicion that the use and choice of "appropriate" identification categories (wife, man, girl, cowboy, etc.) are important to describers and their readers or hearers; for this case, the "wife" apparently is not easily spoken of (or thought of) as an "appropriate *intended* hearer." Conditioning this intuition is a notion that identification categories chosen "ought" to be, or are "expected" to be, *compatible* with a particular interpretation of a scene or parts of a scene. Other identification categories which are perhaps appropriate for a figure in other circumstances[9] are not necessarily suited to or compatible with the way that figure is formulated by the scene depicted/described.

The following excerpt exhibits one type of "compatibility requirement" perhaps governing conversants' selection of identification categories.

M: And the way they're—they're working uh ye know
diving into their
[their hoods ye get the implication
C: [yeah that—that sort of
makes you think they're younger
M: Right, they're
[they're teenagers
C: [(   )
((taken from supplement page 362))

M's first utterance is comparatively unique in that mention is made of both what figures are doing ("working") and how it is "physically" achieved ("diving into their-their hoods"). Inferences that people can make from actions to "physical movements" afford a perspective on how the mentioned "manner of performance" of an action is used in M's utterance. There are several indications that relations between actions and physical movements obtain such that people can infer to an extent, from certain ascribed actions, what the actor's physical movements were: people know how to respond to instructions like "do X" by doing the movements implied (e.g. "X" may be "walk," "take a drink," "sit down," etc.); from a description like "she hurt herself coming down the steps" people can essay guesses at the specific movement that led to the injury; a describer can justify the ascription of an action by noting the occurrence of some physical behavior which it seems to comprise (e.g. "He did climb through the window. I saw his legs disappear over the window sill").

Ascriptions of actions having "usual manners of performances" make a probable range of body behavior inferentially available. Actions bearing these inferences belong to describers' "inventory of recognizably performed behaviors," forming a basic depicter/describer resource. By reference to an action in this inventory certain performances can be understood as "odd" or "irregular" when described or witnessed. A describer who reports, for example, that "she slid down the railing," or "she came down the steps standing on her hands" has reason to expect that the "oddness" of the performance and what is odd about it can be grasped by his readers or listeners if "coming down the steps" is a recognizably performed behavior that is not usually done these ways.[10]

Notwithstanding, within the range of physical behavior inferrable from a particular action ascription are a set of regular, describable, yet distinct manners of performance. "Diving into their hoods" is one of the various manners in which people can engage in "working on their cars," and is here treated as distinctly a "teenage" way. Associations between a distinct manner of performance and an identification category are not unique to this excerpt. Specific manners of performance for an action are associated with an "appropriate" identification category of the figure to whom the manner of performance is ascribed or may require explanation. For example, an "adult" "diving into his hood" to work on his car might be said to be "*acting like*" a "teenager." Other manifestations of the association between distinct "copiable" manners of performance and identities, for example remarks that claim some "X" is "acting like," "imitating," some "Y," are easy to recall—"driving like a woman," etc.

Though "X" may be an "appropriate" identification category for some figure on various occasions, his immediate identity can be, in a sense, reformulated by reference to the way he performs some action, e.g. an "adult" can become a "teenager." At least on occasions in which such a second category for a figure is proffered, that figure's second identity is demonstrably not independent of other things said about that figure, i.e. performances and identities "match"[11] and describers know how and when to do this "matching." This is but one example of describers' provisions for combining "relevant related observables."

VI
PROVISIONS FOR COMBINING "RELEVANT RELATED OBSERVABLES"

Persons' scene depictions/descriptions, inferences, implications, and explanations exhibit features that can be analyzed as their application of general notions of the "compatibility and appropriateness" of the "relevant related observables" mentioned in descriptions. For example, relationships between figures' actions and such observables as "physical objects" and "settings" are repeatedly invoked:

1. M: . . . eh huh huh a—well in this particular
caricature there's this grumpy looking old man
heh heh
2. C: huh huh huh
3. M: with ahh four arrows stuck on his back heh
4. C: Uhuh
5. M: And ah I get the impression that they're they
were shot by a cupid
6. C: Mhm
7. M: because uh he's al-also in this uh
8. C: picture
((extracted from supplement page 364))

For the reference to the "they" in line 5 to be "arrows" in line 3, arrows must be things that can be acted with in the way prescribed ("shot"). Whatever M's reasons for picking out and talking about "four arrows" in the drawing, they can be and are said to be "acted with" objects. "Acted with" or "could have been acted with" features of arrows are not necessarily invoked for all scenes in which arrows can be spotted. Arrows in a quiver, hanging on a wall, lying on a table, etc., are not necessarily always to be mentioned as representative of any action at all, much less representative of some action that got them where they are found.

Countless physical objects can be said to have been acted with, or to be representative of some action, e.g. "cars" and "letters" are treated this way in two of the quips: "Husband opening letter to wife: . . ."; "Wife trying to get car into parking place to husband directing at curb: . . .". However, whether or not physical objects can be treated as an action representative is apparently not the sole criterion that decides whether they are to be treated this way in a description of a scene in which they are visible. Criteria that determine whether objects will be noted, for what they are to be noted, or for what action they have been or are being used, may inhere in the "circumstance" in which they appear; in the above excerpt an object's location (or how it appears) is a tentative circumstance the describer invokes (e.g. "four arrows stuck on his back").

F's use of "settings" and actions exhibits features of their interrelatedness:

.09 M. Oh that's why she was sitting at the other end of the couch, cause she-she was she wasn't far-sighted or she was?
.10 F. Well one would only have to imagine that that wasn't the issue in a setting like that.
.11 M. Well what's the funny part about (heh), ya know I don't see it.
.12 F. The fact that that's not the thing you're supposed to do on a couch. You're supposed to make it on a couch ( )
[in a setting like that

.13 M. [Yeh
((taken from supplement page 359))

The sense of F's remark (lines .10 and .12) is conditioned by the knowledge of the "settinged" character of some activities.

An action that has this "settinged" property is one for which the place of usual occurrence can be inferred, e.g. "brushing teeth—bathroom," "working—office, study, shop," "cooking—kitchen." Utterances like "I am cooking," "brushing my teeth," etc. tell both what the speaker is doing and *where* it is being done, so that they can be adequate answers to a question like "Where are you?"

Relatedly, "action features" of settings serve as directives for understanding when and why certain behaviors are unusual, questionable or inappropriate. For instance, these features perhaps recommend that "playing ball in the kitchen," "brushing teeth in the office," etc. are somehow "exceptional." And comments like "It must be raining outside" and "The bathroom door was locked" need no introduction or explanation when they occur when one is witnessed playing ball in the kitchen or brushing his teeth in the office.

People demonstrate that they know as well that action-setting correspondences can be "subverted." One can pretend to "go to sleep early" by retiring to his bedroom early, at the same time intending to stay up all night. Settings can be used as "fronts" for doing some activities—a grocery store can be a "bookie joint," etc.; a bank "hold up man" can retain an innocuous appearance by performing "appropriate" bank-patron behavior, etc.

There are a number of ways in which depicted scenes can suggest their "settings." In the following excerpt, a figure's attire is used to partially locate the scene's setting as well as mark the location of one of the scene's figures.

1. C. I wonder what this little guy in the background (   )
2. M. [Yeh heh heh heh well he
3. C. [he might
(really know) huh huh
4. M. heh heh heh I guess he he jest uh was jest there when they heh heh took the picture. He looks kinda uh disturbed or something (like) he doesn't know that's happening
5. C. Mhm
6. M. or something I-I don't know. He does seem by the way he's dressed attired—he does seem to be from that country though—a native
((extracted from supplement, page 365))

C's question fragment (line 1) seems to have brought conversational attention to the presence of one of the scene's figures. Alternate designations mark his location throughout the discussion: "background," "that country," "there." In other data, the names of things like a street corner, neighborhood, city, state, country, etc., may all mark the location of the same scene. However, alternative designations for the spot are not necessarily interchangeably used, and there might be some basis for using one designation rather than another. People know, for example, when it is better, more sensible, or relevant to ask what another is doing in, say, a "neighborhood" rather than alternative designations for the location, like a store, county, etc. Furthermore, questions like "What are you doing here (or there)?" are sometimes probably understood to be marking the territory of questionable occupancy with a single one of its possible alternative designations—that is, the interrogated party might understand that his presence at a *museum* rather than the "street" it is on; the "county" it is in, etc. is being questioned; or that his presence in a *country* rather than the "museum" he is in, the "street" it is on, etc. is being questioned. Therefore, it is presumed that there are some manners by which the asker of such a question and its recipient can unfortuitously gain access to the designation of the locational marking being referred to and usually do so without asking what is meant by "here."

Since the noted occurrence of a "settinged" action provides a relevance for one setting as the place of occurrence, on some occasions setting-action relations may be consulted in choosing an "appropriate setting. "Locational identification categories" and/or "locational emblems" can also be used to locate "relevant places." Locational emblems like attire, dialects, last names, license plates, etc. exhibit a "locational belongingness" of its owner. Similarly, there are locational identification categories which, when proffered, indicate one place where the figure identified "belongs" or "doesn't belong" (e.g. native, tourist, German, Okie, etc.). Photographers and cartoonists can use locational emblems, like attire, to provide for a scene's setting, and conversers like C (below), can use emblems to direct their locational inquiries.

> C. Ok now this is a pitcher yeah uhm of two couples and they're probably at uh a beach party or something or something that's (concerned with) a pool or swimming cause they all have on swim suits and stuff

Locational categories, emblems, and actions can be consulted to find out whether a figure belongs where it is, where it came from, or where it might be going. *Clothing* is commonly relied on to conduct such inquiries. People discernibly dress for the beach, for an office job, a uniformed job, a formal dinner, etc. Each kind of dress is ordinarily associated with a particular setting. One can see the "incongruency" of a fellow dressed for the beach in an office, and people tend to form accounts for the "mismatching" by reference to "appropriate" combinations. The figure in the office, for example, can be "on his way to the beach,"[12] "coming back from the beach," an irregular worker, or in an irregular circumstance.

VIII FORECASTING "RESPONSE-RELEVANT" OBSERVABLES

The research has advised that contrivers of scenes, like cartoonists, have reference to describers' resources for anticipating what things describers might pick out of a scene and how they might be mentioned; for instance, resources for finding the scene's place of occurrence, a figure's location, a scene's action, a figure's identity. This kind of anticipation perhaps presumes that some of an observer's "seeing/describing" is done under some predictable procedures.

.01 D. Ok. A man is looking out a window and his wife
his uh wife is sitting on a couch. And he's
.02 looking at his son and he's saying, "Don't ya
think uh Freddy's a little young to be selling
.03 lemonade?" He's telling that to his wife. And
.04 then he says, "It's high time he learned the
(economic) . . ."

The phrase that contains "window" in the excerpt above both locates the "man's" gazing direction and names an object ("window") in the path of that gaze, but does not in itself propose what the man is "looking at" or "sees." Though on some occasion the discernable, notable path of someone's gaze seems to be a partial criterion for finding the focus of that gaze, the apparent distinction between "being within one's sight" and "being seen" do not seem to derive solely from such physical considerations. In fact, sometimes the physical aspects of seeing are dismissed or not even considered as criteria for saying what that figure "sees," or for that matter, whether he "sees anything." One can remark of a vision-possessing person, open-eyed and in full daylight, that he is "walking around stone blind," "not seeing a thing"; an often sensible thing to say is "I can't see a thing," or "there's nothing to see." None of these remarks necessarily imply "inadequate visibility."

The "man" in the excerpt above is said to have a "window" in his line of vision, yet is only said to be "looking at" and perhaps "seeing" "his son." Making out and reporting on what another "sees" can be spoken of as entailing both a "processing" of the observables and some consideration of the "seeing circumstance."

A "seeing circumstance" may involve an interpretation of an

interaction episode. What purportedly interacting figures are said to see can, for example, depend on interpreters' knowledge that "seeing" particular things is part of a figure interactant's business.

Embedded in the construction of G's proposal of a hypothetical circumstance (below) is how persons might be able to know what a figure "sees" or "will see" in a scene as an interactant in that scene.

G. From her expression she looks you know
utterly shocked.
D. heh heh
G. He'll probably be utterly shocked too
when he sees her.

Phrases adjoined in an utterance, and in this utterance, by a "when" (A when B) can be related either merely temporally, or both temporally and in some other way(s). "A when B" can be used to designate the "time" of A's occurrence (*when* B); A can happen "coincidently" when B does, "because" B does, or as a "response" to B. Thus the "when" connector represents a locus of possibilities for the relationship between the A and B it connects. And it is presumed that persons hearing, reading, or using an "A when B" in an utterance usually can tell which relationship obtains. The grounds for an intuition that A is a "response" to B in the line above are to be found in features of the A and B connected.

Earlier in the essay it was noted that interactants' talk (or descriptions of their talk) sometimes reveal that there are things that interactants are expected to "see." In fact, an interactant's remark that purports to inform another of what he "ought to see for himself" might be sanctioned. For example, a scene's interactants or witnesses are expected to notice behaviors without being told about them, and might deprecate remarks that "unwarrantedly" announce on-going behaviors (see pp. 344 ff). The introduction of an actor's *observable presence*, as in the "B" phrase above may be another seeable of this type, i.e. at some point in the episode ("when" the "wife" becomes "noticeable" to the "husband"), she "ought to be noticed" by the "husband."

Some behaviors, e.g. "expressions" (like those noted in an "A" phrase), are recognized as "responses" or "potential responses" to something when they are witnessed/described; for example, second members of a pair of actions ("answers"). The description of a "recognizable response" ("A" phrase) is linked with the reciprocal member of a paired related action sequence ("B" phrase) with a "when," e.g. "He answered politely when I asked his name." In G's utterance above, the "man's" prospective response, "being utterly shocked," is coupled with the observable "her," which seems to exemplify another class of connected events: "seeing X" —"responding to X."

"Excuses" for "failures to respond" can be made by claiming that the candidate responder "did not see," "did not notice," or "was not aware of" the "X" "to be responded to." Thus the occurrence of a responsive act is spoken of as partially contingent on a responder's "seeing" the "X." Therefore, when responses are ascribed, the describers can attribute a specific "seeing" to the responder. Relatedly, if a figure is reported to have "seen" a "response relevant observable," describers can anticipate that there will be a response and, in some cases, what it will be.

Persons expect figures to "see" and "attend" in regular ways specific "noticeable" things in their environment. In a sense, what figures are said to do, think about, be attuned to, and disregard can be understood by reference to fairly well formulated notions of what is relevant for "normal" "predictable" behavers "under the circumstances." The notions alluded to are probably derivatives of a set of "acting procedures" which, among other things, constitute a basis for knowing what behaviors need explanation and what will serve as an explanation.

IX DEPICTED/DESCRIBED BEHAVIORAL EPISODES

We have seen where describers' interpretations of behavior are not necessarily independent of their interpretations of the behavior's situation or circumstance. For that matter, a character's apparent "depicted physical position" need not and does not always by itself seem to imply a single recognizable action. A figure's physically depicted position can hint at a number of alternative actions, the choice of which may be contingent on other things. For example, an apparent physical position like "standing" can accommodate alternative action ascriptions: "looking at something," "coming down steps," "reading a road sign," etc. Describers, in fact, may differ as to what a figure is doing or has done, even though the figure's behavior is or was in full view of the contenders. Again, contentions are probably partially supported by picking out "relevant related observables" (e.g. physical objects, settings, etc.).

Criteria for linking actions and objects, settings, identities, etc., are for cartoonists' as well as describers' use. For example, physical objects can be drawn and manipulated in drawings so as to contrive a scene's action. That there are such resources by which describers can and know how and when to tie certain description/depiction constituents like physical objects into their interpretations adds to what has been one of our ancillary arguments: some of the describers' resources embody means by which cartoonists can know what items to draw, what they can be used to say, as well as characterize persons' instruments for anticipating and/or contriving what they expect viewers of a scene will "see" and talk about. This inquiry has proposed to penetrate persons' facilities for pointing to, drawing, taking a snapshot of a scene with the satisfaction, misery, or indifference of partially knowing what the scene will tell, how it will inform, and what it will "mean" to its viewers.

Describers' action ascriptions have been the focus for our study of persons' procedures in solving observation problems. We have examined some of the relationships that obtain between actions, physical objects, settings, locational emblems, identification categories, etc. and persons' use of these relationships to measure, understand, depict/describe behavioral episodes. Viewed as part of a resource of observation/description knowledge, these findings should find extensive application in the analysis and explication of other data.

DATA SUPPLEMENT

QUIPS

Football coach to alumnus during practice session: "Now there's a lad who's got what it takes to become a star fullback—speed, power, and a girl who makes straight A's."

—*Dick Turner*, NEWSPAPER ENTERPRISE ASSN.

Company president to personnel manager: "Search the organization for an alert, aggressive young man who could step into my shoes—and when you find him *fire* him."

—*Ed Reed*, REGISTER AND TRIBUNE SYNDICATE

One spectator to another at missile range: "It goes faster than the speed of sound or faster than the sound of speed, I forget which."

—"Brother Juniper," Publishers Syndicate

Boss to secretary: "Do you realize, Miss Condon, that counting coffee and lunch breaks this makes the third time you've been late for work today?"

—*Gardner Rea* in LOOK

Middle-aged man to pretty girl in cocktail bar: "My wife doesn't understand me. I'm a nuclear physicist."

—*Lowe* in MALE

Judge giving instructions to jury: "Before we start, I'd like to point out for the Perry Mason fans in the jury that in *this* court the district attorney sometimes wins."

—*Larry Harris* in THE CHRISTIAN SCIENCE MONITOR

One teen-age girl to another: "I developed an entirely new personality yesterday —but my father made me wash it off."

—*Kate Osann*, NEWSPAPER ENTERPRISE ASSN.

Husband, opening letter, to wife: "It's a note from the Friendly Loan Company reminding us they have an alliance with the Unfriendly Collection Company!"
—*Bob Barnes*, REGISTER AND TRIBUNE SYNDICATE

Angry man returning battered book to bookstore clerk: "I was not only able to put it down, I was able to throw it."
—*Interlandi* in NEW YORK TIMES BOOK REVIEW

Baseball manager to player going to bat: "Everything depends on you. Now get up there, and don't think of anything except next year's contract!"
—*Von Riegen* in THE CHRISTIAN SCIENCE MONITOR

Wife, trying to get car into parking place, to husband directing at curb: "Put another nickel in. I'll make it this time."
—*Al Piane* in THE NATIONAL OBSERVER

(from "Cartoon Quips," *Reader's Digest*, October, 1962, p. 281)

CONVERSATIONS

pages 340 and 352

F. It was a picture in the New Yorker
M. In the New Yorker // magazine? (   )
F. To the New Yorker readers . . . sophisticated city folk . . . OOOH it had a picture of a typical looking couple, city folk, in a typical situation //
M. (   )
F. In a typical situation in a typical //
M. Well what was the situation?
F. *courting* situation.
M. A courting situation?
F. A courting situation
M. Ok
F. Sit on a couch (   )
M. [They were both sitting on the couch
F. [In an exceedingly modern sterile room . . . Yeh
M. Yeh
F. Uh . . . both eh sitting on a couch and she apparently had moved to the other end. practically off the couch and he was ((pause)) well, couldn't imag . . . Well she said to him as she was at the other end of the couch she said to him uh that she wasn't far sighted that she did really love him. As he
M. Oh that's why she was sitting at the other end of the couch, cause she she we she wasn't far-sighted or she was?
F. Well one would only have to imagine that that wasn't the issue in a setting like that.
M. Well what's ah what's the funny part about (heh) ya know I don't see it.
F. The fact that that's not the thing you're supposed to do on a couch. You're supposed to make it on a couch (   ) // in a setting like that.

M. Yeh
but she said she said I'm not far sighted // its

F. Yeh but she hadn't he made her he made her say that he made her say that by at least by the reactions on his face and by by the fact that she was in a setting that setting and that's not what you're supposed to do in that setting so she sort of had to excuse herself with something (   )

M. Well an excuse would be "I am far sighted" not "I am not far sighted."

F. Well that was her excuse

M. That she was far sighted // and she could see him better at that distance?

F. Yeh

M. (Aw right) and you say you din't think it was funny?

F. No
((sniff))

page 341

G. Yeh, I see. And this one right here it goes "But how do we know Mrs. Nuggent wouldn't like a part time job?"
Jest

D. [((both laughing)) I don't get it. Isn't that ridiculous?
G. [(   )
((both look at magazine))

D. (How do you know? Who's it from?)

G. So

D. Well

G. Oh, Mrs. Nuggent, isn't that uhm president Kenn//edy's daughter

D. Oh yeah
((both laugh))

G. That's it. Oh so probably they're offering her a part time job since they're only living off her husband's salary.

D. hehheh

G. Yeh, now I get it // Ok. Shall we thumb through this book for more jokes?

D. heh heh

page 342

4.5.7 M. huh Oh in this eh ((whispers)) (match) In this eh
4.5.8 caricature there's—there's this troop uh of Boy
4.5.9 Scouts—uh there's 4 of them and their scoutmaster
4.6.0 and what it is it's uh it's a paper drive.
C. Mhm
M. an heh heh the funny thing about it is that they're
4.6.1 all in back of the ah the truck with all the-the magazines and uh // he's (   )
C. en all
4.6.2 M. the stuff And instead of working they're eh reading huh reading comics

	C.	Yeah
4.6.3	M.	Y'know the-the material itself—they're collecting and they're not really uh putting a lot of effort inta
	C.	yeah
4.6.4	M.	inta collecting all the material
	C.	[and so
	M.	[( )
	C.	the poor scoutmaster is heh heh
4.6.5	M.	Yeah and then he-he looks and he's all de-depressed en ah disappointed en
	C.	Mhm
4.6.6	M.	kinda angry (take a) look at it
	C.	Yeah it's funny that they're sort of it's in Family
4.6.7		Circle y'know—I guess eh I mean that's the name of
4.6.8		I guess who the-the cartoon's by anyway.
	M.	Isn't that the uh // magazine's (name) heh heh
	C.	(the magazine yeh)
4.6.9		en ah I don't know it's just sorta typical because
	M.	uhuh
4.7.0	C.	Y'know being raised in any kinda family this sorta thing happens.
	M.	yeh
4.7.1	C.	They-they're interested in-in probly the results ye know of what's gonna happen
	M.	Right
	C.	the money they're gonna get
	M.	uhuh
4.7.2	C.	from the drive but in the meantime they can't y'know look at it lon—on a long range basis y'know
	M.	Yeh and they're
4.7.3	C.	n' just havin fun
	M.	lookin at hah // the comics
	C.	whereas the
		adult y'know he's all ready ta work
4.7.4	M.	yeah
	C.	That's all he's y'know—he can't see havin any fun while he's,
	M.	right
4.7.5	C.	((mutters)) ( )
		((foot stomping)) ((pause))
4.7.6		en probably another thing too is a lot of them probly had the same magazines or something
4.7.7	M.	( )
	C.	in their house
	M.	in their house
	C.	En they never bothered to watch y'know look
	M.	yeah
4.7.8	C.	at em. This is probly another reason the scout master could be upset—because

4.7.9 M. En they do seem ta be comics
C. Yeah
M. Also
( ). ((clears throat))
M. So that's probably why they're interested in these (now)
C. Mhm
4.8.0 C. En they're just now takin the time to read them
4.8.1 M. En they're just loafin ((pause))
((pages flipped))

page 345

D. Oh, here's some other ones. Ok. Um ok, it's ah a man. Oh let's see, I guess it's a book shop and uh one cu—one customer, he's a really grouchy looking customer with glasses and uh and kinda fat; an he's talking to the salesman, and the salesman looks kinda surprised or bewildered or something; and he says ((pause)) he's talking about his an argument he had with his wife, an' he says "I was not able to put it —not only able to put it down, I was able to throw it."
G. Oh no no, he's talk
D. (   ) yeah
G. He's talking—he's talking about the book.
D. heh heh heh
G. And the salesman probably asked him: well how d'ya like // the book?
D. the book
((both laugh))
G. He says "I was not only able to put it down, I was able to // throw it."
D. throw it huh huh huh
G. I guess that means he didn't like the book very much.

page 350

2.1.9 C. N ((pause)) this (   ) My turn huh huh Now ((pause))
2.2.0
2.2.1 first of all huh this the pitcher the whole setting I
2.2.2 guess is in a neighborhood ye know ye cud see typical houses TV antenae everything
M. mhm
2.2.3 C. and they're just—they're buncha cars all over the place and people are working on em en a few are kinda in the way of what looks to be a
2.2.4 driveway, because there's grass ye know on either side
M. mhm
C. and then ye see a-a man that's he's probly in his thirties or so and he's got a pipe ye know and
2.2.5 (he has) glasses and he's dressed in a suit and it looks as though he's ready to get out ye know he wants to go
M. Out of the car?
C. Out of the driveway
M. Oh out of the driveway
C. Out of the driveway

2.2.6 M. He's in the car uhuh
C. But he can't—no, he's standing outside the car
2.2.7 M. Oh yuh
C. He with his hand on his hip ye know he's kinda upset because how's he gonna get out?
M. right
2.2.8 C. And although ye can't really tell uhm whether or not ye know these people workin on the cars are ye know teenagers, ye kinda—ye might get that idea
2.2.9 M. right
C. Ye could look at it that way uhm ye know the typical teenager who's always tearin his car apart
M. huh huh
2.3.0 C. Ye know so that uh
M. rebuilding
C. perhaps his father or something can't get out a the driveway.
2.3.1 or it could have other uh ye know another meaning.
M. Mhm
2.3.2 C. Uhm because there are just—there are about five cars ye know (here) maybe could mean uhm why do you—why would he *want* to get out ye know if some-
2.3.3 thing's wrong with—if so many people have things wrong with their car. I don't know (   ) heh
M. heh he (it's weird) heh
C. heh huh
2.3.4 M. Let's see here there doesn't seem to be a caption. And he does seem to be ((pause))
C. (a bit upset) heh
2.3.5 M. Uh yeah a little upset and trying to get out and the cars are blocking his way. And uh tch by the looks of things, it looks as though they more or less broke down or something
2.3.7 C. Mhm
M. You can more or less tell they're teenagers uh because of their cars—the way they're fixed up.
2.3.8 C. Yeah uh they could've had uh fixed (a lot) ye
2.3.9 know I mean more exaggerated so that you knew for sure ye know
M. Yeah fer sure (   ) yeah right ye couldn't ye can't really say for sure
C. because as it is (it's kinda) ((pause)) So
M. en
2.4.0 C. it leaves some question
M. And the way heh they're-they're working uh ye know diving into their//their hoods ye get the implication
2.4.1 C. Yeah that-that sort of makes you think they're younger
M. Right they're // they're teenagers
2.4.2 C. (   )
((pause))

2.4.3 M. Maybe uh wh-what they're tryin ta say is that most eh teenagers can't really take care of their cars because of the way they drive around.
C. Yeah
2.4.4 M. how reckless they are they don't really uh pay attention
C. But yet so they get to do more driving
M. (for instance) right
2.4.5 C. And the adult whose cars are in perfect condition
M. heh
C. can't drive uheh heh (   ) I don't know—you can
2.4.6 look at it that way ((pause))

page 352

2.4.9 M. Well in this particular caricature there's this grumpy looking old man heh heh
C. huh huh huh
M. with ahh four arrows stuck on his back heh
C. uhuh
2.5.0 M. And ahh I get the impression that they're-they were shot by a cupid
C. mhm
2.5.1 M. because uh he's al-also in this in this uh
C. picture
2.5.2 M. In this yuh picture and what-what it is is this old uh grumpy looking man he's walking away from cupid with uh these four arrows in his back heh heh
2.5.3 C. huh huh
M. And eh cupid with his bow I guess he ran out of arrows
C. Uhuh huh huh
2.5.4 M. huh is running after the cat
C. a huhh
2.5.5 M. with a—with his bow uh like he's ah y'know about to his him over to ah—yeknow
C. Yeah
2.5.6 M. h-h-hit him over the head with his bow because
C. hm hm
M. because I guess the ah the arrows even though there were four of them
C. Mhm
2.5.7 M. ah didn't have uh too great ah an effect on the guy huh
C. huh huh
M. And maybe the bow will do the trick.
2.5.8 C. Sort of bad (   ) for cupid huh huh huh huh
M. [Well it does a
C. [Somebody better
put him out of his misery hah hah
M. (It) does (an) injustice

2.5.9 C. I know—Yeah that was pretty
M. I guess uh // some
C. (   )
M. Some people maybe uh that doesn't work huh
C. Yeah
M. love arrows
2.6.0 C. huh huh huh
((pause))
M. It is kinda funny
2.6.1 C. Yeah that was good. Well, ye could only take it in that one huh huh way the others (are sorta) (actually)

page 353

1.9.5 M. Let's see—this next picture here uh heh this is
1.9.6 also ah another foreign type uh environment and uh
1.9.7 ye can't really tell where they're at . . . Well you do have some uh some letterings in the background
C. huh huh
1.9.8 M. directions and stuff
C. mhm
M. Oh yeh here it—here it is they're in this foreign
1.9.9 country en there's this uh officer eh of the law I guess uh showin them I guess evidently they're-
2.0.0 they're tourists and they're lost
C. mhm
M. and what-what-what he's doing is eh is eh he has a
2.0.1 map out an he's showing them the direction but eh I guess they're not very observant because
2.0.2 right in the background right in back of em there's this-this huge uh post with all kinds of
2.0.3 arrows pointing which way
C. Mhm
M. [uh with directions on them
C. [mym // so ye
M. so
(   )
2.0.4 C. so yer saying that
2.0.5 mainly uhm if they watched the signs th-that might tell or they failed to watch them or could it be that uhm maybe the signs because they're about
2.0.6 what—probly jest over ten signs we'll say
[(right there)
M. [Yeah they're quite a few yeah
2.0.7 C. So that could be so confusing in itself that uh even with them up there they can't tell which way ta go. And even the uh officer who's probably ye know a native of the country
M. uhuh
2.0.8 C. or whatever he's even // confused

	M.	he's even confused
	C.	So how can ya expect the tourists t-to know
2.0.9	M.	Right, that could be it—it probably is
	C.	I wonder what this little guy in the background ( )
	M.	Yeh heh heh heh well he
	C.	he might
2.1.0		(really know) huh huh
	M.	heh heh heh I guess he he jest uh he was jest there when they heh heh took the picture. He looks kinda
2.1.1		disturbed or something (like) he doesn't know what's happening
	C.	mhm
2.1.2	M.	or something I-I don't know. He does seem by the way he's dressed attired—he does seem to be from that country though—
2.1.3		a native
	C.	trying to figure out what country this could be heh huh
2.1.4	M.	Yeah
	C.	It's // not
	M.	It's not
		English heh
	C.	No it's not German
2.1.5	M.	It's not German? Th it's not French may could it be Spain?
	C.	No it's not Spanish either heh heh
2.1.6	M.	No, not Spanish uh ( ) I've never heard of any of these places heh

ROY TURNER

Some Formal Properties of Therapy Talk

SOME FORMAL PROPERTIES OF THERAPY TALK*

The analysis presented in this essay can be viewed as an attempt to explicate the social-organizational features of group therapy that provide for the possibility of the therapist producing a class of remarks, of which the following are members:

1. Look, before we start.
2. Well, we might as well start.
3. Well, I think what we had better do is start.

* This research was supported by a Canada Council Research Grant, R. A. H. Robson Principal Investigator. Except where otherwise noted, the data come from two sources: transcripts of group therapy sessions under the auspices of the Student Health Service, University of British Columbia; and transcripts of similar sessions held in New Haven, kindly provided by my colleague Dr. Robert Ratner. Stan Persky and Lorne Salutin worked closely with me on much of the preliminary analysis; our thoughts became so interwoven that I cannot identify all of the contributions for which they should be credited.

(*Notes to this selection will be found on pp. 453–454.*)

I anticipate that the reader at this point will react in two ways: first by noting that it is utterly commonplace that an activity should have an announced "start," and secondly by consulting his own members' knowledge to the effect that there are many activities besides group therapy in the course of which it might be entirely in order that some participant should announce a "start." Nevertheless, if we are to come to close grips with the generative features of speech events we must, I would argue, treat such commonplace features as determinate structures to be analysed rather than glossed over, and we can at least note that not all classes of speech events—e.g. conversations between spouses, telephone calls—require or make use of announced openings. It is at least possible, then, that there is some quite powerful social-organizational foundation to be uncovered by an examination of data such as I have reported above.

Kenneth Pike is almost alone, I believe, in noting the importance of identifying and describing the "segmentation" of occasioned activities,[1] as in the following brief treatment of a church service:

> A few days ago I attended the morning service of a young independent church of a rather informal evangelical type—a church which I had attended on numerous previous occasions. Each week as the congregation begins to arrive, the people entering the front door are met by one of the men of the church stationed there, are given a word of greeting, a handshake, and a partially printed, partially mimeographed program or bulletin containing a schedule of the activities for the week.
>
> The early comers enter the auditorium, sit quietly in some pew, or talk to friends in tones low enough as not to disturb any Bible School class whose teacher may have held it too long.
>
> With the start of the organ prelude a few minutes later, talking quiets down, or ceases. A song leader, standing by the pulpit, raises his arms to signal to people to rise as he leads them in singing the doxology to the accompaniment of the small pipe organ and (sometimes) the simultaneous playing of a piano. The doxology is followed by a brief prayer from the pastor, and a couple of hymns.[2]

In providing his characterization of such a "single continuum of constant physical activity" Pike notes that "One segment ends, and another begins, whenever there is an appreciable CHANGE in activity. The most apparent changes are seen when the actors differ."[3] Suggestive as Pike's account is, it begs the question of what constitutes for participants a "change" in activity. But beyond this we must note that the "segmentation" as oriented to and displayed by the participants accords some "segments" a kind of primacy. Thus, to follow Ervin-Tripp, "one strategy in identifying *situations* is to look for folk terminology for them, such as church service, party, interview, picnic, lunch break, conversation, chat, class, discussion";[4] and to extend this framework we can see that when

Pike speaks of "the congregation [beginning] to arrive" and describes the activities of "the early comers" he shares with his fellow-participants an interpretive schema which would warrant our talking of "arriving *for* the service," "being early *for* the service." That is to say, although Pike's obligations as an ethnographer oblige him to describe the "arriving" and the "talking quietly" as part of the "continuum," it is deeply embedded in his description that these are in a sense contingent activities that "merely" preface—but do not essentially *constitute*—a "church service." It is in this sense that I speak of the primacy of some segments of the observed activity. Other sequentially placed segments are warrantably seen as providing for the activity which both names and generates the occasion.

In a similar vein Michael Moerman has described in considerable detail how a "hearing" among the Lue comes off as a social occasion. Like Pike he notes that at some point in time it is possible for the ethnographer who shares the socialized member's orientation to see "arriving" and "waiting," and the persons engaged in those activities as "the participants" in the "hearing" which is as yet scheduled but not realized. Further, in identifying what Ervin-Tripp calls "discourse stages," Moerman notes that:

> Before the hearing opens, no one present ever mentions its subject or, except for an occasional *sotto voce* and/or very brief two-person, exchange, even alludes to it . . . Those who will participate in the hearing sit about . . . talking about crops, prices, weather, lottery results or other common topics of conversation irrelevant to the subject of the hearing.[5]

I take it, then, that the scheduling and concerting of activities makes it an issue for a vast range of social occasions that participants must *assemble* over time before the occasion "begins," and that there may be (a) formal markers establishing when the occasion is warrantably in progress (such that activities which were formerly permissible are now "interruptions" or "disruptions"), and (b) recognized, displayed and sanctioned features of the occasioned activity which are not warrantably available to participants before the occasion "begins," despite the fact that they are already assembled or assembling in the setting—as the Lue, according to Moerman, may be said to "avoid" discussing the business of the "hearing" while "waiting" for it to open. In the pages that follow I shall try to show what it is about therapy talk and the occasion of therapy that provides for the therapist to formulate "starting" as a visible event. This will require (a) some discussion of the assembly of participants, (b) some characterization of the kind of talk that may take place before the session "starts," (c) a characterization of the transformation of routine conversational properties that therapy talk features, and (d) the import of such a formulation as, "Look, before we start."

THE OCCASIONED CHARACTER OF ASSEMBLING

I have suggested in the previous pages that with respect to a variety of social occasions one condition of the occasion's coming off *as* the occasion it is intended to be is the prior assembling of participants. With respect to the possible ways in which the assembling is tied to the core activities of the occasion we may note at least two issues; first, that it is not *a priori* obvious that classes of occasions will be alike in the dependence of the occasion upon some specifiable composition of assembled participants; and second, that assembling activities may be governed in part by notions of their appropriateness as prelude to the core activities.[6]

Taking the latter issue first, I assume that Pike intends his description of assembling as "typical" for such occasions when he notes of "early comers" that they "sit quietly" or talk in "low tones" and that such "behavior" constitutes a display on the part of participants of their recognition of the occasion's properties. Assembling for a church service, a picnic, a wedding or a trial seems to require or permit categories of participants to make such displays as indicate on their part a recognition of both the occasion and the occasioned roles they expect to perform *vis-à-vis* one another. It is part of normal members' competence, apparently, to be able to shape activities in ways that make visible their entry into a setting or their preparedness for activities they are scheduled to concertedly undertake.

With respect to the first issue, the dependence of the occasion upon the categorial composition of assembled participants, it is at least obvious that there may be categories of persons without whom the occasion "cannot" proceed—bridegrooms at weddings, judges in court—and that the duration and character of the assembly period may be responsive to the order in which participants or categories of participants "arrive" in the setting. I shall try to demonstrate the relevance of these issues for a treatment of the properties of therapy talk by first providing some remarks on the assembly of participants in the setting.

ON BEGINNING THE HOUR

Group therapy typically takes place in quite standard settings, under the charge of the practitioner, as for instance private offices in medical buildings or rooms in clinics. There may be a waiting-room attached to the room where the session takes place. In any case it seems to be of some import that participants do not all appear simultaneously, but that before a session begins there is some *assembling* of the participant population. I first wish to discuss some of the features and consequences of such assembling.

Let us suppose that as ethnographers we have identified a *setting* (such as a designated clinic room) where group therapy is scheduled to take place at an announced time, and that in order to obtain an ethnographic record we have set up movie cameras some time in advance, when the setting is unoccupied. At some time minimally a first participant will enter the setting, and at some time later a last participant will depart, leaving the setting unoccupied again. A first question will be: How much of the intervening activity is warrantably to be described as "group therapy"? By asking such a question we allow for the possibility that participants or some participants may engage in activities in the setting which are contrastively identified as *not* "doing therapy." And having provided for that possibility a further question will be with respect to temporal markers: if some part or parts of the time spent in the setting by participants do not constitute "group therapy," how are the boundaries marked and honored by present members?

Members of the society who have never attended or witnessed group therapy will nevertheless, presumably, have available as a cultural resource some notion of the scheduling of occasioned activities which provides for—as a possible description—"before the session begins": a period which properly commences with the arrival of at least a first participant in the designated setting. Even this possibility, however, is culturally elaborated, and there is at least one issue of interest: an activity can be scheduled to begin when some *complement* of participants has assembled, or it can be scheduled to begin at an announced hour. I will try to demonstrate later in the essay that this distinction is consequential for achieving the "beginning" of the scheduled activity. But first we must note that the composition of such a complement may be enumberable in terms of either identifiable *persons* or specified *category-members*. Thus, a "family dinner" presumably is composed of participants oriented to as "persons," whereas a "surgical operation" may require "nurses," "aides" and "surgeons," where persons are and must be regarded as interchangeable. A "cocktail party" routinely begins, given the presence in the setting, of a "host" and a "guest." The arrival of the first "guest" in a sense properly begins the party, i.e. one does not have to wait until, say, 30 per cent of the guests have arrived before offering drinks or making convivial conversation.

Participants in group therapy may have to discover that therapy does not warrantably begin with the minimal presence of a "therapist" and a "patient," and in this respect that an announced beginning time must be oriented to as at least relevant to when and if therapy "begins." Contrastively a party begins, I assume, even if the first guest can be seen (by himself and by the host) to be "early." Group therapists, on the other hand, treat "early" arriving as a sanctionable matter if the early arriver treats his arrival as the warrant for beginning therapy talk. That is to say, therapists are well aware that patients may arrive early "in order to get the therapist to themselves," and there may be explicit rules to the effect that "anything said to the therapist by a patient must be shared by the group." Nevertheless, the presence of a therapist and a patient *at the announced hour* may warrant "beginning" therapy talk.

Though these distinctions may seem pedantic I suggest them as features of the social organization of gatherings with which participants concern themselves. At this point I would like to introduce some data from group therapy sessions.

Excerpt **A**

THER. Hi.
A. Hi. We were just having such a nice conversation.
THER. Oh, about what?
A. Just talking about our jobs.
B. It isn't that we don't like your company.
THER. Uh huh.
A. It's so professional like now all of a sudden you don't know what to say.
/silence of 80 seconds. C. enters/
A. Last one in has to talk first.
C. You mean we've started. Let me catch my breath a little bit.
THER. Look, before we start could I perhaps raise something and that is I'm unable to be here next Monday at four o'clock and I thought it might be a good idea if five perhaps met on an alternate day at four. I wanted to know how you felt about it.
/Discussion of possible meeting times and places follows/
THER. . . . so if you don't hear from me it's Wednesday at four at this very place. OK?
A. Good
/silence of 50 seconds/
C. I'd like to help you out but I don't quite know where to start.

Excerpt **B**

X. Just us merry three?
THER. So far . . . um, Joan won't be here today, or at least she thought she might not because her father was coming down to get her . . . but uh she hoped to be here next week.
A. I hope this is the bit about being got by her parents. (( ))
THER. Well, we might as well start.
?. It's kind of hard to start if our subject's not here today.
/laughter/
A. Well, the subject's got her own troubles ((which)) we don't know whether she's comin or going yet do we? Or goin or stayin.

Excerpt **C**

J. I'm keeping my coat on.
K. Cold?
J. Oh. It is too hot in here. (Hangs up coat.)
K. She took her coat off. So now you can take your jacket off.
L. It's not hot in here.
J. I feel awful empty, don't have anything to say. I don't know why.
K. You're not feeling well. You said you had a cold.
J. I don't even know about this cold. I have this pain in my chest. And I tell myself, it's just my imagination, just my nerves, it's not really a cold, and I know I have a cold. You know, but I think of all the pains I have, and I think, it can't be anything else—just my nerves, it's a very uncomfortable thought you know.
/silence. 45 seconds/
J. What were we talking about last week before we left? You started to say something.

"Starting" as I am talking about it is an activity done and oriented to by participants, and not merely an observer's judgment that, for example, "now they are starting to do therapy." There are standard markers generally available for doing and recognizing "beginning," and some of these may be located in the segments of therapy given above. Examples are, "You mean we've started"; "Look, before we start"; "Well, we might as well start"; "It's kind of hard to start if . . ." In activities such as group therapy where participants must first assemble, I assume there will be issues with respect to the propriety of starting, and further, that those who assemble "early" find that what they are doing may be described as "waiting." It should thus be open for us to observe distinctive activities which properly are located only when the activity has "begun," and some display on the part of early assemblers that they are *doing* "waiting." At least one consequence of this would be that any entering participant could perhaps tell right off that they had or had not "started."

I want now to return to the notion of a complement. I assume that after the first meeting, at least, all participants in group therapy are both competent and required to recognize each other and to membership one another as either "therapist" or "patient." I assume further that during the assembling of the population of participants any one of them can determine when the complement is made up by simple inspection. It follows, then, that at any point during the assembling any participant can "see" the categorical composition of participants already present, and know both the "identity" and categorical membership of those yet to arrive.[7]

Minimally, then, we might suppose that "beginning" is related to "everyone" being present, where "everyone" refers to the members of the complement. In Excerpt B above, note:

PATIENT: Just us merry three?
THERAPIST: So far . . . um, Joan won't be here today, or at least she thought she might not because her father was coming down to get her . . . but uh she hoped to be here next week.

In Excerpt D note:

PATIENT: Well our fourth seems to have (( ))
THERAPIST: Yeah uh she must have got lost or something. Well I think what we had better do is start. And hope that she does come. Uh-h. (( )) is just about twenty after four now. . . .

Noticing that members of the complement are missing, then, is something that participants are entitled to do. Moreover, the categories of the device [patient, therapist] are not symmetrical with respect to the consequentiality of absences: although the absence of a "patient" may be noticeable, it may be come to terms with *within the framework of doing "group therapy"*; whereas the absence of a therapist may require that the hour be canceled. (From time to time participants announce a future absence, since it is usually an expectation that all participants will attend all sessions. If a patient announces a future absence the fact is noted and perhaps an account requested or given. If the therapist announces his own future absence it frequently takes the form "We won't meet next week, I have to go out of town.")

At this point, then, I would like to formulate one of the deep-structural features of "beginning" the session.[8] In this society there are rights and obligations attached to being present when some activity "begins." Thus with respect to some activities—including group therapy—persons who have "not yet" arrived at some point during the assembling are treated as being *entitled* to be present when the session "begins." If that were the case, then we would expect to find assembled participants doing work which gives this fact recognition. Two kinds of work in fact seem to be done: inquiries with respect to "yet" absent participants, and avoidance of therapy-talk before some "proper" beginning. What constitutes a "proper" beginning will be taken up subsequently. Coupled with the entitlement to be present before the session "begins" is an obligation to be present for the "beginning," i.e. to arrive "on time." So not to arrive on time is to be seen as "late"—and other participants may remark this—and to forfeit one's entitlement to be present when the session "begins."

At any point in time when (a) the announced "beginning" time has not yet arrived and (b) some members of the complement are "absent," it may be unknown to some or all presently-assembled participants whether or not those who are "absent" are "planning to come"—after all, they may still arrive on time, they may appear "late" or they may miss the session. If "beginning," then, is an issue with respect to participants' entitlements, and yet on any occasion some participants may be "absent," then it appears that such absences may be properly noticed. Thus we could suggest a first formulation of a rule—all participants must be present in order for the session to "properly begin"—and immediately offer a re-formulation to handle the contingencies that are routinely faced: "All complement-members must be present *or 'beginning' in their absence treated as accountable.*" Remarks on absences and announcements of starts, can then be seen not as simple "descriptions" of the "facts"—i.e. "X is absent is noted since X is absent"—*but as doing the work of providing an account of how presently assembled participants stand with respect to "beginning" the session.*

The therapist's announcement of "planned-and-communicated absences," then, is one method whereby such accounting is done. With respect to persons who have given no advance information of absence it is perhaps sufficient to make visible the concern with their entitlements that presently-assembled persons do not simply "begin"—after all, they might all welcome getting in extra time—but "fill in the time" until that moment which bounds the session, so that those not then present are at least self-evidently "late." A therapist's "Well, we might as well begin," then, is not necessarily simply a recognition of beginning time (as though a bell had rung), but a further recognition that those assembled may be monitoring the situation, "waiting" for the session to "begin," orienting their remarks to the fact that "not everybody is here," etc.

Next I want to consider two matters: the first, how assembled participants display the fact that they are "waiting" or that the session has not "begun"; and second, what seems to be at stake—beyond the issue of entitlements—in marking the "beginning" of "therapy talk."

PRE-THERAPY TALK

The ethnographer who sets up his tape-recorder in the room before any participants arrive discovers that as soon as there are at least two persons present talk may occur. I suppose that *a priori* there is no reason why the beginning of "therapy talk" should not coincide with the beginning of talk; a rule might be formulated that required participants to start doing group therapy as soon as at least two persons were present. In fact this does not seem to be the case. "Early" participants engage in talk which they apparently orient to and mark off as separate from the business of the occasion. At first glance the kind of talk that takes place before therapy talk "begins" may seem to be remarkably uninteresting and trivial. Nevertheless, it is our task as analysts to pose as a problem the question of how such talk gets generated.

In looking at the talk that assembled participants may engage in before therapy begins, we have to remind ourselves that the categorical composition with respect to the [therapist, patient] device is visible to potential speakers and hearers. Let us look at the first interchange of Excerpt A:

THER.:	Hi.
A. 1:	Hi. We were just having such a nice conversation.
THER.:	Oh, about what?
A. 1:	Just talking about our jobs.
B. 2:	It isn't that we don't like your company.
THER.:	Uh huh.
A. 1:	It's so professional like now all of a sudden you don't know what to say.

The transcript represents a point in the assembly of participants where two patients are present in the meeting room and the therapist enters to find them engaged in talk. I take it that "now all of a sudden you don't know what to say" notices his arrival and further notices that he is a "therapist" ("It's so professional"). On entering, the therapist offers a routine greeting which is returned by Patient A, who goes on to say "We were just having such a nice conversation." Now there are a number of ways in which persons can talk about their on-going talk, and these ways seem to be consequential for the interaction. Thus, as Sacks has demonstrated, when a newcomer enters the scene of on-going talk some characterization of that talk can be offered which serves to "invite" or "reject" the newcomer: by characterizing the talk as relevant to members of a category which the newcomer shares in common with the conversers, an "invitation" may be achieved.[9] But clearly that is not what is being done on the present occasion. It develops over the exchange that "having a nice conversation" is contrasted with the kind of talk that might "now" take place, where it is implied that the therapist *will hear talk as a therapist* ("professional"). "We were just having such a nice conversation," then, by indicating that the kind of talk so characterized has terminated, recognizes the relevant cross-category memberships now in operation. When Patient A further characterizes the past "conversation" as "just talking about our jobs" I take it further that the following kind of concern is demonstrable. In replying "Oh, about what?" the therapist has treated Patient A's remark as a pre-invitation. It is now open to Patient A, in talking again, to offer some further characterization which would, after all, invite the therapist to become a co-conversationalist, e.g. "We were wondering how long you've been doing group therapy" or "We were saying how busy the clinic is these days." Now the utterance actually constructed by Patient A can be seen to have quite a different import; first, in that "just" can be heard as playing down the interest or importance of the talk to "others." After all, she's already said that for *them* it was a "nice conversation"—she's now reporting what it might look like to such a category-member as the therapist. And "talking about our jobs" further provides for the restricted relevance of the talk. (Suppose, for instance, they had been comparing their salaries, and noting the pay was good. Then, if she had wanted to do some kind of invitational talk she might have reported, for example, "We were talking about the way everybody's wages seem to be going up these days," providing an entry for anyone who could be seen as part of such an "everybody.")

Patient B's remark underlines the import of the exchange between the therapist and Patient A. "It isn't that we don't like your company" clearly does the work of noticing Patient A's talk as a "rejection," and Patient A then gives the grounds which, as I noted above, tie the present interchange into the relevance of its being "now" talk between "patients" and "therapist" and not, for example, "mere conversation."

On the basis of this interchange, then, it seems that "patients" may engage in some kind of talk which with reference to the therapy situation gets to be seen contrastively as "conversation," and which is oriented to as becoming irrelevant in the face of a possible "beginning" to the session. In this connection notice the course of the talk in Excerpt D:

R.: It used to be a hundred dollars a while ago
S.: It used to be a hundred. But they've knocked it down to twenty-five.
T.: That's bad.
S.: Seventy-five dollars a year.
/Therapist enters/
T.: Well our fourth seems to have (( ))
THER.: Yeah uh she must have got lost or something. Well I think what we had better do is start. And hope that she does come. Uh-h (( )) Is just about twenty after four now. Well what I'd like to do in the beginning is discuss why we're meeting. Uh why each of you think we are meeting and what we can get out of this. And so on. Now uh first of all I'd like to hear what each of you think uh what ideas you have. And then we can go on from there. Do any of you want to start the ball rolling? What do you think, why do you think we are meeting, and uh what do you expect of this. And how do you think/
S.: Well,
THER.: Were going to operate and so on.

This excerpt is from the first meeting of the group, and previous to the interchange above the three "patients" have spent some fifteen minutes "waiting." At the point where I have taken the excerpt from the transcript, they are talking about the advantages of shopping in a town across an international border, and the customs exemptions permitted. Now as soon as the therapist enters the room, one patient (T) addresses him and says "Well our fourth seems to have ((   ))." The first thing to note here is that T treats the previous talk as terminated, and as terminated not because of where they were in the conversation, but on account of the therapist's entry. And given the relation in which they all stand to the therapist, I take it that she effectively terminates the talk for the other patients, and not merely for herself, i.e. in inviting the therapist to speak she is providing for him to speak to "them" and not merely to her. Further, it is arguable that what she is doing is displaying the fact that after all they are "waiting," given that she directs her remark to what can be seen as the possible condition of their starting—the absence of a fourth patient. The therapist then acknowledges that relevance and warrants their starting in the fourth patient's absence.

Now I have stressed the fact that when participants begin assembling for the session, at any point in time they can (and will) determine by inspection the categorial composition of the already-assembled. I assume that one of the ways in which "small talk"—or indeed conversation in general—gets generated is by way of some recognition on the part of the speakers of "relevant" category memberships. So, naively, we could suppose that if several persons assemble for all of whom it is a warrantable fact that it is *as* "patients" that they have assembled, then that could provide some basis for their making conversation while they wait for the session to "begin," or at least for the therapist to arrive. In the same way one could suppose persons who find themselves waiting together for a bus might strike up a conversation by noticing its lateness, that it's a cold day to have to wait at the bus-stop, etc. Nevertheless, this does not seem to hold for any kind of occasion where participants gather and spend some time waiting together for the occasioned activity to "begin." Thus Michael Moerman has noted with respect to "hearings" among the Lue:

> Before the hearing opens, no one present ever mentions its subject, or, except for an occasional *sotto voce* and/or very brief two-person exchange, even alludes to it . . . Those who will participate in the hearing sit about . . . talking about crops, prices, weather, lottery results or other common topics of conversation irrelevant to the subject of the hearing.

With respect to the co-patients of a therapy group it is possible that some known social-organizational features of the sponsorship of the group permit them to membership one another in some way alternative to "patient," as when participants in group therapy sponsored by a student health service may take it that "they" are all "students." But the point I want to make is not merely that they *are*, obviously, all "students," but that they can be seen, perhaps, to invoke this category-bond in alternative to membershipping one another as "patients"—where one consequence of the latter might be that it would be appropriate to compare notes on their "problems." Thus, consider the following interchanges between the three "patients" who also appear in Segment D (the following occurs earlier in the "waiting" than Segment D; recall that these "patients" have not met before):

Segment E

MP1. You two both stay at home?
MP2. No I'm living out, couple of blocks from campus.
FP1. Eh'h. I'm at home! (laughs).
? (( ))
FP1. Are you from Western City?
MP2. I live in North Shore, West Suburb.
FP1. And you board here?
MP2. Yeh.
FP1. Wouldn't it be just as easy to get a carpool from wherever you live?
MP2. Oh I had a carpool for a couple of years now, I think, but/
MP1. (( ))
MP2. Oh it's easy enough. But, uh I far prefer it you know just living here. Its' uh
FP1. Doesn't it cost you more?
MP2. Oh it costs me money but you put money on uh you know what you want. So this is what I want (pause). Ah we got a good deal there's uh five students now an there's two more beds free for a couple more students we sort of live in a coop ((deal)). Big kitchen and uh
MP1. Wha— what's this a landlord charge you so much for the whole
MP2. Yeh.
MP1. place?
MP2. Yeh well there's um a lady running it and she's in the midst of studying to try to get back here. And then her husband works in Squamish. So they stay there, they've got one room. And then uh they sort of rent it out at no cost or no loss to them.
FP1. Oh that's pretty good.
MP2. So uh it's uh (pretty good deal) yeah (pause). I think it's you know sort of got the advantage of the residence in that you can you know get into a University crowd. And uh but then it not so big and/

Without going into a great deal of detail I want to note some of the formal properties of the topic MP1 introduces. In some rough sense the topic is "living situations," but we see that MP1 introduces it via what Sacks calls a correction-invitation device: such a device proposes one member of a possible class of answers, and invites a correction if that is not the appropriate item.[10] Other examples would be, "Where were you, at the store?", "Is it five o'clock?" There may be a number of things that can be done with such a device. In the present instance I take it that MP1 in some sense does not care where they live; he is not, for example, conducting a survey or a census. In the first place I take it that not merely "where you live" but "*whether or not you live at home*" can be a matter of some interest for "young students," and that it can be informative beyond some notion of your address or the composition of your household. In that case, formulating the topic-opener as "You two both stay at home?" provides for them (a) to make the correction if correction is needed—and MP2 immediately makes such a correction; and (b) to talk to an issue that can be assumed to have relevance for any student, i.e. any student will have a "position" on the topic and will be able to direct some remarks to it. Further, the question as formulated provides for both of them to answer.

I take it that when persons are thrown together in a situation where they can see they have time to get through, it can be a problem "what to talk about." And one way of solving the problem could be expressed as a procedural recommendation as follows: provide a topic that selects a membership categorization device embracing the maximum number of participants, and one for which any category-member will have a "value." Any alternative procedure may provide for intended exclusion or rejection or for embarrassment; witness the following account given by a day hospital patient:[11]

> Well, it was kind of a personality problem too, because the other two girls were married. I, I was at the bottom. They were married and they had the better jobs, you know, they'd been there for a couple of years, and I was just new, and I was starting out . . . and then like on coffee breaks and things, they talked about their babies, and I didn't know what to talk about. Cause, uh—well, at the time I was in a rut, cause I, I wasn't dating or anything.

As a first approximation we could say that she hears "the other two girls" membershipping themselves as "wives" and "mothers," and since she is neither she is "excluded." Nevertheless, a slightly more complex analysis seems to be in order. It would be one thing if, for example, being a "wife" or "mother" generated some kind of technical talk that outsiders simply couldn't follow, as a "layman" might expect to be "left out" of the category-generated talk of "nuclear physicists." This does not seem to be the case here. From the way the complaint is formulated it appears not to be a matter of "technical talk" but—at least as she sees it—what we might call "achievement talk": the trouble she had arose from the contrastive membershipping of "mother" and "unmarried woman," where the latter was taken to be in some sense "inferior." Such analysis is warranted, I believe, by her remark "cause, uh—well, at the time I was in a rut, cause I, I wasn't dating or anything." And I assume that the thrust of that remark is that not merely wasn't she a "wife" or "mother" *but that she was without prospects*.

Now I would like to tie this back into the argument by suggesting that for the purposes of "small talk" there are warranted ways of generating participation other than literal membership of the category or device selected by the topic-initiator—in this case, for example, by being a prospective category-member. Other ways are suggested by the following interchanges from the same pre-therapy talk that Segment E is extracted from:

Segment **F**

MP1. I worked all summer, I worked one o'clock to eight o'clock (( )).
MP2. Yeh that's the nice one.
MP1. It's called graveyard (laughs).
FP1. My dad did graveyard twelve to eight (laughs).
MP1. Twelve to eight, yeh. That's worse.

Segment **G**

MP2. . . . And it'll be better this year, you know you were saying for your friend.
FP1. Yeah, my brother wants to get into it too.
MP2. Hmh. Is he old enough?
FP1. How old d'you ((have to be?)).
MP2. What's it, uh, for Workman's Comp.
MP1. As old as you look (laughs). Well for that it's uh. Well different mills, it's usually, the minimum's sixteen/
MP2. Sixteen yeah.
MP1. But some mills start them at eighteen.
MP2. I think it's sixteen (( )). That's right there was a guy working who was in high school there.
MP1. But some guys (( )) when they're and they'll put (( )) and they'll say they're seventeen.
MP2. Yeah.
MP1. But if they're hurt you know they can't get anything for it.
MP2. Oh yeah, they can't claim any compensation.
FP1. Yeh.
MP1. You just take your chance.
MP2. Is he, how big is he? (( )).
FP1. Well he's seventeen, he's pretty tall but he's awfully slim.
MP2. Hm.
MP1. That's all right.
MP2. Yeah ((they)) put the weight on. Yeah that's one good thing we had fantastic meals.
FP1. ((They)) have?
MP1. Yes (( ))
MP2. Yeah, just, yeah. As much as you could eat.
MP1. That's pretty good.
MP2. You know big steaks.
FP1. That's what he needs. He keeps, he's always so, always complaining he's hungry.

At both these points in the talk the two male patients have been discussing summer jobs in logging work and paper mills, comparing mechanical processes in their respective jobs and working conditions. It's fairly obvious that the girl is excluded, and at one point one of the men asks her, "Understand what we're talking about?", and she says, "No, no I'm completely lost." In each of the two segments above she uses a device for hooking into the conversation: in Segment F when the men are talking of the shifts they worked—and it isn't available to her to enter by telling the shift she worked—she ties into MP1's "It's called graveyard" with "My dad did graveyard"; and in Segment G, when MP2 is talking about hiring conditions, which wouldn't apply to her, she says "Yeah, my brother wants to get into it too." I think it is fairly obvious that these instances offer an available procedure, which could be captured as follows: When fellow conversers are exchanging stories of their travels in Europe, and you haven't been there, you can gain entry with, for example, "My parents (sister, son, boyfriend) went to France last summer." And having done that you can then get a share of the talk, so that they can ask you "Did he stay in Paris?", where they might ask each other "Did you stay in Paris?" In short, you can get access to talk on a category-generated topic, where you are not a category member, by proposing that some related person is a category member. And in Segment G she does in fact get into the conversation. I suggest that this is one formal property of small talk—that is, contrastively, it is at least plausible that if you happen to be present at a piece of technical talk by a couple of nuclear physicists, you cannot get into the talk by saying, for example, "My cousin studied physics when he was in college."

THERAPY TALK

The issue, then, is to provide some description of "therapy talk" which clarifies the relevance of "beginning," such that the latter is oriented to as a significant matter by both therapist and patients. I propose to start by considering the concern with accountability.[12]

In the previous section I have argued that "patients" who find themselves "waiting" for the session to begin may engage in some kind of small talk, where categorization devices alternative to [therapist, patient] may be invoked as the identifications participants employ to generate "topics." In particular I suggested that there are interesting ways in which participants may tie their remarks to those of others, where it could be seen that the maintenance of talk was itself a feature of concern, such that persons were free to engage in procedures which allowed them to take a turn despite their lack of membership in some category on which competence to talk might seem to turn.

Group therapy may well have a number of properties which make it a quite different kind of activity from two-person therapy. One of these, I suggest, is that the patient in group therapy is required to talk in the presence of lay hearers, i.e. persons who like himself are laymen with respect to the class of "problems" which legitimate the status of "patient." Another such property is that there seems to be no simple procedure for deciding—for example, by formula—when, how much or in what sequence "patients" should take turns in talking.[13] I want to consider, by way of looking at a small piece of data, how patients may construct utterances that satisfy these requirements of group therapy, i.e. how they accomplish talk that at once solves the sequencing problem and orients to the presence of lay hearers.

Here is a completed utterance produced by a patient within a session, on the basis of which I want to begin to formulate some of the features of "accountable" therapy talk.

BRENDA: I know I-I've stopped going to classes too but it seems to be quite different.

At this point in the session one of the male patients has been discussing the fact that he has stopped going to classes, and he finishes by saying "I've said my two-bits worth for today—somebody else's turn," and there is a pause. Now it is obviously an opportunity for somebody else to talk and it might be an issue for anyone who wants to take a turn how to enter the conversation. It is not difficult to see, then, that Brenda begins by linking her utterance to the last speaker's, in that she roughly says she has "that problem" *too*, and it is therefore open for others to see how she selected herself to talk at that point. And at first sight it might not appear to be remarkable that she has "the same problem"; after all, she is also a "student," and this is group therapy provided by a university health service. Nevertheless, a closer examination of what she says seems to disclose a more interesting problem for analysis, i.e. she says "I've stopped going to classes too *but it seems to be quite different*." (Emphasis added.) What can we make of the fact that while she claims to have "the same" problem she also claims that it is "quite different"?

If we were to take it that "problems" were simply neat psychological units, the formulations of which came ready-made, we might suppose group therapy merely provides an opportunity for everybody to take a turn making his formulation public. As against this I am suggesting that it is of some importance that in tying her utterance to the last speaker's, Brenda has it available to her to do so by similarly tying the formulation of her "problem." We don't know, of course, how Brenda might formulate her "problem" on some other occasion, given some other opportunity to take a turn at talking, and we therefore have to consider the possibility that "problems"—at least the formulations of problems that patients offer—get shaped interactionally in important ways. In other circumstances, then, Brenda might not begin to shape up her problem (for the "group") as that she has stopped going to classes. In formulating it this way she provides herself with an entry into the talk; she is, incidentally, the patient who speaks least during the whole session, and it may be that this is the easiest way for her to make an entry.

But beyond that we have to note that in so formulating her "problem" she is providing a self-identification as a co-category member, i.e. as "also" a student. That the "problem" she presents, then, is a "student's problem" may be a function of the categorical identification patients in the group are entitled to make of one another.

Such a tie of problem-formulation to category membership requires discussion. Minimally, it seems to be the case that "going to a psychiatrist" is a matter that persons in this society find to be accountable; and further, that the "reasons" that are culturally held to be good grounds for needing psychiatric "help" are (a) matters that a layman may not be qualified (at least initially) to know, and (b) matters of some embarrassment to declare, and of a "private" character. It is at least plausible, then, that patients in group therapy will see that they are accountable to one another for their presence in the group, and that categorical identifications may provide the basis for the formulation of "acceptable" troubles. In the instant case, students would presumably "see immediately" the difficulties that might be engendered by failure to go to class.

But the issue of accountability apparently cuts much deeper with respect to the properties of therapy talk. There is a question that recurs in group therapy and appears to be omnirelevant. Either a therapist or a patient may ask it, and apparently at any time, without regard, for instance, to the fact that it has been recently asked and answered. Here are some forms of the question as it occurs in the transcripts:

1. PATIENT: He's got himself last in line actually. (pause). OK, what the heck am I doing here?
2. PATIENT: Uh I'm a I'm in a vacuum . . . I, I don't know what I'm supposed to be getting out of it, I never ah-uh when the idea was first approached to me ((that)) uh you never did tell me what—what I was supposed to be getting out of it, you're supposed to sort of go there and find out, well I haven't been able to find out and I sort of assumed that nobody else has been able to find out either . . . and uh well, maybe, someday you're going to tell us, but it doesn't really look like it.
3. PATIENT: Y'know, but I-I told you why I come back y'know cause this is to me about the last—the last hope I've got. W-why do you keep coming back, I can't understand it.
4. PATIENT: So what the hell are ya doing here?
5. THERAPIST: Well what I'd like to do in the beginning is to discuss why

> we're meeting. Uh why each of you think we're meeting and what we can get out of this. And so on. Now, uh, what first of all I'd like to hear what each of you think uh what ideas you have. And then we can go on from there. Do any of you want to start the ball rolling. What do you think, why do you think we are meeting, and uh what do you expect of this.

I shall refer to the question as "Why are you/we here?" and treat it as a request for an account. Nevertheless, it is not immediately obvious what is involved in such a question, although it is clear that in one form or another it is a question that can properly be raised in a variety of situations. One of its features seems to be that it requires the hearer to see the relevant "where" that corresponds to the "here." Thus, you meet in a store in Paris an old acquaintance from New York, and ask "What are you doing here?" He says, "I live here now," and you presumably take it that he's telling you he lives in Paris, and not in the store. Coming to terms with the "here" requires some sense of what it is that is taken to be accountable; and this will be as much a matter of the relationship of the questioner and the questioned as of geography. In the utterances at hand I take it that the "here" makes reference to the situation of group therapy. In order to explicate the issues involved by such requests for accounts, then, I have first to note some of the social-organizational underpinnings of group therapy sessions:

1. Group therapy partitions its participants as "lay" or "expert" *vis-à-vis* some set of problems. The lay members—"patients"—are taken to be the possessors of such problems, while the "therapist" is an expert for whom the "treatment" of such problems is the rationale of his profession. Patients properly seek out therapists and present their "problems" in search of "treatment."

2. The question "Why are you here?" is properly asked by experts of laymen in consultative situations, and expectably produces a lay description of some relevant "problem." The question, then, may be taken to "stand for" some such expansion as: "I know you are here because you have some problem since that is why anyone comes here. What is the nature of that problem?"[14] This assimilates group therapy to a class of situations where laymen with respect to some domain confront practitioners. In such forms as "What can I do for you?", "What seems to be the problem?", "What brings you here?", or even, "Yes, sir?", it may request the formulation of a rationale for one's presence in a mechanic's shop, a GP's office or an architect's establishment. And I take it that a characteristic of such situations is that the layman is both expected and permitted to offer a layman's version of his "trouble" or business, and that it is seen as the practitioner's responsibility to transform that account into the language of the expertise involved.

3. Upon the layman's formulation of some "problem" as that which

brings him into the relationship, it is in order for the expert to (a) "accept" the formulation and commence diagnostic work or treatment, or (b) "reject" the formulation as not evidencing such a problem, thus terminating the relationship, or (c) make a "referral" to some other practitioner for whom such a problem would be "appropriate." Both (b) and (c) terminate the relationship. Continuance of the relationship, proposing further consultations, etc. warrantably indicates at least tentative acceptance of the "problem's" validity and appropriateness.

4. With respect to group therapy, the therapist's scheduling a program of meetings warrantably provides that in return for compliance, i.e. their narration of their "problems"—which narration constitutes a *first action*—the therapist shall offer some *second action* that shall be seen to have some "treatment" relation to the problems that generate the contact.[15]

These social-organizational properties of group therapy would certainly seem to warrant the therapist's initial inquiry "Why are you here?" as a request for a lay account. The data suggest, however, that the therapist may recurrently produce some version of the question, and hence some deeper analysis appears to be required. Despite the obvious theoretical interest in exploring how psychiatric perspectives properly generate "Why are you here?" as a recurrent question, I shall leave that aside except for a brief mention in later pages. At this point the concern is with the hearing that patients apparently give to the therapist's question. I take it that for patients it is a matter of some importance what practitioners do in response to initial lay formulations of problems. Minimally we have to note that offering an account of one's grounds for consultation with the practitioner offers simultaneously a self-identification, and that there is always the possibility that that identification will be shown to be unwarranted; for example, a person who diagnoses himself as having a minor ailment may hesitate to consult a physician on the grounds that he will be told he has "nothing"—i.e. nothing of consequence—wrong with him, and that he is not entitled to membership himself as "sick" or a "patient." (The availability of the category "hypochondriac" testifies to the recognition that this is a regular problem for physicians.) However the practitioner transforms the layman's account into terms of professional relevance, it seems that an essential feature of the lay-expert transaction is some *recognition* or *acceptance* on the part of the practitioner of the layman's grounds for "being here." Conceivably, then, the "repetition" of the therapist's request for an account may be taken by patients as a rejection of accounts given to date, and as signifying that the patient has yet to adequately answer the question, "Why are you here?". In that the therapist nevertheless "accepts" the patient by continuing the sessions, this may be a genuine instance of what participants might see as a "double bind."

The analysis so far presented suggests that patients and therapists have quite different entitlements with respect to conversational activities, and specifically I want to argue that "What are you doing here?" *addressed by a patient to a patient* does quite different work than the "same" question coming from the therapist. It is at least obvious that patients do not have the same entitlements to make such an initial request as a pre-diagnostic activity. In fact, the data I am presenting in this essay suggests that an appropriate expansion of the question, when both questioner and recipient are patients, is: "Why do you continue to come here?" The puzzle would then be: Why do patients treat continued attendance as an accountable matter?

Given the layman's acceptance by a practitioner as a "client," it is an interesting sociological query to ask how laymen are able to assess the efficacy, necessity and propriety of the "treatment" operations that practitioners bring to bear on the "problem." Presumably it is open to clients to withdraw from the relationship, and it may be an issue for all participants that the relevance and "helpfulness" of "treatment" be oriented to. "Talk" with the practitioner may be acceptable to the client as a necessary prelude for the institution of appropriate treatment routines. With respect to some domains of expertise, however, it seems to be the case that "talk" is also the chief medium of "help," and not merely the pre-diagnostic work whereby the practitioner gathers the "facts" and "symptoms." Patients may be reconciled from the beginning to the notion that in some sense what happens in therapy is "talk," as for example when early in the first session of a group a patient answers the therapist's question "What do you expect we will do here?" by saying:

> Being just from say talking from you, with you, there's no, you know you can say uh you've got a problem, and you should work it out this way. Ah-h, which is OK um but you've got not experience doing this. Ah, but in here y'know you can talk about the problems and work things out right a—right around here. More or less it's sort of uh, sort of that.

In some unexplicated sense, then, the patient takes it that the "talk" in the group will constitute the activity "working things out." As against this I would like to note that in a later session of another group, led by the same therapist, a patient says: "We sit around and talk about things for an hour and a half." Initially, that sounds like a layman's description of group therapy. The problem would be, of course, why the patient should locate a "description" of the activity at some stage in the on-going course of group therapy. It is not obvious that for whole classes of activities—having breakfast, talking with friends, getting money out of the bank—it is any part of that activity that participants should provide a description of what it is they are engaged in.[16] One occasion for offering something that looks like a "description"—particularly a "generalized description," i.e. a description of an activity as recurrent or "habitual"—seems to be in the construction of a "complaint": "Everyday we have hamburger for dinner," "You're always sitting around talking about the weather." If we inquire how such a "description" does the work of "complaining," then I would argue that its "deep structure" can be sketched along the following lines.

Participants in some routine occasion may warrantably take it that co-participants "know" and orient to the "proper activities" of the occasion, what "ought" to take place, given that it's "lunch," a "business conference," etc. In offering a "description" within the occasion, then, one may be seen as possibly "making an assessment"; for example, to propose by means of a "description" that the activity is one which participants can see as "not the business of that occasion," or not the "regular" business of the occasion, or "permissible once in a while but we always do it," is to propose that the occasion is badly conducted, that co-participants are behaving improperly, inadequately, etc. On this basis, then, I hear the description, "we sit around and talk about things for an hour and a half" as formulating a "complaint," and specifically as contrastively suggesting that something other than "sitting around talking" is in order. In short, I take it that here "talk" is intended to characterize the activity as "mere talk," where some other activity that may properly be done through the medium of talk—for example, getting and giving advice, instructing, exchanging ideas, etc.—would be in order. For occasions where such activities were appropriate, then, the claim that what transpires is no more than "talk" may be a methodical way of "complaining" or indicating "failure."

I would like to show the relevance of these remarks for the issue of patients' treating continued attendance in group therapy as an accountable matter. That such attendance is accountable suggests that patients find difficulty in recognizing "talk" as "treatment" for those "problems" that led them into therapy in the first place. Given that the question "Why are we/you here?" is omnirelevant, then, one could argue that patients find it difficult to come up with a description of "what happens in therapy" that *justifies* continued attendance. That this is an issue for participants is evidenced by such exchanges as the following:

STEVE: He's got himself last in line actually. (pause) OK, what the heck am I doing here? (pause)
CHUCK: Obviously you must figure there's some good in it because you're—here—and last year.
STEVE: Well not only here yes but—
CHUCK: (( ))
STEVE: I'm here quite willingly—((don't believe that)) the place is not getting me anywhere. You remember this was asked to me a—at me—to me—asked to me—
AL.: Once before.

?.: (( ))
STEVE: (( )) I said I was here to—I said I was here to—learn party manners. Which was about as brief a way as I could say something fairly complicated. I don't know if I could say anything much better right now.
AL.: What is party manners uh mean? What does it really mean?
STEVE: I've a long history of offending and bothering people.

There are a number of interesting things to note in this exchange. In the first place, it is not simply that the sociologist could pull out of a set of transcripts "evidence" that a question had been previously asked and answered—where it might then be an issue that participants had "forgotten," or that "different" questions were involved—but that here Steve builds into his present account a mention that the question had been asked and answered before, and in addition he recalls what his answer had been at that time. The reader should note that when Steve began by recognizing his turn, he explicitly formulated the concern as "OK, what the heck am I doing here?", and that two utterances later he remarked "I'm here quite willingly." The first remark recognizes the accountability of continuing as a patient, while the second, I take it, is intended to rule out one possible ground for attendance that others might provide—namely, that he might have no choice in the matter. And when Steve does give his account, that he attends "to learn party manners," it is couched in layman's terms, much like the initial accounts patients produce to account for their initial appearance in therapy.

But beyond that, in coming to terms with the accountability of continuing as members of the group, patients may develop formulations that can be seen to be nicely constructed for the task of accounting, in that they make reference to some "obvious" property of interaction in the group and propose that it corresponds to some feature of the patient's "problem." Such accounts have the following structure:

Statement of a "problem" + reference to some property of the group's interaction which accomplishes a "solution" to the "problem" as formulated.

Thus, a little later in the session than the exchange presented above Steve elaborates his "party manners" account in the following way:

> ((I think)) it's an empirical thing—myself, but—the fact is—that obviously if I come here and I start to bother people—one thing I do know about group therapy is that the fact that you—that you shut a bunch of people up—like this—for a fair length of time—uh raises their boiling points a bit. The fact is that if I'm going to be offensive—uh in this place I'll probably get told off.

Chuck provides a similarly structured account:

> Yeah. Well I could tell you why I—why I keep coming—or could tell you why Brenda keeps coming. Simple reason I keep coming is cause—well—uh—I could probably—be more at ease with—with a group of people sitting around talking. So—if I come here—uh—it's good practice to express myself—and uh—be sort of—accustomed to—to sitting in a group of people and expressing my ideas.

I have suggested in these last few pages that patients find their continued presence in the group accountable in that they do not easily recognize that the "talk" that constitutes "doing group therapy" is describable as "treatment." Earlier, I suggested that what is involved here could be seen in terms of the therapist's failure to produce "second actions" in response to patients' offered "first actions." Since I assume that patients' contributions are largely shaped by the therapist's activities I now wish to turn to a characterization of the latter in terms that will further clarify those properties of therapy talk relevant to the issue of "beginning the session."

There is one kind of joke about psychiatrists that has the following structure. For instance, a patient goes to see a psychiatrist and gives a long narration of his problems, and at the end of his narration the psychiatrist says something like, "Why don't you pull yourself together?" And presumably it is a joke because psychiatrists do not say that, but that may be what you would expect to hear from friends or parents if you told them your problem. And an interesting question, then, is: how do psychiatrists attend to problems?

It seems to be perfectly possible for a therapist to live up to his professional obligations while himself contributing little to the talk during the session. One thing it would be nice to show is that whether he talks, or talks very much, or not at all, the therapist controls the talk; and if that were the case we would expect the therapist to have procedures for exercizing that control. The first place to look for such procedures would be in the domain of conversational methods. In undertaking this search it is important to keep in mind that *conversation is not only speaking but hearing*. Sacks has amply demonstrated that the normal progress of conversation provides for hearers to demonstrate that they are hearers, and the intricate interlocking of successive utterances is presumably a feature of talk that permits speakers to monitor others' "understanding" and hence their own entitlement to proceed.

The therapist, then, might conceivably control the talk in important ways by virtue of the hearing that he gives the talk that others produce. If this seems far-fetched, the reader might like to try the following experiment: listen to some talk, involving at least two other participants, strictly to locate opportunities for puns (i.e. disregarding normal conversational obligations); then introduce those puns by taking a turn at talking. To do this systematically, I argue, leads to control of the conversation, for example, by making it "impossible" for others to continue with whatever conversational activities they were engaged in. It is, of course, true that such an experiment depends on the disrupter *talking* disruptively; but it must not be overlooked that in order to do this systematically such a participant must engage in a kind of "subversive listening," searching for ambiguities and *double entendres* that are normally disregarded.

In proposing, then, that therapists "fail" to produce "second actions" as constrained by patients' offered "first actions," I am suggesting that therapists are to be seen as engaged in "hearing" patients' talk in some theory-governed fashion designed to control the talk. Space permits me to present only one class of such activities on the part of the therapist.

I take it that there are many occasions where at least part of the action is achieved through talk that permit some kind of "time out." By this I mean that although that time in some sense is to be seen as part of the occasion in which it is located, it may nevertheless be oriented to by participants as a momentary suspension of at least some of the occasioned rules. It is conceivable, for instance, that within a language lesson conducted in the language of instruction (a French lesson conducted *in* French) there may be momentary "breaks" that legitimate a student's asking in English, for example, "How am I doing?" and receiving an answer to that question—where neither that question nor its answer is treated as part of the lesson. And this despite the fact that any interruption at that point could be seen as "interrupting the class." The point is that if the rule is "speak in French" the rule may be suspended from time to time to permit a student to check out his progress.

It seems to be a matter of some consequence to patients in group therapy that they should check out their "progress" with the therapist. The following three sets of interchanges locate instances of patients seeking to do this within the session:

Excerpt **G**

CHUCK: How long do you figure on on uh keeping this up or what's your idea or do we look like we're benefitting from it or what?

THER.: Well I don't know. I think the only person who can really answer that is uh is yourself, whether you feel you are or whether you feel the group is, I uh, you know. And how long we how long we go is is really up to you.

CHUCK: But as as uh your capacity as a psychologist you oughta be able to tell whether whether we ever got this thing off the ground or whether it's just—not having even been in another one I don't know ((aw)) what to compare it to, maybe we're getting along famously, maybe we're not, I don't know.

THER.: Well, what are your feelings about it?

Excerpt **H**

CHUCK: . . . I just kind of like to know whether whether we're doing what we're supposed to be doing or whether we're way off the track or what. I never get an answer one way or the other I usually get "well, let me ask you" routine, so I end up not knowing any more than before I asked the question. (pause)
THER.: What do you think you should be getting?
CHUCK: Well this is what . . ./
?: What what
CHUCK: This is what I've been asking you, I don't know. I really don't know. Uh I'ma I'm in a vacuum, I, I don't know what I'm supposed to be getting out of it, I never ah-uh—when the idea was first approached to me ((tha—)) uh you never did tell me wha-what I was supposed to be getting out of it, you're supposed to sort of go there and find out well I haven't been able to find out and I sort of assumed that nobody else has been able to find out either . . . and uh well, maybe someday you're going to tell us, but it doesn't really look like it . . .

Excerpt **I**

THER.: Well it seems that Al and Chuck keep coming back to this—question here—uh—y'know—what are we meant to be doing here and what are we doing here and why are we here and uh what's it all about?
AL.: Yeah, I'd like you to spend about five minutes and tell us what it's all about. (laughter).

Excerpt **J**

THER.: Well, what ideas do you have about ((being))—why—why do we come? (pause)
CHUCK: Ya asking me again or?
THER.: Everybody.
? I'm not sure. (pause)
AL.: I w—I would think that—that uh—after—well, the number of times that I've asked—you wouldn't be asking me.
(laughter)

All I want to note in these interchanges for present purposes is the hearing that the therapist gives to patients' questions. Each of these segments provides a patient's account of the reception the therapist has given a request or question. Thus, in Excerpt G, after the therapist's "answer" to his "question," Chuck produces a new formulation that treats the "answer" as "no answer." In Excerpt H, Chuck characterizes some recurrent feature of the therapist's treatment of "questions" as a "well, let me ask you routine." And in Excerpt J, Al similarly comments on a recurrent feature of the sessions by saying "I w' I would think that-that uh-after-well, the number of times that I've asked-you wouldn't be asking me."

For the moment I want to treat these materials as evidence for the patients' discovery that there is no "time out" within the sessions, that whatever "therapy" consists of, the therapist gives a theory-governed hearing to *all* patient utterances "during" therapy. I have sketchily suggested that the therapist's productions can be brought under a rule that provides for him not to produce "second actions" as responses to patients' "first actions." A further characterization would be that patients can find any and all of their talk to be accountable, in that one property of second actions is their recognition of corresponding first actions as warranted. On the basis of these characterizations of "therapy talk," then, I want to return to the issue of "beginning the session."

THE PROCEDURAL RELEVANCE OF "BEGINNING"

At the beginning of the essay I discussed some of the issues relating to beginning the session, with respect to the matter of assembling and the entitlements of patients to be present for the "start." I further suggested that this analysis did not sufficiently provide for the data, and hence I then turned to some characterization of pre-therapy talk and therapy talk. I now want to return to "beginning the session," and to further analysis of the data provided in segments A, B and C.

Granted that there is some issue of there being pre-therapy talk, and further of recognizing the rights of yet-absent patients, so that some talk might proceed between "therapist" and "patients" before the "beginning" of the session, it might then be objected that there is nothing more involved in an announced start than, for example, "calling the meeting to order." Such an objection does not seem to handle the data adequately. Note for example that in Excerpt A the therapist says:

> Look, before we start could I perhaps raise something and that is that I'm unable to be here next Monday at four o'clock and I thought it might be a good idea if five perhaps met on an alternate day at four. I wanted to know how you felt about it.

Announcing a start, then, could hardly be a matter simply of "getting everybody's attention," since here the therapist announces business relevant to all participants to be done "*before we start.*" In order to see what may be involved here we shall call upon the resources of earlier sections of the analysis, and look further at the exchanges of Excerpt A.

An issue so far avoided concerns the possibility, for any activity, of there being "an authorized starter." If participants are oriented to some activity as providing the relevance of the occasion, it may be that the

categorical partitioning of persons provides "who" shall commence that activity. In addition, it may be that by virtue of this same distribution of rights, participants can come to see what constitutes a "beginning," or that a "beginning" has been achieved. In Excerpt A, a patient says "It's so professional like now all of a sudden you don't know what to say," and falls silent. The ensuing silence lasts eighty seconds and is broken by the same patient's saying, upon the entry of the remaining patient, "Last one in has to talk first." Now in some literal sense such a remark seems to be "meaningless," i.e. there has already been talk, first between two patients and then between the two patients and the therapist. "Talking first," I take it, is "talking first in therapy," and such a remark suggests that "talking first" may be an unenviable requirement.

In order for the patient to have produced that remark, then, I assume there must be some procedural way in which it could have been seen to be in order. Inspection of the transcript reveals that the same patient produced that last previous utterance, and that that previous utterance ties back into the pre-therapy talk. Between the two utterances there is a silence of eighty seconds, and it appears that the patient had relinquished her turn at talking before the silence. (That is to say, I do not think that the silence can be heard as her "pause" in mid-utterance; the fact that she talks first after the silence I take to be contingent.) It is the silence we must focus on, I believe, if we are to see how the utterance under scrutiny came to be constructed.

My argument is as follows. Given the presence of the therapist and presumably some approximation to clock starting time, participants can orient to the closure of pre-therapy talk. Given further that after some contribution to pre-therapy talk there is no "response," a "silence" can be seen as the opportunity for any speaker to continue that talk, and an opportunity foregone. That is to say, the lengthening of the silence can be taken by participants as evidence that others have "nothing further to say" with respect to pre-therapy talk, and as an orientation to its closure. Further, if to "talk first" in therapy may be "difficult" or "painful," then the silence can be seen to be one in which "no one wants to start"—*and thus, I argue, the silence can be constituted, by participants, as the boundary between pre-therapy talk and therapy talk*. The patient's remark, "Last one in has to talk first," then, is constructed by her on the assumption that therapy has "started" un-announced. Moreover, the entering patient now says "You mean we've started," and again a literal hearing could not make sense of this as data; it could be objected, e.g. "How could he mean they've already started if she's asking him to start (talk first)?" But if "starting" is oriented to as something to be achieved, and if silences regularly serve as boundary markers for therapy talk, then the entering patient could well see the dilemma the group is in, namely that therapy has "started" but as yet no one has offered a contribution; and he could likewise see the remark

"Last one in has to talk first" as directed to getting the group off the hook of permitting the silence to lengthen indefinitely.

Now with respect to authorized starters, I suggested that an issue could be to see that some event properly constituted a "start." Thus, it need not be the case that an authorized starter must make an announcement. Such a person could perhaps "permit" an occasion to start and this could pre-suppose that participants oriented to monitoring the authorized starter's activities to decide whether or not this was the case. The therapist, for instance, could respect the boundary silence, and any participant could then warrantably "talk first"—i.e. do therapy talk—*on the grounds that the session had already started*. Nevertheless, if control of starting rests with an authorized participant, and if there are issues with respect to social-organizational features of starting, e.g. the presence of a quorum or the dependence of the occasion upon the accomplishment of some other activity, then the authorized starter may undercut what will retrospectively be seen as "attempts" by others to "start."

In this instance, then, I take it that the therapist does rule out what has occurred as having the status of a "start." And given that he has "business" to transact, involving "everybody," i.e. the matter of possibly changing the meeting time for subsequent occasions, he can be seen to have been "waiting" for the third (and last) patient to arrive. The central question can now be formulated: If the therapist undercuts a proposed "start," and if he nevertheless has "business" to transact—where we might assume, after all, that "business" ought to properly occur *after* starting, i.e. as part of the core activity—then the issue is: What is procedurally involved in starting the session? What is at stake, in terms of how therapy talk differs analytically from other kinds of talk which may occur among the assembled participants, which provides for the therapist to treat some kinds of "business" as essentially "pre-therapy" activity?

Consider the following set of interchanges—transcribed from the "business transaction" conducted by the therapist, immediately following his utterance above—in the light of the characterization of "therapy talk" offered in the previous section:

THER.: We could meet Wednesday or Thursday whichever suited you best.
PAT. A: Wednesday is better for me.
PAT. B: Same with me.
PAT. C: Wednesday it is then.
THER.: O.K. I thought I'd like to get this straightened out.
PAT. C: Same time?
THER.: Same time four o'clock. I think it will be all right for the same place. I'll have to check.
PAT. C: Then we'll meet over there?
THER.: No, we'll meet over here, etc.

What is to be remarked here is the "ordinariness" of the talk, and my assumption that the reader can make it out as ordinary not only by its mundane topic but by its perfectly routine employment of, e.g. questions and answers. The therapist appears to be treating questions as "anyone" might, and patients' talk is quite matter-of-factly related to the topic at hand, free of characterizations of their own or the therapist's talk.

In short, I suppose that any psychiatric theory provides therapists with a warrant for hearing patients' utterances as coming under a rule suspending routine conversational constraints. From the moment the session "begins," patients' utterances are to be treated as "data," and not honored as the activities they might be seen by patients as constructed to do. If this is the case, then for the therapist it will be germane to distinguish "business," e.g. social-organizational arrangements respecting meeting times, planned absences and so on, from "therapy" where "anybody" may properly treat any production as therapy-oriented. Thus, to ask patients "how they feel" about the meeting time *within* therapy is to entitle them, for example, to hear the question as inviting such things as an account of "neurotic" problems with punctuality rather than as "face-value" talk concerning scheduling sessions. In this respect, then, "business" resembles pre-therapy talk in that *all* participants are expected to give routine societal-members' hearing to one another's remarks without regard to their cross membership of the device [therapist, patient].

Such an analysis points up the fact that "patients" as well as the "therapist" are expected to attend therapy-talk as possessing distinctive properties. How that is achieved is a topic for further analysis.

MATTHEW SPEIER

Some Conversational Problems for Interactional Analysis

My purpose in what follows is to present some preliminary problems in social interactional analysis having specifically to do with the phenomenon of talk. The first part of my discussion will be devoted to spelling out some relevant problems in what I am calling conversational structure. The second part will focus on a small excerpt of data from my corpus of family household activity field tapes[1] in an attempt to develop some of these problems of conversational structure using a naturally occurring and socially located occasion of talk in family households.

(Notes to this selection will be found on p. 455.)

I
SOME ASPECTS OF CONVERSATIONAL STRUCTURE

1. CONVERSATIONAL EXCHANGE

To begin, I want to propose that everyday social activities of all sorts can be studied by looking closely at one of the main constituents of such daily enterprises, talk. I will address my remarks to that form of talk commonly referred to as "conversation," although I will make no attempt here to explicate why I treat "conversation" as a special class of a larger class of phenomena called talk, except to say it seems intuitively right to me at the moment. The following discussion of some structural features of conversation will hopefully make a preliminary contribution to the study of some of the invariant features of face-to-face interaction.

The first thing one notices about conversation is, of course, that it is a communicative act of speech among face-to-face interactants. They exchange their speech with each other. I want to make a very simple proposal for doing interactional investigations: treat any observable interaction in which a conversational exchange is made as a socially organized set of speech events. These events are accomplished by the members of that exchange by virtue of their knowledge and application of conventional procedures of conversing, to a large extent. Cultural competence in using conversational procedures in social interaction not only displays adequate social membership among participants in the culture, but more deeply, *it provides a procedural basis for the ongoing organization of that culture* when members confront and deal with one another daily. To study interaction, then, I am proposing that we explicate the procedures in conversational exchanges taking place among everyday actors, for they hold a powerful clue to the nature of social organization.

What are some of the basic features of conversational exchanges? I would like to take these up in turn.

First, it is obvious that conversational exchanges take many forms depending upon the composition of the conversational group and the setting and occasion within which it is viable. The first feature I want to consider is a highly general one that precludes even the very central questions of setting and occasion. This pertains to *the number of conversationalists in a conversational gathering*. Intuitively we think of two-party conversations as rather private affairs and more than four or five as larger types of conversational occasions. The larger the number gets, it would seem, the more strenuous it becomes to sustain a single interactional unit of a conversation. The tendency in such situations is to develop multiple conversations going on simultaneously. Persons standing in a crowd for a mutual purpose may engage each other in conversation within that occasion of public interaction, while in the confines of a household living-room a half-dozen persons may at times mutually participate in a single conversational focus, or allow it to dissolve into sub-conversational activity. It appears intuitively clear, then, that it is possible for two-party conversations to develop within a wide range of social settings and within quite disparate kinds of social occasions. The same can be said for three-party, four-party, etc. talk.

The point I am making is that there may be rules or procedures for conversing that are built into a conversational event depending on whether the interaction is indeed two- or four-party. There is, of course, a set of contingent conditions bearing upon these numerical features that emanates from the nature of the occasion and the setting, i.e. two-party talk is more structurally conducive in a bus-seat or a love-seat than at a large round table in a conference room, and in the latter, side conversations during an official meeting would normally involve just two adjacent parties, whereas before the meeting had gotten underway multi-party talk might have taken place across the table, and so on. *But* despite all these possible contingencies of ecology and occasion, there still appear to be conversational constraints that are determined solely by the number of conversationalists *available for a conversation.*

The importance of *constraints of availability* can be appreciated if we consider what speech sequence is possible, as a distribution of speech among the participants, when only two parties are conversing. The sequence of talk would run AB, and if more than one exchange were made, it would run on in similar structural fashion, ABABAB etc. Two-party talk, then, as I will define it here, consists of *those conversational situations in which two, and only two, persons are conversationally present.* This is a hard-and-fast condition I wish to apply to the operational definition of two-party talk. I will explain the reasons for it.

A simple adherence to a quantitative rule for deciding about the number of persons in a given conversation could amount to saying: take the number of persons who actually make speech exchanges in that instant conversation and let that number be the definitive basis for calling it N-party conversation, where if two persons make exchanges N equals two, etc. What is wrong with this rule is that it ignores the structural relevance of total speech availability by all present interactants and whatever constraints upon that availability may exist in the conversation. Therefore, if a group of three is gathered together, but only two of them exchange speech, the third remaining silent from the start to the finish of that occasion, we would not want to call that two-party conversation, because to do so would overlook the structural relevance of the third party *as hearer and as legitimate speaker* (unless of course he were prohibited by the situation from speaking legitimately at all). Silence in such a case would not be a simple quantitative distinction but a socially meaningful act of refraining from conversational participation in the interactional presence of others.

To carry a consideration of the phenomenon of silence a bit further, we will not rule out cases of interaction where two persons come into each other's sole presence and one initiates talk with another but gets nothing in return, e.g. as when one reports, "I said hello to him but he didn't say anything, so I said hello again, louder, and he still didn't seem to hear me, so I just dropped the whole thing and walked away." This might be characterized as an attempted two-party conversation where the interval between the first and second speech of the greeter is treated by him as a slot left noticeably unfilled by the party to whom the speech was directed. We might take this up as an interactional encounter that never came off, or had conversation been previously underway, one which went amiss, the latter being an issue in interactional sustainment and the former an issue in interactional starts.

The structural possibilities of a conversation among three persons is notably distinct from that of one where four persons are gathered, for the following simple reason. When there are four, two persons can focus on each other, leaving an opportunity for the other two to start up a separate stream of exchanges. Such availability for speaking being operant, it provides for different structural patterns of the distribution of speech. Whereas in two-party talk, ABABAB etc. invariably occurs, in three-party talk it is not necessarily, in fact rarely, ABCABC etc., and for four-party speech we can find ABABAB co-occurring with CDCDCD, but always providing for the possibility of a single conversational focus in the gathering such as ACBCBADADB etc. where the order in which the speakers talk is non-determinative by way of a simple rule or set of rules for precedence of speakers, i.e. all four parties do not use a rule that dictates a fixed order of precedence for them, such that B can speak only after A, C only after B, and D only after C, then A beginning again—as in a round of speech.[2]

To summarize the rather simple point I have been making, one structural property of a conversation is the number of individual participants whose presence is normally sufficient in itself to "count" each as a conversationalist and as an available speaker and legitimate hearer of all that transpires in the occasion. This means, in other words, that conversational members are normally always active as both speakers and hearers, and that further, speaking and hearing are procedurally controlled to achieve a sequence of speakers who follow one another in turn and alternatively hold or release the floor when it is their turn. This is so regardless of how "disorderly" conversationalists seem at times to be conducting themselves, e.g. overlapping, interrupting, etc. Even such seeming disorderliness, I will argue, is methodically produced by conversationalists.

What we have to start with, then, is a set of minimal objects for a conversation: a *speaker*, other(s) who are *hearers* of that speaker and who themselves are available for speakership, and the speech delivery of each, a finite string of words and parts of words that are attached to each speaker in the form of his *utterance*. I would now like to take up these components of a conversation in turn, beginning with the utterance as a central structural unit. All of my remarks will be addressed to the practical problem facing students of interaction when they wish to record and analyze the records for the behavior they contain. I take it interactional analysts must come to terms with the problem of making such records. The one I am concerned with here is a speech record, commonly called a transcript. I take it that transcripts of audiotapes (or videotapes) are the "hard data" without which sound empirical investigations are not feasible.

2. SOME STRUCTURAL COMPONENTS OF CONVERSATIONAL EXCHANGES

2.1 *The Problem of Utterances and Turns.* The total content of any conversationalist's speech in one exchange is nothing more or less than what he says when it is his turn to speak. At the moment it appears that nothing more definitive can be said about what constitutes an utterance beyond the following rule of recognition: an utterance may be described as one speaker's turn at talking. This is naturally quite problematic as it stands, since we would have to have a means of recognizing a turn when we see one, which conversationalists presumably are able to do quite regularly without excessive difficulties. Yet as analysts we might find it poses a problem in deciding what in fact is a conversationalist's method for determining when he has a turn, how he takes it, how he takes it away from another, how he recognizes when another has completed his turn, etc. Holding to this view of what an utterance is, even minimal "grunts" or "noises" would constitute an utterance, as in A) "Can I have that?" B) "Uhm" A) "What's the matter?" I will have more to say later on about the various analytic issues that arise when examining transcripts that contain what look like unfinished utterances, regained turns, etc.

Are utterances to be treated the same as sentences? Off hand it seems that they cannot be so treated. Utterances are to conversation what sentences are to a language. Like sentences they are produced under the guidance of grammatical rules that assign syntax to their various component parts. Like sentences, utterances have an internal structure. But unlike sentences they have structural relationships to the interactional circumstances under which they occur and for which they have important consequences as to what takes place next in the field of interactional events. We can imagine a speaker learning a language competently enough to engage in conversations with the natives of the language and in his lessons he recites simple exchanges like "Good morning," "How are you?", "I am fine," etc. But when he is confronted with the actualities of making a practical opening like this to a native speaker, the very same sentences become the basis for an occasion of social interaction and for possible further conversation. He is doing much more than using linguistic skill at producing acceptable and recognizable sentences; he is entering the arena of social action and exploiting some available procedures for social organization by doing so.

The analytic importance, then, of turns that "carry" the exchanged utterances from one party to others is that they are indeed the very basis for conversational participation. A turn at talking commits the speaker to social action. It is an event that occurs with respect to other conversational events, takes them into account, builds on or alters them in methodical ways. A turn establishes the positional relevance of any utterance as a sequence of temporally occurring conversational exchanges. It can be seen by participants as following or coming before another speaker's turn. By means of the flow of turns a conversation gets built. In the course of building it, I take it that conversationalists must have ways of keeping track of what others have said and tying their own utterances to them. By means of turns, conversation becomes a referential activity, not merely to those things in the world that can be named, but to what others say in the course of conversing with their fellow interactants—the "how" being part of the substance of their utterances.

The unit we can call a "conversation," then, must consist of at least one exchange by participants—that is, we can all recognize that some piece of talk among several persons seated about a room, say for a half hour, amounts to this unit: they are having a conversation. But can we call highly mortal speech exchanges conversations? For example, two persons encounter each other on the street. They exchange greetings, then continue on their way. We might not want to say that as far as *they* were concerned a conversation transpired between them. But for our purposes we might want to characterize their talk as a *minimal conversational exchange*. One thing we can feel confident about, and that is that those who engage in such an exchange provide an opportunity to make themselves available for further talk in that interactional instance. We might say they are entering into a state of talk as some kind of *pre-conversational* activity. This would be understood as an exchange by reference to the unit we are calling conversation, which might follow quite naturally from the initial greeting exchange of two utterances. In any case we might arrive at refined descriptions of conversations, sub-classes such as "ceremonial" or "ritual" conversations invariably being minimal exchanges.

2.2 *The Problem of Speaker Identification.* The next component of conversational exchanges I want to discuss concerns a very fundamental problem in social interaction and one which implicitly entails making a transcript of conversation. This problem concerns the "who" of the exchanges. That "who" is posed here as analytically problematic for understanding how speakers go about identifying one another as social actors in everyday conversational life. Two sorts of identification procedures operate. I want to discuss them in some detail.

One is the procedure employed by interactants themselves. The other is a procedure employed by observers who might analyze conversational encounters in a manner such as sociologists or anthropologists often employ when making sense of a social scene.

The two procedural operations are not necessarily interchangeable, indeed are most often not synonymous. By interchangeability I mean that the analyst's procedures for identifying the speakers are the same as those used by the interactants for identifying themselves in the scene under analysis.

I want to clarify how these procedures work. Consider first the procedure an analyst *might* employ to identify speakers in a conversation. It will illuminate the general sociological import and nature of the identificational problem.

There is this object I have mentioned called a transcript. It is a written record of conversational interaction that is best produced from a tape of the speech events. The tape is a sound reproduction of these events and is transformed into a written object by means of certain conventional transcription rules, the basic ones being: Differentiate the voices on the tape as particular speakers whose speaking can be represented chronologically on paper by putting some identifying mark alongside of every sequential utterance to show "who said what." The resulting list of speaker-identified utterances hopefully corresponds to the temporal sequence of natural events. It represents a set of speech occurrences in serial order. The problem I wish to consider is not the possible technical ways transcripts might be produced but what the conventional notational method of identifying speakers involves in the way of making a description of conversational interaction.

To describe the conventional method I will refer to the transcript as an object which has a left-hand and a right-hand column.[3]

The left-hand column contains the identifiers of speakers, e.g. a name, a category like "mother" or "father," or "male" or "female," or one of the previous ones plus age.

The right-hand column contains the utterances that such identified speakers make.

The problem is: How does the analyst decide upon the identifiers that go into the left-hand column?

The answer to this question is contained in the procedures the analyst uses for *categorizing the conversational interactants* relevant to the occasion and the setting within which alternative possible categories of social membership are selected for them. For example, in a family household the conversationalists can be identified as mothers, fathers, children, sons, daughters, infants, grandmothers, housewives, females, visitors, etc. such that they are put into the left-hand column of a transcript as one of those categories of speakers with their utterance being shown in the right-hand column.

Given that analysts use available identifiers in this way *as members of the culture they are observing*, we may conclude that their methods of categorizing conversational interactants shows that a general descriptive principle is at work: any conversationalists may be described as acting towards each other under the guidance of some categorical class of membership they assign to each other within a given occasion and setting—that is, members of a conversational occasion can call or treat each other according to various identificatory terms culturally available as families of membership terms, i.e. some terms naturally group together or are paired like mother, father, and child, or adult-child, and some do not, like mother, friend, and clerk, or mother-supply manager, etc. These families have been called "Membership Categorization Devices" by Sacks.[4] Using Sacks' findings as an analytic resource we can proceed to show the analyst's problem of speaker-identifiability when he confronts an interactional encounter that can be transformed into transcript form.

Consider the following exercise: You are presented with an incompleted transcript. It has only the right-hand column. Your task upon reading that column is to supply the identifiers for speakers in the left-hand column. The restriction on showing the individual utterances, i.e. the turns of each speaker, has been applied and by inspection the utterances are noticeably spaced to show each speaker's turn. The question is, can you supply the identifiers by knowing nothing else than what appears in the utterances?

Now let us reduce the restrictions to allow for at least the sequential identification of speakers qua speakers, i.e. the utterances are identified in the left-hand column to show only by some letter code which speakers go with which utterances in the sequence. With this much recoverable information available, how does the transcript analyst go on to fill in the identifiers, e.g. select for speaker A, "Mother A," etc? Why choose this as against that categorical assignment in the task of identifying the speakers?

Here I would like to refer to what Sacks has called the problem of the relevance of competing ways of categorizing persons.[5] Given that the analyst's problem is to decide which of more than one usable MCD is appropriately assignable to a speaker—since it can be seen by him that no one device is exclusively appropriate to categorizing the speaker such that it is only a question of a correct category for one possible device—his problem is one of deciding by some principled selection procedure the relevance of one as over another device.

To return to our exercise, what information in the utterances and in their sequencing alone would permit us to decide "which identifiers" to select? I take it this is a problem in deciding the competing relevances of speaker's categorical possibilities. To answer our question, it would appear that unless the utterances contained names and categories in "sufficient" display, very limited identifiers could be produced in the left-hand column.

Now a problem can be posed with reference to this assertion. If all that conversational interactants have, as it were, is the right-hand column, i.e. the utterances, how is speaker-identification practically achieved by interactants themselves?

Recall that the purpose of raising a distinction between the speaker-identification operations of interactants and of analysts has been to elucidate the speaker component in the structure of face-to-face talk. This consideration renders problematic what otherwise might be taken as a simple matter, viz. to identify a sequence of conversational exchanges an analyst has only to assign to each utterance the identifier of "speaker's name," for example. The analyst's problem, however, is not that readily solvable. This is so because it is precisely the speaker's relevance for choosing a categorization device that is especially problematic for the analyst, given that the right-hand column is intended to be brought under the categorical auspices of the left-hand column—that is, when men are occupationally organized into a social arrangement called the police, for example, a transcript of their talk would display this organizational arrangement in the left-hand column identifiers—even if the talk should lapse from practical issues or the job into familial or personal ones, such that the policeman is talking to his workmate as "one father to another." We would not alter the left-hand column to show this identification, even though it is categorically at that point in the talk mobilized.

Here is an excerpt of data. It can clarify the analyst's problem regarding competing ways of categorizing speakers: some devices can be seen to operate there in interesting ways.

	Left Col.	*Right Col.*
1.	FATHER A	Sit down on that side.
2.	JOHN 4½ YRS	Do you like lettuce with these? Michael do you like lettuce with these?
3.	PATTY 8 YRS	*I* do.
4.	FATHER A	It's not bad for two dollars.
5.	FATHER B	Quite a bit of work.
6.	FATHER A	Quite a bit of work—many hours of work putting it-it oh are you holding it for me? Thank you.

7.	MICHAEL $3\frac{1}{2}$ YRS	Somebody give me some milk. Please can I have some milk?
8.	MOTHER A	*Oh* yes. Milk.
9.	PATTY	Su said "*Oh* yes. Milk." ((Pause)) Your house is different from our house.
10.	FATHER A	Think so?[6]

The left-hand column shows the categories of mother and father assigned to three speakers in the MCD "family"; other categories in that device which could appropriately be used for the other speakers such as daughter, son, are not found in that column, however. (This observation necessarily uses information that was available to me as the producer of the transcript. I knew that those categories could be appropriately available to members of the conversation.) Further, it can be seen that the other speakers are assigned first-name-plus-age identifiers, indicating the relevance of the MCD "age," given that not all speakers are so categorized. It should be noted also that first names usually can be seen to have the MCD "sex" built into them as do the categories "father" and "mother," but this does *not* entitle us to see these identifiers as of the MCD "sex." Via the use of the device "age" for some of the members, another MCD can be seen to be assignable which permits the categorization of *all* present speakers into the two categories "adult" and "child" of the MCD "stage of life"—that is, it could be systematically re-assigned to replace the left-hand column categories in every case, and for this "population" of interactants it would be referentially adequate. *But* it should be seen that these considerations are not offered as a way of remedying a defective left-hand column. They are raised to show how it is an analyst assigns identifiers to any given set of speakers in an interactional occurrence.

The import of the last remark is to indicate that the analyst's assignment of membership identifiers is a common-sensically natural accomplishment and one not conventionally accorded the status of a first order sociological problem, i.e. when producing a transcript he performs the assignment task by means of implicit categorizing operations whose relevance is decided by some principled treatment of a set of utterances as setting and occasion generated, and under the guidance of the "consistancy rule," as Sacks calls it.

To clarify the operation of the consistency rule consider the following assignment of items to the left-hand column:

1. Adult
2. Boy
3. Child
4. Name
5. Father
6. Man

7. Child 2
8. Female
9. Girl
10. Adult

which are to be read as replacement for the items in the excerpt of data presented above. What would we say about the transcript as an interactional record we could produce by an inconsistent application of categorical identifiers to speakers? (Readers of it could not make proper sense of the record.) That is, it would not appear to be done with any rules for economy since we observe that here the analyst does not select a category for a speaker and stick to the category in further identifying the same speakers in the transcript. It would be a case of "first this speaker is one sort of object and then when I see him again he is another sort of object."

Now the analyst's problem has been taken up, as far as I care to take it for the present. I now want to consider the other problem—namely, a speaker's identification by other speakers as can be partially studied in the right-hand column containing the encounter's utterances.

The following consideration is offered as part of an explication of what appears in the right-hand column of our data. The analyst conceives of the categorical possibilities assigned to this column's utterances according to the same methods of categorizing he presumes to be operating among the speakers.

Another way of putting it might be, as I already suggested: the analyst's principled selection procedures for categorizing interactants *reproduces the procedures employed by interactants who are engaged in categorizing themselves*; or we may say that there is *a convergence* in the methods of both in categorizing speakers.[7]

The question that I wish to raise here is that if the analyst's categorical assignments of identifiers to speakers is a convergence with speakers' assignments of the same and thereby permits their outcome reproducability, what are the observable properties of specific utterances that generate those convergent categorical identifiers? Given the utterances alone as an interactional sequence of talk, what can be generated from them to warrant the analyst's description of those conversationalists as one kind as over another kind of speaker? What provides for the "fit" between the left and right columns of the transcript?

The problem that I have just set up requires consideration of the third basic structural component of a conversation, *the hearer*.

2.3 *The Problem of the Hearer*. As I shall refer to it, the problem of the hearer concerns the method for identifying hearers in a conversation. It is a peculiar sort of problem that can easily lead to insoluble philosophical regressions unless constraints are carefully built into the analysis.

The determinations of how speakers identify each other via categorizational methods that a cultural apparatus makes available to them—these determinations presuppose, of course, that speakers produce utterances to be heard, i.e. that there are objects in the world called "hearers" and such objects can be found in any conversational encounter.

Another way of putting this is: When a speaker takes his turn at talking, at any point in that turn another member of the conversation can be in receipt of his utterance.

Call such a member in receipt of a speaker's utterance, at any point along the course of its delivery, a hearer.

Given that any utterance in a conversation presupposes at least one hearer (hearers and speakers are here treated as mutually exclusive categories although a speaker is, of course, a hearer of his own utterances) namely, the other party in a two-party talk, or numerous parties in multi-party talk, it would seem useful to make the distinction between a potential and an actual hearer by pointing out that a potential hearer is one who usually has a legitimate right to be an actual hearer, i.e. to verbally respond to the speaker or to otherwise show he has heard.

As noted earlier, no universal requirement appears to exist in our culture that *all* present in multi-party gatherings who are potential hearers take a turn at speaking (unlike two-party talk where that requirement is normally in force).

Correlatively, in multi-party talk there does seem to be an existing entitlement by *all* present parties to a gathering to stand as legitimate actual hearers, i.e. there is normally no rule in effect in multi-party talk (unless it is a game built around the suspension of that normal rule) that restricts the rights of another party to hear.

Parenthetically, this availability of hearers to participate in a conversation raises intriguing problems of analysis for such phenomena as "over-hearing," "whispering," "asides," and "inattentiveness," to name a few possibilities. Nothing will be said here about them.

Thus we find there may exist restrictions on both speaking and hearing, although it would appear that restrictions on rights to speak are more elaborated than those on rights to hear. This, of course, is obvious in multi-party talk, where persons can be found to talk *while* others talk, i.e. when sub-sets of conversationalists are exchanging talk, a person can theoretically keep himself "hooked into" two sub-conversations as his hearer's rights might permit, but naturally only in some alternating manner such that he could not both speak in one sub-set and hear in another with continued fluency. His local involvement in one would produce some fractionated participation in both, no matter how hard he tried.

I now raise the problem of deciding in any instant case when a party to a conversation of multi-party type (more than 3) is definitively treated as a hearer by a speaker. How do we determine, in other words, who is in receipt of an utterance in the progressing conversational development?

The first problem confronting our data, then, is: what sorts of determinations can be made about a speaker's utterance as being in receipt of the hearer?

This problem presupposes that any utterance can be treated as a conversational *action* by virtue of its orientation towards another present party, i.e. utterances are normally spoken to others, which is not to say that an utterance *must* be heard, but only that it is made available for hearing. I want to suggest that an utterance is in every case capable of doing something in the world into which it issues forth. I take it that this capability amounts to a performative of social action. To use the language of J. L. Austin, words do things.

Having this power, utterances are very real objects in the world. They possess concrete properties when spoken and these properties are in and of themselves decidedly determinate. That determinacy gets built into utterances and provides an initial range of possibilities that they contain when issued forth in conversation. These concrete properties enter into the selection of how an utterance is taken into receipt by the hearer. The "how" is problematic. On it turns a great deal. I will call the problem of "how" an utterance is taken into receipt the "hearer transformation problem."

The "*hearer transformation problem*" can be formulated as follows: A hearer being in receipt of an utterance can determine from its recognizable properties what those properties provide for in the way of possible next utterances and from them he can make a selection of a next utterance. In order to speak, as a *next speaker*, then, a hearer must methodically decide upon the previous utterance's available determinate ways of being heard, and the sorts of determinations involved pertain to how he can procedurally accomplish "understanding." More should be said on this transformational process.

The "hearer transformation problem" would therefore appear to involve in the most central way procedures that hearers use to both form their own utterances and connect them to previous ones. The phenomenon of tying is a hearer's problem or what we might call a *next speaker's problem*—that is, the way of deciding about how a hearer in fact *is* a hearer at all is to hear him as a next speaker that shows not only that he indeed heard, but also *how* he heard. We noted earlier that one can normally assign the status of legitimate hearer to any present party who is a potential hearer. Now, however, we come onto the notion that what makes a hearer *interactionally consequential* is his own transformation into a next speaker and thereby entering the arena of conversational actions. (Imagine scenes where one shows how he heard another speak without himself speaking—is speech not being called for in some way in the scene?)

To continue, what does the distinction between hearing another speak, i.e. *that* he spoke, and *how* he spoke, look like? Can it properly be said of a hearer: *that* he heard another is a separate sort of phenomenon from *how* he heard him? It appears to be a distinction that has a basis in fact: When a hearer asks of a speaker that he repeat his utterance it can only be that he in fact heard it without hearing how it was said, e.g. the hearers employ what we might call a "repeat what," as in "What did you say?"

To consider the issue posed regarding the transformation of hearing into speech, I refer again to the distinction between two-party and multi-party talk. In two-party talk the problem of hearer transformation is clear cut: A speaker does a first action and then his hearer does a second action. That looks like: *AB*. How *ABA* can occur is in seeing the next transformation from second speaker back to first speaker who is now in receipt of the first hearer's utterance.

Continuing this consideration, a question may be posed: Can we call the hearer's *processing* of a previous speaker's utterance an action *until* he transforms it into speech or other actions? That is, what grounds are there for seeing a next speaker's hearing as an action? It would appear to be the case that only *after* the transformation has occurred can we directly observe the facts of *how* he heard and that for all practical purposes his utterance as a next speaker is a realized transformation of it.

There might appear to be an element of mystery here. The mystery I refer to is: how do we *know* another *hears* speech the way we claim he does? Might he not in fact have heard it one way as opposed to another? Is this sort of consideration that I am proposing—the purported mystery about hearing—a problem we can handle? The only answer that appears satisfactory is to look to what the speaker's utterance provides as possible determinate ways of being heard and to what the next utterance produces by way of hearing it as containing those possibilities rather than ask psychological questions about the hearer's state of mind while processing the speech he hears. He may of course be "thinking" things that we have no clue about at all. In effect, all we care to "know" about his hearing is his subsequent conversational action that is a visible consequence of the other's speech. All else must in some sense remain if not a pure mystery, then at least irrelevant for our interactional analysis.

I want to state at this point in the argument that not all problems of hearing require analytic resolution by looking to actions that are exclusively conversational, i.e. as next utterances. That is the case when we see, for example, that a speaker has been heard by getting some next non-spoken action done, and that in fact this action shows his utterance was in receipt by those who do it. Therefore, there is no mystery about the hearing process when an interactional sequence goes: A) Have a seat, B) ((sits down)). From this we are warranted in saying that B sat down because he heard A's invitation to do so, that he was invited to do so and *that he did so, despite whatever else he might have been thinking at that moment* (i.e. his sitting down shows he accepted and not rejected the invitation, where a rejection might be: B remains standing and says: "No, thanks").

As an interactionally recordable matter, however, we find these considerations lead us to view transcripts as problematic as records of spoken interactions, wherein there can be cases when nothing is put in the right-hand column to show when it is the case that a hearer has done a non-conversational next action. Normally this job is achieved by an analyst's descriptor, e.g. B ((sits down)). Now that is peculiar because the left-hand column must still identify who the descriptor applies to, e.g. B in this case. But B has not taken a turn to speak, so then why list him among the speaker identifiers? He is being nevertheless identified in that column, but in fact *as a hearer* who does some next relevant action, visual if silent. There may, of course, be only silence, no other noticeable action, that yet is slotted in the conversational sequence. Hearers may "remain silent," and that is noticeable.

An assertion can be made that follows from this. If a person does a next action without speaking and that action shows the sufficiency of that person's hearing the first one, then that constitutes an interactional sequence even though there is only one utterance produced in the action sequence. This is to be treated as a special sort of conversational exchange however, a type of sequence found perhaps in many places within a conversational encounter. We might say "silent turns" and non-spoken actions are part of the texture of any conversation.

The problem is a knotty one given the fact that interactional circumstances can involve in numerous ways phenomena that are not covered, so to speak, by utterances. At this point I want to suggest expanding our analysis of a conversational exchange to eventually include such phenomena as silences, pauses, glances, facial movements, gestures, etc. I will not attempt to analyze them here, however, but since they enter into such exchanges they deserve to be at least preliminarily noticed.

Now that I have outlined some of the basic components and some key problems for analyzing conversational structures, I want to pass on to the treatment of an excerpt of data. The reader is asked to keep this part of our discussion in mind when following the arguments presented in Part II.

II
INSPECTING A PIECE OF CONVERSATIONAL DATA: SOME TABLE TALK

I offer the following data for analysis:[8]

1. FA A — Sit down on that side.

2. JOHN, $4\frac{1}{2}$ — Do you like lettuce with these? Michael do you like lettuce with these?

3. PATTY, 8 — *I* do.

4. FA A — It's not bad for two dollars.

5. FA B — Quite a bit of work.

6. FA A — Quite a bit of work—many hours of work putting it-it ((pause)) oh are you holding it for me? Thank you.

7. MICHAEL, $3\frac{1}{2}$ — Somebody give me some milk. Please can I have some milk.

8. MO A — *Oh* yes. Milk.

9. PATTY — Sue said *oh* yes. Milk ((pause)) Your house is different from our house.

10. FA A — Think so?

11. PATTY — Yeah.

12. FA A — How is it different?

13. PATTY — Well our house is noisier and um and in our house Johnny's always fighting/and ((pause)).

14. MO B — Sue, shall I put some lettuce on for you?

15. MO A — Yeah.

16. PATTY — mommie and daddie are always, always talking about/ ((laughter all around))

17. FA B — Well how does that make our house any different? Maybe we just behave differently.

18. PATTY — But their rooms are (   ) and Michael's room is smaller than our room and/

19. FA A — That's Johannisberg Riesling.

20. MICHAEL — Did you see how much books I have?

21. PATTY — Oh *yeah*!

22. MO B — Does this go with that/

23. FA A — I uh don't know. Ask Sue.

24. MO A — Yeah.

25. FA A — Does ((pause)) my goodness look at those fancy mushrooms. Yes have some, have some bread mmm with butter on too.

26. MICHAEL — I'm not gonna have much bread.

27. JOHN — I'm not either.

28.	PATTY	I am.
29.	FA A	Who would like some bread over here?
30.	JOHN	I'm not.
31.	MICHAEL	We don't like those (we love rice)
32.	FA A	Who else would like some bread?
33.	MICHAEL	C'n I have some butter and bread?
34.	JOHN	Me too.
35.	FA A	Here pass this to ((pause))
36.	JOHN	Thank you Sue.
37.	FA A	Why do I have two forks here? I must have took yours. ((laughter))
38.	MICHAEL	I don't want mushrooms!!
39.	JOHN	I don't either.
40.	FA A	Michael doesn't care for mushrooms Rosa.
41.	ROSA, 13	Oh.
42.	MO B	Remove John's mushrooms Rosa.
43.	FA A	He doesn't like mushrooms either?
44.	MO B	Let's not waste them.
45.	MO A	((laughs)) Uncouth little boys.
46.	MO B	((laughs))
47.	FA A	How can you not like mushrooms—you silly boys?
48.	JOHN	Cause they don't taste good to us huh?
49.	MICHAEL	Yeah.
50.	FA A	Some kind of collusion/
51.	MO A	United front over there.
52.	MO B	Yeah. ((laughs))

I want to raise some problems that the student of conversational analysis might generate out of this piece of data. In coming to terms with the data, as is always the case, I must make continual reference to whatever information I have both from my own experience as a participant in the situation and as a transcriber of the tape, as well as to what anyone would find it necessary to employ as common-sense knowledge of the culture in order to make sense of the occasion in which this speech takes place. I do not maintain, however, that the reader is severely handicapped either because he was not a participant in the occasion or because he must rely on my say-so about it. I assume that the reader could do substantially the same conversational analysis as presented here, using the additional information I might supply. I am naturally aware of the problem of objectification that surrounds the use of such information, but I do not believe any defects that might exist on that score seriously prevent my generating some basic issues in conversational analysis. I believe these issues can be judged by the reader on his own with the data before him. I am more concerned at the moment with data analysis than with "methodological" issues in deciding about rules of evidence, which if taken up as a preoccupation can only lead right down the path into the maze of "how do we know what we know," which in the end is not data analysis at all.

To begin, then, I have chosen an excerpt from a tape of a dinner-table gathering. My main justification for selecting this as opposed to other segments of the tape is that we find the dinner-table activity is just getting started. I would like to say something about the opening of an activity as a problem in itself in interactional analysis.

We saw earlier that conversation consists of a sequence of exchanges that naturally develops out of a series of turns at talking. I mentioned that these exchanges take place in a variety of settings and situations and that an occasion of talk can itself be subsumed under an occasion of practical activity for that setting or situation. A structural issue that I hinted at pertains to how any occasioned piece of talk, as we might refer to it, gets under way and is sustained by participants. Just as there are utterances in conversational exchanges, so too there are *activities* in the practical routines of everyday household life. One simple, yet powerful way to cut into analytic issues of how conversations are part and parcel of social activities is to ask: How does an activity start and how does a conversation start with respect to that activity? Interactional openings seem to be a logical place to begin an inquiry of this sort.

First, we should note that the participants consist of two families. One can be identified in the transcript as Mo A and Fa A, and their son, Michael, 3½ years old. I will refer to this family as the *host family*. The visiting or *guest family*, consists of Mo B and Fa B and their three children, Rosa, 12 years, Patty 8 years, and John, 4½ years. The table occasion, then, consists of the interaction of two units of social membership associated with household life, the unit called "family." The occasion is a dinner (which in our culture usually occurs between the hours of 5 and 9 p.m.). It has been planned several days in advance, the guest family having been informed of the day and the time to arrive.

What we have to start with, then, is a routine activity found in households in our culture. But it is to be differentiated from everyday dinner activity by the simple fact that guests are members of this dinner occasion. Thus we may assume that the activity represented in this data is itself part of a larger class of activities that we might think of as "household visiting." Accordingly, the flow of interaction that has transpired from the time of the guests' arrival up to the time they take part in the dinner is presumably an integral part of the visiting activity. There are, to be sure, pre-dinner activities involved in the way the dinner-table occasions open. Pre-dinner interaction, however, is not available in our excerpt, which shows only the beginning of the meal and not, for instance, how all the participants got to assemble themselves in the kitchen. What had in fact happened was the movement of adults from the living-room into the kitchen upon Mo A's announcement that dinner was ready and her simultaneous announcement to the children who were playing in the boy's bedroom. At the time of utterance number one in the transcript, participants were all oriented to the opening of the table activity.

Members of both families assemble around the table, which is set for their use, standing in various positions around it in the kitchen (which serves as a dining-room in this household). It is a large old-fashioned kitchen big enough to accommodate the round dinner-table in it. Very swiftly they take seats at the table:

Mo B
Mo A R
Fa B J
Fa A M
P

I should also add that these families are very friendly and see each other quite often, the two boys playing together every day in the guest family's house in a child-care arrangement while the mothers work. They have had dinner together on numerous previous occasions, only at the guest's home, however, where most interaction between the families has taken place.

With these preliminary remarks in mind, what can we now say about the interaction presented in the transcript as a conversation and an activity? As I see it there are two general strategies for doing some methodical inspection of the transcript. One pertains to the entire conversational sequence of the transcript as a segment of dinner-table activity—that is, as a sequence of co-ordinated actions by the participants who are working their way through the natural order of events of a meal. The other concerns conversational development from one utterance to the next. The two are not the same insofar as there are different analytic issues made relevant by each such strategic examination of the data. I will try to clarify the meaning of this distinction.

A meal has a natural order of its own. One can identify the opening stages. For example, by knowledge of the normal organization of dinner into courses, one can then decide how far into the meal the participants are. The temporal span can vary widely from one such meal to the next, depending upon the speed with which participants take the meal and the number of courses and length of intervals taken between courses. Ultimately, however, the participants come to a point at which they are in its final stages and are mutually finishing up the last item on the menu, e.g. dessert or coffee, etc.

Now these practical actions can sequentially develop in large part quite independently of any conversational exchanges that might take place, indeed a meal can be accomplished in absolute silence. Also, quite obviously, conversations can develop quite differently from meal to meal. There apparently do exist some general characteristics of table talk, however, that are sufficiently uniform to suit the occasion and its practical purposes, i.e. eating a meal. There are types of conversational exchanges that "fit" closely to meal-time actions, that get some of the work of the activity accomplished, so to speak. I take it the core of that practical activity is precisely to open and close a series of stages in the meal. So, for example, conversational exchanges are made that consist of requests for things on the table or to be brought to the table. In each case the request brings about an opportunity for some person's action to fulfill it; and upon hearing it addressed to him or to anyone capable of fulfilling it the request may be ignored or denied. The way of meeting a request is normally to "pass" what is desired to the requesting party. When something is called for that is not at the table, the request seeks to get another to bring it to the table. This phenomenon has special interest for us in dealing with our data. I will explain this momentarily.

Requests, then, are speech events that are understood in terms of their formal characteristics, rather than because of reference to certain "topical" contents in table conversation—that is, I take it that "Please pass the salt" is not a "conversational topic," in the sense that "What happened at school today?" is such a "topic." The notion of "topic" is perhaps the most central means that participants normally have of turning eating activity into an occasion for talk. One can apparently get conversations going at the table by raising some topic presumably of interest to others or capable of being developed into one by the members of the activity. In other words, "topics" are resources for conversationalists in ways that practical requests normally are not. One obvious source of topicality is the menu fare, for example. Participants can comment upon the menu and discuss food preferences, make compliments about the hostess's culinary skill, refer to previous occasions of eating, pass judgments on restaurants, and so forth. I am not suggesting that some exhaustive list of such topics pertaining to the practical purposes of the activity ought to be drawn up for descriptive use in analyzing the activity, nor in fact even that such a list is possible. I frankly doubt that it is possible. I am pointing out only that we see the main purpose of the activity can be tied into the topicality of participants, talk *as a method for developing conversation* in the first place. Naturally there are a vast number of other resources that participants can draw upon to create such topicality—their social relationships, their social positions, their life experience, etc. It is to the methods of using such resources to make topical conversation that we must be looking when trying to spell out the formal properties of participants' talk in whatever occasion they share their speech.

The points I have made so far pertain to two aspects of dinner-table activity. One involves getting participants to orient to the start of the activity, getting them assembled and seated, and the other deals with how the meal conversationally develops in conjunction with the practical actions at hand when participants work through the stages of the meal once it has begun.

One strategy of analyzing our data, then, could consist of examining the natural progression of the meal through its stages to see how that temporal organization also organizes the ongoing speech of participants. The other strategy would be to concentrate entirely upon the utterance-by-utterance exchanges that sequentially occur and treat each participant's turn at talking for the general properties that exist in the exchanges, whether or not they are relevant for the particular type of practical activity at hand, i.e. I assume there are invariant features of conversational structure that are operating in very different sorts of practical activities and occasions—for example, asking questions and getting answers in a procedurally competent way. These strategies are not intended as alternatives, but each yields different problems and findings for an analytic machinery of conversational structure, i.e. one could extract two utterances from a conversation and treat it for some property that requires no analysis of its relation to the setting or activity in which it was produced—for example, the use of pronouns to make referentially adequate group speech. I believe, however, that the analysis of speech actions with respect to locatable practical activities is a very central concern for the study of social organization and how talk is involved in that organization.

I would now like to inspect some of the issues in the data at hand, employing both strategies wherever a pay-off seems most likely to occur in the form of useful findings about conversational structure.

One issue I hinted at earlier pertains to "requestive" activity, as we might call it, in table talk, and how objects can be passed or brought to the table upon request. It is the latter that I want to focus on briefly. We find that once the meal has begun, after Fa A has taken his territorial right as "host" of the occasion to direct others to the table, some talk takes place between the children, followed by an exchange between the fathers. Then, utterance 7 is made by the $3\frac{1}{2}$-year-old boy of the house. He says:

U7: Somebody give me some milk. Please can I have some milk?

He is heard by Mo A, his mother, who answers his request:

U8: *Oh* yes. Milk.

I want to consider the organization of this activity in regards to how family meals are projects managed by adult participants and how they formulate their conversation around their practical tasks of running the meal for the children participants. Likewise, how children formulate their speech for the adults whom they recognize as controlling the activity is equally relevant as an interactional issue.

What is there about family household organization that provides for the child's saying U7? That children make requests for things, services, help, etc. from household adults is a regular occurrence that permits us to see through the conversational actions of the child how he views his own social competence and also his own privileges as a member of the household. Given that a 3½-year-old has restrictions on his rights to perform household actions of various sorts, that he must often seek and gain permission to perform them, he feels entitled to trade on that parentally presumed incompetence by getting a parent to do things for him wherever that is a reasonable possibility. At the dinner-table parents in our culture exert control over children's actions in numerous ways, one of them being to get him to stay at his seat and to ask for something if he wants it. The child's entitlement to be helped is also constrained by his awareness that he ought to show appreciation and gratitude for it.

The 3½-year-old's utterance is formulated, I take it, with these interactional principles as guides. The features of his request are as follows. He asks for milk, but does not address anyone in particular. He leaves it open for a potential hearer to decide to fulfill the request, as a "somebody," when in fact he might have specifically directed his utterance to his mother. There are two parts (or sentences) to his utterance. The shift from the first to the second part involves a re-formulation of his request, but not for the purpose of removing the ambiguity of the utterance's directedness. Instead it is done to include a politeness marker, "please." The form of the request also changes from the more coercive command of "Somebody give me . . ." to the more humble and permission-seeking form, "Please can I have . . ." I see this as the child's willingness to politely cooperate in making a request, but under a rule of reciprocity that holds for adult-child standardized relationships, which says that a child may ask for something and an adult hearer will be under some obligation to recognize and fulfill the request. In other words, despite the openness of the pronoun "somebody," I take it that it is not meant for everyone present, i.e. it does not referentially include all participant hearers in the conversation. Michael does not expect Patty or John to leave the table to get him milk, but he could expect any of the adults, particularly the mothers who have been engaged in bringing things to the table (the mothers cooperate in this project) to fetch it for him.

U8 shows that the utterance has been acknowledged by his mother and that his request will be met. Mo A's utterance also indicates more, organizationally speaking, than just a recognition of her son's request for milk. It also shows her recognition that this item fits into a whole class of items that belong on the menu and on the table. Her utterance is formulated to account for the item's absence from the table. The utterance following it, by Patty, is not entirely clear, but it appears to be the case that she notices Mo A catching herself or thinking out loud about an oversight on her part, and perhaps, as part of the child's orientation to parental control over household activities, she finds such an admission worth remarking upon, and calling to the attention of others. The first part of U9, which is an actual imitation of the intonational pattern of Mo A's utterance, thus *ties back* to U8 and shows one of the structural features of conversations upon which sequenced speech can be built.

To summarize these points, we have seen three consecutive utterances tied together: U7, U8, and U9. They show, first of all, the process of hearing that goes on when a child in the table activity wants to direct a request to a potential hearer without naming or specifying the particular parties who are capable of hearing it as directed to them. The membership of participants according to the basic division between adult and child categories is operative in how the child organizes his formulation of a request for politeness. An adult, in fact, shows recognition of his utterance and also acknowledges a requirement in managing a meal to include the appropriate items. Finally, in U9 the 8-year-old girl overhears the conversational exchange between the mother and her son, and imitates the speech as a way of showing her orientation to the requestive actions and their implications for the competency of the adult to manage the project of running the meal smoothly.

Now U9 clues us into another structural feature of conversations that involves the problems of size in conversational gatherings that I discussed earlier. This is a larger gathering than 4 and therefore the possibilities are strong for the co-occurrence of two or more conversations. The principle of *speaker availability* can be observed in this occasion when various participants engage in *side or sub-conversations*. We find that in U4–6, for example, the two fathers are engaged in some talk that apparently has referential antecedents in the conversation (i.e. we would have to run the tape backwards a bit to find out the remarks that may have led to these). Their remarks are "sandwiched" in between the children's talking about food preferences in U2 and U3 and the child's request in U7. There is no connection between these three utterances and those of the two fathers *despite* their contiguity in time and on the transcript. The two sets of conversational exchanges occur in sequence, but are not related in any other way than through their chronologically sequential order. The stream of talk at the table, then, just from an inspection of the first 9 utterances *appears to be anything but what we might call a single conversational focus of attention among the participants.*

But to return to the clue of U9, I want to point out that it is like U3, which also belongs to Patty. What is structurally relevant about these two utterances is that both provide us with instances of conversationalists enlisting themselves into an exchange in unsolicited ways. Patty is in the position of a legitimate hearer of the talk going on around her. She in both places uses the opportunity of an utterance not directed to her to take a turn at talking. When John asks Michael if he likes lettuce with the food, repeating it so as to include the intended hearer's name as a directiveness marker, Patty answers in the slot that was set up for Michael. She adds emphasis by intonationally stressing the self-distinguishing pronoun "*I*," to show that she has indeed heard the question being addressed to another party. The topicality introduced by John provides her with an opportunity to speak. She has done so, as we see, by *speaking when another has been called upon to speak*. She takes his turn away. Now in U9 she does not speak where another ought to have spoken, but after a remark that did not involve her in the exchange; I presume that she sees the opportunity to "overhear" as a means for conversational involvement. Patty uses two methods, then, for gaining a turn and getting the floor. We may presume that part of the child's socialization to household activity consists in large part of learning various such methods for conversational participation.

The next property I want to point out has to do with the "fit" I spoke of previously between practical activity and conversation at the dinner-table. You will find places in the texture of this conversation where the practical actions of eating together dominate the focus of conversationalists. The domination of these actions manifests itself in various ways in the transcript.

U1 directs others to take seats at a particular place at the table. Fa A is guiding the children, in fact, to one part of the table. (Ecological arrangements that segregate children from adults or, alternatively, space them between parents for control purposes is an issue that might be taken up as an aspect of the problem I originally raised about running a household meal—I will not take it up here.) U2 to U3 is an exchange about the food placed on the table. U6 is an instance of a sub-conversation that is interrupted by the passing activity at the table: after a pause the speaker, Fa A, orients to Patty who holds some food up for his retrieval alongside him. He notices it out loud, so to speak, and does a polite "thank you." U14 to U15 is an exchange between the two mothers, in which the visiting mother offers some help to the hostess. Notice that this exchange effectively produces a stop in the flow of Patty's conversation with the two fathers. She pauses until the mothers complete their exchange. In U19 Fa A points out to someone the variety of table wine being drunk and this utterance interrupts Patty (U18) who is talking to him. Patty never completes her utterance; it ends with "and." Michael, however, picks up on the topic she has raised about the rooms in the host family's house, and uses it to enter the conversation in U20. Once again the practical concerns of eating dominate the conversation when Mo B asks the father of the house about the organization of the table fare. He refers her to Mo A who can be expected to provide that information as the main adult in charge of running the meal. From U25 all the way to the last utterance, U52, the participants become involved in the dominating activity of the occasion, *passing*, *offering*, *receiving*, *rejecting*, all being constituent speech events of the ensuing conversation. In sum, there are good grounds to show that in this occasion, at least, the participants are firmly locked into the practical activities of running a meal. It may be a feature of family household meals that the presence of children and the actions of parental overseers produces an ongoing concern for management that is governed by socialization practices in family life more than by the simple business of serving and passing food around a table which adults alone might have to deal with.

There are several instances of *conversational tying procedures*[9] that are useful to discuss. I will close this analysis of the data with some consideration of each. They involve the following: 1) question-answer sequences, 2) elliptical utterances, and 3) extensions and completions of utterances.

1. Questions-Answer Sequences. One common form of conversational exchange consists of question-answer pairs. Participants can direct questions to others which derive their interactional power from the obligation they place upon a hearer to come back with an answer, or as Sacks puts it, "a proper question gets a proper answer."[10] Further, a structural condition that is established by a simple question-answer (Q-A) sequence is that the questioner gets another chance to talk by virtue of his placing the question in the first place, i.e. he obtains a "reserved right" to speak again, as Sacks notes. In such a manner, methods for putting forth questions and receiving answers can develop into *chain-structures of turns: QAQAQA* etc. This kind of sequencing builds a conversation into a closely tied referential set of interactions. There is, to be sure, room for considerable refinement as to what constitutes an interrogative utterance, given that there are questions that may not be intended for answering, where answering might even in fact be quite inappropriate. Yet there seem to be a vast number of possible utterances that one could empirically locate that do indeed operate on the reciprocity rule of "proper question gets a proper answer." However, I will not go so far as to suggest that any utterance that brings some conversational response can be treated as functionally equivalent to question-answer pairs. This seems flatly wrong to me. I have in mind such things as requests that functionally ask for a service, for example, when their syntactic form is not an interrogative, e.g. calling a plumber and reporting "my hot-water heater is broken" is not a question, despite the obvious fact it may be soliciting a service.

On the issue of the relevance of question-answer pairs of utterances for the occasion or setting involved in their production, I am inclined to view QA structures as independent to a great extent from their settings, in terms of their power to build a conversation. There can, however, be a different outcome for the development of a particular conversation if these interrogative structures are used for initiating a conversation or for sustaining it. That is, their *position in a conversational sequence* may be more relevant in their methodical use than the practical situations and settings under which they may be constructed.

In the data we find in U2 to U3 a child is asking another a question, and not getting a proper answer he repeats the question with a speaker identifier attached to it, thus providing for its directedness—always an issue for the development of QA structures. However, the one to whom the Q is addressed does not answer, so that the outcome is a QA pair produced by another hearer making a legitimate answerer of herself. There are questions, then, it would seem that can be appropriately or possibly answered by another party—perhaps *any* present party. I presume there is also a class of questions that cannot be so freely answered.

Fa A's question in U6 would seem to be in the category of "rhetorical" questions, in so far as it is not calling strongly for an answer, but simply noticing and clarifying a circumstance, where the action involved speaks for itself, as it were. No chain structure gets built up in this instance.

Looking at the sequence U9 to U13 we find that Patty introduces a topic to Fa A and he picks it up with a question, something that provides for the child's going on to speak again. Now this is not a case of the QA "chairing rule," as Sacks calls it,[11] because the first speaker in this exchange is not asking a question. Patty is reporting upon something. Fa A allows her to carry her report further, to elaborate upon it, by putting a question that is entirely open for her to take anyway she wishes. And Patty reaffirms her initial opinion, but with the minimally elaborate "yeah" in U11. To get her to go on to say why she might hold that opinion and report further about the topic, Fa A asks her another question, this time more pointedly calling for a more explicit answer. U13 provides the elaborated answer. The result is a QA chain structure that goes: QAQA, but with the provision that the interactional issue is not that Fa A as the first questioner has a "reserved right" and gets another turn to speak again, but where instead his method for interrogative usage is to induct the child to conversational exchanges. Patty could have elaborated her report at U11, but did not. I take it that a feature of adult-child conversation is precisely the recognition by adult speakers that children require some induction into conversational participation. Parents often assist children to talk to them, particularly those children who are not their own.[12]

2. *Elliptical Utterances.* This class of tying phenomena involves such utterances as found in U2 to U3, where "*I* do" is to be heard as carrying along with it the part of the utterance in U2 that syntactically gives it its meaning, e.g. I (like lettuce). Utterances naturally build on each other by this general sort of operation in many instances. Speakers and hearers tie their productions together by means of the *principle of ellipsis*. I will look at an interesting set of these elliptical utterances for the inter-

actional consequence they have on collaborative speech production, where the alliance of two speakers' intentions to speak as one unit is an important membership phenomenon of this occasion.

I am referring to the two boys who tie their speech together closely in several parts of the sequence. By this method of tying they organize the conversation around their own social relationship *vis-à-vis* the other participants. They perform the tying by elliptical constructions. In the sequence U26–U28, Patty includes herself by ellipsis, but does not membership herself into activity of the two boys. In fact she counts herself out on the food selection issue. Michael announces that he is not going to have much bread, after his father has offered some to others, in his capacity as host, and following his announcement, John says: "I'm not either" = "I'm not (going to have much bread either)." Patty follows with: "I am."

Now another issue arises having to do with the contiguity of utterances in the transcript. Looking at U29 and U30 we find Fa A has offered some bread to some participants (locationally identified with "here") and the next utterance goes: "I'm not." The contiguity provides for hearing these two utterances in sequence as tied, when in fact their syntactical consistency is not preserved from U29–U30. Thus, by ellipsis, "I'm not (liking some bread)" does not appear to make syntactical sense (assuming grammatical competence is underlying the performance of John's speech). What I take to be happening here is that there is tying back to the utterance before the previous, contiguous one. John is carrying on an elliptical construction that began in U26 by Michael, and his saying U30 ties back to the last item in that sequence of elliptical constructions, Patty's remark, "I am"—that is, Patty has said "I am" and John says "I'm not."

In U31 Michael notices a bowl of marinated mushrooms on the table near his place and he comments: "We don't like those (we love rice)." (The use of parentheses in the transcript indicates uncertainty about the transcription.) What this does is to use the pronoun *we* to include another in the referentiality of the utterance. Does he mean everybody at the table? What other persons are included in that reference? The clues to answering this are found in the remainder of the transcript, but before taking them up I want to pass directly to U33 and U34, because in them we see a sequence of the very membershipping between the two boys I am describing as a unit-way or a plurality of conversationalists speaking as one speaker, which in an interactional sense is very strong speaker unity. In U33 to U34 we see that after their common rejection of eating a large amount of bread, Michael asks for some, followed by John's request for the same:

U33	MICHAEL:	C'n I have some butter and bread?
U34	JOHN:	Me too.

It is the feature of "me too" that children often use that I want to show here as a commonplace method of tying by elliptical constructions. Using this particular construction is one method of showing others that what the previous speaker has said holds for oneself. It is one way of allowing another's speech to represent your own speech, such that without his utterance you would not have one of your own.

Moving on to U38 and U39 the boys reject the mushrooms in the same fashion as they have previously done, using an elliptical construction in their collaboration. The following is said:

U38 MICHAEL: I don't want mushrooms!!
U39 JOHN: I don't either.

This exchange is done quite outspokenly to make sure that everyone present hears their rejection, and subsequently the adults orient to that fact. Fa A informs Rosa of his son's dislike of them, because she is passing them to the boys. Mo B tells Rosa to remove John's mushrooms from his plate, adding what I take to be a mild sanction for his having taken them:

U44 MO B: Let's not waste them.

Finally, to show a further sequence in which the two boys collaboratively conduct their speech, the issue of rejecting the mushrooms is now on the floor and brings a humorous criticism from Mo A:

U45 MO A: ((laughs)) Uncouth little boys.

which is followed by some laughter by Mo B. Then Fa A indicates his surprise at their rejection of this food, mildly derogating them:

U47 FA A: How can you not like mushrooms—you silly boys?

The collaborative sequence follows from this question. John answers the "charge":

U48 JOHN: Cause they don't taste good to us huh?

The "huh?" calls for ratification by Michael, John including him along with himself by selecting the pronoun *us*. In other words he takes it he has spoken for both of them and is representing Michael. This is ratified by U49, Michael's "yeah." This collaboration between the boys finally leads to a collaboration among the adults. I want to discuss that in terms of a third tying procedure.

3. Utterance Extension and Completion. One of the ways that conversations are built is for participants to borrow the parts of other speakers' utterances. The elliptical construction does that, as we saw. Another borrowing phenomenon consists of taking a previous utterance and extending it or completing it, not such that it only carries forward what has aelrady been said as in ellipsis, but more than that, it *adds* meaningful elements to the speech on the floor. Thus I can say: "I think he was acting really very ((pause))" and you can add "negatively?" In this case if you are right in *extending* my utterance you might get a ratification utterance from me next. Or if wrong, a modification would be made by me to correct your extension, and then I might go on to complete my intended utterance: "about that issue." Another method would involve *completing* another's utterance. By completing it I mean the one whose speech was extended treats the extension as a completion of his own utterance and goes no further with it. A nice illustration of both extension and completion is found in a recent article in which the author, James Baldwin, is being interviewed:

Q: What you are calling for, then, is a radical change in thinking by government and industry.
BALDWIN: Yes.
Q: And given the inertia plus . . .
BALDWIN: Fear.
Q: . . . fear and whatever else there may be, any such changes seem . . .
BALDWIN: . . . seem improbable.[13]

Now looking at our data we find that the final exchanges in it show a collaboration between the adults who are commenting upon the very noticeable interactional achievement of the two boys speaking in an intimately tied fashion:

U50 FA A Some kind of collusion/
U51 MO A United front over there

Sacks has referred to such instances as "joint sentence production."[14] It is one method of persons talking together as a group of speakers, i.e. they speak with the unity of a group—as one body. They do this by closely fitting each other's speech together. This occurs very swiftly and suggests the power of conversationalists to perform an ongoing analysis of each other's utterances in order to fit their speech in so carefully. The particular rule for completion that Sacks notes involving nominal participalizations[15] is not found in our data, but similar rules presumably operate to provide the conversational mechanisms that enable collaborative speech to occur. In U50 and U51 the second utterance in the pair borrows that part of U50 that precedes the prepositional phrase "of collusion." One says: "Some kind of" and the next speaker can extend it by supplying candidate prepositional phrases to go into that slot, e.g. "Some kind of (alliance between these two)." Now what is happening is that a *deletion* must be made by the second speaker and then a suitable candidate sought and entered as its replacement. The rule, if we can reconstruct it, might be: when a speaker employs a prepositional phrase, use the preposition as a pivotal term to delete the noun that follows it and replace it with some suitable candidate noun. For example, A says "I was (or "we were") thinking of getting" and B comes in with "going out for ice-cream." Some extensions, then, use a deletion procedure as well as one for adding on terms to the previous utterance in order to complete it.

We find another sort of extension in our data at U5 to U6. Here Fa B has begun to comment upon the kitchen table which Fa A has shortly before explained as having been refinished. Fa B begins an utterance and Fa A picks it up and carries it forward on his own, using the same syntactical formula to do so: "Quite a bit of work" becomes "many hours of work."

I have attempted to outline briefly some of the tying procedures conversationalists use to build the mutual activity called conversation. It is my belief that much will be uncovered about the way such procedural operations develop conversations. Once again I point out that these procedures are used as part of the occasion of conversation at the dinner table, but that they are sufficiently general to conversational activity to the extent that I would not want to say they are the exclusively setting products of table talk. I expect, on the contrary, that they can be uncovered in numerous settings and conversational situations. Unlike analysis of the main practical features of getting through a meal that involve cooperative eating behavior, which would take into account setting-specific features, an analysis of the properties of conversational tying are probably structurally deeper than those practical differentia that distinguish one purposefully organized activity from another via setting and occasion. A simple way of putting this idea might be: there exist a number of invariant properties of conversational structure that would presumably hold for any conversations that could be located in societal settings, however situated in social interactional circumstances.

In summary, what I have spelled out in this paper has been a general outline of some key analytic problems for studying conversation and how it gets structured by interactants. The data was presented to consider these problems in a concrete context in which their natural occurrence can be studied. Conversations are part and parcel of practical activities such as we find here in the family household. How conversation gets organized in and by means of such practical activities requires us to examine the basis of the conversational interaction as an occasion located within the setting of such practical activity. But, as we discovered, other elements are built into conversational structure that are not empirically covered, so to speak, by the main purposes of practical activity themselves. The findings of future research in this area of inquiry will hopefully illuminate the relationship between occasioned settings of talk and the conversations that participants can construct within them.

Notes to Selections

[1] The work of Alfred Schutz, cited in footnote 2, is a magnificent exception. Readers who are acquainted with his writings will recognize how heavily this paper is indebted to him.

[2] Schutz, Alfred, *Der Sinnhafte Aufbau Der Sozialen Welt*, Wein: Verlag von Julius Springer, 1932; "The Problem of Rationality in the Social World," *Economica*, 10 (May, 1943), pp. 130–49; "Some Leading Concepts in Phenomenology," *Social Research*, 12 (1945), pp. 77–97; "On Multiple Realities," *Philosophy and Phenomenological Research*, 4 (June, 1945), pp. 533–75; "Choosing Among Projects of Action," *Philosophy and Phenomenological Research*, 12 (December, 1951), pp. 161–84; "Common Sense and Scientific Interpretation of Human Action," *Philosophy and Phenomenological Research*, 14 (September, 1953), pp. 1–37; "Concept and Theory Formation in the Social Sciences," *American Journal of Philosophy*, 51 (April, 1954), pp. 257–74; "Symbol, Reality and Society," *Symbols and Society*, Fourteenth Symposium of the Conference on Science, Philosophy, and Religion, edited by Lyman Bryson and others, New York: Harper and Brothers, 1955, pp. 135–202; *Collected Papers: I. The Problem of Social Reality*, edited by Maurice Natanson, The Hague; Martinus Nijhoff, 1962.

[3] Obversely, a knowledge of how the structures of everyday activities are routinely produced should permit us to tell how we might proceed for the effective production of desired disturbances.

[4] Karl Mannheim, in his essay "On the Interpretation of Weltanschauung," *Essays on the Sociology of Knowledge*, translated and edited by Paul Kecskemeti, New York: Oxford University Press, 1952, pp. 33–83, referred to this work as the "documentary method of interpretation." Its features are detailed in my article, "Common Sense Knowledge of Social Structures: The Documentary Method of Interpretation," in *Towards a Definition of Mind*, edited by Jordan M. Scher, Glencoe: The Free Press, 1962, pp. 689–712.

[5] The concepts of "trust" and "distrust" are elaborated in my article, "A Conception of and Experiments with 'Trust' as a Condition of Stable Concerted Actions," in *Motivation and Social Interaction*, edited by O. J. Harvey, New York: The Ronald Press, 1963, pp. 187–238. The term "trust" is used there to refer to a person's compliance with the expectancies of the attitude of daily life as a morality. Acting in accordance with a rule of doubt directed to the correspondence between appearances and the objects that appearances are appearances of is only one way of specifying "distrust." Modifications of each of the other expectancies that make up the attitude of every-day life, as well as their various sub-sets, furnish variations on the central theme of treating a world that one is required to know in common and take for granted as a problematical matter. See footnote 2 for references to Schutz' discussions of the attitude of daily life. The attitude's constituent expectancies are briefly enumerated below, pp. 15–16.

[6] The term is borrowed from Max Weber's essay, "The Social Psychology of the World Religions," in *From Max Weber: Essays in Sociology*, translated by H. H. Gerth and C. Wright Mills, New York: Oxford University Press, 1946, pp. 267–301. I have adapted its meaning.

[7] *Op. cit.*, Schutz, "On Multiple Realities," and "Common Sense and Scientific Interpretation of Human Action." *Op. cit.*, Garfinkel, "A Conception of and Experiments with 'Trust' . . ." and "Common Sense Knowledge of Social Structures," *Transactions of the Fourth World Congress of Sociology*, Milan, 1959, Vol. 4, pp. 51–65.

[8] I use the term "competence" to mean the claim that a collectivity member is entitled to exercise that he is capable of managing his everyday affairs without interference. That members can take such claims for granted I refer to by speaking of a person as a "bona-fide" collectivity member. More extensive discussion of the relationships between "competence" and "common sense knowledge of social structures" will be found in the Ph.D. dissertation by Egon Bittner, "Popular Interests in Psychiatric Remedies: A Study in Social Control," University of California, Los Angeles, 1961.

The concepts of "collectivity" and "collectivity membership" are intended in strict accord with Talcott Parsons' usage in *The Social System*, Glencoe: The Free Press, 1951, and in the general introduction to *Theories of Society*, by Talcott Parsons, Edward Shils, Kaspar D. Naegele, and Jesse R. Pitts, New York: The Free Press of Glencoe, 1961.

[9] Common sense rationalities are discussed at length in Schutz, *op. cit.*, *Economica*, and in my article, "The Rational Properties of Scientific and Common Sense Activities," *Behavioral Science*, 5 (January, 1960), pp. 72–83. The common sense rationalities were made the basis of a radical criticism and reconstruction of sociological interests in mental illness in Egon Bittner, *op. cit.*

[10] Parsons, Talcott, "Economy, Polity, Money, and Power," dittoed manuscript, 1959.

[11] Wittgenstein, Ludwig, *Philosophical Investigations*, Oxford: Basil Blackwell, 1959.

[12] The *et cetera* clause, its properties, and the consequences of its use have been prevailing topics of study and discussion among the members of the Conferences on Ethnomethodology that have been in progress at the University of California, Los Angeles, and the University of Colorado since February, 1962, with the aid of a grant from the U.S. Air Force Office of Scientific Research. Conference members are Egon Bittner, Harold Garfinkel, Craig MacAndrew, Edward Rose, and Harvey Sacks. Published discussions of *et cetera* by conference participants will be found in Egon Bittner, "Radicalism: A Study of the Sociology of Knowledge," *American Sociological Review* (in press); Harvey Sacks, "On Sociological Description," *Berkeley Journal of Sociology*, 8 (1963), pp. 1–16; Harold Garfinkel, "A Conception and Some Experiments With Trust . . .," *op. cit.* Extended studies dealing with coding procedures, methods of interrogation, lawyers' work, translation, model construction, historical reconstruction, "social bookkeeping," counting, and personality diagnosis will be found in papers by Bittner, Garfinkel, MacAndrew, Rose, and Sacks; in transcribed talks given by Bittner, Garfinkel, and Sacks on "Reasonable Accounts" at the Sixteenth Annual Conference on World Affairs, University of Colorado, Boulder, April 11–12, 1963; and in Conference transcriptions.

[13] Insofar as this is true, it establishes the programmatic task of reconstructing the problem of social order as it is currently formulated in sociological theories, and of criticizing currently preferred solutions. At the heart of the reconstruction is the empirical problem of demonstrating the definitive features of "*et cetera*" thinking.

[1] See 1.1.1 for the meaning of this term.

[2] See, for example, Quotations 1, 5, 22 in the appendix.

[3] The question of what it is that "help" consists of will not be dealt with here.

[4] When "member" is used with an upper-case m it refers to a user of the categorization devices; when with a lower-case m it refers to a category that is a member of some collection.

[5] In the term *collection of categories*, *collection* is not used in a weak sense, as equivalent to the weak sense of *set*, but is only used to refer to groups of categories that Members of the community of users do indeed group together. Thus the issue of whether some particular category is a member of some particular collection of categories is an empirical issue, upon which any particular assertions we may make can be erroneous.

[6] Constraint (b) is introduced largely for purposes of simplicity. We will see (2.2.4 ff.) that there are Pn-adequate devices that do have overlapping members. For our current problem we need two devices that do not have overlapping members.

[7] I choose the example of the collection "age" in order to notice a feature that it and some other collections have: The device is Pn-adequate over a variety of formulations of the categories that are its members. Categories may be replaced from the collection without affecting its ability to categorize any population N. That is not to say that for any given group of categories any given category may be removed and remain Pn-adequate. There are thus alternative groups of categories where it is the groups that are substitutable, or where some particular category is partitionable into a group of categories constituting subsets of it.

[8] If a device is Pn-adequate, it follows immediately that it is also Pa-adequate, where a is some particular natural integer. It is not simply the case then that an uncounted population may be categorized by a Pn-adequate device, but also that any counted population may also be categorized by such a device. Having counted a population, it is of course the case that some devices other than Pn-adequate ones may be adequate to categorize it.

[9] See (2.2.5).

[10] It may be observed that either the first alternative constitutes a version of the second, where part of the research is done by one lacking professional status, or the second constitutes a version of the first achieved by reference to the fact that the professional is a Member of the population of categorization device users or feels competent to act on their behalf.

[11] For the relevance of this rule, see (2.2.4–5).

[12] The consistency rule can only be generally formulated for Pn-adequate devices. However, for partially specified populations, e.g. for those that have been counted, the consistency rule might be usable for non-Pn-adequate devices.

[13] The import of two or more categorizers will be considered in (1.1.6.1, and 4.2 ff.).

[14] First, see (2.2.3). Second, the relation between referential and inferential adequacy is extremely close. I explore the relation elsewhere, and one of the findings of that research especially relevant here may be proposed as follows: Any Member of any of the categories of such a device is a "presumptive representative" of that category. Briefly, the knowledge organized by reference to some category of a Pn-adequate device is presumptively appropriate for some Member given the determination that he is an incumbent of the category.

[15] The materials of this section are quoted verbatim from *Children Tell Stories*, by Evelyn G. Pitcher and Ernst Prelinger, New York, 1963, p. 35, 31.

[16] They also know the device whose collection is the pronouns. The working of this rather central device will be considered elsewhere.

[17] Ibid. p. 31, emphasis added.

[18] For some Pn-adequate devices, their construction is such that for any population Member the categories are mutually exclusive. For some Pn-adequate devices this is not so. For such (latter) devices it is nonetheless possible that a single categorization may reproduceably be provided for by reference to an orderly procedure for considering the applicability of categories and a rule providing for stopping as soon as a category has been found applicable for any given Member.

[19] For some devices, their proper use does not involve repeatable use of categories. Suppose, for example, one is using the device *baseball team* (first base, second base, . . . catcher) to select players from a larger population than nine (or eighteen) potential players.

[20] Or any other correspondence-type criterion.

[21] While we do this introduction without having shown how the relevance of these collections is provided for, that task is not going to be ignored. The reader who would rather proceed by reference first to the indication of relevance may turn to 3 ff.

[22] Recall (1.1.6.1).

[23] By "partially" we mean that such matters as the rules of conventional sequencing by which the relevant interchanges take place have not been constructed.

[24] Recall Note 14, 1.1.5.

[25] Recall 1.1.6 ff. Given Pn-adequacy of K and R, we can see both the possibilities of mutual exclusiveness and of convergence.

[26] The formulation will be seen to be correct for K.

[27] It may be noted that the characterization has been developed from a consideration of a variety of materials other than the suicide materials presented above and in the appendix.

[28] From author's field notes.

[29] G. Bateson, p. 172, *Group Processes*, 1955, ed. Schaffner.

[30] *The Witnesses*, p. 46, testimony of A. Zapruder, Bantam Books, 1964.

[31] Los Angeles Times, 4-14-65.

[32] Genesis, Ch. 19.

[33] Franz Kafka, *The Trial*, pp. 7–8, Knopf, New York.

[34] A. I. Richards, *Chisungu*, pp. 38–9, Faber, 1956.

[35] Mark Zborowski and Elizabeth Herzog, *Life is with People*, p. 289, Schocken edition, 1962.

[36] See further (8 ff.).

[37] From the analysis we have presented, it is quite expectable that persons who find themselves in the binds described may find themselves unable to turn for help, and elect suicide. Several of the suicide notes we have collected or seen evidence that the suicidal had found themselves in such a situation. It is expectable further that persons in such a situation will not leave a note or a note that gives an account of their trouble. Cressey's data, similar as it is to the materials we have been analyzing, and given the fact that it is largely concerned with persons who have failed to find a legitimate way out, i.e. with persons in prison, seems to confirm these expectations. See, for that data, Donald R. Cressey, *Other People's Money*, Free Press, 1953, especially Chapter 2.

I am indebted to Harvey Sacks for calling the phenomenon to my attention.
Sacks (1967 and forthcoming).

[3] A central reason for frowning on invented data is that while it can be easily invented, it is invented only from the point at which it is relevant to the point being made, thereby eliminating a central resource members use in hearing it, i.e. its placement at some "here" in a conversation, after X; in short, by eliminating its conversational context.

[4] By "problem" I intend not that speakers will have pondered the matter, but that what they say is to be seen by analysts, both professional and lay (i.e. hearers), as a solution, as the outcome of work.

[5] On choosing that way of identifying oneself that maximizes status, see Moerman (1967). Suttles (1968) reports for the slum he studied that with the exception of five occupations, persons answer inquiries about their occupations by reporting the place where they work or the industry, rather than their job title, 46 & 100.

[6] A curious appearance of this: if your tobacconist "remaindered" matches you may find yourself with one which advertises "Al's Liquor Shop, 122 Main St.," and wonder where it is.

[7] See, for one attempt in this direction, Lynch (1960).

[8] On componential analysis, see e.g. Conklin (1955), Frake (1961), Goodenough (1956), and Lounsbury (1956).

[9] Garfinkel and Sacks (1969) review the terms and discussions by philosophers, logicians, and linguists. Their paper is relevant to several themes in the present discussion.

[10] Schegloff (1967), Ch. 2.

[11] Although the unit to which "local organization" applies may be quite large. Thus, for example, the "common sense geography" to which we referred earlier involves some knowledge about places never visited, but expectably known by competent members. Whereas asking of one returned from Peru whether he travelled to Colombia does not necessarily exhibit the asker's intimate familiarity with those places, remarking to someone who reports living on West Fourth Street, "Oh, you're in the Village," can be seen to exhibit a knowledge based on personal experience. Which sorts of places are known generally, in the manner of a common sense geography, and which are known "locally" in the sense intended in the text, is a matter for empirical investigation. I am indebted here to Diana Cook.

For one ethnographic report on the variation of naming and knowledge of an area by proximity to it, cf. Suttles (1968), 24–5.

[12] On direction giving, see Psathas and Kozloff (1968).

[13] Schegloff, 1968.

[14] William Labov argues that it would be a good strategy to reserve the term "question" for such utterances as have been traditionally so described by linguists employing syntactic and intonational criteria. In that case, knowledge that linguists have about "questions" would not be diluted by including in that class utterances for which that knowledge does not hold. A_3 would simply be called "a request for information." On the other hand, neither syntactic considerations (such as inverted verb forms) nor distinctive intonations seems to mark adequately the class involved. Perhaps eventually we will understand by "question" utterances that provide the relevance of distinctive sequencing rules for the ensuing utterances. It is with an eye to such a possibility that I use the term "question" here.

[15] Although we have omitted consideration of the following point earlier, it is important to note it here. "Right" formulations need *not* be drawn from the set of "correct" formulations; it is not a set-sub-set relationship. When one office worker says to another at the end of a coffee break, "Well, back to the salt mines," the rightness of the formulation is not precluded by the "incorrectness" of the term as a description of his work place. This is a direct parallel for place formulations to what Sacks calls "intentional mis-identification" for membership identification.

[16] This point is reminiscent of a classic concern of the sociology of knowledge. It has been part of the program of one approach in the sociology of knowledge that accounts, descriptions, theories, etc. are to be examined most importantly not with respect to the objects with which

they seek to come to terms, but with respect to the circumstances of the producers of the account, or its audience. To understand how some account comes to be offered, an investigator should look not to the objects being addressed; they will not explain the production of the account. It is to the circumstances of its production (its environing class structure, Zeitgeist, psychic states, cultural values, professional ambience, etc. in traditional studies) that one must look to understand its occurrence. I have argued here that formulations of location are used by reference to, and hence exhibit or "reflect," the situational or contextual features of their production. That a formulation is "correct" is, in this context, the least interesting of its features, for it would be equally true of a range of other formulations. Not any "correct" formulation will do. "Right" formulations are "right" in part by exhibiting the particulars of the situation of their use. These notes may then be read as bearing not only on issues in the study of conversational interaction, but also (if the two are separable) as an essay in the sociology of common sense knowledge. See Garfinkel, 1967, and, especially, Garfinkel and Sacks, 1969.

[17] Sacks, 1967, and forthcoming.

[1] The definition of discourse analysis with which Harris begins his "Discourse Analysis Manual" shows no relation to the problems to be raised in this paper, nor to any other theoretical problems which I have been able to discover. For Harris, "discourse analysis is a method of seeking in any connected discrete linear material . . . some global structure characteristic of the whole discourse . . ." This global structure is "a pattern of occurrence . . . of segments of the discourse relative to each other." Harris points out that this is the only type of structure that can be investigated "without bringing into account other types of data, such as relations of meanings throughout the discourse." This pursuit therefore forms part of Harris's previous interest in analyzing the phonology and grammar of a language without reference to meaning.

[2] It was an unpublished draft by Bever and Ross on "Underlying Structures in Discourse" (1966) that put the issue most directly. In order to show coherence in a discourse such as "Everyone should read the Bible. Deuteronomy is one of the great books of the world," Bever and Ross thought that it would be necessary to include in the grammar that Deuteronomy is one of the books of the Bible, and that discourse analysis therefore lay outside of linguistics. The rules of discourse developed here are not subject to this problem; they would typically show that some such relation is being asserted by the sequence itself, as listeners unfamiliar with the Bible would infer without difficulty.

[3] Charles M. Schulz, *Peanuts à Vendre* (J. Dupuis, Marcinelle-Charleroi-Belgíque, 1968), p. 64. I happen to have seen this in a French translation, but I am sure that the English original reflects many parallel cases in real life.

[4] From current studies of therapeutic interviews being carried out by David Fanshel of the Columbia School of Social Work and myself.

[5] There are cases where A makes a statement about an AB-event which require an answer; but these seem to be equivalent to rhetorical questions that are not requests for information, and should probably be covered by a different rule.

[6] An adolescent club in South Central Harlem, composed of a number of peer groups of Negro boys 13 to 17 years old, one of the main sources of data for the study of non-standard Negro English as reported in Cooperative Research Report 3288 (Labov et al. 1968). This particular session was the subject of considerable study; it was recorded on video-tape as well as on multiple audio tracks.

[7] At a higher level of analysis, this is a challenge to Rel (see CRP 3288, sec. 4.2.4). However, the rules presented here are aimed at the lowest level of abstraction, closest to the linguistic material.

[8] This work is described in detail in Cooperative Research Report 3288 (Labov et al. 1968); this research, carried out from 1965 to 1968, was supported by the U.S. Office of Education. I am indebted to Paul Cohen, Clarence Robins, John Lewis and Benji Wald for their assistance in this study, and particularly to Benji Wald for suggestions incorporated in the present version of the analysis of sounding. Much of the following material on sounding is adapted from section 4.2.3 of CRP 3288, Vol. II.

[9] While this incident is necessarily anonymous, it was reported to me through close associates who are related to some of those involved.

[10] I am indebted to Dan Swett of San Francisco State College for further data on this incident; he was directly acquainted with some of the principals in this affair.

[1] The equipment and field time for making recordings in Thailand were sponsored by grants from the Center for Southeast Asia Studies, University of California, Berkeley and the Committee on Research of the Academic Senate, University of California, Los Angeles.

[2] The sequenced data required for my arguments are provided in Appendix B. Fragments of that conversation, and of others, are also provided where referred to. The data are referred to by a Roman numeral, which designates the tape number, followed (after a period) by the Arabic number 1 or 2, designating the track. The Arabic number which follows the number sign (#) provides the serial utterance number. This is sometimes followed by a colon (:) which precedes the number of the specific word being referred to. Copies of the original tape recording are available for the cost of dubbing and postage.

[3] An informant, bilingual in Lue and Central Thai, made the initial transcript. We then listened together to modify his transcript. I usually deferred to his hearing of the tape and when I could not, noted both versions. Glossing and translation was done by me after discussion (in Lue, Central Thai, or Yuan) with the informant. The informant, whose assistance I gratefully acknowledge, was Mr. Dheerawatana Wongyai.

[4] My use of "Lue society" or other named societies is as a gloss. Elsewhere (1968a), I have pointed to the oddness of assuming that all predicates about social activities have an ethnic label as their object. There is little reason to regard any of the conversational principles discussed in the enclosed paper as relevantly Lue, and none for considering them peculiar to the Lue.

[5] I accept responsibility, but not sole credit, for this analysis which incorporates detailed suggestions from Anita Krakowski, Jerry Krakowski, Harvey Sacks, and Emanuel Schegloff.

[6] Throughout this essay, material required for intelligible translations is added to the gloss, but enclosed in parentheses (for items which I feel are given by syntax) or brackets.

[7] This is one reason why "a semantic theory [that] cannot be expected to account for the way settings determine how an utterance is understood" (Katz & Fodor, 1964: 486) is insufficient for the analysis of natural conversation.

[8] The plural is not editorial. It refers to the work being done on conversational analysis by the group whose members are occasionally mentioned in this essay.

[9] Anita Krakowski.

[10] In both Thai and English, phrases which are otherwise idiomatic are sometimes given a literal reading. I do not know whether this ever becomes an issue for members, but suggest it as an issue for linguists to investigate.

[11] The reader will observe that #204 lacks actors. That and how participants knew to which actor the activity is ascribed will be developed below.

[12] Given the importance of sequenced context to participants' orientations toward the meaning of an utterance, my use of "repetition" is not analytic. Specifically (and among other features), members may orient to the very fact that an utterance is being said for a second time so as to make its second saying perform a different activity (e.g. reprimanding) from its first (e.g. asking).

[13] Evidence that an utterance of one type requires a subsequent utterance of another type might consist of participants orienting to and interpreting the absence of the second in the presence of the first. That questions require answers can be shown in this way for both Lue and English. That a summons requires a reply has been demonstrated, for English, by Schegloff (1967). The present run of data will not support the claim that a paradox requires (in this strong sense) an explanation.

[14] The voice that says #204 sounds rather like the one that says #228. The voice that says #228 sounds like the one used by the woman who lives in, as "mother of the household" (*mɛ̄· hə·n*), the house where the recording was made. That this observation is phrased so strangely and relegated to a footnote results not from my uncertainty about its accuracy, but from methodological insistence that member's knowledge that a particular individual sometimes is correctly categorized as "occupying" a role does not constitute an analyst's account of what that individual is (perhaps otherwise) doing.

[15] In the present data, see VIII.1 #'s 192–195, 196a'–196d, 198, 200–207, 211, 215, 217, 220, 222–223, 228, 231–232, 234–241.

[16] Paul Newman's discussion of Terra narratives suggests that speakers of that language require social knowledge for aligning actions with the actors indicated by sex-neuter pronouns (personal communication).

[17] If one supposes that the ability to participate in conversations is a member's criterion of competence, capacities that might be required for any conversation (although not necessarily the capacities required for every and all conversations) are among those of all competent members of (a) society.

[18] Instanced by who was scolded, by whom, and for what, as discussed below.

[19] Since ǐ, is a title for females and *pɔ̄·ló·ŋ* one for males, I can facilitate reader comprehension by sometimes using "she" or "her" to refer to A_2 and "he" or "him" for A_1.

[20] The informant's initial transcription was *caj paj*. He revised this to *paj*. In numerous subsequent listenings, I hear *caj paj*. The uses of bad data are considered in the *Discussion* section.

[21] The alignment of actors with actions is somewhat less transparent to inspection in a Lue transcript than in an English one, since a Lue utterance may, like the utterance upon the member-analysis of which it is based, lack actors (whether pronominial or not).

[22] This essay uses *individual* as an analytic object: a human being not formulated with a CL. The data themselves contain no individuals, since any label which members use for a human being, even "human being," is a CL in that the label and its situated use have interactive implications. In this essay, personal names are CLs with no special status aside from intended consistency-of-individual-as-speaker in the transcript and in my references to it, i.e. I hope that an individual speaker categorized in the transcript by a name (e.g., "C," "W_1") in the left margin is always the same individual.

Since many CLs can correctly be assigned to more than a single individual, an unsituated CL is insufficient for the unique designation of an individual. Even such an apparently unique designator as "the present king" requires temporal situation in order to accomplish unique designation. That this is not true of all CLs is suggested by such CLs as "the first king of France" or "Jesus Christ." The apparent uniqueness of the second does not derive from its being a proper name since these, unless conversationally situated and participant analyzed, can rarely do unique designation (see I.1 #99–108).

I.1

#99
mk Yes, [he] really likes trouble.

#100
NA Who?

#101
mk Him. Nan (a title) Phian (name) (and) those (guys) there.

#102
NA W Which Phian.

#103
mK Nan Phian.

#104
K I haven't yet gone to look for the *caw thaw*, but [we] discussed it.

#105
NA Which Phian?

#106
mK on our own.

#107
mK Nan Phian [the son of police] seargaent sɛn there, sir.

#108
NA Exclamation! Those kind (of people) make a lot of trouble.

Because they otherwise behave like CLs, and since their correctness is insufficient to account for their situated use, and since unsituated names can be referentially ambiguous, I see no reason at this point not to regard proper names as a collection of CLs.

The use of CLs is not a subject solely of academic interest. Rather, it is the source of some important unsolved practical problems. Individuals will starve because they are categorized as "Indian" by "Americans." The evil of discrimination consists largely of treating individuals as members of categories which they reject in the situations in which they are so treated (Schutz 1964:259). A large set of dangerous policies (variously termed "imperialism," "tribalism") seem to consist of aggressive (or selfish, or defensive) behavior concerted by means of the enthusiastically shared common categorization labels of those who carry out the behavior against other individuals who are taken to share some other CL. It is these observations (and my dream of subverting their situated automaticity) that furnish the emotional basis for my interest in how CLs are assigned and used and in how behavior is concerted through them.

[23] Those listed (Lue, headman, peasant . . .) are all correct CLs for the individual whom the data of this paper label "K."

[24] I am not fully confident of my argument that information additional to that set out in Appendix A, Section 2 is required for participants to know that the time is unusually long for such a trip. It is clear, however, that even this knowledge is not the same as knowing that A_2 relevantly and sanctionably delayed in returning from market.

[25] Participant knowledge of these things requires them to analyze, not passively record (if such is ever possible) the relevant utterances. This may be suggested to the reader by the absence of actors or quotation markers from the gloss of the relevant utterances.

[26] See Appendix A, Section 2.

[27] See *Taking sides*, below.

[28] The issue of productive knowledge is considered in the *Discussion* section.

[29] "Suggests" because supposing some temporally vague, extensible, and generally ascribable activity may be just the thing to do if one has not attended closely. Nevertheless, I will argue below that #204:1 shows its speaker to have attended to the sequence of tied utterances beginning with #190.

[30] So permitting translation as "[She] (must have) dawdled . . ."

[31] Although the speaker of #204 is female (see *Providing accounts*, above), I have heretofore avoided as analytically unmotivated any reference to "her" and "she." Since my current argument is that W's femaleness is relevant to the feature of #204 now being analyzed, I drop that rather strained practice.

[32] The speaker of #204 might have refused to recognize a delay by saying something like, "It always takes me that long, too."

[33] It may be that justifying the scolding and making use of the normal operations of social institutions provide the "must be" of #204:5.

[34] #204's acceptance of the sparse formulation is not interactionally inert. Its speaker

could have refused to accept the typicality of the actors and asked or supposed such considerations as, "Was *ĭ·naŋxam* a cripple?" This would have both excused the delay and challenged the justice of the scolding which it occasioned.

[35] As a more general matter of social control (Moerman, *in press*) it may be that those who have the right to scold thereby have a duty to scold and, through the folk theory that scolding is corrective, find that their reputations are implicated by the misbehavior of those over whom they have that right/duty.

[36] See *Providing accounts*, above, and especially its comments on III.1 #333–5.

[37] There are a number of related candidate observations about series of stories which I have not yet either fully substantiated or developed into an argument. My impression from the ethnographic literature is that many peoples tell stories and proverbs in rounds or series. My impression of American data is that stories and jokes frequently come in rounds and series. Stories in my Lue corpus are usually in series or rounds. It is my distinct impression that the focus or "point" of a Lue or an American story is heavily informed or constrained by the other (and especially the preceding) stories in the round or series. It is conceivable that the very series of utterances examined in this paper—perhaps until #204 could, were they part of a different series and made by a speaker and before an audience correctly categorizable as "young," constitute a story about how demanding, nagging, unsympathetic, and petty old folks are. If stories and proverb do, indeed, get much of their "point" from the series in which they are told, this would help to account for:

(a) the ambiguity of multiplicity of meanings which natives and folklorists consider to be a feature of (isolated) stories and proverbs;

(b) the observation that these forms do usually come in series or rounds and not in isolation. If it is typical for the "point" of a story or proverb to derive essentially from the series of similar items (together with the category alignments of participants) in which it is told, there is little to recommend the content analysis of isolated stories and proverbs.

Appendix C provides a translation of the stories that C told immediately before and after the one that provides the data for this paper.

[38] Consider the interactive implications of an account of A_2's delay like, "I suppose she was having menstrual cramps, poor thing."

[39] So, for example, componential analysis, as a tool of ethnoscience, can provide a "correct" definition of "mommy" as "informal term for first ascending generation lineal female kinsman." It cannot account for the following real data:

BOY$_1$: Ken, face it, you're a poor little rich kid.
BOY$_2$: Yes, mommy, thank you.

Nor can it permit us to reckon with, let alone account for, the observation that persons who can correctly be categorized "mommy" are not always so categorized (or, at least, always so labelled) during the course of an interaction.

[40] "Minutae" is used here in a folk or commonplace sense.

[41] Readers familiar with the anthropological literature will realize that I cite this as an example of unusually good contemporary ethnography.

[42] I would suppose it to also depend upon such considerations as the relevant statuses of A, B, and C; the presumption that the talk was not "private" or "privileged."

[43] Although I think that it might have been a possible alternative to stipulate the form of tieing and deduce the substantive norms, conventional ethnographic knowledge informed E_1 and E_2. It was part of the lexical knowledge (of *ĭ·* and *pɔ̄·ló·ŋ*) needed for demonstrating the correctness of the possible relationship between A_1 and A_2. It provided some legitimacy for the frequent suppositions which I made about what could have been said other than #196b:1 or #204:1.

[44] One exciting promise of the procedures employed in this research is their potential for self-correction. To suggest this promise, it is more encouraging to point to possible future

modifications of the analysis offered in this paper than to the shortcomings of its earlier versions. The conversational phenomenon this paper calls "providing an account" may well be subsumed under more powerful devices, found in both Lue and American conversation, whereby a speaker can direct the sense that participants make of his topic by requiring them to decide among ambiguous semantic interpretations. This would associate "commonplace paradox" with irony and quotation as they occur naturally.

[45] Translation seems especially problematic. The essential importance of sequencing for member-meaning might suggest that translation is impossible. However, it is a quite obvious and basic fact about the history of human civilization that translation is a possible and normal human enterprise. On the basis of my own efforts, I am at the moment quite partial to (but unable to demonstrate) the view that satisfactory translation consists of (heretofore unconscious) analysis of situated utterances in one language for the interactional activities they perform and their translation into situated utterances in another language which perform those same activities. The possibility of such an enterprise would, of course, rely upon the existence—which there is little reason to doubt—of interactional universals.

[1] The third, which involves the issue of how the properties of things and of persons are mutually implicative, must be deferred for subsequent treatment.

[2] Such a lexical marker of conversational tieing would be interesting in that its usage:

(1) would be in fact (not just in logicians' fancy) be restricted historically, to things previously mentioned.

(2) would be precluded across conversations. Specifically, *NOUN nî· nī* would never begin a conversation or topic as pronouns and proverbs (e.g., do, can, make) can in English conversation.

[3] *pɔ̄·ló·ŋ* as a term of reference, *pɔ̄·ló·ŋ* + *N* and *pɔ̄·ló·ŋ* + *Ø* when used as kinship terms mean "elder brother of my parent" or "husband of elder sister of my parent." A person so categorized, whether or not a kinsman of the speaker, is always male and at least middle-aged. When not a kinsman, he is usually a prominent or wealthy person. *ǐ·* + *N*, *ǐ·* "*which*," *ǐ* + *D* are used for females. The term is sometimes said to be deprecating. After a girl marries, she is typically referred to as a "wife + TN (of husband)." Once she has children, she is typically referred to as "mother + N" or "mother + name of child." I regard *pɔ̄·ló·ŋ*, *ǐ*, and all other title and kinship terms as CLs. For an interesting and ingenious discussion of *ǐ·* as a Yuan term of address and abuse see Wijeyewardene 1968.

[4] Anthropologists will note that "reciprocal" is often used but rarely defined in discussions of kinship terms.

[5] I phrase the issue in this somewhat awkward way (i.e., by referring to #196d:11 and not to *cōmó·ŋ* or to "an hour") in order to remain consistent with our basic orientation to utterances in conversational sequence and not to decontexted lexical meanings of words.

[6] The absence of recorded data from my argument precludes using a more neutral word.

[7] I believe that naming some place physically as close to the central market as Ban Mang is would be less emphatic of how long it took the girl to make the trip.

[1] William J. Goode, "Norm Commitment and Conformity to Role-Status Obligations," *American Journal of Sociology*, LXVI (Nov., 1960), 249, italics in original.

[2] *Ibid.*, 246.

[3] See David Sudnow, "Normal Crimes: Sociological Features of the Penal Code in a Public Defender Office," *Social Problems*, 12 (Winter, 1965), 255–76, and Aaron V. Cicourel, *The Social Organization of Juvenile Justice*, New York: Wiley, 1968.

[4] Goode, "Norm Commitment and . . .," *op. cit.*, 250, italics in original.

[5] Kingsley Davis makes essentially the same point: "How an individual actually performs in a given position, as distinct from how he is supposed to perform, we call his *role*. The role, then, is the manner in which a person actually carries out the requirements of his position. It is the dynamic aspect of status or office and as such is always influenced by factors other than the stipulations of the position itself. This means that from the point of view of the social structure it always contains a certain novelty and unpredictability." A footnote then appears: "What Mead calls the 'me' is the internally perceived position while the 'I' is the actual behavior in the position." *Human Society*, New York: Free Press, 90. Davis then quotes from Mead as follows: "The response to that situation as it appears in his immediate experience is uncertain, and it is that which constitutes the 'I'." G. H. Mead, *Mind, Self, and Society*, Chicago: University of Chicago Press, 1934, 175.

[6] Harvey Sacks, *The Search for Help: No One to Turn To*. Unpublished doctoral dissertation, Berkeley: Department of Sociology, 1966; and dittoed lecture notes, Fall, 1967.

[7] A. Paul Hare, "Interpersonal Relations in the Small Group," in R. E. L. Faris (ed.), *Handbook of Modern Sociology*, Chicago: Rand McNally, 1964, 218. Translating structural notions like a legitimate order of authority into cognitive and behavioral activities at the level of social interaction remains unchartered territory, except for the truncated small groups studies which do not permit an assessment of the relevance of such work if moved to the more complicated stage of everyday life, where persons "keep score" and worry about consequences under different kinds of pressures. I am suggesting that the qualitative differences between currently conceived small group experiments and "spontaneous" and "institutionalized" activities in everyday life are not shown to be in correspondence, and that the relation between our formal theoretical concepts about structure and process and the small group theorist's formulations appear unconvincing.

[8] Robert Rosenthal, *Experimenter Effects in Behavioral Research*, New York: Appleton-Century-Crofts, 1966.

[9] Cf. Edwin M. Lemert, *Social Pathology*, New York: McGraw-Hill, 1951; Erving Goffman, *The Presentation of Self in Everyday Life*, Garden City, New York: Doubleday, 1959; Sheldon L. Messinger, H. Sampson and R. D. Towne, "Life as Theater: Some Notes on the Dramaturgic Approach to Social Reality," *Sociometry*, 25 (March, 1962); Donald J. Newman, "Pleading Guilty for Consideration: A Study of Bargain Justice," *Journal of Criminal Law, Criminology, and Police Science*, 46 (March–April, 1956), 780–90; Howard S. Becker, *The Outsiders*, New York: Free Press of Glencoe, 1963; David Sudnow, "Normal Crimes: Sociological Features of the Penal Code in a Public Defender Office," *Social Problems, op. cit.*; and Aaron V. Cicourel, *The Social Organization of Juvenile Justice, op. cit.*

[10] Goode, "Norm Commitment and Conformity . . .," *op. cit.*, 247.

[11] See Robert E. Ward et al., *Studying Politics Abroad*, Boston: Little, Brown, 1964; and Aaron V. Cicourel, *Fertility and Family Organization in Argentina*, forthcoming.

[12] Ralph Linton, *The Study of Man*, New York: Appleton-Century-Crofts, 1936, 113.

[13] Kingsley Davis, *Human Society, op. cit.*, 86–9.

[14] Talcott Parsons and Edward A. Shils (eds.), *Toward a General Theory of Action*, Cambridge: Harvard University Press, 1951, 154.

[15] Talcott Parsons, *The Social System*, Glencoe, Ill.: The Free Press, 1951. Consider the following quotation: "On the one hand there is the positional aspect—that of where the actor in question is 'located' in the social system relative to other actors. This is what we will call his *status*, which is his place in the relationship system considered as a structure, that is a patterned

system of *parts*. On the other hand, there is the processual aspect, that of what the actor does in his regulations with others seen in the context of its functional significance for the social system. It is this which we shall call his *role*." (25)

[16] George C. Homans, *Social Behavior*, New York: Harcourt, Brace and World, 1961, 337.

[17] *Ibid.*, 379.

[18] Peter M. Blau, *Exchange and Power in Social Life*, New York: Wiley, 1964, 4.

[19] *Ibid.*, 297.

[20] *The Presentation of Self in Everyday Life*, *op. cit.*, 1.

[21] *Ibid.*, 13.

[22] *The Presentation of Self in Everyday Life*, *op. cit.*, 243.

[23] See Goode, "Norm Commitment and Conformity . . .," *op. cit.*, 251.

[24] L. Wittgenstein, *Philosophical Investigations* (trans. by G. E. M. Anscombe), New York: Macmillan, 1953.

[25] See Kaplan, *The Conduct of Inquiry*, San Francisco: Chandler, 1964, 8.

[26] Goffman, *op. cit.*, 15.

[27] G. H. Mead, *The Philosophy of the Act*, Chicago: University of Chicago Press, 1938, 192.

[28] Ralph H. Turner, "Role-Taking: Process Versus Conformity," in A. Rose (ed.), *Human Behavior and Social Process*, Boston: Houghton Mifflin, 1962, 22–3.

[29] Gregory P. Stone, "Appearance and Self," in A. Rose (ed.), *Human Behavior and Social Process*, 88.

[30] T. R. Sarbin, "Role Theory," in Gardner Lindzey (ed.), *Handbook of Social Psychology*, Cambridge: Addison-Wesley, 1953, 225.

[31] John Rawls, "Two Concepts of Rules," *Philosophical Review*, LXIV (1955), 3–32.

[32] Aaron V. Cicourel, "The Acquisition of Social Structure: Toward a Developmental Sociology of Language and Meaning," in H. Garfinkel and H. Sacks (eds.), *Contributions in Ethnomethodology*, Bloomington: Indiana University Press, forthcoming.

[33] Goode, "Norm Commitment and Conformity . . .," *op. cit.*, 254–5.

[34] Tamotsu Shibutani, *Society and Personality*, Englewood Cliffs, N.J.: Prentice-Hall, 1961, 40.

[35] Noam Chomsky, *Aspects of a Theory of Syntax*, Cambridge, Mass.: MIT Press, 1965.

[36] See Basil Bernstein, "Some Sociological Determinants of Perception," *British Journal of Sociology*, 9 (1958); "A Public Language: Some Sociological Implications of a Linguistic Form," *British Journal of Sociology*, 10 (1959); "Language and Social Class," *British Journal of Sociology*, 11 (1960); and "Linguistic Codes, Hesitation Phenomena and Intelligence," *Language and Speech*, 5 (Jan.–March, 1962).

[37] Alfred Schutz, *Collected Papers: I* (edited by Maurice Natanson), The Hague: Nijhoff, 1962; and Harold Garfinkel, *Studies in Ethnomethodology*, Englewood Cliffs, N.J.: Prentice-Hall, 1967.

[38] Alfred Schutz, *Collected Papers: II* (edited by A. Brodersen), The Hague: Nijhoff, 1964, 11.

[39] Y. Bar-Hillel, "Indexical Expressions," *Mind*, LXIII (1954), 359–79; Cicourel, "The Acquisition of Social Structure," *op. cit.*; H. Conklin, "Hanunoo Color Categories," *Southwestern J. Anthropology*, 11 (1955), 339–44; C. Frake, "The Ethnographic Study of Cognitive Systems," in T. Gladwin and W. C. Sturtevant (eds.), *Anthropology and Human Behavior*, Washington, D.C.: Anthro. Soc. of Wash., 1962, 72–85; H. Garfinkel, *Studies in Ethnomethodology*, Englewood Cliffs, N.J.: Prentice-Hall, 1967; and H. Sacks, *op. cit.*

[40] Schutz, *Collected Papers: II*, *op. cit.*, 29–30.

[41] *Ibid.*, 34.

[42] *Ibid.*, 36.

[43] *Ibid.*, 39.

[44] *Ibid.*, 42.

[45] *Ibid.*, 43.

[46] *Ibid.*, 44, italics in original.

[47] *Ibid.*, 49.

[1] Sacks, H., "An Initial Investigation of the Useability of Conversational Data for Doing Sociology," in this volume.

[2] Schegloff, E., "Notes on a Conversational Practice: Formulating Places," in this volume.

[3] For a treatment of such dimensions of settings most readily translateable and amenable to extension in these temporal terms, see Goffman, E., *Behavior In Public Places,* Glencoe, Ill.: The Free Press, 1964.

[1] By the term "being an observable" I mean having, and being aware of having, an appearance that permits warrantable inferences about one's moral character. This use conforms with a usual use of the term "observable" as the object which an appearance permits inferences about. I might note that the use of the range of terms such as "appearances," "inferences," etc. is not a matter of philosophical or other like election. They are used simply because they seem the most empirically appropriate terms.

[2] While I shall not focus on the matter in this essay, the central sociological status of the "possibility of embarrassment" is strongly suggested by its prominence in *Genesis*. Not only is it that the first human encounter with God begins with embarrassment, but the treatment of Cain suggests that, if only to avoid embarrassment alone, a conforming life is recommended. He, we recall, is condemned not to death, but to "observability for life."

That these are not merely arcane issues is accentuated by the concerns of modern literature. For example, each of the major works of the great social analyst Franz Kafka begins with, then develops a description of, what life is procedurally like after the transformation of the hero into an observable.

[3] Although, again, I shall not focus on the matter, some remarks on privacy are in order. For the society under consideration, giving a public accounting is about as serious a situation as one can face. Furthermore, given the concern to use the appearances persons present in public as the materials for deciding their proper treatment, privacy is not merely valued, but is enforced. In routine interaction others need not attend to one's actual grounds of conduct. Indeed, within the bulk of legal situations "actual grounds" are enforceably excluded; one enforceably attends only to the typical grounds appearances suggest. See further the author's *The Lawyer's Work*, mimeo.

[4] Conformity is not sufficient. It is the comfort with which one wears conformity that seems critical, as the ensuing (esp. ss. 4.) shall suggest. If this is so, it may lead to the development of an explanation for such data as Messinger's, *Sociometry*, v. 25, 1962, pp. 98–109, where the trouble ex-mental patients felt was a lack of comfort with their conformity.

The position noted in the text has been expressed most dramatically by Emerson:

> Commit a crime, and the earth is made of glass. Commit a crime, and it seems as if a coat of snow fell on the ground, such as reveals in the woods the track of every partridge and fox and squirrel.
>
> Quoted in *Nightstick*, by L. J. Valentine, 1947, New York.

[5] Let me note, however, that the question "what is to be done" is handled quite widely by requiring of a properly located candidate that he offer an accounting for his appearance. If a person is competent to reasonably answer "why" questions, then that seems to stand as an indicator of his competence to regulate his affairs.

While one might suppose that the term "reasonably" is the sticker here, it does seem to be the case, perhaps curiously so, that even when persons are under interrogation for possibly serious offenses, ones for which their lives may be at stake, confessions can be garnered by saying to them that what they have said at some point is inconsistent with what they have said at another point. One might imagine them to say "How can it be inconsistent; I said both those things," or et cetera. A preliminary investigation of the method of interrogation suggests that while in exploration of what goes on in such situation is of great interest, it is by no means to be supposed that persons take lightly the reasonableness, consistency, clarity, and so on, of their answers, and may well be more concerned with preserving their claim to consistency than their claim to innocence.

Persons whose competency is denied, i.e., who are not given the right to state the sense of their actions seem to find the situation of interrogation tremendously frustrating.

[6] The public-spirited citizen is not simply someone who responds with moral indignation towards perceived offenses; he is one who adopts an organization of observations—and

indeed attends the world—so as to produce and explain with respect to legal system notions, the behavior of his neighbors. Below are some excerpts of what seems to have seemed strange.

> ... A complaint was received to the effect that neighbors suspected that a woman was a "bookie." The complainant, who remained anonymous, indicated that this woman has been boasting of her winnings on the horse races and has been purchasing clothes and furnishings in excess of what she is capable of purchasing on her husband's earnings as a mail carrier. Neighbors also indicated that a man visited the house each morning and left something in the mailbox. vol. 11, p. 61.
>
> ... Some patrons of a bar reported to the local police that they believed gambling was going on there because two or three other patrons seemed to have quite a bit of money and no visible means of support. p. 62.

The above quotes are from pp. 61 and 62 of volume II, *The Administration of Criminal Justice in the United States*, Pilot Project Report, American Bar Foundation. This study will hereafter be referred to as ABF.

[7] See ss. 4.g. below.

[8] See ss. 4.f. below.

[9] This feature is of course crucial to the problem of bribery. Failures to arrest may have low visibility. The surprise situation of halting for interrogation prominent citizens and officials, and the generally negative but occasionally positive gains to the policemen are well known. See further ss. 5.d.

[10] It is perhaps because of this orientation of the police that the most dangerous of persons are felt to be the person who uses his appearance as a policeman to cover his crooked acts. The members of the Denver police force who were also thieves used police cars as look-outs. Gosling, in *The Ghost Squad*, 1959, notes that criminals who presented the appearance of detectives were a matter of tremendous concern because of their effect in undermining public certainty about the import of apparent police status.

[11] While, given the means of routinizing casual public interaction it is expectable that persons need good grounds in order to make the explanations of appearances a project for empirical investigation, this fact that they do need good grounds is by no means of trivial status. The norm "do not investigate, unless a problem is warrantable" may be the practical theorists' correlate of the scientist's norm of elegance. Theorists who warrant their investigations on the grounds that they will have no practical import are perhaps producing a warrant of the sort although there is no good grounds for investigating this, it is investigatable because nothing practical will come of it. If something practical will come of it, then good grounds may be needed. Cf. the emergence of sociology from the study of recognized social problems.

The normative import of knowledge of the world held in common seems such that those who will make of this knowledge a problem must first suggest the troubles we now have with its use.

[12] See ss. 4.g. below.

[13] See McAllister, R., *The Kind of Guy I Am*, New York, 1957.

[14] See e.g., ABF vol. 5, pp. 1–19 to 1–29, or Callan, G. D., *Police Methods for Today and Tomorrow*, ch. 3, Newark, 1939.

[15] Ss. 3.c. above.

[16] "Milwaukee recruits are instructed that if they observe a young man crossing the street with an overcoat on, collar up, and hat pulled down, in warm weather, they are to suspect that he is a burglar." ABF vol. 5, pp. 1–19.

[17] Anderson and Moore, "Autotelic Folk Models," *The Sociological Quarterly*, Vol. 1, pp. 203–16.

[18] If one feels that it is strange that the rate of crime vary with the suspiciousness of the police, one probably has in mind crimes of violence or robbery as typical crimes. And these might be expected to be reported by the public. However, such matters as gambling, prostitu-

tion, dope selling depend for being listed in statistics on the ability of the police to locate arrestable persons.

[19] By significant time I mean only that "the same time" may not be the same clock time. It may be "closing time" or "dinner time" or the like.

[20] Ibid., pp. 115, 123.

[21] ABF vol. 2, p. 118.

[22] Ibid., p. 120; see too Gosling, *op. cit.*, p. 56.

[23] Ibid., pp. 137, 138.

[24] Ibid., p. 160.

[25] For example:

> After an unsuccessful effort to contact a source of supply for narcotics, the following occurred: The agents took Myra to A Street, somewhere near B Street where she was to begin hustling. Myra mentioned that she had not been picked up by the police for the past two weeks for some reason she could not explain, but facetiously guessed that the Detroit police "must know I've been copping for the Feds." Ibid., p. 90.

[26] See O'Connor, Len, *They Talked to a Stranger*, 1957, passim.

[27] Thorp, A., *Calling Scotland Yard*, p. 9, 1954.

[28] Anderson, C. H., *Beverly Hills is My Beat*, 1960, pp. 33–4.

[29] One training manual states the matter neatly:

> "Once a man has chosen police work as a career, he should do his part to make it a profession." Towler, *Practical Police Knowledge*, p. 58, 1959.

[30] "Once or twice he had gotten close to Sutton, but the wily bank robber seemed to have a second sense that told him Phillips was closing in. Phillips had picked up a former partner of Sutton's, and hoping for a lighter term than he faced, he had told Frank a lot about the fugitive. 'I seen Bill Sutton six weeks ago,' the prisoner said earnestly. 'He knows you're after him and he don't like it. Sutton never used a gun in his life, but he swears he'll kill you if he ever catches up with you. He's never forgotten what you did to Eddie Wilson.'

"He didn't tell her about this, but one of his partners did. When she mentioned it to him he laughed, 'Sutton is a professional like I am. He knows I have nothing personal against him. He's a crook; I'm a cop. He knows the rules of the game as well as I do. To Sutton I'm a business rival—nothing more. That punk I collared who sang about Sutton was just trying to make things easy for himself.'

"And so it proved. When Sutton was finally caught he told Phillips about the rumors he had heard about his reported personal vendetta against the detective. 'That bothered me,' Sutton said. 'Sure I was afraid you'd make me some day and grab me, but I knew there was nothing personal about you trying to collar me. Shooting a cop is for these trigger-happy young punks who are loaded with junk. I'm a bank robber, not a killer, Frank. Believe that. Of course,' he added with a grin, 'there were some days when I didn't like you so much. . . .'"

Reynolds, Q., *Headquarters*, pp. 15–16, 1955.

[1] This fragment is excerpted from a collection of field notes made several years ago. Data designated FN are from that collection.

[2] The following fragments were excerpted from transcribed tape-recorded conversations between middle-aged women. This particular corpus is designated S. Data designated DA and NB are also from conversations between middle-aged women. The participants vary within a corpus as well as among them.

It is interesting to note that the apparent alternative to not mentioning some "trivial" matter is not an action which is appropriately described as equally trivial, i.e. "just mentioning it," but involves for example, "hurting someone's feelings."

S:2:2:3:15 B: But y-uh see, when we get used to people we'll just realize with Elaine she's gonna *do* this.
A: Mm hm,
B: *I* don't care,
A: I don't ei // ther.
B: I don't care a *bit*. I mean I wouldn't say anything to her for the *world*. And hurt her feelings.

S:1:12:28 B: And she *did* en*cou*rage me, but uh she said she uh she says "W'l I just had to push Jean into buying that house."
A: Uh(hhh)
B: But uh I—so I never correct her, I // think "What difference does it make, // really," but,
A: Uh huh,
A: No : :
A: None.

S:2:2:2:40 B: But uh she does, and uh she was doing that to me, But I don't pay any '*ten*shun // to her,
A: Mm hm,
. . . . .
. . . . .
B: Or I say you know, . . . I say "What'n the hell're you talkin about,"
A: hehhh hehhh hhhehh hh heh

[3] Barker and Wright have collected volumes of materials by following children through a day and recording what they say and do. The materials include observers' characterizations of the actions, and these characterizations were purposefully done as "lay" work. Among the actions specifically characterized were "repeats."

> Margaret left her mother and ran to Mrs. Thomas. Margaret asked, "Where's Ellen?" Mrs. Thomas said, "She's at the show." HER VOICE SHOWED THAT THIS WAS A REPETITION.

(Roger G. Barker and Herbert F. Wright, *Margaret Reid: A Full Day Record*, p. 318, 1949, unpublished manuscript.)

> She asked seriously and with a soft voice, "Is Ellen coming out?" I DIDN'T HEAR AT FIRST and asked her what it was she said. SHE REPEATED HER QUESTION, "Is Ellen coming out?"
>
> (Ibid., p. 263.)

[4] Sacks has provided some discussion of the phenomenon of the "partial repetition form" as a "locator," specifically by reference to occurrences such as:

A: I wanna fast car so bad,
B: You wanna what?

(Cf. Sacks, Lecture 12, November 14, 1967, p. 2 ff.)

[5] NB:1:10.

[6] "Recognizable complete utterance" is a technical term developed by Sacks. For the purposes of this essay no more is intended by the use of that name than that an utterance appears to be completed. For the issues involved in "recognizable complete utterance" see the transcribed lectures, for example, Lecture 3, October 12, 1967, p. 6 ff.

[7] DA:3.

[8] FD:IV:77. Fragments designated FD are transcripts of tape-recorded phone calls between personnel at a large metropolitan fire department, and various civilian and professional persons.

[9] GTS:1:2:29. Fragments designated GTS are taken from transcribed tape-recorded group therapy sessions attended by teenagers and a therapist in his early thirties.

[10] Schoggen and other students of Barker and Wright have collected materials which include characterizations of objects in this essay called "questioning repeats"; these are characterized as expressing "disbelief," "real surprise," et cetera. In the following fragments it can be seen that they specifically provide for a "self-correction" from the recipient.

> The first boy gets up and says, "If I'm elected vice-president I'll keep the room quiet, I'll be a good sport, and I'll help other people, and I'll ask questions . . ." finishing lamely.
>
> Several children say with disbelief, "*Ask* questions, *ask* questions!"
>
> The speaker smiles broadly.
>
> He corrects himself in a self-deprecatory tone, "Answer them." He looks embarrassed though.
>
> (Schoggen et al., *Sammy Lewis*, Vol. II, 621–622, unpublished manuscript, 1962.)
>
> Patrick leans forward on the table, trying to puzzle out the score.
>
> He holds up his fingers, as though to count, and looks off in a preoccupied way out the window and says hesitantly, "6–8."
>
> "6–8?" repeats Ernie with real surprise in his voice.
>
> "6–4" says Patrick, correcting himself.
>
> (Schoggen et al., *Patrick Taylor*, Vol. I, 312–15, unpublished manuscript, 1962.)

In a corpus designated P356, consisting of calls to a large metropolitan police department, a "questioning repeat" is prefaced with an exclamation of disbelief:

CALLER: She *is* in serious condition, an'—uh—and it could be, *qui*ckest way t'get *help* would be tuh take her *to* the hospital,
DESK: Mm hm, Well ma'am, we don't have a squad available at this time, we are // (   )—
CALLER: Well I heard to beat! You don't have a *squa::d*?
DESK: No, they're all tied up on other runs ma'am, . . . we simply do not have a squad. All of our squans 'r—squads are on runs at this time,
CALLER: Well, I never heard to beat. Okay. Thank you.
DESK: Yes ma'am.

[11] The term "laugh tokens" is used since it is here taken that "laughter" is a socially organized phenomenon not only in terms of its actual production, but that "laughter" is heard in contrast to, for example, "coughing." On some occasions persons apparently hear "laughter" when what has been done is "coughing," and go through an orderly laughter procedure, that procedure regularly involving that one party initiates and others "join in," i.e. overlap with their own laugh tokens:

A: heh // hehh heh heh
B: heh heh heh

This procedure can be observed where what has initiated it is in fact a cough:

A: khakhh//uhkk
B: heh heh heh

The cough can be seen to be generative of the sequence in that a second laugh token is regularly placed in overlapping-adjacency to a first. Also involved in the recognizability of laughter is that what has been on-going is (a) possibly a thing for which laughter is an appropriate next action, and (b) has proceeded far enough that it is seeable as such; i.e. coughing is not so likely to be heard as a possible laugh token when somebody has just started talking.

[12] GTS:1:2:29.

[13] GTS:2:2:89.

[14] One of the base environments of "laughter" is following a joke, where its use demonstrates a hearer's finding that the joke has been successfully completed. Further, laugh tokens are used to signal or to attempt closure of interchanges. The familiar "curtain line" might be given a technical name like "pre-sequence terminator," and one can go through a corpus of conversations to find that quite regularly the occurrence of a curtain line and its associated laugh tokens are predictive of "goodbyes." Consider the following fragments excerpted from transcriptions of a two-way radio talk show, designated C:

C:1:43 A: Maybe he figured thet enny letter from en officer assigned t'the *Pen*tagon to a man working fer ((Radio Station)) might be suspishis en 'e better not d(hh)o (h)i(hhh)t,
B: eh heh heh! hhh
A: hhh
B: Alright Tod, // (   )
A: *Nice* talkin to // you sir.
B: I won' holdjeh enny longer,

C:1:57 A: This is a business exchange. En that means when *you* dial hh *e*nnything beginning with Falbrook *six* you've gotta very *good* chance of winding up talking to en empty *o*ffice building.
B: hhh! hh hmh!
A: Mehhhhh! // *How* ever.
B: [[(   )—
A: [[I'm *so*rry abaht it.
(pause)
B: Thankyou
A: Tha:nk you fer calling,
B: Bye,
A: *Good* night.

C:1:77 B: Don't talk, I've taken to vacuuming this daw(hh)g
A: Ehhhh heh heh hah hah hahhh hah hah hah! Well that's about *it*!
B: Okay Tod,
A: Okay?
B: Thank you very // very much.
A: Thank you dear.
B: Bye bye
A: Mm bye bye.

[15] "Assessments" very frequently occur as tag lines to anecdotes. They mark that the anecdote is completed. In the following case, an anecdote is overlapped by an announcement

that the session is over. Apparently the anecdote is then reduced to its minimal components and proposed to be complete by the addition of an assessment tag line.

GTS:3:82 KEN: Well, up at Camp Montrose one night, we went up there // (on our own)—
DAN: Well let's—
DAN: We're gonna haftuh call // it a day now.
KEN: They were havin a dance, we took the fire hoses an' washed everybody ou(hh)t. hehhh th' last night I was th(hh)ere.
(1·0)
KEN: That was fun.
DAN: Well, I'm sorry we won't be having you back.
LOUISE: I'm soh—I don' know-I-I c(h)an't—
DAN: We : : ll—
KEN: Well honey,—Goodbye.

That co-participants use the "assessment" to see that an anecdote is finished can be seen in the relationship of the pause to Dan's talk, and the relationship of Dan's talk to the assessment, where immediately upon completion of the assessment Dan initiates "goodbyes" to Louise, who is quitting the group.

[16] GTS:1:1:79.
[17] GTS:1:2:45.
[18] S:1:1:12:23.
[19] S:2:2:3:19.
[20] Schoggen et al., *Patrick Taylor*, Vol. I, 311–22, unpublished manuscript, 1962.
[21] GTS:5:29.
[22] NB:1:9.
[23] GTS:4:56.
[24] GTS:2:2:7.
[25] GTS:1:2:15.
[26] GTS:1:2:31.
[27] GTS:2:2:16.
[28] The orderliness of conversational interaction such that it can be described in terms of "rules" is an enormously generative notion developed by Sacks. It serves as a guide for observation of phenomena, for developing and testing analyses, and is a key notion for this paper.
[29] The notion of "utterance pairs" with question-answer as a prototypical instance has been rather extensively developed by Sacks. (Cf., e.g., Lecture 6, October 24, 1967.)
[30] GTS:2:2:23.
[31] GTS:1:1:35.
[32] GTS:1:1:48.
[33] See footnote 4.
[34] FN.
[35] FN.
[36] Schoggen et al., *Sammy Lewis*, Vol. II, 621–629, unpublished manuscript, 1962. The report as it appears in the manuscript uses the participants' first names as the items which, in this paper have been replaced by game-relevant designations, as follows: Pitcher—Sammy; Batter—Brian; Runner—Harry; Baseman—Craig.
[37] NB:2:4.
[38] GTS:1:2:47.
[39] GTS:3:17.
[40] C:2-22-68:62.
[41] GTS:4:22.
[42] GTS:2:2:19.
[43] GTS:5:37.

[44] GTS:1:1:23.

[45] Remarks can be found in Lectures 5 and 6, November 1968, and in one of several yet-to-be-transcribed lectures from December of 1968.

[46] GTS:4:5. In the transcript from which this was excerpted there is a footnote above Roger's "It's a Beatle" explaining that it "refers to GTS 1." This is a lay-observation derived from having heard GTS 1 and talk about the Beatles occurring in it, subsequently hearing GTS 4 with its possibly referential item, and Ken's "It's a Beatle. Oh *no(hhh)o*!" which was heard as a similar object to "Not *that* again!," i.e. recognition of the prior item's doing of reference to GTS 1.

[47] See footnote 11.

[48] GTS:4:23.

[1] See the data supplement at the end of the essay for others.

[2] Harvey Sacks' work with the phenomenon conversation initially influenced my choice of conversation as a source of material for research. Though I am now primarily focusing on descriptions of behavior found in conversations and other places, his techniques and findings with conversation data and his comments on my own related research have been and remain important consultants.

[3] First, the reader is warned that in order to preserve research tactics that rely heavily on actual data, many of the essay's analyses contain detailed discussions of a specific excerpt. A careful preliminary familiarization with each excerpt as well as some focussing on these tactics, hopefully, may diminish, or at least requite, some of the possible reading discomforts inflicted by any resulting disruptions of the paper's continuity. Transcription symbols used:

[indicates overlapping utterances

( ) indicates there was some transcribing uncertainty for what appears inside the parentheses.

(( )) indicates transcriber's addition.

[4] See p. 360 of data supplement.

[5] Other virtues of using this sort of material for such a preliminary investigation shall be noted throughout the essay.

[6] One can even imagine or remember remarks like "He wasn't doing anything, just reading (or smoking, eating, etc.)," where the actions named do not count as "something."

[7] Sometimes, however, such "single party" talk is interpreted into a circumstance so that to say that a relevant *explanation* is being done by the interpreter would be stretching a point, e.g. dictating to a tape recorder, practising diction or a part in a play, etc.

[8] This is one example where "lay descriptions" of conversational episodes reflect some of Harvey Sacks' findings. Sacks has discussed conversants' use of and practices involving "paired utterances" such as question-answers, excuse-pardon, greetings, etc. He points out and describes (in his lectures) the conversants' attendance of the obligatory character of such pairs. Discussion of this and related topics will be published in his forthcoming volume, *The Organization of Conversation*, Prentice Hall, 1970.

[9] "Wife," "woman," "mother," "nurse" might all refer to one figure, yet may not all be "appropriate" identifications for that figure in a particular instance described. Again one can get some feeling for this characteristic of identification categories by substituting "woman" or "mother" for "wife" in the data being considered.

[10] Even though people are said to perform actions in "dissimilar" fashions, it nonetheless must be clear that when an action is ascribed with no explicit reference to the manner of performance these possible dissimilarities have nct been at issue.

[11] Sacks comments extensively in his lectures (and in "Initial Investigations of the Analyzeability of Children Stories" in *New Directions in Linguistics*, Hymes, Gumperz eds., Holt, Rinehart and Winston, 1969) on conversers' uses of the relationship between categories and what he calls "category bound activities." Although, it is not as yet clear from the data how or whether describers attend this feature of "category boundedness" of activities themselves, it is in the above and other instances suggested that the *manner of performance* of activities may have categorical associations (or "boundedness").

[12] Harvey Sacks, who pointed out to me the "on the way to" and "coming back from" accounts attire might bear, also suggested that attire can tell people what the wearer is "going as"; e.g. one goes to the beach dressed like a "teenager," "vagabond," "adult," etc.

[1] I follow Goffman in thinking of social occasions as "the structuring social context in which many situations and their gatherings are likely to form, dissolve, and re-form"; Erving Goffman, *Behaviour in Public Places,* The Free Press of Glencoe, Collier-Macmillan Ltd., London, 1963, p. 18. By occasioned activities, then, I mean to refer to those activities which are seen to occur under the auspices of a social occasion.

[2] Kenneth L. Pike, *Language in Relation to a Unified Theory of the Structure of Human Behaviour, Part I.* Summer Institute of Linguistics, Glendale, California, 1954, p. 29.

[3] Ibid., p. 30.

[4] Susan Ervin-Tripp, *Sociolinguistics.* Working Paper No. 3, Language-Behaviour Research Laboratory, University of California, Berkeley, November 1967, p. 114. Emphasis added.

[5] Michael Moerman, "A Little Knowledge," unpublished paper, p. 19.

[6] By core activities I mean that sub-set of activities which provide the rationale of a social occasion. Thus, I take it that Pike's churchgoers oriented to something called "the service," and that entering church, finding a pew, etc., were undertaken as necessary preliminaries to "the service." Cf. the earlier discussion of segments which have primacy.

[7] In my use of categories and categorial identifications as fundamental analytical tools I draw upon Harvey Sacks, "An Initial Investigation . . ." this volume. Sacks there considers the "natural groupings" or collections of categories which members of a society employ in identifying one another, and refers to any such collection, together with the rules of application involved, as a Membership Categorization Device. I assume that many such devices are generated out of social occasions and/or are employed in rendering the events of occasions intelligible.

[8] I borrow the term "deep structure" from transformational grammar. Although I am not able to provide its sociological use with the kind of technical specification that it possesses in its original domain, I find it useful in the following kind of way: I use it to refer to the social-organizational features which members must be assumed to consult in order to make routine sense of events and activities. I take it as absolutely fundamental in the analysis of transcripts that the analyst shall explicate *not* (or not only) the syntactic properties of utterances and their relations, but primarily such procedures for displaying or invoking social-organizational features as participants must be assumed to employ in constructing their own and "processing" others' utterances. Cf. Harold Garfinkel, "The Routine Grounds of Everyday Activities," this volume; also Harold Garfinkel and Harvey Sacks, "On Formal Structures of Practical Actions"; unpublished paper prepared for *Theoretical Sociology: Perspectives and Developments,* John C. McKinney and Edward Tiryakian Eds., Appleton-Century-Crofts (1969).

[9] Harvey Sacks, unpublished lectures.

[10] Ibid.

[11] Taken from a transcript of an occupational therapy group, most of the members of which were former state-mental-hospital patients.

[12] For sociological treatments of accounts and accountability see Harold Garfinkel, *Studies in Ethnomethodology,* Prentice-Hall Inc., Englewood Cliffs, New Jersey, 1967, esp. Chapter One; Harvey Sacks, unpublished lectures, passim; Marvin B. Scott and Stanford M. Lyman, "Accounts," *American Sociological Review,* Vol. 33, No. 1, February 1968, pp. 46–62.

[13] For lengthy and detailed discussions of sequencing rules in conversation see Sacks, *op. cit.*

[14] On "expansions" see Garfinkel, "Routine Grounds," *op. cit.,* and Roger Brown and Ursula Bellugi, "Three Processes in the Child's Acquisition of Syntax"; in Janet A. Emig et al., *Language and Learning,* Harcourt, Brace and World, New York, 1966.

[15] I borrow the notion of "first actions" and "second actions" from Sacks, *op. cit.* The issue is that some activities have sequential ties, in that on the occasion of some category-incumbent doing an activity, it is then regularly in order for some other category-incumbent to do "in response" some other activity. One import of this tying of activities is that it permits

actions to be seen as "missing" in a warrantable way; e.g. I may engage in a lengthy conversation during the course of which I do not laugh, but to note as a feature of that conversation that I "failed to laugh" may be to produce an odd description or the query "So what?" But should I "fail to laugh" following your telling a joke, then that failure may be properly noticeable and accountable—i.e. "telling a joke" is a first action for which some kind of "appreciation" is a second action.

[16] On "formulating" as a members' activity see Sacks, *op. cit.*, and Garfinkel and Sacks, *op. cit*. By "formulating" I mean, following Sacks and Garfinkel the activity of "describing," "naming" or "characterizing" the activity or occasion *in the course of which* the "description," etc., is offered.

[1] For a detailed analysis of this data see the author's unpublished doctoral dissertation, *The Organization of Talk and Socialization Practices in Family Household Interaction*, Dept. of Sociology, University of California, Berkeley, 1969.

[2] I owe my awareness of this and related problems of turn-taking and speaker sequencing to Harvey Sacks. His formulation of the speaker sequencing problem can be found in connection with his discussion of Ethel Albert's paper on the Barundi. He discusses the ordering principle of ranking by superior caste position, such that conversationalists must follow a round of speech in accordance with the ranking among them: Highest rank first, next highest rank speaks next, and so on, in that order and that order only. The constraint this principle of ordering would produce upon multi-party speech is obviously very powerful: for four it would go: ABCDABCDetc. Cf. E. Albert, "'Rhetoric,' 'Logic,' and 'Poetics' in Barundi: Culture Patterning of Speech Behavior," *American Anthropologist*, Special Publication, Vol. 66, No. 6, 1964. See also Sacks' formulation upon this in Lectures 1–3, Spring Quarter, 1967, UCLA.

[3] This analytic device was given to me by Stan Persky in a discussion about the analyst's problems of treating the participants of a conversation according to the competing relevant ways of categorizing them via social setting, occasion, and standardized social relationships. The analytic device was afterwards subjected to discussion in a meeting of myself, Stan Perskey, Lorne Salutin, Don Zimmerman, Roy Turner, Dorothy Smith, and Tony Crowle, all of whom contributed to my decision to take up this device for further consideration.

[4] Cf. Sacks, "The Search for Help," unpub. Ph.D. dissertation, Dept. of Sociology, Univ. of Calif., Berkeley, 1966. A version of this work can be found in Edwin Shneidman (ed.), *Essays in Self-Destruction*, Science House Inc., New York, 1967. The work can also be found in more technical format in Sacks' Draft 4B, mimeo, UCLA.

[5] Cf. Sacks, "The Search for Help," Ch. 2.

[6] Author's Field Tapes: 24: 1.

[7] Cf. Sacks, "The Search for Help," Ch. 2, on the convergence problem.

[8] This excerpt is from Field Tape 24:1.

[9] I am indebted to Sacks for his discussions on referential tying in conversation. See his Lecture 10, Fall Quarter, 1966, UCLA.

[10] See Sacks, Lecture 2, Spring 1966, UCLA, pp. 15–22.

[11] Ibid.

[12] I discuss this in some detail in Speier, *The Organization of Talk and Socialization Practices . . . op. cit.*, pp. 213–38.

[13] *Esquire*, July, 1968, p. 50.

[14] See Sacks, Lecture 10, Fall Quarter, 1966, UCLA and Lectures 1–3, Spring Quarter, 1967.

[15] The nominal participation rule, according to Sacks, would consist of replacing a previous speaker's noun coming at the end of an independent clause with a participalized version of it and continuing on with another clause, dependent to the first one, by speaking syntactically consistent with it. So what one regularly finds are exchanges like the following, as reported by Sacks:

A. We were in an automobile discussion
B. —discussing the psychological motives for
C. —drag racing on the streets.

This instance is more complex because the entry of a third party who completes the dependent clause produced by B's participalization of A's utterance. Perhaps more common are simpler pairs of exchanges using this rule, e.g. A. "We were having dinner," B. "—dining on roast beef." A participalization of a prepositional noun can be used to replace another participalization, as well, as I illustrate in the discussion by: "of getting" becomes "of going out for . . ."